A HISTORY
of
Rockbridge County
Virginia

Oren F. Morton

HERITAGE BOOKS
2020

HERITAGE BOOKS
AN IMPRINT OF HERITAGE BOOKS, INC.

Books, CDs, and more—Worldwide

For our listing of thousands of titles see our website
at
www.HeritageBooks.com

A Facsimile Reprint
Published 2020 by
HERITAGE BOOKS, INC.
Publishing Division
5810 Ruatan Street
Berwyn Heights, Md. 20740

Copyright © 1920 Oren F. Morton

— Publisher's Notice —
In reprints such as this, it is often not possible to remove blemishes from the original. We feel the contents of this book warrant its reissue despite these blemishes and hope you will agree and read it with pleasure.

International Standard Book Number
Paperbound: 978-0-7884-1026-0

CONTENTS

Part One: General History

Chapter

	Introduction	v
I.	The Local Geography	1
II.	Scenic Features	6
III.	The Ulsterman and the Pathfinder	12
IV.	The Borden Land Grant	21
V.	Early Pioneer Days	33
VI.	Civil Government: 1737-1852	45
VII.	Annals of 1737-1777	54
VIII.	Strife with the Red Men	61
IX.	Rockbridge County Established	76
X.	The Calfpasture	83
XI.	The War for Independence	92
XII.	Middle Period	104
XIII.	A Year of Suspense	111
XIV.	The War of 1861	123
XV.	Recent Period	136
XVI.	The Negro Element	141
XVII.	The Town of Lexington	147
XVIII.	Buena Vista and Glasgow	153
XIX.	Villages, Hamlets, and Summer Resorts	156
XX.	Highways, Waterways, and Railways	161
XXI.	Industrial Interests	168
XXII.	The Churches of Rockbridge	172
XXIII.	Temperance Societies and Other Fraternities	180
XXIV.	Old Field Schools and Free Schools	183
XXV.	Washington and Lee University	188
XXVI.	The Virginia Military Institute	199

XXVII.	The Ann Smith and Other Academies	207
XXVIII.	The Franklin Society	214
XXIX.	Journalism and Literature	217
XXX.	Old Militia Days	221
XXXI.	A Rockbridge Hall of Fame	224
XXXII.	Stonewall Jackson at Lexington	233
XXXIII.	Robert E. Lee as a College President	238
XXXIV.	Family Sketches and Biographic Paragraphs	244
XXXV.	The MacCorkle Family	278
XXXVI.	Rockbridge in the World War	293
XXXVII.	Supplementary Items	299
XXXVIII.	Rockbridge Inventions	307

PART TWO: GENEALOGIC MATERIAL

	Introduction	337
Section I.	Given Names and Surnames	339
II.	Conveyances in Borden Tract, 1741-1780	343
III.	Early Patents Outside the Borden Tract	351
IV.	Secondary Land Conveyances Prior to 1778	355
V.	Tithables of 1778	365
VI.	Taxpayers of 1782	370
VII.	Taxpayers of 1841	378
VIII.	Present Surnames	388
IX.	Militia Officers Prior to 1816	396
X.	Soldiers of the Revolution	402
XI.	Rockbridge Artillery	405
XII.	Soldiers of the World War	444
XIII.	Various Lists	456
XIV.	Miscellaneous Data	469
	Appendices	547
	Errata	568
	Supplementary Items	569

FOREWORD

IN THE summer of 1917 the writer visited Lexington to see if there was a practical desire for a history of Rockbridge. The encouragement was such as to lead him to undertake writing one, and the present volume is the result.

All the magisterial districts were visited. The public records of the county were attentively examined, as were also the early records of the parent counties, Orange, Augusta, and Botetourt. The archives in the capitol and the state library at Richmond were freely consulted, as were likewise various books in public and private collections. The files of the local newspapers yielded much valuable material. The documentary history of Rockbridge is practically continuous, and it proved necessary to make the utmost possible use of it.

County history is either general or genealogic. It is general, when it deals with the people of a county as a community. It is genealogic, when it deals with the same people as made up of families and attempts to trace lines of descent from the pioneer ancestors.

Either of these two aspects of local history is the complement of the other. John Dee may be pleased to find that his great grandfather, Adam Dee, came into the county a hundred and fifty years before the date of his own birth, bought the John Smith farm, and reared ten children, nearly all of whom married and from whom have come grandchildren and great grandchildren. But John Dee should not assume that persons who are neither cousins nor near-cousins will grow enthusiastic in viewing the intricate branches of the family tree. To them it is little else than a dry network of names and dates, unless one or more members of the connection have done something that is a good deal out of the ordinary. But if we seek to know the times in which Adam Dee and his sons lived; to learn how they dressed, labored, and housed themselves, and what was the environment, physical, civil, and social, in which they were placed: we then have begun to put flesh and blood into the skeleton of names and dates, and have created a degree of living interest that is not confined to John Dee and his kinsfolk. An interpretation to them becomes an interpretation to others.

This book is therefore divided into two sections. The one dealing with the general history of Rockbridge begins with a survey of the geographic and scenic features of the county, this being necessary to an adequate understanding of the development of the past two centuries. It then explains whence the pioneer families came and why they came, and in what manner they established themselves in the wilderness. It attempts to trace the civic, social, religious, educational, and industrial unfolding that has since taken place. It tells of the growth of centers of population, and of the steady outflow of people that has been true of this region from the start. So far as could conveniently be done, documents have been allowed to speak for themselves. In a word, this first portion of the volume aims to present the Story of Rockbridge since the beginning of white settlement in 1737. What took place between that date and the war of 1861 is rather unfamiliar to the people who are doing the work of the county today. The sources of information for that long period are fragmentary and are tedious to consult. The compiler has therefore given special attention to the years that lie mainly or wholly beyond the practical recollection of any person now living.

Some explanation of the second or genealogic section of this book may be found in the introduction to Part Two.

As a subject of local history, the annals of Rockbridge are of much more than ordinary interest and value. The presentation of them in book form has been seriously thought of, at one time or another, by several of the native citizens. The matter was urged upon Captain J. D. Morrison in 1894. In the same year it was suggested that a club be formed to gather facts concerning the prominent names in Rockbridge history. But while, with respect to county histories in general, certain things are obviously in favor of the native historian, observation shows that he seldom gets down to the task. This is largely because he sees no end to the material which is constantly coming to light. He may give one, two, or five years to his task, and all the while be turning up fresh soil. But unless the undertaking is in every respect a labor of love, there is a limit to the time and expense which may be given. The historian who is a stranger is not beset with the antagonisms which are nearly sure to affect the labors of the native. The very fact that he is a stranger makes it the more easy to be judicial and to deal with his subject from a broad angle. Nevertheless, he starts in under a handicap of unfamiliarity with his chosen field. He is very much in need of a live coöperation on the part of the inhabitants. This coöperation needs to be active and not passive.

During a number of weeks, reading notices relating to the enterprise appeared in the newspapers of Lexington. The compiler hoped thus to come in touch with many persons who could supplement the data he was gleaning from the public documentary sources. The responses were few and not all the aid promised was forthcoming. Personal calls were made by him whenever they were asked. If the chapters on biography and family history, as well as certain tabulations, are here and there deficient, this paragraph will afford some explanation. However, our country was at war while this work was being done, and the minds of the people were much engrossed by this circumstance.

If this book were to be offered at a "reasonable price," it had to be written within a certain limit of time and printed within a certain limit of cost. It was therefore necessary to be concise in statement. There was a sharp limit to the space which could be devoted to any given topic. The exceptions are where such space has been paid for by specially interested individuals.

Several residents of Rockbridge have aided very materially by contributing oral or written information, donating or loaning books or other published material, or extending courtesies in hospitality or travel. Particular acknowledgement is thus due to William A. Anderson, Mr. and Mrs. Walter W. Dunlap, Frank T. Glasgow, Mr. and Mrs. William G. Houston, Mr. Henkle, of Buena Vista, Mrs. G. A. Jones, Harry O. Locher, Sr., Mr. and Mrs. L. C. Lockridge, Joseph R. Long, James H. McCown, Emmett W. McCorkle, Daniel W. McNeil, Mrs. Graham Montgomery, General E. W. Nichols, J. A. Parker, Earle K. Paxton, J. Sidney Saville, Dr. Henry Louis Smith, Harrington Waddell, and Hugh J. White. The McCormick portion of the chapter on Rockbridge is from the pen of Doctor J. H. Latané of Johns Hopkins University. The material for the sketch of the McCorckle family has been contributed by William A. MacCorkle, ex-governor of West Virginia, and several other members of the McCorkle connection. Other assistance from without the country has been given by J. J. Echols, O. C. Ruley, and Kate M. Jordan.

There is further acknowledgement to Boutwell Dunlap, of San Francisco, who has heretofore furnished the compiler with some data for his histories of Bath and Monroe. He has opened to him all his manuscript material relating to Rockbridge. Mr. Dunlap's manuscript collections on the history and genealogy of the Valley of Virginia and Western Virginia are said to be the largest in America. His interest in this history of Rockbridge is in remembrance of his father, William Dunlap, a native of Rockbridge, a respected California pioneer of 1849, one of the largest landholders of the Sacramento valley, and a member of one of the most prominent family connections of the Valley of Virginia and the West. Mr. Boutwell Dunlap's aid has been especially helpful in affording material for chapters X, XXXI, and XXXIV, and Section XIV.

In making most grateful recognition to all the above named persons, the author does not mean to withhold his thanks from anyone else who has, even if in a small way, shown an active interest in the preparation of this history. This book is the first history of Rockbridge that has been written. It represents eighteen months of hard work. No statement has gone into these pages without a careful scrutiny. Yet it should be borne in mind that there is no claim for immunity from error in statements of fact or in the spelling of proper names. The man or woman who can write a local history and escape censure is not to be found on this side of the millenium, even by the "efficiency engineer." Another craftsman than the one who does write the book could probably do better in some one respect, or in several. The pertinent question is whether in the long run he could have done as well. The person who is keen in looking for flaws in a county history will do well to remember that the reviewers often find glaring misstatements in works intended to be authoritative; and that Joseph E. Worcester, the lexicographer, said that no amount of care will render even an unabridged dictionary exempt from error.

When an omission or inaccuracy is noticed, one reader will at once denounce the entire book and excoriate the author. Another reader will write a correction on the margin of the page. Copies of the book thus annotated are more valuable than others, especially to the local historian of the future. And unlike the generality of books, the county history does not depreciate in financial value. It commands a higher price as it grows scarce. The owner of such a book has made a safe investment, and if he takes jealous care of his purchase posterity will thank him for doing so.

OREN F. MORTON.

Staunton, Virginia, September 28, 1918.

HISTORY OF ROCKBRIDGE COUNTY, VA.

I

THE LOCAL GEOGRAPHY

Position and Size—Boundaries—Mountains—Lowlands—Streams—Geology—Soils—Climate—Plants and Animals—Divisions—Place Names—Natural Advantages

There is but one Rockbridge County in the United States. The unique name is due to a great natural curosity within its limits.

The position of the county is nearly midway in the longer direction of the Valley of Virginia. The latitude—mostly to the south of the thirty-eighth parallel—is that of the center of Kentucky, the south of Missouri, and the center of California. In Europe it is that of the south of Spain and the island of Sicily. In Asia it is that of central Asia Minor and central Japan.

In form, Rockbridge is an irregular rectangle, the longer direction being nearly northeast and southwest. The length of the county is nearly thirty-two miles, and the extreme breadth is nearly twenty-six miles. The area is officially stated as 593 square miles, which is considerably more than is true of the average county in Virginia.

The curving eastern boundary follows for forty miles the crest of the Blue Ridge, and is therefore a natural geographic line. The western line begins on Camp Mountain, and passes to North Mountain, then to Mill Mountain, and finally to Sideling Hill. The short lines by which the boundary crosses from one to another of these elevations are determined by valley-divides, so that the western boundary may likewise be regarded as natural. But the northern and southern boundaries of the county are straight lines, entirely artificial, and they set it off as a cross-section of the Valley of Virginia.

The Blue Ridge is not a single well-defined mountain range. Looking from the high ground along the Valley Railroad, there is seen in the east a succession of bold elevations. The nearest are heavy foothill ridges. Beyond are the higher fragments of interior ridges, marked off from one another by depressions more or less deep. These intermediate heights afford only occasional glimpses of the central range. Consequently, the general appearance of the mountain wall is that of a labyrinth of long and short elevations occupying a considerable breadth of country. But on the western side of Rockbridge, the ranges are single and well-defined, and present sky-lines that are fairly regular. For several miles east of the axis of North Mountain, much of the surface is occupied by short parallel ridges of much the same character as North Mountain itself. Some of these are the House mountains, Camp Mountain, Green Mountain, Little North Mountain, the Jump, and the Loop. The most eastern is the uplift known as the Short Hills. These break down rather abruptly near the course of Buffalo Creek, but beyond they reappear under the name of the Brushy Hills.

The space between the two mountain systems may be termed the Central Lowland. It runs the entire length of the county. On the east it is bordered by the bottoms along South and North rivers, and by Salling's Mountain, which is an outlier of the Blue Ridge, though lying to the west of the James. In the north the breadth of this lowland is more than ten miles. At the south it is scarcely half as much. It is by far the most populous area in Rockbridge.

In general the contour of the county is mountainous. The Blue Ridge section is interrupted only by such narrow depressions as Arnold's Valley and the valleys of Irish Creek and the Little Mary. The surface of the Central Lowland is heavily rolling. Between drainage basins it rises into divides of considerable altitude. Westward is the mountainous belt already mentioned. It includes a number of well populated creek valleys. In the extreme northwest is a section of the basin known as the Pastures. Southward it is prolonged into the wilderness drained by Bratton's Run.

The highest point in the Rockbridge section of the Blue Ridge appears to be Bluff Mountain with an altitude of 3250 feet. The northern point of the Short Hills has a height of 2565 feet. Adcock's Knob in North Mountain has a height of 3325 feet, and the Jump of 3190. Big House and Little House mountains are respectively 3612 and 3410 feet high, and seem to be the most elevated ground in the county.

The entire area of Rockbridge lies in the basin of the James. This river courses ten miles through the southeast of the county. North River, which joins it immediately above Balcony Falls, flows not less than fifty miles within the confines of Rockbridge and drains seven-eights of its area. It rises in Shenandoah Mountain, and as the Great Calfpasture it flows southwardly to Goshen Pass, just above which it is joined by the Little Calfpasture, also running in the same direction. A little farther above are the mouths of Mill Creek and Bratton's Run. A mile below Goshen the river begins to flow squarely toward the Blue Ridge, and below its junction with the Little Calfpasture it becomes known as North River. After passing into the limestone region of the Central Lowland, its course, which is now a succession of large loops, is first southward, then southeastward, and finally southward again. The largest tributary is Buffalo Creek, which is itself entitled to be called a river. It rises near the southwest corner of Rockbridge, and has a broad, rapid course of about twenty-five miles. Hays Creek, the next largest affluent, rises in Augusta, and above

New Providence is known as Moffett's Creek. Its largest tributary is Walker's Creek, which also rises in Augusta. South River, which hugs the foothills of the Blue Ridge and consequently pursues the same general direction, likewise has its source in Augusta. Irish Creek and the Little Mary, both heading in the Blue Ridge, are its only important tributaries. Kerr's Creek parallels the Buffalo, but has a much shorter course. Still smaller affluents of North River are Whistle Creek, Mill Creek, Back Creek, Woods Creek, Borden's Run, and Poague's Run. Below the mouth of North River are Arnold's and Cedar creeks, flowing directly into the main stream.

Small watercourses are rather many in Rockbridge, and even the Central Lowland is better supplied with running water than are some other limestone districts. And because its streams are geologically old, Rockbridge is without lakes or ponds.

The geological structure of Rockbridge is very ancient, although its rocks are not among the very oldest of the stratified formations. The age of the rocks renders it quite useless to expect to find coal, oil, or natural gas, although by the same token we do find the mountains well stored with that most necessary metal, iron. Other metallic and mineral riches are manganese, marble, kaolin, limestone, fireclay, gypsum, barytes, and even tin, a metal with which the United States is sparingly endowed.

The Central Lowland is preëminently the agricultural district of Rockbridge, and here the soil is a heavy loam, intermediate in color between the light and the dark shades, and resting on limestone strata. The rock formation is generally tilted to a considerable angle, and crops out in ledges or in rocky slopes, and an occasional sinkhole manifests its presence. The bottoms along the rivers and the larger creeks are variable in width, and have a soil which is dark in color and somewhat sandy in texture. Much more stony than other soils and the least desirable for general farming are those of the mountain slopes. No large inroad has been made into these, except where they merge into bench or bottom lands.

The climate of Lexington is a fair average for that of the county in general. The mean annual temperature of the county seat is fifty-four degrees, which is slightly below that of the city of Washington, the effect of a more southern latitude being more than offset by the very much greater altitude. With respect to the seasons, the mean temperatures are 34.5 in winter, 53.8 in spring, 72.2 in summer, and 55.4 in fall. The coldest month is February, with a mean of 33.5; the hottest is July, with a mean of 73.7. But during a period of twelve years, the mean of the coldest month varied from 26.4 degrees to 40.8, and that of the hottest month from 63.9 to 78. In the average year, the range of the thermometer is from a minimum of 1.5 degrees to a maximum of 96. But temperatures of 101 degrees above zero and sixteen below have been observed.

The yearly rainfall of forty inches is well distributed among the seasons, yet is heaviest in summer and lightest in the fall. June is ordinarily the wettest month and November the driest. The average period between killing frosts is from April 24th to October 15th.

Two inches of sleet in December, 1907, caused a rare beauty of "icescape." A hailstorm on Colliers's Creek, June 8, 1909, completely destroyed all crops in its path and even killed fish in the stream. In the mountain hollows the huge pellets did not entirely disappear for several days.

But there are wide variations in the climate of Rockbridge. Frost has been known in every month except July, although one fall was so mild as to be without a killing frost till the end of November. In the winter of 1855-56, there was sleighing for six weeks, and the ice in the North River canal interrupted navigation for two months. Two years later, there was no ice in the canal worth mention until March 5th. Snow fell to a depth of eighteen inches, October 24, 1854. There was a heavy fall May 20, 1857, and it lay several days on the Blue Ridge. In the spring of 1859, trees were nearly in full leaf April 23, more than three weeks in advance of the usual time. Fires and warm clothing were needed during the third week of August, 1866. Rain fell to the depth of four and two-third inches, September 22, 1907, and in the Kerr's Creek valley the precipitation for the month was 15.9 inches. High winds are not unknown. Floods are sometimes very serious, as in 1870, 1877, and 1913. There is no proof of any material change in climate since the Rockbridge area* became known to white people. There was a severe drouth in 1758, and another about 1751, the earlier one causing a local famine.

Since the surface is diversified, the drainage nearly perfect, and the average altitude not far short of 1500 feet, the air is bracing and health conditions are naturally very good. The annals of the county disclose many instances of longevity. The ailments of most frequent occurrence appear to be those of the respiratory organs. Typhoid fever, a disease due to defective sanitation, has several times seriously interrupted the schools of Lexington. Smallpox has been an occasional visitor.

The soils of Rockbridge take kindly to a covering of grass, so that the county is well adapted to grazing as well as to the general farm crops. But where nature has her way, she everywhere covers the hills and valleys with a diversified forest growth. The prevailing wood is oak, chestnut, elm, hickory, walnut, poplar, sycamore, and other deciduous trees. Pine occurs in some localities and cedar is still more common. Among the numerous shrubs is the mountain laurel in the high, shaded hollows. The wild fruits include the black-

---

*By "Rockbridge area" is meant the geographic space within the present limits of the county, and as though such limits have existed for an indefinite time.

berry, the common and the mountain raspberries, strawberries, huckleberries, mulberries, and pawpaws. The animal life is of the kinds found in the Valley of Virginia. The buffalo and the elk disappeared soon after white settlement began. The puma and the wolf held their ground much longer, but are now extinct. The mountains shelter an occasional black bear and a few deer. Such predatory pests as wildcats, foxes, and skunks still remain. Groundhogs, rabbits, and squirrels are tolerably plentiful. Still other mammals are raccoons, opossums, otters, and mink. The wooded surface attracts birds in considerable variety, such as turkeys, ducks, cranes, pheasants, hawks, owls, woodpeckers, pigeons, thrushes, crows, robins, partridges, larks, doves, catbirds, and redbirds. In the mountains are eagles, buzzards, and ravens. Fish would be more abundant but for the pollution of some of the streams by sawmilling and mining. There are the usual insects native to this part of America, but the mosquito is not a nuisance. In a single season, a few years ago, the bounty of fifty cents a head on chickenhawks was paid on 469 of these birds of prey. They were about one-half of a flock that came from the west.

Rockbridge is bordered by the counties of Augusta, Nelson, Amherst, Bedford, Botetourt, Alleghany, and Bath. Its magisterial districts are six. Buffalo lies in the southwest, Natural Bridge in the southeast, South River in the northeast, Walker's Creek in the northwest. In the central west is Kerr's Creek, and in the center is Lexington District. The corporation of Buena Vista is a seventh political subdivision.

The names borne by the streams and mountains of Rockbridge have in a number of instances undergone no change since the exploration by the white pathfinders. North River was for a while styled the North Branch of the James. Until about 1760, South River was the River Mary, and Kerr's Creek was Tees Creek. The pioneers seem to have given names to all the water-courses, small as well as large, but some of their designations have gone out of use. In several instances some peculiar happening appears to have suggested the name. Thus, Whistle Creek was at first known as Can't Whistle Creek.

As a place for white occupancy, Rockbridge has natural advantages of a superior character. The climate is temperate and invigorating. Much of the soil is fertile, and the hillsides not brought under tillage are very useful for pasturage and as a forest reserve. The mineral wealth is very considerable, as is also the water power. And finally, the passes at Balcony Falls and Panther Gap have caused the county to be traversed by important railway lines.

II

SCENIC FEATURES

ROCKBRIDGE LANDSCAPES—THE NATURAL BRIDGE—GOSHEN PASS—BALCONY FALLS—HOUSE MOUNTAINS—THE JUMP

Appalachian America is renowned for its scenic beauty, and Rockbridge county has been granted an ample share. The Blue Ridge and the Alleghanies are geologically very old and have been eroded into a very great complexity of outline. Because of this wearing-down process, they do not exhibit the great elevations and the rugged features of young mountain systems, such as the Rockies and the Alps. But on the other hand there is more gracefulness of contour, the effect of which is greatly aided by the loveliness of the Appalachian forests in the summer season.

The five points of interest we are about to describe do not by any means exhaust the list of scenic attractions in Rockbridge county. Monotony is never present in the landscape. In touring this region, the visitor travels many miles in the thriving agricultural expanse of the Central Lowlands, dotted with its scores of comfortable farm homes; he passes through areas of more fertile bottom land, like the "Egypt field" of Kerr's Creek; he crosses the deep valley of the Buffalo, and follows the narrow, thickly populated creek valleys that lie in the evening shadows thrown by the North Mountain. And when his road crosses a mountain ridge, there is likely to be a delightful view that sweeps far out upon the lower levels.

Foremost among the scenic features is the world-famous Natural Bridge, to which the county owes its name. John Marshall, the chief justice, called this natural curiosity, "one of God's greatest miracles in stone." It was almost as well known to the Americans of three-fourths of a century ago as it is to those of the present day. It was represented by crude woodcuts in their school geographies, and in some other books of wide distribution. In the school reader was a thrilling account of how some foolhardy person tried to carve his name in the rock at a greater height than anyone else had reached. Ever since illustrated books on America have been on the market, the Natural Bridge has ranked with Niagara Falls as one of the most prominent subjects of pictorial art. By common consent it is one of the wonders of the Western World. It is, however, no more remarkable than the twin Tower Rocks of Pendleton county, West Virginia; but these are concealed in an almost unknown mountain hollow. It is less stupendous than the recently discovered natural bridges in Utah; but these lie in an arid and almost inaccessible region.

An explanation of the Natural Bridge of Virginia is not at all difficult. The Central Lowland of Rockbridge owes its existence and its peculiarities to the thick stratum of limestone that is not everywhere concealed by the surface soil. This layer, in common with the sandstones and shales of the mountain ridges, has been bent into almost every possible angle by upward thrusts coming from the interior of the earth. These titanic forces seam the rocks with lines of cleavage, both lateral and vertical. Into these narrow openings water forces its way, and when in the form of ice it acts as a lever to pry the seams farther apart. When charged with acids drawn from the air and from vegetable matter, water is a powerful solvent of limestone. The narrow crevice becomes broad; the shallow parting becomes deep. The rock deposit becomes honey-combed with water-channels, small and large. The water from the clouds ceases to flow on the surface, and finds its way into underground passageways. Extensive caverns are thus eaten into the limestone, and as these spread themselves laterally, the roof becomes weak, and here and there it falls. On the surface a limited area of subsidence is indicated by a sinkhole. When the underground stream has grown large and powerful, the roof gives way entirely for long distances. The creek now becomes visible, though flowing in a deep gorge. But atmospheric agencies begin at once to lessen the steepness of the walls of the canyon.

It is to the working of the process just described that the Natural Bridge owes its existence. Cedar Creek is a mountain stream rising in the Short Hills. After a quite direct course of hardly more than six miles it falls into the James at Gilmore Station. At some remote day it behaved like certain of the present watercourses in Monroe county, West Virginia. A short distance below its source it was drawn into a sinkhole and reappeared near the bank of the river. Little by little the roof of the subterranean channel collapsed. Nothing is now left but the arch where the support was thickest and strongest. This fragment is the Natural Bridge. It is significant that for a short distance, above and below, there is a precipitous wall on either side of the little stream. But although the slopes soon become much less abrupt, there is an extent of perhaps three miles within which it would be very difficult to build a road across the valley. The massive arch comes to the rescue by providing a perfectly easy passage, and a county road has used it since a very early day.

To view the bridge from below the visitor starts from the Natural Bridge Hotel and follows a path leading down a ravine to the brink of the creek. Looking upward, a sheet of limestone, sixty to 150 feet broad and with a span of ninety feet, is seen to connect the opposing cliffs. It is 215 feet to the arch, which is forty-eight feet thick. Almost overhanging the upper edge of the arch are the tops of trees and shrubs. Because of these the stranger traveling the county road is hardly aware when he is upon the bridge. The surface of the rock-wall under the arch scarcely permits any foothold for vegetation. The stone presents some diversity of color, the yellowish and reddish tints being due to iron oxide, better known as iron rust. When the trees are in full leaf, the gorge is shaded and cool, and the ruggedness of the canyon is greatly softened. But at any season the visitor can hardly fail to be impressed with the grandeur of the spectacle.

The Rockbridge pioneers must have known of the bridge from an early day, but we have no evidence that it made much impression on their matter-of-fact minds. The earliest published mention is by the English traveler, Burnaby, who wrote in 1759. It was twenty years later that lightning struck the arch and threw down a large mass of rock. The original patentee of the bridge, including some land immediately around, was not an actual settler, but a non-resident living in Albemarle. This was Thomas Jefferson, and the date of his patent is July 5, 1774. During the Revolution the bridge was twice visited by French scientists. The picture made from their measurements and diagrams was widely copied and was about the only one known prior to the invention of photography.

After Jefferson became President, he surveyed and mapped his patent with his own hands. The next year he built a two-roomed log cabin, and left it in charge of a negro named Patrick Henry. One of the rooms was to be kept open for the entertainment of visitors. He also left a large book in which visitors might record their "sentiments." This was written full, but was accidentally destroyed in 1845. The property did not pass out of the Jefferson estate until 1833. It is to be regretted that the author of the Declaration of Independence did not convey this ground to the State, or to the National government, so that it might at all times be freely open to the public, as in the case of the Yosemite Valley of California.

It was in 1802 that Jefferson built the cabin above mentioned. Ever since that time the bridge has been much visited. Marshall, Monroe, Clay, Van Buren, Jackson, Benton, and Houston were among the earlier of the American notabilities who have viewed this "bridge not made with hands."

When he was a young man, the agile and well-muscled Washington climbed to a niche some twenty feet above the waters and carved his name. This exploit was very much exceeded by Thomas Piper, a foolhardy student. He placed his name higher than anyone else had done, and finding he could not return he accomplished the almost incredible feat of climbing to the top. A very narrow ledge, perhaps a hundred feet above the creek level, is pointed out as the place another person reached, but he had to be rescued by means of a rope let down from the top of the cliff. Several other individuals have been less fortunate, and a few fatalities are on record. In 1843 a stranger leaped from the bridge. If he intended to commit suicide, he accomplished his purpose.

Goshen Pass was formerly known as Dunlap's Gap and then as Strickler's Pass. It extends from near the mouth of the Little Calfpasture to Wilson's Springs, a distance of five miles. Just below the mouth of the tributary mentioned, North River begins its sinuous passage of the North Mountain. The heights, which sometimes tower a thousand feet above the swirling waters, are not generally so steep as to be destitute of a growth of wood, and in summer the forest verdure adds much to the grace and beauty of the scene. Yet here and there is a vertical ledge exhibiting the flexures worked into the stratum by the upward pressure of the earth's crust in remote geologic periods. The river is constantly flowing over or among masses of rock and is a continuous cascade. A new vista opens with every bend in the road, and the stranger who goes from one end of the pass to the other and then retraces his steps finds the return nearly as replete with interest as the advance. There is not a house and not an acre of tilled land within the pass, and the view is well-nigh as primeval as it was in the day of the Indian. And yet the road was once a busy thoroughfare, a line of stages running between Lexington and Goshen.

When Matthew F. Maury was a resident of Lexington, he liked to visit this watergap in early summer. His admiration for it was so great that one of his final requests was that his remains should be taken to their permanent resting place by way of Goshen Pass, and when the laurel should be in bloom. This direction was faithfully carried out. In going through the pass the procession halted a while at the foot of a low cliff and below a sharp point of rock projecting over the road. Soon afterward, an anchor, taken from the pontoon bridge left at East Lexington by General Hunter; was suspended from the projection. With a strange want of consideration, this suitable memento was at length taken down by some person and carried away. It was the abundance of rhododendron along the river border that caused a very narrow belt of low ground to be named Poison Bottom. Fresh herbage is so eagerly devoured by domestic animals in early spring that they will eat laurel leaves when nothing else is to be had and sickness is the result.

Another interesting watergap is the pass at Balcony Falls. This is one of the two places in Virginia where the Blue Ridge opens to its base, so as to permit the passage of a river. Looking from the town of Glasgow, a stranger might not suspect the existence of the gap. He will imagine that an exceedingly narrow valley is making a zigzag approach to the west from the axis of the Blue Ridge. As in the case of Goshen Pass, there is not a house in the four miles of the passage. The mountain slopes are unbroken by clearings, and except for the railway and the county road, the scenery is that of the virgin wilderness. The

James falls about 200 feet in going through the defile, and in the days of batteau navigation it was a danger point.

To the person standing on College Hill at Lexington, the view toward the west is dominated by an imposing height of unusual form. This is Little House Mountain, and it has carried this name ever since the day of the white explorer. The name was evidently suggested by the shape of the elevation. The summit, half a mile long, is almost horizontal. At each end there is an abrupt falling away, the mountain terminating in either direction in a concave slope of heavy grade. The eastward and westward slopes are likewise steep, and all the way around the mountain is an unbroken forest rising from a stony surface. When the observer changes his point of observation to Fancy Hill or to the divide between Kerr's Creek and North River, he discovers the existence of Big House Mountain, which from Lexington is almost completely eclipsed by its companion. The two mountains lie side by side, and are parallel to North Mountain. The distance from summit to summit is less than a mile, and the valley between is very deep. Big House Mountain is camel-backed and is the higher of the two, although the difference in altitude is not conspicuous. Since the House mountains rise like islands from the floor of the Valley of Virginia, their isolation, their lofty summits, and their exceptional form render them a striking feature in a Rockbridge landscape. They may be seen to good advantage from the Matthews mansion near Glasgow, fifteen miles away as the crow flies, and on a clear day they are in plain view from Flag Rock on Warm Springs Mountain, almost twenty miles distant. Conversely, a very large portion of Rockbridge may be viewed from the summit of Little House Mountain. The view from its companion is less satisfactory because of its less favorable position. From Lexington the twin heights are so conspicuous and so imposing that the residents regard them with a feeling akin to affection.

Certain legends are associated with the House Mountains. One of these relates to a man named Shepherd, who lived a while at the high-lying rock which ever since has borne his name. He was often noticed poring over a small book carried in a leather pouch. At intervals not frequent he came down to Collier's Creek and paid for provisions in bright new coins. He was at first suspected of being a horse-thief, but he turned out to be a counterfeiter of silver quarters. Shepherd found it expedient to go away, but the credulous continued to see lights on Shepherd Rock which would vanish when approached. Some searching has here been done for pots of silver.

Jump Mountain has a very precipitous face toward the east. It is so named because of a legend of a battle between Indians at the mouth of Walker's Creek. The story relates that an Indian woman watched the conflict from the mountain, and when she saw her husband fall she threw herself over the precipice.

But she must have possessed telescopic eyes to recognize her mate at a distance of at least two miles. As for the alleged battle, it probably rests on no more substantial basis than the former existence of the Walker's Creek mound, an account of which is given in Chapter VIII.

Of Crystal Spring in Arnold's Valley, there is the following beautiful legend. An Indian warrior loved a maid of a hostile tribe, and gave her a gem which his people had brought from beyond the Father of Waters. It was transparent, and she wore it in her necklace of beads. The trysting-place was a spring. A jealous lover of her own tribe found her here and snatched away the jewel. She caught his hand, recovered the crystal, and threw it behind her into the spring, where it dissolved, and gave to the water its purity and its sparkle.

III

THE ULSTERMAN AND THE PATHFINDERS

STRATHCLYDE AND ULSTER—SCOTLAND IN 1600—THE ULSTERMEN—THEIR RELATIONS WITH THE BRITISH GOVERNMENT—THE EMIGRATION TO AMERICA—AMERICA AND VIRGINIA IN 1716—PENNSYLVANIA AND THE IMMIGRANTS—THE AMERICAN HIGHLANDER—SPOTTSWOOD—SALLING

In the story of the world's progress, the American Republic is a colonial extension of Europe. As a white man's country, its history has therefore a European background. This background must be studied if the development of our country is to be properly understood.

For the history of the upper Valley of Virginia the European background is to be sought in the southwest of Scotland and the north of Ireland; in Strathclyde and in Ulster, respectively. In latitude, and in surface, soil, and climate, the two regions are much alike. In each there are mountains, usually deforested and sometimes gaunt and gloomy, which are similar in height to the elevations rising above the floor of the Valley of Virginia. In each there are fine swift streams, comparable in volume to the North River at Lexington, or to its tributary, the Buffalo. In each the surface alternates from mountain to valley, and from broken ridges to small tracts comparatively level. In each the soil is often stony, sometimes excessively so, and in general is not highly fertile or easily tilled. The mean annual temperature is fifty degrees, as against fifty-four at Lexington. The winter temperature is noticeably milder than that of Rockbridge, but the summer is very much cooler, being scarcely so warm as a Rockbridge May. The climate, cool, cloudy, and humid, is suited to grass, oats, and root crops, and either region is better adapted to grazing than to tillage. A domestic rather than an outdoor life is indicated, while the stony and often spongy soil compels habits of industry and thrift. And since the aspect of nature is stern rather than smiling, and the sky more often cloudy than fair, it need not surprise us that these lands have nurtured a sober, thoughtful, matter-of-fact, unemotional race, with a higher appreciation of the obviously useful than of the merely beautiful.

The above description of the countries on the two sides of the North Channel suggests a certain measure of resemblance to the Shenandoah Valley and the Appalachian uplands. The rock formations are of the same geologic periods and the soils are similar in texture. The degree of resemblance goes far to explain why the immigrant from Ulster has so successfully adapted himself to Appalachian America. The sky proved to be warmer and sunnier, yet the new home was not strikingly dissimilar, as was found to be the case with the Mississippi Basin and the plains and mountains beyond.

The southwest of Scotland was once Strathclyde, a petty kingdom about the size of Connecticut. It was at length overrun by the neighboring kingdom of Northumbria, and the native Celtic speech gave place to the Saxon. This circumstance does not imply that the old population was displaced. The prevalent idea that the people of Scotland and England are predominantly Germanic is incorrect, and was disproved before the late war had burst upon the world. Consequently the experts who have investigated the matter did not have this tragedy to bias their conclusions. The population of the British Isles is mainly of the elements that held possession in the days of Cæsar. The invading bands of Anglen, Saxons, and Jutes overran the lowlands on the instalment plan, and full success did not come for many years. By assimilating with the natives they gave the country a new language and new institutions. But whether Highlanders or Lowlanders, the Scottish people are essentially one with respect to origin. The Lowlands gave up the old speech, while the Highlands retained it. And it is worthy of notice that the dialect of English spoken in the Lowlands differs little from the everyday speech of the north of England.

When Jamestown and Plymouth were being founded, Scotland had about one-sixth of its present population, perhaps 200,000 of the number being in Strathclyde. But this corner of Scotland has furnished a disproportionate share of the great names that occur in Scottish history. Its people of this period were tall, lean, hardy, and sinewy. They were ignorant of high living and had good nerves and digestion. They were combative, and not easy to get along with to those who did not fall in with their ways. They were strong-willed and strongly individualistic, and were therefore fierce sticklers for personal liberty. By the same token they were more democratic in thought than the English and were less inclined to commercial pursuits. To challenge this Scotsman's views of right and wrong roused him to speedy action. He was either quite bad or quite good. In the former respect, he fought, swore, was given to gaming and racing, and drank plentifully from his whiskey jug. In the latter respect, his morality had a solid groundwork, being based on general education and on regular attendance at his house of worship. Outwardly he was unemotional and not given to displays of affection. Yet there was more sunshine in his life than is commonly believed.

It had been only a few years since John Knox had caused the Protestant Reformation to triumph in Scotland. Nowhere in Europe was this movement effected more peacefully. In England the Reformation was like an inverted pyramid, in that it began with the sovereign and the court party. In Scotland it began with the common people, and was in reality a return to the form of Christianity first preached in the land. It has been said, and perhaps without much exaggeration, that Scotland emerged from barbarism within the span of a single generation of human life. Knox insisted on a school in every parish. And as thrift has been a watchword of Protestantism from the first, the Scotch fell into the habit of mending their clothes till they would no longer hold together, and of saving every nubbin and potato. From a coarse, rough, unruly horde of semi-barbarians, scornful of steady labor, the Scotch became a religious, industrious, energetic people, mindful of the main chance, and able to hold their own against all comers. Yet the change was slow to make them recognize that a cottage looks better for having a flowering vine climbing up the gable, or that a house of worship should have a higher degree of architectural grace than the "little red schoolhouse" that is not as yet forgotten in America.

Scotland united with England on her own terms. Ireland, on the contrary, was subdued, and to the impoverishment by absentee landlords was added the oppression of harsh laws with respect to religion and industry. Under James the First, whose reign began in 1603, an unsuccessful rising of the Irish was punished by the confiscation of more than 3,000,000 acres of Ulster soil. This area had become partially depopulated, and the English king made successful efforts to re-people it with settlers from the other side of the Irish Sea. Already some lawless Highlanders had flocked in, but they were a most undesirable element, and preference was now given to the Lowlanders.

When the descendants of these colonists began coming to America, they were called Irish for the very practical reason that they came from Ireland. Irishmen of the original stock were scarce in the United States before the enormous immigration caused by the potato famine of 1845. The term Scotch-Irish came into use to distinguish the earlier inflow from the later. This term is firmly fixed in popular usage, and yet it is rather misleading. It implies that the people thus styled are the descendants of Scotchmen who settled in Ireland. This is true only in part. The Scotch of Strathclyde were the most numerous element and they gave their impress to the entire mass. But there were nearly as many settlers from the north of England, and there were a few from Wales. There were also not a few Huguenot refugees from France. It was the talented French Protestants, coming at the instance of William of Orange, who introduced the linen industry into Ulster and made it the basis of its manufacturing prosperity. And finally, some of the native Irish blended with the immigrant population. It is customary to deny any such fusion, and so far as religion is concerned, there was none. The newcomers were Presbyterians, while the natives were Catholics. In Ulster these two elemnts have never ceased to dislike one another. Yet the rather frequent occurrence of native Irish names among the emigrants from Ulster has a very obvious significance. It shows that here and there the native accepted the Protestant faith, and that neither social nor religious barriers then remained. It is not a characteristic of the Ulster people to turn a cold shoulder toward those who agree with them. J. W. Dinsmore observes that the Ulsterman "has the steadfastness of the Scot, the rugged strength and aggressive force of the Saxon, and a dash of the vivacity and genius of the Huguenot." He might have added that when the Ulsterman came to America he spoke the Elizabethan type of English, which the Irish adopted as an incident in their conquest.

It is now necessary to speak of the relations between the Ulstermen and the British government. There was a Church of Ireland, identical except in name with the Church of England. Though it had few adherents, the law was behind it, and it laid a heavy hand on Dissenters as well as Catholics. The Presbyterian minister was expected to preach only within certain specified limits, and was liable to be fined, deported, or imprisoned. He could not legally unite a couple in marriage, and at times he could preach only by night and in some barn. The infamous "Black Oath" of 1639 required all the Protestants of Ulster who were above the age of sixteen to bind themselves to an implicit obedience to all royal commands whatsoever. This display of autocratic tyranny led multitudes of men and women to hide in the woods or to flee to Scotland.

In 1689 the Irish rose in behalf of the deposed king of England, James the Second. Protestants were shot down at their homes. Women were tied to stakes at low tide, so that they might drown when the ocean waves came back. Londonderry was besieged by a large army, but was defended with a desperation unsurpassed in history. Without help from the English, without trained officers, without sufficient food or ammunition, and in the face of deadly fever, the invaders were beaten off with great loss. This staunch support of the new king would seem to have entitled the Ulstermen to much consideration. Nevertheless, the British Parliament enforced its anti-popery laws against the Presbyterians as well as the Catholics. The time had not yet come when a Presbyterian might sell religious books, teach anything above a primary school, or hold civil or military office. There was no general redress of grievances until 1782.

The persecution was industrial as well as religious. English laws discriminated against Ulster manufactures, particularly the manufacture of woolen goods. This flourishing business was ruined by a law of 1698.

In view of such a hounding persecution, it might seem strange that the people of Ulster could retain a shred of respect for their government. Yet, as citizens of the British Isles, they professed loyalty to the crown, which by a figure of speech signified the state in its sovereign capacity. They appear to have had no ill feeling toward the king himself. He did them no harm, because he did nothing at all in a governmental sense. From 1704 to 1760 the English monarch was a figurehead in almost the fullest sense of the term. The resentment of the Ulster people was directed against the corrupt clique that governed in the king's name. However, there was a ruling English party in Ulster. At the present time, Episcopalians are more numerous than Presbyterians, in at least two of the seven counties, and the Catholic population is equal to the Protestant. It is a mistake to think of Presbyterians as outnumbering other denominations in Ulster.

The straw that broke the camel's back for the Ulster people was the display of greed shown about 1723. A large quantity of land given to favored individuals was offered only on 31-year leases and at two to three times the former rental. An emigration to America, which really began about 1718, now assumed large dimensions. During the next half century, or until interrupted by the war for American independence, the aggregate outflow is reckoned by some authorities as high as 300,000. Ulster was thus drained of the larger and best part of its population. The fundamental reasons for the exodus are thus stated in a sermon delivered on the eve of the sailing of a ship: "To avoid oppression and cruel bondage; to shun persecution and designed ruin; to withdraw from the communion of idolators; to have opportunity to worship God according to the dictates of conscience and the rules of his Word."

Throughout this period of heavy emigration from Ulster there was almost as large a tide of Germans from the valley of the upper Rhine, inclusive of Switzerland. But until near the outbreak of the Revolution, the German settlers in Rockbridge were very few. So it is scarcely necessary, at present, to speak further on this parallel stream of immigration.

It is next in order to sketch the America of 1716, so as to observe the effect of the inflow from Ulster and the Rhine.

There were at this time twelve of the English colonies, and their 400,000 inhabitants were scattered thinly along the coast from Casco Bay in Maine to Port Royal in South Carolina. Exceedingly few were the people who were located so far inland as a hundred miles. Boston, New York, Philadelphia, and Charleston were the largest towns, and not one of them had a population of 10,000. The colonies must have presented a very new appearance, but not of a truly pioneer type. The homes of all but the poorest people were as good as the better class of homes in Europe. There was a lively commerce with the British Isles and with the West Indies, the products of the farms, the forests. and the fisheries being exchanged for manufactured goods and for sugar and other tropical supplies. There were but three colleges. Elementary education was general only in New England. Elsewhere, education was regarded as a private interest, and there was much illiteracy. There was no mail service worthy of the name, no daily newspaper, and perhaps not more than a half dozen weeklies. Religion was free only in Rhode Island and Pennsylvania. Elsewhere there was an established church supported by general taxation. The colonials of 1716 were overwhelmingly of English origin, but there was a sprinkling of Scotch, Welsh, Irish, Hollanders, and French Huguenots. Each colony was an independent country with respect to its neighbors. And as roads were bad and bridges few, traveling was slow and difficult. All knowledge of the outside world was elementary. There was no intercourse with Asia or South America, Africa was visited only in the interest of the slave trade, and Australia was unknown. Every sea was infested with pirate vessels.

Turning to Virginia we find that its 100,000 people, of whom one-fourth were negro slaves, lived almost exclusively to the east of a line drawn through Washington and Richmond. Williamsburg, the capital, was merely a village. Norfolk was doubtless smaller than Lexington is now. Virginia was strictly an agricultural region, and the growing of tobacco was by far the dominant interest. The structure of society was not democratic. At the head of the scale was the tidewater aristocracy, feudalistic and reactionary, polite to women, profane among its own kind, fond of horses and sports, and indifferent to books. These people constituted the one and only ruling class, and the public business thrown upon them induced a good degree of practical intelligence. Below them were the professional men, tradesmen, small farmers, and white servants, some of the latter having come to America as convicts.

Such in outline was the America of 1716. Most of its people were American-born and were beginning to look upon themselves as distinct from the British. Nearly all of the new immigration landed at Philadelphia, because the colony of which it was the metropolis was held in high repute across the Atlantic for the liberality of its government. In 1769 the French traveler Cluny declared of Pennsylvania that "its form of civil government is better calculated to promote private happiness and consequently public prosperity than any other with which we are acquainted under the sun." But the immigrants found a difference between its theory and its practice. It is instinctive in the human species to look with suspicion or dislike on those whose ways are different from our own. The comfortable Quakers did not like the idea of being swamped by this deluge of strange people, one portion of whom spoke an unfamiliar language, while the other portion appeared assertive, somewhat uncouth, and not overly particular in costume or personal cleanliness. There was scant welcome for the newcomers in the small settled district, and so they pushed inland, the Germans moving rather to the right and the Ulstermen to the left. Had the Quakers been more inclined to observe the spirit of their institutions, they would have retained most of this immigration and the settlement of the Valley of Virginia would have been much delayed. The Ulstermen were very much inclined to keep together. It was usual for a whole congregation, headed by its pastor, to leave Ireland in a body and to seek to settle as neighbors after coming to America. But a tax was laid on the immigrants, they were kept as long as possible from having any effective voice in the colonial government, and when the war of 1754 broke out, there was a failure to protect the frontier. Thus we are the better able to understand why some of the Ulster people lived a while in Pennsylvania instead of coming directly to Virginia. The liberality of Pennsylvania was largely outweighed by its narrowness, and so the Ulstermen pushed southward as well as westward, gradually occupying all Appalachian America from the Iroquois country south of Lake Ontario to the Cherokee country on the waters of the upper Tennessee. In this way the inland frontier of America was pushed rapidly forward. Otherwise the year 1776 might have found in Virginia but a handful of people west of the Blue Ridge.

In the way we have pointed out, the Ulstermen became a frontier people as soon as they were settled in America. They were well fitted to become such. They were overcomers by nature and did not shrink from facing difficulties. They wanted room and plenty of it, and they wished to bury on their own soil instead of on the domain of some detested landlord.

The Ulstermen were joined by some of the Germans, and by some of the more venturesome spirits among the English and Hollanders of the coast settlements, both northern and southern. The pioneer population of the Alleghany valleys thus developed into a composite stock, that of the American Highlander. This homogeneity moved more rapidly in a blending of customs than in a mixture of blood. But it was the Scotch-Irish who gave a dominant impress to the entire frontier.

Before taking up the settlement of Rockbridge, it is necessary to tell of the discovery and exploration of "New Virginia," this term being applied to that part of the Old Dominion which attracted the Ulster people.

For more than a century after the founding of Jamestown there was no clear knowledge of what lay beyond the Blue Ridge. An exploring party had indeed penetrated as far as the falls of New River as early as 1671, but this spurt of enterprise was not followed up. In a letter to the Board of Trade in 1710, Governor Spottswood remarks that some adventurous men had just climbed the Blue Ridge, hitherto deemed impassable, and would have proceeded down the west slope but for the lateness of the season.

The governor became interested. He thought the distance to the Great Lakes much less than it really is, and he believed it sound policy to keep the

French from getting the fur trade entirely into their hands. He therefore recommended that trading stations be established on the lakes, and that they be connected with the Virginia coast by a chain of fortified posts. To look into this matter in person, he headed an exploring party that left Williamsburg in the summer of 1716, and spent thirty-six days in reaching the summit of the Blue Ridge, probably at Swift Run Gap. The South Fork of the Shenandoah was forded in the vicinity of Elkton, and the next day—September 6th—the gay cavaliers who comprised most of the fifty men held a grand revel on the dozen varieties of liquor they had brought with them. After each toast there was a volley of powder and ball. Spottswood made no attempt to prosecute the exploration, and contented himself with viewing the Alleghany ridges from a distance. We hear nothing more of his zeal in the fur trade. The behavior of the whole party was that of a crowd of young bloods bent on a jollification in the mountains.

Nevertheless, an important result came of this expedition. Now that glimpses by rangers or hunters had been supplemented by a visit from the governor and a delegation of the tidewater aristocracy, it could be announced that the Valley of Virginia was officially discovered. It had been assumed that it was a forbidding land. On the contrary it was found to be pleasant and fertile, and abounding in game and fish. There were no Indian occupants, although a grassy prairie covered the lowlands between the Blue Ridge and the Alleghanies beyond. It was a vision to appeal to the land speculator, and it did not appeal in vain.

It was sixteen years before John Lewis came with his advance guard of Ulster people into the presents limits of Virginia. But although exact information is provokingly scarce, it is very clear that during this interval land prospectors were busy in spying out the country and naming the mountains and streams. It was only eleven years after Spottswood's visit that a company of tidewater promoters petitioned for 50,000 acres on the headwaters of the James, almost before there was a solitary cabin in the Shenandoah Valley itself.

During the period of exploration, the one and only conspicuous name among the known landhunters, so far as the Rockbridge area is concerned, is that of John Peter Salling. According to the usual version of the story, Salling went up the Valley from the Potomac in 1726, in company with John Marlin, a pedler or trapper. On the Roanoke they were attacked by Indians and Salling was captured. He was taken from his Cherokee captors by some Illinois Indians and wandered with them to Kaskaskia, where he was adopted by a squaw. Several times he went down the Mississippi with the red men, and at length the Spaniards bought him to use as an interpreter. From New Orleans he in some way was taken to Canada, where he was redeemed by the governor of that province, and sent by him to the Hollanders of New York. After six years of varied experiences he arrived at Williamsburg. The traditions in the Salling family agree in stating that the pioneer ancestor was several years a captive among the Indians, by whom he was taken to the lower Mississippi. According to Henry Ruffner, who wrote in 1844, Marlin met Salling in Williamsburg and so interested the latter by his description of the Valley that both men went up the James as far as the beautiful bottom immediately above Balcony Falls. Salling was so well pleased that he did not wish to look further. He returned to the capital, patented a choice portion of the bottom, and settled on it with his bachelor brother. Salling's home was so well known as to be marked on a map of 1755.

It was in the summer of 1732 that John Lewis came with his family and built a house a mile below where Staunton now stands. So far as known he was the first settler in Augusta county. According to Ruffner and others, Lewis visited Williamsburg before making any settlement, and there met Salling, whose roseate description of the "back country" led him to choose land on Lewis Creek. But it is known that Lewis fled from Ireland as a refugee from British law. He was at length pardoned, but until this took place he would not have exposed himself to arrest. He is known to have spent a few years in Pennsylvania before coming to Virginia, and it is possible that the pardon was as early as 1732. But he did not acquire title to his land until 1738.

IV

THE BORDEN LAND GRANT

THE McDOWELLS—BENJAMIN BORDEN, SR.—THE VIRGINIA LAND SYSTEM—SETTLEMENT OF
THE BORDEN TRACT—BENJAMIN BORDEN, JR.—DISPUTES WITH
THE SETTLERS—JOSEPH BORDEN

Early in September, 1737, a little party of homeseekers were in camp on Linville Creek in what is now Rockingham county. They were journeying by the trail that was sometimes called the Indian Road, and sometimes the Pennsylvania Road. In the company were Ephraim McDowell, a man now past the meridian of life, his son John, and a son-in-law, James Greenlee. The younger men were accompanied by their families. It is rather probable that a few other persons were in the party, especially one or more indentured servants. The destination they had in view was South River. James, another son of Ephraim, had come in advance and planted a little field of corn in that valley opposite Woods Gap.

The McDowells had come from Ulster in "the good ship, *George and Ann*," landing at Philadelphia, September 4, 1729, after being on the Atlantic 118 days. This was a slow voyage, even in those days of sailing vessels, and yet it was not unusual. As in many other instances among the Ulster people, Pennsylvania was only a temporary home. The country west and southwest of the metropolis, as far as the Susquehanna and the Maryland line, was now well-peopled, according to the standard of that agricultural age. Land was relatively high in price, and so the newcomers, if they had to move inland to the advance line of settlement ,often thought they might as well look for homes in "New Virginia." John Lewis, a kinsman to the McDowells, had founded in 1732 the nucleus of the Augusta settlement, and by this time several hundred of the Ulster people had located around him. Religion was not free in Virginia, but it was doubtless the belief of the newcomers that the planters of Tidewater, who were the rulers of the colony, would not deem it wise to molest them in their adherence to the Presbyterian faith.

To afford the reader some idea of what Pennsylvania was in 1729, we give a synopsis of a letter written about that time by a young man to his sister in Ireland.

The writer pronounces Pennsylvania the best country in the world for tradesmen and working people. Land was twenty-five cents to $2.50 an acre, according to quality and location, and was rapidly advancing because of the large and varied immigration. His father, after a long and cautious search, made a

choice about thirty miles from Philadelphia. For 500 acres of prime land,
inclusive of a small log house, a clearing of twenty acres, and a young orchard,
the purchase price was $875.00. In the meantime the father had rented a
place and put 200 acres in wheat, a crop that commanded fifty cents a bushel.
Oats were twenty-eight cents a bushel, and corn was twenty-five cents. The
laboring man had about twenty cents a day in winter. In harvest time he was
paid thirty cents a day, this service including the best of food and a pint of
rum. At the end of his swath he would find awaiting him some meat, either
boiled or roasted, and some cakes and tarts. One to two acres could be plowed in
a day, which was twice the speed that could be made in Ireland. A boy of
thirteen years could hold the implement, which had a wooden mouldboard.
Horses were smaller than in Ireland, but pacing animals could cover fifteen
miles in an hour's time. At Philadelphia, then a little city of perhaps 5,000
inhabitants, all kinds of provisions were extraordinarily plentiful. Wednesdays
and Saturdays were market days. Meat of any kind could be had for two and
one-half cents a pound. Nearly every farmhouse had an orchard of apple,
peach, and cherry trees. Wheat yielded twenty bushels to the acre and turnips
200. The writer corrects several false reports about the colony which had been
carried to the other side of the ocean. He said there had as yet been no sickness
in the family, and that not a member of it was willing to live in Ireland again.
The cost of passage to the mother country was $22.50.

There must have been some regret among the Ulster people that it was not
easy to secure a foothold in such a thriving district as the Philadelphia region.
But America was a land of opportunity, whether on the coast or in the interior.

It was just after the McDowells had established their camp on Linville
Creek that an incident occurred which led to some change in destination. A man
giving his name as Benjamin Borden* came along and arranged to spend the
night with them. He told them he had a grant of 100,000 acres on the waters
of the James, if he could ever find it. To the man who could show him the
boundaries he would give 1,000 acres. John McDowell replied that he was a
surveyor and would accept the offer. A torch was lighted, McDowell showed
his surveying instruments, and Borden his papers. Each party was satisfied with
the representations made by the other. At the house of John Lewis, where they
remained a few days, a more formal contract was entered into, the phraseology
of which indicates that it was written by Borden. The document reads as follows:

---

*The name is sometimes, but erroneously, written Burden. This spelling doubtless
indicates a very usual pronunciation in the pioneer period. But in their signatures, the
members of the family used the spelling Borden.

Sept. ye 19th 1737

This day John McDowell of Orange County in Virginia have agreed with Benjamin Borden of the same place that he the said McDowell would go now with his family and his father and his Brothers and make four Settlements in the said Bordens land which was granted to the said Borden on this side of the blue ridge in the fork of said River, and said McDowell has also agreed with the said Borden that he the sd McDowell would cut a good Road for Horses loaded with common Luggage and blaze the Trees all the way plain, and also the said McDowell has agreed with the said Benjamin Borden that he the said McDowell would go with the sd Borden and take account of the Settlement of Borden Land on the River at the place called the Chimbly Stone and on Smith Creek and be evidence for the said Borden of all his settlements aforesaid, and in consideration of the premises the said Borden is to give one thousand acres of Land when he the said McDowell build in the sd fork of the sd River and the sd Borden is to give the said McDowell good lawfull Deed as the said Borden can get of the King clear of all charges excepting the quitrents & also the said Borden do here agree to give to these the other three Settlements six hundred acres of Land clear of all charges as before excepted and the said McDowell is to go down with a compt (count) of all the Settlements as aforesaid with Borden to his House by the tenth day of October next to go with said Borden to Colo Willis to price the Settlements as aforesaid as witness my hand

BENJAMIN BORDEN

The lands at the Chimney Stone and on Smith Creek lay in the lower Shenandoah Valley.

Accompanied by John McDowell, Borden went on from Lewis's and camped at a spring where Midway now is. From this point the men followed the outlet of the spring to South River, and continued to the mouth of that stream, returning by a course. Borden could now see that he was within the boundaries of his grant. John McDowell built a cabin on the farm occupied by Andrew Scott in 1806. This was the first white man's settlement in the Borden Tract. The McDowells had never heard of this grant, and it had been their intention to locate in Beverly Manor.

All Virginia west of the Blue Ridge was until the establishment of Augusta and Frederick in 1738 a part of Orange county, and the seat of local government was near the present town of Orange. But so far as treaty engagements had any force, the Borden Tract lay in the Indian country. It was not until 1744 that the treaty of Albany was superseded by that of Lancaster. The former recognized the Blue Ridge as the border of the Indian domain. The latter moved the boundary back to the Indian Road, already mentioned. The red men were within their rights when they hunted in the Valley, or passed through on war expeditions. In point of fact the whites were trespassers. But the American borderer has seldom stood back from this form of trespass whenever he was in contact with desirable wild land.

Borden remained about two years on his grant, spending a portion of the time with a Mrs. Hunter, whose daughter married a Green, and to whom Borden

gave the place they were living on when he left. There is a statement that
Borden sailed to England and brought back a large company of settlers. This
is very doubtful. Such action was not necessary. He did advertise his lands,
and to such effect that more than 100 families located on the Tract within the
two years. But immigrants were arriving at Philadelphia almost every week,
sometimes to the number of hundreds, and efficient advertising was certain to
bring the desired results. When Borden went back to his home near Winchester, he left his papers with John McDowell, to whose house many of the prospectors came in order to be shown the parcels they thought of buying. Three
years later he died on the manor-place he had patented in 1734.

Benjamin Borden, Sr., came from New Jersey, where the name Bordentown commemorates an early settlement by the family. It is manifest that his
education was meager. The language of his will, which resembles that of the
contract given in this chapter, is boyish and crude, and defective in spelling and
grammar. The personalty inventoried in the settlement of his estate made a
total of $487. The house furnishings were simple and primitive, many of them
being listed as "old" and of little value. The items include a servant man, two
stallions and seventeen other horses, seventeen cattle, seven sheep, three small
hogs, a silver watch scheduled at $10.42, a half-dozen chairs, and some carpenter
tools. In ready means Borden did not quite rank with some of the other early
settlers of Frederick. But as a business man he was shrewd, alert, and tactful,
and was what would now be styled a "plunger." Besides "Borden's Great
Tract," and several much smaller patents in the valley of the James, he owned
land in New Jersey and in several localities in the Shenandoah. On his homestead was a mill. It is said that he came to the frontier as a trader, and he
unquestionably knew a good thing when he saw it. His prominence among the
pioneers in the Valley is reflected in the fact that he was a justice of Orange and
afterward of Frederick. William Edmondson relates that "old Mr. Borden
was cunning and polite," and that he had heard older men laugh in telling of
Borden's fertility of resource in meeting all objections. Where the timber was
scanty, he was able to see "a fine young growth." Where the soil was poor, he
"grandly observed fine sheep walks."

Benjamin Borden, Sr., was probably less than fifty years old when he died.
His sons were Benjamin, Jr., John, and Joseph, the last named being a small boy
at that time. His daughters were Hannah, Martha, Abigail, Rebecca, Deborah,
Lydia, and Elizabeth. Four were already married, Hannah to Edward Rogers,
Martha to William Fernley, Abigail to Jacob Worthington, and Rebecca to a
Branson. Abigail subsequently married James Pritchard. After their father's
death, Deborah married a Henry, and Elizabeth a Nicholas. Lydia married
Jacob Peck, who came from Germany in 1745, and lived until 1797, to figure

prominently in the Borden litigation. The will left to Abigail, Rebecca, Deborrah, Lydia, and Elizabeth, "5,000 acres that is all good," out of the grreat tract on the James. The rest of his lands, excepting the homestead, which was willed to the sons, and in dower to Zeruiah, the widow, he ordered to be sold, and the proceeds divided equally between the widow, the sons, and six of the daughters. To Hannah, the remaining daughter, was given 800 acres of the homestead. The executors were the widow, Benjamin, Jr., and William Fernley, whose bond, with William Russell and John Hardin as sureties, was in the sum of 500 pounds. In 1745 the widow gave Benjamin, Jr., a power of attorney with respect to sales in the Great Tract, and the following year the latter came into exclusive control of it. The other sons conveyed their interest to Russell.

According to one writer, the elder Borden was an agent for Lord Fairfax in settling the Northern Neck. This is very possible. But the statement by Henry Ruffner that he was a son-in-law to Colonel James Patton is incorrect.

We are somewhat in the dark as to his prestige in securing so large a grant as the one in Rockbridge. He visited the colonial capital shortly before he met the McDowells. It is affirmed, and probably with truth, that he ingratiated himself with the governor. That official, his son-in-law, and two other men were interested in getting into their personal control some of the land on the upper James. Mrs. Greenlee, sister to John McDowell, says these men assigned their interest to him in the course of a frolic, which of course had its inspiration in liquor. The younger Borden, during his administration of the estate, told Samuel McDowell, the son of John, that the estate was much in debt, especially to one Lauderdale, who seems to have been one of the original grantees. Mrs. Greenlee further relates that one Hardin, who may have been the same as the bondsman to the executors of the will of the elder Borden, offered James McDowell the unsold lands in return for a bottle of wine, provided McDowell would assume the liability for the payment of quit-rent. But Ephraim McDowell counseled against any such transaction, telling his son it might get him into trouble.

A silly story has been repeated time after time to the effect that Borden and Lewis visited the capital with a buffalo calf and presented it to Governor Gooch, causing that dignitary to be so tickled as to sign away the title to 100,000 acres of the public domain. The buffalo never roamed in the Tidewater, yet was plentiful in the Indian meadows of the Valley, and was necessarily known to the governor. Gooch, who was one of the best of the colonial executives, was too sensible a man to be carried off his feet by the present of a shaggy, ungainly, and ungrown beast. As for Borden, he was not the man to lead the calf all the way to Williamsburg, without feeling some assurance that the childish proceeding would be worth his while. A colonial land-grant, like the one made in favor of Borden, was on stipulated conditions and with the concurrence of the Colonial Council.

It is now in place to tell how and for what announced purpose such a large grant came to be made to a private person who was without aristocratic birth or connections.

The immigrant to colonial Virginia, provided he was of age and could prove he had paid the cost of his passage from Europe, could claim a "head-right," entitling him to fifty acres of public land. He was further entitled to fifty acres for each male member of his household. He was required to settle on the land, to improve at least six per cent of the acreage, and to pay each year a quit-rent of one shilling for each fifty acres. On taking up a head-right, he paid a fee of five shillings. The tendency of this law was to fill Virginia with a substantial class of citizens. The working of it was much the same as that of the present homestead law of the Federal government.

But the governor, with the concurrence of the Council, could grant a huge block of land to an individual, or a group of men acting as a company. The theory of the order of council was to settle within a stated time a minimum number of families on the tract. The grantee was supposed to be restrained from charging more than a specified price per acre. He issued deeds, just as though the block was owned by himself in fee-simple. In practice, there was created a proprietorship, usually non-resident, which enabled men influential with the colonial government to levy a burdensome tax on the settler without rendering in return a corresponding benefit. Much of the public domain was thus cornered by these influential men. The settler had to pay their price or go on to the very verge of settlement. Many a person did so, and the frontier was pushed forward too rapidly for comfort or safety. Furthermore, the government is said to have been very lenient in enforcing forfeiture where there was a failure to comply with the conditions attached to the grant. The order of council method was monopolistic in its very nature. The headright method was equitable, and it assumed, which was ordinarily the truth, that the homeseeker was capable of choosing land for himself.

In the case of Borden, there was a penal bond in the sum of 1800 pounds ($6,000). The grantee was to sell the lands at the rate of threepence (ten cents) per acre. Sometimes, indeed, he gave title for a smaller sum. But the rate exacted was sometimes much larger, as will appear from a study of Section III. A petition to the Assembly, dated 1786, would seem to voice the prevalent opinion in Rockbridge. The petitioners believe the survey to contain a good deal of surplus land. In reserving some of the most valuable tracts, the Bordens "accumulated a large fortune." A considerable portion was still unsold at the date of the petition, and like unappropriated land, was in great part free from tax. This was offered for sale at the highest price that could be secured. "Your petitioners have ever considerd this monopoly hard and oppressive, even under a monarchial government, where the natural rights of man are so much abused." They ask that the representatives of the proprietor be compelled to account for all arrears of taxes, and that the lands be disposed of at a reasonable price; and that the grant be resurveyed so that the title to the surplus lands may be vested in the commonwealth.

The patent to Borden was not issued until November 6, 1739. It is based on the representation that a family had been located for every 1,000 acres of the grant. The acreage is set at 92,100, and this would indicate that the number of actual settlements was ninety-one, exclusive of those by the McDowell party. In consideration of building a cabin, the settler was given 100 acres, and had the privilege of buying additional land at the minimum price. Such parcel of 100 acres was called a cabin-right. These cabin-rights were of vital importance to Borden. Each one validated his own title to 1,000 acres of his grant. Mrs. Greenlee relates that the cabin-rights were at length counted and a return made to the governor. Benjamin Borden, Jr., affirmed that the number was 145. But Mrs. Greenlee says one person would go from cabin to cabin, and claim a cabin-right in each instance. It was immaterial where these claim-cabins were built. Mrs. Greenlee adds that she heard much of the doings of a young Milhollen woman, a servant to James Bell. She dressed as a man and saved five or six cabin-rights. She used a different Christian name at each cabin she appeared at. John Patterson, who made the count and kept tally with chalk-marks on his hat, was surprised to find so many Milhollens. Mrs. Greenlee does not commit herself as to whether she believed this sharp practice to have been instigated by the elder Borden. The junior Borden, in his answer in the suit of Bell v. Borden, denies that his father sought any advantage from fraudulent improvement. He says he believes it to be true that Bell "caused a servant wench of his to be dressed up in man's apparel or clothes, and show himself on one of the improvements he pretends to have made," and that at another time, Bell "caused the wife of William McCanliss, his servant man, to appear in his own proper person on a different part of the land, as the wife of another settler."

The surveying of the boundaries of the Tract was not done until after the counting of the cabin-rights. This circumstance will account for the extraordinarily irregular outline. More than sixty angles are described in the patent. The general survey was performed by James Wood, surveyor of Frederick county, assisted by John McDowell. McDowell seems to have surveyed some, at least, of the individual tracts, yet Mrs. Greenlee says one Beaty appears to have been the first man to survey land in the Borden Tract. One John Hart was also a surveyor. Separate parcels, however, were not always surveyed before purchase, but were described by general boundaries. James Buchanan says his father's land was paid for before survey, although certain boundaries were agreed upon. The younger Borden did not observe these bounds, although referees decided in his favor. Mrs. Greenlee says people sometimes squatted in the grant, and without first contracting with "old Borden." William Patton says that parcels passed from hand to hand prior to the making of any deed. This circumstance helps to explain why the names of some of the settlers do not appear in the deeds issued by the Bordens.

The death of Benjamin Borden, Sr., left the proprietary interests in the Tract in much confusion. Many bargains with the newcomers had been reached, but in rather numerous instances the settler was living on land to which his claim was incomplete. Judge McDowell very justly remarks that the business of the estate was intricate and very troublesome. The elder Borden had either sold or given away many tracts that there was no account of among his papers. Disputes arose and some of the contestants made good their claims. The quit-rents coming due every year on the unsold portion of the Tract were a burden to the younger man. One deponent says a parcel was sometimes sold off merely to get the money for this purpose. It was the practice of the Bordens to sign no deeds until the purchase money had been paid in full. For some cause, the land purchased by Ezekiel Clements in 1746 reverted to the Crown seven years later.

In 1742 Benjamin Borden, Jr., visited the Tract, spending his time at the home of John McDowell. When he came back, the year following, his father and John McDowell were both dead. The junior Borden was a young man and was at first viewed with coldness and suspicion. There seemed to be nothing in his bearing to set him above the generality of the settlers themselves. It was said that he was illiterate, but this could hardly have been the case. He was not at first held in respect by Mrs. McDowell, whom he married about 1744. On his reappearance he entered upon the management of his inheritance. He lived at Thorn Hill, afterward the Bowyer estate, which lies on Woods Creek two miles southwest of Lexington. That his home was just outside the Tract is explainable on the supposition—which is almost a certainty—that his wife, whose maiden name was Magdalena Woods, was a sister to Richard Woods, who settled in this beautiful valley in 1738. Here in April, 1753, the younger Borden died of smallpox. The disease was epidemic that spring, and Borden was the first person at his own home to contract it. His three daughters, his brother Joseph, the children of John McDowell, and several negroes also fell ill, and one or two of his children died. Martha Borden, then a girl of about eight years, had a slow and tedious convalescence. About 1779 she married Robert Harvey. Mrs. Greenlee, who was probably immune, nursed the patients at the Borden home.

The appraisement of the junior Borden's personality makes the following exhibit, the values being given both in Federal currency and in the colonial money of Virginia.

Roger (slave)	40p	$133.33
Mill (slave)	30p	100.00
Other slaves—value not given		
13 horses	63p 10s	211.67
26 sheep	6p 10s	21.67
One yoke of oxen	6p	20.00
8 milch cows	13p	43.33
3 calves	1p 4s	4.00
32 hogs	6p	20.00
Nails	1p 11s	5.17
Case of pistols and holsters	1p	3.33
Still and vessels	23p	76.67
Implements, traps, smith's tools	14p 3s 6d	47.25
Wagon gears	10p	33.33
3 linen sheets	1p 16s	6.00
Large table	8s	1.33
One dozen chairs	1p 8s	4.67
Bed and furniture	2p 10s	8.33
Silver watch	4p	13.33
3 wigs	1p 10s	5.00
Books	3p 6s 6d	11.08
128 pounds steel, 77 of iron	4p 19s 8d	16.58

Total, 235 pounds, 16 shillings, 8 pence; equivalent to $786.11.

During the ten years he lived in the Tract, Benjamin, Jr., rose in the estimation of the settlers. In 1746 he became a captain of the militia, and in 1752 he qualified as a justice of the county court. He was somewhat frequently called upon to perform public business. Mrs. Greenlee says he appeared to be a good man and disposed to do justice to the settlers. His stepson, Samuel McDowell, says he was honest and upright, generally well spoken of, and gave satisfaction in his management of the estate. Such testimony is very strong, and yet there are statements that seem to conflict with those given by the stepson and his aunt. In 1748, the younger Borden was convicted by the Augusta court for giving false receipts for the payment of quit-rents. Three years later, Martha, the wife of James Dunlap, was fined for saying she would not believe him on oath. John Patterson, in making his will in 1749, claims seventy pounds as due him from Borden, and instructs James Patton to see that Borden does not wrong his wife and children. Borden's sister Deborah deposed in 1790 that her brother had treated Mrs. Worthington with much cruelty in word and manner. From the tenor of the declarations in a number of chancery suits, one is driven to conclude either that the plaintiffs were trying to "do" Borden, or that the latter was evasive and dishonest in his dealings with them. We cannot lightly believe that all the complainants could have been tricky and untruthful.

The suit of Downing v. Borden is a quite typical specimen of the litigation that arose after the death of the elder Borden. John Downing sets forth that John Patterson was a duly authorized agent to act for Benjamin Borden, Sr.; that through the said Patterson he purchased 300 acres on Galway Creek; that one-half the purchase money was to be paid as soon as Borden should execute a good deed, and one-half at the end of twelve months. The elder Borden having died before title had passed, Downing asked the son to make out a deed, complaining at the same time that his neighbor, George Moffett, had a mind to come over the creek running through the land. Benjamin, Jr., replied that Moffett should not come over, that Downing was in control and should go ahead with the improvement of his land. Downing says he has made considerable improvement, and has offered to pay the purchase money, but that Borden insists there was no bona fide purchase; that Patterson was without authority, unless in case of a lease-right; that the agreement between Patterson and Downing was oral only, and that the proprietor is under no obligation to convey.

In the suit of Young v. Borden, Robert Young says Robert Crockett bargained with the elder Borden and paid one pistole* to bind the contract; that he himself, to whom Crockett had assigned his right, has paid in $10.82, yet without being able to get a deed. In 1750 Young petitioned that Borden should not acknowledge title to any of the land without his consent. The petition was allowed. In Patterson v. Borden, James Patterson says that the senior Borden made a verbal agreement with John Patterson, whereby the latter was to act as agent; that when Borden visited the Tract, which he did frequently, he lodged with Patterson, who found his own provisions and also entertained landhunters; and that Patterson attended the surveyor, for which service he was to have three and one-half shillings (fifty-eight cents) a day. Borden refuses to pay any of these claims, falling back on the technicality of an English law of 1689 and saying that a writing was necessary. The case was dismissed in 1760 without award. In Mitchell v. Borden, 1747, John Mitchell says that in consequence of a rumor, after the death of the elder Borden, that the son would not give title to the places his father and the agents of the latter had agreed to convey, he himself and several others made preparations to move from the Tract. The younger Borden, finding his land would be depopulated, and in danger of lapsing for want of cultivation, publicly announced that he would perfect and confirm all such agreements. Mitchell remained, but Borden sometimes offers some excuse for not making title and sometimes absolutely refuses. Borden rejoins

---

*$3.92.

that Mitchell did no more than make an entry with Patterson, whom he looks upon as an intruder. In Bell v. Borden, which was abated in 1751, James Bell says that eighteen cabin-rights were taken by himself and his servant, John Milhollen, and sixteen other men: Thomas Armstrong, George Henderson, John and Quentin Moore, Alexander, George, James, Robert, and Adam Breckenridge, John Bell, William McCanless, John Walters, Robert and Seth Poage, John Grove, and Daniel M'Anler. These settlers were to build and improve by April 1, 1738, and to be at no expense except the drawing and recording of deeds, and a fee of eight shillings for laying off each tract. The deeds were not forthcoming, and the settlers concerned threatened suit. The proprietor then agreed to make conveyance, but died before the deeds were executed. The younger Borden says he does not know of any improvements by these men, and denies that Bell has any right to the 200 acres claimed in behalf of himself and Milhollen.

The McDowells themselves had trouble with the proprietors. The senior Borden wanted John McDowell to select on Hays Creek the 1,000 acres he was to have for surveying. McDowell would not accept brushy upland which he deemed barren. He brought suit for a selection on Timber Ridge and won, to the chagrin of Borden, who wanted the land himself. Mrs. Greenlee's husband purchased on Turkey Hill, but the younger Borden resisted giving a deed, alleging that the whole parcel was choice land, and "for the sake of peace" a portion of it was given up. Greenlee's title was confirmed by the court.

The lands remaining unsold after the death of the younger Borden were considered of inferior quality. Yet for a long while, sales continued to be made by the executors, of whom Archibald Alexander was chief. A report of sales that ends in the year 1780, shows that up to that date nearly 300 parcels had been disposed of.

But Benjamin Borden, Jr., was not always the defendant in this maze of litigation. He himself brought many suits, usually to enforce the payment of purchase money.

As to Joseph Borden, Judge McDowell says he was a man "not of the best sort." The younger brother came to live with Benjamin, Jr., and went to school. The fall after the latter died, he went away by dark, not very well liked, and not made very welcome. After his recovery from the smallpox, he explored his brother's papers. His sister-in-law missed a bond of some 300 pounds, and when she accused him of the theft, he asked her in effect, what she was going to do about it. About twenty years later he again appeared in the Tract and told Samuel McDowell that he had bought out the claim of his sister, Mrs. Worthington. McDowell replied that Benjamin, Jr., had bought out the rights of his sisters—three of whom had spent about ten days in visiting him—

because he could not get the lands laid off according to the terms of his father's will. Joseph Borden insisted that Mrs. Worthington had never acknowledged the deed. To Joseph Walker, the absentee explained his abrupt departure in 1753. He told Walker he could not get on with his sister-in-law. A friendly servant took his clothes to the woods and caught for him a mare that was the leader of a herd. As he rode away he was followed by a drove of horses. Walker told him such conduct was very dishonest, and asked him where he had been that he had not attended to his claims earlier.

However, Joseph Borden did pay the sister $300 for her interest in her tract of 1,000 acres, and because of this land he brought suit against his niece, Martha Harvey, and her husband, Robert. The almost interminable depositions and other proceedings during the period 1790-1807 fill two large volumes in the office of the circuit clerk at Staunton. The controversy centered for a while about a tract of 448 acres owned by an Edmondson, in the "New Providence barrens." The kernel of the whole trouble was the provision in the will of Benjamin Borden, Sr., that five of his daughters should have 5,000 acres that was "all good land." Judge McDowell deposed that as a boy he was a chain-carrier for the surveying parties in the Tract, and thus became very familiar with the ground. He said it was not possible to embrace 1,000 acres of choice land in a single survey, and that it would require from fifteen to twenty surveys to cover the total of 5,000 acres. Joseph Borden died in 1803 at his home in Iredell county, North Carolina, but the suit dragged its weary length along, and was at length merged into the suit of Peck v. Borden. It appeared in the docket term after term with monotonous regularity. The Borden heirs became more numerous, year by year, and the case never seemed ready for settlement. About 1885 the circuit judge ordered the funds in the hands of the court, amounting with interest to some $5,000, to be paid to the army of heirs. The case was then stricken from the docket. It had involved the legality of all the Borden titles, but no landholder in the Tract was dispossessed.

Passing the entire Borden matter in review, it appears in the light of a long-continued nuisance and an unjustifiable and injurious monopoly. The elder Borden had performed no public service to warrant so large a benefit from the public domain. The heirs, with the one exception of Benjamin, Jr., were nonresidents. There was never any sound reason why the individual purchases should not have been patents issuing from the state. A vast amount of litigation and other forms of annoyance would thus have been avoided.

V

EARLY PIONEER DAYS

SOCIAL DISTINCTIONS—A VIRGIN WILDERNESS—HOUSES—PREDATORY ANIMALS—CHURCHES, TAVERNS, AND MILLS—STAUNTON—LITIGATION—WILLS—
NATURE OF THE TIMES

The eighteenth century was less democratic than our decade of the twentieth, and the English were less democratic than the Ulster people. Yet even on the old frontier, where leveling tendencies came into play from the very outset, social lines were somewhat closely observed. More than a century after the settlement of Rockbridge, we are told by Alexander S. Paxton that there was little or no social intercourse between the planter on the one hand and the mechanic or the ordinary tradesman on the other. In land deeds the social rank, or the occupation, of one or both parties was frequently mentioned. The institution of nobility, universal in Europe in our colonial period, never took formal root in our soil. The recognized gradations in social rank were fewer in the Valley of Virginia than in Tidewater. In the former district the number of those who were technically known as "gentlemen" was quite small. This term did not have in 1737 its present rather indefinite application. The gentleman was understood to be one of the upper middle class, coming between the nobility and the yoemen. He was descended from freemen, had a coat of arms, and had the privilege of wearing a sword. But on the frontier, a prominent person, a member of the county court for instance, would be given the title as a matter of courtesy.

The yeoman, according to the British usage, was a freeholder, and was qualified to vote and to serve on a jury. In old Augusta this class was numerously represented, and it was the backbone of its society. Below the yeoman was the freedman, who had emerged from servitude and was now in the full enjoyment of the ordinary civil rights. On a level with the freedmen were a considerable number of people who were penniless or nearly so. These were sometimes worthy members of society and sometimes very unworthy. At the bottom—and still on the white side of the scale—was the indentured servant. With the exception of his larger legal rights, he was practically as much a serf as the negro. These white servants were numerous in Augusta and require special mention.

Some of these people were convicts. But the convict of those days was not necessarily a "hard case." The person who purloined a coat or loaf of bread to fend off cold or starvation was marked for the gallows by the letter of the savage English law. The British judge would order him to be transported to America, where he had to undergo servitude a number of years. Some other members of this class, especially boys, had been kidnapped from the British seaports. Still others were debtors, poor relations, and ne'er-do-wells, sent away by their "friends," so as to be out of sight if not out of mind. But many a person sold himself to some shipmaster in order to reach America. Such a person was known as a "kid." On arrival at an American seaport the servants, whether voluntary or involuntary, were sold by the captain, the usual price being about $65. The average age at indenture was nineteen, and the average term of servitude was five years. They were beetter fed than in Europe and did not work so hard. They were entitled to free time, medical attention, commutation from punishment, the right to sue and to complain by informal petition, and protection from service to colored persons. When the servant's time was out, his freedom dues would help him to get a start in the world. If he ran away—and he often did—he was advertised, and if retaken he might be branded and whipped. The county court would also decree that he should serve his master a year or more of extra time, by way of indemnification for the cost of recovery. On the other hand, there are instances where the servant agreed to serve a year longer for being purchased from a disagreeable master. In 1761, a servant to Sampson and George Mathews agreed to serve them three years extra time in return for their consent to her marrying the man of her choice. If in that time there were no issue the brothers were to pay her $10 a year, less the cost of her clothes.

The indenture system, with respect to immigrants, came to an end during the Revolution. It was a mode of colonization and it promoted a democratic feeling. But with its decline negro slavery grew in favor. The moral influence was bad, and not a few of the women servants were of loose character. When, as often occurred, one of these women had a child by another man than her master, she would be required to serve him extra time.

There were native apprentices as well as imported servants, and with respect to the general character of the servitude there seems to have been little difference between the two classes. The master was not infrequently summoned to answer the complaint of an apprentice. A petition of 1811 asks for a more efficient means of effecting recovery of the many apprentices that try to abscond.

In the next paragraph we give a specimen of the colonial form of indenture. The John Roseman mentioned therein was a settler of the Raphine neighborhood. The McBride name appears in the same locality.

THIS INDENTURE made the twenty fourth Day of ——— in the year of Our Lord Christ one thousand seven hundred and fifty five WITNESSETH that Daniel McBride of the County of Augusta in the Colony of Virginia hath Put himself apprenting Servant and by these presents Doth Voluntarily Put himself and of his own free will & accord put himself apprenting servant to John Roseman Cordwainer or shoemaker of this sd County of Augusta in the Colony aforesd to Learn his art and Trade or Mystery after the manner of an apprenting servant to sarve him or his assigns from the Day of the Date hereof for & During the full Term and Time of two full years next ensuing, During all what time the sd apprentice his Said Master faithfully shall Serve his secret Keys his Lawfull Commands very —— gladly obey he shall Do no Damage to his said Master nor see it Done by others with out Letting or giving notice thereof to his said Master he shall not wast his said Master's goods nor lend them unlawfully to others he shall not Commit fornication nor Contract Matrimony within the sd Term at Cards or Dice or any other unlawfull games he Shall not play whereby his said Master may be Damaged with his own goods or the goods of others During the sd Term without the License of his sd Master he Shall Nither Buy nor Sell he Shall not absent himself Day nor Night from his sd Master's Service without his Leave nor haunt ale houses still houses Taverns or play Houses but in all things Behave himself as a faithful apprentice Savant ought to Do During the sd Term & Time and the sd Daniel McBride doth hereby Covenant and Declare himself Now to be of the age of Nineteen years a single Person & no Covenanted Indented or Contracted Servant or apprentice to any persons or persons whatsoever and the sd Master Shall use the utmost of his Indeavors to Teach or Cause to be Taught & Instructed the sd prentice in the Trade and Mystery he now professes Occupieth or followeth and procure and provide for him the sd apprentice sufficient meat Drink apparel washing and Lodging fitting for an apprentice During the sd Term and at the End & Expiration thereof the sd master shall pay unto the sd prentice the sum of Ten pounds Current Money of Virginia or the value thereof in goods or Chattels and for the true performance of all & every this sd Covenant & agreement Either of the said Parties binded them selves to the other firmly by these presents IN WITNESS whereof they have hereunto Interchangeably set their hands and affixed their seales the Day and Year first above written

The newcomers spoke English of the Elizabethan type that was current in Ulster. Words peculiar to the Scotch dialect were also heard. The old pronunciation vanished in the second or third generation, on American soil, yet there is abundant evidence of its everyday use in the colonial age. The broad sound of the first letter of the alphabet was much more often heard than it is now. A number of conversational expressions, such as "cow-beast," have gone out of use, but when our ancestors committed their thoughts to paper, their meaning is perfectly clear to ourselves; more so than our own breezy, snappy speech would be to them, if they were here to listen to it.

Though we speak of Rockbridge as being on the old American frontier, it was never, unless to a partial extent for a few years, a section of the backwoods fringe. The immigrants continued to clothe themselves very much as they had been doing. The dress suit of the gentlemen and yeomen was more elaborate than a costume of this character is now. The colors were brighter and more diversified. We read of green and plum colored broadcloths and of bright red fabrics. The coat of a certain militia captain was valued by himself at $13.33, and it would have taken two or three of his cows to pay for it. We find a tailor's bill of $7.67. In the settlement of the estate of Adam Dickenson, a pair of silver knee buckles is listed at one pound, a set of silver breeches buttons at the same figure, a silk bonnet at $11.33, and a lawn handkerchief at $1.25. The man for whom Jackson's River is named lived on the very edge of settlement, yet he wore a wig and a stock and buckle. The statue of Andrew Lewis at Richmond presents that general in hunting shirt and leggings. This is a violation of historical fact. He had little to do with the conventional garb of the scout and is known to have been particular in the matter of raiment. The Reverend Samuel Houston was old-fashioned in his attire, which was representative of the epoch under consideration. He wore short breeches buttoned and buckled at the knee, long stockings, large shoes with heavy silver buckles, a dress-coat rounded in front and with its many buttons on one side only, and a standing collar. His broad-brimmed, three-sided cocked hat was made by John Ruff, a famous hatter of Lexington. His riding boots that reached nearly to the knees and had white leather tops were made by Colonel Jordan of the same town.

In many an instance the settler was master of some handicraft, as is often noticed in reading the early land deeds. One man was a weaver, another a millwright, another a cooper, another a rope-maker, and still another a carpenter or cabinet-maker. A very important man was the blacksmith. He did not limit himself to repair work, but was really a manufacturer. He made nails, horseshoes, edged tools, and cooper-glazed bells. He also made farm implements, except such as were wholly of wood.

When immigration began to flock into the Rockbridge area in the fall of 1737, it was not into an unknown land. Governor Gooch had given wide publicity to what had been seen by Spottswood and his companions. The prospectors who spied out the choicer portions of the Valley, with the intention of covering them with orders of council or with patents of less ambitious size, were desirous of seeing people come in. John Lewis, who arrived at Lewis Creek in 1732, very soon had a hundred families of the Ulster folk around him, and when Augusta attained to separate county government in 1745, the population of its vast area was about 4,000.

Nearly coinciding with the line of the present Valley Turnpike was an Indian warpath, which, like all the more conspicuous trails of its class, could be used by a wagon as well as by a pack-horse. This "Pennsylvania Road" was the one thoroughfare by which a stream of immigration poured into Augusta. The court of Orange adopted it as a county road. The latter portion of its order reads as follows:

And that the said road continue from Beverly Manor line to Gilbert Campbell's ford on the North Branch of James River, and that Capn Benjamin Borden, Capn William

Evins, and Capn Joseph Culton be overseers of the same, and that the gang to clear the same be all the inhabitants above Beverly Manor line to the said Gilbt Campbell's ford.

And that the road continue from Gilbt Campbell's ford to a ford at the Cherrytree Bottom on James River, and that Richard Wood, Gilbt Campbell, Joseph Lapsley, and Joseph Long be overseers, and that all the inhabitants betwixt the said rivers clear the same.

And that the said road continue from the said Cherrytree Bottom to Adam Harmon's on the New, or Wood's, River, and that Capn George Robinson and James Campbell, and Mark Evins, and James Davison be overseers of the same, and that all the inhabitants betwixt James River and Wood's River clear the same.

And that a distinct order be given to every gang to clear the same, and that it be cleared; as it is already blazed and laid off with two notches and a cross. Given under our hands this 8th day of April, 1745.

The settlers of this county found that much of its area was covered with brush, or with "Indian meadows," in which the coarse grass and peavine is spoken of as quite luxuriant. A forest growth was confined largely to the mountains, as in the case of Timber Ridge, which derives its name from this circumstance. So far from being compelled to clear the land, the settler had sometimes to go a mile to find logs for a cabin. And yet, as the "brushy barrens" were considered poor, they were passed over in favor of the timbered localities. The early comers were particular in refusing all lands they thought to be poor, but afterward found their judgment had sometimes been at fault. Thus Timber Ridge was settled in preference to open ground that was actually better.

The country being generally open, it was a comparatively simple and expeditious matter for the homeseeker to view the land, determine his individual preference, and assist in making what were called roads in that early time. If any of his open ground went back to its natural forest covering, it was because he permitted it so to do.

The purchases within the Borden grant averaged nearly 300 acres, and this was rather less than the customary size of the individual patents around it. And since labor-saving machinery was unknown in that day, so large a holding was a plantation rather than a farm. As a rule the purchaser was a substantial yeoman, and he often had a tenant on his place or one or more indentured servants in his household. Under circumstances like these, the normal development of the region would be at a quite rapid pace.

The very first dwelling houses were undoubtedly primitive. They were round-log cabins, and sometimes the floor was nothing better than the naked earth. There is no doubt that the bark hunting-lodge left here by the red man was occasionally used. But by all except the moneyless and the easy-going, the rough and ready shelter was intended only as a makeshift. The man of property who felt that he had come to stay did not lose much time in building a larger and better dwelling of hewed logs. The house of Captain William Jameson, of the Calfpasture, built in 1752, was probably a fair specimen of a home of the permanent type. It was eighteen by twenty-four feet in the clear, one and one-half stories high, and had a shingled roof. The contract price was $22.50.

The Indian peril, which first manifested itself at the close of 1742, must have been a powerful incentive to build houses of strength and a fair degree of security. Several structures of this kind are still in existence, but with enlarged windows and some other alterations.

Log houses were the rule for several decades. The immense chimney was of stone, the supply of which in Rockbridge is abundant. Before the close of the Revolution there were few houses of stone or brick. As the years went by, the brick house became increasingly frequent, but it was some time before the log house was outnumbered by the framed dwelling. Even yet, the log house is far from being extinct in Rockbridge.

The tilled acreage was small. Grain could be marketed only in the form of flour, and then only to a limited extent. Consequently, the pioneer grew little more than the supplies consumed on his place. Indian corn, unknown in the British Isles, was the only staple he had to learn how to grow. Since only the well-to-do could afford clothes of imported cloth, there was much weaving of linen and linsy-woolsy. The flax patch was consequently a feature of the frontier farm. Hemp was a staple crop, and it was the one most immediately a source of ready money. The cultivation of it was encouraged by the colonial government. The fiber brought $5 a hundredweight, and there was a bounty of $1. More hemp seems to have been grown in Rockbridge than in other parts of old Augusta. Orchards were begun with young apple and peach trees brought from Pennsylvania. Kitchen gardens are said to have been unknown before the Revolution. The hint was taken from the Hessian prisoners-of-war at Staunton, who were permitted to plant gardens in the vicinity of their camps. Wagons were at first scarce, but were rather common during the Revolution. The farming tools were few and simple. Almost the only implements drawn by horses were the brush harrow and the plow with wooden mouldboard.

Rockbridge is well suited to grazing, and the early farms were well stocked with horses, cattle, sheep, and hogs. These animals were not so large as the breeds of the present day. The immigrants were not slow to see the advantage of irrigating the level meadows along the large streams. Such artificial watering was practiced on Walker's and Kerr's creeks. There is mention of the "Egypt field" on the last named watercourse. The dams and ditches are now gone, and corn is king rather than hay.

The early comers found the wilderness infested with several predatory animals, the most troublesome of which was the wolf. For many years it was necessary to pen the calves and sheep by night to protect them from the bear and the puma, as well as the wolf. It is a noteworthy fact that crows, blackbirds, and honeybees were not known in this region before the arrival of the white men. The Indians called the bee the "white man's fly."

It was provided that the settlers in Augusta should be exempt from levy so long as they remained under the jurisdiction of Orange. This was found to be a disadvantage, and in response to a petition from them a poll tax of two shillings was authorized. This was to provide a fund for paying wolf bounties. The oath administered to a claimant of the bounty read as follows:

I, —————, do swear that this head by me now produced is the head—or heads— of a wolf taken and killed within the county of —————— in Virginia; and that I have not wittingly or willingly spared the life of any bitch wolf in my power to kill. So help me God.

The whole head of the wolf had to be shown to the magistrate, who clipped the ears, administered the above oath, and issued a certificate. In one month of 1752, 225 wolf-heads were brought to the Augusta court-house. In 1790, forty wolf-heads were presented to the magistrates of this county, the bounty then being 100 pounds of tobacco ($3.33) for a grown animal, and fifty pounds for a cub. A petition of 1809 says wolves are increasingly numerous, and asks that the bounty be raised to $8 and $6. There was the same complaint in 1823. In 1831, the bounties were $12 and $6 for wolves and $1 and fifty cents for red foxes. In 1834, only one wolf-head was produced, but there were 110 fox scalps. Squirrels as well as crows were destructive to the corn, and a law of the Revolutionary period imposed a penalty on each tithable for failing to present a specified number of scalps each year. Deer, on the contrary, were protected by law. A statute of 1792 made it illegal to kill a deer with a bell or collar on its neck.

Except for a few communicants of the Established Church, the pioneer population of Rockbridge was Presbyterian, so far as it adhered to any creed at all. The earliest meeting houses are spoken of in another chapter. The Sunday services continued from 10 o'clock in the morning until sunset, but with an interval of one hour for dinner. At a time of communion the meeting continued four days, and several ministers were present. People then came from a wider radius than usual, and the families living near the meeting house were duly hospitable. Some persons walked barefoot to church, putting on their shoes and socks after crossing the last branch on the road. To serve hot coffee on Sunday was considered a desecration.

According to Howe, there was little social intercourse, except within the churchyard, and there were no gay amusements at any time. In fact, social intercourse was largely of a religious character. The presbytery was the chief festival occasion. Dancing lay under a ban, and the "cavalier vices" of Tidewater Virginia did not flourish within the mountains. But at length some of the

Rockbridge people grew idle, merry, and dissipated, and this element was more conspicuous on the very front line of settlement.

Prior to the organization of Rockbridge as a county, there was no town or village. The store, the ordinary, and the mill were the weekday places where the male element was most likely to congregate. There may have been a few stores previous to 1777, but we have no knowledge of them. The distance to Staunton was not prohibitive, and an occasional visit by a pedlar could be counted upon. The ordinary, or tavern, had a name which was painted on a board placed near the front entrance. There were a few of these in Rockbridge, but they were usually styled houses of private entertainment. There was a fine of ten pounds for keeping a tavern without a license. The guest could not be made to pay unless there were an agreement in advance. "The White Horse" was the name of the McClenahan hostelry in Staunton.

The first mill, according to Mrs. Greenlee, was that of Charles Hays. It was probably built not later than 1740. It was soon followed by the mill of James Young at the mouth of Kerr's Creek. Other mills, dating from about 1752, were those of David Moore, Joseph Long, and Joseph Kennedy. But in 1747, James Allison and Henry Gay had petitioned for leave to build water gristmills. Before 1788, and perhaps a little before the opening of the Revolution, Thomas Paxton had put up a mill at the mouth of the Buffalo. The earliest of these concerns were probably on a par with the tubmills of William Wilson and Adam Dickenson in the Bath area. The former was built in 1750 at the contract price of $20. The labor put into the second mill on the Dickenson plantation was in 1763 adjudged to be worth four pounds cash, or $13.33. The tubmill had a wheel five feet in diameter.

Staunton was the seat of government for the Rockbridge area during two-score years, and therefore deserves a few lines of mention. Nine years after the coming of the McDowells there was nothing around the little log courthouse and prison except two cabins, one of these being tenanted by a woman of questionable character. The colonial capital was at that time a village of about thirty houses. "Stantown" was surveyed in 1750, and three years later contained about twenty houses. Two years later yet, a new courthouse, twenty-six by forty feet, was completed. In 1761, Staunton was designated as a town by legislative enactment, and wooden chimneys were no longer to be permitted. Fairs were authorized in June and November for the second Tuesday of the month. When the Revolution broke out, Staunton was one of the few important towns in Virginia and had several stores and taverns.

The doings within the courtyard were not always tame. The justices were repeatedly disturbed by rioting outside the building or by ball playing. They were sometimes "damned," or otherwise insulted, while on the bench. In 1754 a woman called one of them a rogue, and said that on his "coming off the bench she would give it to him with the devil." Neither was there the best of public order away from the precincts of the court. In 1754 John Clark went into the house of Robert McClenahan and demanded satisfaction for a decision given by McClenahan as a magistrate. Two years later, three men entered the house of Alexander Wright, broke doors and windows, and beat and abused Mary McDonnell, an inmate.

In fact, instances of assault and battery were rather numerous. It was a frequent occurrence for a person to complain of standing in fear of bodily hurt from some one else, and to ask that the person in question be bound over to keep the peace. A certain woman of Kerr's Creek was an offender in this particular. But notwithstanding the many unruly characters, there seems to have been an honest effort to enforce a high standard of conduct, including a strict observance of the Sabbath. A certain man, one of whose sons may have been responsible for the House Mountain tragedy, was repeatedly summoned to show cause why "he does not bring up his children in a Christian-like manner." Samuel Dale was presented for taking wheat or flour and mixing it with his own in John Wilson's mill. For stealing a blanket from Samuel Houston and a bed quilt and a shirt from some other person, Elizabeth Smith asked for corporal punishment and was accommodated with thirty-nine lashes on the bare back at the public whipping post.

The settlers of old Augusta were very much given to litigation. The number of their lawsuits, prior to the subdivision of the county, runs into the thousands. Very many of the suits were for debt, and the jail was principally used as a boarding house for delinquent debtors. Some of the suits were for slander. The charges set forth in these are at times very gross and are described without any mincing of words.

The will of the colonial period usually begins with a pious preamble varying in length, yet with so much general resemblance as to indicate that set forms were commonly used. The maker then asks that he be given Christian burial, and the executors are to see that all claims against the estate are paid or adjusted. Provision is next made for "my well-beloved wife," and the items of personalty left her are minutely mentioned. She is to live with a son, "if they can agree." The son is to furnish her, year by year, a stipulated minimum of garden space, firewood, flour, corn, bacon, etc., and perhaps a stated area in flax. "If she chooses to live in a house by herself," a small one is to be built by the son who inherits the homestead. "If she marry again," her interest in the estate is to be curtailed. The children are generally mentioned by name, sometimes in the order of age, but as married daughters are commonly spoken of as "Margaret Smith," or "Liddy Black," one is not always certain whether a daughter is really meant. Sometimes a son is given only a nominal consideration, perhaps with the explanation that "he has received his sheer already." Personal property—and also real estate, where there is much of it—it apportioned with much exactness. Occasionally the homestead is divided, or a son is given lands patented or purchased on the "western waters"; on the "Canaway" River or in Ohio, or "Caintucky." If there are grandsons bearing the grandparent's given name, they are remembered with a small legacy, and when the will is by a grandmother, the granddaughters bearing her own given name are similarly remembered. Where there are several slaves, they are distributed among the members of the family. To "my beloved John" will be left accounts due the parent by outside parties. To a son will be left "my best suit of close," and to a daughter a horse and saddle. Frequently, the children, or a portion of them are minors, and there are directions for their support and schooling. Quite often, all the children are small, and there is sometimes another birth to be expected. Not seldom was the pioneer cut off by acute illness while in the prime of life. Nevertheless, the merchants sold "Lockyer's Pills" and "Duffey's Elixir," just as the drugstores dispense various proprietary cure-alls today.

Light on a well-nigh forgotten burial custom is afforded in the following petition by the "widow Allison," who lived at a ford of North River near the mouth of Kerr's Creek:

15th March 1773 To Ye Vestry Whereas Joel Millican came to my house in a very low condition destitute of any help for himself either in body or goods Therefore provided a bed for him and attended him nine days and he died. I therefore provided a Coffin and sheet and a gallon and a half of liquor and had him buried in a decent manner according to his station which I hope you will take into consideration as I am not of great ability to be at so much expense and trouble which is from your Humble Servant

In 1767 we find the vestry allowing for one "bare skin to lay under Cummings and dig Cummings grave."

Until 1755 there was no regular mail service with the British Isles, and if a letter weighed more than one ounce, it cost a dollar to have it delivered there. So late as 1775 there were but fifteen postoffices in all Virginia. There were no envelopes, and postmasters read the letters, just as gossip now claims that country postmasters read the postal cards. The first newspaper in the colony was the *Virginia Gazette,* started in 1736. The size of its page was six inches by twelve, and the subscription price was fifteen shillings. There was no other paper in Virginia until 1775.

The purchasing power of the dollar was several times greater in the colonial era than it is now. This fact has to be taken into consideration when we read of the seemingly very low prices for land and livestock. But some articles were relatively more expensive than they are now. Whether, on the whole, living was easier in those days is a question on which a study of the paragraphs below will throw some light. The values are taken from those chancery papers of Augusta which are of a date anterior to the disturbing effect of depreciated currency in the latter half of the Revolutionary struggle.

The rental for three years on a certain farm of 517 acres was $6.46. For the same time, James Gay was to pay four pounds a year for 149 acres. A mare could be had for $15, although an extra good horse might come as high as $40. One to two pounds would purchase a cow, although a young woman, perhaps through sheer necessity, sold two cows and a yearling for $10. In ordinary instances, a sheep or a hog could be had for a dollar. Common labor ran from thirty-three to fifty cents a day, yet corn could be gathered and husked for twenty-five cents a day, while thirty-three cents would command the services of a person who could tend store and post books. A man with his wagon and two horses could be hired for fifty cents a day. Rails could be split for thirty-seven and one-half cents a thousand, although they might sell as high as $5. A blacksmith would make a mattock for sixty-seven cents. A carpenter charged eighty-three cents for making a churn, $2.50 for laying a barn floor, $6.67 for covering a house, and $10.00 for covering a barn. Two pounds would build one of the big stone chimneys of that day, and four pounds would build a log dwelling. A bedstead could be made for $1.25, a loom for $5.00, a coffin for $2.17, and a lintekiln for eighty-three cents. A month's board could be satisfied for $3.00, and $10.00 would pay for a year's schooling. The maid-servant of a man on the Cowpasture worked for $20.00 a year.

Wheat and rye varied little from fifty and thirty-three cents a bushel, respectively. Rye was worth twenty-five to forty-two cents, corn twenty-four to thirty-eight cents, and potatoes twenty cents. Flour by the barrel ran all the way from $3.25 to $8.33. Butter was five to eight cents a pound, and tallow two cents. Beef and mutton averaged hardly more than two cents a pound, although we once find 400 pounds of bear meat, bacon, and venison billed at $25.00. A half of the carcass of a bear is mentioned at eighty-three cents, and a whole deer at thirty-six cents. A "haf buflar" was sold in 1749 for $1.25. Salt varied much. We find it as high as sixty-seven cents a quart in 1745. Coarse salt could be bought for $2.00 a bushel in 1763, and it cost eighty-three cents to have it brought from Richmond. As to sugar, we are sometimes in doubt whether maple or cane sugar is meant. White loaf sugar from the West Indies was generally twenty-five cents a pound. Brown cane sugar was much cheaper.

A weaver was paid six cents for each yard of linen that came from his loom. But Irish linen cost $1.08, flannel forty-one cents, sheeting $1.25, velvet $3.33, and ribbon seventeen cents. The handkerchief cost twenty-five to thirty-three cents if of cotton, but seventy-five cents if of silk. Men's stockings, which came above the knee and were there secured under the trouser-leg with a buckle, cost eighty to ninety cents. Worsted hose for women was fifty cents, and plaid hose thirty-three cents. Leggings were $1.04, pumps $2.00, and men's fine shoes $1.41. A blue broadcloth coat is quoted at $5.42. Gloves are listed at fifty-eight cents, a necklace at thirty-three, and a fan at twenty-five. Leather breeches, very generally worn by laboring men, cost $3.17. Common buttons were forty-two cents a dozen, silk garters, forty-two cents a pair, and thread was half a shilling an ounce. Headgear was high or low in price, according to the means of the wearer. A woman's hat is named at $5.00, and a boy's at eighty-three cents. But a cheap felt hat could be purchased for thirty-three cents.

A very creditable specimen of the colonial will is this one by a pioneer settler of Kerr's Creek:

In the Name of God Amen the 25th March 1786 I Robert Hamilton of Kerrs Creek in Rockbridge County, being very sick and weak in Body but of perfect Mind and Memory thanks be given to God therefor. Calling to mind the Mortality of my Body and knowing that it is appointed for all men once to die, do make and Ordain this my last Will and Testament, that is to say principally and first of all, I give and Recommend my Soul into the hands of God that gave it, and for my Body I recommend it to the Earth to be Buried in a Christian like and decent mannor, at the direction of my Executors, nothing doubting but at the General Resurrection I shall receive the same again by the mighty power of God. And as Touching such Worldly Estate, wherewith it hath pleased God to bless me with in this life, I give and devise and dispose of the same in the following manner and form, to Witt. first I give and bequeath to my wife Margaret a free Room where our bed is with all its Furniture thereunto belonging with her Wheel & Reel with all her Cloathing of whatever kind or sort it is likewise One horse called Wilkenson with a Side Sadle and Bridle (new) with suitable Intertainment for her Station and Seven pounds ye Year to uphold her in Necessaries she finds Needfull for herself during life. But in Case should not to live in that Station she is to have a liberty of Spending her days among either her Children, and in Case she should be so disposed, I bequeath her fifteen pounds ye Year to be paid out of my real Estate during Life, or while she continues my Widow, and no longer. Also I will and Bequeath to my son William Two cows & two Calves to my son Archibald Five Cows and two Calves, and Four Sheep. To my Son Joseph Twenty pounds to be paid out of my Real Estate. I give and bequeath to my son John the place where I now live with all the Improvements thereunto belonging (he paying all these Legacies as the Will Specifies) to him and his heirs forever but in Case he should dye a Batcheler, in that Case the Estate to be sold and Equally Divided among the Rest of his Brothers. To Moses Gwynn I bequeath Ten pounds to be paid out of my Real Estate. To my Daughter Jennett that fifty Acres of Land in Caintuck'y To Mary Erwin my Daughter the 2d Vol. of Askins works, to Miriam my Daughter One Cow & Calf & four Sheep, to my Daughter Margaret, I give or allow a Horse Saddle & Bridle with all her Cloathes, also two Beds and Beding suitable with one Case of Drawers, three Cows and three Calves with six Sheep—also I give to my wife Sarah Callman to wait on her during her Servitude and Hannah her Sister to Margaret, my Daughter on Condition of their performing their duty to them as their Indentures Requires. I constitute Wm. Hamilton & Archibald, my Sons to be my Sole Executors, and I do impower them to collect all Debts due to me & to Discharge all my Lawfull Debts Revoking all Wills and Testaments heretofore made, I confirm this to be my last Will and Testament, This and only this to be my last Will and Testament and none other, in Witness whereof I have hereunto set my hand and Seal the day and Year above Written

VI

CIVIL GOVERNMENT (1737-1852)

CONSERVATIVE INFLUENCES—STATE AND LOCAL GOVERNMENT—LAWS AND PUNISHMENTS—WRITS AND RECORDS—LAND SYSTEM—MARRIAGE REGULATIONS—MONEY

For about forty years after the beginning of settlement, the laws and institutions under which the people of Rockbridge lived were those of Colonial Virginia. For almost twice as long a period, or until the constitution of 1851 went into effect, there was no very striking change. In cutting loose from England, the American did not throw away an old suit of clothes and immediately don a new suit of quite different pattern. It was more as if the old suit were still worn, after being dusted and having a few of the wrinkles pressed out. The coming in of the new order is an illustration of the fact that progress is ordinarily by easy steps and not by jumps.

After independence, the law-making body was the General Assembly, but it was the House of Burgesses under a new name. From certain official forms the king's name was left out. There was still a Governor's Council, and it was very much like the old one. The governor was now a Virginian instead of a Briton, but like the colonial governor he lived in style, and in attending to his official business he followed much the same routine. The Constitution of 1776 left things a good deal as it found them. There was indeed a re-statement of the source of Virginia law, so that there might be a definite recognition of the fact that the state was no longer a part of the British Empire. Juries no longer said that "we find for our Lord the King."

The independence party had a conservative and a progressive wing. The former wanted independence, but with the least possible change otherwise. The latter also wanted independence, but it also wanted to make Virginia a republic, so that it might be no longer a constitutional monarchy. The early years of independence showed that the conservative element was in control and that the progressives had scored only a few points in their program. As the years went by, there was a slow but rather steady yielding in the conservative viewpoint. The dis-establishment of the state church came early, yet only after strenuous opposition. The penal code was ameliorated. Modifications crept here and there into the working of the machinery of government. But the constitution of 1829 was dictated by the conservatives, whose stronghold lay east of the Blue Ridge. To the progressives the new instrument was like a stone instead of a loaf of bread. It was not until 1852, when the third constitution came into effect, that the progressives won anything like a general victory. Until that date, and with respect to economics as well as institutions, the people of Virginia continued to live under conditions that were essentially colonial. The modern era was not fairly under way until the middle of the last century.

Until 1776, the common law of England, supplemented by the enactments of the House of Burgesses, was the law of Virginia. The statutes passed by the colonial legislature were expected to conform to the British practice. The king's veto, which was dictated by the Board of Trade, was freely used, and it went so far as to frustrate the attempt to incorporate some town or village. After independence these annoyances were a thing of the past.

Under the foreign régime, the governor was an appointee of the British crown and acted as its personal representative. Sometimes he remained in England and enjoyed the actual title, the duties of the office being performed by a deputy. But the official that appeared in Virginia lived in pomp and drew a very large salary, even for that age. He was able to wield a great influence, although he was commonly an overbearing aristocrat, who took little pains to acquire the Virginian point of view. After 1776 and until 1852, the governor was an appointee of the Assembly and was not elected by the people. The royal governor could remit fines and forfeitures, and he could veto any bill. He could grant pardon for any crime except treason or wilful murder, and in these instances he could reprieve.

In colonial times there was a Council of eight members, who were appointed and not elected. They served an indefinite time and had a monopoly of most places of honor and trust. They assisted the governor and acted as a supreme court. This council of eight was continued after independence. The members of the House of Burgesses were chosen by popular vote, and there were two from each county. Until 1830, there were likewise two members from each county in the House of Delegates, regardless of the matter of population. After 1830 there was a more equitable arrangement, and it was based on the number of people in the various counties. The Senate of 1776 contained twenty-four members.

Under colonial rule the elective franchise was much restricted, and this continued to be the case until 1852. In effect, there is as much restriction now as there was then, even among the whites. But whereas the small vote now polled in the average county of this state is largely due to indifference, it was formerly due to a property qualification. Voting was viva voce. Until 1852 the burgess or delegate was almost the only public official, state or local, who was dependent on popular vote.

For a long while there was no higher judicial tribunal than the Council. Under independence, there was a State Court of Appeals, any three of its five members constituting a minor court. Rockbridge formed with Augusta, Rockingham, and Pendleton a judicial circuit, its judges having full jurisdiction in civil and criminal causes, and original jurisdiction in all causes involving a consideration of more than 100 pounds.

With the exception that we shall presently note, the affairs of each county were looked after by the county court, a body which until 1852 was almost the same thing that it was in 1737. It was a self-perpetuating, close corporation, and had more extensive powers than those of the present Board of Supervisors. When a new county was established, its first board of "worshipful justices" was nominated by the court of the parent county. When vacancies occurred, or when there was a desire to increase the membership, nominations were made by the court and commissions were issued therefrom by the governor. The county court was therefore not responsible to the people. The system was not democratic. The justices were chosen from the most influential families, and were often related to one another. The office often descended from father to son. It was in the power of the court to use partiality toward its friends and its own membership, and to be arbitrary and tyrannical. But in practice the working of the system was in the direction of good government. The justices felt the responsibility of their position and were in touch with the people. They were not only justices of the peace, but acted collectively, or by classes, as a board of county commissioners. They served without pay. They held office for an indefinite time, but the governor might remove a justice for cause. Until 1830 there was no positive limitation on the number of justices. Four justices made a quorum and opinions were decided by a majority vote.

Until 1776 a county court was opened by the reading of the royal commission: "Be it remembered (date here given) his majesty's commission directed to (names of commissioned justices here given) to hear and determine all treasons, petit treasons, or misprisons thereof, felonies, murders, and all other offenses or crimes, was openly read." The county court had general police and probate jurisdiction, the control of county levies, of roads, actions at law, and suits in chancery. It passed judgment on all offenses except felonies and high treason, these coming before the Governor's Council, to be there examined by a grand jury before the final trial in the home county. But in the case of such criminals as were negro slaves, it could decree the death penalty and order the sheriff to execute it. It appointed the constables and the overseers of the roads, no acting justice being eligible in the latter capacity. After independence it appointed the county clerk. Under British rule, the county clerk was the deputy of the secretary of state, and was appointed by him. A single justice had jurisdiction in matters not exceeding the value of twenty-five shillings. In 1788, suits at common law and in chancery might no longer come before the county court where the consideration was in excess of five pounds.

Jurors were ordinarily chosen from the locality of the issue they were to pass upon. Tavern-keepers, surveyors of roads, and millers were exempt from grand-jury service. In 1793 the allowance to a witness was fifty-three cents a day, in addition to four cents for each mile of travel.

In 1808 the court day for Rockbridge was changed to the Monday after the first Tuesday in each month.

A petition of 1802 complains that the recovery of small debts is difficult, and asks that the jurisdiction of single magistrates be extended to $20.00. It also asks that constables be required to give security for the faithful discharge of their duty, and for the same service as a sheriff to be allowed the same fee.

Each year the court sent to the governor the names of one to three of the senior members, one of whom was commissioned by him as sheriff. But the high sheriff sold out the office to the highest bidder—sometimes at auction—so that the actual work was done by his deputies, while he enjoyed the honor and something of the emoluments. The court also nominated the coroner, who served during good behavior. His office was more important than it is now, since the incumbent was a conservator of the peace.

The county lieutenant was an appointee of the governor and might be regarded as his deputy. He had charge of the militia of the county, and ranked as a colonel in time of war.

An auxiliary medium of county government was the vestry, one of which existed in colonial times in every parish. The parish might be co-extensive with the county, or the county might contain two or three parishes. When a new county was formed, the members of its first vestry or vestries were chosen by the qualified voters. But with a curious inconsistency, the vestry was thenceforward self-perpetuating like the county court. Its executive officers were the two church-wardens selected from its own membership. Their duties were both civil and ecclesiastical. They built chapels and rectories for the established church and levied taxes for that purpose. They also looked after moral delinquencies, and bound out orphans and bastards. The parish clerk and the sexton could be appointed by the rector as well as by the vestry. The vestry fell into disuse during the Revolution, and was never revived. It passed out of existence with the dis-establishment of the Episcopal Church. A petition from Rockbridge, dated May 20, 1780, asks permission for a levy for poor relief. It says that as there has been no vestry for some time, the poor have had to trust to humane contributions.

The courthouse known to the people of Rockbridge in 1746 was the one first built in Augusta. It was of hewed logs, and was eighteen by thirty-eight feet in size. There were two little windows unprovided with glass or shutters, but some light came in through unchinked spaces between the logs, a number of these openings being several feet long and several inches wide. The jail was smaller and not very secure. The first courthouse authorized at Lexington was almost as primitive as the one at Staunton. Prisoners might walk about within the jail limits, which covered five to ten acres. A prisoner for debt might live in a house if it were within such limits.

Previous to the French and Indian war small printed forms were used for legal writs. From then until the Revolution legal papers were written out by hand, usually in a neat, legible manner. Very small pieces of paper were used and the lines of writing are near together. As for the old record-books, they contain many more words to the page than do those of our time, even with the use of the typewriter. The lines are near together, but when a coarse-pointed quill was used, the writing may be more easily read than the hurried scribbling that is customary today. The copyist not only made his small letters of uniform height, but he often took time to begin a long entry with a highly ornamental initial. Indexing was done on the fly-leaves and with great economy of space. The ink was of a very durable kind. None but quill pens were known or used, and unlike steel pens, their action is not corrosive to the paper.

The laws of the colonial era were harsh. Virginia was more humane in this respect than England, and yet twenty-seven offenses were recognized as punishable by death. In 1796 this number was reduced to one. Lashes at the public whipping-post, on the bare back and "well laid on," were frequently ordered, thirty-nine being the limit at any one time. Women were thus punished as well as men. Imprisonment for debt continued until the middle of the nineteenth century. By this time the pillory, the whipping-post, and the practice of branding the hand had become relics of a past age. The spirit of the time demanded a more humane administration of the criminal code.

The constable's path was not one to be envied. A writ of 1765 has this endorsement: "Not executed case of by a hayfork." Another constable says he was "kept off by force of arms."

Taxes were seemingly low, yet no easier to meet than they are today. The poll-tax varied a good deal from year to year, and when new county buildings had been contracted for, it must have seemed rather formidable to many persons. Before the Revolution and for a while afterward, hemp was generally grown on the farms of this county, the state paying a bounty of one dollar per hundredweight. The certificates therefor, issued by the county court, were receivable for taxes. The bounty on a single wolf-head would pay the taxes for almost any man.

Each year several men were appointed by the court to list the "tithables," this term being given to those individuals who were subject to head-tax. Aged men, any men who were objects of charity, and boys under the age of sixteen were exempt. Old or infirm servants were also exempt, but a widow who was the head of a household was subject to levy.

British law followed the Roman in holding that the crown is a personification of the state. Therefore, by virtue of a legal fiction all public lands were held to be the property of the king. Patents for them were made out in his name and signed by the royal governor as the king's deputy. The Revolution swept away this rubbish and recognized the public domain as belonging to the state instead of a theoretical person. The landseeker, armed with a warrant from the state treasury, perhaps the result of military service, applied to the county surveyor and had a tract set off. This survey was the basis on which a patent was issued after the lapse of one or two years or perhaps a much longer period. The survey might be assigned to another man, and several assignments might precede the patent. A transfer of this sort had to be attested by two witnesses. There was much trading in land warrants, and some money was made in these transactions. Regularity in surveying was seldom observed. The first comer ran his lines in any fashion that would give him a maximum of good land and a minimum of cull land. The surveyor held office during good behavior.

In land conveyances before the Revolution, there was followed the English practice of drawing two instruments for the same transaction; a deed of lease and a deed of release, so that deeds are recorded in pairs in the deed-book. The consideration named in the first is usually five shillings. The deed of release, which is the real and effective instrument, is dated one day later and names the actual consideration. There is sometimes mention of the purchaser receiving from the seller a twig in token of possession. The Revolution also did away with this clumsy practice of issuing deeds in pairs, each one stuffed full of verbose legal technicalities.

Until 1776, a quitrent of one shilling for each fifty acres was exacted from purchasers of the public domain. This requirement was very much disliked, and was regarded as a cloud on the title. After American independence was declared, the quitrent was speedily abolished.

The processioning of private holdings of land was begun in 1747. Every four years, men appointed for that purpose by the vestry, and afterward by the county court, marked the corners of the surveys. This had to be done between October 1st and April 1st. In 1797 the payment per day for this service was fifty cents. The practice fell into disuse, but was revived by a law of 1865-6.

Religion was not free in this state until just after the close of the Revolution. The established church was the Church of England, known to us as the Episcopalian. It was supported by general taxation, and each parish owned a farm known as a glebe. On this the rector lived. In theory, and to a limited extent in fact, attendance at the parish chapel was compulsory. Other Protestants were known as Dissenters. Their houses of worship had to be licensed and registered by the county court, and their ministers had to take various oaths. But west of the Blue Ridge, where few people adhered to the Establishment, there was and could be no persecution of the Dissenters. To learn the attitude of the Virginia government, the Presbyterian Synod of Ireland addressed a memorial to Governor Gooch in 1738. It brought this reply:

> As I have always been inclined to favor the people who have lately removed from other provinces to settle on the western side of our great mountains, so you may be assured that no interruption shall be given to any minister of your profession, who shall come among them, so as they conform themselves to the rules prescribed by the Act of Toleration in England, by taking the oaths enjoined thereby, and registering the place of their meeting, and behave themselves peaceably toward the government.

This letter has been construed as a letting down of the bars. Yet the governor promised nothing to the Ulstermen that the laws did not already permit. He merely said in effect that the newcomers would be let alone, so long as they obeyed the laws. There was no limitation on the number of their houses of worship, yet they had to contribute to the support of the Establishment just the same as if they had settled on the other side of the Blue Ridge. Their ministers were not permitted until the close of 1781 to unite couples in marriage. John Brown married two couples in 1755, but finding he was violating a law, he did not again perform a marriage ceremony for twenty-six years. The people of the Valley were restive under the disabilities imposed on them, and were nearly unanimous in helping to secure religious freedom for Virginia, this end being accomplished in 1784. It is claimed, and probably with reason, that the lack of express toleration kept thousands of intending immigrants out of colonial Virginia.

The ruling element in colonial Virginia held that education is a private and not a public interest, and that schooling is to be purchased like clothing or groceries. The constitution of 1776 is silent on the subject. The mention of schools in the public records is accordingly very meager and incidental. We find mention of a schoolhouse in 1753, which was sixteen years after the coming of the McDowells. It is not at all probable that it was the only one, or that it had just been built.

During the colonial time a marriage was solemnized by the parish minister or parish reader, but the certificate he gave was not deposited with the county clerk. The public recording of marriages did not begin until about the close of 1781, and it is therefore difficult to secure definite knowledge of unions that took place before that date. By the new practice, the groom was required to sign a bond of fifty pounds. His surety was commonly the bride's father. If either groom or bride were under the age of twenty-one, and this was very often the case, the consent of the parent or parents had to accompany the bond, which served as a license. The consent was ordinarily written on a narrow scrap of paper, and often with poor ink. The signature, if not in the form of a mark, is usually crabbed and more or less difficult to make out. This scrap, not always unsoiled, was folded into a small compass, making it look like a paper of epsom salts as put up by a doctor before tablets and capsules came into use. The bonds were filed away in bundles. This system was in force until 1852.

Personal liberty was so highly prized on the old frontier that a certain statute of 1661 must have seemed irksome to the settlers. This law made it illegal for any person to remove out of his county until after setting up his name for three Sundays at the door of the church or chapel of his parish. This notice had to express his intention and certify where he was about to go. It was then attested by the minister or reader and the church-wardens, who gave him license to go. The order-books of Augusta indicate that this law was not a dead letter.

The house of entertainment was called an ordinary. The prices the tavern-keeper might charge were regulated by the county court with great exactness. These rates had to be posted in the public room and not above a specified height from the floor. This care was not needless. Extortion would otherwise have been more possible than it is now.

Money was computed, as in England, in pounds, shillings, and pence. But on this side of the Atlantic these names applied to values and not to coins. In the "current money of Virginia," the pound represented $3.33, the shilling sixteen and two-third cents, and the penny one and seven-eighteenths cents. Because of the depreciation of the colonial money, British coins did not freely circulate here. The hard money in actual use came from the West Indies, and was of Spanish, French, and Portugese coinage. Thus we read of the pistole, the doubloon, and the louis d'or, or "loodore." These were gold coins worth, respectively, $3.92, $7.84, and $3.96. It was by way of the West Indies that the Americans became acquainted with the "piece of eight," or Mexican dollar. Eight reals made a dollar, the real being a silver coin of the value of nine pence, or twelve and one-half cents. The earliest mention of the dollar by name, in the Augusta records, is in 1752. The fact that the Mexican dollar subdivided so readily into the terms used in computing the colonial money, is the leading reason why the dollar, a well known coin, became the unit of Federal money. Under the names of "levy" and "fip," the real and half-real were legal tender in the United States until near the beginning of the war of 1861.

CIVIL GOVERNMENT (1737-1852) 53

Since the gold and silver coins that passed from hand to hand were of so varied a character, it was tedious and inconvenient to turn their values into Virginia money. A sum of money is spoken of in 1750 as made up of one doubloon, one pistole, two moidores, and two pieces of silver. The value of these Spanish and Portuguese coins was about $24.00. It was customary to compute the foreign money by weight, and hence money-scales are often mentioned in inventories of personal property. Copper pennies were coined for Virginia in 1733. This coin was worth almost exactly one cent. Paper money of colonial issue began to appear in the colony in 1755. The ten-pound note was not quite one-half the size of a postal card, was crudely engraved, and was too easy to counterfeit. Warehouse certificates for tobacco also passed from hand to hand as money and did not need endorsement. When a money consideration was written into a legal document, the sum usually mentioned is five shillings. The legal rate of interest was five per cent. There were no banks, and when a large stock of money was on hand it was secreted. There is very frequent mention of Pennsylvania currency, in which the pound was worth $2.50 and the shilling twelve and one-half cents.

Money, whether of metal or paper, could be counterfeited with more impunity than is possible today. We not infrequently find mention of bad bills and suspicious doubloon certificates.

VII

ANNALS OF 1737-1777

SELECTIONS FROM THE RECORDS OF ORANGE, AUGUSTA, AND BOTETOURT

ORANGE ORDER-BOOK, 1735-1745

1111 tithables—Nov. 18, 1735.
Road surveyors to set finger-boards at every crossroads in large letters.
The Rev. Richard Hardwell presented for being drunk.—1741.
James Phillips fined ten shillings for non-attendance at his parish church, and for not appearing to answer the charge against him.
Poll tax, fourteen pounds of tobacco—1744.
Andrew Campbell takes out a pedler's license—1740.
Wolf-heads turned in by Charles Campbell, James Hamilton, John James, and Richard McDowell.
Constables: 1741, James McDowell; 1742, Hugh Cunningham; 1743, Joseph Lapsley, John Mitchell, William Moore, and James Anderson; 1744, Samuel Gay.
Militia officers: John Mathews and Patrick Hays appointed captains in 1742; William Jameson, captain, 1745; Alexander Dunlap, captain of horse, 1743; Henry Gay, lieutenant in 1744, and Andrew Hays in 1745.
People of Borden Tract petition for a road from James Young's on to Borden's Tract by a gap in Blue Ridge called Michael Woods' Gap. Francis McCown, Samuel Walker, Captain Charles Campbell, and Captain Patrick Hays among the overseers. Colonel James Patton to lay off the precincts. South River to be crossed at the plantation of Samuel Davis.
Tavern rates, 1742: Hot diet, one shilling; cold diet or loging, sixpence each; corn or oats, per gallon, sixpence; stabling and fodder for one night, or pasturage for twenty-four hours, sixpence; Barbadoes rum, per gallon, eight shillings; New England rum, per gallon, two shillings and sixpence; Virginia brandy, per gallon, six shillings; claret, per gallon, four shillings; Virginia cider, per quart, four and half pence.

AUGUSTA ORDER-BOOKS

1745

Robert Young appointed constable in Richard Woods's militia company, and James Greenlee to succeed William Moore in Benjamin Borden's company. Greenlee afterward excused on account of illiteracy.

1746

Joseph Lapsley and John Peter Salling sworn in as captains, Robert Renick as first lieutenant.
Statements of losses by Indians certified to in case of Richard Woods, John Mathews, Henry Kirkham, Francis McCown, Joseph Lapsley, Isaac Anderson, John and James Walker.—Feb. 19th.
James Huston and three other men presented for being vagrants, and hunting and burning the woods; on information given by John Peter Salling, James Young, and John McCown. Huston fined three pounds for illegally killing three deer.

Constables: William Taylor from Benjamin Allen's to the lower end of the county; William Gay on the Calfpasture; Michael O'Dougherty in Woods's company; John McCown, Michael Finney, and Thomas Williams in the Forks of James. Samuel Dunlap, John Ramsay, and John Campbell succeed, respectively, Nathaniel McClure, William Gay, and Robert Gwin. Alexander McCroskey is also a constable.

1747

Henry Gay, James Allison, John Hodge, and John Edmondson petition for leave to build gristmills.

The road formerly cleared from James Young's mill to Woods's Gap to be altered.

John Allison given license for a ferry between his landing and Halbert McClure's.

Robert Patterson and James Allen to view a road from John Picken's mill to lower meeting house.

Petition by James McCown for road from crossroads below Patrick Hays. Hays is on north side of South River.

1748

Richard Burton to take the list of tithables in the Forks.

Roger Keys and Sarah, his wife, win in a slander suit against Ephraim McDowell. John Lyle is a witness.

George Campbell presented for striking and beating Joseph Walker in the courtyard. Henry C——— presented for assaulting and beating Joseph M——— in a meeting house yard at a time of burial service.

Constables: David Dryden and William Lockridge succeed Samuel Dunlap; William Woods succeeds John McCown; Alexander Walker succeeds Michael Dougherty.

1749

Archibald Alexander, Benjamin Borden, William Jameson, Samuel Gay, John Lyle, John Mathews, and Richard Woods are on the list of justices.

Benjamin Borden to take the list of tithables from North River to the end of the county; David Stuart, from the courthouse to North River.

1750

A road has been cleared over the Blue Ridge at "Woods's old gap"—May 25.

Road ordered from John Hays' mill to Providence meeting house. Posts of direction to be set up.

Richard Burton, Robert Renick, John Poage, Peter Wallace, are to survey a road from Looney's Ferry to North River; Benjamin Borden, John Thompson, Isaac Taylor, and William McClung are to survey to the intersection with the county road.

Road ordered from William Gay's to Robert McCutchen's and thence to Robert Campbell's. McCutchen to build the road with the help of William Elliott, Thomas Fulton, John Fulton, John Meek, Thomas Meek, John Williams, and John Gay.

John Maxwell, James McDowell, and Edward Hogan were in a canoe on the James, Sunday, May 13 (Old Style). The boat upset and Hogan was drowned. Coroner's jury at James Greenlee's, five days later: Michael Dougherty, Josiah F. Hendon, John Hitchins, Joshua Mathews, James Montgomery, John Poage, John Ramsey, John Vance, Matthew Vance, Samuel Walker, Joseph Walker, and ——— Walker.

1751

William Lusk a justice.

Archibald Alexander, Michael Finney, John Hargrove, John Maxwell, and John Peter

Salling are surveyors for a road from David Moore's Mill to Robert Poage's mill.
Order for road from Hays' fulling mill to Timber Ridge meeting house.
Constables: James Phillips vice Samuel McCutchen; William Elliott vice James Gay; Richard Cousart vice James Greenlee; John Gilmore vice John Allison.

1752

James Young, miller, presented for taking toll twice.
Road ordered from William Cleghorn's to Purgatory.
Benjamin Borden to lay off a road from his house to Providence meeting house. John Patton, surveyor.

Petitioners for a road from Kennedy's mill to John Houston's, and from Houston's to the great road from Timber Grove to Woods' Gap: Robert Alexander, Andrew Duncan, Robert Dunlap, Walter Eakin, James Eakin, John Edmondson, John Handly, Patrick Hays, James Hill, John Houston, Joseph Kennedy, William Lockridge, William McConnell, John Montgomery, Andrew Steele, Robert Stuart, John Stuart, William Wardlaw, and John Wilson.

Petition of settlers on the lower Cowpasture petition for a road over the mountains to the Borden Tract—Oct. 19.

1753

225 wolf-heads turned in—Nov. 22.
Cornelius Bryan given permission to cut a road at his own expense from the "bent" in Buffalo to Michael Dougherty's.
Members of grand jury, Nov. 20: Robert Bratton, James Lockridge, John Anderson, William Caruthers, Archibald Alexander, John Paxton, and Samuel McClure. James Trimble, foreman.
John Paxton road overseer from Edmondson's mill to Fork Meeting House.
Order for a road from Campbell's schoolhouse to the Renick road. Samuel Walker, overseer. Workers: John Allison, Samuel Allison, Stephen Arnold, Richard Burton, William Burt, William Byers, James Frazier, Henry Fuller, John Hutchings, Sr., John Hutchings, Jr., John Maxwell, John McColley, Richard Mathews, Sampson Mathews, William Noble, John Peteet, Joseph Ryan, Thomas Shaw, John Smith, Joseph Smith, John Sprowl, John Peter Salling, George Salling, Mathew Vance, Samuel Walker.

1754

Several runaway servants taken up.
Joseph Tees fined twenty shillings for saying, "he got nothing in this court but shuffling."
Lancelot Graham constable on Great Calfpasture, William Ramsay on Little Calfpasture. Thomas Paxton constable to succeed John Lowry.

1755

James Lockridge appointed a lieutenant.
Mary McDonald bound over to keep the peace for putting John Cunningham in fear of his life. Cunningham has tavern license.
Order for a road from Isaac Taylor's to Tarr's shop.
Abraham Brown constable below Brushy Hills in Forks of James.

1756

Mary, wife of William Whiteside, refused separate maintenance. The court blames certain of her relatives for the breach.

ANNALS OF 1737-1777

Many claims for ranging and for the impressment of horses are ordered certified.
Valentine Utter and Mary, his wife, servants of John Paxton, are set free on consideration of their paying him twelve pounds.
Constables: David Doak vice Samuel Braford; Samuel Steele vice James Walker; Moses Whiteside in James Kennedy's company; Samuel Wilson vice Alexander McNutt.

1757

Constables: John Shields vice John Henderson; William Logan vice Andrew Campbell; William Rhea vice Samuel Steele; John Paxton vice Abraham Brown; Thomas Kirkpatrick vice Thomas Berry.

1758

James Alexander becomes a captain.
John McCroskey road overseer from Alexander Miller's to the line of Beverly Manor; Charles Hays, from Andrew Hays' mill to Captain Kennedy's.
Order for a road from Hays's mill to Timber Ridge meeting house. Overseers, Alexander Miller, Joseph Culton, and Archibald Alexander.

1759

Richard Woods, sheriff.
Samuel McDowell, captain, James McDowell, lieutenant, John Lyle, ensign.

1760

Joseph Culton granted mill license.
John Dickenson and James Lockridge to survey a road from John Wilson's to Panther Gap.

1761

John Paxton granted tavern license.
John Buchanan to take the list of tithables on the south side of the James, Richard Woods in the Forks, Archibald Alexander from North River to Beverly Manor, and James Lockridge in the Pastures and on Jackson's River.
John Mathews is road surveyor from North River to the junction with the road near Sharp's.
Archibald Alexander, Felix Gilbert, Andrew Hays, John Tate, John Buchanan, to survey a road from Stuart's to the top of the mountain near Rockfish Gap. Tithables to turn out from Woods Gap to Jennings Gap, and from between North Mountain and South Mountain to North River.—Aug. 19.
John Moore of Borden Tract presented for staying away from public worship.

1763

John Houston overseer of road from Timber Ridge to Providence.
James McDowell, captain, William McKee, lieutenant.
For having two children taught dancing Israel Christian is sued for five pounds.
Thirty-three justices, inclusive of Richard Woods, John Bowyer, James Buchanan, Archibald Alexander, John Maxwell, and Samuel McDowell.

1764

John Paxton certifies to 7720 pounds of hemp.
John Anderson made oath to an account of five pounds expense in taking up his servant, Edward Lochan, who was absent twenty-nine days. Ordered that Lochan serve Anderson fifteen months extra time.

Daniel Lyle, William Ramsay, and James Simpson to view a way from North River to James Stinson's (Stevenson) on Buffalo.

Samuel and David Lyle to view from William Davis's to Timber Ridge.

John Mathews with wife and six children were burned in and with their house according to a statement by Sampson Mathews. Christian Godfrey Milliron is bound on suspicion of being guilty of the deed.

George Lewis is held for trial because of driving a wagon on Sunday.

1765

For provisions and impressed horses for the use of the militia, claims are turned in by Thomas Alexander, Robert Bratton, John Dunlap, William Elliott, John Finlay, Hugh Fulton, James Mateer, Samuel McCutchen, William McKemy, William McNabb, Daniel O'Freel, Thomas Poage, John and Mary Trimble, and Joseph Walkup.

Judith Ryley convicted of killing her bastard child.

John Greenlee road surveyor from John Mathews, Jr's., to Sinclair's Gap.

1766

James Cloyd overseer of road from lower end of John Bowyer's plantation on James, by Cedar bridge, to Mathews road. Workers: John Berry, Matthew Hair, John Hall, William Hall, John Jones, John Logan, James McClure, James Skidmore, George Skillern, Christopher Vineyard, Conrad Wall, George Wilson.

1767

Old and new roads from Isaac Taylor's to Timber Ridge meeting house.

Andrew Hays, captain, James Cloyd, captain, James Lapsley, ensign.

Samuel Todd asks for a mill license on Whistle Creek.

View for a road ordered from Hanna's mill on Collier's Creek to George Gibson's at House Mountain.

Road open from Cowpasture to Gilmore's Gap.

1768

Thomas Paxton is making grape brandy.

Robert Steele has a mill.

1769

James Cowden has a stone house near Samuel McDowell's.

John Summers constable in place of Alexander Dale.

Jacob, a slave, ordered to have thirty-nine lashes for shooting at the children of Alexander Moore.

1770

Charles Hays certifies to 2293 pounds of hemp.

George Mathews, sheriff.

John Hays, James McDowell, Samuel McDowell, and Archibald Houston are vestrymen.

John Caldwell has leave to build an oil mill on South River.

1771

Brice Hanna, contractor to do work at New Providence, failed and ran off. Charles Campbell, Alexander Moore, William Walker, and James Walker, commissioners.

1773

Order for a road from Thomas Lackey's to Timber Ridge meeting house.

Alexander Stuart, neighbor to William McClung, granted mill license on Mill Creek.

Samuel McDowell qualifies as justice.

For illegal selling of liquor, Thomas Mathews asks for corporal punishment in place of a fine. Twenty-one lashes to be given at once and costs imposed.

Road ordered from head of Kerr's Creek to North River. In 1774 the bridle-path is reported to be the most convenient way.

Hemp certificates given: to James McKee for 2290 pounds; John McKee, 2415; Isaac Anderson, 2863; John McCown, 2566; Andrew Hays, 3300; James Kerr, 2372; James Lindsay, 1070.

Dr. George Parker, servant of Samuel McChesney, agrees, with the approval of the court, to pay McChesney 100 pounds for his freedom, on condition of being given a horse and saddle worth ten pounds, and drugs and medicines worth thirty pounds, and is to pay ten pounds a year for his board until the sum of 100 should be paid up. Parker is to keep the horse at his own expense.

1777

John Gilmore, John Lyle, and David Gray are captains.

Nat, an Indian boy in the custody of Mary Greenlee, complains that he is held in unlawful slavery. A stay is granted until Mrs. Greenlee's son in the Carolinas can be heard from. Meanwhile, Nat is hired out until it can be determined whether he is slave or free. The court considers that Mrs. Greenlee has treated him in an inhumane manner.

Zachariah Johnston and Andrew Moore, captains.

Liberty to inoculate for the smallpox is granted to the people of Staunton and for three miles around.

BOTETOURT ORDER-BOOK

1770-1777

Richard Woods is first high sheriff, and James McDowell and James McGavock and John Bowyer are his undersheriffs. John Maxwell is sheriff in 1773.

James Bailey and Joseph Davis are constables on Buffalo, and William Hall on Cedar.—1770.

Salary of king's attorney is 4000 pounds of tobacco, the equivalent of sixteen pounds thirteen shillings four pence, or $55.55 in Federal money.

Surveyors of roads, 1770: Audley Paul and Hugh Barclay, from Renick's to James Gilmore's; James Simpson, from Gilmore's to Buffalo; John Paxton, from Buffalo to North River Ferry; James Templeton, from Buffalo ford to North River; George Francisco, from Fork of road below Barclay's to the Buffalo; James Templeton, from ford of Buffalo to North River.

William McKee to take the tithables from the county line to the Buffalo and from mountain to mountain; Benjamin Estill, from the Buffalo to the James and from mountain to mountain.

John Bowyer, John Maxwell, James Trimble, William McKee, James McGavock, and Robert Poage are among the first justices.

Hugh Barclay has license to keep an ordinary—1770.

Wolf-heads, 173—1770.

Charles Given certifies that his left ear was bitten off by Francis McDonald—1771.

Elizabeth Collier agrees to serve her master, James Green, one year extra time, provided he employs her as house-servant—1773.

Head-tax, sixty-seven pounds of tobacco ($2.00); Tithables, 1494, of whom 229 are delinquent—1773.

Allowance of $40.00 for furnishing courthouse with candles and firewood—1773.

Tavern rates: Warm diet with good meat, one shilling; cold diet, seven and one-half pence; lodging in good bed with clean sheets, six pence; lodging with two or more in bed, four pence each; grain, per gallon, six pence—1775.

Samuel Wallace, road surveyor from Paxton's ford on North River to ford in Buffalo.

Benjamin Estill and John Bowyer among the persons appointed to administer the oath of allegiance to the free white inhabitants, as per Act of Assembly; Estill for the companies of John Paxton and James Hall, Bowyer for the companies of William Paxton and Samuel Wallace—August 13, 1777.

Contract let for building a prison sixteen by twenty feet, logs squared to the dimensions of fourteen by fourteen inches to form the walls and the upper and lower floors.

VIII

STRIFE WITH THE RED MAN

An Empty Land—Indian Mounds—Indian Meadows—Relations Between the Races—
The McDowell Fight—Blockhouses—The Renick Affair—The
Kerr's Creek Raids—Dunmore War—The Long Hunters

The Rockbridge area was a vacant land when found and explored by the whites. That such had always been its condition does not follow by any means. There have been inhabitants in America since a day that makes the voyage of Columbus seem as but an occurrence of last year. In the Western Hemisphere as in the Eastern, we may be sure that war, or pestilence, or some other catastrophe has here and there emptied a region of its human occupants.

It is true enough that the arrowheads, pipes, scrapers, and other relics, which have been numerously found in various localities, do not necessarily point to a period of settled occupation. Hunting operations continued for centuries, varied by an occasional tribal fight, are sufficient to account for these. It was possibly by hunters alone that the Indian path was made which may be seen on Jump Mountain opposite Wilson's Springs. It was possibly by hunters alone that the stone-pile on North Mountain was built up.

But all these suppositions are not enough to account for the mound which used to stand on the Hays Creek bottom, a very short distance below the mouth of Walker's Creek. At the time it was dug away and examined by Mr. Valentine, it was almost circular, averaging sixty-two feet in diameter at the base and forty feet on the flat top. The vertical height was then four and one-half feet, but the *Gazette* in 1876 speaks of it as having been ten or twelve feet high. The encroachments of cultivation had undoubtedly much diminished the original bulk. The excavators found eighty perfect skulls and more than 400 skeletons. In all instances the legs were drawn up and the arms folded across the breast. Shell-beads and pendants were found on the necks of twenty-eight of the skeletons. A few pieces of pottery and some other relics were found, and there were eight skeletons of dogs, several of these being almost perfect. The site is now completely leveled, and the exact spot is in danger of being forgotten.

To those who know something of the customs of the Red American, it is evident that this mound was a burial mound, and that near it was once a village. Indian huts were of very perishable materials, and it is not at all strange that no trace of the village can now be found, unless by a trained investigator. At the time of white settlement—about 1738—there may have been a very low earth-ring, marking the site of a palisade, and this could soon have been destroyed by repeated plowings. At all events, no recollection of such a ring seems to remain.

White people are very prone to imagine that the native mounds were built over the corpses of the braves slain in battle. But the Indian war party rarely comprise more than a few dozen men, and often it was exceedingly small. The victors would lose but a few of their number, if any, and these were buried in individual graves marked by little mounds of loose stones. The vanquished dead were left to be devoured by wild beasts. It is to be remembered that until a quite recent time the European nations held themselves to be under no obligation to bury the dead of a defeated army. The fact that many of the skeletons in the Hays Creek mound were of women and girls, and the conventional mode of interment, show that the burials distributed over a considerable period of time. As to the age of the mound, there is no answer but conjecture. Earthworks tend to endure indefinitely, and in this instance the bones began to crumble on exposure to the air. This burial mound may have antedated the coming of the white man by several centuries.

A tradition of uncertain authenticity tells of a battle between Indians at the mouth of Walker's Creek. It further tells of a squaw who witnessed the fight from the end of Jump Mountain, and leaped over the precipice on seeing the fall of her companion. The tradition may be correct. The battle could not have resulted in the mound, though it may have resulted in the extinction of the village. The Indian's eyes were good, yet not keen enough to identify a man from the top of the precipice several miles away.

The Ulster people were very disputatious, particularly as to the meaning of texts from the Bible. An old resident of Hays Creek contended all his life as to the name of the tribe that built this mound. He made a solemn request to be buried on the hill facing it, so that at the resurrection he might be the first one to see his theory vindicated.

Within the memory of men still living, a mound stood near Glasgow close to the position of the lowest county bridge on North River. On the Buffalo was a burial mound. No other earthmounds, extant or leveled, have been named to the writer. It is surprising that there is no knowledge of any mound on the bottom near Kerr's Creek postoffice. Such a spot would have appealed to the Indian as a place of settlement.

Mention has been made of the stone-heap on the very summit of North Mountain. It stands close to the Lexington and Rockbridge Alum Turnpike. It used to be twenty feet long, six feet wide, and four feet high, but the two holes dug into it have lowered the height and disarranged the once nicely rounded top. The pieces of rock are wholly of brown ironstone, such as is found abundantly on the western face of the mountain. Isaac Taylor, a Rockbridge man who went to Ohio, was told by an Indian that it was the work of a war party from the West. Each brave, while passing over, was to throw down a stone, and on the return each survivor was to pick one up, so that a count of the remaining ones might determine the loss. The expedition was disastrous and the heap remained quite intact. If the tradition be correct, it must apply to some other and smaller stone-pile. Before being tampered with, this mound must have contained several thousands of rock-fragments. Much more reasonable is the conjecture that it grew up little by little, and was due to a custom of the passing red man to drop a stone as an act of propitiation to the Great Spirit, and as the expression of a wish that his journey might have a favorable outcome. It was in fact a practice of the red man to rear a mound where his trail went through a mountain pass. This pass was used by him and when the trees are leafless it commands a view of the Kerr's Creek valley.

When the white explorer came the Rockbridge area, like the Valley of Virginia in general, was largely occupied by tracts of prairie. These were known as Indian meadows, or as savannas, the word prairie having not yet come into the English language. These meadows were fired at the close of each hunting season so as to keep back the forest growth and thus attract the buffalo and other large game. This practice had undoubtedly been going on for centuries. Throughout all Appalachia nature strives to keep the surface clothed in forest. A large expanse of open ground could only originate in the little clearing that always surrounded the native village. The persistent firing of a deserted clearing would make the meadow steadily increase in size.

After white settlement began, parties of Indians continued to come here to hunt, or to pass through on some war expedition. The Iroquois of New York were the native claimants of the district, and they were at feud with the Cherokees and Catawbas to the southward. Hunting parties would build bark cabins for temporary shelter, and these were sometimes temporarily used by the whites.

John Craig was for a third of a century the minister at the North Mountain Meeting House near Staunton. He lived five miles away and walked to church carrying his gun on his shoulder. He wrote that the Indians "were generally civil, though some persons were murdered by them about that time (1740). They march about in small companies from fifteen to twenty, and must be supplied at any house they call at, or they become their own stewards and cooks, and spare nothing they choose to eat and drink."

While he was hunting, the Indian took food wherever he found any, and he considered that animals running at large were lawful game. If he expected free and liberal entertainment, it was because he was ready to treat others as he expected to be treated himself. There were no bounds to his hospitality, because in the usage of his race food was not private property. But the points of view of the two races were very divergent. The native thought the paleface uncivil and unhospitable, and was not attracted to his manner of living. Neither did he like being elbowed step by step out of the hunting ground which for generations had belonged to his fathers. The white man despised the Indian as a heathen and was contemptuous of his rights. He regarded him as a thief and wished he would keep out of the way. He deemed it "contrary to the laws of God and man for so much land to be lying idle when so many Christians needed it." But notwithstanding the sources of distrust, the tribesmen were in a general way friendly until 1753. They learned to express themselves in English, and it is significant that they became very familiar with terms of insult and profanity. In their own languages there were no "cuss words," and they did not comprehend the real nature of them.

The first clash between the settler and the aborigine took place near the mouth of North River, December 18, 1742. Our information as to the cause itself is meager and obscure. The current account is the one written by Judge Samuel McDowell, sixty-five years after the time of the tragedy. But the judge was only seven years old when it occurred, and the most definite impression made on his mind was the sight of the lifeless bodies of his father and the other men who were killed, after they had been brought to Timber Ridge for burial. In a practical sense, his knowledge of the matter was derived from older persons and not until he had reached a mature age.

The judge relates that thirty-three Iroquois came into the Borden tract on their way to fight the Catawbas, and gave the settlers some trouble. They were entertained a day by Captain McDowell, who plied them with whiskey. They then went down South River, lay in camp seven or eight days, hunted, took what they wished, scared the women, and shot horses running at large. Complaint being made, Colonel Patton ordered McDowell to call out his militia company, and conduct the Indians beyond the settled area. McDowell took about thirty-four men, these being all the county could furnish. Meanwhile, the Iroquois moved farther southward. McDowell overtook them and conducted them beyond Salling's, then the farthest plantation. One Indian was lame and fell behind, all but one of the militia passing him. This man fired upon the native as he went into the woods. The native then raised the war-cry, and the fight was on. The Indians at length gave way, took to the Blue Ridge, and followed it to the Potomac. Seventeen of them were killed, several others died on the retreat, and only ten got home. Of the militia, the killed were eight or nine. Jacob Anderson, Charles Hays, Joseph Lapsley, Solomon Moffett, and Richard Woods were in the battle.

Another and more trustworthy version is that which was unearthed by Mr.

Charles E. Kemper from the colonial records of Pennsylvania and New York. This account states that Colonel Patton reached the battlefield three hours after the fight. He wrote that very day to the governor of Virginia, reciting the particulars and asking his intervention to avert a war. That official wrote to the governor of New York, inclosing Patton's letter. This letter recounts that the Indians had appeared in the settlements in a hostile manner, committing the annoyances already spoken of; that on coming up with them, McDowell and Buchanan sent forward a man with a signal of peace, upon whom the Indians fired, precipating a fight that lasted forty-five minutes. Eleven whites were killed and others wounded, and eight or ten Indians were killed. The governor of New York sent an agent to see the Iroquois, who claimed the Valley of Virginia by right of conquest. The Indians were restive and the authorities were apprehensive of trouble. The governor of Pennsylvania undertook to act as mediator. An Indian who was in the fight told him his party consisted of thirty-two Onondagas and seven Oneidas. They were treated well while passing through Pennsylvania, but in Virginia they were given nothing to eat and had to kill a hog once in a while. As they went up the Valley they were several times interferred with by the whites, but avoided difficulties with them. They rested a day and two nights near the spot where the fight took place. On resuming their march, some of the militia, riding horseback, fired on two boys but did not hit them. The Indian leader told his men not to fire because of the white flag. But the whites fired again, killing two of the party. The chief then ordered an attack, and the Indians fought with tomahawks at close quarters. Two of their number were killed and five wounded. The whites were worsted, ten of them being killed. Ten of the Indians went up the river to the mountains, and were pursued to the Potomac, barely escaping with their lives. The mediator ruled that the whites were the aggressors, and by way of reparation Governor Gooch paid the Iroquois 100 pounds. The trouble was finally adjusted by the treary of Lancaster in 1744, the Iroquois then renouncing their claim to Virginia.

In a suit for slander brought by James McDowell against Benjamin Borden, Jr., and which was decided in favor of the defendant, there is an obscure allusion to the responsibility for the affair. According to McDowell, Borden applied these words to him, August 17, 1747: "Thou art a rogue and a murdering villain and I can prove it. * * * He is a murderer and brought the Indians upon the settlement." Thirteen claims for losses by the Indians were presented in the February court of 1746. Among the claimants were Isaac Anderson, Domick Berrall, Joseph Coakton, Henry Kirkham, Joseph Lapsley, John Mathews, Francis McCown, John Walker, James Walker, and Richard Woods.

The following is the roster of John McDowell's company. Not all these men were in the battle:

Aleson, John; Beaker, Hen; Campbell, Gilbert; Campbell, James; Cares, John; Corier, John; Cunningham, Hugh; Cunningham, James; Dredin, David; Finey, James; Finey, Michael; Gray, John; Hall, William; Hardiman, James; Kirkham, Hen; Lapsley, Joseph; Long, ———; Long, ———; Mason, Loromer; Matthews, John; McClewer, Alexander; McClewer, Holbert; McClewer, John; McClure, Alexander; McClure, Moses; McCowen, Fran; McDowell, Ephraim; McDowell, James; McKnab, Andrew; McKnab, John; McKnab, Patt; McRoberts, Samuel; Miles, William; Miless, John; Miller, Michael; Moore, James; Patterson, Edward; Patterson, Erwin; Quail, Charles; Rives, David; Saley, John Peter; Taylor, Thomas; Whiteside, Thomas; Wood, Richard; Wood, Samuel; Wood, William; Young, Robert; Young, Matthew.

The French and Indian war broke out in 1754, and continued, so far as the Indians were concerned, until 1760. The advance line of settlement had passed the Alleghany divide, and the greatest havoc was in the valleys along the frontier. A local cause for the outbreak was the outrage at Anderson's barn on Middle River. The date is not exactly known, but seems to be the month of June, 1753, or possibly 1754. Twelve Indians were returning from a raid against the Cherokees, and lodged with John Lewis near Staunton. Some men were present whose families or friends had suffered some loss at the hands of the natives. A beef was killed and whiskey provided. The guests were induced to stay till nightfall and give one of their dances. After they left they were followed in the darkness to Anderson's barn, where all but one were murdered. For this act of treachery in a time of at least nominal peace, a heavy toll of vengeance was exacted. The colonial government sought to punish the perpetrators, but the effort was ineffectual. One of the faults of the Ulstermen was their propensity to make trouble with the "heathen."

The Rockbridge area was by no means safe from attack, and there were several blockhouses for the protection of the people. William Patton mentions a stockade at Alexander McClary's, a mile and a half from his home, and says there were several others in the Borden grant. One of these must have been the Bell house, which is still standing and occupied. It is about two miles south of Raphine and very near a branch. Another was a log structure on Walker's Creek, used as a dwelling until a recent date. The floor was of walnut puncheons. The roof, which was too steep to scale, fell in during the winter of 1917-18. In several other instances, the pioneer blockhouse still exists, with widened windows and some other alteration, or the logs have been used in a building of later design. In all instances, the walls and doors were bullet-proof against the weapons of that age, the windows were too narrow for a man to crawl through, and there were loopholes in the walls. The loophole was cut in the shape of the letter X, so that a considerable breadth of vision might be commanded by the gun pointed through the opening. A spring or other water supply was always within easy distance. In some instances the water was reached through a covered way, which was practically a narrow tunnel, high enough for a person to pass through. The Indian was unwilling to storm a blockhouse. The cost might be severe, and the defenders were comparatively safe from his bullets. So he endeavored to gain his end by stealth or strategem, and when he did make an attack it was usually by night. If he could set fire to the roof he did so.

A council of war held at Staunton, May 20, 1756, mentions that "the greatest part of the able-bodied single men of this county is now on duty on our frontiers, and there must continue until they are relieved by forces from other parts." Sitting on this council were these captains: Joseph Culton, John Moor, Joseph Lapsley, Robert Bratton, James Mitchell, and Samuel Norwood.

The only conspicuous raids belonging to this period were the occurrences in the Renick settlement and the first foray into the valley of Kerr's Creek. The latter will be spoken of in connection with the second.

The date of the attack on the Renick house is July 25, 1757. A party of Shawnees, said to have been sixty in number but probably much fewer, came through Cartmill Gap to Purgatory Creek, where they killed Joseph Dennis and his child, and took prisoner his wife, Hannah. They also killed Thomas Perry. Then they went to the house of Robert Renick, where they captured Mrs. Renick, her four sons, and a daughter. The next blow was at Thomas Smith's, where they killed both Renick and Smith, and took away Mrs. Smith and her servant, Sally Jew. George Mathews, Audley Maxwell, and William Maxwell,* who then were young men, were on their way to Smith's, and thought a shooting match was in progress. As soon as they saw the bodies of the two men, they wheeled their horses about, and the four bullets fired at them at the same instant did no other harm than to wound Audley Maxwell slightly and take off the club of Mathews' queue. One party of the Indians started away with the prisoners and booty, and the others went to Cedar Creek. An alarm was given and the people of the neighborhood gathered at Paul's stockade near the site of Springfield. The women and children were left with a guard of six men, while George Mathews went in pursuit with a force of twenty-one men. He overtook and fought the enemy, but the night was wet and dark, and the foe got away. Next morning nine dead Indians were found on the battleground and were buried. Benjamin Smith, Thomas Maury, and a Mr. Jew were killed, and were buried in the meadow of Thomas Cross near Springfield. Mrs. Renick was released a few years later. Her daughter died in captivity, and her son Joshua became a chief of the Miamis. The other children returned with their mother. Mrs. Dennis was a woman of much resourcefulness and determination. She learned the Shawnee tongue, painted as the red men did, and because of her skill in treating illness she was given much liberty. She

---

*This name should probably be Paul instead of Maxwell.

thereby found a chance to escape, crossed the Ohio on a driftwood log, and made her way back to her frontier home. This was in 1763.

It is very probable that several minor raids took place, no clear recollection of which has been handed on to the present day. An occurrence can easily be given a wrong setting by its being accidentally merged with some larger event. Sometimes a single Indian would go on the warpath for himself, and when the party was very small only depredations on a small scale were likely to be committed. There were instances where some white scoundrel would disguise himself as an Indian and perpetrate an outrage. Such may be the explanation of the tragedy at the home of John Mathews, Jr., the nature of which recalls the Pettigrew horror of 1846. Sampson Mathews made oath that his brother John, with his wife and their six children, were burned to death in their house. A neighbor named Charles Godfrey Milliron was arrested on suspicion and held for trial at the capital. We do not know the result, but Milliron seems to have been acquited.

An incident which took place in Botetourt is worthy of mention here. Robert Anderson and his son William—grandfather to William A. Anderson of Lexington—went to a meadow to look after some livestock, and passed the night in a log shelter, the door of which could be strongly barred. Before morning Mr. Anderson woke up and roused his son, telling him the animals were restless and that he feared Indians were near. Bear oil and cabin smoke gave the redskins an odor that was quickly noticed by domestic animals. Voices were presently heard, and father and son held their weapons in readiness for an emergency. The prowlers tried the door, and seeing it did not readily yield, they used the pole as a battering ram, but without visible effect. Much to the relief of the persons within they then desisted and went away. In the morning it was seen that another blow would have forced the door.

The red terror threatened to depopulate the Valley of Virginia and the settlements beyond. Writing in 1756, the Reverend James Maury makes this observation: "Such numbers of people have lately transported themselves into the more Southerly governments as must appear incredible to any except such as have had an opportunity of knowing it. By Bedford courthouse in one week, 'tis said, and I believe, truly said, near 300 inhabitants of this Colony past on their way to Carolina. From all the upper counties, even those on this side of the Blue Hills, great numbers are daily following."

What is known as the Pontiac war broke out very suddenly in June, 1763, and continued more than a year. It was a concerted effort, on the part of a confederacy of tribes, to sweep the whites out of the country beyond the Alleghanies. To a band of Shawnees was assigned the task of operating in the Rockbridge latitude. Their first blow completely destroyed the Greenbrier settlements, and their next attention was given to Jackson's River and the Cowpasture. Thence a party crossed Mill and North mountains to devastate the valley of Kerr's Creek.

There were two raids into this locality and there has been some doubt as to their chronological sequence. That one of them took place July 17, 1763, is evident. There is agreement as to the day and month of the other event; October 10th. Samuel Brown says the second raid occurred two years after the first, and he places it in 1765. In this he is followed doubtfully by Waddell in his *Annals of Augusta*. Mr. Brown wrote his account a long while ago, and when people were living whose knowledge of the massacres was very direct. Nevertheless, he is in error. His informants were confused in their recollection of dates.

The record books of Augusta contain no hint of any Indian trouble in the fall of 1764 or 1765. A raid of serious proportions would have constituted a renewal of the Pontiac war, and further military events would be on record in frontier history. But in 1759 and 1760 the number of wills admitted to record, the number of settlements of estates, and the number of orphan children put under guardianship is deeply significant. However, our evidence is more conclusive. In the suit of Thomas Gilmore against George Wilson, recorded November 19, 1761, the plaintiff makes this declaration: "During the late war the Indians came to the plantation where plaintiff lived, and after killing his father and mother, robbed them and plaintiff of almost everything they had. * * * Defendant and several others pursued the Indians several days and retook great part of the things belonging to the plaintiff. The inhabitants of Car's Creek, the plaintiff not being one of them, offered to any persons that would go after the Indians and redeem the prisoners, they should have all plunder belonging to them." The records further tell us that John Gilmore was dead in 1759 and that Thomas Gilmore was his executor. We may therefore affirm that the earlier raid occurred October 10, 1759, and the later, July 17, 1763.

We now proceed to relate the two occurrences, as the particulars have been given to us.

With respect to the first there was a forewarning. Two Telford boys, returning from school, reported seeing a naked man near their path. Little serious thought seems to have been given to the matter. A few weeks later, twenty-seven Indians were counted from a bluff near the head of the creek. The war party first visited the home of Charles Dougherty and killed the whole family. The wife and a daughter of Jacob Cunningham were the next victims. The girl, ten years of age, was scalped, but made a partial recovery. Four Gilmores and five of the ten members of Robert Hamilton's family were afterward slain. The Indians did not go any farther. Accounts differ as to whether any prisoners were taken by them. They killed twelve persons, and according to one statement, thirteen were carried away.

With his usual promptness and energy, Charles Lewis, of the Cowpasture, took the lead in raising three companies of militia, one headed by himself, the others by John Dickenson and William Christian. The Indians were overtaken near the head of Back Creek in Highland County. It was decided to attack at three points. Two men sent in advance were to fire if they found the enemy had taken alarm. They came upon two of the enemy, one leading a horse, the other holding a buck upon it. To avoid discovery the scouts fired and Christian's company charged with a yell. The other companies were not quite up and the Indians escaped with little loss. However, they were overhauled on Straight Fork, four miles below the West Virginia line, their camp being revealed by their fire. All were killed except one, and the cook's brains were scattered into his pot. Their carrying poles were seen here many years later, and ancient guns have been found. In the first engagement the loot was recovered, and it was sold for $1,200.

On the second visitation the Indians were in greater force, and made their approach more cautiously. They concealed themselves a day or two at a spring near the head of Kerr's Creek. But moccasin tracks were noticed in a cornfield, and some men detected the camp from a hill. A rumor had come to the settlement that Indians were approaching, but there was little uneasiness. It is nearly certain that the savages first seen were an advance party, and that this was waiting for a reënforcement. Another probable motive for delay in an attack was to scare the settlers into gathering at some rendezvous, so that they might be fallen upon in a mass. If such was the purpose it was accomplished. The people flocked to the blockhouse of Jonathan Cunningham at Big Spring.

Meanwhile the house of John McKee was attacked and Mrs. McKee was killed. There are differing accounts of this incident. According to Alexander Bane, Mr. McKee started with his wife and a dog to reach a wooded hill. Their children were at Timber Ridge. Because of her condition, Mrs. McKee was unable to walk fast, and she insisted that her husband should go on and effect his own escape. Before doing so, he hid her in a sinkhole filled with bushes and weeds, but the barking dog betrayed the place of concealment. After the redskins had gone on, she was taken to the house, where she soon died. This statement is challenged by the author of *The McKees of Virginia and Kentucky*. He construes it as a reflection on John McKee's courage and his duty to his wife. He says that some of the settlers did not like this pioneer for his bluntness, and that they set afloat a garbled version of the facts. The author of the book prefers to believe that John McKee had gone to a neighbor's to look after some sick children, and finding on his return that his wife was scalped, he took her to the house. Be this as it may, the murder could not have occurred in the first raid, as some statements affirm. The family Bible gives July 17, 1763, as the date of Mrs. McKee's death.

We must now return to the assemblage at Big Spring. A number of the people of the valley were attending a meeting at Timber Ridge, the day being Sunday. Those gathered at Cunningham's were in a field, saddling their horses in great haste, in order to join their friends at the meeting house. The secreted foe seized the coveted moment to cut them off from the blockhouse. The scene which followed was witnessed by Mrs. Dale from a covert on a high point. When the alarm reached her she mounted a stallion colt that had never been ridden, but which proved as gentle as could be desired. The foe was gaining on her, and she dropped her baby into a field of rye. In some manner she afterwards eluded the pursuers, but was too late to reach the blockhouse. A relief party found the baby lying unhurt where it had been left. Such is the story, but it is more probable that the mother recovered the child herself after the raiders had gone away.

While the saddling was going on two men started up the creek to reconnoiter, but were shot down, as were also two young men who went to their aid. The onslaught of the foe was immediate, and each redskin singled out his victim. Mrs. Dale said the massacre made her think of boys knocking down chickens with clubs. Some tried to hide in the big pond or in thickets of brush or weeds. All who attempted to resist were cut down. Cunningham himself was killed and his house was burned. There is no record that the Indians suffered any loss.

According to Samuel Brown, sixty to eighty persons were killed in the two Kerr's Creek raids, and twenty-five to thirty carried away. This is an overstatement. William Patton, who was at Big Spring the day after the massacre, helping to bury the dead, says these were seventeen in number. He adds that the burial party was attacked. Among the prisoners, according to Mr. Brown, were Mrs. Jenny Gilmore, her two daughters, and a son named John; James, Betsy, Margaret, and Henry Cunningham; and three Hamiltons, Archibald, Marian, and Mary. One of the Cunninghams was the girl scalped in the first raid. She returned from captivity and lived about forty years afterward, but the wound finally developed into a cancerous affection. According to a rather sentimental sketch in one of the county papers, Mary Hamilton was among the killed, and John McCown, her lover, died two years later of a broken heart and was buried by her side at Big Spring. Mr. Waddell says she had a baby in her arms when she was captured. She threw the infant into the weeds, and when she returned from the Indian country she found its bones where she had left it.

Mention has been made of a meeting at Timber Ridge the day of the second massacre. A rumor of the attack reached the congregation at the noon recess, but little was thought of it, since similar alarms had often been given. But an express arrived when the second service was beginning. There was immediate confusion and speedy flight. Some of the Kerr's Creek families sought safety in the Blue Ridge.

On the afternoon of the second tragedy, the Indians returned to their camp on North Mountain, where they drank the whiskey found at Cunningham's still. They became too intoxicated to have put up a good resistance to an assault. Yet they had little to fear, as there was a general panic throughout the Rockbridge area. Next day two Indians went back, either to see if they were pursued or to look for more liquor. It seems to have been on this occasion when Mrs. Dale saw them shoot at a man who ventured to ride up the valley. When he wheeled they clapped their hands and shouted. This incident constituted the attack mentioned by William Patton. During the march to the Shawnee towns, the Indians brained a fretful child and threw the baby on the shoulders of a young girl who was killed next day. At another time, the prisoners were made to pass under an infant pierced by a stake and held over them. On still another occasion, while some of the prisoners were drying a few leaves of the New Testament for the purpose of preserving them, a savage rushed up and threw them into the camp fire. When the column arrived at the Scioto, the captives were ironically called upon to sing a hymn. Mrs. Gilmore responded by singing Psalm 137 as she had been wont to do at Timber Ridge. It is related that she had stood over the corpse of her husband, fighting desperately and knocking a foeman down. Another Indian rushed up to tomahawk the woman, but his comrade said she was a good warrior, and made him spare her. She and her son were redeemed, but she never knew what became of her daughters. Several other captives were also returned.

Some account of the massacres on Kerr's Creek was related many years afterward by Mrs. Jane Stevenson. She was then living in Kentucky, and her story was reduced to writing by John D. Shane, a minister. Mrs. Stevenson, who was born November 15, 1750, speaks of a girl four months older than herself taken at the age of seven years and held until the Bouquet delivery in 1764. The children had gone out with older companions to gather haws, and the narrator escaped capture only by not going so far as the others. At the first raid an aunt who had two children escaped into the woods, the Indians going down the river. But on the second occasion, this aunt and her three children were taken and an uncle and a cousin were killed. Two of the children died in captivity, but the aunt and the third child were restored. In this second raid Mrs. Stevenson thinks the Indians "had the ground all spied out," and followed a prearranged program. She says they "came in like racehorses," and in two hours killed or captured sixty-three persons. One of the prisoners was James Milligan. He escaped on Gauley Mountain and reported having counted 450 captives, as the total collected in the entire raid. Two small boy-captives were James Woods and James McClung, and after their return they had the condition of their ears recorded in the clerk's office at Staunton. Cropping the human ear was in those days a form of punishment, and the person who had an ear mutilated by accident or in a fight went before the county court to have the fact certified, so as not to be regarded as an ex-convict.

Mrs. Stevenson was a daughter of James Gay, who lived seven miles from Kerr's Creek. Her mother, whose maiden name was Jean Warwick, was killed by the Indians about 1759. Mrs. Stevenson relates that the adult male members of the Providence congregation "carried their guns to meeting as regular as the congregation went." Alexander Crawford was killed about fifteen miles from the meeting house in the direction of Staunton. The narrator says that when "the Indians took Kerr's Creek settlement a second time they were greatly bad," and that it "almost seemed as though they would make their way to Williamsburg." They "shot the cows mightily with bows and arrows." She moved to Greenbrier in 1775, "where there was never a settlement of kinder people," these being "great for dancing and singing." But her statement that William Hamilton and Samuel McClung were the only Greenbrier settlers who were "not Dutch and half-Dutch," cannot be correct at all, unless true of the particular locality where these men settled. It is also to be remembered that she was not yet grown at the time of the doings on Kerr's Creek. As for Milligan, he must have been able to see more than double in order to count 450 prisoners led away by probably not more than one-fifth as many warriors.

It is not known that the settlers on Kerr's Creek had themselves given cause to make their valley a special mark for Indian vengeance. The native venerated the home of his forefathers, and would make a long and perilous journey for no other purpose than to gaze upon a spot known to him only in boyhood or perhaps only by tradition. It may have been resentment, pure and simple, that led him to visit his fury upon the palefaces who had crowded him out of a choice portion of his hunting grounds. So it is not to be wondered at that the children attending Bunker Hill schoolhouse near Big Spring had a superstitious horror of the field where the massacre took place.

The treaty which ended the Pontiac war stipulated that the Indians should return their white captives, and these were delivered to Colonel Bouquet in November, 1764. However, there were instances where the return did not take place until some time later. According to William Patton, the foray of 1763 was the last that took place on Rockbridge soil. Yet in the Dunmore war, and in the hostilities that continued intermittently from 1777 to 1795, there was always the possibility of still other incursions. The Indian peril was forever removed from Rockbridge by the treaty of Greenville, in 1795, which was secured by General Wayne's victory in the battle of the Fallen Timbers.

The Dunmore war of 1774 was caused by the extension of white settlement into the valley of the Ohio. It was waged between the Virginia militia and a confederacy headed by the Shawnees. Rockbridge men served in the companies from Augusta and Botetourt, and helped to gain the memorable victory of Point Pleasant.

We find only one recorded instance where an Indian was held in slavery in Rockbridge. This was in 1777, and is mentioned in Chapter VII.

It is said that several of the family names on Kerr's Creek were blotted out as a result of the scenes in 1759 and 1763. The record-books for 1758-60 indicate an exceptional mortality in the Rockbridge area. We append to this chapter some names that appear to belong to this region, but we do not know that violence was the cause of all the deaths indicated.

    Jacob Cunningham—will probated March 18, 1760.
    Isaac Cunningham—died 1760*—Jean, administrator.
    Benjamin, orphan of John Gray—1760.
    Samuel, orphan of Alexander McMurty, becomes ward of Matthew Lyle, 1759.
    James McGee—will probated August 20, 1759—Erwin Patterson, administrator.
    Robert Ramsay—will probated November 21, 1759—Robert Hall, administrator.
    James Rogers—died 1760*—Ann Rogers administratrix with Walter Smiley on her bond.
    James Stephenson—died 1760*.
    Thomas Thompson—died 1760.*
    John Winyard—will probated, November 15, 1758—Barbara, executor.
    Samuel Wilson—died 1760*.
    James Young—died 1760.

An episode made much note of in the pioneer history of Kentucky and Tennessee is the story of the "Long Hunters" of 1769-1772. Some writers throw doubt on the narrative, yet it seems founded on fact. From a concordance of the various accounts, it would appear that in June, 1769, a party of over twenty men, several of whom were from Rockbridge, started from Reedy Creek on an extended hunting trip in the valley of the Cumberland. They found a grassy prairie and plenty of game. No Indians were found living in that region, although there were numerous Indian graves. In June, 1770, several of the hunters returned, the others building boats and floating down to Natchez on the Mississippi, where they sold their cargo. A portion of the party remained there and settled, the others returning by way of Georgia. In the fall of 1771, a party of twenty-two went out again. At least five of these

---

*The date is that of record. The person may have died in 1759.

were members of the first party. This second party was so successful that it could not take back all its pelts, and a portion was deposited in a "skin-house" in what is now Greene county, Kentucky. Ammunition ran low, and all but five returned the next February. One of the five fell ill, and a comrade took him to the settlements. Two of the remaining three of the camp guard were captured by Indians. The seventeen returned after about three months, and continued to hunt and explore, some of the names they gave to certain localities enduring to the present day. Late in the summer of 1772 their camp was plundered by Cherokees at a time when they were absent from it, but hunting continued till the end of the season. The only names we can certainly identify as belonging to Rockbridge are those of Robert Crockett and James Graham, of the Calfpasture. Another member was James Knox, who lived at the mouth of the Bullpasture and finally settled in Kentucky. The claim is made with much show of reason that it was this James Knox, and not General Knox, of Washington's army, for whom Knoxville in Tennessee is named. Crockett, who lost his life during the first expedition, is said to have been the first white man killed in that state. The wives of Governor Bramlette and Senator J. C. S. Blackburn, of Kentucky, were granddaughters of Graham.

IX

ROCKBRIDGE COUNTY ESTABLISHED

NEW COUNTIES—ACT OF ASSEMBLY—THE CORNSTALK AFFAIR—ANNALS OF 1778-1783

The house that John Lewis built near the site of Staunton in the summer of 1732 was not within the recognized limits of any county. Until 1744 the Blue Ridge was the treaty line between paleface and redskin. The first county organization to cross that barrier was Spottsylvania, which became effective in 1721. Yet it came only to the South Fork of the Shenandoah, one extremity of the line touching the river in the vicinity of Elkton, the other about midway between Front Royal and Bentonville. Orange was created in 1734, and organized in 1735. It was defined as extending westward to the uttermost limit claimed by Virginia. Four years later, the portion of Orange west of the Blue Ridge was divided into the counties of Frederick and Augusta by a line running from the source of the Rapidan to the Fairfax Stone at the source of the North Branch of the Potomac. The present boundary between Rockingham and Shenandoah is a portion of this line.

During the westward march of population in Virginia, the practical area of a county has always been co-extensive with its settled portion. The fact that Augusta once extended potentially to the Mississippi, did not mean that a juryman might have to travel hundreds of miles to attend court. When the first division of Augusta took place in 1769, probably not less than three-fourths of the inhabitants were living within a radius of fifty miles around Staunton. Of the other fourth, nearly all were within a few miles of a trail leading from Buchanan to Abingdon.

The first county to be set off from Augusta was Botetourt, which became effective January 31, 1770. The line separating it from the parent county is thus described in a report by James Trimble, the surveyor:

Beginning at two Chestnuts and a Black Oak on the South Mountain by a Spring of Pealer Creek on Amherst Line and running thence 55 degrees West 4 Miles 240 Poles to a Spanish Oak marked AC on the one Side and BC on the Other Side where the South River or Mary's Creek empties into the North Branch of James River, and up the North River to Kerr's Creek and up Kerr's Creek to the Fork of the said Creek at Gilmore's Gap. Then beginning at a chestnut and three Chestnut Oaks and a Pine at the upper Fork of Kerr's Creek and runneth the same Course to wit North 55 degrees West, 23 and one-half miles, Crossing the Cowpasture in Donally's Place at a Large Poplar on the River marked AC and BC.

The course beginning on the top of North Mountain continued to the Ohio, which it touched a little below Parkersburg. It is an exact parallel to the present line between Rockbridge and Augusta. It does not appear that the surveying of this line was ever carried beyond the summit of the Allleghany Divide. The cost of the survey by Trimble was $37.15.

From this old boundary between Augusta and Botetourt, the airline distance to Fincastle does not vary much from thirty-five miles, and is slightly less than the distance to Staunton. To the people of the present Rockbridge area, the journey to a courthouse in 1777 was not excessively long. The need for a new county was very much less than in the case of Rockingham or Greenbrier, all three of these counties being authorized by the same Act of Assembly, which was passed at the October session of 1777. The sections relating to Rockbridge are these:

Section Three. And be it further enacted, That the remaining portion of the said counties and parishes of Augusta and Botetourt be divided into three counties and parishes, as follows, to wit, by a line beginning on the top of Blue Ridge near Steele's mill, and running thence north 55 degrees west, passing the said mill, and crossing the North Mountain to the top, and the mountain dividing the waters of the Calfpasture from the waters of the Cowpasture, and thence along the said mountain, crossing Panther's Gap, to the line that divides the counties of Augusta and Botetourt, and that the remaining part of the county of Botetourt be divided, by a line beginning at Audley Paul's, running thence south, 55 degrees east, crossing James River to the top of the Blue Ridge, thence along the same, crossing James River, to the beginning of the aforesaid line dividing Augusta county, then beginning again at the said Audley Paul's, and running north 55 degrees west till the said course shall intersect a line to run south 45 degrees west, from the place where the above line dividing Augusta terminated. And all other parts of the said parishes of Augusta and Botetourt included within the said lines shall be called and known by the name of Rockbridge.

Section 4. (A court for Rockbridge, first Tuesday of every month, the first court to be held at the house of Samuel Wallace. The justices, or a majority of them, being present and duly sworn, shall fix on a place as near the center as the situation and convenience shall admit, and proceed to erect the necessary public buildings).

Section 5. (Making it lawful for the governor with the advice of the Council to appoint the first sheriff.)

Section 6. And be it further enacted, that at the place which shall be appointed for holding court in the said county of Rockbridge, there shall be laid off a town to be called Lexington, 1300 feet in length and 900 in width. And in order to make satisfaction to the proprietors of the said land, the clerk of the said county shall by order of the justices issue a writ directed to the sheriff commanding him to summon twelve able and discreet freeholders to meet in the said land on a certain day, not under five nor more than ten days from the date, who shall upon oath value the said land, in so many parcels as there shall be separate owners, which valuation the said sheriff shall return, under the hands and seals of the said jurors, to the clerk's office, and the justices, at levying their first county levy, shall make provision for paying the said proprietors their respective portions thereof, and the property of the said land shall on the return of such valuation, become vested in the Justices and their successors, one acre thereof to be reserved for the use of said county, and the residue to be sold and conveyed by the said justices to any persons, and the money arising from such sale shall be applied towards lessening the county levy; and the public buildings for the said county shall be erected on the lands reserved, as aforesaid.

Section 7. (Relates to suits and petitions now depending. Dockets of such to be made out in Augusta and Botetourt.)

Section 8. (No appointment of clerk of the peace, nor of place for holding court, unless a majority of the justices be present.)

(Another section dissolves the vestry of Augusta, and instructs the inhabitants of Augusta, Botetourt, Rockbridge, Rockingham, and Greenbrier to meet at places appointed by their sheriffs before May 1, 1778, to elect twelve able and discreet persons as a vestry for each county.)*

The boundaries of Rockbridge, as set forth in the above act, have since undergone but one change. In October, 1785, all the county west of the top of Camp Mountain was annexed to Botetourt.

There is a belief that the killing of Cornstalk at Point Pleasant led to the establishment of Rockbridge. The perpetrators of that deed were some of the Rockbridge militia, and as there was an attempt to punish them, the trial would have been at the county seat of Greenbrier. The erection of a new county would insure a trial among friends and not among strangers. But the killing of Cornstalk took place November 11, 1777. It would have taken several weeks for the news to reach Williamsburg and for a movement to take shape in Rockbridge which would bear fruit in legislative action. The act authorizing Rockbridge had been passed in October of the same year.

Nevertheless, the event should have mention in this chapter.

The Shawnees, "the Arabs of the New World," were a small but valiant tribe dwelling on the lower Scioto. In mental power they stood much above the average level of the red race, and it was an ordinary occurrence for a member of the tribe to be able to converse in five or six languages, including English and French. According to the Indian standard, the Shawnees were generous livers, and their women were superior housekeepers. They were so conscious of their prowess that they held in contempt the warlike ability of other Indians. It was their boast that they caused the white people ten times as much loss as they received.

At the time of which we write, the most eminent war-leader among the Shawnees was Cornstalk. It is not probable that he headed the band that struck Kerr's Creek in 1759, although the warriors may have been of his people. We do know, however, that he was the leader in the terrible raid of 1763. Within a few days his band blotted out the settlements on the Greenbrier, won a victory over two companies of militia at Falling Springs in Alleghany county,

---

*The first vestry for Rockbridge included James Buchanan, Charles Campbell, Samuel McDowell, John Gilmore, John Lyle, Samuel Lyle, Major William Paxton, Alexander Stuart, and John Trimble.

raided the valleys of Jackson's River and the Cowpasture, and then crossed Mill Mountain to work still further havoc on Kerr's Creek. With slight loss to themselves, they killed, wounded, or carried away probably more than 100 of the whites. At Point Pleasant, the Shawnees were the backbone of the Indian army, and Cornstalk was its general-in-chief. It was only because of loose discipline in the camp that the Virginians were not taken by surprise. Technically, the battle was little else than a draw. Cornstalk effected an unmolested retreat across the Ohio, after inflicting a loss much heavier than his own. But his men were discouraged and gave up the campaign. Cornstalk was not in favor of the war, but was overruled by his tribe. During the short peace that followed, he from time to time returned to Fort Randolph at Point Pleasant horses and cattle that had been lost by the whites or stolen from them.

In 1777 the Shawnees were again restless. They had been worked upon by British emissaries and white renegades. Cornstalk came with a Delaware and one other Indian and visited Fort Randolph under what was virtually a flag of truce. He warned Captain Arbuckle, the commandant, of the feeling of the tribesmen. His mission was an effort to avert open hostilities. According to the Indian standard, Cornstalk was an honorable foe, and he knew he ran a risk in putting himself in the power of the whites. Arbuckle thought it proper to detain the Indians as hostages. One day, while Cornstalk was drawing a map on the floor of the blockhouse, to explain the geography of the country beyond the Scioto, his son Ellinipsico hallooed from the other bank of the Ohio and was taken across. Soon afterward, two men of Captain William McKee's company, a Gilmore and a Hamilton, went over the Kanawha to hunt for turkeys. Gilmore was killed by some lurking Indian, and his body was carried back. The spectacle made his comrades wild with rage. They raised the cry of, "Let us kill the Indians in the fort," and without taking a second thought they rushed to the door of the blockhouse. They would not listen to the remonstrances of Arbuckle, and threatened his life. When the door was forced open, Cornstalk stood erect before his executioners and fell dead, pierced by seven or eight balls. His son and his other companions were also put to death. The slain chieftain was about fifty years of age, large in figure, commanding in presence, and intellectual in countenance. Good contemporary judges declare that even Patrick Henry or Richard Henry Lee did not surpass Cornstalk in oratory.

By the people of Kerr's Creek the raids into their valley were remembered with horror. Homes had been burned. Families had partially or wholly been blotted out. Women and children had been tomahawked and scalped. Friends and relatives had been carried away, and some of these had never returned. Even at the present day, the scenes of 1759 and 1763 are referred to with more impatience than is usually found along what was once the frontier.

The Indian method of making war was unquestionably cruel. The impulses of the native were those of the primitive man. Like the child, he was sometimes swept by gusts of passion. Deceit has ever been deemed legitimate in warfare. The Indian played the game without restraint and was consistent. The white man assumes to conduct war according to rules suggested by Christian civilization and laid down in time of peace. But in time of war he does not live up to these rules. It had been little more than a century since Cromwell had carried fire and massacre from one end of Ireland to the other, and with a fury that would have made Cornstalk "sit up and take notice." It was within the memory of living men that the Highlanders of Scotland gave no quarter in their murderous clan fights. It seems instinctive for nations of the Baltic stock to hold the colored races in contempt. To the frontiersman of America, the Indian was not only a heathen but an inferior. The comparatively humane treatment to which he thought the French and the British were entitled, because of their color, he held himself justified in withholding from the redskin. The practical effect of this double standard was most unfortunate. It reacted with dire effect upon the white population. It was more often the white man than the Indian who was responsible for the cause of border trouble. The Indian's version is much less familiar to us than our own.

Despite his proclivity to tomahawk the woman as well as the man, the child as well as the adult, the Indian in his war-paint was a gentleman when compared with the German soldier in the present war. The latter, who professes to be a civilized man, wars against the very foundations of a civilization that the red man knew next to nothing of. The Indian kept his word. He respected bravery. The children he spared and adopted he loved, and not infrequently the adult captive was unwilling to return to his own color. Women were never violated by the Indians of the tribes east of the Mississippi, and when a child was born in captivity to the white female, the mother was looked after as though she were one of their own kind.

The deed of Hall's men at Point Pleasant is a painful incident in Rockbridge history. It bore the same relation to open warfare, whether civilized or savage, that a lynching does to a fair trial in a courtroom. There was nothing to show that Cornstalk had anything to do with the killing of Gilmore, or that the perpetrator of that deed was a member of his tribe. Had Cornstalk been a British officer, his government would have pronounced his murder an inexcusable assassination, and would have avenged it with the execution of some captive American officer. The plea, which is not confined to the book by Kercheval, that it was right for the frontiersman to lay aside the restraints of civilization when dealing with the Indian, would, if it had been used in the present war, been made a justification for matching German atrocity by allied atrocity. Even at Point

Pleasant, where we might expect the feeling against the native to be acute, it was long considered that the town lay under a curse. So late as 1807 it had only a log courthouse, twenty-one small dwellings, and a few ague-plagued inhabitants. It now contains a monument to Cornstalk.

Only a few years since, a contributor to one of the Lexington papers spoke rather harshly of Colonel Roosevelt for mentioning the killing of Cornstalk as "one of the darkest stains on the checkered pages of frontier history." Roosevelt is no apologist for Indian cruelty. The writer was probably unaware of the fact that Patrick Henry, who was then governor of this state, denounced the deed in words that were much more vehement. He regarded it as a blot on the fair name of Virginia, and announced that so far as he was concerned, the perpetrators should be sought out and punished. But as will appear later in this chapter, his efforts were nullified by the friends of the persons responsible.

A sequel to the episode deserves mention. In an attempt to avenge the death of their chieftain, the Shawnees besieged Fort Randolph in the spring of 1778. An Indian woman known among the whites as the Grenadier Squaw, and who was understood to be a sister to Cornstalk, had come to the fort with her horses and cattle. By going out of the stockade and overhearing the natives she was able to tell their plans to Captain McKee, then the commandant. McKee offered a furlough to any two men who would make speed to the Greenbrier and warn the people. John Insminger and John Logan undertook the perilous errand, and started out, but not seeing how they could get past the Indians, they returned the same evening. John Pryor and Philip Hammond then agreed to go. The Grenadier Squaw painted and otherwise disguised the men, so that they would look like Indians. The two messengers reached Donally's fort a few hours in advance of the Shawnees, and though a severe battle quickly followed, the foe was repulsed and the settlement was saved.

We will let the order-book tell the story of the organization of Rockbridge and relate the local annals during the remaining years of the War for Independence.

First court at the house of Samuel Wallace, April 7, 1778. Justices present: Archibald Alexander, John Bowyer, John Gilmore, Samuel Lyle, Samuel McDowell. Archibald Alexander qualified as sheriff, Andrew Reid as clerk, John Bowyer as county lieutenant, and John Gilmore as lieutenant-colonel. Sheriff's bond, 1000 pounds. Next day James McDowell qualified as surveyor, and the following constables were appointed: Richard Williams in Captain James Hall's company; Samuel Wilson in Captain Samuel Wallace's company; Robert Robertson in Captain John Paxton's company; Robert Faris in Captain John Lyle's company; William Dryden in Captain David Gray's company; Isaac Anderson in Captain Alexander Stuart's company; William McCampbell in Captain John Gilmore's old company. John Ward was also made a constable.

Moses Collier was continued as road surveyor from John Thompson's to David Logan's.

New road surveyors appointed: Andrew Taylor, from North River to Stuart's store; Captain John Taylor, from Stuart's old store to Colonel Samuel McDowell's; John McClung, from said McDowell's to the forks of the road at John McClung's; Andrew Moore, from said forks to the county line; James Gilmore, from Buffalo Creek to his own house; Charles Campbell, from Robert Kirkpatrick's to the county line; Hugh Barclay, Sr., from said Gilmore's to the county line; Samuel McCampbell, from head of Kerr's Creek to Andrew McCampbell's; William McKemy, from Andrew McCampbell's to ford on North River; Alexander Tedford, from Robert Kirkpatrick's to North River; Alexander Willson, from Captain Charles Campbell's to Hugh Weir's; Samuel Caruthers, from Buffalo Creek to the forks of the road above James Gilmore's.

Captain John Lyle, John Lyle, Henry McClung, and James Lyle, or any three of them, to view a way from Robert Kirkpatrick's, by way of Alexander Stuart's merchant mill, to Stuart's store.

April 9.—Survey of the town site ordered given in at next sitting.

April 18.—Called court to examine Captain James Hall, bound in recognisance for felony, the specific charge being the murder of Cornstalk. Hall did not appear.

April 28.—Hall appeared, there were no witnesses for the commonwealth, and he was acquitted. Hugh Galbraith bound in recognisance on the same charge.

May 5.—No witnesses appeared against Galbraith and he was acquitted.

Thomas Vance appointed road surveyor from the great road below William Sprowl's to the other great road near James Thompson's.

Grand jury: David Gray (foreman), Joseph Moore, Thomas Wilson, William Porter, Alexander Tedford, David McClure, Samuel McCorkle, William Walker, David McCroskey, James Patton, Hugh Weir, Doctor Patrick Vance, Andrew Hall, Samuel Paxton.

Citizens appointed to take the lists of tithables: Captain John Gilmore, for his own and John Paxton's companies; John Trimble, gentleman, for the companies of William Paxton, Samuel Wallace, and James Hall; Samuel Lyle, gentleman, for the companies of John Lyle and David Gray; Alexander Stuart, gentleman, for the Calfpasture and for the companies of Samuel Steele and James Gilmore; Charles Campbell, gentleman, for his own company and Andrew Moore's.

Rates to be observed by keepers of ordinaries:

"Hot "diett" with small beer ....3 shillings
Cold "diett" with no beer ....2 shillings
Stablage and hay or fodder for twenty-four hours ....2 shillings
Good pasturage for twenty-four hours ....1 shilling 8 pence per horse
                                                             1 shilling 3 pence per cow
Lodging with feather bed and clean sheets ....1 shilling
Lodging with chaff bed and clean sheets ....6 pence
Corn per gallon ....1 shilling 3 pence
Oats per gallon ....1 shilling

Samuel Wallace granted ordinary license.

May 14.—Mary, wife of John Walker, found guilty of uttering words sustaining the authority of king and parliament. Damage penalty of fifteen and one-half pounds and costs.

May 19.—Malcolm McCown bound on the same charge as in the case of Captain Hall, and with the same result.

July 7.—Malcolm McCown acquitted on the charge of raising an alarm on Kerr's Creek.

Mary and Richard, orphans of William Butt, ordered bound.

John Kirkpatrick granted ordinary license.

Joseph Moore, William Paxton, and John Gilmore, Jr., qualify as justices, John Trimble as coroner, Harry Innis as attorney, and William Stuart as constable. William Rowan bound as implicated in the murder of Cornstalk, but with the same result as in the other instances.

August 5.—Samuel Lyle, John Lyle, and Alexander Stuart instructed to let a contract for a courthouse, the specifications being as follows: twenty feet long, sixteen wide, and ten in pitch; well-framed, and weatherboarded with feather-edged plank; roof of lap shingles; house well floored above and below with pine or oak plank one and one-half inches thick; two plain wooden doors; two windows of twelve lights each, and shutters; iron hinges for both doors and windows; house set two feet above the ground on good oak blocks; at one end of the room a convenient bench for the magistrates to sit on; other benches for jury and lawyers; a seat and a table for the clerk; the house to be finished in a workmanlike manner by November 1st.

September 1.—John Houston qualifies as justice.

November 3.—John Gay qualifies as justice.

Ordinary license granted to William Alexander and Alexander Stuart.

Presented for selling liquor without license: William Alexander, William Montgomery, John Lyle, Mary Greenlee, John McClung, John Paul, James Thompson, Jane Lakin, William Paxton.

November 14.—Christopher Meath and Hannah, his wife, acquitted of stealing some linen cloth, but thirty lashes on the bare back were ordered for each of the other parties called up.

February 13, 1779.—A charge against Catharine Coster of stealing goods worth $110 in specie was not fully proved, but the circumstances appearing against her, she was ordered to be given twenty-five lashes on the bare back at the public whipping post and then discharged.

March 2.—Michael Bowyer, Esq., qualifies as attorney.

March 3.—William McKee qualifies as justice.

April 6.—James Buchanan qualifies as justice.

April 7.—Plan for the new courthouse ordered approved and contract let.

Bastardy charge by M—— C—— against W—— J—— made good.

June 2.—John Lyle qualifies as justice.

July 6.—John Greenlee qualifies as justice.

August 3.—John Bowyer, gentleman, qualifies as escheator.

Smith Williamson, Richard Williamson, and Henry Black, having served in Colonel William Byrd's regiment—in French and Indian war—were each given an order for fifty acres of the public land.

Robert Edmondson and Abraham Gasden qualify as assessors.

October 5.—John Trimble, Esq., qualifies as assessor.

Isaac Campbell given ordinary license.

Josiah East, who served in Colonel Washington's regiment, given an order for fifty acres of public land; the same to Richard Walker, a private in Captain John McNeil's Grenadiers. William Alexander, a non-commissioned officer of the Second Virginia under Colonel Byrd, given an order for 200 acres.

James Grigsby and William Brown given ordinary license.

John Bowyer qualifies as sheriff and William McDowell as his deputy.

December 7.—Levy, 2376 pounds, 8 shillings, 6 pence ($7921.42).

Poll tax, $7.00.

March 9, 1780.—Tavern rates: hot dinner, $10; hot breakfast, $8; cold diet, $7; lodging, with feather bed, $2; lodging, with chaff bed, $1; corn or oats, per gallon, 44 cents; whiskey, per gallon, $80. (These sums were in depreciated paper money).

Samuel Wallace allowed $40 for twenty-eight days spent in making roads.

May 2.—Samuel Jack presented for saying, "God damn the army to hell."

June 6.—Isaac Campbell, jailor, ordered to be paid $1179. George Kelly allowed $70 for making a table for the clerk and sundry repairs on the courthouse.

June 6.—Lashes, "well laid on," to the number of twenty-five, were ordered to be administered to Elizabeth Berry.

John Templeton and Robert Ewing granted tavern license.

December 5.—Samuel McDowell, sheriff, protests against the insufficiency of the jail.

Tavern rates: hot dinner, $15; hot breakfast, $12; cold diet, $10; lodging, with feather bed, $6; lodging, with chaff bed, $2; pasturage for twenty-four hours, $4; corn or oats, per gallon, $6.

Joseph Walker qualifies as justice.

Jonathan Whitley bound in his own recognisance on a charge of disloyalty.

George Campbell excused from further payment of county levy.

March 7, 1781.—Tavern rates: hot dinner, $20; hot breakfast, $15; cold diet, $12; rum, per gallon, $200; whiskey, per gallon, $60; all good wines, per gallon, $160.

July 3.—Archibald Stuart qualifies as attorney, Samuel Wallace as lieutenant-colonel, and William McKee as sheriff. Sheriff's bond, $5000.

Samuel Lyle and John Caruthers appointed commissioners of the specific tax.

October 2.—James Gilmore given tavern license.

November 6.—Captain John Bowyer presented for preventing men from going on militia tour when lawfully called.

Samuel Todd, gentleman, allowed $90.42 in specie and two per cent. of the tax for collecting the specific tax, the rent of storehouses, and finding barrels and packing them with flour.

December 4.—Roger McCormick, servant to Robert Campbell, presented for speaking disloyal words. No witnesses. Remanded to jail and soon discharged.

January 1, 1782.—View ordered from Samuel Carter's near the county line to McDowell's.

April 3.—Tavern rates: hot dinner, one and one-fourth shilling; hot breakfast, one shilling; cold diet, one shilling; corn or oats, per gallon, six pence; lodging, with feather bed, seven and one-half pence; lodging, with chaff bed, four pence; wine, per gallon, fifteen shillings; cider, per gallon, one and one-fourth shilling.

May 4.—Samuel Todd qualifies as justice.

October 1.—Robert Eastham ordered to pay John Ramsay, for one day as witness for Andrew Ramsay and eighty miles travel, 185 pounds of tobacco.

November 5.—James Bailey presented for saying that "the sending of the eighteen months men was the doing of the damn'd Congress."

November 8.—Tithables, 1145. Poll tax, sixteen pounds of tobacco. Levy 18,320 pounds of tobacco ($610.70).

Tavern rates: hot dinner, twenty-five cents; hot breakfast, twenty-two cents; cold diet, seventeen cents.

January 7, 1783.—Adam, the mulatto bastard of Catharine E———, ordered to be bound out.

May 6.—William Gray, living near Barclay's mill, presented for "driving his wagon on the Sabbath Day," and Israel C—— presented for having two wives.

November 2.—For stealing fodder, Henry Navils ordered to be given twenty lashes.

X

THE CALFPASTURE

THE PASTURES—EARLY SETTLEMENT—THE PATTON AND LEWIS SURVEY—PIONEER HISTORY—EMIGRATION

Geographically distinct from the rest of Rockbridge, and not properly a part of the Valley of Virginia, is the section of the county west of North Mountain and above the lower Goshen Pass. In the very dawn of settlement it became known as the Calfpasture, or simply as "the Pastures," because it already comprised a large area of open ground. Its leading watercourses were first known as "the Great River of the Calfpasture" and "the Little River of the Calfpasture." It will thus be seen that the valley named the streams and not the streams the valley. In what manner the names Calfpasture, Cowpasture, and Bullpasture came into existence is not clearly known. The Cowpasture was first known as Clover Creek and the Bullpasture as Newfoundland Creek.

Great and Little rivers head in Augusta and Mill Creek in Bath. But the larger and more important share of the Calfpasture basin lies in this county, and with respect to the pioneer families it will be treated as a whole. In the timbered and sparsely peopled valley of Bratton's Run is the resort of Rockbridge Alum Springs. At the mouth of Mill Creek is the town of Goshen. A little above is Panther Gap, utilized by the first railroad to cross the Alleghanies in this latitude. On Great and Little rivers is a considerable area of low-lying land, somewhat thin, but otherwise well suited to agriculture.

Why this section of the Pastures should have been included in Rockbridge is not at this day very obvious. It was doubtless the work of influential men. We do know that some of the inhabitants did not like being placed in this county. We also know that when the people of the Bath area began moving for a new county in 1777, they wished the Calfpasture to be a part of it. The people of the Pastures seem to have been about evenly divided on that question.

The author of *Annals of Augusta* asserts that the Calfpasture was settled about as early as the country around Staunton, yet offers no evidence in support of this claim. The records of the parent county, especially the muster rolls of 1742, do not indicate such early settlement. From another source we learn that the first settler was Alexander Dunlap, who came in 1743. He was accompanied by his wife, four children, and an indentured servant, Abraham Mushaw. At this date there was no settler any farther west. Dunlap's cabin stood near the spot now occupied by the Alleghany Inn.

Next year, James Patton and John Lewis, acting under an order of council, surveyed a tract nearly fifteen miles long, but nowhere more than about one and one-eighth miles broad. Their map shows it cross-sectioned into twenty-three lots. The lower end of the grant included the site of the town of Goshen. The upper end extended rather to the north of Deerfield. With a single exception every lot had been entered by some settler. From this circumstance we may infer that these other people came almost as soon as Dunlap.

The following tabular statement shows consecutively the number of the lot, the name of the settler, the acreage, the purchase-price—when stated in the deed—and the early transfers of title. When the deed was issued to a successor of the original settler, such other name is given in brackets.

Names of consorts are also thus shown:

1. Alexander Dunlap (John Dunlap)—625—$68.69—295 acres sold Robert Dunlap, 1761, for $333.33.
2. William Jameson—170—$20.87.
3. Thomas Gilham—168—$18.86—sold, 1752, by Thomas (Margaret) Gilham to James Lockridge for same price—resold, 1767, by John Dickenson to William Thompson for $200.
4. Robert Crockett—370—$41.15—sold, 1760, by pioneer's sons—James (Martha) and Robert, Jr., (Janet), both of Mecklenburg county, North Carolina—to William Thompson for $200—295 acres sold by Thompson, 1767, for $166.67.
5. David Davis—290—$29—sold, 1749, by Patton and Lewis to John Poague.
6. Thomas Weems—525—$31.10—sold, 1768, by Thomas (Eleanor) Weems to William Given for $723.33.
7. Henry Gay—694—$33.39—100 acres sold, 1769, to James Frazier for $33.33.
8. Francis Donelly—266—$30.02.
9. Robert Gay—519—$57.89.
10. Samuel Hodge—449—$47.97.
11. John Miller—316—$70.08—sold by John (Ann) Miller to John Ramsay, 1757.
12. Loftus Pullin—252 (240?)—$26.92—sold to James Shaw, 1760, for $30—sold by Shaw to John Ramsay, 1768, for $150.
13. Robert Bratton—834—$96.67—400 acres sold to James Bratton, 1771, for $133.33.
14. James Lockridge—280—?—sold by James (Isabella) Lockridge to Andrew Lockridge (son), 1764, for $66.67.
15. John Graham—696—$79.58—150 acres sold to James Graham (son), 1768, for $16.67.
16. Robert Gwin—544—?—sold by William (Agnes) Gwin to Robert Lockridge, 1766, for $575.
17. John Preston—1054—$31.15—520 acres sold by William (Susanna) Preston to Mary Preston, 1762, for $333.33. The same sold by Mary Preston to Robert Lockridge, 1763, for $366.67.
18. William Warwick—106—$118.67—sold, 1745, to John Kincaid.
19. James Carlile—600—$65.39—250 acres sold, 1753, to John Carlile, and sold by him, 1762, to Thomas Hughart for $166.67—200 acres sold by John (Mary) Carlisle to Thomas Adams, 1796, for $391.67.
20. Jacob Clements—457—$51.67—202 acres sold, 1751, by Jacob (Mary) Clements to

John Campbell for $66.67, and sold by John (Ann) Campbell, 1768, to James Carlisle for $250.
21. John Campbell—308—$34.17—208 acres sold by Samuel Campbell to William Lockridge, 1769, for $713.33.
22. James Carter—300—$33.38—sold to Robert Gay, 1768.
23. John Wilson—600—$66.

Other patents in the Calfpasture, prior to 1770, are these: acreage, date, and description being given consecutively:

Adams, Thomas—(1) 190—1769—Bratton's Run. (2) 235—1769—Calfpasture.
Beverly, William—700—1743—head of Great River.
Bratton, James—90—1769—Bratton's Run.
Campbell, John and Samuel—100—1761—branch of Great River.
Crockett, Margaret and Andrew—(1) 48—1749—David Mill place on Calfpasture. (2) 44—1749—adjoining James Poague.
Dunlap, John—125—1760—Dunlap Creek (Bratton's Run).
Dunlap, Alexander—90—1769—Calfpasture above Jameson.
Jameson, William—80—1755—east side Great River.
Kincaid, Andrew—45—1769—Calfpasture above Tinker.
Lockridge, Andrew—22—1755—branch of Great River.
McKittrick, Robert—110—1759—branch of Great River.
Patton, James and John Lewis—600—1743—Elk Creek of Calfpasture.

Still other early settlers were the Armstrongs, Blacks, Blairs, Clarks, Craigs, Elliotts, Fultons, Hamiltons, Hendersons, Johnstons, McConnells, McCutchens, McKnights, Meeks, Mateers, Moores, Risks, Smiths, Stevensons, Walkups, and Youells.

Alexander Dunlap, a man of some means, was appointed a captain of horse in 1743, but died the following year. He was succeeded in this position by William Jameson. Thomas Gilham qualified as captain of foot in 1752, and James Lockridge and Robert Bratton in 1755. James Lockridge and William Jameson are named as members of the first county court of Augusta in 1745. The latter acted as a justice in 1747, but it is not known whether Lockridge qualified.

According to a statement by a daughter of James Gay, the pioneer, there was a stockade on the Calfpasture during the French and Indian war.

The first mill seems to have been that of James Carter. It was probably built about 1745. Some ten years later, Andrew Lockridge had a gristmill.

Charles Knight is mentioned as a schoolmaster in 1755. He was to have $60.00 a year, every half Saturday or every other Saturday to be free time. In case of an Indian alarm he was to enjoy the privilege of being lodged in the settlement. But it is not probable that he was the first teacher.

Rocky Spring Church was built on an acre deeded by Andrew Kincaid, 1773, to the "trustees of a congregation of dissenters." These trustees were James Bratton, Lancelot Graham, Andrew Hamilton, Thomas Hughart, William Kincaid, and Andrew Lockridge. Lebanon Church was organized in 1784 at the home of William Hodge. The first elders were William Youell, Alexander Craig, John Montgomery, John McCutchen, Joseph McCutchen, and Samuel McCutchen. The first meeting house stood close to the Augusta line, the second a half-mile to the south and in Rockbridge. As a consequence there are two cemeteries. The will of John Dunlap, written in 1804, provides a sum to build a gallery for the negro worshippers. John Montgomery, for a while a teacher in Liberty Hall Academy, was the first minister. John S. McCutchen was a successor. But the first congregation on the Calfpasture was that of Little River. The "meeting house land" is mentioned in deeds about 1754. John Hindman preached in the vicinity as early as 1745.

Partly as a result of its only moderate fertility, the Calfpasture has been a great fountain-head of emigration to newer localities, especially Kentucky and Tennessee. Some of the pioneer names have thus been nearly or quite extinguished. Not a few of the men who went from the Calfpasture, or their descendants, have achieved some renown in Western history.

Major Samuel Stevenson, who had lately moved to the Greenbrier, headed in 1776 an expedition to the Bluegrass region of Kentucky. He was accompanied by James Gay, William Elliott, and Benjamin Blackburn. William Campbell, a wheelwright, was picked up as the party went through the wilderness. One of the members said "Blackburn was so stiff with fear we could hardly get him along." In the spring of 1784, Stevenson settled in Woodford county, the "Asparagus Bed" of the Bluegrass State. He was preceded a few weeks by Alexander Dunlap, Jr., and James Gay, Jr. The wives of Stevenson and Dunlap were sisters to Gay, who was a son of James Gay and his wife, Jean Warwick. Pisgah Church, said to be the first Presbyterian organization in Kentucky, was founded the same year. Its first minister was Adam Rankin, who came from Rockbridge. Pisgah Academy, founded by Gay, Dunlap, and Stevenson, developed into Transylvania University, as Liberty Hall Academy developed into Washington and Lee University. The region around was settled almost wholly from Rockbridge and its neighboring counties. The following names, from the membership of Pisgah Church in 1808-1826, will be recognized as occurring in the pioneer annals of Rockbridge: Aiken, Alexander, Allen, Brown, Campbell, Carr, Dunlap, Elliott, Gay, Hamilton, Holman, Kinkead, Kirkham, Logan, Long, Martin, McClung, McClure, McCullough, McPheeters, Renick, Ritchie, Smith, Steele, and Taylor.

We close this chapter with special mention of several of the Calfpasture families.

The Bears sprang from Blastus Baer, a Mennonite who came from Germany in 1740 and settled in Page county in 1763. Jacob, a son, married a daughter of a Mennonite minister and came to the Calfpasture in 1788. Their sect was but slightly represented here, and the Bears attached themselves to other churches.

Robert Bratton, who married the widow of Alexander Dunlap, Sr., was one of four brothers. Samuel remained in Mifflin county, Pennsylvania; James, who married Dorothy Fleming, settled near Christiansburg. Three sons of another brother, went to South Carolina. Captain Robert Bratton was a man of wealth and distinction.

Archibald Clendennin lived in this valley before moving to the lower Cowpasture, where he died in 1749. Archibald, Jr., was the most conspicuous victim in the Greenbrier massacre of 1763. Charles, another son, gave his name to the capital of West Virginia.

Captain James Coursey came from Orange and married as his second wife the widow of Robert Dunlap. A great grandson is Major O. W. Coursey, of South Dakota, a soldier, educator, and historian.

Robert Crockett, son of the pioneer of that name, was one of the "Long Hunters" spoken of in Chapter VIII. The eccentric Davy Crockett, of Tennessee and Texas history, was of another family, although in his youth he worked for a German farmer in this county.

Samuel Ebberd came from Maryland.

Captain Thomas Gilham had seven sons and two sons-in-law in the armies of the Revolution. The family moved first to South Carolina, but afterwards to the north of Illinois.

John Graham and his family experienced a great storm during their voyage from Ulster. John appears to have been a brother-in-law to William Elliott and John Armstrong of the Calfpasture. Elliott was born in 1699. William and Graham was a brother to John. Christopher Graham, who died in 1748, was probably the father of Robert Graham of the Bullpasture, and the wife of Joseph Walkup.

John Hepler came from Pennsylvania.

Daniel Hite—otherwise Hight—was a son of Daniel Heydt, a German who settled in the Luray valley.

William Jameson was commissioned coroner in 1753, and seems to have died the same year. A grandson of the same name owned valuable property on the border of the city of St. Louis. Timothy Flint, the historian, calls one of his daughters a "rose of the prairie," and says of the Jameson family, "a group of more beautiful children I have never known."

The pioneer Lockridges were the brothers, James, Robert, and William. William lived first in the Borden grant. The descendants are most numerous in the West. Colonel John Lockridge was a pioneer of Sangamon county, Illinois. Another Colonel Lockridge figures in early Texas history. Andrew Y. Lockridge, a grandson of Major Andrew Lockridge, son of James, was a noted missionary to the Cherokee Indians.

Five brothers of the name of McCutchen came to this part of Virginia. Robert settled on Little River, Samuel in the Borden grant, and William, James, and John in Beverly Manor. James died in 1759, and his sons, James, John, and Patrick went to Washington county. The descendants of the five pioneers are numerous, widely scattered, and include persons of mark. One of these is Robert Barr McCutchen, a distinguished writer.

The McConnells, who founded McConnell's Station, now Lexington, Kentucky, previously lived on Kerr's Creek, as well as the Calfpasture.

Moses McIlvain located in this valley in 1763. While prospecting in the Bluegrass region of Kentucky, in 1779, he was captured by Indians, but was released at the intercession of a trader by the name of McCormick, who had known McIlvain in Ireland. McIlvain married Margaret, a daughter of Samuel Hodge, of the Calfpasture, and settled anew in Woodford county, Kentucky.

Timothy McKnight came from Ulster. His son John, merchant of St. Louis and trader to Santa Fe, was a heavy owner of realty in and near the Missouri metropolis. Robert, another son, settled in Chihuahua, Mexico, as a merchant and mine owner, and married a Spanish lady. Thomas settled in Iowa and was the first candidate for governor of that state on the Whig ticket. James remained on the Calfpasture, but his son John joined his uncle at Chihuahua and became a wealthy merchant. Rebecca, a daughter, married William McCutchen, and the wife of William W. Rucker, Congressman from Missouri, is a great-granddaughter.

Five Walkups, James, Joseph, John, Margaret, and the wife of John Graham, Jr., were brothers and sisters and came to Little River about 1748. Captain James moved to the Waxhaw settlement, North Carolina, 1755, where he was a large planter and slaveholder. Samuel M., a grandson, was an antiquarian of that state. Joseph, son of John, was a lieutenant-governor of California, and is said to have refused an election to the senate of the United States. For several decades there was much confusion in the spelling of the family surname. Professor Wauchope, a distinguished literary critic of the South, has returned to the orthodox Scotch orthography. The appropriateness of doing so is very much open to question. The form Walkup is free from strangeness, and to the American ear is the closest possible approximation to the Scottish pronunciation. The phonographic value of the word Wauchope is unmistakable in Scotland, but not in America. In this connection it may be remarked that those German families who in years past modified the spelling of their surnames pursued a wise course. It was a practical step in Americanization.

William Warwick had four children. Jean and Martha were killed by the Indians about 1759. John settled in Kentucky in 1784. Jacob was an extensive owner of realty and livestock in Pocahontas. The widow of William Warwick married Andrew Sitlington of Bath.

J. Fulton Whitlock, otherwise Tarleton Whitlock, came from the east of Virginia.

William Youell settled on the Calfpasture about 1771.

XI

THE WAR FOR INDEPENDENCE

CAUSES OF THE WAR—THE FINCASTLE AND AUGUSTA RESOLUTIONS—VIRGINIA IN THE REVOLUTION—CAMPAIGN OF 1781—SUNDRY PHASES OF THE CONTEST—PENSIONERS

The underlying cause of the American Revolution was similar to that which forced our country into her present struggle with Germany. It was a protest against autocracy. The American colonies were founded when the relations between the king and his people had not reached a settled basis. It had always been the English practice for the people of each community to manage their local affairs. This principle was followed by the immigrants who peopled the colonies. Trouble began during the conflict between king and Parliament in the time of Cromwell. It assumed serious dimensions during the reign of James II (1685-8), but did not become acute until the accession of George III in 1760. For several decades before the beginning of the outflow from Ulster, few people had been coming to the colonies. The Americans of 1725 had begun to feel that they were already a people distinct from the English. During the quarrel that began with the ending of the Old French war, the colonies held that they were a *part of* the British Empire. But the British government viewed them as *belonging to it*, and consequently as possessing rights of a lower grade.

To the colonials the person of the monarch was the visible tie that joined them to the British Empire. By a legal fiction the king was an impersonation of the state, and only in this sense did they consider that they owed any allegiance to him. The Americans understood Britain to be made up of king, Parliament, and commons; each American colony to be made up of governor—a representative of the crown—legislature, and people. Under Anne and the first and second Georges, the monarch was a mere figure-head. The actual government was in the hands of a corrupt oligarchy. George I was a German, and could speak no English, except when he swore at his troopers. George III began his reign with German ideas of divine right and absolutism, and these he determined to carry into practice. Local self-government had declined markedly in England. It was only a few persons who enjoyed the elective franchise. Parliament was not representative of the people, and by open bribery the king was able to control legislation. The general mass of the English people were at this time ignorant, brutal, and besotted, and they were apathetic toward their political rights. There was a higher level of intelligence in America than in England.

Under kingcraft, as interpreted by George III, the people were to obey the crown and pay taxes. Functions of a public nature were held to inhere in the sovereign. Activities were to start from above, not from below. The Americans contended that the central government could properly act only in matters concerning the empire as a whole. They did not concede that Parliament had any right to tax any English-speaking commonwealth that had its own law-making body. On the one side of the ocean there was a rising spirit of democracy. On the other, there was an ebbing tide, and a "divine-right" monarch was in the saddle. A clash was inevitable.

To the Americans there were several particular sources of annoyance. It was an anomaly for any other person than an American to be the governor of an American colony. But in the crown colonies, of which Virginia was one, the governor was an imported functionary, and on retiring from office he usually went back to Britain. As a rule he was a needy politician, did not mingle socially with the Americans, and in his official letters he was nearly always abusing them. Another annoyance was the Board of Trade, a bureau which undertook to exercise a general oversight in America. It cared little for good local government. It sought to discourage any industry which might cause a leak in the purse of the British tradesman. Its one dominant aim was to see that the colonies were meek and to render them a source of profit to the British people and the British treasury.

Even after the controversy had become one of bullets instead of words, the prevailing sentiment in America was not in favor of political separation. The colonials felt a pride in their British origin. They recognized that a union founded on justice was to the advantage of every member of the British Empire. At the outset, the Americans fought for the rights which they held to be common to all Englishmen. In this particular they had the good will of a large section of the people of England. It was the autocratic attitude of the king that made separation unavoidable.

American independence was proposed and accomplished by a political party known in Revolutionary history as the Whig. It was opposed by a reactionary party known as the Tory. But in the Whig party itself was a conservative as well as a progressive wing. The former consented to a separation, but otherwise it wanted things to remain as they were. The progressives had a further aim. They were bent on establishing a form of government that was truly democratic.* The progressives prevailed, and yet the work they cut out was only well under way when independence was acknowledged. "The Revolution began in Virginia with the rights of America and ended with the rights of man."†

The basic origin of the Revolution was political. In the Southern colonies

---

*This term is not to be construed in a partisan sense. When the present political party of that name is mentioned in this book it is with a capital letter.
†Eckenrode.

there was not an economic cause also, as was the case in New England. The exports from Virginia touched high water mark in 1775, in spite of the long quarrel between the governor and the people.

We have entered into a rather extended discussion of a topic that belongs more to national than to county history. Yet the interest in the issue was so keen in the Scotch-Irish settlers that our explanation of it may not seem out of place. The Ulster people were naturally more democratic than the English, and nowhere in America was the democratic feeling more pronounced than along the inland frontier. The Scotch-Irish element generally rallied to the support of the Whig party, and was a most powerful factor in its ultimate success. The Tory influence was strong in the well-to-do classes along the seaboard, particularly among men in official and commercial life. Virginia was somewhat exceptional in this regard. It was practically without any urban population. The planter aristocracy upheld the Whig cause, and as it was the ruling class, it carried the colony with it. It must be added, however, that the planters of Tidewater cast their lot with the conservative wing of the party. It was under the lead of such men as Jefferson and Madison, residents of Middle Virginia, that the state capital was taken away from the tidewater district in 1779. The progressive Whigs east of the Blue Ridge found a strong ally in the population west of that mountain.

The resolutions adopted at Fort Chiswell, the county seat of Fincastle, were so closely in harmony with the views of the people in the Rockbridge area that we present them in this chapter. The address by the Committee of freeholders is signed January 20, 1775, and is directed to the Continental Congress. The chairman was William Christian. Other prominent members of the committee were William Preston and Arthur Campbell. Of the fifteen men, all were officers except the Reverend Charles Cumings.

We assure you and all our countrymen that we are a people whose hearts overflow with love and duty to our lawful sovereign, George III, whose illustrious House, for several successive reigns, have been the guardian of the civil and religious rights and liberties of British subjects as settled at the glorious revolution (of 1688); that we are willing to risk our lives in the service of His Majesty for the support of the Protestant religion, and the rights and liberties of his subjects, as they have been established by compact, law, and ancient charters. We are heartily grieved at the differences which now subsist between the parent state and the colonies, and most heartily wish to see harmony restored on an equitable basis, and by the most lenient measures that can be devised by the heart of man. Many of us and our forefathers left our native land, considering it as a kingdom subjected to inordinate power and greatly abridged of its liberties; we crossed the Atlantic and explored this then uncultivated wilderness, bordering on many nations of savages, and surrounded by mountains almost inaccessible to any but those very savages, who have incessantly been committing barbarities and depredations on us since our first seating the country. Those fatigues and ravages we patiently encounter, supported by the pleasing hope of enjoying those rights and liberties which had been granted to *Virginians*, and were denied us in our native country, and of transmitting them inviolate to our posterity; but even to these remote regions the hand of unlimited and unconstitutional power hath pursued us to strip us of that liberty and property, with which God, nature, and the rights of humanity have vested us. We are ready and willing to contribute all in our power for the support of his Majesty's government, if applied to constitutionally, and when the grants are made to our representatives, but cannot think of submitting our liberty or property to the power of a venal British parliament, or to the will of a corrupt British ministry. We by no means desire to shake off our duty or allegiance to our lawful sovereign, but on the contrary, shall ever glory in being the lawful subjects of a Protestant prince, descended from such illustrious progenitors, so long as we can enjoy the free exercise of our religion as Protestant subjects, and our liberties and properties as British subjects.

But if no pacific measures shall be proposed or adopted by Great Britain, and our enemies will attempt to dragoon us out of those inestimable privileges, which we are entitled to as subjects, and reduce us to slavery, we declare that we are deliberately and resolutely determined never to surrender them to any power upon earth but at the expense of our lives.

These are our real though unpolished sentiments, of liberty and loyalty, and in them we are resolved to live and die.

The opening lines of the address do not make the impression now that they were intended to make in 1775. The portraiture of George III is the direct opposite of that given in the Declaration of Independence. The latter document censures only the king, while the address vents its indignation on the king's ministry and on Parliament. But the committee appear to draw a distinction between the king as a man and the king as a sovereign. In the former respect, George III was a very mediocre person, obstinate and narrow-minded. In the latter respect he was an impersonation of the state, and to the state every patriotic citizen owes allegiance.

Thomas Lewis and Samuel McDowell were delegates to the Virginia Convention of March, 1775. The instructions given to them by Augusta county, February 22, contain the following sentences:

We have a respect for the parent state, which respect is founded on religion, on law, and the genuine principles of the constitution. * * * These rights we are fully resolved, with our lives and fortunes, inviolably to preserve; nor will we surrender such inestimable blessings, the purchase of toil and danger, to any ministry, to any parliament, or any body of men upon earth, by whom we are not represented, and in whose decisions, therefore, we have no voice. * * * And as we are determined to maintain unimpaired that liberty which is the gift of Heaven to the subject of Britain's empire, we will most cordially join our countrymen in such measures as may be deemed wise and necessary to secure and perpetuate the ancient, just, and legal rights of this colony and all British America.

A memorial from the committee of Augusta, presented to the state convention May 16, 1775, is mentioned in the journal of that body as "representing the necessity of making a confederacy of the United States, the most perfect, independent, and lasting, and of framing an equal, free, and liberal government, that may bear the trial of all future ages." This memorial is pronounced by Hugh

Blair Grigsby the first expression of the policy of establishing an independent state government and permanent confederation of states which the parliamentary journals of America contain. The men who could draw up papers like these were not the ones to stand back from sending, as they did, 137 barrels of flour to Boston for the relief of the people of that city in 1774. A savage act of Parliament had closed their port to commerce.

Even during the Indian war of 1774 there were very strained relations between the House of Burgesses and the Tory governor. In the spring of 1775, the administration of Dunmore was virtually at an end, and the Committee of Safety was managing the government of the state.

With respect to Virginia soil there were three stages in the war for American Independence. The first was confined to the counties on the Chesapeake, continued but a few months, and closed with the expulsion of Dunmore soon after his burning of Norfolk on New Years day, 1776. The invasion by Arnold began at the very close of 1780, and ended with the surrender of Cornwallis in October, 1781. The warfare with the Indians continued intermittently from the summer of 1776 until after the treaty with England in 1783. Except in the southwest of the state, the red men rarely came east of the Alleghany Divide. The British did not come across the Blue Ridge, and only once did they threaten to do so. Consequently the Rockbridge area did not itself become a theatre of war.

Nevertheless, Rockbridge took an active part in the Revolution. At the outset of hostilities Augusta agreed to raise four companies of minute men, a total of 200 soldiers. William Lyle, Jr., was the lieutenant of the Rockbridge company, and William Moore was its ensign. We do not know the name of the captain, but the colonel was George Mathews, a native of Rockbridge. As the commander of the Ninth Virginia Regiment in the Continental service, Mathews distinguished himself in Washington's army until he and his 400 "tall Virginians" were outflanked during the fog that settled on the field of Germantown and compelled to surrender. Probably a number of Rockbridge men were in this regiment, but we have no positive information. [We do not know of the men then living in the county, or who subsequently settled therein, there were some who enlisted in other Continental regiments.] It was in the militia organizations, and then only for two or three months at a time that most of the Rockbridge soldiers saw military duty.

Probably the first active service on the part of men of this county was in the summer of 1776, when the militia under Captain John Lyle and Captain Gilmore marched under Colonel William Christian in his expedition against the Cherokees. He was gone five months, and accomplished his purpose without actual fighting, although five towns were destroyed. The companies of John Paxton and Charles Campbell were in the column of 700 men that reached Point

Pleasant in November, 1777. Major Samuel McDowell was a line officer in this force, and his men began their march from the mouth of Kerr's Creek. General Hand was to march against the towns on the Scioto. But deciding that it was too late in the season and that provisions were too low, that leader contented himself with announcing the surrender of Burgoyne and then dismissing the militia, who reached home late in the next month. Next spring, Captain William McKee was in command at Point Pleasant. It was another Rockbridge company, under the command of Captain David Gray, that marched to the relief of Donally's fort when the news came that it was attacked by the Shawnees. Captain William Lyle also campaigned on the frontier.

The British invasion of 1781 was a more serious menace. But it is necessary to preface our account of it with a glance at the fighting south of Virginia. After the battle of Monmouth in the summer of 1778, the British leaders made no serious demonstration against Washington's army, and their fleet made them quite safe at New York, which was almost the only ground they held in the North. The war in this quarter was a stalemate, and the British turned their attention to Georgia and the Carolinas. In these colonies the Tories were as numerous as the Whigs. Savannah was taken and then Charleston. After the second disaster there was no field army to contend with the enemy, and South Carolina and Georgia were overrun. While General Lincoln was besieged in Charleston, the Seventh Regiment of Virginia Continentals under Colonel Buford were on their way to reënforce him. But they were surprised at Waxhaw, no quarter was given, and they were cut down by the dragoons of Colonel Tarleton. After dusk some of the troopers, who were generally Tories, returned to the scene of the massacre, and where they found signs of life, they bayonetted the hacked and maimed. Captain Adam Wallace was among the slain. Several other Rockbridge men were either killed or wounded. The inhuman cruelty shown on this and other occasions by Tarleton made him an object of bitter hatred. He thought German methods of warfare the proper ones to use against the Americans, and the resentment he did so much to arouse was not entirely extinguished at the outbreak of the war of 1917.

A few months later a new American army, advancing from the north, was overthrown at Camden. At the close of 1780, when the fortunes of the Americans in the South were at a low ebb, General Greene, a leader of signal ability, was given command in all the colonies south of Pennsylvania and New Jersey. But the wreck of the army defeated at Camden was small, half-naked, and poorly equipped. The British and Tories were in much superior numbers and did not lack for clothing and munitions. Nevertheless, there was a turn in the tide. At the Cowpens, the right wing of the American army nearly destroyed a force under Tarleton, and 600 prisoners were sent to Virginia. Greene made a masterly retreat across North Carolina, closely pursued by Cornwallis, the British commander-in-chief in the South. After Greene crossed the Dan, Cornwallis gave up a chase that was bringing him no result, and fell back to Hillsboro, then the capital of North Carolina. Greene was joined by large numbers of militia, until his army was 4400 strong, but only one of his little regiments was of seasoned troops, and the militia organizations were an uncertain reliance. The force under Cornwallis was only half as numerous, yet his men were veterans, well-equipped and well officered. Greene recrossed the Dan and took position at Guilford, where he was attacked by the British, March 15th. Cornwallis held the battleground, but one-third of his army was put out of action by the American rifles. He could neither follow up his nominal advantage nor remain in North Carolina. He made a rapid retreat to Wilmington, pursued a part of the way by Greene, who then advanced into South Carolina. Cornwallis dared not follow his antagonist, and led his shattered army to Virginia. In four months Greene nearly freed South Carolina and Georgia from the enemy, except as to the seaports of Charleston and Savannah.

Rockbridge men under Captain James Gilmore helped to win the brilliant victory at the Cowpens. Their time had nearly expired, and they were used to escort the captured redcoats to their prison camp. In this fight Ensign John McCorkle was wounded in the wrist and died of lockjaw. But Gilmore seems also to have been present at Guilford, where soldiers from Rockbridge were much more numerously represented. In this battle, Major Alexander Stuart was wounded and captured, and Captains John Tate and Andrew Wallace were killed. Among the other officers were Major Samuel McDowell, Captain James Bratton, and Captain James Buchanan. Tate's company was composed almost wholly of students from Liberty Hall. They acquitted themselves so well as to extort a compliment from Cornwallis. After the action he asked particularly about "the rebels who took position in an orchard and fought so furiously." Samuel Houston, then a youth of nineteen, kept a diary while his company was on its tour. James Waddell, the preacher who was so noted for his eloquence, addressed the command at Steele's Tavern, the place of rendezvous. The company left Lexington January 26th, joined Greene's army five days before the battle of Guilford, and got home March 23rd. Houston fired nineteen rounds during the engagement. The men had orders to take trees and several would get behind the same tree. The redcoats were repulsed again and again. At Guilford, as at the Cowpens, the conduct of the Virginia militia was exceptionally good. Greene said if he could have known how well they would act, he could have won a complete victory. In that case the battle of Guilford might have decided the campaign.

Meanwhile the traitor Arnold had landed 1600 men at Westover on the

James. Two days later—January 5th—he burned Richmond. Finding his flank threatened from the direction of Petersburg, he retreated to Portsmouth, where he was closely watched by a small army under Steuben and Muhlenburg. Colonel Bowyer had a regiment under Muhlenburg, the clergyman-general. The company of Captain Andrew Moore marched from its rendezvous at Red House, January 10, 1781.

Virginia had been stripped of her trained soldiers, and Washington sent Lafayette to take command. The young Frenchman arrived in March with 1200 light infantry. To offset this help, General Phillips left New York with two regiments and occupied Manchester, April 30th. The British much outnumbered the Americans, but were not aggressive. Phillips died of fever at Petersburg, and Arnold was again in chief command. When Cornwallis arrived he brought the British army to a strength of 7000 men. Having no use for Arnold, he sent him away. The odds against the Americans were now serious. Late in May, Cornwallis moved from Richmond to gain the rear of Lafayette's army. He wrote that the boy could not escape him. Yet the boy did escape him, although he was pursued nearly to the Rapidan. Cornwallis then sent out marauding expeditions under Tarleton and Simcoe, while his main army moved upon Orange. Lafayette, reënforced by 800 veterans under General Wayne, recrossed the Rapidan. Cornwallis thought he would cut him off, but Lafayette opened an old road and marched by night to Mechum's River, where, with his back to the Blue Ridge, he made a stand to protect his stores. The British leader did not try to force a decision, and fell back to the Peninsula below Richmond. Tarleton had burned Charlottesville, then a very small place, and the Assembly fled from it to Staunton, where it sat from June 7th to the 24th. Tarleton made a threat of coming over the Blue Ridge. The legislators fled from Staunton so precipitately as to take no measures to defend the place. But the militia assembled in force, their ranks swelled by old men as well as boys, and meant to give Tarleton a hot reception, in case he should attempt to force Rockfish Gap. But as Tarleton had only 250 men, his threat could have been no more than a bluff.

Lafayette, gradually reënforced by the Virginia militia to the number of 3,000, followed the British. Washington came down from the Hudson with 2,000 of his American troops and 5,000 Frenchmen. The sequel is familiar to every reader of American history. Previous to the siege of Yorktown, the two small battles of Hot Water and Green Spring, fought near Williamsburg, were the only engagements in the Virginia campaign that rose above the dignity of mere skirmishes. But during his almost unobstructed march, Cornwallis inflicted a loss of $10,000,000 in looting and burning, and the kidnapping of slaves.

Not only did the Valley men have to contend with the British east of the Blue Ridge and the Indians west of the Alleghany, but in the spring of 1781 they had also to watch the Tories in Montgomery. The latter were threatening to seize the lead mines near Fort Chiswell, and then join Cornwallis, when, as was expected, he would follow Greene into Virginia.

Among the men from this county who turned out to fight the invader in 1781 were companies under Colonel John Bowyer and captains Andrew Moore, Samuel Wallace, John Cunningham, William Moore, David Gray, James Buchanan, and Charles Campbell. Captain William Moore helped to guard the prisoners during their march from Yorktown to the detention camp at Winchester.

There was little active disloyalty in Rockbridge. Archibald Alexander says there were few Tories, and he intimates that these found it advisable to seek a change of climate. One was John Lyon, who had been a servant to Alexander's father. He deserted to the British, and was one of the miscreants who bayoneted the hacked and helpless men on the field of Waxhaw, although he still had enough humanity to spare the life of John Reardon. Lyon was killed at Guilford. Tory Hollow, near the head of Purgatory Creek, derives its name from the Tories who fled into it and were not molested. Doubtless they were wise enough not to make their plight needlessly severe. There is another Tory Hollow between Collier's and Kerr's creeks, and it may take its name from the Tory branch of the Cunningham family. Robert Cunningham, a son of John of Kerr's Creek, became a brigadier-general in the British army in South Carolina. His conduct made him so odious that his estate was confiscated, and although he petitioned to be granted to return, he had to spend the rest of his life under the Union Jack. He was granted an annuity by the British government. His brother Patrick, although a colonel in the British army, was not exiled from South Carolina.

But there was discontent, and there was sometimes a disinclination to perform military service. It is related of Edward Graham that he found the militia assembled near Mount Pleasant about 1778, quite unwilling to volunteer instead of being drafted. Special inducements were offered, but without visible result. Graham addressed the men to induce them to supply the quota with volunteers. Captain John Lyle and a few others stepped forward, and marched and countermarched before the militia, but without effect. Graham then joined the volunteer squad himself, and was followed by enough of the unwilling crowd to make out the number desired. Like some other persons, this minister did not think well of the headlong flight of the legislators from Staunton. He was on his way home from attending a presbytery, and at once set about raising a force of respectable size, acting as its leader.

The most serious disaffection seems to have taken place in May, 1781. It grew out of an Act of Assembly of October, 1780, whereby the counties were to be laid off into districts for the purpose of procuring a quota from each to serve in the Continental line for eighteen months. A petition was sent to the capital from Rockbridge, representing that an absence from home for that length of time meant ruin to the family of the soldier. Districts had been laid off in this county, and in two or three instances the quota had been procured. Jefferson, then governor of the state, pursued a vacillating course and hesitated to enforce the conscription law. Then he wrote a letter taking off the suspension, but by that time the day appointed for the draft had gone by. A date was set for another laying off of the districts. A hundred people gathered at the county seat, May 9th. Hearing that the Augusta people had prevented such action in their county, and seeing Colonel Bowyer getting lists from the captains, a crowd went into the courtroom and carried out the tables. The men said they would serve three months at a time in the militia and make up the eighteen months in that manner, but would not be drafted as regulars for the term mentioned in the law. After tearing up the papers the crowd dispersed.

Virginia was prosperous when the Revolution broke out, but there was much distress during the war. Trade with England came necessarily to an end, and was carried on with France at great risk. Specie was scarce, and there was a tendency to keep it hidden. The currency issued by the Continental Congress to pay its war claims rested on a very insecure basis, and Henry Ruffner relates that it operated as a tax because of its rapid depreciation. In March, 1780, the ratio of paper to specie was forty to one, and in May, 1781, it was 500 to one. Taxes were high and hard to meet, and the collecting of them was an unpleasant official duty. Almost everything was taxed, even the windows in a house. A petition of 1779 complains not only of the high assessment, but says that a still greater grievance is the separate taxing of houses, orchards, and fencing, these items aggregating more than the land itself. It was made legal for taxes to be paid in certain kinds of farm produce. This form was called the specific tax, and it required storehouses for the produce levied upon.

The return of the specific tax for April, 1782, mentions 342½ bushels of wheat, 1,282 pounds of bacon, and $12.58 in specie, turned in by 702 tithables. There were 338 tithables in arrears for 165 bushels of wheat and 676 pounds of bacon. Samuel Lyle and John Wilson, the commissioners, were allowed ten per cent. for their services. A petition of 1784 says there is little or no hard money, and that the number of horses and cattle had been much reduced during the war. The only merchantable staple was hemp, and this had fallen in price very much.

Under the Federal pension law of 1832, the applicant was required to make his declaration before the county court, and his reminiscences are often of interest and value. The declarations below are by men who were living in Rockbridge in the year indicated. Only a synopsis is given here. A less abbreviated account —of more service to genealogists—may be found in *McAllister's Data on the Virginia Militia in the Revolutionary War*.

Ailstock, Absalom: born a free mulatto about 1795. Marched from Louisa about December 1, 1780, it being rumored that the British were going to land on the Virginia coast, and was out four weeks. About April 1, 1781, joined the Second Regiment under Colonel Richardson. The ruins of the tobacco warehouses in Manchester could be seen from the

Richmond side. The brigade was stationed a while at Malvern Hills. The enemy were in the habit of coming this far up the James in boats, each with a gun at either end, the purpose being plunder. Two such boats and seventeen men were taken by the regiment. During the siege of Yorktown the applicant dug intrenchments for batteries and made sand baskets.

Cunningham, John: Born in Pennsylvania in 1756. Served in that state in 1776, 1777, and 1781.

Davidson, John: Born in Rockbridge, 1757. He was willing to go out in the spring of 1778, being then unmarried, but was induced by his mother to hire a substitute. In the summer of that year, as a drafted man, he served in Greenbrier. Under Captain William Lyle he drove packhorses loaded with flour and bacon to the troops on the frontier. In January, 1781, he marched from Red House, his company commanders being Captain Andrew Moore, Lieutenant John McClung, and Ensign James McDowell. At Great Bridge, near Norfolk, two twelve pounder howitzers and about twelve prisoners were captured. There was another skirmish near Gum Bridge, near the Dismal Swamp. He went out again, August 7, 1781, under Captain David Gray, who tried to induce him to be orderly sergeant. At Jamestown the militia were ferried across the James by the French, who were 5,500 strong on the north side.

East, James: Born in Goochland, 1753. In 1779 he was guarding Hessian prisoners at Charlottesville. Left Fluvanna county, 1792.

Fix, Philip: Born near Reading, Pennsylvania, about 1754. Was living in Loudoun county, 1777, and served that year in his native state.

Harrison, James: Born in Culpeper, 1755. In the fall of 1777 he served under Captain John Paxton, marching to Point Pleasant by way of Fort Donally. He witnessed the death of Cornstalk, Red Hawk, Petalla, and Ellinipsico. He reached home shortly before Christmas. In 1781 he was engaged six months in Amherst, his duty being to patrol the county twice a week to thwart any effort by the Tories to stir up disaffection among the negroes.

Hickman, Adam: Born in Germany, 1762, and came to America five years later. Served under Captain James Hall in 1780. That company and Captain Gray's marched about October 1, and was absent three months around Richmond and Petersburg. He went out again in May, 1781, and the Appomattox at Petersburg was crossed on a flatboat, the bridge having been burned by the enemy. He was in the battle of Hot Water, June 28th.

Hight, George: Born in King and Queen, 1755. Was in Christian's expedition against the Cherokees. In August, 1777, he enlisted in Rockbridge for the war, serving in Colonel George Baylor's Light Dragoons. In October, he joined the regiment at Fredericksburg, and the following winter was at Valley Forge. The troop to which he belonged was employed in preventing the people of that region from furnishing supplies to the enemy, and in watching the movements of the latter. He was in the battle of Monmouth. Next September, at a time when the regiment was asleep in barns on the Hudson, it was surprised by General Grey, and no quarter was given except to the members of his own troop. He and another man escaped by getting in among the enemy. In the spring of 1779 the regiment was recruited, and Colonel William Washington took command. It was again employed, this time in New Jersey, in watching the enemy and preventing trading with him. Near the close of 1780 the regiment marched to Charleston, South Carolina. Shortly after his arrival in March, Washington defeated Tarleton, taking sixteen prisoners, but a while later was himself defeated at Monk's Corner. The horses were saddled and bridled, but there was no time to mount them. Applicant was taken prisoner and was exchanged at Jamestown, in August, 1781.

Hinkle, Henry: Born in Pennsylvania, 1750. Served three tours in the militia of Frederick county, 1779-1781.

Kelso, James: Born on Walker's Creek, 1761. Drafted, January, 1781, into Captain James Buchanan's company of Colonel Bowyer's regiment, and was in skirmishes near

Portsmouth. When Tarleton made his raid on Charlottesville, he volunteered and served one month. In September he was at the siege of Yorktown, under Captain Charles Campbell, and after that event he was detailed to guard the prisoners to Winchester.

Mason, John: Born in Pennsylvania, 1740. Was in the battle of Brandywine, serving in a company from Berkeley. In 1781 he was in the battle of Guilford as a member of John Tate's company.

McLane, John: Born in Ulster, 1757. In 1778 served in Greenbrier under Captain David Gray. In January, 1781, he went out on a tour of three months under Captain Andrew Moore. It took about fifteen days to get home from Norfolk.

McKee, James: Born in Pennsylvania, 1752, died in Rockbridge, 1832. Declaration by Nancy, the widow. John T., a son. Total service, seventeen months, twenty-nine days. His first service was three months with Christian in the Cherokee expedition. The second was when he marched under Captain Charles Campbell and Lieutenant Samuel Davidson to Point Pleasant in the fall of 1777. The third was a tour of three months in Greenbrier, just after the Shawnees attacked Donally's fort. The fourth was as an ensign in the spring of 1781, at which time he marched to Portsmouth. In the summer of the same year he served on the Peninsula. In the fall he served his last tour, and was at the siege of Yorktown.

Miller, William: Born in Pennsylvania, 1757, and came to Rockbridge about 1770. October 9, 1780, he went out under Captain James Gilmore, Lieutenant John Caruthers, and Ensign John McCorkle, and was in the battle of the Cowpens. For four weeks he was guarding Garrison's Ferry on the Catawba.

Moore, William: Early in 1781 he served under Captain Samuel Wallace and Lieutenant Edmondson of Bowyer's regiment. Later in the year he marched to Richmond as captain of a volunteer company. In September he went again as a captain. From Yorktown he marched with the prisoners to Winchester, and was discharged there in December, going home with not over twenty of the men he had taken out.

Shepherdson, David: Born in Louisa, 1763, came to Rockbridge, 1815. In June, 1780, he marched to join the army of Gates, and at Deep River himself and comrades nearly perished, having nothing but green crabapples to eat. A detail of 200 men was sent out to thresh some grain. Was in the battle near Camden, August 16th. After the retreat to Hillsboro, provisions became so scarce that the captain advised the men to go home and get provisions and clothing, their clothing having been lost at Camden. They did so and returned, were advised to go home again, and on their second return were honorably acquitted by a court-martial. Next year he served six months on the Peninsula, and was present at the surrender of Cornwallis.

Vines, Thomas: Born in Amherst, 1756. Served at Charlottesville and Winchester, guarding prisoners. Was in the battles of Hot Water and Green Spring and at the siege of Yorktown.

Wiley, Andrew: Born in Rockbridge, 1756. Absent forty-two days in 1777, driving cattle to the mouth of Elk on the Kanawha. In 1778-79, he served twelve months in the Continental line under General Morgan. In the fall of 1780, he was a substitute in Captain James Hall's company. This company and those of Campbell and Gray joined General Muhlenburg at Deep Run Church near Richmond. In the spring of 1781, he joined Greene's army at Guilford as a member of a Botetourt company. The Carolina men, who formed the first line, ran at the outset. The riflemen to which applicant belonged formed the covering party at the left, and when the Carolina men fled, the British came down on a ridge between this party and the command of Colonel Campbell. The enemy were swept off by the Virginia riflemen, but formed again and again, and compelled the party to ground their arms. Captain Tilford was killed.

Andrew Wiley was one of the Virginians who marched against the "Whiskey Boys," in 1794.

XII

MIDDLE PERIOD

A COMPARISON—AFTER THE REVOLUTION—DISESTABLISHMENT—LIFE AND TIMES IN 1850—
PETTIGREW TRAGEDY

The Middle Period in Rockbridge history begins with the peace of 1783 and continues until the outbreak of another American war in 1861. The Recent Period begins with the cessation of hostilities in 1865 and comes down to the present year. The first covers the lifetime of an old man. The second covers the lifetime of a man of middle age. A feature common to the two periods is that each lies between two great wars.

But while, as we shall presently see, the Recent Period is that of an almost revolutionary change in industrial methods, and even in everyday life, the Middle Period is that of a slow and partial unfolding. Labor-saving machinery was virtually unknown when the earlier period opened and was little more than a novelty when it closed. Men wore homespun in 1780, and were still wearing it in 1860. Men were still shooting with flintlocks in 1860. There was no change in agriculture, aside from the discontinuance of hemp about 1825. The Middle Period was well under way when canal navigation entered Rockbridge, and was almost at its close when a railroad crossed the northwest corner. It was almost at its close before people began to use envelopes and stamps in mailing their letters. Brick manor-houses, very rare at the close of the War for Independence, multiplied in the more fertile neighborhoods. But throughout the eight decades the log house was the typical home in Rockbridge. All in all, the impress of the pioneer days was much in evidence, even so late as 1860.

In 1775-1781, few of the men of this county went to war except for two or three months at a time, and as no invading host came to burn academies and plunder smokehouses, the work of the farm could not have suffered in anything like the same degree as in 1861-1865. But in each instance there was a depreciated paper money, a chaos of values, and commerce was almost on a vacation.

When John Greenlee became sheriff in 1785 he found the taxes for the two preceding years uncollected, although the people were permitted to pay them in hemp at the rate of $5.00 per hundredweight, delivery to be made at designated places at any time before December 20, 1785. In collecting the tax Greenlee used a number of hemp receipts which the treasurer of the State was unwilling to receive. Six years later a petition to the Assembly mentions tobacco, hemp, and flour as the chief things available for paying taxes and buying necessaries. It goes on to say that the roads were rough and bad, and the price of tobacco so low that the farmers would have to abandon the crop unless it could be inspected nearer than Tidewater. The petition asked that inspection might be made at Nicholas Davis's below Balcony Falls.

The closing decades of the eighteenth century were a time of fermentation in America. Religion and mental improvement were much neglected, and there seems to have been more coarseness in word and action than in the pioneer epoch. Matters political kept in the lime-light and promoted the noisy assertiveness that sprang from American independence.

The disestablishment of the Church of England was one of the first reforms of the Revolution. One-half of the Virginians of 1775 were dissenters or in sympathy with the dissenters, and they could no longer be made to support a state church in addition to the church of their choice. Accordingly, no taxes were paid to the Establishment after New Year's Day, 1777. In 1802 the parish farms were ordered to be sold. Yet the clerical party fought to the last ditch, and full religious liberty was not secured until 1785. The conservatives argued that conduct is governed largely by opinion, and that it was proper for the legislature to enact measures calculated to promote opinion of a desirable sort. In 1783 they urged that in place of the old Establishment each citizen should be assessed for the support of some church, in order that public morality might be maintained. The counties west of the Blue Ridge were a unit against any such half-loaf. As compared with Tuckahoe Virginia they were new, poor, and radical.

To the people of Rockbridge, the war of 1812 and the war with Mexico were much less serious than the Revolution, and the casualties in battle were exceedingly few. Yet in 1814 there was much illness and a number of deaths among the soldiers from the mountain counties. They were stationed on the coast, especially around Norfolk. To them the climate seemed hot and sultry, and the drinking water inferior to that of the mountain springs.

About 1822 there was a strong agitation for the removal of the capital to Staunton. The Assembly was bombarded with many petitions to this effect from the counties of the Western District. This movement was one of the symptoms of the discord between the two sections of the state. The feud led to the Staunton Convention of 1816 and its demand for reform in the state government. But the Constitutional Convention of 1829 was dominated by the reactionary element, and there was little relief until the Constitution of 1851 became law.

Until 1789 there was no mail schedule south of Alexandria. No envelopes were used with letters. The rate of postage was governed by the distance, and for a long while payment was made by the person to whom the letter was addressed. Three-cent postage did not come until 1855.

Until 1792 values were often computed in terms of tobacco, 100 pounds of the weed being equivalent to one pound—$3.33—in Virginia currency.

In the 30's, and onward until the war of 1861, the country was flooded with banknote currency, much of it of the "wildcat" variety. The national banking system was still a thing of the future, and the man traveling from his own state into another had to exchange his home paper money for that of the other state, and undergo a "shave" in doing so. He had also to be on his guard against counterfeit bills. A copy of the *Counterfeit Detector and Banknote List* was indispensable to any merchant who was doing much business.

The goods for the merchants of Lexington came by the Tennessee road wagon, a huge vehicle drawn by six horses in gay trappings. The cover was sometimes of bearskin instead of canvas. The wagoner was somewhat like the boatman of the Western rivers. He was a hardy, swaggering personage, but the state driver would not tolerate the idea of lodging in the same tavern with him.

The polling places in 1830 were four: Joseph Bell's at Goshen, H. B. Jones' at Brownsburg, the tavern at Natural Bridge, and the house of one of the numerous Moores. Four years later, the tavern of John McCorkle became a voting place, and in 1845 the tavern of John Albright at Fairfield.

Outside of the county seat and the few villages, Rockbridge had in 1835 three furnaces, six forges, ten stores, and twenty-four gristmills. Of the thirteen country churches, nine were Presbyterian.

Before the Revolution, the gentleman appeared on state occasions in a dress suit of broadcloth, often dark-blue, but sometimes plum or pea-green. His long waistcoat was black and his trowsers of some light color. His tall black hat was similar to the "stove-pipe" of a later day. At the top of his ruffled short-bosom appeared a tall, stiff collar of the type known as a stock, and around this was fastened a black silk handkerchief. His hair was cropped short to make room for a powdered wig. Women wore towering bonnets. The low-necked dress had a cape or collar and enormous mutton-leg sleeves. By the close of the war of 1812, tight breeches had just gone out of fashion. The coat was "high in the collar, tight in the sleeve, short in the back, and swallow-tailed. The hat was narrow-brimmed and bell-crowned." The cravat was a white handkerchief, stiff-starched and voluminous, the flowing ends resting on a ruffled shirt-bosom. The pocket handkerchief was a bandanna. Gloves were not much worn. Woman's dress was "plain in color, short in waist, narrow in skirt. As soon as a woman was married she put on a cap." Imported goods were not in general use, but were worn year after year. "In the country, grandchildren could see the wedding coat still on granddaddy's back on state occasions." In the 50's a certain citizen of this county was wearing linen trowsers forty years old, yet seemingly as good as new. A few moccasins were still worn. Work-shoes were of cowhide, dress shoes of calf-skin. The farmer's boy had to make one pair last a year.

In 1810 not less than 5,000,000 yards of homespun linen were manufactured in Virginia, and much the greater share of this output originated west of the

Blue Ridge. Until about the middle of the century it was only the people of aristocratic tastes who wore clothing made of imported cloth.

The hemp that was not sent to market was made into sacking, or into a hard, strong cloth of a greenish hue that slowly turned to a white.

The flax patch was seldom of more than one acre. The stalks were pulled when the seeds were fully ripe, and were laid out in gavels, the stem-ends forming a line. After a while the bundles were set up, and when dry were put into the barn. In the winter season the stalks were broken to loosen the fiber. This was done by laying them against slats and giving a few blows with a wooden knife. Scutching was the next step, and was performed by holding the broken stems against an upright board and striking them obliquely with the same knife. Then came in succession the spinning, the weaving, and the bleaching. The unbleached cloth was of the color of flaxen hair. The homemade linen was of two grades, one for fine and one for coarse cloth. Six yards a day was about the utmost the weaver could accomplish, if the weaving were to be tight enough.

The imported dyestuffs were indigo, logwood, and madder, used respectively for blue, black, and red shades. The root and hulls of the hickory made a dark-brown; the bark, a yellow. Walnut bark made a brown color, sumach a black, and dogwood a dogwood berry tint.

The log house of "ye olden time" had a floor of pine or poplar puncheons, made smooth and level with the adze. As spaces appeared in the process of drying, the puncheons were moved closer together. The building of the roof has taken its place among the lost arts. The first gable-log projected one foot at each end, and was held in place by strong locust pins. The upper gable-logs, or eave-bearers, were held by the rest-poles on which the clapboards were laid. Stretching between the first gable-logs was the eave-pole, which held the first course of clapboards. Rest-poles were laid between the upper gable-logs. The clapboards were three feet long and eight inches wide, and were laid with twelve inches of lap. Each course was held down by what was sometimes called a weight-pole and sometimes a press-pole. This fitted at each end into a notch in the gable-log and was further secured by a peg. Between each weight-pole and the one above it was a support called a knee. The uppermost weight-pole was heavier than the others and was pinned to its position. A rustic way of securing the top courses was with a pair of split poles, one of the halves lying against one side of the crown and one against the other. The ends were tied together with grapevine or hickory withes. When the pins in a press-pole rotted, the pole with its course of clapboards would slide to the ground. The chimney was of short logs well daubed inside with clay. Near the fireplace was the opening called the light-hole. When not in use it was covered with a sliding board. One lazy man broke a hole in the back of his chimney, so that he could poke his firewood through it instead of bringing it in by the door.

The loghouses of the larger and better class had chimneys of stone, sometimes containing an enormous amount of masonry. In this county the stone house generally appeared earlier than the one of brick, and was sometimes intended to answer the purpose of a defense against the Indians. Limestone is abundant in Rockbridge, but has been little used in house-walls. Colonel John Jordan, a native of Hanover county and a builder of many brick mansions and other structures, is said to have introduced the colonial style of architecture into Rockbridge.

The bill of fare was more simple than it is now. Corn pone was much in use. The other ordinary forms of the staff of life were spoon bread, batter bread, and sponge bread. Stoves began to come into use about 1850, and at first were not well thought of. The loom-house was an adjunct of the prospering farm. Elsewhere, the loom was a feature of the living-room or the kitchen. Girls who learned to weave were able to make some money by going from house to house.

The country store was a very plain affair and was destitute of showcases. Only the most common goods and necessaries were on exhibit. The business of the store seemed to move at a slow pace, yet the merchant was prosperous. After the war of 1816 there was a more rapid gait.

There were two types of garden; one with beds and herbs and one without. The climate of Scotland is not quite favorable to the kitchen garden, which was not generally adopted by the Scotch-Irish settlers of the Valley of Virginia until they took a hint by seeing the gardens put out by the Hession prisoners of war at Staunton. The herbs were sage, ditny, boneset, catnip, horsemint, horehound, "old man," and "old woman." These were used as home remedies, especially by the "granny woman," who in no small degree stood in the place of the doctor. She used lobelia as an emetic, white walnut bark as a purgative, snakeroot for coughs, and elder blossom to produce perspiration. The bark of dogwood, cherry, and poplar, steeped in whiskey, was used for fever and ague. For the much dreaded dysentery, she employed Mayapple root, walnut bark, and slippery elm bark. A favorite way of treating a cold was for the patient to warm his feet thoroughly before a fire and then cover up in bed.

Trials of strength entered more largely into the sports of the period than they do now. Wrestling, jumping, and boxing were popular. A very common game was bandy played with turned balls of lignum vitæ.

The "frolic" was a vital feature of the "good old times." One form of it was the corn husking. The corn was shucked in the field, hauled into the farmyard, and thrown into a single pile. At the frolic, two captains were agreed upon, and these worthies, by choosing alternately, divided the crowd into two rival companies. The pile of corn was divided, and there was a race between the companies to see which side would come out first. The defeated company then had to pick up the victor-captain, and "tote" him around the pile of ears. A red ear entitled the finder to a kiss from his companion of the other sex. A big supper followed the husking, after which the floor was cleared by taking the furniture and other impediments out of the room, and then came dancing, sometimes kept up until daybreak. Charges of unfairness were occasionally hurled by one company at the other, and the small boys did well to get out of harm's way. "Black Betty" was passed around. The whiskey inflamed the jealousy aroused by rival admirers and rosy-cheeked girls, and serious affrays were liable to be the outcome. Besides the husking frolic, there were log-rollings, singing schools, shooting matches, and hunting with hounds. Christmas was made much of. "Bring your knitting and spend the day," was the invitation often extended by one woman to another.

A century ago women sometimes wielded the two-pronged wooden fork in the hayfield. Corn was rarely shocked, and yet more rarely topped and bladed. The cradle had just come into general use, but some of the older men still looked with more favor on the sickle. Threshing was sometimes done with horses. The first threshing machines often got out of order. On one occasion a flying tooth tore a hole in the roof of a barn. There was no market for hay. Peavine and "rich-weed" made good pasture. Fertility was maintained by rotation and by the use of lime and clover. There was an independence in the simple life of the Rockbridge farmer of the antebellum period, which has largely passed with the altered conditions of the twentieth century.

Writing in 1844, Henry Ruffner strikes a pessimistic note. He says that "our free mountain air has become tainted; the labor of our fields is done in great part by fettered hands; our manners have become more refined than our morals, and instead of the sturdy but intelligent simplicity that once reigned through all the land, a half-savage ignorance has grown up in its nooks and dells, while in the open country a mixed population shows much that is excellent, but upon the whole a failing spirit of energetic industry and enterprise." It was Ruffner's belief that between 1790 and 1840 Virginia lost more by emigration than all the free states. "She has driven from her soil at least one-third of all the emigrants who have gone to the new states." After Ohio and Kentucky had begun to attract settlers, the more thrifty and enterprising of the Rockbridge farmers acquired lands in that quarter, and the disposal of such tracts is often mentioned in wills.

A brief pen-picture of Rockbridge is given by the Duke of Saxe-Weimer Eisenach, who crossed this county in the fall of 1825. He observes that he traveled from Staunton to Natural Bridge in a miserable stage and over a very bad road. The wooden bridge over the Buffalo was used only in time of very high water. The only "decent places" he passed were Fairfield and Lexington. Yet the foreigner mentions "many very handsome country houses," at one of which he noticed eight eagles sitting on a fence. These were cared for by the proprietor. By seeing snipe fly into the tavern yard at Fairfield, the stranger thought the people were not fond of shooting. He found that game was plenty, and that a whole deer could be purchased for $1.50. He had little to say of Lexington, then a town of 1,100 people. He wondered that all the coachmen were white. There was much travel on horseback. The road from Lexington to Staunton by way of Fairfield was generally through a forest. The traveler was a German and was an object of some interest to the few German people he met in this county.

The most distressing tragedy in the history of Rockbridge took place in the earlier half of the night of December 16-17, 1846. John Petticrew, a native of Campbell county, fell into straitened circumstances, and in 1843 moved into a log house in the southward-facing cove between the two House mountains. The wife of Petticrew had been Mary A. Moore, of Kerr's Creek. The oldest of the six children was sixteen, the youngest was six, and all were healthy and strong. The evening of December 16th was snowy, and by midnight there was a high wind. Next morning the snow was much drifted, and for several days the weather was very cold. The fourth day was Sunday, and in the morning Mr. Petticrew came home according to his custom from his work at the distillery of William Alphin. To his horror he found his house burned to the ground. Lying near by were the frozen and partially clad bodies of the wife and all the children except the oldest, a daughter who was with her sick grandmother on Kerr's Creek. Strong men wept when they saw the corpses laid out for burial. Foul play was suspected on the part of James Anderson and his wife Mary, who lived a half-mile away. The Andersons did not bear a good name. The husband was not one of the crowd that gathered on the Sunday that Petticrew made his grewsome discovery, nor was he present at the burial. Pettigrew had had some trouble with the neighbor because of Anderson's cows breaking into his field. He was knocked down by Anderson, who tried to choke him. Armed with a search-warrant, a brother to Mrs. Petticrew visited the Anderson home and found therein a coverlet and some other articles that had belonged to her. The silverware of the Pettigrews was not found. Anderson was tried in Bath, but was acquitted on the ground of insufficient evidence. He went to Craig and never again lived in Rockbridge. It remained the common opinion that Anderson was really guilty, and there is a story that in a fit of remorse he made a deathbed confession. And yet an examination of the corpses was inconclusive as to whether death came from violence or from the intense cold following a fire either accidental or intentional. Within two years Pettigrew died of a broken heart. The daughter who was away from home subsequently married James G. Reynolds and had two children. The victims of the tragedy were buried at Oxford. The stone over the grave was shattered by lightning and was replaced with a monument paid for by friends of the family.

XIII

A YEAR OF SUSPENSE

Causes of the War of 1861—Presidential Campaign of 1860—Meetings in Rockbridge—Discussions in the Local Newspapers—State Convention at Richmond—A Flag Raising at Lexington

A county history is not the place to dwell at length on the causes of the great American war of 1861. It cannot spare much room for topics essentially national in character.

But in the case of Rockbridge, this theme is of more than ordinary interest. Because of its prominent public men, its educational institutions, and its rank as a Valley county, the people of Rockbrdge took a keen interest in the political events of the year ending in mid-April, 1861. A resident of the county was governor of Virginia; an instructor in its military school was to win great renown as a Confederate general; the beloved leader of the Army of Northern Virginia was to become the president of its college. And during the months in which the storm-cloud was coming to its full dimensions, the issues of the day were discussed at much length, and very ably, in the newspapers and literary societies of Lexington.

In this chapter, therefore, we first take a comprehensive glance at the general causes of the war, and follow it with an account of what was taking place in Rockbridge during the presidential campaign of 1860 and the opening months of 1861.

The thirteen American colonies that shook off their allegiance to Britain in 1776 were politically independent of one another. Not one of the group had the power to absorb the others, and the United States of America is the only country on earth without a distinctive name. The term by which our country is known is a definition, and is not properly a name. Since the colonies used the English language, and derived their laws and institutions from England, they could not do otherwise than act together in effecting the separation that was generally desired. But the Continental Congress was not the same thing as the Federal Congress that succeeded it. The former body was merely a central committee representing the state governments. One state had as much voice in this committee as another. The Congress could advise, but it might not command.

When the states set about forming a "more perfect union," it was much as if the eleven countries of South America should declare a United States of South America. Each country would bring into this union a pride in its four centuries of Caucasian history. It would be jealous of its own rights and suspicious of what the future might develop. The new name would carry no suggestion of nationality. The only nationality the South Americans could feel would be the nationality of Brazil, or Peru, or Argentina. Any member would resent at attempt at military coercion in the name of the union.

What could thus happen in South America is precisely what did happen in North America. The popular opinion among the Americans of 1788 was that they were entering a confederation. For many years they commonly spoke of their union as such. But they were really entering a federation. Now in a confederation, the central government acts on the people through the medium of the various state governments, while in a federation it acts on them independently of the state governments. The framers of the Constitution did not attempt to be entirely explicit. They were practical men, and if they had expressed themselves dogmatically, their labors would have been in vain. The constitution was adopted only after strenuous opposition in a majority of the states. That the Americans of the Revolutionary period generally regarded the new government as a confederation, is because they did not then, nor for some years afterward, have the mental attitude for viewing it in a different light.

The two groups of colonies separated by Delaware Bay were either founded by Englishmen, or soon came under English control. But the motives leading to the colonization of the two regions were not quite the same. The differences were accentuated by economic distinctions. The Southern colonies were almost wholly agricultural, and their population was so dispersive that it took the lead in settling the West and Southwest. The New Englanders were a village people and slow to scatter. Their soil was poor, and because they turned to manufactures and commerce, most of the American cities arose in the North. The Middle Colonies had the economic features of both sections, but their deciding interests were those of the New England corner.

Had the Union never outgrown the area of the thirteen original states, the confederate interpretation of it might have prevailed in the North much longer than it did. The scale was turned by the vast plain of the Mississippi, which is a geographic whole. The West has always been more homogeneous than the seaboard, and its political point of view has always been nationalistic. From the very first, state lines have been of minor importance to the Western man. The coming of rapid travel and labor-saving machinery operated powerfully to link the commercial North to the agricultural West. There was an increased pride of country in these sections. Their people came to look upon the Union as no longer a nation in promise, but a nation in fact. But the South was still almost wholly agricultural, and its mode of life was much the same as in the period of the Revolutoin. It was a perfectly natural outcome that the political point of view of the South had undergone no material change.

The principle of secession, as found in American history, rests primarily upon the idea of a Union based on the free consent of its members. It was first put forward in the North and not in the South. But it is significant that a serious discussion of it in one state would be viewed with immediate disapproval in all the others.

In 1790 there was a balance in population between North and South. For several decades later, people did not feel that this balance was being disturbed. As for slavery, it was not liked in the upper South and was not actively opposed in the North. But by 1850, the North was far in the lead. A rising spirit of the age was antagonistic to slavery. To protect its vast slave property, the South put itself in a defensive attitude.

Until 1861, the control of the Federal government had been almost all the while with the South. This power was voiced by a relatively small class of people. In the North there was a subconscious feeling that its much superior population and its industrial development gave it a better title to lead the nation. For this purpose it organized a new political party and won the election of 1860. The South instinctively recognized this result as a challenge to a trial of strength and acted accordingly. The one great issue, reduced to its lowest terms, was whether the Federal Union had grown into a nation of indivisible sovereignty, with a conceded power to coerce a reluctant member. To the North this time had arrived. To the South it had not arrived. Within a few more decades the South would have thrown out slavery and adjusted itself to the economic civilization of the North. The war of 1861 was a short cut in this direction, and because the measure was drastic it wrought great destruction and great hardship. But when the storm-cloud was about to break, it was only a few far-sighted men who could grasp the issue in its larger aspects. The majority of people feel rather than think, and such persons in 1860 could perceive little more than the outward symptoms. And because thinking was subordinated to feeling, waves of excitement seized the multitudes, both North and South, and hurried the country into domestic war.

The one section could see little else than a wicked attempt by an arrogant oligarchy to pull down the best government on earth, and thus cause either half to occupy a lower rank in the family of nations. The North flew to arms to preserve national unity at any cost, and to see to it that rivalries of a European nature, sidetracked by the Constitution of 1787, could not again spring into life. The other section could see little else than an unholy attempt to overturn its local governments, to destroy the value of a large class of its property, and to adopt without time for adjustment a mode of life prescribed by the victor. Hence the South flew to arms to maintain its local self-government at any cost, and to prevent an abrupt transition from entering into its ecoonmic life. The men on each side of the controversy were honest, sincere, and determined. In the light of the conditions confronting him, neither the typical Northerner nor the typical Southerner could have acted otherwise than he did.

The "year of suspense," as we style the present chapter, began with the nominating conventions of 1860. There were four candidates for the presidency, Lincoln, Douglas, Breckenridge, and Bell. Lincoln stood for the extreme Northern position, and Breckenridge for the extreme Southern. The conservative elements supported Douglass and Bell. Southern votes for Lincoln were very few and were wholly in the border states. That Breckenridge had a considerable support in several Northern states was because of considerations of party regularity. Douglas and Breckenridge were both Democrats, but the former was regarded as a bolter by the supporters of the other candidate. Douglas had a rather large following in the border slave states, and quite a number of the old line Whigs in the coast states of the North cast their votes for Bell. But in general terms, the voting was sectional. The North supported the northern candidates, Lincoln and Douglas. The South supported the southern candidates, Breckenridge and Bell.

In the days before the war, Rockbridge was counted as a Whig community, whereas the state almost invariably gave a majority for the Democratic nominee for the presidency. In 1856, Buchanan's majority over Fillmore was only eighty-eight votes, but seemingly for the reason that 286 votes went to Fremont. When viewed in the light of the next campaign, it seems rather strange that a ninth of the total number of votes should have been given to the first Republican candidate. But Fremont was son-in-law to Senator Benton, of Missouri, and Benton was reared and married in Rockbridge.

The following table shows the vote by precincts in Rockbridge, November 6, 1860:

	Bell	Douglas	Breckenridge
Lexington	290	148	49
Kerr's Creek	96	79	9
Collierstown	76	20	66
Dryden's	37	22	32
Wilson's Shop	62	45	18
Paxton's Schoolhouse	77	15	29
Trevy's	68	63	9
Natural Bridge	111	47	84
Hamilton's	70	50	18
Fairfield	102	85	27
Brownsburg	183	36	8
Goshen	59	31	16
Total	1231	641	365

An analysis of the table shows that Bell carried every precinct, and had almost twice as many votes as Douglas. It also shows that Douglas had almost twice as many votes as Breckenridge. Natural Bridge, where several leaders of public opinion were in favor of secession, was the Breckenridge stronghold.

It is one of the curiosities of that exceptional campaign that the next highest vote for Breckenridge was in the present Republican stronghold of Collierstown. No votes for Lincoln are on record. Bell, the choice of the Rockbridge voters, was the standard bearer of the Constitutional Union party, which was the successor of the Whig party in the South. The only plank in its platform was "the constitution, the union, and the enforcement of the laws."

It is an interesting fact that Bell's leading competitor for the nomination was Samuel Houston, a native of Rockbridge. Bell was nominated on the second ballot, receiving 138 votes. Houston had sixty-nine, and all others, forty-six.

In its issue of November 29th, the *Lexington Gazette* makes this comment on the election, referring to the Democratic party when it speaks of Conservatives:

> Now that he (Lincoln) has been elected, what can he do? The Conservative party have a majority in both houses of Congress. The Supreme Court is Conservative. The Executive can enforce no law prejudicial to the institution of slavery, if Congress enacts none. Every act he does is done under the solemn oath which he takes at his inauguration. Had we not then better try him? It may be that he will prove to be a conscientious and a law-abiding man. Mr. Jefferson went the full length Lincoln goes against slavery. We have not had an ultra pro-slavery president, unless Mr. Tyler may be called so, and yet all the time the institution of slavery has been safe from executive interference.

One day later, the *Staunton Vindicator* published the following editorial comment on secession:

> To our mind the secession of the cotton states is a fixed fact. It is this for which the politicians of those states have been planning and scheming for years. It is no oppression that they feel, but a willful, deliberate, and criminal purpose to dissolve the Union and reopen the African slave trade. The clear and unequivocal policy of the Middle (border) States is to keep aloof from them. In the course of time the seceders may seek a reunion upon such terms as will be granted. If they do not, we venture the prediction that they will become conquered provinces before ten years. The devilish spirit which will have brought this destruction upon the Union can never rest contented after the Southern Confederacy is established, and will be certain to plunge it into war.

Nevertheless, a meeting held at the courthouse in Lexington November 26th shows the intense excitement in Rockbridge. The chairman was directed to appoint a committee of twelve to prepare a circular letter to the people of the county. This committee was made up of Hugh Barclay, J. B. Dorman, Samuel Gilbert, E. L. Graham, T. J. Jackson, J. R. Jordan, David E. Moore, J. W. Paine, E. F. Paxton, J. T. L. Preston, J. McD. Taylor, and William White. The courtroom was filled to its utmost capacity. A discussion on the state of the country lasted from noon until four o'clock. The *Gazette* speaks of a disposition to ignore party differences and to act unitedly. It adds that "the interest felt by the people was such as we have never witnessed before." The call formulated by the committee was couched in the most earnest language. It asked the people of the county to convene at the courthouse on Monday, December 3rd.

Of this second meeting, Hugh Barclay was chairman. There were speeches by the ministers, John Miller and W. N. Pendleton, and by Colonel F. H. Smith, Major J. T. L. Preston, J. W. Brockenbrough, and J. B. Dorman. At an adjourned meeting, December 15th, the leading grievances against the South were enumerated as the aggressive anti-slavery agitation in the North, the personal liberty bills, and the appeals to the spirit of insurrection and murder. The personal liberty laws mentioned were those interfering with the capture of runaway slaves on free state soil. The clause alluding to insurrection and murder relates to the fanatical raid of John Brown at Harper's Ferry, which took place fourteen months earlier. Ten resolutions were adopted, one of which states that "we cannot deem it the part of wise and brave Christian patriots even yet to despair of the republic. We feel it to be a high duty as well as the dictate of true policy on the part of Virginia to struggle for the redress of her grievances within the Union." Another declares it "highly inexpedient in the present crisis to resort to coercion against any seceding state."

South Carolina, the first of the cotton states to act, passed her ordinance of secession December 20th. The movement in that quarter was watched in Rockbridge with much interest, which for the most part was unsympathetic.

A contributor to the *Gazette* makes this comment:

A great deal of rash talk and inconsiderate action certainly characterizes the conduct of the South at this time. There is no deliberation, save the deliberate treason that has long been cherished in the breasts of the leaders of the movement. A disruption of the union of these states reads the doom of African slavery in the South. While the Union exists, there is an influence in the North itself that nearly if not altogether cancels the mad efforts of the abolitionists. While the Union exists, there is a United South, to a man ready to protect the South against aggression. But let the South consummate a severance, then the South stands isolated. Disunion will unsettle the line that divides slave from free territory. Its first immediate effect is to de-Africanize a broad belt of the border slave states, equal in extent to one-fourth of the slave territory. The mere anticipation of disunion has already turned thousands of operatives out of employment in the North. The real event will increase this number by tens of thousands. Desperation will drive these hordes down upon us, either in a hostile raid or to seek a living in a friendly manner. Secession secures non-intercourse, and non-intercourse compels the South to manufacture. She must either do it by these discarded employees or by men from abroad. The result is the same; it brings in contact with slavery a population poisoned to it in all its aspects. The idea of manufacturing by the aid of slave labor is simply absurd, not only from the fact of the incapacity of the negro, but from the fact that there are no slaves to be spared from the planting interests. The African slave trade has been pronounced piracy, and an attempt to reopen it would bring down upon the Southern Confederacy the vengeance of all the great powers of Europe. Moreover, a manufacturing and a slave community are antagonistic and dangerous to each other. It cannot be denied that slavery creates distinctions in society; a laboring and a leisure class. The mechanic and the negro would constitute the former, and the nabobs the latter.

An editorial of the same date as the South Carolina ordinance, and written before the news of that event could have reached Lexington, speaks in this manner of the secession movement:

> We do not desire to see this government broken up upon a point of honor more shadowy, more imaginary, more unreal, than any ever alleged by the professional duelist as a ground for demanding satisfaction. There is no dishonor in submitting to Lincoln's administration, because he is legally and constitutionally our president. Secession is a voluntary and complete relinquishment of the rights we hold in virtue of the Union. * * * Peaceable secession is nothing less than a surrender of these rights (to slave property in the territories). * * * To break up the Union upon a mere presumption that the president-elect intends to trample upon the constitution is to drive our Northern friends into union with our enemies. There were more votes against Lincoln in the North than in the entire South. Peaceable secession is really cowardly submission. * * * There is a well-considered policy of a few plotting Catalines to precipitate the cotton states, and ultimately all the slave states, into revolution.

It is interesting to note the parallelism between the above paragraph and the following extract from a letter written from Lexington, January 1, 1833, concerning the proclamation on nullification by President Jackson. The letter was written by Doctor Archibald Graham:

> In this region it has been received with loud and almost universal applause. A meeting was held yesterday in the courthouse, Reuben Grigsby in the chair. I am told they adopted resolutions approving the proclamation. There is a strong feeling in this county against nullification, and a very general disposition to put it down *vi et armis* (by force of arms). I believe a strong volunteer company could be raised here, at a moment's warning, to march against them.

The editorial further pointed out that secession would work a forfeiture of the interest of the South in the District of Columbia and the public lands, and that the South could not reëstablish this interest without going to war.

The influence on business of the secession talk is thus sketched in a letter in the *Gazette:*

> Money has become so scarce that debts can no longer be collected. Slave property has fallen in value from a third to a half. The indebtedness of the citizens of Rockbridge to the banks is not short of $100,000. The costs of goods brought in for sale is about $200,000. How are they to be paid? The flour sold out of the county this year does not exceed 1,000 barrels, worth about $5,000. The proceeds of other commodities except slaves are about $50,000. The slaves sold out of the county the last three years have brought about $400,000. That source of revenue seems at an end. The people must give up their habits of extravagance. Every lady must have a new bonnet every six months costing $20 to $50 apiece. There is doubt if the flour sold in the last twelve months would pay for the bonnets and silk dresses sold here in the same time.

A proposed local organization was the "Rockbridge Economical Society." If possible, the members were to attend the Rockbridge fair of 1861 in clothes made in Virginia, to buy in that year no cloth not made in Virginia, to discourage bringing in any goods except those of prime necessity, and to promote domestic manufacturing.

It is also significant that the advertising columns of the county papers contain somewhat frequent requests for debtors to "fork over."

An extra session of the legislature was called for the purpose of determining "calmly and wisely what ought to be done." This body met January 7, 1861, and decided to call a state convention, for which delegates were to be elected February 4th. There had never yet been a convention in Virginia not authorized by a popular vote. An editorial of January 3 would appear to reflect the prevailing sentiment of Rockbridge. It makes these declarations:

> We hope the people to a man will vote against a state convention. A convention will be a piece of machinery that will be operated by secessionists to carry Virginia out of the Union. No government such as ours was ever before devised. If we allow it to go down, we believe that with it will go down the last hope of civil and religious liberty. Let us not follow the example of South Carolina, who seeks to put an unanswerable argument into the mouths of despots. South Carolina has said by her action that a republican government can be dissolved at any time, that it is a government without power, that it is no government at all.

Meetings of workingmen at Lexington and Brownsburg were largely attended, and passed resolutions that were "moderate and patriotic." A meeting at the courthouse, January 7th, failed to vote any resolutions, and broke up in disorder, some sixty persons cheering for South Carolina. This element was principally made up of cadets. Many of the citizens were indignant at the rowdyism, and it was denounced in a meeting at Old Monmouth presided over by John Anderson, Sr. The last named meeting resolved that "we refuse to sanction the attempt of any state to secede from the Union, believing that such an act would be no remedy for the grievances of which we complain."

Another meeting at the courthouse, January 21st, adjourned with three cheers for the Union, after resolving, "that in the opinion of this meeting the plan of adjustment proposed by Hon. J. J. Crittenden, and now pending before the Senate of the United States, is a just and honorable basis for settlement of our national difficulties." The same meeting nominated Samuel McD. Moore and James B. Dorman to represent the county in the convention. Three days later, Mr. Moore and Mr. J. W. Brockenbrough, another candidate, published their appeals to the voters. In the event of a dissolution of the Union, Mr. Moore was in favor of Virginia being independent of all the other states. He expressed the opinion that "Virginia never can become very prosperous except as a manufacturing state." He declared in favor of excluding New England from a new confederacy, and was "strongly in favor of the proposed convention being submitted to the people." He added that "the example of the Alabama convention, which has passed a secession ordinance, should be a warning to the people of Virginia." He saw reason to apprehend that a majority of the convention may be elected as disunionists, although a large majority of the voters might be friendly to the Union. Mr. Brockenbrough thought secession would come, and asserted that "the Union that the constitution gave us no longer exists." C. C. Baldwin, a fourth candidate, favored immediate secession if the difficulties with the North were not settled when the convention met.

The short campaign was very animated. An editorial of January 31st urges that the voters insist on a ratification at the polls of the decision of the convention. It remarks that "there is no limit in the law to the powers of the convention," which "may bind you against your will to a monarchy or aristocracy instead of a republic." It points out disapprovingly that "an able writer in the Southern press has proposed the adoption of a monarchy," while another, in letters to the English papers, suggests asking for one of Victoria's sons as a king. It further observes that Mr. Spratt, of South Carolina, had come out boldly for an aristocracy, alleging that there is an irrepressible conflict between democracy and aristocracy; that equality is not a right of mankind in the mass but of equals only.

In the election there were 1,869 votes for Dorman, 1,839 for Moore, 293 for Brockenbrough, and seventy-two for Baldwin. There were no votes for Baldwin in six precincts out of the twelve. The result rather upheld the contention of the *Gazette* that there were not more than 250 secessionists in the county.

The state convention met February 13th, little more than a fifth of the delegates going to Richmond as avowed secessionists. By a vote of more than two to one the people of the state reserved the right to pass upon the action of that body. By the decisive majority of more than 1,500, Rockbridge declared in favor of submitting such action to the people.

The following letter by Alexander H. H. Stuart, of Staunton, throws an interesting light on the atmosphere in which the convention worked.

Since the first day of the session, Richmond has been the scene of unexampled excitement. The disunionists from all parts of the state have been here in force, and have sought to bring every influence to bear to precipitate Virginia into secession and civil war. * * * Secession is a doctrine of New England origin. It is at war with the whole theory of our institutions, and is subversive of every principle of popular government. * * * In my opinion, there is no natural antagonism between the Northern and the Southern states. They (the sections) are the complements of each other. The present alienation is the work of designing men. I believe that all our wrongs can be most effectually redressed in the Union. Secession, instead of being a remedy, would be an aggravation. It would lead to emancipation, and probably to emancipation in blood. Should the Union be dissolved peaceably, the policy of the new government will be shaped by the cotton states. Free trade, and direct taxation for the support of the Federal government, will be the cardinal features of that policy. The expense of maintaining the present government of the United States, ranging from $60,000,000 to $100,000,000 a year, is raised by duties and is voluntarily paid in the form of increased prices by those who buy foreign goods. Under the other system, the tax would be involuntary, and Virginia's part would be about $5,000,000. * * * This would be a very heavy burden. South Carolina's causes of dissatisfaction are financial and not the same as ours.

Samuel McD. Moore, a gentleman now sixty-four years of age, of commanding presence and mature convictions, took a leading part in the proceedings of the convention. He was a member of the Committee on Federal Relations. Jeremiah Morton, of Orange, introduced a resolution declaring against coercion of the seceding states on any pretext whatever, and stating that while Virginia was ardently desiring to restore the Federal Union, she would unite with her sister states of the South if the efforts then under way should not avail. Mr. Moore, in reply, said the cotton states had not consulted Virginia, and he did not intend to be bound hand and foot by them. He would neither be hurried out of the Union, nor kept in it by precipitate action. If compelled to go anywhere, he was determined to know first where he was going, who he was to go with, and what was to be his condition after he did go. He was ready to resist sending troops through Virginia to attack the seceding states, but if the latter thought proper to attack any United States fort, they would have to abide the consequences. He would at a proper time undertake to show that there was a conflict of interest between Virginia and the cotton states.

These five resolutions were introduced by Mr. Moore, February 25th: 1. That in resisting the fugitive slave law, refusing to give up refugees, trying to deprive the South of common territory, in circulating incendiary pamphlets, and furnishing arms to bands of assassins, the South demands full and ample security that these wrongs shall not be repeated. 2. Virginia can never join a confederacy with the African slave trade. 3. Virginia refuses to endorse government by direct taxation. 4. Approval of the Crittenden program. 5. "If such amendments are not adopted, Virginia will enter into a compact with such states as will agree to adopt them, whereby the present government of the United States will be dissolved as to the states so agreeing."

Mr. Dorman introduced an additional resolution to the effect that the Federal Union can rightfully be dissolved only by the power that made it, and that Virginia should work for a vote in *all* the states upon the decision of the Peace Conference. Several speeches were made on the Moore resolutions. A band of fifty to sixty men serenaded the seccessionists who had replied to Moore, and gave three groans while passing Moore's hotel. There was talk of burning him in effigy, and yet there was a motion in convention to adjourn to Staunton.

Meanwhile the people of Rockbridge were expressing their sentiments in word and in act. The *Gazette* had made this comment on the slavery issue, February 7th: "To us it seems clear that in the event a Southern Confederacy is formed, slavery must inevitably be driven from the states of Maryland, Virginia, Kentucky, and Missouri, which will give rise to another dissolution." Just one month later it gave these reasons for not going into a Southern Confederacy: "We are devoted to the institution of slavery. We believe its general tendency is to elevate the condition of the African. A few masters maltreat their slaves, but just as many husbands maltreat their wives. Public sentiment frowns upon both. If the Southern states unite in a Southern Confederacy, slavery will be driven out of Virginia. Fifty negroes would run off then for one that runs off now." In such a contingency, the Canada line would in effect be brought down to the frontier of Virginia.

In a meeting at Natural Bridge, March 30th, with Edward Echols as chairman, secession resolutions were passed with but three dissenting voices. Yet the *Gazette* expressed its belief that if the resolutions were to be offered in a meeting of all the citizens, there would be a majority against them of 1,500. Of Lincoln's inaugural address, the *Gazette* had these words to say: "We are not disposed to complain of the tone of this document. It maintains the doctrine of coercion, but there is not the slightest intimation that he would recommend to Congress the adoption of any coercive measures."

The final day of the period we are considering came perilously near being a day of bloodshed. On receipt of the news that Confederate batteries were firing upon Fort Sumter, a Confederate flag was run up in front of the courthouse. This was at eleven o'clock, on the morning of April 13th. There were speeches by Major Colston, J. G. Paxton, J. W. Massie, J. C. Davis, and J. W. Brockenbrough. The Unionists of Lexington, who were numerously represented among the mechanics and working people, determined to show their resentment by flying a Federal flag from a still higher flagstaff. The pole, which was of unusual length, was brought to the courtyard at too late an hour to set it in place. In the morning it broke while being raised, because of holes that had been bored into it. It was then necessary to splice the pole, and this work occupied some time. Meanwhile, a few cadets had come into town, and hot words passed between them and several of the townspeople. In the scuffle that ensued the cadets were very roughly handled. It is in the nature of youth to be radical, and the cadets of the Institute were generally ardent in their enthusiasm for the Southern Confederacy. On the part of the students of Washington College, such feeling was less in evidence.

After the mauled youths had returned to their quarters and related their adventure, their comrades were hot with rage. Almost at once they shouldered their muskets and began marching up Main Street with the avowed intention of storming the town and exacting satisfaction by force of arms. They were very soon met by Major Jackson, afterward the celebrated Stonewall, who told them they were not marching properly, and they fell into a more regular alignment. He accompanied them to the hollow that crosses the street between the Institute and the courthouse. They were now confronted by Major Colston, one of their instructors and a person of magnetic influence. By a few brief words of command he made the column face about and march back to the barracks. A little later the hotheads were reprimanded by General Smith, who told them it was a flagrant violation of good order, whether civil or military, to take the punishment of their grievance into their own hands and perhaps cause innocent persons to suffer. Meanwhile, Captain E. F. Paxton, of the local militia company, had received notice that the cadets were on their way. Though a secessionist himself, he did not flinch from his duty. His men, seventy-five in number, were given their arms, and were posted in windows and at other points of vantage with orders to fire if the cadets persisted in their rash design. The cadets would probably have experienced a terrible loss of life and limb if they had not been brought under control by Colston. Besides the militia, there were some experienced marksmen in the town who had gathered in from the mountains. Had firing once begun it would have been well aimed.

Francis T. Anderson, who was to speak at the raising of the Federal flag, was slow to appear and was sent for. His son found him in a law office closeted with perhaps twenty-five of the citizens. One of the number had received a telegram from Richmond with the news that Lincoln had called on each of the unseceded states for a quota of men to put down the secession movement. All the persons in the room had a very grave air and were engaged in earnest conversation. Their conclusion was that there was only one thing to do, and that was for Virginia to take her stand with the South. Mr. Anderson presently went out upon the courtyard, and said in substance as he stood by the flagpole: "I love that flag. For eighty years it has been the flag of my country. Under its folds, that country has grown rich and prosperous. But, fellow-citizens, that flag is now in the hands of our enemies." At this point the speaker was hissed, no inkling of the telegram having yet reached the throng. But after he had related the import of the message, and had given his view of its significance to the Southern people, he was cheered to the echo. Unionism had come to a sudden end in Rockbridge. May 23rd, the people of Virginia voted on the ordinance of secession that had been adopted by the convention. In Rockbridge there was only a single negative vote in a total of 1,728.

In reviewing the momentous year that came to such a well-defined close, it remains clear that the people of Rockbridge felt no general enthusiasm in the doctrine of secession; that they deeply disapproved the conduct of the cotton states; that their affection for the Union was sincere; and that they took up arms against the Federal government with regret. But their heritage of political thought taught them that the Union of their fathers was founded by consent and could not rightfully be maintained except by consent. The coercion of a state by the central government was therefore foreign to their creed. They felt that the Union was virtually dissolved, that it was now their duty to stand by their state, and they took up this duty with a resolution worthy of their ancestral stock.

XIV

THE WAR OF 1861

OPENING SCENES—MILITARY ORGANIZATIONS—EVENTS OF 1861-2—FEDERAL RAIDS—HUNTER AT LEXINGTON—THE WAR YEARS IN ROCKBRIDGE—THE CLOSE—DOCUMENTARY PARAGRAPHS

When the news of the firing on Fort Sumter reached Washington, President Lincoln called upon Virginia for 2,340 men as her quota for enforcing Federal jurisdiction in the seceded territory. The date of the proclamation was April 17, 1861. The reply of Governor Letcher was a prompt refusal. The reply of the state was the passage by the state convention of an ordinance of secession. The news of these events reached Lexington the morning of Saturday, April 20th, and this county found itself ushered into a war.

In each section it was the prevalent opinion that a determined stand, backed by a display of military force, would overawe the other. Only those discerning men who best understood the temper of their opponents felt assured that actual war was inevitable and that it would be severe and devastating. No one dreamed that 1,340 engagements would be fought in the Virginias, that more than 600,000 American soldiers would lose their lives, and that 400,000 others would be more or less crippled for life. Some persons regarded the coming clash of arms as though it were like an exciting picnic. Others regarded it with the most serious feelings.

With the people of Rockbridge the leading issue was home rule as against the paramount authority of the Federal government. In the other issues, secession and slavery, they were less interested. Of the four presidential candidates of the preceding year, Lincoln was looked upon as an enemy, Buchanan as a dishonest coward, Breckenridge as a man who truckled to Kentucky Unionism. Bell was a passive spectator, yet gave his assent to the Confederate movement, and his followers in the Gulf states were active in its behalf.

The situation between the free and the slave states had been tense an entire decade. Colonel Smith and several others of the faculty of the Virginia Military Institute, and nearly 100 of their cadets had formed part of the armed force of 1,500 men that was assembled at Charlestown in the fall of 1859 to prevent any attempt to rescue John Brown. It was Colonel Smith himself who superintended the execution of Brown. A year earlier than this, he had been given orders under secrecy to double the guard of the arsenal, since there was a supposed plot to arm the negroes at the Pewe Iron Works near Lexington and set in motion a servile war. In the winter of 1860-61 there had been intense restlessness and some turbulence among the cadets. In the early half of April they were almost daily hoisting secession flags in spite of vigorous efforts to the contrary by the authorities.

About this time a bachelor makes this comment in the *Gazette* on the attitude of the women:

> We believe that it is a historical truth that the ladies of the South have from the beginning of our trouble been in favor of secession. They see by virtue of their superior intuition the propriety of the measure long before the dull and stolid brains of man could receive and respond to the impression of the necessity. Whilst men were reasoning upon the subject and striving in vain to solve the difficult problem, the intuition of the ladies cut the Gordian knot.

J. B. Smith and J. E. Carson were advertising in the county papers that they had $100,000 to spend for likely young negroes.

On Sunday, April 21st, the governor ordered Major Jackson to take a number of cadets to Richmond to act as drill sergeants at Camp Lee, and on Monday the order was complied with. On Saturday an order had come for the volunteer companies of Rockbridge to turn out. At one o'clock p. m., on a date given as Sunday, but which was probably Monday, the Rockbridge Rifles, 103 strong, started from Lexington. The Reverend Mr. Tibbs and the venerable Doctor McFarland gave them a benediction, all heads being uncovered and all eyes moistened with tears. Doctor White pronounced the benediction at the departure of the two companies of Rockbridge Dragoons, each about sixty strong. The destination of these commands was Harper's Ferry. The officers of the Rifles were these: Captain, S. H. Letcher; First Lieutenant, E. F. Paxton; Second Lieutenant, J. K. Edmondson; Third Lieutenant, W. W. Lewis; Fourth Lieutenant, D. L. Hopkins; Orderly Sergeant, J. C. Boude. The following were the officers of the First Dragoons: M. X. White, Captain; J. S. Cumings, First Lieutenant; Charles Jordan, Second Lieutenant; M. Burks, Third Lieutenant; J. W. Moore, Orderly Sergeant. J. R. McNutt was Captain of the Second Dragoons, R. McChesney was First Lieutenant, and John Gibson was Third Lieutenant.

When the cadets, about 150 strong, started to Richmond by way of Staunton, the Rockbridge Greys, about 100 in number, were quartered at the Institute, awaiting orders. The Silver Greys were prompt to form a company and elect officers. The streets of Lexington took on an unusually active appearance. The citizens were very liberal in equipping the soldiers, and a committee of them stood pledged to look after the families of those who had gone to war. According to the *Gazette,* a respected man of color set about raising a fund for this purpose.

A meeting at Natural Bridge, presided over by Colonel J. H. Paxton, adopted these resolutions: That a committee of seven men, one from each magisterial district, be appointed to receive subscriptions of money and materials for clothing; that R. H. Catlett be quartermaster and J. H. Myers, treasurer; that able-bodied young men, to the number of not more than 200, and who desire to serve their country, be requested to report at once to Colonel Davidson at Lexington; that William Dold be a commissary to secure supplies for the soldiers awaiting orders in Lexington.

May 3rd, a flag was presented to the Artillery Company, J. D. Davidson making the speech. Responses were given by Captain Pendleton and Sergeant J. C. Davis. June 8th, the ladies of the Falling Springs congregation presented a beautiful flag to the Liberty Hall Volunteers, who were pronounced "one of the finest looking bodies of men sent from this portion of the state." The company marched the same day with Professor White as their captain. At this time, Washington College, with sixty-nine students on its roll, closed for the remainder of the session. Three days earlier, the Rockbridge Guards, seventy-five strong, left Brownsburg under command of Captain David P. Curry. In a little more than a week the ladies of that village and its vicinity had made coats, trowsers, knapsacks, haversacks, cloth caps, and covered canteens for eighty men, besides ten tents and 140 fatigue shirts of gray cloth. All the men were provided with shoes and socks.

Within twenty weeks from the marching of the cadets, the Lexington papers could announce that Rockbridge had supplied her full quota of volunteers.

All in all, the following organizations were furnished by this county to the Confederate service: two batteries of artillery, four companies of cavalry, seven companies of infantry, a company of rangers, senior and junior reserves to the number of ninety, and 206 men on miscellaneous duty, making a total of 2,343. Of these, 250 were killed in battle, 169 died in service, and 463 others were wounded, making a total in casualties of 882, or 37.7 per cent.; almost precisely three men out of eight. Included in this number, however, are 288 men of other counties who enlisted in the Rockbridge organizations. Another statement places the number of Rockbridge men at 2,154.

In 1900, after six years of toil, J. P. Moore, J. S. Moore, and W. T. Poague compiled a list of the Rockbridge soldiers. They announced that absolute accuracy could not be assured; that several names probably appear twice in their list, that the miscellaneous list is probably deficient, that not all the names of the Senior Reserves could be secured, and that the enumeration of casualties may be incomplete. But since the list is quite nearly accurate, it is a monument to the diligence of these veterans. The senior reserves did not include men under forty-five, and few of them could have been living. Junior reserves were under eighteen years of age.

The Rockbridge commands were in the Virginia campaigns, and most of them were in many battles. The first to respond was the Rockbridge Rifles, which was organized November 17, 1859, immediately after the John Brown affair. It was first assigned to the 5th Virginia, but was soon transferred to the 4th, and just after First Manassas, in which it lost fifteen men, to the 27th. It was in twenty-four engagements, Falling Waters being the first and Appomattox the last, where it surrendered thirty-three men. It had contained in all 140 men, and the preceding casualties were fifty-six. This company was often employed in sharpshooting service.

The Rockbridge Battery marched from Lexington, May 10, 1861, with about seventy men and two small six-pounders from the Institute. Two other guns were given to it at Harper's Ferry. One of its guns was all the Confederate artillery in the affair at Falling Waters, and its fire was very accurate and effective. This command had the reputation of being one of the best in the Army of Northern Virginia, and at no time did it lack for recruits. Of its membership forty-five were commissioned as officers and assigned to other companies. John McCausland, its first captain, rose to the rank of major-general. The command was in twenty-one battles and sustained 147 casualties, yet surrendered ninety-six men at Appomattox.*

The First Dragoons was organized at Fancy Hill May 16, 1859, by Captain L. V. Davidson.

The Liberty Hall Volunteers—Company I of the 4th Virginia Infantry—were organized at Washington College and served in the Stonewall Brigade. The company was in thirty-two battles and lost 146 men, one of whom—A. B. Ramsay—was wounded on four different occasions. At First Kernstown the Volunteers were almost annihilated. At Sharpsburg they lost three out of the five who were engaged. At Chancellorsville they lost nineteen out of twenty-eight, and after the engagement of May 12, 1864, at Spottsylvania, only two men were left.

Company H of the 25th Virginia Infantry, organized at Wilson's Springs, won fame as good marksmen and hard fighters. In the battle of McDowell, it lost twenty men out of thirty-five, every commissioned officer being put out of action.

The Rockbridge Greys of the Stonewall Brigade came principally from within a radius of five miles around Buffalo Forge. They were armed at the start with the very light cadet musket, but later with the Enfield. Their first battle was First Manassas, where they lost nineteen men out of sixty-four.

Company E of the 52nd Virginia Infantry was composed entirely of Rock-

---

*The Story of a Cannoneer, by Edward A. Moore, of the Rockbridge Artillery—a descendant of General Andrew Moore—is a vivid and realistic presentation of war as seen by a private soldier, and has been kindly mentioned by literary critics.

bridge men from the 8th and 144th regiments of the militia. It was organized at Staunton, August 1, 1861, upon the disbanding of the militia organization. It fought under Jackson and was in fourteen battles, losing fifty-two men.

Company G of the 58th Virginia was mustered in at Staunton, also on August 1, 1861. All but about nine of its members were from Kerr's Creek. This company served under General Edward Johnson in Pocahontas and Highland, and was in the battle of McDowell. Thenceforward it was in Jackson's corps. Its leading engagements were twenty-three, and it numbered sixty men at Appomattox.

Company G of the 14th Cavalry, organized in 1862, included nineteen men from this county, twelve of whom were original members of the Greys.

Company C of the same cavalry regiment was organized in 1862, and was largely made up of men who had already served in the Rockbridge Second Dragoons and the Churchville Cavalry. It was larger than the army regulations permitted, and a portion was formed into Company H.

For more than three years Rockbridge was not penetrated by any Federal column. Yet as early as the June of the first year of the war there was a wild rumor that a force of Federal cavalry was on its way from Ohio to destroy the Virginia Military Institute. There were then no hostile troops nearer than the vicinity of the Ohio river, and still the report was enough to bring out about 120 men at Brownsburg and fifty-five at J. W. Youell's on Walker's Creek. July brought anxious moments. Men from this county fought at Falling Waters, the opening engagement in the Shenandoah, at Rich Mountain, where the first serious fighting took place in West Virginia, and at First Manassas, where twelve Rockbridge men were killed and thirty-six wounded. During the remaining months of 1861 there was but slight military activity in the Virginias.

At the opening of May, 1862, the army of Banks, nearly 20,000 strong, was lying at Harrisonburg, only forty miles from the Rockbridge line, and Staunton was threatened. The cadets were called out to aid in the successful repelling of the Federal advance, and after the battle of Port Republic on June 9th, the county was relieved of further apprehension for some months. The field crops were good, both in 1861 and 1862. But the depreciation already creeping into the Confederate currency was reflected in the rise of the private soldier's pay to $15.00 a month.

With one exception the principal threats to the county were from the Federal cavalry under General Averill. The first of these raids was late in August, 1863. Averill left Winchester the 5th of that month and reached Callaghan Station near Covington twenty days later, after destroying the saltpeter works along his route. Colonel W. L. Jackson had 900 men at Millboro, and intended to make a stand at Panther Gap. Two companies of cadets and one company of home guards marched to Goshen, but as Averill did not turn eastward, the reënforcement returned to Lexington after an absence of two days.

Early in November Averill was again at Callaghan. Imboden took position a mile east of Covington, where he was joined on the morning of the 9th by Colonel Shipp with 225 cadets and one rifled gun and by Colonel Massie with 575 of the home guards. Eight companies of these were mounted. Averill retired toward Huntersville, but thinking a flank movement was the real purpose, Imboden took a diagonal course and marched to Goshen. He thus saved the six or eight very necessary blast furnaces. At Armentrout's, Imboden dismissed the cadets and the guards.

Only one month later there was a third and more serious raid. With both cavalry and artillery, Averill was once more at Callaghan, December 14th. Defeated in the battle of Droop Mountain, November 6th, General John Echols had fallen back to Union, where on the night of the 14th he was joined by McCausland from the Narrows of New River. A Federal force under Colonel Scammon had occupied Lewisburg. But Averill found Jackson's River unfordable. General Fitzhugh Lee with two of his brigades advanced from Charlottesville to cover Staunton, and was joined by Imboden on Shenandoah Mountain. General Early came also to Staunton and took command. Averill was at Sweet Springs on the 15th. By marching eighty miles in thirty hours, he struck the Virginia and Tennessee Railroad at Salem and did great damage. Meanwhile, Lee was ordered in pursuit. Colonel Jackson was directed to take position at Clifton Forge, and Echols on Sweet Springs Mountain. Again Shipp and Massie marched with the cadets and the home guards. The latter reached Goshen on the 17th, but was ordered to countermarch in haste and guard the bridges over the Buffalo. By noon on the next day he was joined at Lexington by Lee with 2,700 men, and by Imboden. The combined force advanced to Collierstown and camped. Averill circulated the report that he would return by way of Buchanan and Lee was ordered to that town. But Averill moved to Newcastle, which he reached on sunset of the 18th. He was told that Lee was at Fincastle and Jones between him and Sweet Springs. By great nimbleness of movement, and with the help of a doctor whose knowledge of the mountain roads proved exceedingly inconvenient to the pursuers, Averill slipped between the Confederate commands and escaped by way of Covington. These operations covered one week, which was a time of cold rains and swollen rivers, and consequenlty of great hardship to all the soldiers concerned.

During the winter of 1863-64, the Laurel Brigade of General Rosser was quartered at Buffalo Forge. It broke camp April 11th.

Early in May, 1864, General Crook was joined by Averill at Union. General Jenkins was defeated by him at Cloyd Mountain and at New River Bridge, where

BRONZE STATUE OF STONEWALL JACKSON IN LEXINGTON CEMETERY

Recumbent Statue of Lee in Lexington

the railroad to Tennessee was again damaged. Crook then marched to Staunton by way of Greenbrier.

General Sigel, who commanded the Federals at New Market, was of German birth, and his record as a military leader is indifferent. He was superseded by General David Hunter, who won a victory at Piedmont, June 5th, where General W. E. Jones, the Confederate leader, was killed. Two days later Hunter occupied Staunton without opposition, the Confederates falling back to Rockfish Gap to protect Charlottesville. The railroad for three miles on each side of Staunton was destroyed. The next day he was joined by Crook and Averill, who struck the Virginia Central at Goshen and wrecked it as they came along. June 10th Hunter began his advance to Lexington in four parallel columns, and reached the Rockbridge line by nightfall. Soon after noon the next day he had come to North River, the 1,400 cavalry under McCausland being too light a force to hinder his progress in any marked degree. The Confederates fell back through Lexington, leaving the bridge over North River in flames. The blackened timbers were falling into the current as the Federals came up. Their passage was disputed by some artillery and by sharpshooters on the bluff at the Institute and in storehouses near the river. In his report Hunter calls McCausland unsoldierly in risking the destruction of the town by a superior force. He had thirty guns, some of which unlimbered on high ground and dropped a few shells around the Institute and into the lower course of Main Street. But the skirmish at the river was a small incident, the Federals losing only four men. A pontoon was thrown across below the road, and before the close of the day the town was in their possession. Two of their officers, Colonel Hayes and Major McKinley, were subsequently presidents of the United States. The retreat of McCausland was hastened by Averill, who crossed the river eight miles above the town.

The next morning witnessed the most regrettable incidents of the raid. General Hunter was a stern soldier, harsh toward a foe, and had an almost irresistible propensity to burn private as well as public buildings. Soldiers are quick to take their cue from their commander-in-chief, and the rudeness shown by many of Hunter's men was largely a reflection of the vindictiveness for which the general was well known.

On this day, and not so soon as Hunter had intended it, the Virginia Military Institute and the house of Governor Letcher were burned. The cadets had been sent against the Federal forces whenever opportunity presented itself. Under the generally accepted usages of the civilized nations of 1864, it was permissible to render the buildings unserviceable to them in a military sense. But this school is and always has been fundamentally scientific, the military feature being as incidental as it is in many of the colleges and academies of the present day. That the burning of the recitation rooms, the library, and the scientific apparatus was unwarrantable was officially admitted by the National government subsequently paying the Institute $100,000, which, however, was less than one-half the estimated damages. Nevertheless, Hunter made an almost clean sweep, sparing only the house of the superintendent, where two sick girls were lying. Hunter intended to burn Washington College also, but finally yielded to the representations of one of the oldest of the alumni. Nevertheless the buildings were plundered and damaged, especially with respect to the library and the laboratory equipment, but restitution was made in 1887 to the extent of $17,000.

The burning of the fine residence of John Letcher was a wanton act. Hunter alleges that it was done by way of reprisal, and because of an "inflammatory proclamation" urging the people of Rockbridge to turn themselves into bushwhackers. But Letcher was no longer governor of Virginia. His appeal was that of a private citizen. We have not seen the document, but we feel assured that it did not sanction any form of resistance not generally recognized as legitimate. Mr. Letcher could not have been so unwise and shortsighted as to advise a course of action that would cause needless suffering to his people. General Hunter made the most of some very poor excuses, and his incendiarism was against the express instructions of President Lincoln. It was discountenanced by many of his own officers, so far they could do so without exposing themselves to a charge of insubordination.

Hunter's army remained in Lexington until about daybreak on the morning of June 14th. It made beefsteak of the cows in and around the town, and developed an extraordinary appetite for the acres of onions planted for the Confederate soldiery. The cadets, about 250 strong, had marched to Balcony Falls to assist in holding that pass. The Federal army pushed on to Buchanan, on its way to Lynchburg, in an attempt to capture that important place. In its march through the rural districts it caused much uneasiness, but we are told that the behavior of the soldiers was better than in Lexington. Hunter burned about a half-dozen each of furnaces and canal barges, and carried away a few prisoners, five guns, some ammunition, and the statue of Washington that was on the college tower. Whether the bell of the Institute was carried away or was buried in the debris of the ruins we are not informed. By the standards of 1861-64, the treatment of Lexington by Hunter was severe. Yet it was not a circumstance to what would have been its fate had it been entered by a German army of the present war. The town would have been burned to the ground after the residences had been looted; scores of the inhabitants, without distinction of age or sex, would have been maimed or massacred; the able-bodied males would have been carried away into virtual slavery, and many of the females would have been carried away for a purpose not necessary to particularize.

In the brief interval between the firing on Sumter and the first passage at arms in Virginia, the *Gazette* took occasion to deprecate "the tarring, etc., of those voters who are against the ordinance of secession, as subversive of law and order. If a free citizen is not to be allowed to exercise his free will in casting his vote, then the submission of the question is mere mockery. Many of our best citizens still believe the border states have not adopted the best method of redressing their grievances. Whilst they cannot conscientiously change their opinion, toss up their caps and huzza for secession, they are ready to defend Virginia with the last drop of their blood. We are personally acquainted with the sentiments of some sterling men, whom we have heard assailed as abolitionists by flippant coxcombs and silly misses."

At the close of 1864 the War Department of the Confederacy estimated that there were 50,000 deserters from its armies in the mountain districts of the South. Some of these were in this county. In August, 1863, Lieutenant Wise was sent out with fifty of the cadets to scour the hills, but returned the next day without meeting any success whatever. The mountain paths were far more unfamiliar to them than to the refugees.

More than one-seventh of the white population of Rockbridge was absent in the Confederate army, and as the greater portion of the farmers were not slaveholders, there was a distressing shortage of labor. The hardships which the people at home were called upon to undergo were very great. Fencing was burned for campfires, and fields thus became commons. There was a progressive deterioriation of the roads. Many of the people became very poorly clad, even after bedding had been made into wearing apparel. Maple sirup and sorghum sirup took the place of sugar. Many a meal consisted only of corn bread, roasted potatoes, and rye coffee, and even then there was a scarcity of corn. Foodstuffs were hidden to escape the thief as well as the impressing agent, and it was very unsafe to tell where such articles were concealed. The informant was sometimes put out of the way. Deserters and slackers were tolerated because of the fear that they would burn the home of the one who would tell about them. As for the hungry soldier, he was much the same, whether Federal or Confederate.

As early as August, 1862, the depreciation in the paper currency was causing prices to soar. But in the summer of 1864, a yard of linsey sold at $25 00, and other articles in proportion. Postage was five cents for a less distance than 500 miles, and ten cents for a greater distance. However, depreciation was not the only trouble with the prices. Governor Letcher's message of September 26, 1862, contains this vigorous denunciation of the profiteer:

> A reckless spirit for money-making appears to have taken entire possession of the public mind. Patriotism is second to a love of the Almighty Dollar. The price of everything is put to the highest point. What must be the feelings of a man who is fighting the

battles of the country, when he is receiving but $11.00 per month, is informed that a pair of ladies' shoes costs $16.00, with everything else in proportion? With what heart can he fight our battles under such circumstances?

There were other complaints of extortion. A local paper said Rockbridge was overrun with speculators and hucksters, who were stripping the country of almost everything necessary to human existence. Provisions of any kind could hardly be had for love or money. Thousands of barrels of flour, purchased at $15.00, were stored at Lynchburg and Richmond for sale at $30.00.

After four years of progressive privation, the return of peace was a relief. A meeting held at Staunton, May 8, 1865, declared the people of Augusta county ready to conform to the laws of the United States. Even before Appomattox, one of the men representing Virginia in the Confederate Senate had expressed himself in favor of a reunion of the states. Wreck and ruin were visible in every direction, and it was a large task to remove the signs. Yet such was the energy and the recuperative power of the Rockbridge people that the process of restoration was rapid, and in five years it was fairly complete. In commerce the recovery was faster than in farming. But during the twelve months following the surrender of General Lee, little money was to be seen except specie, and there was a tendency to hold coin in reserve.

In the first years of the war the rich could purchase exemption for their own sons, and it was due to this discrimination that even yet the war is sometimes referred to as "the rich man's war and the poor man's fight." But substitution was at length abolished. The outcome of the great conflict put the aristocrat on his mettle and he went to work.

If 1870 found economic recovery measurably complete in Rockbridge, it also marked the end for Virginia of that unsavory episode in American history known as the Reconstruction Period. In 1868 Virginia was Military District Number One, and it was not able to take part in the general election of that year. A few months later the carpet-bag régime was overthrown, and in January, 1870, the state was again a member of the Federal Union.

To give a further insight into the events of the four years of war, we devote the remainder of this chapter to extracts from the county order-books and the newspaper files.

EXTRACTS FROM THE ORDER-BOOKS
1861

All justices present, May 9th, to consider the subject of arming the militia, according to the Act of January 19th. The following orders were issued:

An issue of county bonds to the amount of not more than $25,000, and in sums of not less than $100. The bonds to be registered and numbered, signed by the presiding justice and countersigned by the clerk, and made payable to the treasurer. Interest payable semi-annually.

William Dold, Joseph G. Steele, and John D. Paxton constituted a committee to carry the above order into effect, and to deposit the money thus realized with the Bank of Lexington.

Whenever the colonel, lieutenant-colonel, and first major—or any two of them—of either militia regiment shall certify that at least sixty efficient men are organized into a volunteer company, and that the assistance of the county is needed to equip the company, a warrant to that effect is to be issued, but not for more than $25.00 per soldier.

The commissioners shall provide quarters and subsistance while such companies are drilling, such expense not to exceed $20.00 per soldier; likewise subsistance, and transportation to rendezvous if ordered into service.

The justices of the several districts—or any two of them—may ascertain the wants of the families of men who are in service, and see that requisite necessaries are supplied, and make report monthly. The sum to be thus used is not to exceed $5,000.

Reports to be turned in at each term of court.

The foregoing orders to be published in the *Lexington Gazette* and the *Valley Star*.

Ordered, June 3rd, that a Home Guard be organized, the same to include all the white males able to serve and who have taken the oath of fidelity to the Commonwealth. The Guards to patrol their several neighborhoods with a view to the preservation of peace and quiet, and to be empowered to arrest and bring before a justice all persons, white or black, whom they may have reason to suspect of improper purposes, or violation of the Ordinance of Secession.

Abraham Doubt, slave of Mrs. Hennetta Ruff, cleared of the charge of inciting servile insurrection, but not of that of making seditious speeches. Ordered that he be given thirty-nine lashes on the bare back at the whipping post.

A levy ordered of six cents per $100 on land and personalty, and eighteen cents on each slave over twelve years old, the avails to be applied to the interest on the bonds and the payment of the first instalment. Another levy, of seventy cents per $100 of land and personalty, was to pay interest on the county's subscription to the North River Navigation Company.

The road levy was fixed at $1.50 in money or two days in labor.

The July court reduced the minimum bond to $20.00.

1862

In March and April 385 men were exempted from military service because of physical disqualification. Ninety-six others were exempted as being millers, overseers, blacksmiths, etc. There were ninety-three refusals.

A bond issue of $10,000 ordered in May to relieve the families of volunteers and the militia.

Robert J. White was appointed salt agent, and was authorized to buy not more than 10,000 bushels, the faith of the county being pledged to the payment.

1863

In January there was a further issue, by a vote of eleven against ten, for the relief of soldier families. In the further distribution of relief, ordered that the weekly allowance, paid in money, be $1.25 to a wife, seventy-five cents for each girl over the age of twelve, and fifty cents for each child under twelve.

An order of $10,000 in county notes was ordered, the issue to be in the denominations of one dollar, fifty cents, twenty-five cents, fifteen cents, and ten cents.

In January there were 608 slaves in the county between the ages of eighteen and forty-five, who were liable to be drafted for work on fortifications. The apportionment was to be made by a committee of justices, one from each district. The slaves were to be valued. The number actually drafted was 266.

In September the sheriff was to enroll all male slaves, including rfugees, between the ages of eighteen and fifty-five, to fill a requisition for work on forts. 292 were furnished, out of the 701 who were liable.

1864

Substitution was abolished in January by an Act of the Confederate Congress.

A. S. Bacon, forty-seven years of age, was appointed General Agent and Storekeeper for Rockbridge, giving bond in the sum of $50,000. He was directed to borrow, on the faith of the county, to the amount of not more than $50,000, and to purchase cotton yarns and cloths, and other articles of prime necessity. While thus employed he was to have a salary of $200 a month, over and above his expenses, and was to make a report at each term of court. In February he asked whether, in the existing condition of the country, he should continue his efforts. He was directed to use his own discretion.

There was a call, February 1st, for ninety slaves to work on the forts around Richmond. The court thought they should be kept at home to work the farms, fortify the mountain passes, and aid in preventing the raids that were always threatening the county. Raids had already taken place in the preceding year in the months of June, August, November, and December, and another invasion was likely to occur at any time. The governor of the state was asked to exempt the county from the requisition.

Supplies extremely scarce in April. Agents cannot buy enough for the indigent families. 1,300 persons are dependent on public support. 4,950 bushels of corn and 660 barrels of flour are needed before August 1st. The court certifies that the supplies asked are necessary. It is represented to that body that corn and wheat may be purchased at the depots of the tax-in-kind of the Confederate government. Bacon is instructed to spend as much of the $50,000 as will relieve the want, refugees and sojourners being included.

The court asks that the deputy sheriffs now liable to service be exempted. Three are required, outbreaks being daily on the increase. For more than thirty years four deputies have been constantly engaged. The county has over 18,000 people, and is broken and mountainous.

In April it is stated that certain citizens are believed to be evading the impressment of supplies. Impressment agents are required to call upon the sheriff, or any constable, and such official is authorized to summon any number of citizens to take impressed articles by force. A refusal to so assist will be contempt of court.

Several murders and attempts at murder during the year.

A committee was appointed June 6th to visit the battlefields near Staunton and Richmond to look after wounded Rockbridge soldiers. Another committee is in the field to collect supplies and forward them to the first committee.

During Hunter's raid, thirty or more barrels of flour—left in certain mills—were carried off.

In November another issue of $50,000 in bonds for the relief of indigents.

Severe drouth in the summer and very meagre crop. Scarcely enough supplies in the county for home needs.

(FROM THE NEWSPAPER FILES)
1861

1,500 men in the county on government wages.

Complaint in October that tanneries are paying only five cents per pound for hides, but asking from sixty cents and upward for leather.

Schools languishing.

1862

Prices in August: flour, $8.00; corn, $1.00; oats, fifty cents; butter, twenty-five to thirty cents; bacon, thirty-five cents; beef, nine to twelve cents; eggs, fifteen cents.

"If every part of the Confederacy has as many idle young men in it as this quiet little town of Lexington, we might raise a splendid army in addition to the forces now in the field."—*Gazette,* August 14.

The Natural Bridge Aid Society sent $150 to the relief of the wounded of the 12th Georgia at McDowell.

Public schools partially or entirely closed for more than a year. Private schools fully sustained. Ann Smith Academy reorganized with Mrs. George D. Baskerville as principal. The Rev. Mr. Trimble's school at Brownsburg now in its third year and more flourishing than ever before.—August 21.

Good crops in the Valley of Virginia.

Candles seventy-five cents a pound. Why not substitute an hour of the morning for an hour of the evening?

About 150 of the Rockbridge Dragoons surprised and captured in the west of Greenbrier, about December 1st, by the Federal cavalry.

1863

Farm produce five times as high as usual. Things purchased, ten times as high.—February 2.

Wood, per cord, $12.00.—March 5.

Native dyes, copperas being a requisite in each instance: The root and bark of sassafras, a beautiful yellow and orange; kalmia (dwarf laurel), a drab; willow bark, a deep blue-black on wool and linen, a dark slate on cotton; bark and root of red oak, a chocolate brown; pine bark, a slate (on cotton); pine with kalmia, a dove; sweet gum bark, a dove; maple, a purple; beech bark, a dove; leaves and berries of sumach, a black; white oak, a lead (on cotton), but will not dye wool.

200,000 pounds of bacon in the county—April 15.

As a candidate for the Confederate Congress, Baldwin has 676 votes and Letecher 526.

253 cadets in the Virginia Military Institute, May 6th, and more wish to come in. Sixty students at Washington College.

Seventy-five families in Lexington will need bread this winter, and 100 will need fuel to the amount of 500 cords. 150 families in the corporation produce no foodstuffs.

1864

Lexington House sells for $100,000 in January.

Many farmers on half rations of meat so as to send meat to the army.

Matrimonial advertisement by one of Rosser's soldiers.

Several smokehouses robbed in April.

English stationery on sale at one of the stores.

Large wheat crop, considering the reduction in the supply of labor.

XV

RECENT PERIOD

Progress During the Period—Local Politics—Economic and Social Changes—
War of 1917

More than half a century has now elapsed since the great war of the 60's. In this county the period has brought a progressive transformation, greater and more striking in its aggregate results than was witnessed in the equal number of years just preceding.

In October, 1868, a local paper remarks that greenbacks were becoming fairly plentiful and that the merchants were laying in heavy stocks of goods. In the same month the Rockbridge Agricultural and Mechanical Society roused itself from its war eclipse and held a fair continuing three days. The new beginning was kept up, and notwithstanding the fact that the whole country was in 1874 in the throes of a severe business depression, the fair of that year was quite successful.

In 1890 Rockbridge fell a victim to the speculative mania known as a boom. The visitation created an important town at Buena Vista and was not entirely unsuccessful at Glasgow or at the county seat. The amount of money that was forthcoming to be invested in "development" stock and town lots was a significant commentary on the rapid recuperation that had taken place in twenty-five years. In fact, the assessed valuation for 1877 was greater by $2,000,000 than the value of farms, farm machinery, and livestock in 1850. By 1917 the valuation of real and personal property had risen from $5,785,786 to $8,533,920, exclusive of Buena Vista.

During the reconstruction episode the "Yankee" was not a popular personage. In 1869 we hear the complaint that pedlers from the North were representing themselves as Englishmen. However, when Colonel Waite came from Batavia, New York, in 1873 to visit his old friends the Davidsons, he could report that he was treated in the most friendly and courteous manner, although he saw many ex-soldiers who were lame or otherwise disabled. He observed that the negro was inclined to flock to the towns, thus causing a scarcity of labor, although many were still in the employ of their former masters. He found slavery unregretted, yet found the opinion general that the enfranchisement of the blacks, in the way it was accomplished, was a political blunder. Two years after the visit of Colonel Waite, John Leyburn remarked that "no well disposed Northerner need fear as to a kindly reception." Two years later yet, a county paper was wishing that more results might come from efforts to attract immigration from the North. It remained for the dastardly shooting of President Garfield to elicit the following remark from the *Gazette:*

> No event in American history has so unified the people as the shot at Garfield. We have discovered all at once that we are Americans. The Union has been restored. The Republic lives. Guiteau's bullets have done more to show the people of these United States what manner of men they are than anything that has happened in their history. The spontaneous outburst of Southern indignation speaks too plainly to be misunderstood.

In announcing the death of the president, C. M. Dold, mayor of Lexington, requested that business be suspended for the day, and that at four o'clock the citizens should assemble at the Presbyterian church, the largest in the town. The schools were also suspended, minute guns were fired at the Institute, and the religious services at the church were largely attended.

By a majority of forty-four votes, one precinct not reporting, Rockbridge declared itself adverse to the Constitutional Convention of 1902. But the changes embodied in the state constitution of that year met with general approval. Three years later the *County News* deprecated airing the race issue on the stump.

During the few decades that the Whig party was a factor in American politics, Rockbridge gave majorities for that ticket. We are without precise knowledge of the political complexion of the county in the early period of the nineteenth century.

The close of hostilities in 1865 found the Whig party in high favor in the South because of its far-sighted attitude respecting secession in 1860-61. Its opponent, generally in the lead in these states, was under some reproach because of the results of its sponsorship of that issue. The way seemed open for two strong parties to exist in the South as well as in the North. But with a profound lack of broad vision, the ultra partisan element that came to the front after the assassination of Lincoln pursued a course which almost solidified the whites of the South in a support of the Democratic party. In 1873 the Democratic candidate for the governorship had more than twice as many votes in Rockbridge as his opponent, the latter carrying only one precinct. In the presidential contest of 1876 Tilden had 2505 votes and Hayes only 903. When the Democracy of Virginia divided on the state debt issue, the Readjuster wing was the stronger in this county, and its majority in 1879 was about 200. Yet in 1881 the Readjuster candidate as governor ran behind his popular opponent by ninety-one votes, although he carried seven precincts.

Many of the Readjusters went over to the Republican party, and for more than twenty years Rockbridge lay in the doubtful column. In 1880 the Republican candidate for the governorship had a majority of sixty-eight. In 1884 the Democratic majority for Cleveland was 101, and in 1892 it was 230. But McKinley's majority was 660 in 1896, and 553 in 1900. In 1901 the state ticket showed a Republican majority of 142. In 1893, Yost for Congress had a majority over Tucker of seventy-seven.

The constitution of 1902 had in Rockbridge a twofold effect. It caused a great reduction in the aggregate vote, and as this reduction made a heavier inroad upon the Republican column than upon the Democratic, the county no longer stands in the doubtful list. Thus in 1894, 1900, and 1901, the combined votes for the two leading candidates were respectively 3,945, 3,968, and 3,450. It is therefore evident that the average election brought out fully eighty per cent. of the voting population. But in the first election under the new system—that of 1903—the total vote had fallen to 1,895. In 1913 it was only 780. In 1912, however, it rose to 1,837, 1,106 votes going to Wilson, 474 to Taft, and 257 to Roosevelt. In 1916 the Democratic candidate for the Assembly carried thirteen precincts and had 1,030 votes. His Republican competitor carried eight precincts and had 835 votes. In the same year Wilson had 1,205 votes and Hughes 678. The west side of the county remains a Republican stronghold.

The period we are considering has brought a number of important changes. The census of 1870 was defective in the Southern states, but on the face of the returns there was a significant loss in population in this county for the decade 1860-70 of 1,190. Between 1870 and 1910, there was a gain of fifty-two per cent., or, if the figures for 1860 be compared with those for 1910, the gain was forty-two per cent. However, much the greater share of this gain is absorbed by the increase in the town and village population. In the neighborhoods strictly rural the gain has been small.

The canal has gone into disuse, there have been great inroads upon the forest supply, and the smelting of iron keeps in the closest touch with the railway siding. But with the exception of the old line of the Chesapeake and Ohio, all the railroad mileage in the county has come into operation since 1880. If mining has relatively decreased, manufacturing has greatly increased. If there is no conspicuous increase in the tilled acreage, the local agriculture has advanced in output, and there is a more general recognition of scientific methods. The silo and the commercial orchard have appeared, and the canning industry is gaining a foothold. The log house is not extinct, and inhabited specimens will be found in Rockbridge about as long as anywhere in Virginia; but very many of the farm homes are roomy, comfortable, attractive, and modern.

The pay school has yielded to the free school, and the latter is efficiently administered. The higher educational institutions of the county were never in a more prosperous condition.

The telephone, the automobile, and free rural delivery, unknown in the early years of the period, are deeply modifying the habits of the people. The taxable wealth is greater than in the most palmy days of the antebellum era, even with its slave valuation.

With a colored laboring class nearly one-third as numerous as the white population, there was necessarily a jar in the adjustment to the changed labor system that began in 1865. But the whites went to work so manfully that in a few years the deeper traces of the war were obliterated. Hired service is no longer under any social ban. Between 1900 and 1910, the colored element decreased nearly one-third, and Rockbridge has assumed much of the appearance of a community that is wholly white. Yet it does not by any means follow that the negro will totally disappear. In the Rockbridge of today the colored people are, on the whole, orderly, industrious, and prosperous.

In a larger degree than was usual in the Valley counties, the old Rockbridge was noted for its fine country estates, owned by an old family element that was numerous, cultured, and influential. This class has relatively declined, much of it having been attracted to the cities and to other states. The less wealthy class of whites has perhaps come nearer to holding its own, and a new element has slowly yet steadily been coming in. In consequence, there is a very perceptible difference between the Rockbridge of yesterday and the Rockbridge of today.

The citizen of this county is industrious and hospitable, and is conservative in thought and action. His local patriotism is deep, and it leads him to draw a distinction between the descendant of the early settler and the resident born in some other community.

In 1914 the world was prosperous. With only one conspicuous exception all the members of the family of nations had a sincere desire to live in peace with one another. Yet a rich and thriving country of Europe, acting through a subservient neighbor, deliberately provoked a general war, and waged it with a studied cruelty which would have shamed the North American Indian of the eighteenth century. There was a contempt for the good opinion of the world. No considerations of truth, honor, or humanity were permitted to stand in the way of the German program. The horrible crimes perpetrated by the German armies were by order of the German leaders, and seemingly with the general consent of the German people.

The colossal vanity of the kaiser made him aspire to be another Alexander the Great. Behind him was a feudalistic group of military leaders, land barons, and captains of industry. Below him and them were the millions of the German people, trained from infancy to obey the nod of the man in authority, and without any practical voice in their government. The conceit, arrogance, and greed of the war lords was boundless. By means of a domestic propaganda, adroit and persistent, the German had for years been indoctrined with the myth of his superiority to anyone else whomsoever. The clergyman, the schoolmaster, and the journalist were permitted to teach only what would encourage the opinion that it was the God-given mission of the German to overcome other nations by the sword and rule the entire earth. The world was not to be conquered for the world's good, but that it might be plundered and domineered over. That nation the German saw fit to deem degenerate was to be blotted out. This propaganda developed the "bighead" in a most acute form. It led to an insufferable contempt for the rest of the world. Consequently, the German has utterly failed as a colonizer, or in gaining the good will of the Europeans who are not German, yet hitherto under German rule.

Germany has posed as a highly civilized nation. Her industrial organization was very efficient. She already had an enviable "place in the sun," but wanted a monopoly of this privilege. The Germans have some commendable traits and have great possibilities for good in the upbuilding of the world. But they are as yet a young people, only superficially weaned from barbarism and paganism, and without the acquirement of the habit of good manners. Napoleon said that if one scratched a Russian he found a Tartar. Were he alive now he would say that if one scratches a Prussian he finds a savage. Under autocracy, the civilization of Germany was an effort to accommodate the twentieth century to the spirit of the Middle Ages. It was worn as a garment and not as a part of her being. It was materialistic and without a soul. It scoffed at the reality of any power except brute force. The war which the criminal leaders of Germany set in motion in 1914 has been a conclusive demonstration of the unfitness of present-day Germany to lead the world in the path of real civilization.

That war was not a war in the ordinary sense of the term. It was the overpowering of an outlaw who was running amuck. A more righteous conflict was never waged. Germany was fought that the world might be made a decent place to live in. There is no place for that country in the household of civilized nations until her people cease to bow down to the false gods they have so assiduously worshipped the last half century. It is entirely against a growing spirit of the age for one nation to throttle another by a resort to arms, particularly when this recourse involves the plunder or destruction of mines and factories, the enslavement or massacre of the operative population, and indiscriminate piracy and murder on the high seas. It is not for any nation to assume that it is a law to itself and that whatever it does is justifiable.

The United States was forced into this war to assist in the rescue of civilization. The people of Rockbridge have the consciousness that they loyally upheld their country, and that their sons were numerously represented on the battle-front that ended the war.

XVI

THE NEGRO ELEMENT

SLAVERY IN VIRGINIA—GROWTH OF SLAVERY IN ROCKBRIDGE—MAINTAINING ORDER AMONG THE NEGROES—CRIME—EMANCIPATION EFFORTS—THE NEGRO IN THE WAR OF 1861—THE ROCKBRIDGE NEGRO OF TODAY

African slavery was almost as unfamiliar to the British people in their own land as it was in the whitest county of the Old Dominion. It was not legalized in Virginia until more than fifty years after the founding of Jamestown. White servants were preferred to colored ones until after 1700. Negroes of American birth were more satisfactory laborers than those coming direct from Africa. Slavery grew in favor, and when American independence was declared, the negro population of Virginia was already so large that it seemed likely to exceed the white at an early day.

The more far-seeing of the ruling class in Virginia perceived the undesirability of this inundation. The House of Burgesses repeatedly asked the British government to cease bringing negroes to the colony. All these efforts were set at naught by the greed of the mercantile classes of England. On the eve of the Revolution, Lord Dartmouth said England "cannot allow the colonies to check or discourage in any degree a traffic so beneficial to the nation." This forcing of slaves upon Virginia was one of the grievances named by Jefferson in his original draft of the Declaration of Independence. It must be conceded, however, that slaves would not have been brought to Virginia unless there was a willingness to buy them. A stern boycott would have ended the traffic. No British ministry would have dared to break down such a weapon by sheer force.

The fact that the summer climate of Virginia is considerably warmer than that of Britain had very little to do with the importation of slaves. Black slaves as well as white servants were purchased because the society of Tidewater was essentially aristocratic. Where there is an aristocracy, there is inevitably a menial class. The Tidewater was a land of tobacco plantations, and these could not be carried on without a large class of laborers. It is interesting to note that above the Tidewater and below the Blue Ridge, slaves were fewer than in the former section. In the Valley they were still fewer, and in many of the counties beyond the Alleghany Divide they were almost non-existent. Slaves and large farms grew fewer and yet fewer as one journeyed toward the Ohio.

There never was a time when the opponents of slavery in America were not numerous. The institution was vehemently denounced by the delegates from Virginia to the Federal Convention of 1787. A Virginia law of 1784 encouraged the freeing of the slaves. In the same year the Methodists of America became an independent church, and one of their first official acts was to petition against slavery, although most of their membership was then in Virginia and Maryland. Slavery tended to make manual labor discreditable unless it was performed by slaves. It thereby degraded the lower classes of society and contributed to idleness in the higher. It was a Southern man who tersely described slavery as "a curse to the master and a wrong to the slave." It was another who defined it as "a mildew which has blighted every region it has touched from the creation of the world."

Colonial Augusta was almost a white man's country. In 1756 it had only about eighty slaves; perhaps not more than one per cent. of the population. But thence forward they became increasingly numerous in the better agricultural districts of the Valley. In Rockbridge they were few prior to the Revolution, and they were confined to a small number of the wealthier families. When the iron industry arose and made a demand for labor, negroes were hired from masters east of the Blue Ridge. "By 1861," remarked Colonel Preston, "we were quite a slaveholding people; a few more years, and we would have had to undergo much that Tuckahoe did on that score. It was well the unpleasantness came as soon as it did."

So completely have the outward vestiges of the reign of slavery passed away from Rockbridge, that only a few of the original negro quarters remain. A notable exception in the Weaver estate at Buffalo Forge, where the houses for the slaves were of an uncommonly substantial and comfortable kind. The institution was milder in Virginia than in the cotton belt, and the relations between master and slave were as a rule kindly. The main highway to "the darky's heart was down his throat." The slave was given a holiday week at Christmas time and he enjoyed it as much as his master did. He was in his element when playing banjo and bones and patting his knee.

But since the African came to Virginia as a child-race, and was not used to any softer argument than brute force, it was felt that slavery could not be maintained by treating the negro in the same manner as the white man. The slave was supposed not to carry a gun or to go outside his master's premises without a pass. Poisons might not be put into his hands, and this restriction was necessary. In 1839 a Rockbridge slave attempted to poison several persons. He might not be taught to read or write. But between himself and his own slaves the master did not think the law had any claim to interfere. Accordingly, if he saw fit, he taught a favorite slave to read and write.

The patrol system was one means of keeping the slaves in order, and it occasioned a good deal of expense. Captains were appointed by the county court, each having a force of some six or eight men. A captain and his squad were to patrol a specified area at specified times. For this service the patrolman was paid thirty-three cents a night in 1782. In 1822, he was paid six cents an hour. The penal code was not the same to the slave that it was to the Caucsaian. His ears could be cropped. He could be hanged for burning a barn, or for stealing, and the county court was empowered to decree the death penalty. But before the negro was hanged, his valuation as a slave was determined, and this sum was paid by the county to the master.

A considerable share of the crime in Rockbridge has been committed by the negro. The first civil execution of a white man in this county took place August 3, 1905. It was preceded by the legal hanging of five negroes at five different times. York, a slave of Andrew Reid, was adjudged guilty December 1, 1786, of killing Tom, another of Reid's slaves. It was odrered that he be hanged one week later, that his head be severed from the body, and that it be set on a pole at the forks of the road between Lexington and John Paxton's. Rape was not at all unknown before emancipation. An execution for this crime took place in Rockbridge in 1850. For assaulting and beating Arthur McCorkle, Alexander Scott was ordered to be hanged April 5, 1844. The master was to be paid $450.00. Cyrus, a slave of Robert Piper, was ordered to hang in 1798 for burning his master's house. In 1840, Nelson, a slave, was ordered to be hanged for burglary. Outlaw slaves might be put to death with impunity. But the penalty for burglary was sometimes changed to transportation to Liberia. Whipping was administered in less serious matters, as when thirty-nine lashes were ordered for Peter, a slave of John Hays, in 1800. He had stolen leather worth $3.25. In 1804, Jinny, a slave of John Dunlap, threatened his wife, Dorcas. The woman was ordered to be kept in jail until her child was born, and thirty lashes, well laid on, were to be given. A negress was occasionally guilty of infanticide.

Before 1861, and particularly before 1830, there were somewhat frequent instances of manumission. But restrictions were imposed on the freedman. He was registered as to height, color, markings, etc., and a duplicate of the paper given him. Registration had to be repeated every five years. To live in the county he had to have the consent of the county court. But he had a surname as well as a given name, and his marriages were recorded among those of the white people. It was the policy of Virginia to discourage the free negro from remaining in the state. He was too frequently idle and worthless, and his presence tended to make the slaves restless and demoralized. Yet a request to remain, if by a freedman who stood well with the whites, was not likely to be turned down.

In 1830 the desire to get rid of the institution of slavery had become very strong in Virginia. The state was declining in wealth, and emigration to the West and South was very heavy. About this time, 343 women of Augusta county signed a petition for immediate emancipation. A petition to the Assembly, dated 1827 and sent from Rockbridge, asks the removal of free negroes from the state, and favors manumission and colonization. It goes on to say that "the evils, both political and moral, which spring from the difference of color and condition in our population, are great and obvious. The blacks, in proportion to their number, are a positive deduction from our military strength, an impediment to the wealth and improvement of the country, and to the general diffusion of knowledge by schools; a source of domestic uneasiness and an occasion of moral degeneracy of character. Separated by an impassable barrier from political privileges and social respectability, and untouched by the usual incentives to improvement, they must be our natural enemies, degraded in sentiment and base in morals." Another Rockbridge petition exhibits the contrast between 1790 and 1830, with respect to the section of the state east of the Blue Ridge. The whites had increased from 314,523 to 375,935, but the blacks had increased from 288,425 to 457,013, being now in a large majority. The tendency toward an Africanization of the Eastern District was causing much emigration of the whites. It was prophesied that a race war would result and cause a blotting out of the negroes. The petition asked for a special tax to create a fund to remove such blacks as were willing to go, and to purchase some others to send with them. It also asked that private emancipation be followed by removal.

In 1832 a bill for a general emancipation passed the lower house of the legislature, and lacked only one vote of going through the senate. The Western District of Virginia was almost unanimous for the measure. The value of the slave property was about $100,000,000. Shortly after the defeat of this bill came the tragic insurrection in Southampton, whereby sixty white people lost their lives. An anti-slavery feeling spread in the North, and the many anti-slavery societies in the South were disbanded. The institution was given a new lease of life, and yet there was still a strong economic opposition to slavery in the Western District, this name being given, until 1861, to the portion of Virginia west of the Blue Ridge.

A petition from this county in 1847 says it is believed there are 60,000 of the free colored in the state, and it asserts the opinion that there will be 250,000 of them in the year 1900. It recommends deportation to Liberia, and says that with few exceptions the freedmen are idle, worthless, and increasingly injurious to the slaveholders and the slaves. Henry Ruffner, himself a slaveholder, put forward a plan the same year. He found that slavery was driving away immigration, driving out white laborers, crippling agriculture, commerce, and industry, imposing hurtful social ideals upon the people, and that it was detrimental to the common schools and to popular education. His plan was to divide the state along the line of the Blue Ridge, eliminate slavery on the west side, and on the east side to introduce a policy of gradual emancipation, deportation, and colonization. John Letcher was also in favor of eventually keeping slavery out of the Western District. In the course of an interview at Washington College, General Lee said he had always favored gradual emancipation. He had considered the presence of the negro an absolute injury to the state and a peril to its future. He thought it would have been better had Virginia sent her negroes into the cotton country.

In 1860, the imminence of civil war depreciated slave values and gave a stimulus to a more active selling of them in the cotton states. In the *Gazette* for January 24, 1860, William Taylor advertises for 1,000 negroes for the Southern market. Another advertisement, dated May 10, 1860, reads thus: "I wish to purchase 500 likely young negroes of both sexes for the Southern market, for which I will pay the highest market prices in cash. My address is Staunton or Middlebrook, Augusta County, Va. J. E. Carson." About this time advertisements of runaway slaves were somewhat a regular feature of the newspapers.

During the war of 1861 the conduct of the negroes was highly creditable to the race, and there were few misdemeanors among them. Many of the slaves showed great fidelity in staying with the families of their masters and working the farms. In one instance a master was about to join the Confederate army and had to leave five children behind him. His man-slave told him to go on and he would himself see that things at home were attended to. The master was killed in battle, but the negro was faithful to his trust, and the children were enabled to go to school. A monument marks the grave of the old servant in the Timber Ridge burial ground.

American slavery was doomed by the war of 1861, no matter which side might triumph. The Federal government resorted to emancipation as a war measure, and it was made permanent by a constitutional amendment. Yet it is not generally known that an emancipation act was passed by the Confederate Congress in the closing days of the war.

The slave was commonly known by a single name, instances of which are Mingo, Will, Jerry, Jude, Pompey, Dinah, Daphne, Rose, Jin, Nell, Let, Phœbe, Phillis, and Moll. One effect of emancipation was to ensure him a surname, which was often that of the family in which he had worked.

An interesting exception to a general rule was that of the Reverend John Chavis. In 1802 it was certified that he was free, decent, orderly, and respectable, and had taken academic studies at Washington College. Another was Patrick Henry, for whom Thomas Jefferson built a cabin on his land at Natural Bridge and left him in charge of the property, so that it might be adequately shown to visitors. Jefferson conveyed some land to him in fee simple and he lived on it till his death in 1829. Henry's will is on record at Lexington. He had the unique distinction of being a colored slaveholder, as the following document will show:

> Be it known to all whom these presents may come, that I, Patrick Henry, of the County of Rockbridge and State of Virginia having in the year of our Lord one Thousand eight hundred and fifteen purchased from Benjanin Darst of the town of Lexington a female slave named Louisa, and since known by the name of Louisa Henry; now, for and in consideration of her extraordinary meritorious zeal in the prosecution of my interest, her constant probity and exemplary deportment subsequent to her being recognized as my wife, together with divers other good and substantial reasons, I have this day in open court in the county aforesaid, by this my public deed of manumission determined to enfranchise, set free, and admit her to a participation in all and every privilege, advantage, and immunity that free persons of color are capacitated, enabled, or permitted to enjoy in conformity with the Laws and Provisions of this Commonwealth, in such case made and provided. And by these presents I do hereby emancipate, set free, manumit, and disenthrall, the said Louisa alias Louisa Henry from the shackles of slavery and bondage forever, for myself and all persons whomsoever, I do renounce, resign, and henceforth disclaim all right and authority over her as, or in the capacity of a slave. And for the true and earnest performance of each and every stipulation hereinbefore mentioned to the said Louisa, alias Louisa Henry, I bind myself, my heirs, executors, and administrators forever. In testimony whereof I have hereunto set my hand and affixed my seal this second day of December in the year of our Lord one thousand eight hundred and sixteen.
>
> Patrick Henry.

In 1910 the negroes of this county were sixteen per cent. of the population, and paid taxes on land and personalty assessed at $237,505. The gregariousness of the race is indicated in the fact that of the aforesaid amount, $155,653 belonged in Lexington town and district.

It is worthy of mention that Amy Timberlake, daughter of a negress brought from Africa, lived to a greater age than any other resident of Rockbridge, so far as our information goes. She died in 1897 at the age of 107.

In the middle course of Irish Creek is a considerable community sometimes known as the "brown people." They live the simple life in their little log cabins which dot the valley and the bordering hillsides. In the veins of many of them is the blood of the Indian as well as that of the African, but the Caucasian type is dominant.

XVII

THE TOWN OF LEXINGTON

Founding of the County Seat—The Town Site—County Buildings—The Fire of 1796—
Lexington in 1816 and 1835—Lexington in Recent Times—
A Letter of 1781

When the county of Rockbridge was authorized in 1778, the population was probably not less than 4,000. It must have been well distributed, except that it had not penetrated so deeply into the mountain coves as was the case a century later. The Rockbridge people of that day were altogether rural. The nearest approach to a village was the school-hamlet at Timber Ridge. One cannot find in the United States nowadays an area so large as Rockbridge with its then population and without a full-fledged town.

But for the creation of the new county, ten and perhaps twenty years would have elapsed without placing a village in the center of the Rockbridge area. The county had to have a center of local government, and west of the Blue Ridge a county seat has always meant a town. The selection of the plateau at the mouth of Woods Creek was governed partly by the general attractiveness of the spot, but still more because of its central position and its being on the main line of travel between Staunton and the settlements on and beyond the Roanoke. It was also on a direct line of travel to the Kanawha and the West.

Thus we find that the same Act of Assembly which created Rockbridge also provided for laying off into streets and lots a tract of about twenty-seven acres. The net return from the sale of lots was to be applied to lessening the county levy. In the Act the statute-made town is called Lexington. We do not know who was particularly responsible for the choice of name, but the Lexington of Virginia, like the Lexington of Kentucky, appears to be a namesake of the village in Massachusetts, where the first battle of the Revolution was begun.

The first private owner of the tract was Gilbert Campbell, who left a new "hoose" and personalty of $179.41 on his decease in 1750. The property then passed to his son, Isaac, the possessor at the time of the War for Independence. The rectangle of 900 feet by 1,300 feet, provided by the statute, was divided into thirty-six lots, two of these being reserved for the county buildings. The original lots are 128½ feet broad and 195 feet deep. The three streets running in the longer direction were named Randolph, Main, and Jefferson. The cross streets were called Henry, Washington, and Nelson. With one exception these streets bear the names of Virginia statesmen of the Revolutionary period. An alley all around the circumference of five-sixths of a mile is indicated in the original plat. The courthouse reservation was defined as fronting Main and extending from Henry to Washington.

The boundaries of Lexington were extended in 1847, 1850, 1874, and 1916. It is a curious fact that the title of the Act of 1850 conveys no hint that the statute concerns any other town than Clarksburg, the birthplace of Stonewall Jackson.

The first care of the county court was to provide for the public buildings. The specifications for the first courthouse are given in Chapter IX. The building was to have been completed by November 1, 1778. Nothing appears to have been done, for next year we find the court ordering a courthouse twenty-five by thirty feet, flanked by two jury rooms, each twelve feet square. A stone foundation was to support a brick wall nine feet high. The roof was to be in the form of a T and covered with joint shingles. The courthouse now ordered appears to have been burned in 1787. In that year we find the justices contracting with William Brice to build a courthouse twenty-four by thirty feet on the ground, and with a wall eighteen feet high. Again the foundation was to be of stone and the wall of brick. Again the courtroom was to be flanked by a jury-room twelve feet square and provided with a chimney. In front there was to be a lobby twelve feet by twenty-four. The courtroom was to contain a gallery, and was to be lighted by two windows taking glass eight inches by ten, but with twenty-four panes instead of eighteen. Pine flooring and chestnut shingles were to be used. This second courthouse perished in the great fire of 1796. The justices to draw the plans for still another courthouse and jail were John Bowyer and John and James Caruthers. In 1798 a pillory and stocks were ordered. We are not informed as to the size of the original county "boarding house," but in Rockbridge, as elsewhere, an "insufficiency of the jail" was for years a complaint entered by every incoming sheriff. In 1815 a stove was ordered for the "dungeon of jail." A new office for the clerk of the court was ordered in 1845. The present commodious and quite modern courthouse was opened in 1897.

April 11, 1796, the young village was scourged by the fire-fiend. According to one version of the occurrence, some resident had burned the trash in his garden, and the coals were given new life by a rising wind. By another statement the fire began on the lot above the one occupied by the Methodist Church in 1889. The hay in a stable took fire, either from the pipe of a negro hatter or from the embers under a wash-kettle. Both accounts agree that there was a westerly wind. Little could be done to check the conflagration, and it extended as far eastward as the intersection of Main and Henry streets. The courthouse burned down, and for a while the residence of Andrew Reid was used as a substitute.

The disaster of 1796 stimulated the people to devise a means for being less helpless in the event of another fire. So we find fifty citizens signing in the same year the following petition:

We, the inhabitants of the town of Lexington and its vicinity, under the impression of our late misfortune by fire, and sensible of the great danger to which we are dailey exposed from many unavoidable circumstances; do hereby mutually associate ourselves for the purpose of forming a fire company, to be known by the name of the Lexington Fire Company.

About thirty years later, another petition says there is an engine and hose, but no fire company. It remarks that the town levy on all real property is three per cent.

A petition of 1801 mentions an Act of Assembly whereby certain persons named therein were authorized to raise by a lottery $25,000 for the relief of the sufferers by the fire. It goes on to suggest, that as the Act was not carried into effect and the townsmen had in some measure recovered from their loss, the sum named be reduced to $5,000, and be used in building a schoolhouse in the town and in opening roads over South and North mountains.

A much better class of houses appears to have succeeded those destroyed in the great fire. One Isaac Burr, of New York, who kept a diary on his trip up the Valley of Virginia in September, 1804, says that "Lexington is a handsome little village with good buildings." Burr must have been very fond of pie. He complains that he could get none except those made of apple or peach, and even these were exceedingly scarce.

A petition of 1805 finds a grievance in the playing of "long bullet," the nature of which seems now forgotten. It was played so much on the highways and near the town as to endanger the safety of people traveling about. Gambling was a feature of the game. Convictions were hard to secure, and that the practice might be stamped out, the aid of the Assembly was invoked.

For a quarter of a century there was no church building in the town, and religious services, as well as literary societies and singing schools, were held in the courthouse. On Washington's birthday, 1796, the sum of $2,500 was subscribed by forty-five men to erect a Presbyterian Church. The fire which quickly followed was probably responsible for some delay. At all events the church was not completed until the fall of 1802. It had an outside gallery and could seat 800 people. It stood near the main entrance to the present cemetery, and in 1844 was succeeded by the one now in existence. This, however, has been remodeled since the war of 1861. The Presbyterian house of worship has been followed, in the order of their mention, by the Methodist, Baptist, Episcopal, and Roman Catholic churches.

Unless the "Campbell schoolhouse" of 1753 stood near or on the site of

Lexington, the one built by William Alexander near where the union station now is would appear to have served the needs of the village in its earlier years. Apart from the Ann Smith Academy, the first pretentious effort in the educational line seems to have been in 1819, when the "Central School of Lexington" was built by an association at a cost of $1,100. In 1834 it was still in use and incorporation was asked.

In 1811 there were eleven mechanics asking leave to incorporate as an association.

In his semi-centennial address before the Franklin Society in 1873, Colonel J. T. L. Preston gives an interesting picture of Lexington in 1816. The town was still nearly or quite within the limits decreed in 1777. Main Street was not compactly built up, and there was but one brick building on its southward side. The finest structure was the Ann Smith Academy. Beyond it was a cornfield. At opposite sides of the college campus were two brick halls two stories high. The water supply was from a pump and from Back Spring. Hauling water by sled was "quite an institution." Ice-houses were unknown. The Presbyterian was the only church. There were two services separated by an "intervale" of one-half hour, and nearly as many people were present in the afternoon as in the morning. The large oak grove then reaching from the church gate to Woods Creek was a rambling ground during the noon intermission. There were many merchants for a town of not over 600 people, but the trading was on a small scale. The store of William Caruthers was the largest. Goods were purchased in Philadelphia. Prices were higher than in 1873, and money was scarcer. The town physician was Samuel L. Campbell, an eccentric gentleman of fine sense, kind heart, good culture, and liberal views. His field was a large one, yet there was less sickness than in later years. The able and very genial bar, of which riotous stories were told, consisted of Chapman Johnson, Daniel Sheffey, Briscoe Baldwin, and Howe Peyton.

In 1832 the lottery was still hardly thought of as a form of gambling. In that year Lexington was authorized to raise $12,000 by such means and use it in paving the streets and bringing water into the town.

Martin's *Virginia Gazetteer* of 1835 tells us that Lexington had Presbyterian and Methodist churches, a printing office, five shoemakers, five saddlers, four taverns, four carpenters, three hatters, two tanneries, two tinplate works, two cabinet-makers, two wheelwrights, two jewelers, two blacksmiths, and one bricklayer. Three libraries were open to the public. There were about 150 dwellings and nearly 900 inhabitants.

Howe, in his *Sketches of Virginia,* dated 1845, reports that the town had four churches, two printing offices, and 1,200 people. He quotes an English traveler as saying that "the town has many attractions. It is surrounded by beauty, and stands at the head of a valley flowing with milk and honey. House rent is low and provisions are cheap, abundant, and of the best quality. Flowers and gardens are more highly prized than in most places."

American opinion in the 50's sounds less appreciative. An observer of 1855 calls Lexington "an indifferent town and rather small, with muddy streets." Speaking of the town in 1859, Florence McCarthy, the Baptist minister, says it then looked as though it had been finished twenty years earlier, a new house being a very rare event. Yet in 1855, J. W. Paine was keeping a bookstore, and two years later Samuel Pettigrew had a daguerreotype studio. In this period the drinking habit was unpleasantly conspicuous. A petition of 1852, signed by 182 persons, says there are six unlicensed drinking places, and it asks for a search-warrant law. Just before the war of 1861 there were eight groggeries, and court day was no time for a self-respecting woman to appear on the street.

After the return of peace Lexington roused itself to a considerable degree of business activity, yet in 1873 a local newspaper said the streets were uncleanly and the sidewalks unworthy of the name. Eight years later there were paved streets, brick sidewalks, waterworks, and sanitary arrangements, but no railroad. It took eighteen hours to come from Lynchburg, a distance of fifty miles.

Before there were banks in the Valley of Virginia it was a custom to conceal money. It is said that when Major William Dunlap died in 1834, there was the sum of $12,000 in specie lying buried on his farm near Goshen. In later years much time was spent by residents of the neighborhood in searching for it. The first bank in Rockbridge was the Lexington Savings Institution, incorporated in 1843, but chartered under a longer name in 1834. It was still in operation in 1860, and gave five per cent. interest on time deposits. The Lexington Building Fund Association was organized in 1854. In 1860 its assets were $51,611.75, and its expense account for the year was $1,114.94.

The coming of peace in 1865 found the town cemetery in a very much neglected condition. Few stones had been set up during the war, and much of the inclosure was a jungle of grass, weeds, and tree-sprouts. During the war there were 108 interments of Confederate soldiers from other states than Virginia. More than one-half were North Carolinians. But the cemetery is now well cared for. It lies high and level, commands a fine outlook, and is much beautified with flowers and shrubbery. It is the resting place of many of the eminent dead of Rockbridge. The most conspicuous feature is the pillar surmounted by a statue in heroic size of the great Confederate leader, Stonewall Jackson.

Lexington was incorporated December 18, 1841. On the first Saturday in January, 1842, and every second year thereafter, the free white male house-keepers and freeholders, twenty-one years of age or upward, were to elect seven trustees, these serving two years and four constituting a quorum. They were enpowered to appoint a board of three assessors. They could also adopt rules and regulations for the maintenance of order, grade and pave streets, put in waterworks, and proceed against delinquents. Their jurisdiction extended one mile beyond the town limits. They appointed a town sergeant, who acted as constable within the corporate limits.

During the last fifty years Lexington has been a place of about 3,000 inhabitants. The business quarter is chiefly on Main street, and is quite compact. The business and professional interests are about such as may be looked for in an American town of this size. Yet Lexington has never been an industrial center. It is supported by a considerable country trade and by the two great educational institutions within its confines. The streets are generally paved, and the residence sections include many modern cottages setting back from the sidewalk in very attractive grounds. The improvement since the 50's is due more to the changed conditions of the postbellum era than to a marked increase in population. In 1850 the county seat was credited with 1,105 white and 638 colored inhabitants. In 1860 the total population was 2,135. In 1870 it had risen to 2,873, which is well-nigh as large as the figures for 1910. In 1874 the assessor found 1,451 white and 1,251 colored citizens and 501 students.

We close this chapter with a letter written from Lexington while it was yet an infant village.

Lexington 1st Feb. 1781

May it please your Excellency:

Accounts from all quarters lead us to expect vigorous Measures from our Enemies the next Campain. I have just received Duplicates of Letters sent from our Officers of Ilinois to others at Louisville which inform that the Spanish & American Ilinois Settlements are preparing defensively for heavy attacks. The original Letters I hear are sent forward to your Excellency. On conferring with Cols Bowmans & Trigg we concluded it expedient to send 150 Men to Garrison the Mouth of Licking until Crockett shall arrive which we shall expect weekly. We apprehended the Expenxe wd be less to Government than to wait until the Enemy arrived at our Settlements and better conduce to the Security of the people.

Inclosed are Recommendations for certain officers in this County. Would there be any Impropriety in sending out some Blank Commissions as formerly? I wd engage that no abuses be committed. There are many vacancies for other Officers than those recommended whose Ranks are as yet unfilled.

I have the Honor to be with the greatest Respect,

Your Excellency's
Most obedient and
humble Servant

To Gov. Jefferson

JOHN TODDYS

XVIII

BUENA VISTA AND GLASGOW

At a point where North River exchanges an easterly for a southerly course, is a long and tolerably broad expanse of river-bottom. Immediately eastward are the high and broken foothills of the Blue Ridge. Westward is the rapid flowing river, and beyond is the rolling upland that extends to the North Mountain. The locality was long known as Hart's Bottom, because a portion was patented by Silas Hart, a pioneer magistrate whose home was near Staunton. John Robinson came here shortly after the close of the Revolution, and by adding to his original purchase acquired a large estate. In 1889 the bottom was owned by Samuel F. Jordan, B. C. Moomaw, and one Gurney, of New York. By this time it was known as Green Valley. Near the flag station on what was then the newly built Shenandoah Valley Railroad was the Appold Tannery. Near this small industry were a half dozen dwellings for the employees.

About thirty years ago, a "boom fever" was spreading like an epidemic the entire length of the Valley of Virginia. "Development companies" sprang up like mushrooms, each one announcing that it designed to transform some old town or village into a hive of industry, or to create a brand-new town on a tract of farming land. Finely printed prospectuses were scattered broadcast, lot sales were held, bonuses were given to industrial "plants," and speculation ran riot until the inevitable reaction came. The result ranged all the way from moderate success to utter failure.

The effort launched at Green Valley was the earliest in the Valley of Virginia with the exception of Roanoke, and to this priority is largely due the fact that Buena Vista is an actual town and not a memory. A development company was organized with J. T. Barclay as its president. The issue of capital stock was fixed at $600,000. Within nine days this was oversubscribed by nearly twenty-five per cent. The land purchased and laid off into lots amounted to 900 acres. The streets, which are seventy-five feet wide, generally conform to the cardinal points of the compass. Those known as avenues bear the names of trees. The cross-streets are known by number. The blocks are of uniform size. Lots are 125 feet deep. Business lots are twenty-five feet wide and residence lots are fifty feet wide. The business quarter is next the river and along the railroad tracks. The residence section lies toward the Blue Ridge and rises into some of the lower foothills.

The stock was sold in shares of $50, two shares entitling the holder to a residence lot, and seven giving him a business lot. Some of the industrial enterprises that came brought skilled workmen from Pennsylvania, but otherwise the people are almost wholly Virginian. Much of the early influx was from Amherst on the other side of the Blue Ridge. During the early years in the history of the town, a rough, disorderly element, partly white and partly colored, was too conspicuous.

In 1891 Buena Vista was incorporated as a city and thus became politically independent of Rockbridge county. It is alleged, and it would seem with reason, that the count of the inhabitants was padded. At all events, the town has never yet had the 5,000 people that the statute law asks as a requisite to incorporation.

Buena Vista has had its ups and downs. Nearly one-half the buildings in the place appeared in 1890. Next season a reaction came, and for six years the town was at a standstill. Since that period of ebb there has been a slow but rather steady progress. The present population is about 3,500, and only about 150 persons are colored.

The leading industries of Buena Vista employ about 550 workmen. They comprise the Columbia Paper Company, the Alleghany Iron Company, the Buena Vista Tannery, and the Buena Vista Extract Company, all but the last named being owned in Pennsylvania. Smaller industries are a firebrick company, a stationery company, a silk mill, a saddle factory, a canning company, a building supply company, planing and lumber mills, and a brick plant that uses slag. The silk mill is owned in the North. Several of the early industries succumbed. One of these was a glass company, which sold out to the Armour Fertilizer Company. Another was a concern for the manufacture of wire fencing.

As in other boom towns of the period in question, one of the very first things set on foot by the promoters was a hotel on a scale entirely unwarranted by the probable support it would have. The Buena Vista Hotel was built at a cost of $85,000, yet was placed on an elevation at the very edge of the town, and thus could not attract commercial travelers. It did not burn down under the suspicious circumstances that were true of several other boom hotels of the Valley. It was at length sold for $10,000, and was converted into a very prosperous seminary. The churches of the little city are Methodist, Presbyterian, Baptist, Lutheran, and Episcopal, and two of differing branches of the Church of the Brethren. There are three hotels, a bank, about fifteen mercantile houses, and a local newspaper, the *Buena Vista Weekly Times*. The public schools are independent of those of the county. The chief commercial outlet is the Norfolk and Western Railroad, but the town is also served by the Lexington Branch of the Chesapeake and Ohio.

The town derives its name from the Buena Vista furnace which was operated by the Jordans in the near vicinity, and which, as its name suggests, antedated the town some forty years. Buena Vista is the industrial metropolis of Rockbridge, and is sustained by the metallic ores and the timber resources of the vicinity. Additional forest products are drawn from as far as North Carolina. The town has a pleasant situation, and makes a much better appearance than many of the new towns of its class.

Glasgow has naturally a more favorable situation than Buena Vista. It lies on a still more magnificent bottom girt with beautiful mountain scenery, and the James was formerly navigated to Richmond below and Buchanan above. It has the further advantage of being not only on the same branch of the Norfolk and Western, but also on the freight-carrying line of the Chesapeake and Ohio that extends from Clifton Forge to Richmond. But its attempt to become an industrial town has beeen less fortunate. Its own boom was not launched early and had to contend with the many other booms of 1890. In that year a development company was organized with General Fitzhugh Lee as president, Major M. M. Martin as vice-president, and R. H. Catlett as secretary-treasurer. These gentlemen, with William A. Anderson, of Lexington, and Joseph Davis, of Lynn, Massachusetts, constituted the board of directors. The purchases of land aggregated several thousand acres, and included the Salling and Glasgow homesteads. The large area was laid off into villa sites and town lots, and several enterprises were induced to come. A power and light plant was built, but was never operated, and was at length dismantled. A costly hotel was built, but never opened, and has lately been torn down. Much money was lost and much of the town survey has returned to agricultural use. Aside from a corn mill at the Locher flag station, the only present industrial concerns in the vicinity are two. One is the Glasgow Clay Products Company at Locher, one mile west of the town. This new corporation is the successor of the James River Cement Works, operated by the Lochers for sixty years. The new concern manufactures brick, tiling, and other clay and shale products, and they are of superior quality. The raw material for the new plant comes from the same deposits used by the cement works. The plant of the Virginia Western Power Company is just below the confluence of the two rivers at Balcony Falls. It is new and up-to-date, and its 150 miles of transmission wire reaches as far as Hinton, West Virginia. As in the case of boom towns started on a very ambitious scale, the buildings at Glasgow are considerably scattered. The population is probably under 500. The churches are Presbyterian and Episcopal, in addition to two Baptist churches of the colored people.

Willow Grove was the name of the first postoffice at Balcony Falls. It was kept in the fine brick mansion built by Peter A. Salling and used as a hotel as well as a private residence. It is now the property of George P. Locher.

XIX

VILLAGES, HAMLETS, AND SUMMER RESORTS

Brownsburg and Fairfield—Country Hamlets—Railroad Villages—Goshen—Raphine—
Wilson's Spring—Rockbridge Baths—Rockbridge Alum—Natural Bridge

An aggregation of homes can scarcely be termed a village unless it includes a schoolhouse, one or more churches, two or more business houses, a resident minister or physician, a repair shop, and in this modern age, a garage. When it falls much below this standard, it is a hamlet and not a village.

In speaking of towns and villages, the local history often attempts to make itself also a business directory. But any directory almost at once begins to grow out of date, and after a very few years it reads like ancient history. It is for this reason that we shall attempt no more than a general description of the small centers of population in Rockbridge.

A petition of 1793 asks the legal establishment of the town laid out on the lands of Robert Wardlaw and Samuel McChesney. Five years later another petition mentions the town as Brownsburg, and asks an extension of time for the improvement of lots. In 1835, Martin's *Gazetteer* speaks of the village as containing twenty dwellings, three stores, two shoe factories, three wheelwrights, two smith shops, two tailors, a tavern, a tanyard, a saddler, a cabinet-maker, a carpenter, a hatter, a gristmill, and a mercantile flour mill. Ten years later Howe speaks of it as having about thirty houses. That Brownsburg has scarcely increased in size, even in seventy years, is obviously because a village which in our present time is not a county seat and is not on a railroad, is very much circumscribed as a commercial and manufacturing center. It does well if it can hold its own in population. It may be a very comfortable place to live in from the viewpoint of the old resident, yet the dwellings are likely to assume a look of age, and the society is probably staid and conservative. In our day, however, such a village will probably have a bank and a garage, as well as at least one or two quite modern cottages, these contrasting somewhat oddly with the plain, old-fashioned dwellings. Brownsburg lies in the well populated valley which above is styled Moffatt's Creek and below is called Hays' Creek. It is consequently the trade center of a considerable district. In a former day it was noted for its high-grade private schools. The academy building yet stands on a rise of ground and recalls the fact that the village and neighborhood have figured to a regrettable extent in the matter of homicide. It was in ths old schoolhouse that Doctor Z. J. Walker killed Henry Miller, November 8, 1889, at the close of the examination of the former before a justice. Walker was speedily killed by

Miller's sons. During the confusion, Mrs. Walker received a fatal bullet said to have been meant for the husband, and one of the sons of Miller was severely wounded. The most conspicuous of the other occasions was when two young men were shot dead by a youth they were teasing.

Fairfield, like Brownsburg, lies on a well traveled automobile highway. It is of similar size, age, and general appearance, yet stands on somewhat higher ground. Its one street is the turnpike along which it stretches a considerable distance. In 1835 Martin says it had twenty dwellings, one union church, two taverns, one store, one tannery, two doctors, and 130 people. Howe mentions twenty-five homes in 1845, and it will thus appear that the village has long been stationary. Following the National Highway toward Lexington, we soon pass Cedar Grove, the mansion-home of the McDowells. A little beyond is their brick-walled family burial ground, perhaps the oldest place of interment in the county, but now very much neglected. Still farther on is a brick house dating from the Revolutionary period, and once the locally famous hostelry known as the Red House. It was in this territory that the first homes were reared in Rockbridge.

Six miles north of Fairfield, where the turnpike enters Augusta, is the hamlet of Midway, formerly known as Steele's Tavern. David Steele had a disfiguring gash on his face, and in his skull was a silver plate, both injuries being due to sword-cuts in the Revolution. In the winter season his guests sat around a blazing fire in the barroom. In the summer they sat on plain benches on the verandah. To the Virginian of his time, the bench in front of a tavern was a necessity. At the dinner table there was plenty of hot coffee, biscuit, and fried chicken. Near Midway, but on the road to Raphine, is pointed out the birthplace of Cyrus H. McCormick, and near by is the stone shop in which his trial machine was built.

West of North River is an absence of true villages. Collierstown is an extended section of well-peopled creek valley. Fancy Hill, though much associated with the names of private academies, is but a hamlet. Mechanicsville, two miles west of Buena Vista, is even less a hamlet than it used to be, and the same is true of Buffalo Forge. Springfield, very near the Botetourt line, was laid out into forty lots as far back as 1797.

Riverside, Midvale, and Vesuvius are small points on South River and the Norfolk and Western railroad, and lie five, ten, and seventeen miles, respectively, north of Buena Vista. Buffalo Forge Station is another little railroad place at the mouth of Buffalo.

The one town in the northwest of Rockbridge is Goshen, at the confluence of Mill Creek with the Great Calfpasture, and within sight of the upper entrance to Goshen Pass. As a point on the main line of the Chesapeake and Ohio railroad, thirty-three miles from Staunton and twenty-four from Clifton Forge, Goshen essayed a boom during the epidemic of 1890. The principal reminder of the visitation is Alleghany Inn, built in the Queen Anne style and perched on a hilltop. The little town lies in the valley below, astride the course of Mill Creek. In 1873 there was a proposal, never tried out, to make it the seat of government of a new county. Notwithstanding the iron deposits and the smelting interest in the vicinity, Goshen lost a third of its population between 1900 and 1910, and now has under 200 inhabitants. A mile southward and not in view from the station is the Victoria furnace, and just beyond is a cluster of small, red tenement houses.

The fourth town in Rockbridge is Raphine, which dates from the coming of the Valley Railroad in 1883. It was named by James E. A. Gibbs and laid out on his lands, although he did not expect more than a hamlet to grow up. The first passenger car to make a stop was attached to a work train, and left September 18th of that year to take his daughter on the beginning of her trip to Arkansas. The first store came the same year. An elevator was opened in 1886 and a bank in 1906. Presbyterian and Methodist chapels were built in 1889 and about 1890. The boom fever paid a visit to Raphine and held out the prospect of a shoe factory, as well as making the place a health resort because of its lithia waters. The town now has about 350 people. The high school has six rooms, five teachers, and more than 100 pupils. The commercial interests of the place include a bank, four stores, a fine garage, and an automobile agency, a wagonmaker, a blacksmith, and a firm handling grain, hay, and fertilizer.

A little more than a mile south of the town is a low stone house situated near a bold spring and built as a fortified house in the Indian times. It is still occupied as a dwelling house, but the windows have been widened. Many years ago mysterious occurrences held sway her for three months. It is related that the poker and fire shovel waltzed across the room, a trunk flew out from under a bed, hot stones fell upon and smashed dinner plates on the table, and hot pancakes fell in the meadow as manna did for the Hebrews in the wilderness of Sinai. A woman who was the mother of a child was the reputed witch. The only actual sufferer was a colored girl on whose person welts appeared as if from blows, and who screamed from what she believed to be pin-thrusts. The spell was broken when the girl was sent South. Such tales are seemingly absurd, yet in this instance are believed to rest on a basis of fact. The manifestations appear to be due to what is called *poltergeist* by the Germans.

The summer resorts of Rockbridge have enjoyed much renown. A contributor to the *Gazette* in 1874 writes in a very interesting manner of old times at Wilson's Spring at the lower entrance to Goshen Pass. The strong sulphur waters issue from a rocky islet in the midst of North River, and consequently the spring is temporarily overwhelmed in time of flood. By virtue of a land deed these waters have been made accessible to the public for all time. The first land patent was in the name of William Porter in 1755. The next owners were the Stricklers, whose name attached itself for a while to the spring and the pass through the mountain.

The writer we have referred to says that "most of our springs began business as deer licks. By accident or otherwise, a curative value was found, and then some one built a hut." Other people built huts, and in July and August there was a lively concourse of the rural yeomanry. Visitors put up their horses at Wilson's stable, fed the animals themselves, washed their hands and faces at the spring branch, and perhaps slept in the barn. They ate their lunches while sitting on benches on the front porch, and tossed their corncobs into the front yard. When harvest was over, visitors would come in a covered wagon drawn by four horses, and containing a bed or two, provisions, and sundry paraphernalia. All the family went, except that one or two of its members took turn in staying at home to attend to the farm chores and bring supplies to camp. The cooking in camp was done under an arbor covered with pine brush. Some slept in the wagon, some in the arbors. The visitors did little at dressing up. The old ladies assembled in some cabin and talked. The old men met in squads under the large oaks. The grown girls made parties, swung, went after huckleberries, and cast eyes at the young men. Children played in the sand or waded in the river.

The picnicking thus described as being true of eighty years ago continues in principle, even if not identical in manner. Wilson's Spring is still a popular resort for the people of the county. Guests from a distance board at the farmhouse. The much greater number of county people occupy a considerable cluster of very unpretentious cottages built by themselves. But on certain days many hundreds of people visit the spot, coming in the morning and returning at the close of the day.

Little more than a mile down North River is the hamlet of Rockbridge Baths, eleven miles from Lexington. It has grown up around a small hotel on a level lawn very near the stream. The magnesia waters are thermal, have a temperature of seventy-two degrees, and act favorably on the digestive organs. They are also useful in cutaneous affections. In the spring is a growth of algae that reproduces itself when cut back. A mass of this applied wet to a sore has a tendency to heal it. This resort was opened by the Jordans. The guests are city people of a class not much attracted to the sulphur spring above. The vicinage is not very broken, and is typically rural in appearance. It is pleasant and attractive.

Nine miles above Goshen, well toward the source of Bratton's Run, and in the narrow valley between Mill and North mountains, is Rockbridge Alum. Five springs, varying somewhat in their mineral strength, issue from the base of a slate bluff. The waters contain iodine, magnesia, sulphuric acid, and the sulphates of iron and alumina. The waters are purgative and diuretic, and they relieve congestion and inflammation. They are also tonic, and they improve the appetite. Their action on the skin is secondary, and like the waters at Rockbridge Baths, they are very serviceable in cutaneous affections, including indolent sores. Formerly something was done in bottling the waters and in separating the mineral ingredients by evaporation. In addition to the five alum springs there is one of chalybeate water.

The realty including these springs was first owned by John Dunlap and a Campbell, each man holding a half-interest. It was opened as a resort about 1834. The property is said to have been considered at one time as the most valuable single piece of real estate in the South, and was sold in 1853 for $150,000. The spot used to be frequented by throngs of people from all the former slave states, as many as 400 guests being registered in a single day. The various buildings of the hotel property form a quite extensive array, but are of a type that is now antiquated. The lawn, which lies in the creek valley, is fairly level. For several miles around there is almost no settlement. The scene is very nearly as primeval today as it was in the time of the pathfinder. A more healthful and restful spot can scarcely be found in America.

A much less important resort is Cold Sulphur Spring, about two miles southwest of Goshen. John Dunlap was also the owner of this spring, and he permitted visitors to camp around it without charge. All the buildings were burned some years ago.

The Funstaine was a resort on the old Major William Dunlap farm near Goshen. It was afterward owned by the Bells. A part of the old building is yet standing in the Bell orchard.

No later than the summer of 1887 there were 1,700 summer visitors in this county. But the present reign of the automobile has robbed the resorts of Rockbridge of much of their oldtime popularity. The mineral springs are comparatively remote from railway, are not reached by macadamized thoroughfares, and during the recent years their patronage has very much fallen off.

Natural Bridge is without mineral waters, but maintains itself by reason of the great natural curiosity within the bounds of the hotel property. It is also on the main automobile route through the Valley of Virginia, and is but two miles from Natural Bridge Station on the Norfolk and Western and Chesapeake and Ohio railroads. A macadamized highway connects the hotel with the station. The hotel itself is a quite pretentious structure, and is pleasantly shaded by trees. There is a swimming-pool at the head of the hollow, down which a footpath leads to the brink of Cedar Creek. At the railroad station the tracks of the Norfolk and Western and the Chesapeake and Ohio cross, and somewhat of a village has been called into existence.

XX

HIGHWAYS, WATERWAYS, AND RAILWAYS

Aboriginal Paths—Pioneer Roads—Road Improvement—Turnpikes—Canals—Railroads

The Rockbridge of 1737 was largely open country carpeted with grass. The area in prairie was a grazing ground for the herds of buffalo and deer. The former animal always went about in herds. When the grass was nibbled too close in one spot the herd moved to another place, taking a very straight course, and the well-defined path was used season after season.

At first blush it would look as though the buffalo was the first road-builder in Rockbridge. But the Indian was here before the buffalo. That shaggy beast was not a denizen of the forest. His original habitat was the vast grassy plain that sweeps eastward from the base of the Rocky Mountains. But until he possessed the mustang, which came to him by way of the Spaniard, the Indian found the Great Plains a very unsuitable land to occupy. The few red men who lived here dwelt only along the larger watercourses. To attract the buffalo eastward, and thus have a more abundant supply of food, the forest tribes of the Mississippi Basin created artificial prairies. The original small opening grew steadily larger in consequence of burning the grass at the end of each hunting season. In this way the buffalo was lured farther and farther eastward until he reached the Valley of Virginia. The moundbuilding tribes of the Ohio valley fell away from their agricultural habits and depended in an increased degree upon the bow and arrow. The Indian of the historic period was a wholesale burner of the woods, and Hugh Maxwell, a forestry expert, declares that in a few more centuries Virginia would have become either a meadow or a desert.

The Indian often used the buffalo trail, but his network of footpaths in the wilderness antedated the work of the buffalo. His own trail followed valleys and crossed ridges. If at all possible, a creek was crossed where the fording was easy. The larger paths were called war trails, and they were like trunk lines of railroad. They were worn rather deeply into the earth, and were often wide enough to admit a wagon. As a matter of course the path of the aborigine was adopted by the white pioneer. The latter saw no reason to cut out a new road where there was already a serviceable one. It is therefore easy to understand why the "Indian Road" of the early settlers soon became known as the "Pennsylvania Road," and why with some modification of route it developed into the Valley Turnpike and its connecting links to the southward. The section of this thoroughfare passing through Rockbridge was accepted as a public road by the court of Orange in the spring of 1745.

The Indians had other paths in this territory, one of which came from the Ohio and crossed North Mountain into the valley of Kerr's Creek. A section of still another path may be seen on Jump Mountain opposite Wilson's Spring. In occasional instances the present county roads undoubtedly follow some of the minor trails of the red man. The fact that it was nearly fifteen years after the beginning of settlement before a second public road was authorized, would seem to indicate that the settlers were quite well accommodated with the paths they found awaiting them.

In October, 1751, nine settlers on the lower Cowpasture petitioned for a road over North Mountain to the Borden grant. Next year there was a petition for a road "from Kennedy's mill to John Houston's, and from Houston's to the great road from Timber Grove to Woods Gap." The twenty names appended are chiefly or wholly those of settlers in the north of the Borden land. About this time, twenty-one men living toward the west of the present county ask for a road from Joseph Long's mill to James Young's mill, and to William Hall's on North River, and into the great road on James Thompson's plantation. They explain that it was their course "to meeting, mill, and market." In 1753 a road was ordered from Campbell's schoolhouse to the Renick road. The twenty-five tithables mentioned therewith were in the lower part of the present county, or within the present Botetourt line.

The first road precincts were necessarily few and large, and all that the small working force could accomplish was to open a rough and ready path capable of admitting a wagon. When Botetourt began local government in 1770, there were only thirty-nine road precincts in the long distance from Kerr's Creek to the Tennessee line. But in 1859 the road precincts within Rockbridge were 102.

The old roads were "straight, steep, narrow, and rocky." An undated petition, probably of near the year 1880, says that the mountain roads were unpleasant, and for carriages dangerous, because much obstructed by rocks, for the removal of which the law made no provision. Nevertheless, the public opinion of the colonial age required that the public highways be kept up to a certain standard. Many a road overseer was presented by the grand jury for failing to keep his track in order, or for not putting up "indexes" at the forks as required by law. An acting justice was ineligible as a commissioner of roads.

Until just after 1840, the roads were worked by compulsory labor. The road levy, which now became law, seems to have caused considerable dissatisfaction. In 1843 the surveyor was allowed $1.00 a day, the common laborer fifty cents. A man with a plow, two horses, and a driver was paid $1.50. In 1845 the rates were advanced to $1.25 for the surveyor, and seventy-five cents for the workman. For cart, horse, and driver, the allowance was $1.25. In 1861 the levy was $1.50 per capita, or two days in labor.

According to a petition of 1802 there were several forges west of the Blue Ridge, and yet all wagons had to go to Rockfish Gap in order to cross the mountain. From this and other authorities, we glean some idea of the cost of travel a century ago. The petition just named says it took twelve to fifteen days for a wagon to make a roundtrip to the markets east of the South Mountain. About thirteen barrels of flour made a load for four horses, and it usually sold at $5.00 a barrel. Merchandise to the amount of 5,000 to 6,000 pounds was hauled back at a charge of $1.30 per hundredweight. A load of flour was often retailed before coming to Richmond. The teamsters had regular stands where feed was left to be used on the return. In 1806 William Wilson spent $21.40 in a round-trip to Richmond. T. Wayt turned in a bill of $56.50 for an absence of thirteen days, while taking a patient to the hospital for the insane at Williamsburg. Wayt went with a guard and an impressed horse. When J. D. Davidson set out from Eagle Tavern in Lexington, in 1836, he paid $50.00 in stage fares before he reached the Ohio at the mouth of the Guyandotte. Thence, to New Orleans, his steamboat fare was $120.00. When this book was begun, a person could journey from Goshen to the Ohio river for about $4.90, and in less than a tenth of the time that Davidson had to use. And furthermore, the $4.90 was easier to get hold of than it was eighty years earlier. Even in 1848, which was before the iron horse had cut any figure west of the Alleghanies, it took the family of Cyrus H. McCormick twelve days to go to Chicago, then a city of 20,000 people.

As for postal rates, six cents would not carry a letter even thirty miles in 1838. If the distance were from thirty to eighty miles, the postage was ten cents; if it exceeded 400 miles, the charge was twenty-five cents.

Between the wars of 1812 and 1861 there was great interest in turnpike roads. The railroad was unknown in America until 1829, and not until 1848 did it reach the Alleghanies at any point. The country was vast, and unless good wagon roads were to be had, the interior districts were doomed to be most seriously handicapped. But the United States was poor as well as vast, and "metaled" roads, such as were being extended over populous Europe, were seldom possible. Most of the turnpikes of that period were simply well-graded "dirt roads." A petition of 1836 tells us that what was styled a piked road cost $784 a mile, or forty-four and one-half cents a yard. Several of the longer lines were usually built by private companies. The funds were raised by subscription or by lottery, and the stockholders looked to the tollgate for their dividends. But the charter for a turnpike was not always followed by a visible highway. There were paper turnpikes in those days, just as there were paper railroads at a later time. One of these was chartered in 1853. It was to take form as a macadamized way from Collierstown to the mouth of North River.

The Lexington and Covington Turnpike Company was incorporated in 1829 with an authorized capital of $20,000, a sum which today would scarcely make a respectable beginning. The width was to be sixteen feet on North Mountain, and twenty feet elsewhere, but in 1851 there was permission to reduce the width to eighteen feet if livestock were exempted from toll. The route was surveyed by Claude Crozet, and the road was completed in August, 1832. About the same time the pike from Lexington to Millboro was built. In 1830 a lottery was authorized for the raising of $30,000 for a road from Lexington to New Glasgow in Amherst. Five years later a survey was ordered for a road from Lexington to Richmond by way of White's Gap. The capital was placed at $75,000, and the tollgates were to be fifteen miles apart. A petition of 1847 asks for a macadamized road between Staunton and Buchanan. The road along the base of College Hill from Lexington to North River was piked with stone as early as 1820. Until the railroad appeared, this seems to have been about the only piece of road within the county that was actually macadamized.

While the furor for planked roads held possession of Virginia, a highway of this description appeared in the southeast of Rockbridge. The road in question is still sometimes known as the "Plank Road," but it is hardly necessary to add that the planking soon rotted away.

It appears to have been somewhat earlier than 1820 that fifty-four petitioners ask the amendment of a recent law, so as to exempt them from working the highways outside the limits of Lexington, except with respect to the ford in North River. They also ask that it be made unlawful to gallop horses in the streets of the town. They announce that they would rather pay in due proportion for the repair of the streets than be called upon to work them.

It was a long while before the fords and ferries in the larger streams were superseded by bridges. In 1834 Colonel John Jordan contracted to bridge North River near his mill at a cost not to exceed $1,500. The bridge was to have two passage-ways. Yet it was twenty-five years earlier that Jordan and his partner, John Morehead, asked leave to put in a toll-bridge near their new flouring mill.

A century ago the stage was what the rail-car and the motor-car are now. The early carriages had an attachment underneath that was in the form of a hayfork. It could be let down to serve as a brake. Stages of an improvised type appeared about 1825. By 1820 a stage came to Lexington three times a week. In 1836 there were stages twice a week on the Lexington and Covington pike. The tollgates east of the Alleghany line were at Armentrout's, at the foot of North Mountain, and at Hugh Mackey's, midway between Lexington and Armentrout's. The species of gentleman known in the Old West as the "road agent" sometimes paid his respects to a stage, and the merchant who went to the city to buy goods carried a pistol.

The waterway has always been a cheap means of transportation. Attention was early directed to the outlet afforded by the James and North rivers. A petition of 1810 states that North River has been cleared out, and it asks that the county court be given authority to levy not more than $200 a year to keep the channel open. An Act of 1811 gave the necessary authority, but roused the wrath of certain of the inhabitants. They say the benefit was not general, and declare many of the people knew nothing of the measure until it became law.

Sluice navigation from Richmond to Balcony Falls was open in 1816, and to Buchanan in 1827, but the James River and Kanawha Canal, incorporated in 1831, did not reach Balcony Falls until about 1850, nor Buchanan until 1851. During the intervening third of a century the batteau was used in moving produce from Rockbridge to Tidewater. This craft was a narrow boat about ninety feet long, and it was propelled by poles. In the center was a canvas awning eight to ten feet long. Three negroes made a crew. As cargo, seventy-five barrels of flour could be taken on. If tobacco were the load, the hogsheads—seven to ten in number—lay lengthwise with the boat. It was comparatively easy to go down stream, but since it was difficult to "shove back," after getting above the smooth waters in the lower James, the batteau was sometimes disposed of at Richmond. The nightmare of the voyage was Balcony Falls. In this four-mile pass the James falls some 200 feet, and the channel is beset with rocks. The few steersmen who could put a craft through "Bal-co-ny" were in much demand at high wages, yet in time of high water not a few of the batteaux were broken on the rocks. Pig iron, of which from five to eight tons made a cargo, was recovered in some quantity in after years, at times when the water in the pass was very low and clear. During the reign of the batteau, boat building was quite a business at several places in the county. The leading boat captains were John Hamilton, Samuel McCorkle, and Elisha Paxton. It was during this period that Cedar Grove, as the head of navigation on North River, was almost the metropolis of Rockbridge. After the coming of the canal it fell into utter decay.

By a majority of 217 in a total vote of 615, this county subscribed $15,000 to the North River Navigation Company in an election held June 1, 1850. A further subscription of $29,950 was carried August 23, 1851, 687 citizens voting for it and 385 against it. At the close of the war of 1861 the interest on the principal of $26,115.44 amounted to $2,856.75.

From Glasgow to Lexington the canal was built in sections, arriving at East Lexington in 1852. As each section was opened to travel, a warehouse was built. The first one above Balcony Falls was at Miller's, half way to Buena Vista. Another was at Thompson's, several miles farther on, and a third was at the mouth of South River. Until a warehouse ceased to be a terminal it was a very important place. Goods were wagoned on to Lexington and more remote points in the county. The canal boat would stop anywhere to take on or put off freight. The crew would even help a farmer to thresh, so as to secure the moving of his wheat. Freight was paid to the owner of the boat, and a toll to the canal company. In 1855 more than 7,000 tons went down the canal. This included 18,879 barrels of flour, 7,500 bushels of wheat, and 2,226 tons of pig and bar iron. In 1860 the freight to Richmond on a barrel of flour was sixty cents. In 1853 there went down 150,000 bushels of corn and 60,000 gallons of whiskey.

In all, there were six canal dams on the two rivers. There were five locks on the James, within the limits of this county, and fifteen on North River.

The first packet boat to reach Lexington arrived November 15, 1860.

These passenger conveyances made three trips a week. The packet was drawn by three horses, a shift being made every twelve miles. The speed of four miles an hour was much more rapid than that of the freight boat.

The canal continued in use until put out of business by the railroads soon after 1880. As late as May, 1878, it was repaired by convict labor. In 1876 iron and whiskey were still the chief items of export. Ruined dams, grass-grown locks, and empty sections of canal bed remain as landmarks of a vanished era.

Almost thirty years before the railway locomotive entered Rockbridge, the Virginia and Tennessee—now the Norfolk and Western—had passed to the southward, and the Virginia Central—now the Chesapeake and Ohio—had come to Staunton. In 1860 a company was chartered to build a line from Goshen to Rockbridge Alum. But it was not until after the war of 1861 that a serious effort was made to bring a railroad to Lexington.

A subscription of $100,000 was voted to the Valley Railroad in November, 1866. This was followed by one of $300,000 in December, 1868, and by one of $125,000 in July, 1871. To the third subscription Lexington added $30,000, making a grand total of $555,000. A contract for building the railroad from Staunton to Salem was let in May, 1873. A financial crash came the same year and nearly paralyzed industrial activity all over the United States. It was ten more years before the Valley Railroad reached the county seat of Rockbridge. The sum of $1,250,000 was spent on the stretch of thirty-six miles between Staunton and Lexington, and $800,000 was sprinkled over the eighty-six miles between Lexington and Salem. The cuts, fills, and abutments that are scattered between these two points are mute witnesses to a waste of good money. To Rockbridge the result was doubly unfortunate. The county had only a partial return for its investment. Instead of the central portion being crossed by an important track, it is merely entered by the now isolated and unimportant Valley section of the Baltimore and Ohio. The possibility of its completion was fondly discussed in the county papers as late as 1906.

A very important freight-carrying branch of the Chesapeake and Ohio system was built between Clifton Forge and Richmond under the name of the Richmond and Alleghany Railroad. The Lexington extension was completed October 14, 1881, the main line along the James a month earlier. In the same year the Shenandoah Valley Railroad was built through the eastern side of the county. Two years later, as we have seen, the Valley Railroad finally came to Lexington. The Richmond and Alleghany line was at length acquired by the Chesapeake and Ohio Company, and the Shenandoah Valley by the Norfolk and Western. During the period while all the railways entering Rockbridge were dominated by the Pennsylvania system, the Lexington extension of the Chesapeake and Ohio was made to connect with the Norfolk and Western track at Glasgow. The ten mile section between Balcony Falls and Lock Laird was then dismantled. From the very first all the trains entering the county seat used one track between that point and East Lexington. The main line of the Chesapeake and Ohio had crossed the northern corner of Rockbridge as early as 1856.

The total mileage of the Chesapeake and Ohio within this county is 30.36 miles, and it is assessed at $657,208.70. The Norfolk and Western mileage is 36.45 miles, and its assessment, $620,892. The Baltimore and Ohio mileage is 17.38 miles, and it is assessed at $154,950. Consequently, there are 84.19 miles of railway in Rockbridge with an assessed value of $1,433,050.70. This aggregate does not include about eighteen miles of lumber railway up Irish Creek to the county line. This spur will be in use some years, and if the tin ores in that valley are successfully developed it may become permanent. There was formerly a railroad track up Bratton's Run to Rockbridge Alum, thus realizing for a while the project of 1860.

When the year 1918 began, the passenger fare of two and one-half cents a mile on the Norfolk and Western and the Chesapeake and Ohio lines, and three cents on the Valley line was a striking reduction from the five cent rate charged in 1881.

XXI

INDUSTRIAL INTERESTS

ROCKBRIDGE AGRICULTURE—MANUFACTURES—MILLS—THE IRON INDUSTRY—TIN MINE

Of pioneer agriculture something has already been said. It was crude and laborious, and was carried on for a century in almost entire ignorance of labor-saving machinery. The conservation of soil fertility was little appreciated. Was there not still a large amount of uncleared ground? And was there not a well-nigh boundless wilderness of virgin soil in the direction of the setting sun? So long as considerations like these seemed a sufficient answer, there was little incentive toward intensive farming.

But the methods in use were not entirely wasteful. Before and during the Revolution a great deal of hemp was grown, and this crop requires good soil. After Kentucky was comfortably open to settlement, hemp culture disappeared from Virginia, and migrated to the Bluegrass State and to Missouri. Yet with this drain on the virgin fertility, Rockbridge has continued to produce a very considerable surplus of wheat, wool, and dairy products, and an ample amount of corn and hay. In 1850 it was growing twice as much wheat as was needed at home, and its cornfields yielded twenty-three bushels per capita. It was not until the coming of the canal and afterward the railroad that this county had a convenient access to the markets of the outside world.

Flax growing disappeared with the arrival of the great city factory, and is now but a fast fading recollection. The fiber crops have become extinct, yet the other staples remain substantially the same as they always were. They comprise corn, wheat, hay, and oats, and small amounts of rye, buckwheat, and barley. The chief innovation is the growing of apples on a commercial scale. For this purpose the high-lying and relatively thin lands are well suited.

The farms of the colonial period were quite well stocked with domestic animals, which, however, were not so large as the improved breeds of the present day. Yet the pioneers were not indifferent to good stock. In 1752 James Fulton mentions a pacing mare purchased in New England.

By 1877 a very perceptible improvement in farming methods was noted. Yet as early as 1839, we hear of the Rockbridge Agricultural Society, which under the style of the Rockbridge Agricultural and Mechanical Society, was still in existence in 1860. In the year last named an agricultural department was appearing regularly in the *Gazette*. A two pound tomato in 1857—before improved varieties had been thought of—and a turnip of four and one-half pounds indicate that the antebellum tillage was not to be despised.

In 1910 the production of corn and the cereals was about 1,000,000 bushels, grown on one-eighth of the county's area. The yield of corn was at the rate of almost thirty bushels to the acre, which is distinctly above the average for the United States in a series of years. The showing with respect to potatoes and the cereals was not quite so favorable. Yet yields of wheat of thirty to thirty-six bushels to the acre are sometimes obtained, and in 1917 the value of the wheat threshed from twelve acres near Raphine was $1,000. In the Boys' Corn Club contest of 1911, the prize winner grew 104½ bushels on one acre, demonstrating the possibilities that lie in thorough and well-directed work. But the unsightly gullies and the galled spots seen on occasional slopes are evidence to a former neglect.

Despite the great inroads into the uncleared surface, both for farming and the marketing of lumber and other forest products, there is still a large wooded area in Rockbrdge. In the Blue Ridge an extensive acreage has been taken over by the National government as a forest reserve.

Rockbridge has been little conspicuous as a manufacturing district. What was true of the early period was true of Appalachian America in general. The farm home was more or less a workshop. There were hatters as well as tailors and shoemakers; the blacksmith was a small iron-worker; the wheelwright made wagons as well as repaired them; the cabinet-maker made tables, bureaus, and bedsteads. But the great factory, aided by rapid transit, has driven the home mechanic to a dependence on repair service. In 1850, the census could report only $22,018 as the value of home manufactures.

Nevertheless, this page of the industrial chapter was not a blank one. The first McCormick reapers were made near Midway. This county was the pioneer in building iron plows to supersede those with the wooden mouldboard. Such a one, known as the Lexington plow, was being manufactured at Riverside in 1832. Two years later was chartered the Rockbridge Manufacturing Company with a minimum capital of $10,000 and a maximum of $100,000. It was to build on North River, on the lands of John Jordan and the heirs of John Morehead a mill for cotton, woolen, and hemp goods. In 1856 there is mention of the Rockbridge Woolen Factory. The wool clip of this county is placed at 30,469 pounds in the census of 1850.

The gristmill came early and has been well represented ever since. The first in the county was that of John Hays. It was built about 1740, and must have been a specimen of the primitive affair known as the tubmill. But Hays had a fulling mill by 1751, and probably earlier. It was perhaps the same fulling mill which was carried on at a somewhat later date by Joseph Kennedy. Petitions for leave to build gristmills were sent in to the county court in 1747 by Henry Gay, James Allison, John Hodge, and John Edmondson. David Moore, Joseph

Long, and James Young had mills in 1751. Young's mill was at the mouth of Kerr's Creek. The first we hear of on the lower Buffalo was that of Thomas Paxton, probably built a little earlier than the Revolution. By 1820, grist and saw mills had become rather numerous. Outside of South River and Walker's Creek districts—from neither of which we have any report—there are now eleven flouring mills and two other mills that grind corn.

When we come to the iron industry there is a larger story to tell. The smelting of iron began west of the Blue Ridge in 1760, and the beginning seems to have been in Rockbridge. By 1779 we know that Daniel Dougherty was operating a forge near the mouth of Irish Creek. It is said that cannonballs made here were fired at the British in Yorktown in 1781. In 1799, there is mention of the forges of McCluer and Nicholas Vanstavern. The former seems to have been near the site of Buena Vista.

In 1835 Martin speaks of the Bath Iron Works as making thirty tons of pig a week. This furnace employed sixty-five workmen and had a dependent population of 150. A petition of 1850 speaks of seven furnaces on or near North River with a capacity of 7,000 tons of metal a year. To argue the importance of river improvement, the petition says it was costing $2.00 a ton to haul iron from Lexington to Balcony Falls, and $5.50 to have it sent thence to Richmond. With navigation all the way, it was believed the cost of freight could be reduced one-half. In 1853 there were four furnaces, with a capital of $90,000 and a yearly output of 4,000 tons of pig metal; three forges, with a capital of $30,000 and an output of 500 tons; and two foundries making 400 tons of castings.

In the old days of the iron industry, the metal was shipped as pig and sold at about $20.00 a ton. The workmen were mostly slaves from east of the Blue Ridge, hired from their masters for $60.00 to $80.00 a year. Merchants traded for a good deal of the metal and hired farmers during their slack season to wagon it to Scottsville. The round trip consumed a week. On the return the wagons brought goods for the Rockbridge stores. The coming of the canal facilitated the marketing of iron, but at the present moment the iron industry in this county is carried on only at Buena Vista and Goshen. From the latter point a railway was built up the valley of Bratton's Run to reach the deposits of ore in the bordering mountains. This line has been dismantled, yet is likely to be rebuilt.

The Bath furnace stood at the south end of Little Goshen Pass, a short distance above the mouth of the Little Calfpasture. A mile below was a foundry, and near Rockbridge Baths was still another. A third foundry, last known as Weaver's, stood on the Buffalo, a mile above the mouth of the stream. In its palmy days Buffalo Forge was a busy industrial place. The Buena Vista furnace stood near the town of that name. The Vesuvius furnace was twelve miles above on South River. Mount Hope, built about 1850, was on Bratton's Run near Rockbridge Alum. A mile from Mount Hope was the California furnace. The Rockbridge Foundry was on the south side of Irish Creek, a half mile above its mouth. In 1856 it was operated by T. B. Taylor and T. P. McDowell.

The furnaces of Rockbridge were blast furnaces and used charcoal. Little was then known of the coal deposits west of the Alleghany, and they were practically inaccessible. Some day the iron industry will assume greater proportions than ever in this county, but we cannot expect this to happen so long as the sand-like ores of Lake Superior, which may be scooped up with a steam shovel, are sufficient for the needs of the country.

In the files of the *Richmond Times-Dispatch* is the following paragraph relating to the antebellum iron industry of this county:

As the tourist rides through the mountains, he will see close to some roaring torrent the ruins of old stone blast furnaces overgrown with ivy and bright with the fiery-tinted trumpet flower, gentle and dainty reminders of the ruddy glare of other days, of the sparks and flames from these forgotten shrines of Vulcan. The famous Jordan family, iron kings of the antebellum days, freighted their product down the James to the foundries and machine shops of Richmond. After the Union blockade of Southern ports, the Confederacy found almost its entire supply of iron in the Virginia mountains.

Well up the valley of Irish Creek is what is known as the tin mine. Here is a deposit of tin ore, which has been traced some distance along the axis of the Blue Ridge. Machinery was put in place some time ago, but shipping facilities proved to be too inconvenient, and the mine has never yet come into practical operation. However, it has lately come under the control of some Boston capitalists, and may be rehabilitated. There are methods of handling the ore which were unknown at the first attempt to exploit the deposits. The lack of this knowledge was a great obstacle to success.

XXII

CHURCHES OF ROCKBRIDGE

Presbyterianism in Rockbridge—New Providence—Timber Ridge—Other Early Meeting Houses—The Methodist Church—The Baptist Church—The Episcopal Church—Rural Churches

Ever since the Protestant Reformation took root in Scotland, the Presbyterian has been the national church of that country. The pioneers of Rockbridge were staunch upholders of this faith, and brought its creed with them. The first regular Presbyterian sermon in Augusta was preached in 1738 in the house of John Lewis near Staunton. The minister was James Anderson.

When American independence was declared, the Presbyterians and the sects allied to them in religious belief constituted the strongest religious force in the land. The New England section was overwhelmingly Congregationalist. The Dutch Reformed and the German Reformed churches were conspicuous in the Middle Colonies. Presbyterianism was heavily represented wherever the Ulsterman had gone. All these sects were at one in creed and differed only in methods of church government. It was mainly because of the democratic spirit pervading this group of churches that the War for Independence was successful. The Presbyterian minister was a leader of opinion. His church would not ordain a man who could not teach, and from its clergy it exacted a high order of educational attainment.

Before the Revolution, according to the Reverend Samuel Houston, the people of New Providence kept Sunday with great strictness. Howe adds that the gay amusements of Tuckahoe Virginia were here unknown. There was little social intercourse outside of the churchyard. But the influence of camp life during the Revolution was very demoralizing, and the change for the worse thus set in motion was not counteracted by certain of the new families that settled in Rockbridge. Yet there were no revivals in the Valley of Virginia until the fall of 1788, and they were not well thought of by the Ulster-Americans. However, there was a schism among the Presbyterians in the colonial period. The conservative wing was known as the "Old Side," and the progressive as the "New Side," or "New Lights." The Rockbridge congregations allied themselves with the progressives. These differed with the Old Side in approving the outdoor, unconventional, and revivalistic preaching of George Whitefield, who made a tour of the colonies in 1739-41. The breach is said to have been healed in 1758, yet something of the rift remained.

The perfervid, emotional campmeeting oratory of a century ago sometimes caused that nervous derangement in the hearer which was known as the "jerks." Ann Henderson was seized with this manifestation in Timber Ridge meeting house, Sunday, August 4, 1805. Major Samuel Houston told her it would not do to dance during the preaching, and he took her outside. He was assisted by James Decker and resisted by Daniel Lyle. Houston was presented for disturbing public worship, but his course was upheld by the pastor and the congregation generally.

For sixteen years there was no settled minister in Rockbridge, although the immigrants were visited by Alexander McDowell and others. Three ministers, McDowell, Alexander Craighead, and William Dean, acquired land in the Borden grant or on the South River. Craighead lived on the Cowpasture a little below Millboro Springs, and Dean on Brandywine Creek in Pennsylvania. In 1746 John Blair effected church organization at New Providence, Timber Ridge, Monmouth, and Falling Springs. But for seven years longer there was no resident minister at any of these places.

The log meeting houses at New Providence, Timber Ridge, and Falling Springs were accepted as houses of worship by the court of Augusta, May 20, 1748. And as the order-book informs us that the one at Timber Ridge was in place in February of the same year, it could scarcely have been built later than in the fall of 1747. The statement we have seen that it was built in 1742 is very doubtful. The log Timber Ridge church had high pulpit, split-log seats, and earth floor. The pioneer church in this county was always a log structure. It was usually succeeded by a stone building, and then by a brick.

There seems to be some fogginess as to how New Providence came by its name. Archibald Alexander said his grandfather worshipped at a Providence church near the site of Morristown, New Jersey. Some families of that congregation came to "New Virginia," built a New Providence, and when it had become inconveniently small, another New Providence was put up on Timber Ridge. On the other hand, the name Providence is said to have been adopted at the suggestion of John Houston, because of the harmonious spirit shown by the people in selecting a site. Yet the name New Providence is used in the call refused by Mr. Byram in 1748. Another call was at once presented to William Dean, but he died the same year. In 1753 the call extended to John Brown by 114 attendants at New Providence and Timber Ridge was accepted.

The first home of the New Providence congregation stood close to the log academy of Robert Alexander. The location was at length deemed unsatisfactory, and after some discord it was decided to move into the valley of Hays Creek. About 1789 some of the members took offense at the singing of the hymns by Isaac Watts, and built a stone meeting house on the old site, which became known as Old Providence. It lies a mile beyond the Rockbridge boundary.

For a good will consideration, Joseph Kennedy conveyed three acres and 118 rods of ground to the trustees of New Providence meeting house. The deed is dated August 21, 1754, and says the building is already under way. It was not then known that sand for the mortar could be found any nearer than South River. A supply was brought from that watercourse in sack-loads, each horse in the train carrying a girl as well as a sack. An armed escort was in attendance. A sycamore seed brought from the river took root in the sand-pile, and grew into a tree that is yet standing. Nails and glass came by packsaddle from Philadelphia, and were paid for with butter carried to market in the same way. But for want of means, the meeting house was not finished for about seventeen years, and swallows made nests inside. In 1771, Brice Hanna, who had contracted to complete the building, failed and went to parts unknown. The brick structure which now serves the congregation dates from 1859, and is the fifth in the series. Its immediate predecessor, also of brick, was erected in 1812.

John Brown was pastor forty-five years. His first elders were John Houston, Samuel Houston, James Wilson, Andrew Steele, and John Robinson. The salary promised Mr. Brown was 120 pounds, or $400. The most liberal giver at the start was Andrew Steele, who contributed $7.22. John Bowyer subscribed two pounds. The minimum was five shillings, or eighty-three cents. John Brown went to Kentucky and was very soon succeeded by Samuel Brown. The third pastorate was that of James Morrison, who was here from 1819 to 1857. E. D. Junkin, was pastor from 1860 to 1871, C. R. Vaughn from 1871 to 1881, and G. A. Wilson from 1890 to 1908. The wife of Samuel Brown was Mary Moore, whose second daughter wedded James Morrison, the next pastor. The wife of H. W. McLaughlin, pastor since 1909, is a later descendant of Mary Moore Brown, whose grave in the extensive and well-kept churchyard is often inquired for by visitors.

A Sunday school was organized at New Providence in 1830, the first superintendent being James, a son of Samuel Brown. The revival of June, 1834, caused the membership to rise to 591. It was here that the Synod of Virginia was organized in 1788, and the centennial of this event was observed in October, 1888.

Until suspended in 1917, on war considerations, there had for some twenty years been an annual chrysanthemum exhibit at New Providence. The money derived from a small admission fee and from suppers and other adjuncts was used in the expenses of the church. The fine floral displays became widely known, and drew crowds of people from within a radius of more than twenty miles. A further attraction was the opportunity for social intercourse.

It is worthy of mention that the New Providence built at McAfee Station, Kentucky, in the dawn of Kentucky settlement, and the New Providence of Blount county, Tennessee, were in reality daughter churches of the New Providence of Rockbridge. Another New Providence arose in the west of North Carolina.

The log Timber Ridge meeting house stood some distance north of the present church. The spot is on rising ground, about 100 yards east of the nine-mile post on the turnpike, and near a log schoolhouse no longer in use. Nearby is an early graveyard, now almost indistinguishable. The logs of the pioneer church were built into the dwelling house of M. H. Crist, which was standing until after 1906. The stone church was built in 1756 by the efforts of about fifty families. There was a puncheon floor, high-backed pews with very narrow seats, and stone stairways to the gallery. The clerk stood at a desk in front of the pulpit and led the singing, the lines being given out in couplets or by verses. As in other houses of worship of the pioneer day, there was a sounding-board above the pulpit, which was placed much higher than in the present custom. With considerable enlargement and modernizing, the old stone church is still a part of the one now in use.

The Hanover Presbytery met at Timber Ridge in 1784 and licensed John Blair, pastor of the first organized Presbyterian church in Richmond. Two years later was held the first session of Lexington Presbytery, attended by twelve ministers. The first elders of this church were Archibald Alexander, John Davidson, Daniel Lyle, William McClung, Alexander McClure, and John McKay. The first pastor was John Brown, who resigned in 1767. William Graham was pastor from 1776 to 1785, Daniel Blair from 1802 to 1814, Henry Ruffner from 1819 to 1831. The later pastorates number fourteen.

Hall's Meeting House in the "Forks of the James" stood an hour's walk west of Lexington. A deed for the ground was given in 1754. William Dean was called in 1748, but there was no regular pastor until William Graham came in 1776. During this long interval there was occasional preaching by John Craig, John Brown, and others. Graham also preached at John McKee's, where Doctor Archibald Alexander gave his first exhortation in 1790. The meeting house is supposed to have been built about 1748, and is said to have been a large building in a beautiful grove. The second was of stone, appeared in 1789, and was given the name of New Monmouth. It was torn down in 1902, at which time the locust frame and walnut facings were still sound. The present New Monmouth, in the valley of Kerr's Creek, is the successor of a brick structure completed in 1853.

Doctor John Leyburn has left us an account of the blue limestone Monmouth, which in his boyhood stood in a dense grove of oak. A steep outside stairway led to the gallery. Above the large pulpit was a sounding-board. The pews were very high, and therefore unpopular with the young people. To accentuate this peculiarity, the aisles were so low that only the heads and shoulders of standing people could be seen. Some came from Lexington, either afoot or mounted, and carried dinner baskets. They entered the meeting house two abreast. Outside, the people stood in groups or sat on stones or rude benches. The dinner baskets were deposited in the session house. Mothers who could not leave their babies at home remained outside and listened. At communion time, in spring and fall, religion was a very prominent theme of conversation.

In 1788 the Presbyterians of Lexington secured one-fourth of William Graham's time, thirty-six members subscribing $71.75. The first meetings were in a grove on East Washington Street. In 1792 a tent was used. A meeting house, begun 1797, was not completed until 1802, and was enlarged in 1819, when the membership was ninety-four. The Forty-Third General Association of the Southern Presbyterian Church was held in Lexington, May 21, 1903.

Falling Springs, in the valley of Poague's Run, one of the best farming districts in Rockbridge, is a reminder of the olden time. The brick church lies on the border of an extensive burial ground, in which the lettering on some of the headstones is quite ancient. No historical sketch of this organization has come to our hand.

Ben Salem, southeast from Lexington, arose in 1834, or according to another account, not until 1846. The present church was built in 1884.

The organization at Bethesda was effected at Wilson's Spring in 1821 with fourteen members. The first church was dedicated in 1843, the second and present one in 1876. The first regular pastor was W. W. Trimble, who served from 1853 to 1865. There were 209 members when W. W. McElwee closed his long pastorate in 1901. The McElwee Memorial Chapel on Oak Hill was dedicated in 1905.

Oxford is not within the Borden Tract, as is sometimes affirmed. The Henry Borden who is associated with its history was a stonemason living on Collier's Creek. There seems to be no evidence that he was related to Benjamin Borden, the patentee. An "eight-cornered" meeting house is said to have been built as early as 1763. A limestone structure followed in 1811, and the present brick church was completed in 1867. The first minister was James Power, who declined a call and returned to Pennsylvania in 1773. Samuel Houston, Daniel Blain, and Andrew Davidson preached here from 1794 to 1843, Mr. Davidson's long term beginning 1803. Altogether, this church has had twenty pastorates. There are no continuous records prior to 1843.

A church at Collierstown was built in 1837 and was followed by a brick building completed in 1856.

The wills recorded in this county throw some light on the philanthropic and missionary spirit among the early people. John Mathews, Sr., left $10.00 in

New Providence Church
In the cemetery adjoining is buried Mary Moore, the "Captive of Abb's Valley"

"Willow Grove," the Home of G. P. Locker, Glasgow, Va.
One of the most up-to-date country homes in Virginia

1757 to the poor of the parish of Augusta. Hugh Weir in 1821 left $150.00 to the American Board of Foreign Missions to educate a Hindoo boy, who was to bear his name after baptism. Cynthia Cloyd in 1830 gave to foreign missions and other church work $500.00 in money and five shares of stock in the Bank of the Valley.

A church census taken in Lexington a few years since gave the following result: Presbyterians, 899; Methodists, 713; Baptists, 350; Episcopalians, 198; Roman Catholics, forty-two; Associate Reformed Presbyterians, twenty-eight; Lutherans, twenty-three; Mormons, eighteen; Jews, sixteen; other denominations, ten; no preference, thirty; total, 2,327. Perhaps the tally for the Presbyterians and the Methodists at the county seat fairly indicates their proportions for the county in general. With respect to the Baptists and Episcopalians, it would appear to exceed the proportion. At all events, a vast majority of the church members of this county are of the four communions above named.

Methodism began as a society within the Church of England, and for the upbuilding of a higher type of religious character than was commonly found in the England of the eighteenth century. When the war of the Revolution came on, the Methodists of America were as yet almost insignificant in point of number. Their leaders took the unwise course of urging them not to uphold American independence, and in this way a reproach little deserved was cast upon the society. American Methodism took its stand as an independent church in 1784. To its flexible itinerant system and its adaptability to frontier conditions are due its wonderful progress.

The first Methodists to preach in the Valley of Virginia were John Haggerty and Richard Owen, who came about 1770. They do not seem to have penetrated as far as Rockbridge, and we have no definite mention of a Methodist preacher of any sort until 1793, when William Craven, a stonemason and also a local preacher, came from Rockingham to build the stone academy on Mulberry Hill. But in the *Gazette for* 1873 we are told that John Burgess and his large family were the first Methodists in Lexington. They came in 1823, and the first Methodist sermon at the county seat was preached in the Burgess home. A plain frame church soon appeared, and Presbyterians and others assisted in building it. About this time John Sheltman and his bevy of rosy-cheeked daughters came from Rockingham. The first meeting house proving too small, a brick building—later occupied by colored Methodists—was built in the south side of the town. A larger one was then put up on Jefferson Street. The cornerstone of the present church was laid August 21, 1890. The congregation in Lexington was at first a part of a circuit. It is the mother church of Methodism in Rockbridge. Previous to the war of 1861, the Methodist Church was in some disfavor in this county because of its anti-slavery leaning. The formation of the Methodist

Episcopal Church South was little felt in Rockbridge for some time, and there is still a congregation of the Methodist Episcopal Church in Buffalo District. Otherwise, the white Methodists of Rockbridge are of the Southern branch. In 1855 we hear of the Rockbridge Bible Society, which met in the Methodist Church of Lexington.

The oldest Baptist church in the Augusta Association is Neriah, about five miles from Lexington. It dates from 1816. The Baptist church of Lexington was organized May 9, 1841, by a council of three ministers—Cornelius Tyree, William Margrave, and James Remley—and sixteen constituent members, nine of whom were of the Jordan connection. Colonel John Jordan may be regarded as the founder of this church, and he was one of its first deacons. Cornelius Tyree, the first pastor, was followed by seventeen others. The first Sunday school superintendent was Professor George E. Dabney, who became a member in 1843. The first member to be received into fellowship was Milton, a negro, and so far as known, he was the first person ever baptized in Lexington by a local Baptist pastor. He was a deacon for the colored membership, and seems to have been the Milton Smith who was the first pastor of the colored congregation after its separation from the white in 1867. Until 1866 the pastor of the Lexington church divided his time with other congregations. The house of worship built on Nelson Street has been continuously in use, though with some enlargement. Since this book was undertaken, a new, modern, and commodious house of worship has been in course of erection on Main Street. Since 1876 the congregation has been a member of the Augusta Association. In 1867 the colored members, excepting one woman, were granted letters of dismission to organize a church of their own, which took effect September 22, 1867, as the Lexington African Baptist Church. The congregation has prospered. Its large building cost $25,000, and in 1918 an organ was installed at an expense of $2,000.

There was a Church of England party in Ulster, and it had an influential following in Augusta. Thomas Lewis, the founder of the Augusta settlement, was a churchman. A house of worship at Staunton was completed in 1763, and in it was held in 1781 a session of the Virginia Legislature. In 1757 there was a "chapel of care" in the Forks of James, and Sampson Mathews drew a stipend as reader. In that year his services were discontinued, because of the number of people who had fled the locality in consequence of Indian alarms. We have no information where this chapel stood, but it must have been in the far south of the county or even within the Botetourt line. Possibly it was the "Fork meeting house" to which a road from Edmondson's mill was ordered in 1753. In 1804 John Cowman and Molly, his wife, deeded one and three-fourths acres on Walker's Creek to the trustees of the Episcopal and Presbyterian congregations, each to have equal use and benefit. There seems already to have been a house on the lot. The property was sold in 1828 to James McChesney. The first Episcopal church in Lexington was built a litle prior to 1845, and has been superseded by the handsome Lee Memorial church in a corner of the University campus.

In Lexington District, outside the limits of the county seat, are Poplar Hill and Liberty Hall Presbyterian churches, both of very recent organization. In Buffalo District are the Presbyterian and Methodist churches of Collierstown, both of brick. The former was organized in 1843, the latter about 1850. Another early Methodist church is the North Buffalo. At Rapp's Mill is a union church used chiefly by the Methodists. The first building here was erected about 1830. Oakdale Baptist church was not organized until about 1916. At Hamilton's schoolhouse there has been preaching about a century. The building was given by Robert Hamilton for the free use of all denominations. The carpenter work was done by the father of Governor Letcher. In Kerr's Creek District are Kerr's Creek and Chestnut Grove Presbyterian churches, the first organized 1845, the second, 1910. Ebenezer is a house of worship of the Associate Reformed Presbyterian Church, and Bethany, of the Lutherans. The Methodists and Baptists have each a church in the district, but there has been no organization of the Church of the Brethren for more than 30 years. In Natural Bridge District are 13 church buildings. At Glasgow and Glenwood are Presbyterian churches. Broad Creek is Associate Reformed Presbyterian. The Episcopalians have St. Johns, Trinity, and High Bridge, the first at Glasgow, the second at Natural Bridge Station. The Baptists have churches at Glasgow and Natural Bridge, and at Glasgow and Buffalo Forge are two others for the colored people. The Methodist churches are Elliott's Mill, Wesley Chapel, Mount Zion, and Beth Heron, the last named being at Natural Bridge Station. At Gilmore's Mill is a union church. We have no report for the other districts of the county.

A modern custom that is well nigh universal is to inter the dead in public and church cemeteries. The private burial grounds have fallen into disuse and sometimes into great neglect. A resident of Kerr's Creek tells us he knows nearly 40 of these in that district alone.

XXIII

TEMPERANCE SOCIETIES AND OTHER FRATERNITIES

The Liquor Habit—Temperance Reform in Rockbridge—Secret Orders

It is conceded that in the days of our grandparents the drinking habit was very general, and yet it is maintained that actual drunkenness rarely occurred. This claim is a fallacy. It flies in the face of fact and will not stand a serious investigation. The illusion on which it is based is well set forth in this couplet:

> 'Tis distance lends enchantment to the view,
> And robes the mountains in their azure hue.

No one but the hidebound apologist for the liquor traffic any longer holds that alcohol is a food in any true sense of the word. It is a drug, and a drug is a poison when used outside of medical limitations. Any drug is out of place when the body is in health. Alcohol is invariable in its nature, and among all peoples its effect is substantially the same. Whether the effect is slow or rapid is a matter of temperament and modes of living. That men persist in making an exception in favor of alcohol, and are not willing to class it with such habit-forming drugs as opium, cocaine, and the loco weed, is because its indiscriminate use has been strongly intrenched in social custom.

The nations of the Baltic stock have ever shown a proneness to the use of intoxicants. The people of Ulster, as a branch of this stock, have been no exception. Their inclination to distill whiskey as well as to use it in liberal amount, has caused that beverage to displace rum as the leading American intoxicant. The drinking habit appears to have been well-nigh universal among the immigrants from Ulster, just as it was among the people of English origin east of the Blue Ridge. Alexander Craighead, a minister who owned land in the Borden Tract, had his punch-bowl. When James Morrison came to preach at New Providence in 1819, all but one of the eight elders of his church had their stills.

Yet only ten years later a temperance society was organized here as the result of a letter to the pastor by Captain Henry B. Jones.

In 1754 a petition to the Augusta court, signed by 91 of the settlers, condemns the "selling by ordinaries of large quantities at extravagant rates whereby money is drained out of the country." The signers say they intend to produce their own liquor and keep their money in the country. There is not the least hint that they are bolstering up a bad business. They thought it as necessary a business as any, and believed their aim was most praiseworthy.

The colonial tavern invariably kept liquors in much variety, even to various kinds of wine and brandy imported from France and the Spanish peninsula. All stores likewise kept liquors in stock. For the years 1762-1768, the books of William Crow, a merchant of Staunton, show very few long accounts that do not contain several charges for drinks. Presentments for the illegal selling of liquor are exceedingly common in the court records prior to the civil war. The persons who thus exposed themselves to fine were often some of the leading members of the community.

It would be very illuminating if we could know what part was played by intoxicants in the innumerable brawls in the courtyards and outside of them; in the careless behavior of both combatants and non-combatants during the years of the Indian war; and in the conduct of the Indians themselves, the aborigines having a weakness for what they expressively called firewater.

Bad as the situation must have been before the Revolution, it was even worse after that event. The demoralization bred in camps was carried home by the returned soldiers. Doctor Archibald Alexander relates that a certain Continental purchased a house in Lexington, where he collected all the vagrants around. Many of the ex-soldiers had been convicts, and were now living in dissipation on their certificate money. At his resort, drinking bouts would be kept up for weeks, and these affairs were enlivened with hard fights. Henry Ruffner adds his testimony that in 1844 the Valley had not yet recovered from the disorganizing effects of the Revolution. Between 1790 and 1810, the increase in the consumption of distilled liquors was one-half greater in the United States than the increase of population. In 1825, 39 pints per capita were consumed, irrespective of the matter of age or sex. It was about this time that an English visitor—coming from a land of grogshops—said that "intemperance is the most striking characteristic of the American people."

Whether Robert McElheny would succeed his father in 1799 as possessor of the parental homestead on Kerr's Creek, was made conditional by a clause in the will saying it depended on whether the son "refrained from drinking to excess."

Speaking in 1873 at the semi-centennial of the Franklin Society, Colonel J. T. L. Preston said of the days of his youth that there was "more of open and gross drunkenness than now." Here is straightforward testimony from an excellent source; all the better because the speaker's personal recollection began in the opening years of the last century.

In 1853 sixty thousand gallons of whiskey were sent ont by the canal, and in 1876 iron and whiskey were the chief items of export from this country.

A reformation began in Rockbridge about 1829, some societies demanding no more than moderation in the use of liquor. No very beneficial effect could come from such a half-loaf as this. The then president of Washington College called a temperance society of this sort "a well-organized drinking club." The first teetotal speech in the county was by C. C. Baldwin in the lecture room of the Lexington Presbyterian church. This was in 1836. Within the next twenty years a strong sentiment in favor of the extinction of the liquor traffic had developed. In 1854 a petition of this character was signed by two hundred and forty people. Another petition of the same year says a majority of the citizens will vote for a prohibitory law. Two years earlier we find much indignation at the way the liquor business was carried on in the county seat. A petition signed by one hundred and eighty-two of the people asked for a search-warrant law. It states that there were six joints in Lexington, that fifty negroes had been seen entering one of them in an afternoon, and that all efforts to punish the seller had failed. But in 1856 no licenses were issued.

During the war of 1861, the Confederate government passed stringent laws against distilling, with a view to the conservation of grain. These efforts were much evaded, and after this war, as after the Revolution, there was for a while a great slackening of practical interest in the matter of temperance. An editorial in the *Gazette* for December 26, 1873, thus speaks of the holiday revel in Lexington. "Christmas was celebrated in Lexington by an unusual amount of noise and a profuse liquoring. Main Street was blocked up several times by crowds of boisterous negroes. No lady dared to come on the street without running the risk of being jostled by staggering men or hearing profane, vulgar "Could the excessive use of whiskey be abolished and the carrying of pistols stopped, three-fourths or more of the crime of Rockbridge would be eliminated."

In 1914, this county gave prohibition a majority of 414 votes in a total of 1790. Of the twenty-three precints, seventeen supported the measure, and there was a tie vote in two of the others.

During the decade of the 50's, the efforts to curb the drinking habit largely took the form of what were known as temperance societies. They were patterned after the secret orders, and had constitution and ritual, signs and passwords. Their fraternal and social features made them attractive, and they exerted a wholesome influence. But the lodges, or "divisions," were lacking in permanence. Before the war, the Friends of Temperance and the Sons of Temperance were most in favor. During the 70's and 80's, they were succeeded by the Good Templars with their more elaborate ritual and their regalia.

XXIV

OLD FIELD SCHOOLS AND FREE SCHOOLS

EARLY EDUCATIONAL IDEAS—THE LITERARY FUND—JOHN REARDON—THE OLD FIELD SCHOOL—THE PUBLIC SCHOOL SYSTEM—STATISTICAL

During the two centuries that Virginia held to the idea that education is a concern of private interest only, the training of the young was left wholly to private effort, and wherever indifference ruled illiteracy was the result. A law of 1809 created a Literary Fund, into which were to be paid certain fines and other odds and ends of the public money. The income was to pay the tuition of those children whose parents were unable to send them to school. The intent of the law was benevolent, but it made the beneficiary a species of pauper and thus was galling to people of ambition and self-respect.

A law of 1846 enabled any county to initiate a public school system within its own territory. Several of the counties within or beyond the Alleghanies availed themselves of this privilege, although it met with little favor in the remaining portion of the state. Rockbridge does not appear to have been one of the counties to take advantage of this law, although in the 50's we find the agent for the Literary Fund styled the County Superintendent. But he was only a clerk and did not exercise any supervision over the schools.

The income from the Literary Fund was apportioned among the counties according to their respective numbers of free white inhabitants. The disbursement within a county was in the hands of a board of trustees, one of whom acted as a bonded treasurer. It was the duty of this board to ascertain the number of indigent children, how many of these would go to school, and for how many of the latter number it could pay tuition. With the consent of their parents such children were sent to school. Books and other necessaries were provided, but the instructions given them did not go beyond the three R's.

Under this system the people of a neighborhood built a schoolhouse and employed the teacher. The latter did not have to get a license, nor attend an institute, nor was he sandbagged into subscribing for several educational books and journals. If, in the judgment of the patrons, he was sufficiently qualified, that was enough. The school was open to all pupils whose parents were able and willing to pay tuition. The local board entered into a contract with the schoolmaster to teach the indigents for whom it had made provision. The teacher had to fill out a blank for each pupil in order to draw the public money thus coming to him.

During this intermediate period, that lay between the reign of the strictly private school and the coming of the full-fledged public school, attendance was voluntary. The ratio was high or low, according to the degree of educational interest in the neighborhood. The time was not ripe for a compulsory law. This would have been deemed an encroachment on personal liberty.

Every since the Protestant Reformation took root in Scotland, the people of that country have been noted for their zeal in the cause of general education. John Knox, the apostle of Presbyterianism, insisted on a school in every parish. Education was in fact regarded as growing out of a religious need. The ability to read the Bible and the catechism was almost an axiom in the Presbyterian practice. And since the pioneers of this county were almost wholly from Ulster, they were very generally able to read and write.

As a matter of course the schoolhouse quickly appeared in Rockbridge. But as education was then altogether a matter of private effort, such mention of schoolhouses or teachers as we find in the public records is purely incidental. What is said of them in tradition and miscellaneous sources is very nearly as meagre. But schools there were, and the one spoken of in 1753 could not have been the earliest. The first teacher in the Borden tract is said to have been a man named Carrigan. James Dobbins is named in 1748 as the teacher of Alexnader McNutt. Robert Fulton was a teacher in 1765.

In 1775 William Alexander came from South River and built a dwelling in the fork at the mouth of Woods Creek. There was already a school in the forest a half mile north of Clifton, the recent home of F. W. Houston. Within a year, and probably with the help of some neighbors, Mr. Alexander built a schoolhouse near a spring a little below the railroad station at Lexington. John Reardon, then a servant to Alexander, presided over the school, which was a large one. Reardon was a young convict who wrote a fair hand and understood bookkeeping. He had read Latin as far as Virgil and had a reading knowledge of the Greek Testament. The teacher did not pretend to exercise any authority over the large boys, but he used his switch on the small children. While learning their lessons the pupils read as loud as possible, and some of them could be heard a quarter of a mile away. Reardon went into the Continental service and nearly lost his life in the Waxhaw massacre. Yet he came home, reared quite a large family, taught at Timber Ridge, and appears to have lived to old age.

Except for the quasi-public feature of the Literary Fund, the old field school of the period that came to an end just after the civil war was essentially the same as the school of the Revolutionary days. The method of instruction was nearly the same, the building itself was scarcely better, and its equipment was litle different. Neither was the old field teacher so very much better paid. In the colonial time, Charles Knight, a teacher on the Calfpasture, was to have

$60 for teaching one year, every half-Saturday or every other Saturday to be free time. In case of an Indian alarm, he was to be lodged in the settlement. But this does not seem to have been a liberal salary, even for that period.

The day will soon arrive when the old field school will live only in tradition and in the accounts that have been thrown into type. One of the most readable of the latter is "Memory Days," by Alexander S. Paxton. The writer gives an extended account of a school of his boyhood in Arnold's Valley. We use his narrative to supplement the reminiscences given to us by Mr. J. A. Parker, of Raphine.

We are told of a log cabin 16 by 18 feet in dimensions, but with a chimney that was able to devour a cartload of wood in a day. Except when the door was open, all the light that came in entered through a space in one side of the room where a log had been left out of the wall. Into this opening was fitted a row of window lights. Just below was the writing-board, set at a slant and held in place by pegs. The benches were peg-legged puncheons. The school dinner was brought from home in a basket. The attendance was large, and it was not then considered a hardship to come to school from a distance of two and one-half miles. The tuition was $1.25 a month for each pupil, but with a higher rate for advanced studies. The term was occasionally ten months long. There was neither blackboard nor wall-map. Webster's "blueback" was the spelling-book, and there were drills in this study. Sometimes the spelling was "by plank," the speller advancing one step for every time he turned another pupil down. There was no uniformity in text-books, and for this reason the instruction was largely individual. The ink, made of copperas and maple bark, was good but it soon used up the noisy quill pens. Discipline was enforced with "hickory oil," well rubbed in, and this medicine was sanctioned by public opinion. Frequently the teacher "boarded round." It was also a custom to go home with a delegation of pupils and spend the night at their house. The schoolyard games were quoits, hop scotch, corner ball, and town ball. The great event of the term was for the scholars to arrive some morning before the teacher, and barricade the door until he would sign the articles drawn up by them. These usually requested a holiday or a treat. But in this contest of wits the victory was often with the teacher. Mr. Parker was once handed some articles he was to "except," and the misapplied word was used to impart some advice the school did not forget.

The minimum required of the old field teacher was to be good in elementary English, to write a fair, round hand, to make goose quill pens, and to use the rod freely and with emphasis. Nevertheless, there was many an old field teacher who could give instruction in the classics, if this was desired. The pedagogue of that age was nearly always a man, and as he was often of mature years he had some prestige in the community.

The "schoolma'am" was an infrequent personage, yet she was not non-existent. Colonel Preston speaks of "Granny Brownlow," grandmother of the war-famous "Parson Brownlow," of Tennessee. She taught an elementary school in Lexington. It was her habit to pet the little ones, coax the older ones, give the small ones apples and cakes, and when they were sleepy, lay them on her trundle-bed.

The colonel also tells of Charles Tidd, a Connecticut man brought here by Captain Leyburn. He was almost illiterate at first, but made a good teacher, and a good brick schoolhouse was built for him. When a new educational era began to creep in, he retired to the head of Collier's Creek. Tidd was one of the pedagogues who did not spare the rod and strap. Another popular and successful teacher from the North was Giles Gunn, who taught in the 50's on and around Kerr's Creek.

The free school, fathered by W. H. Ruffner, a native of Rockbridge, became an institution of Virginia in 1870. In this county as in some others, it won its way only in the face of long-continued opposition. The change from the old system was abrupt, and was viewed in the light of a distasteful innovation. For a considerable time the free school was a vexed topic, friends and foes airing their views in the county papers. But the complete disappearance of the pay-school reveals a tendency of the age.

Out of 4369 whites and 1492 colored persons in 1870, between the ages of five and twenty-one, 700 were receiving elementary instruction in 35 schools. Two years later the annual expenditure had reached only the small sum of $952.07. But in 1875 the expenditure for schools had grown to $12,971. There were now 86 schools with 89 teachers. The average length of term was 5.4 months. The salary of the superintendent was $350. In 1894 there were 99 white schools with 109 teachers and an enrollment of 3182 pupils, and 24 colored schools with 28 teachers and an enrollment of 1092. Nine years later, there were 3833 pupils in school out of a school population of 6647. However, the number of illiterates among the children was 1875.

An interesting relapse to a once popular and still useful institution was the spelling bee held at the county seat, March 6, 1911. The number who took part in it was about 600.

The school year that closed in the summer of 1918 showed an expenditure of $82,114.73. All the ninety schoolhouses were frame buildings, except three of brick, and the two log structures that hold over from the olden time. In the schools for the white were nine male and 143 female teachers. In the schools for the colored people were two male and sixteen female teachers. The teachers who had been in service at least ten years were thirty-five. The length of the school year was nine months in the town of Lexington, eight months in the other high and graded schools, and seven months in the schools of one or two rooms. The school libraries were forty-seven, and had approximately 7,000 volumes. In the rural districts the monthly salary varied from $35 to $50, according to the grade of certificate. With respect to the white population, the figures for school age, enrollment, and attendance were respectively, 5,779, 4,151, and 2,732. For the colored population, the corresponding figures were 1,305, 656, and 462. The pupils in the high school department were 341, and all were white. It is noteworthy that in the matter of attendance, girl pupils are considerably in the majority in each race, although with respect to the total population, Rockbridge has an excess of males.

Since 1905 there has been a progressive consolidation in the rural schools, and it has now gone about as far as it is possible. During this period, ten rural and several graded schools have been established. Schools of three or more teachers have taken the place of the former one-room schools, and several school wagons are in use. There is now much emphasis on a thorough and well-graded course of study, and there is special effort to secure well-trained teachers for the primary rooms as well as for the upper grades.

In the fall of 1911 was held the first school fair in Rockbridge. It proved so interesting and successful that a fair has been held every year since, in the first or second week of November. In 1914, and again in 1916, at least 2000 children marched in parade and were viewed by a much larger number of spectators. The prizes offered in the latter year amounted to nearly $1000. The exhibits were literary, domestic, and in the line of manual training. Exhibits by boys' corn clubs are shown in connection with the school fairs. In 1914, Logan C. Bowyer won the first prize by growing 208 bushels on two acres.

The first county superintendent we find mentioned as such, was John M. Wilson in 1851. His bond was for $3000. John W. Barclay was a successor. Since the arrival of the public school system, the list of superintendants is as follows:

John Lyle Campbell, 1870-1882; J. Lucian Hamilton, 1882-1886; J. Sidney Saville, 1886-1900; A. Nash Johnston, 1900-1904; G. W. Effinger, (acting), 1904; Robert Catlett, 1904-1908; G. W. Effinger, 1908-1913; Earle K. Paxton, 1913-.

XXV

WASHINGTON AND LEE UNIVERSITY

The Alexander School—Mount Pleasant—Timber Ridge—Mulberry Hill—The Stone Liberty Hall Academy—Removal of Lexington—College Era—The University Period

The first classical school west of the Blue Ridge was opened in 1749 by Robert Alexander. The log cabin, doubtless of a single room, is said to have stood on the farm immediately north of the churchyard of Old Providence. Alexander was a graduate of Edinburgh University. Some of the copies of the Greek and Latin authors were in his own handwriting. He came to Augusta in 1743 and remained here until his death in 1787. His school must have been fairly successful, for he continued to teach it four years. We know the names of only two of his students. These were James and Robert, sons of James McNutt.

Then, for 21 years, the school was continued by the Reverend John Brown, and seems to have been taught at his home. His students were probably few and did not make very exacting demands upon his time.

The year 1774 registered a distinct advance. In October, the Hanover Presbytery ordered that a public school be established in Augusta. Six persons were authorized to take subscriptions, these to be payable not later than the following Christmas. William Graham was designated as the instructor, and he was to be under the supervision of John Brown. Next April, which was the month in which the battle of Lexington was fought, the Presbytery declared that it would not limit the school to the students from Presbyterian families.

Mount Pleasant Academy, the school thus established, was a log cabin of one room. It stood on a small belt of tableland a short mile north from Fairfield Station and perhaps an eighth of a mile west of the railroad track. Between the upland and the railroad is a fine spring. The field in which the cabin stood is on land now owned by William G. Houston, and even at that time must have been partially cleared. The exact site, not apparent to a stranger, commands an extensive mountain prospect, especially toward the east. For a school amid rural surroundings the situation is pleasing and interesting. "All the features of the place," remarks Henry Ruffner, "made it a fit habitation for the woodland muse." A horn answered the purpose of a bell. The students carried their dinners, and their sports were mainly gymnastic. They studied within the schoolroom or under a tree. The spring was necessarily one of their resorts, and it was here that James Priestly, a student and afterward an instructor, used to "spout" the orations of Demosthenes in the original Greek.

Graham had been graduated from Princeton College the year before coming to Mount Pleasant, and one of his classmates was Richard Henry Lee, the statesman and orator. In October, 1775, John Montgomery, who was afterward minister at Deerfield, in Augusta county, became his assistant.

The school seems to have prospered during the two years it remained at Mount Pleasant. In fact, the time was now propitious for an embryo college. This section of the Valley of Virginia had now been settled nearly forty years. Many of the families were in comfortable circumstances. Furthermore, the Valley had acquired such a degree of maturity as to create an appreciable demand for professional men. The distinctions conferred upon a man trained to some profession was understood by the youths of the Valley and appreciated by them.

In May 1776, the Presbytery accepted the gift of eighty acres of land, contributed in equal amounts by Samuel Houston and Alexander Stuart. The weight of authority is that the schoolhouse, twenty-four by twenty-eight feet on the ground and one and one-half stories high, stood near the stone church built at Timber Ridge in 1756. Persons living in 1844 remembered a log house answering the description. At Philadelphia, Graham purchased books and philosophical apparatus to the value of 160 pounds ($533.33.) These articles were paid for with 128 pounds raised by subscription, and 32 pounds made up in some other manner. The library thus begun contained 290 volumes. The apparatus included a small reflecting telescope, a solar micsroscope, an airpump, an electrical machine, a barometer, a quadrant, a very small orrery, a pair of twelve-inch globes, and instruments for surveying. Graham went as far as New England in his canvass and obtained some help from that section. Doctor Archibald Alexander says that "several small, neat buildings were erected for the use of the students, and a good house on the New England model was reared for the rector. Students came in goodly numbers, mostly grown young men." The various buildings were completed late in 1777, the property, all told, costing about $2,000. Graham was a very good scholar in the classics and was fond of the natural sciences. He gave much attention to the science of government although censured by some people on the ground that he was thereby meddling in politics. He wanted to pattern his school after Princeton College. The cost of board and tuition was $35 a year. Tuition alone was 4 pounds ($13.33.)

The name now given to the academy, Liberty Hall, was adopted May 13, 1776. It is believed to have been suggested by Graham. The Revolution was now in progress. Rockbridge did not come within the theater of military operations, and the school was not closed on their account. But in another way the effect of the war was disastrous. The Continental currency began to depreciate and this process went on with accelerated speed. Prices rose correspondingly. At length the steward was no longer to give board at the original figure of $21.67 a year. The price was raised, but he resigned. Board was then given at the rate of $50 a year in the homes of Samuel McDowell, Alexander Stuart, David Gray, Samuel Lyle, and John Lyle. The financial embarrassment compelled Graham to remove to the farm he had purchased at Mulberry Hill near Lexington. He left the school to be carried on by his assistant, whose name was Willson and who became a minister. Willson was an excellent classical scholar and could repeat hundreds of lines from Homer. But partly because of his ill-health and partly because of the bad times, the number of students sank to five or six. The school was suspended in 1780 and was never resumed at Timber Ridge.

As early as 1777 Archibald Alexander often saw companies of militia from the backwoods pass the academy wearing brown hunting shirts and deer-tail cockades. The company of Captain John Tate, that served in the Carolinas in 1780-81, was composed almost wholly of students from Liberty Hall. On the field of Guilford they fought with the proverbial bravery of students, and their gallantry drew words of praise from the British commander-in-chief.

The next chapter in the history of the institution carries us to Mullberry Hill, a mile northwest of Lerington. It was only by bringing the school to the vicinity of his home that Mr. Graham was able to reopen it in 1782. Incorporation was granted in October of this year. The petition asking for it states that "your petitioners believe that a seminary may here be conducted to very general advantage,—when (we) consider the extensive fertile country around the place, the fine air, and pure water with which it it blessed.—120 acres (have been) procured in the neighborhood of Lexington for the Academy, also a valuable library of well-chosen books, and a considerable mathematical and philosophical apparatus. They ask incorporation, also exemption to the professors and master from militia service." Incorporation took the school out of the hands of the Presbytery, and it was thenceforward undenominational. Though styled only an academy, the institution was placed on a level with colleges in its ability to confer degrees.

The first trustees were John Bowyer,* William Alexander,* Arthur Campbell, Alexander Campbell,* William Christian, John Hays,* Samuel Lyle,* James McCorkle, Samuel McDowell, William McKee,* William Graham,* George Moffett,* John Montgomery, Andrew Moore,* Archibald Stuart, John Trimble,* Joseph Walker,* Caleb Wallace, John Wilson, * William Wilson. Those whose names appear with a star were present at the first meeting of the board, January 30, 1783. Graham, Montgomery, Wallace and William Wilson were ministers of the Presbyterian Church. Bowyer and Moore held the title of general.

The site on Mulberry Hill was where three farms came together, each owner contributing a portion of the ground. The new schoolhouse stood on a high spot and in a grove of oaks. It was soon destroyed by fire, and incendiarism was suspected. Another building, sixteen by twenty-four feet, was put up in the same place in 1784. The Timber Ridge property does not seem to have realized more than one-third of its cost. Mr. Graham canvassed for help, and outside of his expenses he collected $2589.67 in paper money. But in specie it was worth only three cents on the dollar. A new subscription effort was productive of little result.

When the academy was opened under the charter, it was with William Graham as rector and James Priestly as assistant. Priestly, who has already been mentioned, was a good teacher and an eager student. But because of the demoralization bred in the camps, there was a great change for the worse in the character and behavior of the young men who now presented themselves. Profanity, drunkenness, card playing, and malicious tricks were the order of the day among them. A better standard of behavior was slow to appear.

It was in November, 1784, that the trustees petitioned the Assembly for help. They speak of their school as having "very flattering prospects," and that its greatest need was funds. But their appeal fell on deaf ears.

The first commencement was held on September 13, 1785, and the degree of Bachelor of Arts was conferred on the following young men: Samuel Blackburn, Samuel Corrick, Moses Hoge, Samuel Houston, William McClung, Andrew McClure, John McCue, James Priestly, Adam Rankin, Archibald Roane, Terah Templin, and William Willson. Corrick, Hoge, McClure, McCue, Templin, and Willson became Presbyterian ministers. Hoge at length became president of Hampden-Sidney College, and Corrick of Blount College in Tennessee. General Blackburn settled as a lawyer in Bath county. He was an eloquent orator and a master of ridicule and sarcasm. Roane was governor of Tennessee in 1801-3. McClung was a circuit judge in Kentucky, and Priestly became president of Cumberland College.

Lexington wished the academy moved within its boundaries. The trustees declined at this time, thinking the students were unruly enough where they were without placing them in a less favorable environment. The town was much infested with quarrelsome drunkards, by whom the few earnestly religious citizens were feared and hated.

In 1793, a stone building was erected, William Cravens of Rockingham being the contractor. It was thirty by thirty-eight feet in the clear, three stories high, and contained twelve rooms, each nearly fifteen feet square. The cost was about $2,000. The academy was now given a more respectable standing, and the moral tone began to improve. The average attendance was about twenty-five.

For seven pounds ($23.33) a year, the steward furnished meals, made beds, and cleaned the rooms twice a week. At this time, wheat was fifty-eight cents a bushel, rye fifty, and corn forty-two. Beef was two and one-half cents a pound, and pork three and three-fourth cents. Breakfast consisted of bread and butter with tea, coffee, or chocolate; dinner, of bread, vegetables, and either beef or pork; supper, of bread, butter, and milk. Room rent in the academy building was fifty cents a session for each student, unless there were five or more students in the same room. In this case the charge was $2 for all.

Tuition was 5 pounds. Aside from the ancient languages, the subjects taught were arithmetic, algebra, geography, logic, criticism and rhetoric, trigonometry, navigation, surveying, and, probably, natural philosophy.

In 1796 the library and apparatus were valued at 2000 pounds. But the academy was in much financial embarrassment. It was pressed by its creditors, and the trustees paid some of the debts out of their own pockets. The legislature was again appealed to but in vain. The trustees remonstrated against being divested of their office. The price of board was advanced fifty per cent.

Relief came at a most opportune time. In 1784 the legislature of Virginia incorporated two companies, one to improve the navigation of the James and the other that of the Potomac. It authorized the treasurer of the state to subscribe for 100 shares in the James River Company and fifty in the Potomac Company, these 150 shares to stand in the name of General George Washington, and to be a gift for his personal benefit. Washington replied that inasmuch as he had declined to accept any pay during the Revolution, he could not consistently accept the shares for himself, but would apply them to some public benefit after they had become productive. Andrew Moore and Francis Preston called the general's attention to Liberty Hall Academy, the name of which may have influenced his decision. Mr. Graham also called a meeting of the trustees, and prepared an address to Washington, who in September, 1796, deeded the James River share to Liberty Hall, the Potomac shares going to Leesburg Academy. The transalleghany region was already showing that it would be a great factor in American development, and Washington understood it better, probably, than any other statesman east of the Blue Ridge. He fully appreciated the services which the men west of that mountain had rendered the cause of American independence. He was, furthermore, a great friend to education, and he knew that the struggling academy at Lexington was the only higher institution of learning within the mountain country. In giving Liberty Hall this help, Washington desired that it should be a school of the purest patriotism. He could not but have known that the adoption of the Federal Constitution by Virginia was decided by the votes of the delegates who were at the same time trustees of Liberty Hall.

The par value of the stock donated to Liberty Hall was $20,000. The first dividend—of three per cent—was paid in 1802.

Partial View, Washington and Lee University, Lexington, Va.

Virginia Wilson McCorkle

William H. McCorkle

On Christmas eve, 1802, there was another disaster at the hands of the fire fiend. The academy took fire on the roof and burned to the ground, the side walls and a portion of the ends remaining in place. The building had just been insured and the sum of $2,563 was thus realized. The movable property, such as books, apparatus, and bedding, was saved, but the seal of the academy was not discovered until 1893. The building experts of Lexington gave an unfavorable report as to a reconstruction on the old site. In the opinion of Henry Ruffner, their motives were not disinterested. Yet even if they were not biased, it would look as if their judgment was at fault. The walls continue to stand even after the lapse of 116 years. They form a picturesque ruin, visible from some distance, and are witness to the excellence of the masonry.

Lexington, now a town of 100 families, made another effort to secure the school. A reluctant consent was given. Andrew Alexander took the old site in exchange for his house and its lot of two acres in the town. He sold 28 acres additional for $180, the trustees paying about $1700 for the exchange. Less than $3,000 was available for new buildings. It was decided to erect two wings, twenty by seventy-five feet on the ground and two stories high, containing sixteen rooms in all. These were built hastily and of poor materials, and within twenty years had become insecure. Alexander's house became the rector's home. It was a two-storied wooden structure and was where the president's house now stands. One of the two academic buildings was on the site of the present Newcomb Hall, while the other was at the east end of the University group. The steward's house, a very plain affair thirty by forty-two feet, stood at the front entrance to the grounds. All of these were constructed of poorly burned bricks made on the academy lot. But temporary quarters were needed for about a year, and a building for this purpose was rented on Jefferson street.

In a material point of view, the change was for the better. The attendance rose, and in 1805 there were seventy students. A four-year course of study, nearly like that of Princeton, was adopted, and it remained in force until 1821. However, a preparatory school was maintained. In 1808, the steward system broke down, and was not again resorted to except for a brief period beginning in 1821. With this exception, the students took their meals among private families. W. H. Ruffner considered that the change was beneficial, remarking that in a mixed society students strike for the best families. But for a long while the removal to Lexington was unfavorable to good conduct. The students often took part in the numerous street fights, and the townsmen came to their side when the faculty tried to enforce discipline. But Lexington has always had a circle of good society, and in time its atmosphere very greatly improved.

In 1798 there was a change of name to Washington Academy. In the same year Mr. Graham resigned, having been associated with the academy twenty-four years. He was succeeded by George A. Baxter, who came from New London Academy to fill the chair of mathematics. Daniel Blain also joined the faculty and some students came from a distance. The salary of Doctor Baxter was about $900, that of Blain about $700.

In 1812 Washington Academy became Washington College, and this continued to be its name almost sixty years. In 1818, while a state university was taking form, the trustees of the college tried to have it adopted as the University of Virginia. Its claims were presented by Colonel James McDowell.

A memorial sent to the Assembly in 1821 states that in addition to the James River stock the college has seventeen shares in the Bank of Virginia, these having been purchased out of savings from the endowment. The bank stock was yielding three per cent. a year, the James River stock, $1200 to $1800. The tuition was $30 a year, of which one-third went to the president, and two-thirds to the two professors and the tutor of the grammer school. During the three years past, the average attendance had been forty-four. The students were generally between the ages of sixteen and twenty-one. About thirty were taking the college course.

In 1821 the rector became the president. The other professors were Daniel Blain and Edward Graham. Between 1803 and 1821 there were three schools of study: one of mental philosophy, chemistry, and astronomy; and one of Latin, Greek, French, English, Hebrew, and geography. The teaching was wholly from text-books. There was at this time a popular prejudice against the dead languages. During the college year 1816-17, $600 was spent for books and the library was put under strict regulations. Until 1820 the high-water mark in the income from the James River stock was $3,200. In 1832 and later, there was a guaranteed income of $3000.

Other help came to the college. John Robinson's estate, which ultimately yielded $46,000, came productive in 1829. In 1807 the Society of the Cincinnati turned over its funds to Washington College on condition that fortification and gunnery be taught. The money, however was not deposited with the state treasurer until 1824. That officer failed and more than one-half of the fund was lost. Not until 1848 did the college receive the $25,000 due it. The donations previous to the war of 1861 aggregated about $100,000. But while this sum looks very small when compared with the benefactions in recent years, the importance of the early help, particularly the canal stock, was inestimable. The Washington fund did not become steadily productive until 1811, and during the years when there was a deficiency of income, the rector allowed the shrinkage to fall upon himself.

The Center Building cost $9,000 and created a debt of $4,000. At the laying of the cornerstone, which toook place in 1824, John Robinson sent up from his distillery at Hart's Bottom a barrel containing forty gallons of his best rye whiskey. This reservoir with all its intoxicating potentialities was set on the campus. The day of temperance reform had begun to arrive, and although the college authorities viewed the present with disfavor, Robinson was too good a friend of the institution to be treated with discourtesy. Some of the trustees and professors did not partake at all, and others did so only in a nominal way. But among the spectators were a large contingent of the would-be "Tight-Brigade." The agonies of thirst impelled them to an onset that was irresistible. With cups, dippers, gourds, and every other obtainable thing of the sort, they proceeded to drain the barrel, but before they could complete the process it was intentionally upset. The wreckage around the spot, human and inanimate, was suggestive of a battlefield. Robinson, who was a man of a past age with respect to his ideas of conviviality, was much chagrined. He had intended his present for the élite and not for the mob. But he was making a most generous estimate for the capacity of the élite.

In 1829 there were breaches in the fence around the college grounds caused by hauling wood, brick, and building materials. Domestic animals were free to come in and were in partial possession of the buildings, sometimes climbing to the second floor. These four-footed "students" were now expelled and the gaps closed.

In 1845, according to Howe, the yearly expense to the student did not necessarily exceed $150. His board was about $8 a month and his washing and sundries about $3. The cost of matriculation, tuition, room rent, and sundry deposits was $42. But poor students were remitted their tuition and could get along on $80 to $100 a year. In 1855, eight students took the degree of Bachelor of Arts.

In 1840 the late Joseph A. Waddell was a student at Washington College. His student life, as he describes it, was not overburdened with attractiveness. The young men had to lodge in the college building unless there was good reason for the permission to sleep elsewhere. The college inclosure was primitive and rude, and the buildings were as primitive and unadorned as possible. There were four instructors. At bedtime one of them would call at every door, to see if all the students were in and to mark the absentees. But the professors did not try to get acquainted with the students and had little to do with them except at times of recitation. The hour of prayers at the chapel was announced with a tin horn by "Professor" John Henry, the negro janitor. The chapel was as cheerless as a barn and as cold in winter as an ice-house. When Professor Calhoun offered prayer, he put both his hands into his pockets to keep them from getting numb. The chapel hour was before breakfast, and in winter the only light was a tallow candle. Roll-call was next in order. There were Bible classes on the afternoon of Sunday; an English class by Professor Armstrong, a Greek class by Professor Dabney. But in the latter class there was no word of exposition or exhortation; all that each member of the class had to do was to read one or more verses from a chapter in the Greek Testament. The students generally attended the Presbytrian church bcause the Ann Smith girls went there. Some of the young men did not go to church at all, and this did not seem to make any difference to anyone.

President Baxter was followed by Lewis Marshall, a brother to John Marshall, for many years Chief Justice of the Supreme Court of the United States. He in turn was followed, though only for a year, by Henry Vethake. In 1836, the latter was succeeeded as president by Henry Ruffner, who was graduated from this college in 1817, and had been a professor since 1819. Of him the following anecdote is related. On entering his class-room one morning, he found his armchair in possession of a calf, which saluted him with a "ba-a," perhaps from a willingness to be relieved from managing a recitation. "Young men," said the doctor, "I see you have an instructor fully competent to teach you, so I'll bid you good morning." The calf was soon nibbling grass on the campus and an apology was sent to the victorious president.

The Graham Society—later the Graham-Lee—was founded in 1809 by nine students, all of whom were men of force. In its early years it discussed and condemned secession and slavery. In 1840 its library contained 2,000 volumes. Some years after the Graham arose, there came the Washington, and there was much rivalry between the two societies.

George Junkin came to the head of affairs in 1848, and resigned in the spring of 1861, because of his uncompromising stand against secession. During the four years of the civil war, the doors of the college were closed, the students being generally with the Confederate army. There were twelve in the senior class of 1861. All were given degrees, whether present at Commencement or in the army. Two of the graduates, Joel W. Arnold and Alexander S. Paxton, were of Rockbridge county. The pillaging that took place during the occupation of Lexington by the army of General Hunter is elsewhere spoken of. The end of this suspension of activities found the campus a commons and the buildings out of repair. The resources were hardly enough to pay the four professors who were needed when General Robert E. Lee took charge in the fall of 1865. But at the time of his installation, which was of the simplest character, the "five brick buildings, all in a row," were freshly painted inside and out. About 100 students were present at the reopening, and a year later there were 320. There was no graduating class until 1866, because a senior class could not be gathered together.

With the incumbency of the ex-commander-in-chief of the Confederat armies begins the modern period in the history of this institution. For want of space we must pass over it briefly. It has been our aim to dwell on the earlier history of the school, not alone because of its great interest, but because much of the material for this history is not readily accessible.

Very soon after the death of General Robert E. Lee, and in memory of him, Washington College became the Washington and Lee University. General G. W. C. Lee was at the head of the institution until 1897, and was succeeded by William L. Wilson, whose short incumbency was marked by the inauguration of the School of Applied Science. Doctor Wilson died in office, and Harry St. George Tucker acted as president for the remainder of the college year. The administration of George H. Denny, which closed in 1912, gave place to that of the present incumbent, Henry Louis Smith, who is of Rockbridge parentage, though a native of North Carolina.

The grounds belonging to the university now cover ninety acres. Most of the trees that shade the campus are not of primeval growth, but have been set out. General Robert E. Lee was very instrumental in thus beautifying the inclosure. The buildings number forty-three, and include the largest and best equipped gymnasium in the South. The recent structures vastly eclipse the plain, inexpensive ones of the ante-war period. The library houses about 50,000 volumes. The endowment has risen to several millions of dollars, and has been contributed chiefly by Robert P. Doremus, George Peabody, W. W. Corcoran, Thomas A. Scott, Andrew Carnegie, and Cyrus H. McCormick.

The schools of instruction are four; the Academic, and those of Commerce, Law and Equity, and Applied Science. The School of Law and Equity grew out of the school of law founded in Lexington in 1849 by John W. Brokenbrough. The school year of thirty-seven weeks is divided into three terms. During the session of 1917-18, there were thirty-six members of the faculty, and there were also several student instructors. There were 523 students, Virginia contributing 194. The others came from thirty-two states of the Union, and Hawaii, Porto Rico, China, Japan, and Persia were also represented. During the same session the cost of room and board varied from $24 to $37 a month. The tuition and fees, other than those relating to labaratory work, amount to $105 a year, except in the Law School, where the total is $120.

In review, it may be mentioned that Washington and Lee University is neither a state nor church institution, but is controlled by a self-perpetuating board. The influences are nevertheless Christian, and the student branch of the Young Men's Christian Association was developed during the presidency of General R. E. Lee. At the close of his administration, 105 students were members of some church. An honor system is in force and this is strengthened by the social relations subsisting between the faculty and the student body.

The individual student is not subjected to espionage nor to vexatious restrictions. It therefore goes without saying that the annoyances that hindered the working of the school for several decades after the Revolution have passed into the limbo of local history.

The little school founded by Robert Alexander has grown, step by step, into a university of broad scope and of national influence.

XXVI

THE VIRGINIA MILITARY INSTITUTE

The Lexington Arsenal—How the Institute Arose—The Opening—Antebellum History—War Record of the Institute—Later History—General Smith—Other Instructors

A state arsenal was established at Lexington in 1816, where 30,000 stand of small arms were kept for the militia of the southwest counties. The arsenal itself was a substantial brick building four stories high, "from which every architectural beauty was scrupulously excluded." The roof was surfaced with zinc. In the basement was a mess-hall, lighted when necessary with whale oil lamps. In front were the commandant's house and the barracks, the latter a brick building containing nine rooms. The two structures formed one side of a quadrangle, a brick wall fourteen feet high forming the other three sides. The barrack windows were grated and the place was suggestive of a prison. The grounds were not so extensive as those of the school that succeeded the arsenal. On the slope of the hill were a few cedars and some deep gullies. A cornfield surrounded by a worm fence occupied a portion of the present parade ground. The only tree on the plateau was a hickory known as the "guard tree."

The first commandant was Captain James Paxton, a native of the county and a thorough soldier who had served with much credit in the war of 1812. The second commandant was Captain D. E. Moore.

To look after the burnished muskets stored on the upper and well scoured floors of the arsenal, there was a guard of twenty-eight enlisted men, who were paid $9 each a month, or $3,024 in all. They were under strict discipline. Reveille at daybreak and the drum at nine or ten o'clock at night were a part of the established order of things. Drill and guard duty constituted the legitimate duty of the men. With a few exceptions, they were not of much character, and had accepted this mode of life as being on the "line of least resistance." They were much addicted to liquor and to stealing ripe melons and fruit. One of the letters by "Civis" in 1835 says that, "as a body they are respected by none, considered obnoxious by some, and disliked by all." Eight years earlier, one of the guards was killed by a companion soldier.

Andrew Alexander is said to have been the first citizen to suggest turning the arsenal into some kind of school, and thus getting rid of a nuisance. The idea was at length taken up by the Franklin Society, and in December, 1832, it was twice debated in its halls. The second evening there was a unanimous vote in favor of the proposition. So great was the interest now aroused, that before the members had left the hall steps were taken to set the ball to rolling.

In August and September, 1835, three letters signed "Civis" appeared in the *Gazette*. These articles explained what the proposed school ought to be in the judgment of the writer. Their author was Colonel J. T. L. Preston, but he never claimed to have originated the views he advanced.

The real originator appears to have been Claude Crozet, a native of France who was educated in the Polytechnic School of Paris. He became a captain of artillery in the army of Napoleon, won the Cross of the Legion of Honor, and soon after the downfall of the empire he came to America. Shortly after his arrival he was appointed to the chair of engineering at West Point. This position he filled seven years, and he was the first man to teach the highest branches of mathematics in that institution. Excepting the five years he was president of Jefferson College in Louisiana, Crozet spent the rest of his long life in Virginia. As state engineer he laid out a number of important turnpikes. One of his achievements is the Blue Ridge tunnel on the line of the Chesapeake and Ohio railroad.

The measure was put before the Assembly, but as there was considerable opposition, success was not speedy. The Act first passed made the proposed school "a part and branch of Washington College." This was repealed in favor of the one passed March 29, 1839. This made a yearly appropriation of $6,000, which was the same as the cost of maintaining the arsenal. It created a Board of Visitors, appointed by the Governor. From twenty to forty cadets, between the ages of sixteen and twenty-five, were to be admitted yearly, and these were to constitute the publice guard of the arsenal. The officers and the cadets were to be held responsible for the arms. Any non-commissioned officer of the militia of the state was permitted to have free tuition for not more than ten months, but was not to be recognized as a regular student.

The members of the first Board of Visitors were Cononel Claude Crozet. General P. C. Johnston, General Thomas Botts, General C. P. Dorman, Captain John F. Wiley, Governor James McDowell, Doctor Alfred Leyburn, and Hugh Barclay. It will be observed that nearly all these men carried military titles. Colonel Crozet was chairman. The board was a very able one, and the action it took was in line with these words of our first president: "However pacific the general policy of a nation may be, it ought never to be without an adequate stock of military knowledge for emergencies." The school these men were to establish was to have military features, and yet it could not strictly be another West Point. The great function of the United States Military Academy is to provide thoroughly trained army officers. Each graduate becomes at once a lieuenant, and so long as he does not resign from the military establishment of the nation, he enjoys a salary for life. Virginia could not thus provide for the graduates of her military school. The chief purpose of the new school was to impart a superior scientific training and supply well-equipped teachers. A parallel purpose was the better defense of the state in case of war. "Practical utility, thorough discipline, and formative training" were to pervade every department, and the military feature, with its thoroughness in instruction as well as discipline, was to be a most useful help in securing these ends. "Energy, efficiency, and reliability," remarks General Smith, "have been characteristics of its graduates in every pursuit of life."

Thus arose the second military school in the United States, West Point being the first. Without additional current expense, a most useful school took the place of the semi-idlers who had been a pest to the community.

Francis H. Smith, a recent graduate of West Point and now professor of mathematics in Hampden-Sidney College, was unanimously chosen as the first superintendent. The man thus selected was ambitious. The new school was in the nature of an experiment, and it did not look clear that an acceptance was a promotion in the educational field. After a little hesitation he accepted, and he remained at the head of the institution the very long period of 50 years. His salary at the start was $1,500. The rank of colonel was given to him, and that of major to a full professor. The only other instructor at the start was John T. L. Preston, who took the chair of modern languages.

In September, 1839, twenty state cadets and thirteen pay cadets were appointed, and thirty-one of these formed the corps of 1839-40. John S. L. Logan was the only member from this county. The opening of the Institute, which took place November 11 of the same year, was very unpromising. The barracks had been raised one story to provide more space, but the work was not yet finished. The roof was not in place and no fuel had been laid in. There were no uniforms. There was no banner and the roll was not called. The youths were strongly minded to desert and go home, but the calmer second thought prevailed.

The annuity was gradually increased until in 1860 the annual appropriation was $20,000. During the first twelve years three instructors were added to the faculty. The first was Thomas H. Williamson, who taught drawing and tactics. The second was Lieutenant William Gilham, professor of the physical sciences. The third was Thomas J. Jackson, whose chair was that of natural and experimental philosophy. A library was begun by the state library sending the second copy in those instances where it possessed two copies of the same work. There was next an appropriation of $500 a year for five years, and the valuable scientific library of Colonel Crozet was thus purchased.

In the first graduating class were sixteen cadets. The Institute commencement used to come on July 4, which was a great day in Lexington. A feature of the exercises, which were held at the Presbyterian church, was the reading of the Declaration of Independence by a graduate. By an Act of 1842, each graduate was required to teach two years, in order to return to the state some direct benefit for his free tuition. The first teachers went out in 1843. Teaching was then thought unworthy of a young Virginian, and much of the educational work of the state had been done by Northerners or by Europeans. But this feeling was gradually overcome, and in 1860 the college students in Virginia numbered 2500, the ratio to the white population being larger than in any other state.

The first student organization was the Society of Cadets, which arose in 1840. It was followed in 1849 by the Dialectic Society.

In 1854 occurred the killing of Blackburn by Christian. There was ill-feeling between these two cadets, and Blackburn was fatally stabbed near the Presbyterian church. Christian was acquitted at Lynchburg on the ground of self-defense.

During the first seven years of the Institute, there was an arrangement with Washington College, whereby the cadets received instruction in chemistry at the college, while a body of college students, known as the Cincinnati Class, drilled with the cadets. This system did not work well and was terminated in 1846. The officers of the Institute could not exercise any direct control over the Cincinnati Class, and as the uniform of the latter was nearly like that of the cadets, some confusion resulted.

Beginning about 1844, there was for several years, a lack of harmony between the Institute on the one hand and Washington College and the town of Lexington with its Presbyterian church on the other hand. The town showed an unfriendly spirit in certain ways, as when the superintendent was presented by a grand jury for selling goods without a license. He had been compelled to provide uniforms for the cadets owing to the inferior goods and extortionate prices of the town merchants. Neither the Institute nor the College was denominational, although the former was in some degree under Episcopal supervision, as was the College under Presbyterian influence. A charge of sectarianism was brought against the management of the Institute. As for the college itself, it chose to look upon its neighbor as a rival institution intruding into a field which it should have to itself. These jealousies were outgrown. They reflected a narrowness of outlook which was not uncommon in America seven decades ago. Yet the removal of the Institute to some other town was seriously considered and the matter was significantly mentioned in the Act carrying an appropriation of $46,000 for new buildings. The people of Lexington and the College authorities also, now took alarm and exerted their influence in favor of a retention of the military school.

The appropriation just named was in response to an appeal by the Board of Visitors and a long auxiliary petition by the cadets. It was pointed out that when the Institute began there were only four rooms in which to lodge thirty-one cadets. In 1849 four or five cadets had to study and sleep in a room only sixteen feet square. Because of this congestion, not more than half the students that applied could be admitted. Day and night fifty wood fires were burning, a constant danger to the state property, the value of which was estimated at $350,000. The cornerstone of the new building was laid July 4, 1850. By 1860 the appropriations for building purposes aggregated $151,000.

In 1858 the superintendent visited Europe on a leave of absence. After his return he made important recommendations bearing on the further growth of the Institute. One of these was the founding of a School of Scientific Agriculture.

In 1850 the cadet corps was present at the laying of the cornerstone of the Washington Monument at the national capitol, and on the return by way of Richmond it was the bodyguard of President Taylor. The fine appearance and soldierly bearing of the cadets won for them much praise, and one result of the excursion was a battery of six pounders given by order of the president. In 1858, the superintendent had charge of the execution of John Brown at Harpers Ferry, and nearly 100 of the cadets were present as a portion of the infantry and artillery force.

The war with Mexico came only six years after the opening of the Institute, and yet twenty-five of the ex-students took part in that conflict, generally as commissioned officers.

We now come to the important part played by the Virginia Military Institute in the war of 1861. During the winter that preceded the actual clash of arms, there was intense restlessness and some turbulence among the cadets. Nearly all of them were ardent partisans of the Confederate side of the controversy. As soon as Virginia seceded, the superintendent was summoned to Richmond to serve on the Council of Three, and subsequently to take part in organizing a system of defense for the lower Chesapeake. April 21 Major Jackson was ordered to take to Richmond as many of the cadets as were available as drillmasters. There were left behind forty-eight of the younger and less experienced of the corps, and these were consolidated with the Rockbridge Greys. At Camp Lee, near Richmond, the other 200 cadets did excellent service in drilling the green volunteers. The more than 20,000 Confederates who were presently to fight under Johnston and Beauregard on Bull Run and the lower Shenandoah were so rapidly and so effectively put into a good degree of discipline, that in the first years of the war they were superior in this respect to the troops opposed to them. President Lincoln found occasion to remark that the Federal armies were not fighting raw militia, but soldiers drilled by highly trained officers.

Most of the cadets who went to Richmond were soon commissioned as officers, and as we have seen, those who were left behind went into the service with a local organization. The Institute did not reopen until January 1, 1862, and a month later 269 students were present. With several interruptions due to military exigencies, work was carried on at Lexington until the close of June, 1864. The military feature was now more prominent than ever, since the present function of the school was chiefly to furnish additional drillmasters to the Southern armies. Recitation work was carried on at a disadvantage, since the cadets were restless and eager to get to the front. After the burning of the Institute by General Hunter, the cadets were for a brief while quartered in the buildings of Washington College. They were then furloughed, and they reassembled at Richmond, where they were placed in the vacant Almshouse. A semblance of classroom work was there carried on nearly four months, or until the evacuation of Richmond, April 3, 1865.

In 1860 there were 433 living graduates of the Virginia Military Institute, to say nothing of the larger number of eleves, or students who did not complete the course of study. Among the graduates were nine governors, two United States senators, twelve college presidents, more than twenty congressmen, and more than forty judges. Of graduates and eleves, 810 were commissioned officers in the Confederate army as against 282 from West Point, although, as a matter of course, the West Pointer was the more likely to attain high rank. However, the Institute was represented in the Confederacy by three major generals, eighteen brigadier-generals, and 263 regimental officers. Of the fifteen regiments that took part in Pickett's famous charge at Gettysburg, thirteen were commanded by Institute men. The importance to the Confederate government of the "West Point of the South" thus becomes strikingly apparent. Out of the 810, there died in military service 249, and a larger number were wounded. In the Federal army were fifteen officers who had been trained in the Institute.

It is next in order to tell something of the military services of the student corps itself. The first was in May, 1862, when General Milroy was threatening Staunton from the west, and was likely to be joined in a few days by a larger force under General Fremont. General Jackson, who was watching from the south end of Peaked Mountain another Federal army under General Banks, summoned to his aid the force under General Ewell on the eastern side of the Blue Ridge. Leaving Ewell to confront Banks, Jackson made a roundabout and stealthy movement upon Milroy. At his request, the cadets were sent to join his army at Staunton. They left the Institute at noon, May 1, 1862, bivouacked that night at Fairfield, and reached Staunton on the third day of the march. Under Major Shipp they marched to the battlefield of McDowell, but did not take part in the engagement. Yet they marched in the pursuit to McCoy's mill, near Franklin, and studies were not resumed until May 20. In August of the following year, Lieutenant Wise with fifty cadets scoured the mountains of

Rockbridge to arrest deserters. Two days were thus spent but without any success whatever. A few days later the cadets turned out to assist in repelling a force of Federal cavalry under General Averill. Two companies carrying four guns and rations for seven days marched as far as Goshen, but as Averill did not move eastward from Covington, the cadets were absent little more than forty-eight hours. A more serious task came the following November, when Averill made another raid on nearly the same course. But this time Major Shipp marched by way of Longdale to the vicinity of Covington, where General Imboden proposed to make a stand. Averill moved toward Huntersville, and thinking only a feint was intended, Imboden proceeded to Goshen. But the movement was not a feint, and as before, the cadets returned without a share in any action and after an absence of five days. Only one month later, Averill set out on still another raid and penetrated as far as Salem, where he did great damage to the railroad. Well-planned efforts were made to cut off his retreat, but Averill escaped the toils that were closing around him. The cadets, 180 strong and with their rifled cannon, marched again under Shipp, but found Bratton's Run unfordable and went into camp on its bank. Next day they managed to get across and bivouacked at Colk Sulphur Spring, where they received orders to return, and their next camp was at Wilson Spring. Returning to Lexington after an absence of four days, they expected to have to march to Buchanan, but were ordered to join Colonel Jackson, and after a further absence of two days they were again at their old barracks. This six days of service was very severe, a long, continued cold rain being followed by freezing weather, and the roads were icy as well as rough.

The only battle in which the cadets were actually engaged was that of New Market, May 15, 1864. At that point, General Breckenridge with 4,500 men attacked the 6,000 Federals under General Sigel. The engagement was very severe and at times the result was in doubt. At a critical moment the 221 cadets made a brilliant charge that contributed very materially to Sigel's defeat. The casualties were 57, including nine who were either killed or mortally wounded. The highly creditable behavior of the cadets in this action has been written up by several pens and rather voluminously. It is therefore quite unnecessary to give a detailed account of the battle in this chapter. But it is quite erroneous to assume that the cadets were mere boys and without any practical experience in campaigning. On the contrary they were of quite mature age, were thoroughly drilled, and were able to march as well as seasoned troops. The brief tours we have already mentioned had given them no little amount of experience. In short, the morale of the corps could hardly have been surpassed. One week after their battle the cadets reached Staunton almost barefoot, and were at once ordered to Richmond, but were again at Lexington, June 9.

The raid by General Hunter is related in Chapter XIII, as is also the share of the cadets in the military operations connected therewith. The final and very brief service of the cadets in the war of 1861 was when they were sent to the front from Richmond, to help in repelling Sheridan, March 11, 1865, followed by their trench duty in front of that city on the day of the evacuation. In the afternoon of the same day they were marched into Richmond and disbanded.

The fall of 1865 seemed a very unpromising time to reopen the Institute, particularly in view of the fact that its equipment was gone, and that nothing remained of its buildings but a mass of ruins. Neither was there any money in hand with which to rebuild. But failure was a word the superintendent would not accept. In such temporary quarters as could be made available, the school was reopened October 1, 1865, with a full faculty and about twenty cadets. The number of the latter rose during the year to fifty-five. But the professors did not receive more than $400 apiece, by way of salary, whereas the cost of board to the cadets was $25 a month. A year later there were lecture rooms and mess hall, and 147 cadets. In 1869 the burned buildings were restored. All this was not accomplished without acute financial embarrassment.

At the time of the reopening in 1865, 2,000 students had matriculated and 510 of these had been graduated. Of the 2,000, the state cadets numbered 527, and 177 of the latter were graduated. The graduates who had taught numbered 146. Before the war the average expense to the pay cadet was $375 a year.

General Smith resigned as Superintendent in 1889, and was succeeded by General Scott Shipp. The third and present incumbent is General Edward W. Nichols, whose administration began in 1907.

XXVII

THE ANN SMITH AND OTHER ACADEMIES

A GIRL'S SCHOOL FOR LEXINGTON—ANN SMITH—FINANCIAL EMBARRASSMENT—LATER HISTORY—OTHER PRIVATE SCHOOLS

The opening years of the nineteenth century did not find the people of Rockbridge limiting their interest in higher education to the collegiate training of young men. In the spring of 1807 they were taking practical steps to provide secondary instruction for the other sex.

The subscribers to the school of this character held their first formal meeting at the courthouse, April 20, Colonel James McDowell acting as chairman and John Leyburn as clerk. The other men present were Dr. Samuel L. Campbell, James Caruthers, John Caruthers, William Caruthers, Cornelius Dorman, James Gold, Edward Graham, Reuben Grigsby, John Irvine, Henry McClung, Joseph Paxton, John Robinson, Alexander Shields, John Sloan, and William Willson. Dr. Campbell was proxy for William Lyle.

Almost the first act of the meeting was to select a committee to choose a suitable site, and to submit a plan for the building, together with an estimate on the probable cost of both land and schoolhouse. The members of this committee were John Leyburn, Andrew Reid, Edward Graham, Alexander Shields, James Caruthers, and Dr. Campbell. Other duties devolving on this committee were to see whether a convenient house could be used as temporary quarters, to formulate the rules for the government of the school, and to petition the next General Assembly for an act of incorporation. The report was read at a meeting held August 1, other subscribers present being Daniel Blain, Thomas L. Preston, and Arthur Walkup. Andrew Reid was called to the chair. Edward Graham was appointed treasurer of the organization. As secretary of the above-named committee, he announced that no suitable house had yet been found, but that Miss Ann Smith had tendered her services for one year without charge. The meeting voted an appropriation of $1,800 for grounds and buildings, and $500 for enabling the school to be opened in the fall of the same year. It was further ordered that globes and other apparatus be provided.

The committee on organization reported October 9, that a house should be rented at once and maps and other necessaries purchased; that of the two vacations, the first should extend from the third Wednesday in April to the third Wednesday in May, and the second, from the third Wednesday in October to the third Wednesday in November; and that a steward, giving proper security, should at once be employed to board the students at a cost of not more than $50 a term. Tuition was not to exceed $20 a year.

Thus it is probable that the first session of the Ann Smith Academy began November 18, 1807. Joseph Dilworth was engaged as steward, January 9, 1808, and was required to give bond in the sum of $1,000. The schoolroom was found to be too small, and John Galbreath, Jr., came to the rescue by offering the use of the large room in the steward's house of the Washington Academy. The offer was accepted, and at a cost of $25 Mr. Galbreath agreed to lay a plank sidewalk between the two school buildings.

While these adjustments were being affected, the Assembly passed, January 9, 1808, the needed act of incorporation. This was in response to a petition by nineteen persons, who say they selected Lexington as a school for female education, "as it is going forward under favorable appearances, but we are under the disadvantage of not being legally authorized to manage its funds." The first clause of this quotation seems to refer to the town rather than the school.

The first section of the Act is of the following tenor:

"Be it enacted by the General Assembly, That Samuel L. Campbell, John Preston, Edward Graham, Thomas L. Preston, William Caruthers, Alexander Shields, Daniel Blain, James McDowell, John Leyburn, Andrew Reid, James Caruthers, William Wilson, John Robinson, and the principal teacher, for the time being, be appointed trustees of an academy for the education of females, hereby established in the town of Lexington, and county of Rockbridge. And the said trustees are hereby constituted a body politic and corporate, by the name of "The Trustees of the Ann Smith Academy, and by that name, shall have perpetual succession, may sue and be sued, and have common seal, with the power to take and hold any estate, real or personal, for the use of the said academy."

Miss Smith was known to the trustees before they organized the school, and it was their aim to secure her if possible. She was a cultured lady, a born teacher, and was highly successful in her new position. Her terms were liberal in the extreme. She declined to accept any salary, but her board and her incidental expenses were to be paid by the trustees. There has been an opinion in Rockbridge that she contributed to the school in a pecuniary way, but there is nothing to indicate that she gave assistance of this tangible sort. It is more than a century since Ann Smith closed her labors in this community, and little is now known of her. It is believed that she came from Fredericksburg, although there is some ground for thinking she was a native of Maryland.

At the beginning of 1808 Edward Graham was hired as assistant teacher on a salary of $150 a session. Already, one student had been expelled after a lengthy trial. The girl was Nancy Miller, whose offense was smashing a bonnet. But she was soon reinstated.

In June 1808, a two-acre lot was purchased from John Moore and his wife, Polly, at a cost of 100 pounds ($333.33). It lay just outside the town limits, and ran down to Nelson street to the Franklin Library lot. The lower portion was afterward laid off into building lots and the proceeds applied on the indebtedness that we shall presently mention. The academy building was begun the same year, but the completion does not seem to have taken place until the following spring. It was a brick structure and rather imposing for those early times. The center was of three stories and the wings of two. Colonel Jordan was the contractor for the brick work and John Chandler for the wood work. The bills they presented were for $4302.67, and here was a beginning of long continued trouble.

Aside from a miscellaneous item of $106.50, the face value of the fund subscribed by 113 persons was $3894.50. John Preston headed the list with $500. James McDowell, Andrew Reid, and John Robinson followed with subscriptions of $200, $160, and $150, respectively. John Leyburn, Alexander Shields, William Caruthers, Carter Beverly, Gordon Cloyd, and John Taliaferro gave each $10. The remaining pledges were of sums varying from $5 to $60. The subscriptions were not fully paid in, even so late as 1827. Thus the school was heavily in debt from the start. The income from tuition was scarcely more than sufficient for the ordinary expense, and very little could be done toward paying off the indebtedness. A judgment was at length secured by Jordan, but he allowed a rebate of $250 on account of the damage resulting from the use of inferior brick. By the close of 1821, his claim with interest had grown to $2321.66. In March, 1824, a sale of the schoolhouse and lot was decreed, the personal property of the academy, amounting to less than $100, having already been applied to the indebtedness. John Robinson, the benefactor of Washington College, now interposed, bought off the claimants, and executed a release to the trustees. There were no further financial difficulties of a serious kind, and the property was kept in repair from the income from the rents.

Relief had vainly been asked of the legislature. A memorial by the trustees, dated 1821, proposed to turn the school over to the state, This paper gives some interesting facts. The buildings had cost $5255.51. They had a capacity for 100 students, besides room for the principal and the steward, and lodging for forty-five boarding students. The high-water mark in the attendance had been seventy, but for several years past the average had been about twenty-five. Instruction was given in reading, writing, and arithmetic, grammar, geography, natural philosophy, chemistry, astronomy, belles lettres, French, painting, instrumental music, and embroidery. Tuition in the lower branches was twenty-five dollars a year. The extra tuition for geography and other advanced studies, and for painting, embroidery, and music, varied from $5 to $20. The students were generally between the ages of thirteen and sixteen. All had to eat at the steward's table, unless there were special arrangement otherwise. The rules of government were unwritten, the discipline being on a parental basis.

It was pointed out that Ann Smith was the only school of its kind in the state, and so far as known to the trustees, it was the only one of its kind in the entire South. In Virginia the education of females had hitherto been left to the schools of a transient sort. The trustees remarked that an institution of a permanent character would tend to break down local prejudices and create something like uniformity in sentiment, habits, and manners. Under Miss Smith hundreds of girls from Virginia and other states had been educated at Lexington, who otherwise might never have enjoyed anything better than rudimentary training. But because of the suit threatened by the principal creditor, students were discouraged from coming, and the teachers had found employment elsewhere. As a private residence the academy building was not worth what it cost. The school had no productive funds whatever, and in default of outside help there was no future for it. John Ruff and Samuel McD. Reid were made a committee to back up the statements in the memorial with evident facts. But as already observed, the Assembly turned a deaf ear to the appeal.

Ann Smith severed her connection with the Academy in 1812. Her reasons for doing so are not clearly shown. Perhaps she thought that after working five years for no other financial return than her board and other primary expenses, she had done her part in putting the new school on its feet. Under her supervision the academy had been very prosperous, and her departure was sincerely regretted by the community. The average attendance had been thirty-four, and during sixteen sessions the charges for tuition amounted to $6525.96. In the expense account, the following are a few of the items charged to the principal:

One pair of "Dogg irons"	$22.39
One pair shoes	1.75
One pair black stockings	2.92
30 yards dimity	18.75
One yard blue satin	2.00
Mending an umbrella	.19
Hauling a trunk from Colonel McDowell's	.25

Yet the loss of the first principal was unfortunate. The attendance fell off in a marked degree. From 1821 to 1839 the building was simply rented out for school purposes. But after the latter date there was a regular succession of principal, and the school recovered something of its early prestige. Under the Reverend John W. Pratt, who took charge in 1871, there was an advanced course in which the tuition was $50. Boys were admitted about 1877. Then for about a quarter of a century, the academy was a good day school with classical features. The last principal was Miss Madge Paxton whose administration continued from 1879 until 1892. The last trustees were John L. Campbell, Addison Hogue, W. T. Shields, General Scott Shipp, and W. C. Stuart.

In 1903 the building was rented to the public school board. Fve years later the trustees offered to convey the property to the town of Lexington, on condition that the town would,—by October 1, 1909,—erect a school building of not less than $15,000. For this purpose there was a bond issue of $20,000, and the venerable building was torn down to give room on the same spot for the High School of Lexington. On New Year's day, 1910, the trustees turned over to the public school board its unexpended fund of $730, and in return for this gift two perpetual scholarships were established in the high school These, known as the Ann Smith scholarships, are awarded by the principal to two meritorious girl students of Lexington or Rockbridge county. The above act closes the official history of the Ann Smith Academy. The school had endured more than a century, and had imparted secondary education to many hundreds of girls, especially those of Rockbridge.

We now present in its actual form, Miss Smith's letter of acceptance at the end of the first and experimental year. The original is well preserved and is written in a clear, bold, and rather masculine hand. It is followed by a letter of farewell from the trustees, who then, as always, were among the leading men of Rockbridge. The two letters not only throw some light of their own on the history of the academy, but they are interesting specimens of the precise and formal epistolary language of a hundred years ago:

Col. McDowell, Captn. Preston, Captn. Wilson, E. Graham Esqr.
Gentlemen

The favorable sentiments toward me, expressed in your polite address, have diffused over my mind a considerable degree of complacency, and I beg you to accept my thanks, for your esteem and approbation, with which you are pleased to honor me. Your solicitude for the prosperity of an institution, that has for its object, the enlargement of the female mind, excites my gratitude; and prompts me to a concurrence in a zeal so laudable. My peculiar turn of mind, renders it disagreeable to me, to enter into a positive engagement, or to say, or to do any thing, that would oblige me to *fix here;* yet for a continuance of my exertions, I think you may with *safety rely*, on my habits of industry, and the friendly sentiments, with which I am impressed, toward the inhabitants of the place.— As to pecuniary matters, my accompt at the post-office, and small demands which casualties may oblige me to make, will be all I shall ever ask:— However Gentlemen, as you seem inclined to respect whatever may be interesting to me, I will mention a subject that has engaged my attention, ever since an unexpected number of students, promised success to our seminary.— I have been informed, that the Washington Academy, is much indebted to the exertions of the late revd. Mr. Graham, and that he was the friend of genius, and of literature. Now, could we extend the advantages of this institution, to his family, it might be pleasant to the feelings of the benevolent, and grateful, to see an *old debt* noticed, and the virtues, of a father, visited on his children.

The peculiar circumstances, of one of the Miss Grahams, have disposed me much in her favor, and I think it would give me pleasure, to have an opportunity, of showing her attention.

I hope, Gentlemen, what is here suggested will be agreeable to you, if otherwise, remember I am to *receive,* not to *give* directions.

ANN SMITH.

Lexington April 8th 1808.

Miss Ann Smith:

Madam, The Trustees of the Seminary which bears your name, have heard with regret that you have expressed an intention of leaving the institution at the end of the present session. Although the Trustees have never expected you to continue with them longer than would be consistent with your comfort and convenience, yet having been led to believe that you had some time ago, made up your mind to continue at least until next Fall, they have not made those efforts to procure a suitable successor which perhaps they might otherwise have done. The interests you must naturally be expected to feel for the future prosperity of an institution which has grown up into eminence under your patronage and care, will doubtless induce you to endeavor to leave it in such circumstances as will afford a reasonable prospect of its permanent usefulness. Your continuance another session would enable the Trustees to collect the greater part of the outstanding subscriptions, to pay the debts of the institution, to procure a good set of maps & globes, & perhaps to obtain a reputable female successor. But on this subject the Trustees cannot insist. You have already done more than, at first they could expect; and if your determination is fixed they must in silence acquiesce. It is a duty, however, which they owe to you & to themselves to express, as they on several occasions have done heretofore, the high sense they entertain of the assiduity & skill which you have always manifested in conducting the seminary, and which had so large a share in raising it from small beginnings to its present eminence. And they have the satisfaction to reflect, that it has been their constant endeavor to promote your comfort & convenience, so far as it could be done by any effort on their part. If there has been any failure, it has arisen from want of skill or want of means, and not of want of inclination.

To whatever part of the world you may remove or whatever mey be your future destiny, you will carry with you their best wishes for your happiness & they will hope that you will always entertain a maternal solicitude for the interests and prosperity of the Ann Smith Academy.

So long as education was usually regarded in Virginia as a private interest, the pay school had a monopoly of educational efforts. And since the well-to-do were the most willing as well as the best able to pay tuition fees, it is easy to understand that much stress was laid on a better training than could well be given in the old field school itself. The men who conducted the schools of higher rank were frequently college graduates, and were often of superior qualifications for the school room. The effect was to diffuse a considerable degree of scholastic culture among the more prosperous members of the community. The private academy had lost none of its repute in the decade following the war of 1861. But the opening years of the twentieth century found the free school system so well intrenched, and doing so efficient work in the higher grades, that the private institution could no longer compete on equal terms with the public graded school. It was because of this fact that the Ann Smith Academy passed out of existence.

The antebellum academy schools at Lexington, Brownsburg, Fancy Hill, Kerr's Creek, and Ben Salem could fit the student for college or give him a respectable start even without college training. Many of the old field schools were able to give instruction in the classics.

Lexington, Fancy Hill, and Brownsburg have been the most conspicuous seats of private academies. The record of the county seat is to be found in the history of Liberty Hall and Ann Smith Academy. Yet in 1834, incorporation was asked for the Central School of Lexington, founded in 1819 by John Leyburn, John Perry, John Jordan, Andrew Wallace, William H. Letcher, Reuben Ross, Samuel Darst, Phoebe Caruthers, John Ruff, and Joseph Blair. These persons bought a lot and built a house upon it at a cost of $1100. But it would appear that primary rather than secondary education was the purpose.

In the Lexington *Gazette* for 1855 are the advertisements of four schools of academic rank. One of these was the Brownsburg High School, under the care of James Greer. Another was the Lexington Classical School, conducted by Jacob Fuller, A. M. Its tuition was $40. There was also the announcement of the Lexington Mathematical and English Academy, to be presided over by G. A. Goodman. The tuition was $8 for five months. The same paper advertised that James B. Ramsey would open a classical school at Highland Bell schoolhouse near New Monmouth.

In 1860 the Brownsburg Female Seminary advertised a nine months session, with tuition at $20 to $40 and board at $100 to $110.

In 1856 the *Valley Star* contained a notice of the Rural Valley Seminary, three miles north of the Natural Bridge. The principal was the Reverend Samuel Emerson, A. M. In 1860 the Brownsburg Seminary announced a session of nine months, with board at $100, and tuition at $20 to $40. The same year Miss Laura Ball was teaching a term of ten months in Lexington.

The same fall that brought General Lee to Lexington witnessed the opening of the Lexington Classical School by C. P. Estill, a graduate of Washington College and an accomplished scholar. Another laborer in this field at the same time was W. B. Poindexter.

In 1866, the Brownsburg High School, now in charge of Captain H. R. Morrison, was still at work. The same year the county papers advertised the Fancy Hill Classical School by Colonel W. T. Poague, and the opening of an English and Classical School by S. C. Smith. A select school, conducted at the county seat for several years by the Misses Baxter, was still at work. His house "Seclusaval," near Fancy Hill, Robert C. McCluer, who died in 1881, maintained for many years a classical school for girls. David E. Laird, who won a Robinson prize medal in 1856, opened a classical school at old Fancy Hill, and continued it for nineteen years. Colonel Poague was associated with him for six years.

Palmer's Academy, near the junction of the north and south forks of the Buffalo seems to have been the last school of this class. A joint stock company was formed in 1903. The following spring, the cornerstone was laid with Masonic ceremonies and was followed with an educational address by Doctor J. A. Quarles of Washington and Lee University. After three quite successful sessions as a high grade private school, the academy was in 1907 converted into a public high school, the first to be organized in this county outside of Lexington.

XXVIII

THE FRANKLIN SOCIETY

No history of Rockbridge would be at all complete without a sketch of the Franklin Society. For nearly a century it was foremost among the debating clubs of the county, and it provided a public library to the town of Lexington.

The exact year of its origin is not certainly known. According to the *Valley Star* of 1856, it took its rise in 1800. We find also a belief that it was in existence as early as 1796. Both these statements may be correct. During several successive winters the men of Lexington may have maintained a debating club in an informal manner and without giving it a distinctive name. They would soon have come to feel the need of definite organization.

Be this as it may, Colonel J. T. L. Preston, in his address before the Franklin Society in February, 1873, tells us that it was first known as "The Belles Lettres Society." Four new names succeeded one another within the next dozen years. In 1804 the organization was called "The Union," in 1807, "The Republican Society"; in 1808, "The Literary Society of Lexington"; and finally August, 1811, "The Franklin Society."

The following persons are named as the leading members—probably for the year 1800—John Alexander, Andrew Alexander, Doctor S. L. Campbell, John Caruthers, James Caruthers, Cornelius Dorman, John Leyburn, Thomas L. Preston, Alexander Shields, and Layman Wayt.

Colonel Preston says the society made its first purchase of books in 1813. The thirty-eight volumes were mainly on historical subjects. In 1801, however, a library, disticnct from the debating society, was organized on the share-holding principle. This library was sold in 1825.

Incorporation came January 30, 1816. The first meeting under the charter was to effect an organization, and was held in the hall of Washington College. Ten years later, ground was purchased at the corner of Nelson and Jefferson streets, and a building was erected at a cost of $1,800. Several years later the lot was enlarged. The original charter expired by limitation, February 1, 1850, but a renewal was granted and this was to remain valid until 1870. The petition asking for the renewal informs us that in 1849 the house and lot were worth $2,500. and that the 1400 volumes in the library had cost $3,000. But seven years later, the *Valley Star* tells us there were forty shareholders, and that the real estate and the library were each worth $4,000. A meeting held January 27, 1851, decided to ask that the society be given leave to enlarge its quarters, its building not being sufficiently commodious. The Franklin Hall was twenty-four by fifty feet on the ground and two stories high. The upper floor was occupied by the hall for debates, which were held every Saturday night. The library was also kept in the room, and for more than fifty years John W. Fuller was the librarian. By 1873, $10,000 had been expended for ground, house, and library. The books came through the war of 1861 unscathed.

The questions for debate were scientific as well as literary, and were exceedingly varied in their scope. "Since 1850," remarks Colonel Preston, "no subject of interest, of national, or state, or county importance, has failed to be discussed in the Franklin. In 1860-61, how wide the difference of opinion, and how sternly those opinions were held!"

Some of the questions for debate in the pre-war period were these:

"Would a separation of the states be preferable to a limited monarchy?" Decided in the negative.

"Are theatrical amusements prejudicial to morality?" Decided in the affirmative

"Does man consist in two substances, special and distinct from each other?" Decided in the negative.

"Can any heathen be saved who never heard the name of Jesus?" Decided in the affirmative by a unanimous vote.

"Ought the Scriptures to be used as a classbook in the schools?" Decided in the affirmative.

"Would it be polite to repeal the hog law in this town?" Decided in the negative.

From the first there was a good feeling between the Franklin Society and Washington College. It is also worthy of note in this connection that the establishing of the Virginia Military Institute was first publicly discussed by this society.

The weekly debates came to an end in 1891, and in the same year the hall and library were transferred to the Washington and Lee University on condition that a Franklin Society scholarship be founded for the benefit of some student from Rockbridge. In 1909 the hall was sold by the university. It was destroyed by fire January 8, 1915.

The Franklin Society flourished almost a hundred years. It was indeed a wise foresight that purchased the lot and built the hall. Without such an anchor a debating society will languish and at length dissolve. But real estate is held to with tenacity, even though it may not put back a dollar into the pockets of its owners. The hall was a place for lectures and entertainments as well as debates. It was frequented by the ablest talent of Lexington, and among the attendants, despite the fact that the automobile had not yet arrived, were men from the rural districts. The society exerted a wide and beneficial influence in Lexington and its vicinity, and even outside of Rockbridge county.

Interest waned after the coming of the iron horse to Lexington. The debates languished. There seemed to be only one thing for the society to do, and that was to close its doors. In our day there is a greater inclination to scan the daily newspaper in its headlines, to gallop through the "latest book," and to go joy-riding in a Ford than to take time for the more substantial benefit that comes through the perusal of the world's classics, or the threshing out of some topic of interest by debaters who prepare themselves for the fray. Ours is a time of transition, a hurried, feverish time. But all fevers burn themselves out, and as our new century becomes more "stabilized," the debate may once more come into its own. It may also be that some of the people who knew the old Franklin will know a new one.

XXIX

JOURNALISM AND LITERATURE

THE REPOSITORY—ANTEBELLUM NEWSPAPERS—THE NEWER JOURNALISM—ROCKBRIDGE IN LITERATURE

At the outbreak of the War of the Revolution, there were only two newspapers published in Virginia and both were published at the capital. Neither of them contained more reading matter than one of our present four-page Sunday School papers.

On first glance it is almost a wonder that within thirty years a weekly newspaper of a still larger size should appear in distant Lexington. But at the opening of the nineteenth century the county seat of Rockbridge was one of the more important of the few and small towns of this state. It was also a time when political feeling in America was running high. This was a powerful incentive to the multiplication of partisan newspapers.

In the library of the Washington and Lee University is the only copy of the *Rockbridge Repository,* known to be in existence. It bears the date, Wednesday, January 19, 1804. The title-page carries the motto, "Truth our Guide, the Public Good Our Aim"; and as a vignette, a bust of the Goddess of Liberty. A further scrutiny of the heading shows that publication began October 21, 1802. The size of the page is that of a five-column paper of the present day. Long primer type is used. The publisher was James McMullin, and the subscription price was $2 a year. The editor claims that his patronage is widely distributed. A recently established opposition paper was the *Telegraph*, which McMullin, like a true knight of the quill, excoriates in his editorial column. The *Repository* was still in existence in 1805.

It is related in Foote's Sketches of Virginia that in October, 1804, the first number of the *Virginia Religious Magazine* was issued from the press of Samuel Walkup in Lexington. That periodical, which was of sixty-four pages, continued to appear every other month for three years. It is said to have been the first of the kind to be published south of the Potomac.

A dark age with respect to our knowledge of Rockbridge journalism now appears to set in. In 1835, a paper calling itself *The Union,* and published by C. C. Baldwin, changed its name to the *Lexington Gazette* and under the latter title it has appeared ever since, excepting that it was *The Gazette and Banner*, in 1866, *The Virginia Gazette,* in 1869-70, and for a while in after years, *The Lexington Gazette and Commercial Advertiser.* Until after 1873 its editors were O. P. Baldwin, C. C. Baldwin, James Patton, Alphonso Smith, David P. Curry, James

K. Edmondson, John L. Campbell, W. W. Scott, Josiah McNutt, Samuel H. Letcher, John J. Lafferty, and A. T. Barclay. In 1839, *The Valley Star* came into existence and was published until after the presidential campaign of 1860.

For more than twenty years these well-matched journals occupied the local field. Each had an ornamental title-head, this being a quite universal feature of the American weeklies of that period and also for some years after the war of 1861. The page is of seven columns. The type is smaller than is now customary in papers of this class, so that the amount of reading matter is very considerable. Fully two pages are devoted to Congressional doings, national politics, stories, and miscellaneous matter. The proceedings in the halls of Congress are given at such great length, and such liberal extracts are taken from the speeches of "Timothy Tremendous" and his contemporaries, that this department of either paper reads like the *Congressional Record*. So much space is given to politics—of the nation even more than of the state,—that the local news is very meagre. The person who is delving into local history consequently finds little to reward him for his search. The advertising matter, which covers nearly two pages, is set almost solid. Capitals and heavy-faced type are counted upon to catch the eye of the reader. The art of display was little understood.

The *Valley Star* supported the Democratic party. *The Gazette* supported the short-lived American Party, which in a large degree supplanted the Whig, and disappeared in 1860 after changing its name to the Constitutional Union party. Some features of the advertising columns look strange to us now. There are advertisements of runaway negroes, while certain persons announce that they are in the market for the purchase of slaves. Occasional mention of the Maryland Lottery calls to mind the fact that it has not been so very long since the Louisiana Lottery was excluded from the mails after a long fight with its large corruption fund. A little earlier in the century, even churches did not scruple to raise funds by resorting to lotteries. But a healthier moral tone at length drove this form of gambling to cover.

To the historian of the war of 1861, the Lexington papers of the years 1859-1865 will repay a close examination. Particularly is this true of the twelve months ending with May, 1861. The issues of the day are ably and lengthily discussed in the editorial columns, in articles contributed by prominent citizens, and in letters coming from a distance. Even the four years of actual combat did not induce the editors to cut out very much of the space they had formerly allowed to poetry, fiction, travel, household items, and paragraphs of general interest. In pursuing this course the editors were wise. Such reading was a relaxation from the strain which was sure to follow a too absorbing interest in the events which persisted in occupying the foreground.

The *Gazette* appeared quite regularly throughout the war period, even though it reduced its pages from four to two. It was more fortunate than some other journals of the South, for it was often compulsory to resort to the most indifferent materials, even wall paper, in order to come out at all.

Until after the clash of arms in April, 1861, the Lexington papers were temperate in the language they used when speaking of the North and its people. But after that occurrence there was an abrupt change.

That the close of that conflict indeed marked the "end of an era," is perhaps nowhere more evident than in a comparison of the journalism of the 50's with that of the decade following the war. The earlier style simply passed out of existence. In the latter period there is a new point of view. The minute reports of Congressional proceedings are a thing of the past. Matters of state, and particularly of county interest, receive a greatly increased share of attention. In this is reflected a desire to repair the waste caused by the war. Economic change compels some change in mental attitude. There is a greater activity of the social consciousness. The literary feature is by no means neglected, and is indeed better than in the earlier time. There now begins a "fighting them over" of the campaigns of the war, articles of this class embracing biographies of Confederate leaders, controversies relative to military operations, and incidents of camp, march, and battle. The editorials are fiery and speak of the Federal administration as though it were a foreign government. The general effect of these on a Northern reader would have been much like that of rubbing a cat's back in the direction which is not agreeable to that animal. But in this respect there was little to choose in the political editorials of America, whether written north or south of the old Mason and Dixon line. On neither side was there any lack of ginger. The partisan journalism of that period, irrespective of section, has had much to answer for in keeping alive the coals of distrust and misunderstanding. However, this peppery style of editorial writing was not often rebuked.

Wit and humor were more characteristic of this period in Rockbridge journalism than either before or since. Conspicuous in this line are snake stories and other "yarns" of a like degree of extravagance; mention of orations by "Furiosus Bombasticus" and the "Reverend Theodore Swellhead"; the "Intercepted Letters" that were appearing about 1877. A forecast of the year 1874 we transfer to this chapter, using a slight amount of editing.

Careful calculations based on the respective situations and appearances of the heavenly bodies, by a competent astrologist, led to the following conclusions concerning coming events in this county during the year just begun.

The year will open with snows and the consumption of immense quantities of eggnogg. The shire-town of the county will experience a political revolution and consequent change in its administration policy and municipal officers. It will rain persistently for one week and then freeze and cause people to "slick up." The Franklin Society will disestablish the English Church. People will get drunk at court and other days, chew tobacco and smoke, and dip snuff. Some will be put in the "cage." It will snow and sleet and rain some more. One hundred and fifty people will get tired living singly and agree to do so doubly. Some will die. The wheat will look dreadfully bad. It will certainly turn out to be "winter-killed," taken by the fly, or rust. There will be no corn in the land. The taxes will be high. The dogs will kill some sheep. The roads will be in a miserable condition. Some people will eat possums and coons. A few will quarrel with our representatives in the legislature, and many will want to go there themselves. There will be preaching in all the churches tolerably regularly. People will sue and be sued. There will be court once a month and four times a year, too. The bank will not honor your check when you haven't any money there. The railroad won't come this year. Money will be hard to get. Children will be born with red, black, light, curly, and kinky hair, and some without any. None will be born with teeth. Some will be born good and some bad. There will be fights, fusses, and frowns.

In 1874 the *Gazette* thus speaks of its veteran typesetter:

There is a printer in the *Gazette* office, Burgess by name. He has been "setting" from scrawly type for half a century. The arrowhead inscriptions would be as plain as pica to him. He can put in type the curious marks made by the county court lawyer. He never failed on Judge McLaughlin's writing, fine as if made by a cambric needle, with one good letter beginning a word and the balance a wavy line. Colonel Allen couldn't balk him with microscopic manuscript looking like the fuzz on a flea. But the law class sent up Mr. Tucker's notes to print. For two hours Burgess tried in vain to start a single line on any paragraph. The unrappy printer felt his head to find if it was too hot or out of gear. A walk in the cool air gave him no aid. After we had examined them ten minutes, Burgess looked over our shoulder and said we had them upside down.

All in all, the Rockbridge newspaper of this period was a distinct advance over that of the 50's and had a general solidity that has not since been surpassed.

The *Rockbridge County News,* appearing as a non-political paper, made its bow November 7, 1884, and from that time to the present has been a well-printed local newspaper, substantial in its contents, and strong in its presentation of matters that are of fundamental interest to the people of its county.

When we compare the Rockbridge paper of 1918 with its predecessor of 1858, the contrast is striking. Local news predominates in the former over all other kinds, and even state news occupies a subordinate place. Very long articles are infrequent, unless in the case of an address at the University or the Institute. Miscellaneous reading, unless it may feature as a topic of the day finds little room. The open spaces in the advertisements contrast strongly with the closely printed advertising columns of the earlier period.

In most instances the literary record of a county is soon told. Occasionally, in fact, there is no record to tell. But the list of books by natives of Rockbridge, or long-time residents of the county, is of quite formidable length. So difficult would be the task of constructing a full and accurate biography, that we have not felt warranted in undertaking it. Such titles as have become known to us are in general to be found in the sketches comprising Chapter XXXIII.

XXX

OLD MILITIA DAYS

THE COLONIAL SYSTEM—THE MILITIA IN THE REVOLUTION—THE ROCKBRIDGE ORGANIZATION
—MUSTER DAYS

Before the Revolution there was no standing army in any of the American colonies, and the exclusive reliance in time of war was upon the militia. In this contingency, all the white males in Virginia, if adult and able-bodied, were supposed to be subject to the call of the county lieutenants. The commissioned officers were nominated by the county court and confirmed by the governor.

The day of general muster was the fourth Tuesday of September. There was a company muster every three months. The private went to muster or to war in his ordinary clothes. The hunting shirt, sometimes of one color and sometimes of another, and the coonskin cap were so typical on the frontier as to serve the purpose of uniform. The militiaman took his own rifle or smooth-bored gun, and in his belt were a hunting knife and a tomahawk. The company officer seem generally to have dressed like the privates and to have carried his rifle and powder-horn, the same as his soldiers.

A commission in the military service was esteemed very honorable, and was regarded as a stepping stone to something higher. Yet it was only the officer with a strong inborn power of leadership who could exert much influence over the frontiersman. The latter was almost without any sense of military ethics, and could not see why his neighbor should have any designated right to give orders. He was not inclined to obey except when it suited his pleasure to do so. His lack of precaution as well as discipline often caused him to run into an ambuscade, or to permit the Indian to get close to his stockade without being seen. His "tour of duty" was seldom for more than three months, and frequently it was for not more than one or two months. While thus absent the pay of the private was from a shilling to a shilling and a half a day.

During the Revolution there was no radical change in the method of public defense. A standing army was held in so great suspicion that it was all but impossible to convince the leaders of affairs of the unwisdom of pitting an insubordinate militia against trained regulars. Nevertheless, a considerable number of men were enlisted in the Continental service. When trained by professional drillmasters, many of whom were foreigners, they could hold their own against the best of the redcoats. This shows that it was not the men themselves who were at fault, but the system, or rather the lack of system. Occasionally, as at King's Mountain and the Cowpens, and to a partial extent at Guilford, the militia fought to good purpose. But in general their propensity to take to their heels caused them to be held in contempt by the Continentals and to be sworn at by the higher officers. No militiaman could tell how his comrades might act. They were easily demoralized, and when this was the case, each person looked out for himself. Few of their officers had a practical knowledge of the art of war, and were consequently the less able to turn raw, willful material into good soldiery in a month or two. Washington, Morgan, Henry Lee, and other leaders understood the situation perfectly, but had to contend with opposition from men like Jefferson, who, with respect to military matters were impractical and inefficient. But for the influence of men like him, the war might have ended in 1777 instead of 1781.

Some light on the comparative merit of the trained and untrained soldiers of the Revolution can be gathered by reading their applications for pension. In the case of a veteran who had served in a Continental regiment, we find that he usually had seen considerable of the war. Not infrequently he was wounded or captured in some important engagement. But when the militiaman was out on several tours, the aggregate seldom amounted to a year of service, and we come upon the very frequent statement that the applicant "was in no battle."

The militia companies of Augusta were expected to consist of expert riflemen. Each soldier was to "furnish himself with a good rifle, if to be had, otherwise with a tomahawk, common firelock, bayonet, pouch or cartouch box, and three charges of powder and ball." If the rifleman made an affidavit that he could not supply himself as above, the equipment was to be furnished at public expense. For providing his own equipment, he was to be allowed a rental of one pound a year. His daily pay was to be twenty-one cents. From this was deducted an allowance for "hunting shirt, a pair of leggings, and binding for his hat."

After American independence was accomplished, Virginia was divided into divisions, brigade, and regimental districts. The militia of this county belonged to the Thirteenth Brigade District, which lay in the Third Division District. In 1794 there were five companies in each of the two battalions of the Eighth Regiment, but in the year following there were six companies in each battalion. A grenadier and a rifle company are mentioned in 1794, and one company each of cavalry, artillery, and light infantry in 1815. A division into two regiments seems to have taken place in 1807, in which year we find mention of the Third Regiment.

To each division were attached one regiment of cavalry and one of artillery. The regiment, consisting of at least 400 men and commanded by a colonel, was divided into two battalions, one commanded by the lientenant-colonel and one by the major. Each battalion had a stand of colors. In each company were one captain, two first lieutenants, two second lieutenants, five sergeants, and six corporals. The ensign, a commissioned officer having charge of the colors and ranking below the second lieutenant, was dispensed with after the war of 1812. On the staff of the colonel was one quartermaster, one paymaster, one surgeon, one surgeon's mate, one adjutant with the rank of captain, one sergeant major, one quartermaster-sergeant, two principal musicians, and drum and fife majors. Each company had one drum and either a fife or a bugle. A failure to attend muster meant a fine, usually seventy-five cents, and this was put into the hands of the sheriff for collection.

Regimental muster came off in April or May, and was preceded by a three days, training of the officers, who were gaily appareled. Their costume included a hat with dangling feathers and a long, swallow-tailed dark-blue coat with eqauletts and brass buttons. The privates were uniformed and sometimes carried canes or umbrellas in place of arms.

The day of general muster was the event of the year. It brought to town a great crowd of both sexes and races and all ages. The costumes presented all the colors imaginable. There were sheet-covered wagons with little tables in front, loaded with sweet cider, ginger ale, half-moon pies, lemonade, coffee, and cup-shaped pound cakes. There was the military strut of the officer, the proud prancing of ribbon-decked stallions, and the soul-stirring music of drum and fife. The hour of muster was ten o'clock. As the time approached, a detachment of cavalry was sent to escort the colonel and his staff to the parade ground. Guards were posted around it to keep the field clear. After two hours of drill, during which each man kept his own step the procession came back to town, and was dissolved with the long roll, concluded with "Yankee Doodle," or some other quick, lively tune. The colonel then complimented his men and told them how interesting they would make it for an enemy if ever they should have to meet him. There was finally the command to "break ranks, march." The sequel was a general imbibing of liquids much stronger than those vended at the tables in front of the wagons. This had its inevitable accompaniment of fights and bloody faces. There was noise and fuss of every description. It was a day of "rare frolic for the boys, a scary time for the mothers, and a busy time for the magistrates and constables."

As a practical instrumentality, the militia system of that period was little better than a farce. Its inefficiency appears in the fact that before the middle of the century it had broken down and continued to exist only on paper.

XXXI

A ROCKBRIDGE HALL OF FAME

Emigration From The County—Notable Names

Almost from the very dawn of settlement there has been a persistent emigration from Rockbridge. Like all agricultural communities of its class, this county has been a nursery ground for the peopling of newer portions of the Union. For a long while the outflow was almost wholly toward the points in the western half of the compass dial. Emigrants from this locality were in the forefront in peopling the Bluegrass region of Kentucky. So many of the sons and daughters of Rockbridge poured into the Valley of East Tennessee as to make some of its counties—Blount, for instance—look like colonies of Rockbridge. Some of the later emigrants did not pause until they reached the Pacific coast or the vicinity of the Rio Grande.

But during the last quarter-century the eastern half of the compass dial is claiming some attention. The Great West has lost its pristine newness, and the Atlantic seaboard presents certain attractions. There is an appreciable reflex movement felt even as far as the Pacific. The outgoing tide from Rockbridge may be termed cosmopolitan, so far as the boundaries of the American Republic are concerned.

It is significant that from the center of the county, where there was the most slavery as well as the most wealth, the emigrants used to find the greatest attraction in the planting districts of the South and Southwest. But from the western border the emigrant has been much more inclined to settle west of the Ohio.

The people of Rockbridge have been a rather prolific stock. Had the rate of increase which was true of all America until 1840 been maintained to the present year, and had there been an iron law to keep any person from moving out, this county would now contain as many inhabitants as the city of Washington. It will thus appear that the people of Rockbridge birth or ancestry who live outside our borders are vastly more numerous than the people actually within them.

The colonial imigrants from Ulster were the pick of that region. The other people who took part in the subjugation of the Rockbridge wilderness were among the more energetic of the dwellers along the Atlantic coast. The fusion of these elements produced a stock virile, forceful, and intellectual. That from it should come statesmen, soldiers, explorers, professional men, writers, and inventors, was a more natural consequence. Of the celebrities from Rockbridge

Rev. Henry W. McLaughlin, D. D.
Pastor New Providence Presbyterian Church
October, 1909
There have been only eight pastors of New Providence Presbyterian Church in 173 years of its history.

Southern Seminary, Buena Vista, Virginia. Founded 1868
Devoted to the education of Girls and Young Women. In its fifty-third year.
Principals: Rev. E. H. Rowe, Prof. R. L. Durham

named in "Augusta County, Virginia, in the History of the United States," fifty-three are contributed by four families: the McDowells, the Dunlaps, the Logans, and the McKees.

No attempt to construct a Rockbridge Hall of Fame can result in completeness. To sift out from the major and minor celebrities of America all the names traceable to a Rockbridge source is a hopeless undertaking. In this chapter we mention only such names as have come to our notice.

Furthermore, Rockbridge has been much honored by men and women who were born and reared elsewhere, yet came here to live, sometimes not until the evening of their days had arrived. The influences that drew them here lay very much in the two great educational institutions of Lexington. Conspicuous among the personages of this class are Robert E. Lee, the foremost chieftain of the Confederacy; Stonewall Jackson, the right arm of Lee; Matthew F. Maury, the "Pathfinder of the Seas"; John Brown and William Graham, founders of Liberty Hall Academy; Henry Ruffner and George Junkin, presidents of Washington College; Francis H. Smith, fifty years the head of the Virginia Military Institute; John W. Brockenbrough, jurist and teacher of law, David H. Hill, the soldier-professor; J. Randolph Tucker, authority on constitutional law; William L. Wisson, congressman, cabinet officer, and university president; John M. Brooke, the professor who planned the ironclad Merrimac and made ocean cables possible by his device for determining the depth of the ocean; and finally, the authoresses, Margaret Junkin Preston and Susan P. Lee.

It would be very interesting to know to a certainty how many counties, cities, and towns in our forty-eight states have been named for Rockbridge men. As to counties, we know of more than are to be found in Arizona, Delaware, Nevada, or Wyoming, or in any of the six New England states.

Four counties, a great commercial city, and towns and villages in twelve states bear the name of General Sam Houston, the Washington of Texas. Allen county, Kentucky, was named for Colonel John Allen, killed in the battle of the Raisin in 1813; Anderson county, South Carolina, for General Robert Anderson, Campbell county, Kentucky, for Colonel John Campbell. Carlisle county, also in Kentucky, bears the name of an eminent son of the Bluegrass State, whose first American ancestors lived on the Calfpasture. Carson county in Texas was named for Samuel P. Carson, and Craighead county in Arkansas for Thomas B. Craighead, a descendant of Alexander Craighead, a pioneer divine who owned a farm in the Borden Tract. Dale county in Alabama was named for General Samuel Dale, whose parents left Rockbridge in 1775. "Big Sam" was a great scout and Indian fighter. In eight days and without change of horse, he rode from Georgia to New Orleans to deliver a message for General Andrew Jackson. He sat in the legislatures of Alabama and Mississippi, and in 1831 superintended the removal of the Choctaw tribe to Oklahoma. Edmondson county, Kentucky, contains Mammoth Cave and was named for Captain John Edmondson, another soldier killed in the battle of the river Raisin. Estill county in the same state was named for James, a brother to Benjamin Estill, ancestor to the Estills who used to live in Lexington. Hays county, Nevada, commemorates the name of Colonel John E. Hays, the first sheriff of San Francisco. Jo Daviess county, Illinois, was named for Colonel Joseph H. Daviess, a rival of Henry Clay as an orator and the first Western lawyer to appear before the Supreme Court of the United States. McDowell county in West Virginia and the town of McDowell in Virginia were named for Governor James McDowell. Meigs county, Tennessee, was named for Return J. Meigs, who lived a while on the Calfpasture. The county of Rhea in Tennessee derives its name from a member of the Rhea connection of this county. In Mississippi is a Tate county. Warrick county, Indiana, is named in honor of Jacob Warrick, who was born on the Calfpasture in 1773 and fell in the battle of Tippecanoe. He was a son of John and grandson of William Warwick. His descendants figure in Western history. The counties in Kentucky and Indiana that are known as Whitley derive the name from William Whitley, born in Rockbridge in 1749. He heard glowing accounts of Kentucky, to which his wife, whose maiden name was Esther Fuller, made this comment: "Billy, if I were you I would go and see." Billy made his tour of investigation by traveling afoot. He was killed at the Thames in 1813, where he was serving as a volunteer, although sixty-four years of age. Two of his descendants were William and Milton Sublette, who achieved some fame as explorers in the Rocky Mountain region. Captain William Sublette built Fort Laramie in 1834.

At least five governors of states were born in this county; James McDowell and John Letcher, governors of Virginia, George Mathews, twice governor of Georgia, Samuel Houston, governor of Tennessee and later of Texas, and Alexander G. McNutt, governor of Mississippi. The governors of Rockbridge parentage or rearing are much more numerous. The list includes Henry C. Stuart, of Virginia, Milliam A. MacCorkle and Henry M. Mathews, of West Virginia, B. Gratz Brown and Herbert S. Hadley, of Missouri, Joseph M. Brown, Joseph E. Brown, and Nathaniel E. Harris, of Georgia, William G. Brownlow, Robert L. Caruthers (not inaugurated), and Robert G. Taylor, of Tennessee, Orion Clemens, of Nevada, James M. Harvey, of Kansas, J. Proctor Knott, of Kentucky, Eli H. Murray, of Utah, Thomas Posey, of Indiana, and William A. Richardson and William Walker, of Nebraska. Clemens, Murray, Posey, Richardson, and Walker, were territorial governors. Knott was a scion of the McElroy family.

As to Federal senators we are able to name B. Gratz Brown, of Missouri, James Brown and Thomas Posey, of Louisiana, Robert H. Adams, of Mississippi,

Joseph E. Brown, of Georgia, William G. Brownlow, and Robert L. Taylor, of Tennessee, Joseph M. Dixon, of Montana, James M. Harvey, of Kansas, William Lindsay and William Logan, of Kentucky, George S. Nixon, of Nevada, Miles Poindexter and John L. Wilson, of Washington, and William A. Richardson, of Illinois. Dixon, Nixon, Poindexter, and Wilson are respectively of Hadley, Estill, Alexander, and McKee lineage. Landon C. Haynes, who sprang from the Taylor family was a Confederate senator from Tennessee.

Among members of the Federal House of Representatives we find Simon H. Anderson, William A. Anderson, John Boyle, George W. Dunlap, Samuel McKee, and Thomas Montgomery, of Kentucky; Augustus A. Chapman, Henry A. Edmondson, Archibald Stuart, Edgar McC. Wilson, and Thomas Wilson, of Virginia; William C. Dunlap, Abraham McClellan, and Nathaniel G. Taylor, of Tennessee; William McK. Dunlap, of Indiana; Joseph W. McCorkle, of California; Joseph J. McDowell, of Ohio; John McKee of Alabama; John T. Stuart and Medill McCormick, of Illinois; Edward J. Gay, of Louisiana; Charles B. Timberlake, of Colorado. Boyle, Chapman, Edmundson, and Stuart are respectively from the Tilford, Alexander, Reyburn, and Walker families.

Men who have held the rank of major-general or brigadier-general in the Continental, Federal, Confederate, or foreign service are these: John C. Bate, Jeremiah T. Boyle, James P. Brownlow, Robert Cunningham, Henry C. Dunlap, James Dunlap, William McK. Dunn, Samuel L. Glasgow, Harry T. Hays, Felix Huston, Albert C. Jenkins, Edward J. McClernand, John C. McFerran, William L. Marshall, Thomas Posey, Eli D. Murray, John D. Stevenson, J. G. Tilford, J. E. B. Stuart, James A. Walker, and Lucien Walker. Boyle sprang from the Tilfords, Dunn and Jenkins from the McNutts, Huston and Murray from the Allens, McClernand from the Dunlaps, Marshall from the Paxtons, and Stevenson from the Houstons. John M. Bowyer and John C. Fremont, Jr., attained the rank of rear-admiral. Joseph E. Montgomery was a commodore in the Confederate navy.

A further list of the sons of Rockbridge who have reached high position in public life embraces these names: John McKinley (from Logan family), Justice of the Supreme Court of the United States; Jacob M. Dickenson (McGavock family), Secretary of War; Richard G. Dunlap, Secretary of War of the Republic of Texas; James Guthrie (Dunlap family), Secretary of the Treasury; William H. Jack (Houston family), Secretary of State of the Republic of Texas; James Brown, Minister to France; James G. Birney (McDowell family), Minister to the Netherlands; Charles Denby (Harvey family), Minister to China; William C. Dunlap, Minister to Mexico from Texas; John Hays Hammond (Hays family), special Ambassador to Great Britain; Alexander K. McClung, Minister to Bolivia; Robert S. McCormick, Ambassador to France, Russia, and Austria-Hungary;

Thomas A. R. Nelson (Paxton family), Minister to China; Henry L. Wilson (McKee family), Ambassador to Mexico; James Wilson (McKee family), Minister to Venezuela.

We now come to a list of rather less prominent names. These are William Y. Allen, chaplain of the Congress of the Republic of Texas; H. S. Beattie, the first man to build a house in Carson valley, Nevada; Major Lancelot Armstrong, second in command of a Kentucky regiment in the battle of New Orleans, J. W. Bashford (Dunlap family), bishop of the Methodist Episcopal Church; Ishom Gilham, sheriff of Madison county, Illinois, when it covered the north half of that state, and instrumental in keeping slavery out of Illinois; Edward J. Glasgow, overland trader and captain under Colonel Donaphan in the battle of the Sacramento; Doctor Alfred Y. Hull, editor and legislator in Iowa; Stephen D. Logan, an Illinois jurist; John McKee, register of the United States Land Office in Illinois; Colonel John McKee, a native of Rockbridge, who in 1813 induced the Choctaws and Chicamaugas to side with the Americans; Robert McKnight, leader of what was probably the first private trading expedition to Santa Fe; Colonel Joseph L. Meek, relative to James K. Polk, who helped to establish a civil government in Oreogn in 1843; James Moore, a native of Rockbridge and president of Transylvania Unifersity; William McC. Morrison, missionary to the Congo; Joel P. Walker, who in 1841 piloted the first emigrant family to the Pacific coast, Joseph Walkup, a lieutenant-governor of California; William M. Todd, a founder of the California Republic of 1845 and painter of the famous Bear Flag of that state.

The writers of more or less prominence are numerous. They include Archer Anderson, Joseph R. Anderson, Marian P. Angelotti (Walker family), Oswald E. Brown, Nettie H. Bringhurst (Houston family), O. W. Coursey, Samuel McC. Crothers, (Dunlap family), Maria T. Daviess, (Houston family), Fanny C. Duncan (McElroy family), Jesse B. Fremont, Ellen Glasgow, Hiram Hadley, James A. Hadley, Mary G. Humphries, (Gay family), Anne B. Hyde (Taylor family), Louisa P. Looney, Benjamin McCutchen, John T. McCutchen, Robert Barr McCutchen, Robert M. McElroy, Joseph W. McSpadden, Benjamin C. Moomaw, John B. McFerrin, Lanier McKee, Lannie Haynes Martin (Taylor fabily),Maud L. Merrimom (Paxton family), John G. Paxton, William M. Paxton, Hannah D. Pittman, (Hamilton family), John Rankin, Edwin D. Royle (Peebles family), Ripley D. Saunders (Dunlap family), Charles A. Smith, Egbert W. Smith, Henry Louis Smith, John R. S. Sterrett, Givens B. Strickler (Walker family), James I. Vance, Joseph A. Vance, Sue L. A. Vaughan, George A. Wauchope, Emma S. White, Bert E. Young.

The wives of several notable men were of Rockbridge origin. They include the consorts of Edward Bates, Secretary of War, General N. B. Forrest, General

R. E. Colston, General G. J. Pillow, General Thomas Posey, General John A. McClernand, William O. Bradley, Senator from Kentucky, General Hugh L. White, Rufus W.Cobb, Governor of Alabama, and Frank White, Governor of North Dakota. It is believed that the wife of President Lincoln should be included.

In the field of invention the names of Cyrus H. McCormick and James E. A. Gibbs easily stand foremost. McCormick made a practical invention when only fifteen years old, and manufactured sixty-eight of his reapers at Walnut Grove. William A. Seward declared that this machine advanced the line of Western settlement thirty miles a year. Until it appeared America was not the granary of Europe. In 1836-37 there were bread riots in the city of New York, and grain was imported from Europe to the amount of 1,300,000 bushels. It is one of the ironies of history that a native of a slave state should give the free states an industrial weapon which in the war of 1861 outbalanced the negro labor of the South. The rotary hook devised by Gibbs was one of the fundamental things in the evolution of the perfected sewing machine of the twentieth century.

We next give in alphabetical order some facts relating to persons of note of Rockbridge, or who are connected with Rockbridge families.

The founder of Decoration Day was Mrs. Vaughn, of Missouri, whose maiden name was Sue L. Adams. Another member of the Adams family of this county was Robert H., who settled at Natchez, Mississippi, in 1819. He was elected to the Federal Senate in 1830, but died the same year. Still another was Hugh, very prominent in the business circles of Chicago.

Isaac Anderson, born near New Providence, March 26, 1780, was the oldest of the seven children of William Anderson. He was educated at Liberty Hall, studied theology under Samuel Brown, and in 1801 accompanied his father to East Tennessee, where he died January 28, 1857. Isaac Anderson was indefatigable as a minister, teacher, and student. His most enduring monument is Maryville College, the outcome of the log academy he opened in 1802. This institution has modern buildings on its campus of 250 acres, an enrollment of more than 800 students, and is one of the few present day colleges where young men and women can be educated at a low cost.

Archibald Alexander, a founder of Union Theological Seminary, was one of the foremost theologians and theological educators of America. His son, William C., was a lieutenant-governor of New Jersey, and was narrowly defeated in a contest for the governorship. Eben, a son of Adam B. Alexander, professor of Greek in the University of North Carolina, was United States Minister to Greece, Rumania, and Serbia.

Simon H. Anderson, congressman, was a son of James and Margaret.

John Bell, of Tennessee, senator, secretary of war, and in 1860 a candidate for the presidency, was a son of Samuel and Margaret (Edmiston) Bell and was related to the Bells of Augusta and Rockbridge.

The biographers of Thomas H. Benton assert that he was a native of North Carolina. On the contrary he was not only born on Walker's Creek but he was married in this county. Benton represented Missouri thirty years in the Federal Senate. He was a statesman of the first rank and was the author of a valuable contribution to American history.

Scions of the Bowyer family are Rear-Admiral John M. Bowyer and Brevet Brigadier-General Eli Bowyer of Missouri. From George Poindexter, who married Frances, a granddaughter of Michael, came Senator Poindexter of the state of Washington, who is also related to the Andersons.

William G. Brownlow, of East Tennessee, known in the civil war as "Parson Brownlow," was a picturesque character, vitriolic in tongue and pen. At the outbreak of the war he was editor of the Knoxville *Whig*. After its close he became governor of his state. He was the oldest son of Joseph of Rockbridge.

Mrs. Fannie K. Costello, a daughter of Porter Johnson and native of Rockbridge, contributes poems and short stories to *Harper's*, the *Century*, and the *Atlantic* magazines, and to the *Youth's Companion*. She is also the author of "The Beloved Son," published in 1916.

Olive Tilford Dargan, one of the greatest literary women of the South, appears to be descended from the Tilfords, of this county.

John P. Davidson, who died at Richmond in 1911, was a specialist in diseases of the eye, ear, nose, and throat.

James Gay, born in the Pastures, was the first man to import blooded cattle into Kentucky. His sister was the first white woman in Lexington, Kentucky.

James Grigsby, who went to California in 1845 and was temporarily at the head of the Bear Creek revolt against the Mexican government, was a native of Tennessee, but apparently of Rockbridge descent. Hugh Blair Grigsby, son of Benjamin of this county, achieved a more than state-wide reputation as a scholarly educator and historian.

Haysborough, six miles below Nashville, Tennessee, on the Cumberland River, was once a rival of that city. It was founded by Colonel Charles Hays, and was the seat of Davidson College, which grew into Peabody Normal College.

John A. T. Hull, congressman from Iowa, is a grandson of John, who went from Rockbridge to Ohio in 1813.

James Johnson was one of the thirteen children of James Johnston, Sr., who married Margaret Bay in 1776. One of the wife's sisters first married James Gold, of Lexington, and later a Maxwell. She went with him to Kentucky. Robert Johnston, son of James, Jr., was born on Buffalo Creek in 1818. He settled first at Clarksburg, and finally at Harrisonburg, where he died in 1885. Mr. Johnston was a lawyer of high repute, but was much in public life, serving in the General Assembly, as Auditor of Virginia, and as a member of the Confederate Congress throughout the war of 1861.

The storage reservoirs now under construction in the Miami valley of Ohio form one of the greatest engineering enterprises ever undertaken in this country, and the master builder is Charles H. Locher, who was born at Balcony Falls.

William Lindsay, a son of Andrew, left Rockbridge while a young man and began the practice of law at Frankfort, Kentucky, in 1858. He served four years in the Confederate army and was chosen state senator in 1867. For two years he was Chief Justice of the Kentucky Court of Appeals. From 1893 until 1901 he was in the United States Senate. Judge Lindsay was a member both of the Columbian Exposition Commission and the Commisssion of the Louisiana Purchase Exposition. He declined an appointment to the Interstate Commerce Commission. His grandfather, James Lindsay, was born near Glasgow, Scotland.

General John A. Logan, of the Federal army, and later a senator from Illinois and a candidate for the vice-presidency, was a descendant of Joseph D. Logan, whose wife was a descendant of Pocahontas. The general was noted for his Indian-like appearance.

General George Mathews, twice governor of Georgia, was a gallant officer against the Indians and the British.

General James H. McBride, of the Confederate army and a citizen of Missouri, was a grandson of William McBride, killed at the battle of Blue Lick, July 19, 1782. The latter seems to be identical with William McBride, of Rockbridge.

Daniel McCoy, Jr., of Ohio was in twenty-seven battles in the war of 1861 and five times severely wounded. For gallant and meritorious conduct, particularly in the battle of Nashville, he rose from the rank of private to that of brigadier-general.

Colonel James McDowell and his son, Governor James McDowell, are elsewhere mentioned. Among the descendants of their ancestor, John McDowell, were Irvin McDowell, David B. Birney, and John Buford, all of whom held high rank in the army of the Potomac. Brothers to Major-General Birney were James Birney, acting-governor of Washington Territory, 1861-63, and Brigadier-General William Birney. Humphrey Marshall, minister to China and brigadier-general in the Confederate service, was another descendant of Captain John McDowell, as was also the wife of General John C. Fremont.

Michael Miley learned photography while a prisoner of war. His practical discoveries in color photography were in no sense dependent on those of the French investigators in this line. Miley maintained that there were only three primary colors.

Major-General Samuel F. Patterson, born at Brownsburg in 1799, went to North Carolina in 1814, and was fifty years in public life in that state, sometimes occupying high position. In 1833 he was Grand Master of the Masonic Order.

There is a strong probability that the grandfather of James K. Polk was for a while a resident of the Raphine neighborhood. The names Poague and Polk are variants of Pollock. Leonidas Polk, the bishop-general of the Confederate army, was a kinsman to the president.

General Thomas Posey, senator from Louisana and in 1813 governor of Indiana Territory, was reared in this county and married into the Mathews family. Posey was the only man to whom George Washington ever gave a portrait of himself, or to whom he ever made a gift of realty.

William H. Ruffner was the father of the free school law of Virginia. He was also the chief founder of the Virginia Polytechnic Institute and the Farmville State Normal College.

John D. Sterrett was a metaphysician as well as farmer, and was the author of "The Power of Thought." John R. S. Sterrett, a professor in Cornell University, was an eminent archeaologist in the Orient.

General J. E. B. Stuart, a famous cavalry leader of the Confederate army, and Alexander H. H. Stuart, Secretary of the Interior, 1850-53, were of the Stuart connection of Rockbridge, and so is Henry C. Stuart, an ex-governor of this state.

William Taylor, first missionary bishop of the Methodist Church, preached in more parts of the earth than any other man before his time. Of a different family was General Nathaniel Taylor, who left Rockbridge to become a wealthy planter and manufacturer of Carter county, Tennessee. Robert L. Taylor and Alfred L. Taylor, the brothers who made a spectacular race for the governorship of that state in 1886, the one as a Democrat, the other as a Republican, were great grandsons of General Taylor.

There have been many Trimbles in the medical and legal profession. John, the congressman, was the son of James, who left this county with his mother and step-father to settle at Nashville.

"Big Foot" Wallace, a picturesque character in Texas history, was born one mile from Lexington.

Captain Joseph R. Walker was a guide to Bonneville in 1831-36, and afterward to Fremont in their explorations in and beyond the Rocky Mountains.

James Wilson, member of Congress and minister to Venezuela, was a grandson to William McKee. John L. Wilson, a son, was United States senator from Washington. Henry L., another son, was ambassador to Mexico and minister to Chili. Thomas Wilson, born in Rockbridge in 1765, settled in Morgantown, now in West Virginia, and took up the practice of law. In 1811 he was elected to Congress as a Federalist.

Almost as this book is going to press, our attention is called to a notable coincidence. In the general election of 1918, Medill McCormick, of Illinois, and E. J. Gay, of Louisiana, were chosen to the United States Senate. Both these men are of Rockbridge ancestry, and both are members of millionaire families. The latter is not the same as Congressman E. J. Gay.

XXXII

STONEWALL JACKSON AT LEXINGTON

EARLY LIFE—HIS TEN YEARS AT LEXINGTON—CAREER AS GENERAL—BURIAL AND MONUMENT—
PERSONAL CHARACTER

In a four-roomed cottage, near the courthouse at Clarksburg, West Virginia, was born Thomas Jonathan Jackson. He was the only son of Jonathan Jackson, a lawyer, and he had but one sister. While yet a small boy he became an orphan, and he was reared chiefly by a half-brother to his father.

At the age of sixteen he was made a constable, but when ordered to enforce an execution against a poor widow, he paid the claim out of his own pocket and resigned his office. Two years later, and very largely through his own efforts, he entered the United States Military Academy at West Point. To secure the appointment he walked all the way from his home to the city of Washington. His educational preparation was deficient, yet by dint of hard, persistent study, he attained a very respectable rank in his class. He learned slowly, but never forgot, and would never give up an undertaking. From the Academy he passed to the Regular Army as a second lieutenant of artillery. He served in the war with Mexico, and by meritorious conduct rose to the rank of major by brevet.

In May, 1851, Jackson applied for a position in the faculty of the Virginia Military Institute. He was chosen in preference to several competitors, and entered the school as instructor in the natural sciences, the theory of gunnery, and battalion drill. It was the most difficult chair in the Institute. Jackson had never before taught, and he was not naturally a teacher. Yet in this, as in all other places, he was conscientious in endeavoring to perform his duty. He had the highest respect of his fellow teachers, exerted much influence over the cadets, and expected to remain at this post the remainder of his life.

Jackson was a resident of Lexington almost ten years. The house he lived in here was the only one he ever owned. During his occupancy it was a commodious stone cottage of eight rooms. In 1906 it was purchased for $2,000 by the Mary C. Lee Chapter of the Daughters of the Confederacy. It was now converted into the Jackson Memorial Hospital, and as such it was opened June 1, 1907. Jackson worked his garden himself and grew an ample supply of produce. He also farmed a tract of twenty acres that he purchased a little distance from the town.

When the war of 1861 broke out, Major Jackson was little known in Virginia, and still less outside of the state. Except to a limited circle of acquaintances, he was an obscure, eccentric professor. But the governor of

the state at this time was also a resident of Lexington, and he recognized that
Jackson was eminently a man for the occasion. He ordered Jackson to lead to
Richmond such of the cadets as were likely to make good drillmasters for the
raw recruits assembling at Camp Lee. Punctually at a set hour on April 21,
1861, the march began. Jackson never again saw Lexington, and never for
even a night was he absent from his command.

From Richmond the as yet almost unknown man was soon sent to Harper's
Ferry as a colonel of infantry. In June he took command of what was afterward known as the Stonewall Brigade. This was a part of General Joseph E.
Johnston's army in the Shenandoah Valley. His first engagement in the war
took place July 2, 1861. It was the affair at Haines' Farm, or Falling Waters,
on the south bank of the Potamac six miles north of Martinsburg. On this
field Jackson had only about 400 men and one gun of the Rockbridge Battery.
The fight was in the nature of a reconnoisance. Jackson lost twenty-five men,
but took forty-nine prisoners.

Shortly afterward, Johnston led his army across the Blue Ridge to re-enforce Beauregard. It was on the momentous field of Manassas that the steadiness of Jackson's men gained for their leader the appellation of "Stonewall."
Thenceforward, this adjunct name clung to him. The same month he was
commissioned a brigadier-general. Early in October he was a major-general and
was placed in command in the Shenandoah. Jackson was a man of few words,
but in parting with the Stonewall Brigade he made a very earnest speech.

Until the following March there were no movements of much importance
in his military department. It was not until the warm months of 1862 that
Jackson really won his spurs. In March he lay in camp near Woodstock. He
advanced with his 3000 men and fought 7000 Federals at Kernstown, a few
miles southwest of Winchester. This battle was a defeat, and the only one that
Jackson experienced. Yet the audacity of the attack was disconcerting to the
authorities at Washington. It produced the very effect that Jackson desired.

Greater events were soon to follow. At the opening of May, 19,000 Federals under Banks had occupied Harrisonburg. Fremont with 15,000 more was
advancing up the South Branch of the Potomac. Milroy and Schenk were
across the Alleghany divide with 6,000 and were threatening Staunton. Jackson
was at the south end of Massanutten Mountain with only 6,000 men under his
immediate command. Just across the Blue Ridge was Ewell with 9,000. Edward
Johnson, who had fallen back before Milroy, had 3,000. The odds against
Jackson were more than two to one with respect to numbers.

It was now that he began to display a capacity for unexpectedly rapid marching that gave his soldiers the name of "foot cavalry." Banks wished to join
Milroy before Staunton, but was checkmated by Jackson, who was where he

could speed down Luray valley and fall upon the Federal communications. Jackson took his column across the Blue Ridge and to the Virginia Central at Mechum's River. He then hurried it to Staunton and picketed the roads leading toward Harrisonburg. Meanwhile, Ewell came over the mountain and occupied the abandoned camp. Jackson had slipped away from Banks and was now free to deal with Milroy. The battle of McDowell, May 8, compelled Milroy and Schenk to fall back upon Fremont's army for support, and they were pursued nearly to Franklin. The road running east from this town to Harrisonburg was so obstructed that Fremont was compelled to move much farther down the South Branch to find an open way to the Shenandoah valley. He did not reach Wardensville until the last day of the month. Jackson hurried back the way he had himself come. Banks had fallen back to Strasburg, placing, however, a small detachment at Front Royal. His army had been depleted to 8,000 men in order that a strong force might be assembled at Fredericksburg and march thence to the support of McClellan before Richmond.

With 17,000 men Jackson swept down the Luray valley and made short work of the outpost at Front Royal. He was now as near to Winchester as was Banks, and there was a race for that point. By fighting a rear-guard action just beyond Winchester, the Federal general succeeded in taking the greater part of his army across the Potomac. Yet he lost 2,000 men as prisoners and so large quantities of supplies that he became known as "Jackson's commissary." Four days after the fight at Winchester, Jackson was at Halltown, only six miles from Harper's Ferry and within sixty miles of Washington. Jackson's aim was to relieve the pressure upon the main Confederate army at Richmond. The Federal administration fell into the trap set for it. McDowell was ordered to detach one-half of his 40,000 men and throw it in Jackson's rear. While this column was advancing from the east, Fremont was coming on from the west. But by superior speed Jackson escaped before the jaws of the trap could close upon him. At the south end of the Massanutten he turned upon his pursuers and defeated them separately, Fremont at Cross Keys and Shields at Port Republic. The Shenandoah was thus so nearly cleared of Federal troops that there was nothing to interfere with marching to the aid of Lee at Richmond. The Valley campaign of 1862 was a striking success, and it established Jackson's fame as a military leader.

Jackson and his corps now became a part of the Army of Northern Virginia. In October of the same year the hero of the Valley was advanced to the rank of lieutenant-general. After joining General Lee he figured prominently in the battles of the Peninsula and Fredericksburg, and with very special prominence at Second Manassas, Sharpsburg, and Chancellorsville. In the last named conflict he was accidentally wounded in a volley fired by his own men. He was taken to a little house near Guinea Station, where he succumbed to pneumonia, May 10, 1863, at the age of thirty-nine.

The remains of the general reached Lexington by packet-boat in the afternoon of May fourteenth, and lay in state next day in his lecture room, the casket being draped and also nearly hidden by a mass of floral offerings. The funeral was on Saturday, May 16th, and he was buried by the side of his first wife in the town cemetery. Lexington was temporarily in possession of Hunter in 1864, and the report became current that the flag at the head of Jackson's grave was cut down by Federal soldiers. According to Colonel Schoonmaker, who commanded a brigade under Hunter and visited Lexington forty years later, the circumstances were these, Three elderly men called at the colonel's headquarters and asked permission to remove the flag. They said it had been left at the grave inadvertently, no disrespect being intended. The colonel said the flag might remain in place until sunset. At that hour he rode to the cemetery with his staff, twelve soldiers, a bugler, and the three citizens. Flags of the Twelfth Pennsylvania and Fifth Massachusetts were set on opposite sides of the mound and three volleys were fired over it by way of military salute. The Confederate flag was then given to the three men, who seemed visibly affected.

When the war closed there were only two dark boards at the grave, but next year the plain slab was set up that may still be seen at the original grave. In July, 1891, a monument was unveiled in the presence of 10,000 people, among whom were the general's widow and many other distinguished guests. The orator of the day was General Jubal A. Early. There was music by the Stonewall Band, and a salute of fifteen guns was fired. The unveiling was by a golden haired granddaughter, four years of age. In 1912 a statue, the gift of Sir Moses Ezekiel and Thomas F. Ryan, was unveiled at the Virginia Military Institute.

Stonewall Jackson was nearly six feet in height. His eyes were grey, his hair was light-brown, and during his campaigns he wore a long, full beard. His voice was soft, and in his personal relations with people he was kind and gentle. As a military leader he had an iron will and an abounding firmness. His intimates were few. He walked the streets of Lexington with a methodical stride, looking neither to the right nor to the left. His customary air was a dignified reserve and he was lacking in a sense of humor. He had no use for liquor or tobacco, saying of the former that he was more afraid of it than of Federal bullets. One of his mottoes was, "Never take counsel of your fears." His decisiveness of character is shown in his response to an urgent request to speak in the Franklin Society, of which he was a member. The occasion was in February, 1861, during a political debate. His reply was as follows: "Mr. President, I have learned from Old Hickory when I make up my mind never to do a thing, never to do it. I made up my mind before coming here not to make a speech, and I don't intend to do it."

Jackson was ever a close student of military science. A townsman remarked of him that he was "as exact as the multiplication table, and as full of things military as an arsenal." His successes were gained by the insight that goes with the professional soldier, by the energy that is a part of the born leader, and by unusual nimbleness in the conduct of a march. He insisted on discipline, and the topography of the Valley of Virginia was an open book to him. His achievements caused him to be idolized by his soldiers and have given him a high place in the military science.

Stonewall Jackson was a deacon in the Presbyterian church at Lexington, and attended to his religious duties with his customary punctuality and conscientiousness. He sought to make all the acts of his daily life conform to his conception of Christianity. In giving a tenth of his income to the support of the Church he followed literally the Biblical rule. The church building has been remodeled since his day, but the position of his pew is indicated by a tablet.

Jackson's concern in the moral betterment of the negroes led him to open a Sunday school for them in 1855. It met in the afternoon and he himself opened each session with prayer. His absence in the army and his death did not halt the work thus begun, and the outcome was a stalwart church organization. The morning after the first battle of Manassas although inconvenienced by a wound in his hand, he punctiliously took time to send his pastor $50 to be used for his Sunday school. Jackson's name is revered by the colored people of Lexington.

The first wife of Jackson was Eleanor Junkin, daughter of a president of Washington College. The second was Mary A., a daughter of the Reverend Robert H. Morrison of North Carolina. Their daughter Julia was born in wartime, November 23, 1862, married William E. Christian, and died of typhoid fever in 1889, leaving two children, Julia J., wife of Edmund R. Preston, and Thomas J., an officer in the army of the United States. Wife and daughter were with the general when he died.

XXXIII

ROBERT E. LEE AS A COLLEGE PRESIDENT

THE FATHER OF GENERAL LEE—EARLY LIFE OF ROBERT E. LEE—LEE AS A CONFEDERATE GENERAL—HIS PRESIDENCY OF WASHINGTON COLLEGE—CLOSING DAYS—HIS PERSONALITY

It is necessary to begin the present chapter with some mention of the father of Robert E. Lee. Henry Lee, whose own father was a first cousin to Richard Henry Lee, a celebrated statesman of the Revolutionary period, was a graduate of Princeton College, and he intended to enter the legal profession. The war for Independence breaking out before he had reached his majority, he became an officer in Washington's army. When twenty-two years of age, he was put at the head of a band that became famous as "Lee's Legion." For his exploit on the present site of Jersey City, where he took 160 prisoners with the loss of scarcely a man, he was given a gold medal. At the close of 1780, when he had attained the rank of lieutenant-colonel and when the American cause looked dark, he led his legion, 300 strong and composed of both cavalry and infantry, to join General Greene in the South. During the campaign of 1781 his services were invaluable. In 1791 he was chosen governor of his state, and a county was named for him. In 1794 he was commander of the army of 15,000 sent to put down the Whiskey Insurrection. Four years later, when war with France seemed imminent, he was advanced to the rank of major-general. While serving in Congress, he delivered the address on Washington that contains the well-known phrase, "First in war, first in peace, and first in the hearts of his countrymen." During the war of 1812 he was severely injured in Baltimore while defending an editor-friend from a mob. From this hurt there was no full recovery. In the hope of benefit he visited the West Indies, but growing worse, he asked to be put ashore at Cumberland Island, Georgia, so that he might die at the home of his late commander-in-chief. He was hospitably received by the widow of General Greene, and ended his days in her house, three weeks later, at the age of sixty-two. This event took place March 25, 1818. Pursuant to an Act of the General Assembly, the remains were removed to Lexington in 1913 to rest by the side of those of his still more distinguished son. The Honorable Hugh A. White, of Lexington, was chairman of the legislative committee that personally superintended the removal.

General Lee was almost a neighbor to General Washington, and enjoyed his confidence and esteem. As an alumnus of Princeton he was brought into close acquaintance with the founders of Liberty Hall. When Washington was studying what to do with the canal stock donated him by the state of Virginia, Lee was instrumental in directing his attention to the struggling academy. Lee sent his fourth child, Henry Lee, Jr., to study at Lexington, and the son was one of the early graduates of Liberty Hall. He died in France in 1837 at the age of fifty. He was able and well-informed, and was the author of several books. But the father himself owned land in Rockbridge and spent some of his time here. Lee was a planter, the tidewater soil was growing poor, and the unsettled period lasting from the beginning of the Revolution to the close of the war of 1812 was not conducive to material prosperity. Like many other men of his class, Lee was in debt, but it is alleged that he did not allow such a matter to engross his thoughts. Several anecdotes along this line are told of him. One of these is to the effect that a Rockbridge creditor needed his money, became impatient, and went with a constable to the general's home in Arnold's Valley. Light-Horse Harry, by which name he was familiarly known, was at home, and the callers had a delightful social hour. They left without saying a word about the writ, and the creditor was indifferent as to whether he should get his pay or not. The general's attitude might be styled an instance of unconscious and unpremeditated diplomacy.

Robert Edward Lee was born at Stratford, his father's manor-house in Westmoreland county, the date of his birth being January 19, 1807. He was the youngest of the sons of Light-Horse Harry, and his mother was a second wife. He passed through West Point without a demerit, graduating in 1829 at the head of his class. His first service was in the Engineer Corps of the army of the United States. He entered the war with Mexico as a captain, and won such distinction under General Scott as to attain the rank of colonel at the close. In 1852-5, he was superintendent of West Point. He remained with the regular army until the spring of 1861, spending only portions of his time at Arlington, the estate near the city of Washington which was inherited by his wife, Mary Custis, a great-granddaughter of Martha Washington by her first husband. It was during a leave of absence that he was put in charge of the Federal troops sent to deal with John Brown at Harper's Ferry.

In the opening months of 1861 Lee was again at home at Arlington. He was now fifty-four years of age and in the full maturity of his powers. General Scott loved him as a son, and not only had the highest opinion of his military skill, but predicted that Lee would greatly distinguish himself if circumstances should ever place him at the head of an army. It was because of this reputation that he was offered the command of the field army that was to invade the South. Lee was very much opposed to secession. As to slavery, he said that if he were to own all the slaves in the United States he would set them free as a means of preserving the Union. The political storm that was now breaking caused him great distress of mind. A Union that could not be vindicated except by an appeal to force was repugnant to him as it was to all others nurtured in the same school of political thought. He believed that when the Lincoln administration adopted a coercive policy, the Union of 1788 was virtually dissolved, and that each of the competent states was at liberty to shift for itself. Looking at the situation in this light, he conceived that his first duty was to serve his native state, which from 1775 to 1788 had enjoyed a career practically independent. He therefore resigned his commission in the army. That he was entirely conscientious in this step is now conceded gy all students of American history. He decided his problem for himself and without attempting to influence even his sons.

Going to Richmond, Lee was made a major-general of the Virginia troops. The last day of August he was advanced to the rank of full general in the Confederate service. In September he was in command on the Greenbrier. His operations in this quarter were inconclusive and of short duration. The following winter he was in charge of the engineering details of the defense of the Atlantic coast, particularly in South Carolina. This work was so well done that Charleston was not occupied by the Federals until flanked by Sherman's army in the closing months of the war. In the spring of 1862, Lee was called to Richmond to act as military advisor to the Confederate president. When General Joseph E. Johnston was wounded at Seven Pines, May 31st, Lee was appointed to succeed him. Lee was now in his element, and for almost three years he remained at the head of the army of Northern Virginia. The story of that superb organization is almost the story of the war itself. It was the spearhead and most successful factor of the Southern resistance. The great battles of the Peninsula, Second Manassas, Sharpsburg, Fredericksburg, Chancellorsville, Gettysburg, the Wilderness, Spottsylvania, Cold Harbor, the siege of Petersburg, and the campaign of maneuver against Meade in 1863 were all fought under the immediate direction of Lee. Sharpsburg was a drawn battle, and Gettysburg a reverse, but neither of these actions took place on the soil of Lee's native state. Worn down by relentless attrition and cut off from its supplies, the army of Northern Virginia gave up the struggle at Appomattox, April 9, 1865. A few more weeks and the Southern Confederacy ceased to exist.

Lee's home had been appropriated by the Federal authorities. The summer of 1865 found the great Confederate chieftain living quietly on a plontation in Powhatan county. He turned down all inducements to begin a career in Europe, believing it his duty to remain with his own people and share their fortunes. Neither would he listen to any overture which had no other primary object than the capitalizing of his name. Yet some mode of breadwinning was necessary.

At a meeting of the trustees of Washington College, held August 4, 1865, Bolivar Christian nominated General Lee as its president. It is said that when

J. W. Brockenbrough was selected to carry the offer of the trustees to the general, he declined on the ground that neither he himself nor the college had any money for the traveling expenses, and furthermore, that his clothes were not good enough. But the necessary money was raised and a friend loaned a new suit. Lee accepted the proffered office August 24th, stipulating that his duties were to be executive only, and that he was not to be asked to give classroom instruction. The following month he came to Lexington, riding his famous battle-horse, Traveler, and was quietly inaugurated October 2nd. During the five years that covered the final chapter of his life, General Lee was president of Washington College and a resident of Lexington. His salary was $1,500 and a cottage was built for himself and family.

The fortune sof the college were at this time at a low ebb. The building had been partially looted and the grounds were in disorder. The small endowment was unproductive, and the fifty students who presented themselves were wholly from Lexington and the country around. The magic of Lee's name, coupled with the affection in which he was held, would alone have swelled the student body to a goodly size and lent a great measure of success to his administration.

But Robert E. Lee was not the man to treat his office as a sinecure. A college presidency seems a far remove from the leadership of a great army. Yet it was in the educational field that Lee felt that he could be most useful to his people. The day of warfare was past. A period of transition had come to the South. The great present need of the time was constructive work, and nowhere was this more applicable than to the young men of student age. Lee applied himself to his new sphere with assiduous diligence. He had been a soldier by profession, but he was also a man of sound scholarship. His eye was everywhere. His system of reports, instituted by himself and almost military in its exactness, caused his spirit and his influence to pervade every department. In this way he kept himself informed of the progress and standing of every student. In administering reproof he was firm, yet gentle and fatherly. Under his executive skill, the attendance rapidly increased, the school prospered, and improvements were made in the college property. One of his earlist tasks was to build the chapel, in the basement of which was his office. This room is kept as nearly as possible in the same condition as when he last used it.

In the third year of the war General Lee had a severe attack of laryngitis, followed by a rheumatic periodical inflammation. For some time he could not exercise on foot or ride fact without being inconvenienced by a pain in the chest or by difficult breathing. There was gradual improvement, although he continued to have occasional attacks of muscular rheumatism. In the winter o 1869-70, his health began sensibly to fail, and in the spring he visited Georgia. There was some relief, but not for long. His final illness, which seized him as he was about to say grace at his dinner table, was a passive congestion of the brain resembling concussion, but without paralysis. After lying unconscious several days he died October 12, 1870. Interment was in the mausoleum under the college chapel, in which other members of the Lee family now lie. June 24, 1883, a recumbent statue was placed in the chapel in the rear of the platform and within view of the audience.

Robert E. Lee was six feet tall, faultless in figure, and unusually handsome in feature. His coal-black hair became very grey during the progress of the war. Until his second campaign he wore no beard except a mustache, but afterward his face was unshaven. An aged resident of this county speaks of his countenance as noble and benignant, and not suggestive of the warrior. Yet he had temper, as was shown in the case of the dispatch that was dropped in a street of Frederick and fell into the hands of McClellan. He avoided all display and ostentation, and set before young men an example of simple habits, manners, needs, words, and duties. He wrote his daughters that "gentility, as well as self-respect, requires moderation in dress and gayety." The most distinguishing feature of his educational career was the moral influence he exerted on the student body. He abstained from the use of both liquor and tobacco. At Lexington he led a retired life, and did not mingle in society. His pastime was to ride about the country. He once remarked that "Traveler is my only companion. He and I wander out into the mountains and enjoy sweet confidence." In these expeditions he did not go inside the farm homes, but as he was very fond of buttermilk he often called at them for a glass.

Students of military science give Lee a very high place among the great generals of the world. His personal influence over his men was most unusual. He was always daring, and if he sometimes took great risks, it was because he had taken the measure of the commander opposed to him. His usual tactics were the offensive-defensive, in which a stand technically defensive is converted at an opportune moment into an energetic offensive. He intended to write the history of his campaigns, and collected some material for this purpose. Yet he never carried out the plan, thinking he would cause pain by presenting his narrative before there had been time for much abatement in sectional feeling. His advice to his people of the South was to use silence and patience: to "avoid controversy, allay passion, and give scope to every kindly feeling."

There has long been general agreement respecting the spotless private character of Lee, the purity of his motives, his earnest Christianity, and the good faith with which h accepted the downfall of the Confederate cause. Some words he wrote on hearing of the assassination of Lincoln are touching in their magnanimity and in their accurate appreciation of the kindly qualities of the president.

They also convey his abhorrence of the crime. His tolerant spirit is further shown in his opinion that the Democrats should have nominated Chase in 1868, although Chase had been a member of Lincoln's cabinet.

The centennial of Lee's birth was observed at Washington and Lee University, June 19, 1907. The central feature was the address by General Charles Francis Adams, a grandson of John Quincy Adams. Adams was seventy-two years of age, had fought in the Federal army, and was a scholar as well as a man of affairs. His sketching of Lee as eminently a man of character was an amplification of these words of Thomas Carlyle: "Show me the man you honor; I know by that what sort of man you yourself are. For you show me then what your ideal of manhood is." A letter from President Roosevelt was read, the writer having already stated his belief that Lee was the foremost general that America has produced. At the luncheon t othe Confedrate veterans, there were toasts to Lee, the Union army, and the Confederate soldier.

The children of General Lee were seven. Three sons served in the Confederate army, two of them attaining the rank of major-general.

XXXIV

FAMILY SKETCHES AND BIOGRAPHIC PARAGRAPHS ARRANGED ALPHABETICALLY

Alexander. Archibald, Robert, and William, sons of William Alexander, Sr., came from near Londonderry, in 1737, and lived about ten years near Philadelphia. The brothers were well-to-do for those days, and were men of character, education, and influence. Robert, a Master of Arts of the University of Dublin, founded the school which finally grew into Washington and Lee University, but was himself a resident of Beverly Manor. Archibald removed in 1747 from the bank of the Schuylkill and settled on South River nearly opposite the mouth of Irish Creek. His son, William, born on the Schulykill, settled about 1775 at the mouth of Woods Creek, and there opened the store which he seems to have conducted until his death in 1797. He also established the first school to be taught within the present confines of Lexington, making one of his own man-servants the teacher.

As a captain of rangers, "Old Arsbel" had a share in the Big Sandy expedition of 1757. Under orders from the governor of the colony, Andrew Lewis led an expedition against the Indian towns on the Scioto, but did not cross the Ohio, and his men suffered terrible hardships from inclement weather and inadequate rations.

A daughter of William Alexander married Edward Graham of the faculty of Liberty Hall Academy, and another married Samuel L. Campbell, the first resident physician of Rockbridge. Archibald, still another of the eight children was born in a house of squared logs on the family homestead on South River. His schooldays began in the log structure his father had built on Woods Creek, and were continued at Liberty Hall. Coming under the influence of the Great Revival of 1739, he resolved to become a Presbyterian minister, and was licensed in 1791. For several years he was engaged in itinerant work, and thereby acquired a remarkable facility in offhand speaking. With a brief intermission he was president of Hampden-Sidney College from 1796 until 1807, and then became pastor of Pine Street Church, Philadelphia. In 1812, he was made first professor in the Princeton Theological Seminary of New Jersey. The title of Doctor of Divinity had already been conferred upon him by the College of New Jersey. The school had just been opened and Doctor Alexander had taken a very active part in its establishment. He remained at Princeton until his death, October 22, 1851, at the age of seventy-nine. Like his father he was short and compact in stature, and he had brown hair and hazel eyes. His memory was remarkable, and he was a delightful companion. As a pulpit orator he was unrivalled. As a writer on theological subjects he was quite prolific, his principal works being these: "A life of John Knox," "The Way of Salvation," "A History of the Israelitish Nation," "An Outline of Moral Science," "A Brief Outline of the Evidences of the Christian Religion," "The Canon of the Old and New Testaments Ascertained," "Biographical Sketches of the Founder and Principal Alumni of the Log College," "A Selection of Hymns," "Practical Sermons."

In 1802 Doctor Alexander was married to Janetta, a daughter of James Waddell, a blind minister who lived some years in Augusta, and whose eloquence was highly extolled by William Wirt. His sons, Joseph A. and James W. were also eminent as ministers, writers, and teachers of Theology. The former was an eloquent orator and remarkable linguist. The latter was at the time of his death in 1859 pastor of the Fifth Avenue Presbyterian Church in the city of New York.

Anderson. Francis T. Anderson was unrelated to the Anderson connection of Rockbridge. He was a son of Colonel Thomas Anderson of Botetourt, and was born in 1808 at Walnut Hill, the family homestead. His mother, Mary A. Alexander, was a sister to Doctor Archibald Alexander, of Princeton. The son was educated at Washington College and was admitted to the bar in 1830. He practiced the legal profession with great success, was many years a member of the Supreme Court of Appeals, and upon his death in 1887, the Bar of the State and the Supreme Court remembered him with eulogistic resolutions. Mr. Anderson was a leader of the Whig party of Virginia, a rector of Washington and Lee University, and a ruling elder of the Presbyterian Church. He removed from Botetourt to Lexington, but lived some years on his large estate of Glenwood, his home then being near Natural Bridge. He was a brother of General Joseph R. Anderson and Colonel John T. Anderson of the Confederate army. His children who grew to adult age are Anna A., wife of William F. Junkin; Mary E., wife of Alexander Bruce, of Halifax county; Frances M., of Washington, D. C.; Josephine A., wife of William B. Poindexter; William A.; Isabella G., wife of William B. Bruce; and Francis T., whose wife is Rosa Bruce, of Halifax county.

William A. Anderson, son of Francis T., Sr., was born May 11, 1842, and is the senior member of the Rockbridge bar. He has been Attorney General for his state and has twice represented his county in the Assembly. Major Anderson, who was made a cripple for life at First Manassas, is a Virginia gentleman of the old school and his courtesy is unfailing. He has been twice married; first to Ellen G., daughter of General Joseph R. Anderson, and second, to Mary L. Blair. His children are Ruth F., Anna A., William D. A., Judith N., and Ellen G. Besides being active in his chosen profession, Major Anderson has been a leader in the industrial development of Rockbridge.

Baldwin. John C. Baldwin was a son of Cornelius C. Baldwin of Balcony Falls, one of the original secessionists of 1860-61. The son, who died unmarried in 1881, at the early age of thirty-four, deserves mention for his assiduous and succesful efforts to educate himself. His book studies began when he was seven years old. He took up Latin at sixteen and became able to read it almost as readily as Shakespeare. He also studied Greek and French, the mathematics, and several branches of the sciences. Perhaps he was the only boy in Virginia who made himself by solitary endeavor a fine classical and English scholar, a good writer, and one of the best informed country gentlemen in the state. Mr. Baldwin was retiring, fond of home, devoted to a simple life, and he enjoyed the society of his few intimate friends. He adopted as his own this motto by Bishop Berkeley: "I had rather be master of my time than wear a diadem."

Joseph G. Baldwin, the brilliant author of "Flush Times in Alabama," is said to have been related to the Baldwins of Rockbridge.

Barclay. Elihu H. Barclay, almost thirty years a force in Rockbridge journalism, was a member of an old and prominent family. He was a son of Alexander T. Barclay and his third wife, Mary E. (Paxton) Barclay. The father was a son of Elihu Barclay, who married Sarah Telford. Elihu H. purchased the *Rockbridge Citizen* in 1873, when he was twenty-seven years old. Next year he acquired the *Gazette,* which he conducted until his death in 1902. The maiden name of his wife was Margaret S. Rowan.

Baxter. The Reverend George A. Baxter, whose name is long and honororably identified with what is now the Washington and Lee University, was born in Rockbridge in 1771. From New London Academy he came to Lexington in 1798 to fill the chair of mathematics at Liberty Hall. A year later he became rector of the academy. Two very prominent events are associated with his administration. The school was moved from Mulberry Hill to Lexington, and it was advanced from the rank of academy to that of college. As rector, and later as president, the income of Doctor Baxter was small, and he supplemented it with active labor in the Presbyterian ministry. He is remembered in our local annals as a faithful and conscientious educator and as a preacher of power and effectiveness. His wife was Anna C., a daughter of Colonel William Fleming. Their son, Sidney S., was likewise an educator of note.

Brockenbrough. John W. Brockenbrough was a native of Hanover county, where he was born December 23, 1806. After graduating from the University of Virginia, he entered the legal profession, in which he became very eminent. From 1846 until 1860 he was judge of the United States Court for the Western District of Virginia, and in this capacity none of his decisions was ever reversed.

In the crisis of 1860-61, he was a secessionist, and was defeated as a candidate for the State Convention of 1861. He represented Virginia in the futile Peace Conference which sought to avert the calamity of war. He also served a term in the Confederate Congress. In 1849 Judge Brokenbrough had opened at Lexington a school of law, and when General Robert E. Lee came here as a college president, he became the head of the newly created law school in Washington College. Judge Brockenbrough was a man of very estimable qualities. He died in Lexington, February 21, 1877.

Brown. John Brown, the first resident minister in Rockbridge, came in 1753 in response to a call signed by a great number of his future parishioners. He was then but twenty-five years of age. He was pastor at Timber Ridge and New Providence until 1767, and served New Providence twenty-eight years longer. In Kentucky, to which state he removed in 1797, he was pastor of Woodford church. He died there in 1803, and his grave lies between those of two men who had been his elders at New Providence. During his early years in Rockbridge, his salary was but little more than $200. It is related of him that he used to walk around the New Providence church with head uncovered and Bible in hand, and pray for the various families. He left Timber Ridge somewhat abruptly, and in consequence of a slight which seems to have been quite unpremeditated, although his sensative nature did not permit him to excuse it. In 1755 he purchased a farm, the position of which is on the line of the Valley Railroad and a little north of Fairfield. Between the resignation of Robert Alexander in 1753 and the coming of William Graham in 1774, Mr. Brown taught the classical school begun by the former. His wife was Margaret, a sister of Colonel William Preston. The careers of several of the children reflect the substantial quality of their parentage. John, Jr., was a member of the First Congress, Samuel was a professor in Transylvania University, James was a United States senator from Louisana and minister to France, and William was a physician of South Carolina. The daughters, Elizabeth and Mary, married, respectively, the Reverend Thomas B. Craighead and Doctor Alexander Humphreys. Samuel, who died in 1830 at the age of seventy-one, took the degree of Doctor of Medicine from the University of Aberdeen. He then entered upon an eminent career as physician and chemist. At Lexington, Ky., he organized a medical society which is said to have been a pattern in constitution and in ethics to all such American societies of later date.

The Samuel Brown who came to New Providence as its pastor in 1796 was not related to John Brown. He was a native of the east of Virginia. In 1789, when twenty-three years old, he went to Kentucky with some friends. The journey was made on foot as far as Kanawha Falls, and by a dugout canoe the rest of the distance. After teaching a year at Paris he returned, and was licensed as a minister in 1793. His salary at New Providence was $400. Mr. Brown was feeble in constitution, yet in addition to ministerial effort he taught a classical school, and among his divinity students were several who attained distinction. He owned and lived on a farm two miles north of Brownsburg. In 1816 he went West with a view of locating, and for $1600 was offered a tract of land within the present limits of the city of St. Louis. Yet he turned down the offer, deciding that his family would be better off in the West only in a material point of view. He died two years after his visit to Missouri. In 1798 Mr. Brown was married to Mary Moore of Abb's Valley, some account of whose captivity is given in Chapter VIII. She was an affectionate wife and loving parent. The pair had eleven children, the difference in age between the oldest and the youngest being seventeen years. Seven sons and three daughters grew to maturity. Six of the former were Bachelors of Arts of Washington College, three of them graduating in the same class. In 1918 a reunion of the descendants of Mary Moore Brown were held at New Providence, the wife of its present pastor being one of them.

Campbell. One of the very oldest and most numerous of the group-families of Rockbridge is that of the Campbells. It includes a considerable number of persons who have attained some degree of prominence. Samuel R. Campbell, a son of Alexander, was born between Brownsburg and Fairfield in 1766 and died at his country home, Rock Castle, in 1840. He was a graduate of Liberty Hall Academy in 1788 and studied medicine at Philadelphia. His medical practice was large, and he was much respected in his profession. Yet he found time to bring his strong civic spirit into play. He was a firm friend to Washington College and he took a leading part in establishing the Franklin Society. Doctor Campbell was a witty, cultured gentleman and good writer. In his later years he lost his eyesight, although he continued to ride the highways, humorously cautioning those he met to look out or he would ride over them. It was he who built the Stone Rock Castle which was burned. In 1794 he was married to Sarah, a sister to Doctor Archibald Alexander. His four sons were graduates of Washington College. All went West and all became eminent. His daughter, Sophia, married Robert McCluer in 1816. The other daughters married John S. Wilson and the Reverend Nathaniel C. Calhoun. Two of the three husbands were also graduates of Washington College.

Caruthers. The Caruthers name was once very conspicuous, but has long been extinct. The male members were residents of Lexington or its vicinity and were much inclined to commercial pursuits. Isaac migrated to Monroe, married there, and was one of the proprietors of Salt Sulphur Springs. Yet a literary vein was present in the family, as is indicated by the very active part taken by it in founding the Franklin Society and Ann Smith Academy. In

William A. Caruthers this trait had a special development. He was educated at Washington College, and though he went into the medical profession, he was a prolific writer of historical romances and a frequent contributor to the magazines. His literary work is full of spirit and animation. He was the author of "Knights of the Horseshoe," a work of fiction founded on Spottswood's expedition to the Shenandoah Valley in 1716. In 1838 Doctor Caruthers wrote a vivid account of a hazardous ascent of the Natural Bridge. He died at Savannah, Ga., about 1850, and at the age of about fifty-five years.

Davidson. Andrew B. Davidson, a native of Botetourt, does not seem to have been of the Kerr's Creek connection or of the family that migrated to Ohio from the lower course of North River. He was born in 1779 and died in 1861, spending all but the earliest years of his life at Lexington. He was graduated from Liberty Hall Academy in 1807, and was licensed as a minister the same year. In the same year, also, he was married to Susan Dorman, apparently a sister to Charles P. Dorman. In 1814 he returned to Lexington as a pastor, and was a principal of Ann Smith Academy. All his four sons were alumni of Washington College. General Alexander H. became a resident of Indiana. Charles B. was an Episcopal clergyman. James D. and Henry G. remained in this county, the former being a lawyer and the latter a physician.

Dorman. The Dormans have been very few in number, yet influential. Charles P. Dorman, a lawyer and editor, was in the Virginia Assembly thirteen years and was an adjutant in the war of 1812. His son James B., born 1825 died 1893, graduated from the Virginia Military Institute in 1843 and became an attorney. The war with Mexico aroused his spirit of adventure, and he served as sergeant-major in the Texas Rangers of Colonel Wood. He was present at the capture of Monterey. Returning to Lexington, he was sent in 1861 to the State Convention as a Union man. After war came on he went into the Confederate army as a major in the 9th Virginia Infantry. Major Dorman was a fluent speaker and a man of unusual ability. He had strong literary tastes and was a master of the English language, whether written or spoken. He was married in 1871 to Mrs. Mary L. White Newman. During the last ten years of his life he was Clerk of the Supreme Court of Appeals and lived in Staunton.

Dunlap. Alexander Dunlap, the first settler on the Calfpasture and first owner of the site of Goshen, died in 1744, leaving four children, John, Robert, Alexander, and Elizabeth.

In 1776 John Dunlap visited Ohio on a prospecting tour, and acquired 7,000 acres in Ross county, the smaller of the two tracts including the old Shawnee town of Chillicothe. He also secured 1436 acres in Kentucky, but was furthermore the largest landholder in Rockbridge. He was married to Ann Clark, who was related to General George Rogers Clark, the "Hannibal of the

West," and his brother, Colonel William Clark of the famous Lewis and Clark expedition. Both these celebrities made visits to the Dunlaps. The family home was a large three-story brick mansion, built soon after the Revolution and on the site of the Victoria furnace near Goshen. The house was torn down many years ago. The only member of this Dunlap family to stay in Rockbridge was James.

Robert, second son of the pioneer, fought at Point Pleasant and was an ensign in the battle of Guilford, where he was killed. It is said he refused to obey an order to retreat. He owned Aspen Grove and one other plantation in Rockbridge. His widow married James Coursey. Of the seven children of Robert Dunlap, Alexander settled in Monroe and Robert and John in Augusta. Anne and Margaret went with their husbands to Kentucky and Missouri, respectively. Only William and Agnes remained in this county, but the children of William went to Missouri. Robert, Jr., organized the first temperance society in the Valley of Virginia. William, Jr., a son of William, was one of the first men to explore Kansas. A grandson of William, Jr., is Boutwell Dunlap, of San Francisco, a lawyer and historian and formerly consul for Argentina. He is the author of a valuable contribution to American history: "Augusta County in the History of the United States." Among the progeny in the female line, in this family of the Dunlaps, are the Reverned O. E. Brown, of Vanderbilt University, church historian, and the Reverend W. M. Morrison, the missionary to Africa, whose exposure of the atrocities on the Congo roused the government of the United States and Europe to take action against the king of the Belgians.

Alexander Dunlap, Jr., went in early life to Kentucky, and later to Brown county, Ohio, where he built one of the very first houses of worship in that state of the Disciples communion.

The four Dunlaps, Samuel, David, Robert, and John, who purchased land in the Borden Tract are believed to have been related to Alexander of the Calfpasture. They seem to have moved to the Carolinas.

John Dunlap came from Campbelltown, Scotland, in 1775, and settled at Chambersburg, Pennsylvania. Robert, one of his seven children, was born just before the family came to America, and located near Middlebrook in Augusta. Madison Dunlap, his son, came to Kerr's Creek about 1830. John Dunlap was grandfather to Major-General John D. Stevenson, of the United States army. He was great grandfather to Brigadier-General Robert N. Getty, of the same army, and to John R. S. Sterrett, the Greek scholar and archæologist.

Few families in the South can surpass the Dunlaps of Rockbridge in exhibiting so many members who have been large landowners, or have been conspicuous in public, professional, or military life. The Dunlaps dispute with one other Rockbridge connection the honor of furnishing the most ministers to the Southern Presbyterian Church.

Echols. Captain Edward Echols, who lived at the mouth of North River, was a brother to General John Echols, of the Confederate army, and consequently an uncle to the late Edward Echols, of Staunton. He was a citizen of considerable local prominence, and died in 1874 at the age of fifty-seven. An incident in his career illustrates his unselfishness and his generous impulse. It also brought suddenly to the front an unexpected power of vivid narration. The account of the incident which has been furnished to us we quote entire.

In January, 1854, a large covered freight boat with a cargo of nearly 100 negro men who had been hired in the vicinity of Richmond to work in the furnaces above Buchanan was swept over the dam on James River at Balcony Falls, in consequence of the breaking of the tow-line, as the boat was struggling across the mouth of North River then swollen by a heavy freshet. Most of the negroes as soon as the boat began to drift down the stream plunged into the river and swam to the bank. About a dozen of them who probably could not swim stuck to the boat and were dashed over the dam into the boiling and foaming whirlpool below. The boat was broken into fragments, and half the men drowned. The others clung to a fragment of the wreck and were drifted down the surging and roaring torrent about a mile and a half, until they struck a large rock called the "Velvet Rock," from the carpet of soft green moss which covered it, when they jumped off and after much scrambling secured a precarious foothold on the narrow surface of the wet and slippery stone. One of these men was William G. Mathews, uncle to William G. Mathews of the Virgina Western Power Company. The river was rising, the spray dashed over the rock. The weather was freezing, a dark night was closing in, and it was impossible to send a boat through that surging torrent to bring off the shipwrecked sufferers, whose doom seemed to be sealed. To encourage them to hold on to their perilous position and to cheer their desponding spirits, a large fire was kindled on the opposite bank of the canal, about 100 yards off, by a body of rough, but kind-hearted men, who sang and danced and shouted around it all that dark and gloomy night. Above the loud roar of the turbid waters as they rushed through the narrow gorge of the Blue Ridge, their trumpet voice could be heard ringing on the midnight air, "Hold on, hold on; dance and sing; we'll save you; we'll save you; day is almost here; hold on; hold on; the river is falling; you're safe; you're safe." Thus animated and encouraged, the imprisoned men did hold on through that awful night until the first faint streak of day, when the river having fallen during the night, a canoe danced over the foaming tide and brought the half-frozen men to the bank. And there was such a scene, such hugging, and dancing and laughing, and crying and shouting and rejoicing. A few days later Captain Edward Echols, who resided in the immediate vicinity and was an eye-witness of most of these thrilling scenes wrote a most vivid and graphic account of them, which was published in the *Lexington Gazette* and copied by many papers in and out of the state. Captain Echols almost literally photographed the whole catastrophe, from the breaking of the rope to the rescue of the men in a series of living pictures taken fresh from nature. You almost saw the boat as it plunged over the dam, and heard the shrieks of the drowning and drifting men. The style was perfectly simple and unpretending— like naive Isaac Walton in his "Compleat Angler"—a style which every school boy thinks he can write until he tries, but which the critics say has never been successfully imitated,—

fresh, racy, nervous, pictorial, and yet familiar, colloquial, easy and natural. Captain Echols's success in that happy effort is easily explained. He felt warmly, the scenes were distinctly pictured on his heart, and his pen naturally copied them. Feeling is the source of eloquence, and simplicity is the source of refinement. It is but simple justice to a man to say that Captain Echols was untiring in his efforts to save these unfortunate men and that they probably owe him their lives. The same praise is due to another worthy man, Peter A. Salling. A negro named Frank Padgett, who belonged to a gentleman of that name in Amherst, was drowned in a voluntary and heroic effort to save some of these imperilled men. The humane and martyr-like conduct of this poor slave, who simply yielded to his natural sympathies for his suffering fellows made a deep impression on Captain Echols's susceptible heart, and most justly encited his warm admiration. To commemorate this noble deed he erected at his own cost an enduring monument to Frank's memory at the lock opposite the "Velvet Rock" about a mile and a half below the dam, in the midst of the wildest and grandest scenery in Virginia, where the gurgling and foaming river dashes in tiny cascades through the overhanging mountains, and sweeps off in a glittering stream of silver. The traveler may observe a stout obelisk of dark marble bearing the following inscription:

> "IN MEMORY OF FRANK PADGET"
> "a colored slave who during a freshet in James River in January, 1854, ventured and lost his life by drowning in a noble effort to save some of his fellow creatures who were in the midst of the flood from death."

If the hearty admiration and commendation of noble and generous action is the next thing to performing them, then when Captain Echols so generously erected this monument to this poor, humble negro, who deserved it far better than many an overpraised and vulgar hero who dies on the field of battle, he illustrated the nobleness of his own heart and built for himself, let us hope, an enduring monument in the hearts of his countrymen.

When the canal was sold to the Richmond and Alleghany Railroad Company, it was stipulated that the monument should not be disturbed, and a railing was placed around it.

Edmondson. During a long while the Edmondsons were numerously represented in this county. The name is now extinct, although it maintained itself more than a century and a half. James K., a son of James and Margaret, was a lawyer by occupation and was county judge from 1870 until 1881. In the Secession war he was colonel of the 22nd Virginia Infantry and lost an arm at Chancellorsville. He was married to Emily J. Taylor. No children were born to the union. Colonel Edmondson died in 1898 at the age of sixty-six.

Estill. The Estills who have been identified with Lexington, and have distinguished themselves in literary and professional lines, are of the numerous progeny of Wallace Estill, a grand nephew to the first white child born in New Jersey. Wallace lived in the Bullpasture valley from 1745 to 1773, and was high sheriff of undivided Augusta. When seventy-five years of age he moved to what is now Monroe county, a region then on the very border-line of settlement.

At the time of this migration to Indian Creek, all—or all but one—of the nine children of his last wife were under age. The Estills have been people of strong mental power, and many of them engaged in public or professional life. The Estills of Lexington, sprang from Benjamin, the oldest son of Wallace, and a member of the first county court of Botetourt. Doctor Andrew D. Estill was born in 1853 in Tazewell, but married Lavellette Davidson, of Rockbridge. Henry Estill, who died in 1880 at the early age of thirty-five, was a graduate of Washington College. He edited the *Virginia Educational Journal,* and was an author of school books. In 1878 he became McCormick Professor of Natural Philosophy in his alma Mater.

Gay. William Gay, who fought at the siege of Londonderry, had at least six children who came to the Calfpasture. These were William, John, James, Robert, Samuel, and Eleanor. Robert and Samuel did not long remain in this locality. Eleanor married William Kincaid. William Gay, who owned 900 acres on what is wrongly called Guy's Run, died in 1755. His wife, who was Margaret Walkup, aftreward married William Hamilton. James Gay, son of the pioneer James, and his brothers-in-law were the first men to introduce cattle of an improved breed into Kentucky. The Gays of Kentucky are derived from the Rockbridge families. They are among the largest landholders in the Bluegrass region and are connected with scores of the historic families of that state. Henry Gay, who married Jane Henderson, was a brother to the pioneer Gays, or at least a near relative, and he lived a while on the Calfpasture. His son, John H., born in 1787, became a millionaire merchant of St. Louis. Edward J. Gay, son of John H., was the largest sugar planter in Louisiana, and left an estate worth $12,000,000. The sugar mills and plantation are still in the Gay family.

Glasgow. Three brothers of this name, Arthur, Robert, and Joseph, came to America late in the eighteenth century. They first settled at "Green Forest" within the present limits of Buena Vista. The second located at Max Meadows, while the third went with his large family to Ohio in 1806. The wife of Arthur was the widow of John McCorkle who fell in the battle of Cowpens. Of the three sons, Joseph settled at Balcony Falls, John at "Tuscan Villa" at the mouth of South River, and Robert on his father's homestead. Alexander McN., the only son of John who attained his majority, inherited his own father's estate. He and his two sons were educated at Washington and Lee University. Of the four sons of Robert who arrived at maturity, Joseph R., and William A., settled at Fincastle as lawyers, but the latter removed to Lexington in 1887, living here till his death in 1910 at the age of eighty-five. Frank T. settled at Richmond, and during nearly all of his business life was superintendent of the Tredegar Ironworks. Robert died of fever in the Confederate service. The sons of William A., who was many years a trustee of Washington and Lee University, are Frank T., and Robert of Lexington, the former an attorney, the latter a physician. With few exceptions the Glasgows have been Presbyterians, and the record of the family is very honorable in every respect. They have been very strongly attracted to the professions, particularly that of the law. Quite a number have been graduated from college, in several instances with much distinction. The town of Glasgow derives its name from the family.

Graham. William Graham, so prominent in the pioneer history of Liberty Hall Academy, was born at Harrisburg, Penn., Dec. 19, 1746. In his youth he was inclined to be wild, but his viewpoint changed as he neared his majority. Aided more by his mother than by his father, he then began to prepare for the ministry, and was graduated from the College of New Jersey in the same class with General Henry Lee. About the same time he was licensed to preach. In the fall of 1774 he came to Rockbridge to act as principal of the Presbyterian school that had just been authorized. He remained its head until 1796, when he resigned and went to the Ohio River with the intention of settling. But he was injudicious and the result was financially disastrous. He died at Richmond in 1799, while on a visit to the state capital in behalf of his land title. Some years later his remains were interred on the campus of Washington and Lee University. As the head of Liberty Hall Academy for twenty-two years, Graham had to struggle against some very untoward circumstances, and it is much to his credit that the school did not succumb. For the ministry he seems to have been rather less adapted. His strong point was in the teaching of political science, and he was a member of the convention that drafted the constitution of the state of Franklin, a commonwealth that had only a brief existence. It is unfortunate that this state did not come fully into being. It was not coterminous with the present state of Tennessee. The proposed boundaries, as stated by Arthur Campbell—a trustee of Liberty Hall,—included that part of Virginia sometimes called Little Tennessee, all of North Carolina west of the Blue Ridge, very small slices of West Virginia, Georgia, and Alabama, and rather less than one-half of Tennessee. It would have made a mountain state, homogeneous in geography and population.

Greenlee. In all the annals of Rockbridge there is no individual of more striking personality than Mary Elizabeth McDowell, who became the wife of James Greenlee. So far as we have positive knowledge, she was the only woman in the little band of homeseekers, who in October, 1737, made the first actual settlement in Borden's Great Tract. At this time she was thirty years of age, and two of her eight children had been born. She lived many years a widow, and displayed much ability in managing a considerable estate. Its appraisement by William and John Paxton and Jacob Hickman showed that the personality was $2,970, inclusive of eight slaves, these being valued from $100 in the case of a child to $500 for an adult. No books are mentioned. Illiteracy relieved her husband from serving as constable, and it would seem that the wife cared little for the printed page. Yet her mental faculties were keen and alert to the end, she used good language, and in a verbal passage at arms, she appears to have been a match for all comers. Various legends cluster about her name, and it has been handed down that her wit and her nimbleness of mind came near causing her to be proceeded against for witchcraft. This is not impossible, since it was in her own girlhood that a woman was ducked by the civil authorities in Princess Anne county on a charge of being a witch. In certain Alleghany valleys a belief in the delusion exists to this day among people of German descent. In her widowhood Mary Greenlee kept a tavern, and as hostess she showed her eye for the main chance by flouting the regulations of the county court relative to the sale of ardent spirits. She moved from Timber Ridge to Greenlee's Ferry in 1780. If Mrs. Greenlee was keen in business, she was also something of a shrew. It was perhaps a victim of her caustic tongue who perpetrated the following lines of doggerel, which, let us hope, were written in pleasantry and not in malice.

> Mary Greenlee died of late;
> Straight she went to Heaven's gate:
> But Abram met her with a club,
> And knocked her back to Beelzebub.

As a result of a lawsuit instituted by Joseph Borden, Mrs. Greenlee was called upon for a deposition. When asked how old she was, she made this tart rejoinder: "What is the reason you ask my age? Do you think I am in my dotage? Ninety-five, the seventeenth of this instant." It is evident that her mental processes were in extraordinarily good working order, even at another deposition, taken at her home four years later, November 10, 1806. Two-thirds of a century had elapsed since she came to Rockbridge. Her reminiscences of the early pioneer days are numerous and precise, and of much historical importance; more so than any other statements given by the old residents. Mary Greenlee became a centenarian, since her span of life reached from November 17, 1707 until March 14, 1809. This tendency to longevity seems to have been inherited from her father, who reached a great age, and to have been passed onward to her grandson, John F. Greenlee, who died in 1915, when in his ninety-ninth year. Mr. Greenlee never married and was the last of the name in this county. Like his ancestress, he was in his old age a great source of information on local history. His habits were favorable to a long life, since he used no tobacco and rarely touched liquor. James, the husband of Mary Greenlee, died about

1764, leaving an estate appraised at $2,767.67. By owning six slaves he was the heaviest slaveholder of that period of whom we have any certain knowledge. Exceptional items in the inventory are seven silver watches, valued at $20 each eight geese, and five pounds of beeswax. Yet the watches were not so low priced as they would seem, since it would have taken a very good horse, or three cows, to buy a single one of them. John, the oldest son of James and Mary Greenlee, disregarded his privilege under the British law of entail, and took steps to divide the estate equally among the five brothers. He had no issue, and as only one or two of his brothers remained in Rockbridge, the Greenlee name was never extensively represented here.

Grigsby. The Grigsby family appeared in this county at the close of the Revolution, having come from the other side of the Blue Ridge and being of English derivation. The members of the connection were well-to-do, able, and influential, and owned several large farms, each with its distinctive name. As in several other instances, the name is now entirely gone. Benjamin Grigsby, son of James, was graduated from Liberty Hall Academy in 1789, and was licensed as a Presbyterian divine in 1792. He died at Norfolk in 1810 at the early age of forty. His only son was Hugh Blair Grigsby, who achieved more than a statewide reputation as scholar, educator, and historian.

Houston. The most famous character to come out of Rockbridge was General Samuel Houston, whose name and fame are inseparably associated with Texas. He was a grandson of John, the founder of the Rockbridge line of Houstons, and a son of Samuel and Elizabeth (Paxton) Houston. In a log house that stood seventy years ago in the rear of Timber Ridge meeting house, the future general was born March 2, 1793. He lost his father in 1806, and three years later he accompanied his mother and his younger brothers and sisters to Blount county in the valley of East Tennessee. He was daring and ambitious from the first, and in his new home he soon showed the venturesomeness which does not seem characteristic of the Houstons as a family. He went for a while to the Cherokees, and was adopted as a son by one of their chiefs. After his return he taught school. When nineteen years old he enlisted to serve against the Creek Indians, and in the battle of Tohopeka he was several times wounded, both by arrow and ball. His gallantry in this engagement made the youth a lieutenant. About 1820 he took up the practice of law. In 1823 he was elected to Congress and served two terms in the lower house. Houston was a born leader of men. So rapidly and effectively did he rise in the attention of the public that in 1827 he was elected governor of Tennessee. He did not serve out his first term. Just after his first marriage he suddenly resigned his office, not making public any reason for doing so. He went beyond the Mississippi to live with an Indian chief whom he had known eleven years earlier. This chief owned a large plantation worked by a dozen slaves. Houston lived among the Cherokees at least three years. This period must be regarded as the low-water mark in his varied career, since it was now that he gave way to the vice of intemperance. But the friendship between himself and the Indians was never broken, and where they were wronged he was always ready to uphold their cause. So far back as 1817, he acted as a sub-agent in the removal of the Cherokees from Georgia, but resigned the following year because of some reflections on his official conduct, and also because of a reproof from Calhoun, Secretary of War, for coming into his presence in Indian attire. During his present residence among the Cherokees he twice visited Washington to protect them from fraud and greed.

At the very close of 1832, when Houston was in his fortieth year, there began the most eventful period of his life. By request of the Federal government he visited Texas to make treaties with the border tribes for the protection of traders. Deciding to remain, the Texans sent him to their constitutional convention of April 1833, and he took a leading part in its deliberations. Near the close of 1835, when there was war with Mexico, Houston was made commander-in-chief of the armies of Texas. April 21, 1836, he won the decisive battle of San Jacinto, fighting 1800 men with 700, and inflicting a loss of 1690 against thirty-one on his own side. The invading army was annihilated. Santa Anna, who was not only its leader but also president of Mexico, was taken prisoner. It shows a humane spirit in General Houston that he did not cause the Mexican commander to be executed because of his atrocious cruelty on several occasions. The victory of San Jacinto established the independence of the republic of Texas and is a holiday in that commonwealth. When Texas was admitted as a state in the Federal Union, Houston was chosen senator and in this capacity he represented his state at Washington from 1846 until 1859. He was then elected governor of Texas, but because he was inflexibly opposed to secession, General Houston was removed from office in March, 1861. He ignored the secession convention, refused to swear allegiance to the Confederacy, and believed in fighting within the Union if there was to be any war at all. In 1860 he ran next to John Bell in the presidential convention of the Constitutional Union party. After being deposed, Houston went to his home at Huntsville, where he lived quietly until his death, July 26, 1863.

General Houston was of commanding presence. He was six feet three inches tall, large-framed, and well-proportioned. In manner he was courteous and pleasing. As a senator he wore coat and breeches of the best broadcloth, a tiger-skin vest, a sombrero, and a bright-colored blanket. He did not care to make money, although he did not lack opportunity. His habits were simple. He lived plainly in a log house and went to bed at nine o'clock. Houston had a melodious voice and was a fine orator. He was a good stump speaker, and could address the borderers in their own dialect. As a legislator he was noted for impartiality and unusual foresight. In the Senate chamber at Washington, he had the curious habit of whittling all day long, fashioning darts, crosses, and other objects that he gave away as curios. As a military leader he was wary, yet brave, able and resolute. In 1854, General Houston became a member of the Baptist Church. By his second wife, Margaret M. Lea, he had four sons and four daughters. Of these, Nettie P. has a record in prose and poetry, while Samuel, Jr., a physician has written for the periodicals.

John Houston, the pioneer, figured in an exploit during his voyage from Ireland to Philadelphia. He and his fellow passengers became convinced that the captain and crew meant to rob them. So the passengers put the suspects in irons and navigated the vessel themselves.

Samuel, Sr., the father of General Houston, was himself a soldier, having served in the Revolution as one of the famous riflemen of Daniel Morgan. Afterward he was an inspector-general of troops on the frontier and held the rank of major. A first cousin was the Reverend Samuel Houston born on Hays Creek, January 1, 1758. He was a graduate of Liberty Hall and was licensed as a Presbyterian minister about 1784. He spent several years in the proposed state of Franklin, which he took a leading part in trying to establish, being a member of the committee that drafted its constitution. Returning in 1789 he now became pastor of the churches at Falling Springs and Highbridge. Mr. Houston was a polished writer and for about twenty years he taught a classical school in a building on his own place. He was original in his ideas and was the inventor and patentee of a threshing machine. His house and barn were built on plans of his own, and his farm of six hundred acres was tilled on more scientific methods than were usual in his day. During his long pastorate he perhaps united more couples than any other minister in Rockbridge. He became blind near the close of his long life, but was to have preached the day he died, which was January 29, 1839. He was tall, erect, and square-shouldered, dignified in manner, and was both particular and old-fashioned in the matter of dress.

A son of the last-named, and therefore a second cousin to the general, was the Reverend Samuel R. Houston, born March 12, 1806. He was graduated from Dickenson College in 1825, and after teaching six years at Philadelphia in a school for the deaf and dumb, he was ordained to the Presbyterian ministry, and sailed in 1835 as a missionary to Greece. At historic Sparta he conducted a large mission school. In 1841 he returned to America because of ill-health in his family. During forty-four years he was pastor at Union, W. Va. The diaries that Doctor Houston kept during his residence in foreign lands and as a non-combatant in the war of 1861 are of much historical and descriptive value. He was the father of the late Judge William P. Houston, of Lexington, a gentleman who was a cyclopedia of the local history of Rockbridge. Doctor Houston was also the author af "A History of the Houston Family." In this work he relates that of the progeny of John, the pioneer, nearly fifty were Presbyterian elders, and more than thirty were ministers of the same or other communions. Many of the connection had held civil or military office, while many in the female line married men engaged in the learned professions, or who were otherwise of force and influence. Few had become wealthy and none had fallen into gross crime.

Jordan. Colonel John Jordan came from Hanover county soon after his marriage to Lucy Winn in 1802. His home, "Jordan's Point," now known as "Stoner," was built in 1818. It is a fine mansion in the colonial style, with handsome grounds. Rockbridge was almost wholly rural when he came to Lexington. Colonel Jordan had much to do with its industrial development. He became interested in iron smelting, flour and grist mills, lumber mills, blacksmith shops, and the weaving of woolen and cotton goods. As a contractor, he built Washington College and Ann Smith Academy, and for near a half century practically all the other large buildings in and around Lexington. He constructed the batteau canal at Balcony Falls, and was the first president of the construction company. He also took part in the building of the James River and Kanawha Canal. Colonel Jordan was also a road builder. In 1826 he built a road across North Mountain from near Collierstown to Longdale. When the county court hesitated, the colonel made this characteristic reply: "Give me the men and I will build the road." The road was constructed. Twelve furnaces were owned and operated by Colonel Jordan and his sons. Four of these were in this county. The others were chiefly in Alleghany and Botetourt. The Victoria furnace was in Louisa, and the Westham was near Richmond. Ironmaking was in fact a family pursuit, the colonel's father having made cannonballs for the American army in the Revolution. Colonel John Jordan was six feet three inches tall, and had dark hair and fine dark eyes. He was not only of commanding appearance, but was kindly, affectionate, honorable, and charitable. Both himself and wife were Baptists, and when the Lexington Baptist church was organized, one-half of its membership came from the Jordan household. Colonel Jordan was a close personal friend to General F. H. Smith. The two men would sit for hours on the veranda at Jordan's Point, talking on affairs relating to the Virginia Military Institute.

Mrs. Jordan, a very handsome blonde, was six feet tall. She was a woman of unusual strength of character, very industrious, and personally superintended the affairs of her large household. Spinning, weaving, dyeing, sewing, and the care of laundry, dairy, storeroom, smokehouse, orchard, and garden were but some of the activities of the estate, much of the work being done by slave labor.

Colonel and Mrs. Jordan had twelve sons and two daughters, nearly all of whom grew to maturity. Like their parents they were handsome in person, and the sons were generally of superior size and stature. Edwin J., the oldest, lived at White Haven in Alleghany. John W., was the founder of Rockbridge Baths. Samuel F., was particularly interested in the iron business, and it was under the colonel's sons that the industry attained its greatest development. The sons generally migrated from Rockbridge, sooner or later, and very few of the later descendants are now residents here. A number of the present generation are serving in the war now closing. Colonel Jordan was himself a lieutenant in 1812, and twenty silver dollars were used as mountings on his sword. Several of his grandsons were in the war of 1861 and Captain Charles H., son of Samuel F., was severely wounded at Fisher's Hill.

Junkin. George Junkin was born at Carlisle, Penn., October 1, 1790, and was graduated from Jefferson College in 1813. The first Sunday schools and temperance societies in central Pennsylvania were organized by him. He was the founder and the first president of Lafayette College, and for three years was president of Miami University. In 1848 he came to Lexington as president of Washington College, and held this position until April, 1861, when he resigned because of his inflexible opposition to secession. Doctor Junkin returned North, where he died, May 20, 1868. He was a prolific author, especially of religious works. The father's antagonism to secession was not shared by all of the six sons and three daughters. Margaret, the eldest—born 1825, died 1897—married Colonel John T. L. Preston. Mrs. Preston had remarkable literary and scholastic gifts. While yet a child, she thought in verse, and she learned the Hebrew alphabet at the age of three. In her adult life she was one of the best among American writers of sonnets. Several volumes of poems, rather of the Browning type, came from her pen. In 1856 appeared "Silverwood," a novel. To promote Southern literary effort, Mrs. Preston gratuitously edited several papers. Of the other daughters of Doctor Junkin, Elinor was the first wife of Stonewall Jackson, and Julia M. married Prof. J. M. Fishburne, of Washington College. Three sons, George, Ebenezer, and William F., entered the ministry. The last named—born 1831, died 1900—married Anna A., the oldest sister of William A. Anderson. He was for some time pastor of Falling Springs Church. His children are Mary E., (wife of General Edward W. Nichols, of the Virginia Military Institute), Julia T., Anna D., Francis T. A. (a lawyer of Chicago), Elinor J., (present wife of Doctor John H. Latané, of Johns Hopkins University), Isabel S., and William D. A., a lawyer of New York City.

Laird. James Laird, Sr., was living in 1756 with John Craig in what is now Rockingham county. The house he built in 1760 on his purchase at the foot of Laird's Knob and at the head of Smith Creek is still an occupied dwelling and is in a good state of preservation. The pioneer died here in 1803. His children were James, David, and Mary. The first of these served in the French and Indian War and both were in the Revolution. In 1805, James, Jr., was living in Rockbridge near Fancy Hill. Mary a sister to James, Sr., married James Craig, Sr., who was a member of the Augusta court in 1771-78. David E. Laird conducted at Fancy Hill one of the best preparatory schools in Virginia. In central Kentucky is an emigrant branch of the Rockbridge Lairds, and it includes people of wealth and position.

Lee. George Washington Custis Lee was the oldest son of General Robert E. Lee. In 1854 he came out of West Point at the head of his class, and was in the engineering corps until the outbreak of the war of 1861. As a captain of engineers he was then employed on the forts around Richmond. In the summer of 1861 Jefferson Davis made him an aide-de-camp with the rank of colonel of cavalry. Near the close of the war he had risen to the rank of major-general. He saw little active service, although this was not according to his desire. In the fall of 1865 he came to Lexington as professor of civil engineering and applied mechanics. February 1, 1872, he succeeded his father as college president, and was the first to preside over Washington and Lee University under its present name. In 1897 he retired. As president emeritus he was offered $2,000 a year and the use of the house he was occupying. This was declined and he went to live at Ravenwood, a family estate in Fairfax county. There he died in 1913 at the age of eighty. General Lee was unmarried.

Susan P. Pendleton, sister of General A. S. Pendleton, married in this county Edwin G. Lee, a native of Jefferson county, West Virginia. In conjunction with her father and sisters, she carried on a classical school in Lexington. Mrs. Lee, who wrote "A School History of the United States" and "Memoirs of William N. Pendleton," died in Lexington in 1911, aged seventy-nine.

Letcher. John Letcher came to this county from Fluvanna. He was an uncle to Robert P. Letcher, who was governor of Kentucky in 1840-44. After coming to Rockbridge, John married Mary Houston, an aunt to General Sam Houston, of Texas. Two of his sons remained in their native county, John, Jr., operating a tannery ten miles south of Lexington, and William H., living at the county seat and keeping a boarding house for students. John, a son of William H., was born March 28, 1813, and was educated at Washington College, afterward studying law at Randolph-Macon College. He was highly successful in his chosen profession, and won a renown that sent him to the Constitutional Convention of 1850. From 1851 to 1859 he was a member of the House of Representatives at Washington, where he sat in the Committee on Ways and Means. His Congressional career was conscientious and useful. It was here that he became known as "Honest John Letcher," and as the "Watch-Dog of the United States Treasury."

In 1859, Mr. Letcher was elected governor of his state by the comfortable majority of 5,569, although he failed to carry the Eastern District. His administration covered the years 1860-63 inclusive, so that he was one of the war governors of the period. After this responsibility and trying experience, Mr. Letcher returned to his native town to resume the practice of law, but after the close of hostilities he was repeatedly sent to the General Assembly. Politically, Governor Letcher was a Democrat and for some time he was editor of the *Valley Star*. During the months of suspense prior to the firing on Fort Sumter, he was not one of the original secessionists and his views were conciliatory. Even after the wanton burning of his fine residence by order of General Hunter, and while the memory of it must still have been fresh, he could use these words in an address at the Virginia Military Institute, September 19, 1866: "The war has ended. We are again a united people. Let the passions, the prejudices, and the revengeful feelings, which have existed between the sections, and which were intensified by the civil war, be consigned in solemn silence to a common grave, there to sleep forever. The past is gone and should be forgotten. The present is upon us, and should be wisely improved with a view to the future and all it has in store for us." The governor's death took place January 26, 1884, closing a long period of invalidism. The wife of Mr. Letcher was Mary S. Holt, of Augusta county. The children born to the couple were William H., Elizabeth S., Ann H., Andrew H., John D., Mary K., Virginia L., Fannie P., and Greenlee D.

Leyburn. John Leyburn graduated from the College of New Jersey with two honors and prepared for the ministry at Union Theological Seminary. His first pastorate was at Gainesville, Ala. For nine years he was co-editor of *The Presbyterian*, at Philadelphia. He was also secretary of the Publication Society of the Presbyterian Church. The Secession war found him traveling in Europe and called him home. Just after the close of the war he was serving a church in Baltimore. In 1874 he again went abroad, having already visited the British Isles as a delegate to the Ter-Centenary Celebration of the Presbyterian Church of Scotland. His wife was Mary L. Mercer, a granddaughter of General Hugh Mercer of the Revolution. There were no children. Doctor Leyburn was born in Lexington and in the evening of his life he wrote some very entertaining reminiscences for the Rockbridge papers. He died in 1893 at the age of seventy-eight.

Locher. Charles H. Locher is a son of Charles H. Locher, Sr., a native of Maryland who came to Balcony Falls about 1852 to manufacture cement. This business he pursued on a large scale until the plant was demolished by a flood in the James. He died at Glasgow in 1889. The son, who is a younger brother to Harry O. Locher of Glasgow, obtained a very practical knowledge of railroad construction, and drifted into contract work in which he has made a nationwide reputation. He is the owner of several patents, inclusive of an aerial dump used in excavation. The principal undertakings which Mr. Locher has carried to completion are these: the Chicago Drainage Canal the; Wachusett Dam in Massachusetts; the Shoshone Dam in Wyoming; the Livingstone Ship Channel in Detroit River; and the I. and O. Viaduct at Richmond, Virginia. Without his knowledge or solicitation, Mr. Locher was selected as manager to place a system of dams in the basin of the Miami River of Ohio. By an expenditure of $25,000,000, it is hoped to so impound the flood waters of that valley that such a disaster as befell the city of Dayton in 1913 is not at all likely to recur. Mr. Locher is ingenious, a good organizer, rather careful in making a promise, but scrupulous in the fulfilment.

Lusk. William Lusk, a justice of this county, was a self-made man, and incidentally was an ingenious mechanic.

Maury. Matthew Fontaine Maury, one of the foremost scientific men of the nineteenth century, was born in Spottslyvania county in 1806. At the age of nineteen, and as a midshipman, he began a voyage that extended around the world. In 1843 he was given charge of the National Observatory at the city of Washington, and the present Weather Bureau grew out of his suggestions. His knowledge of things maritime was so profound as to give him the title of "Pathfinder of the Seas." He instituted deep sea soundings, pointed out to Cyrus W. Field where an ocean cable should be laid, and wrote a standard work on physical geography. Offers of knighthood by the British government were refused, and he declined invitations to Russia and France. The last named country offered him the superintendency of the National Observatory at Paris. During the war of 1861 he supervised coast defenses for the Confederate government. After the surrender of Lee he went to Mexico, where he had a seat in the cabinet of the Emperor Maximilian, and he introduced the plant from which quinine is derived. From Mexico he went to England, where he was given the degree of Doctor of Laws by the University of Cambridge. In 1868 he was recalled to his native land, and he settled at Lexington as professor of meterology in Washington College. After five years of usefulness in this final position, he died at the age of sixty-seven. By his special request his remains were afterward taken to Richmond for re-interment, and by way of Goshen Pass during the rhododendron season. For this beautiful watergap he had a particular admiration. The will of Commodore Maury is noteworthy for its Christian spirit and for the way in which it distributes among his children the many medals he received from the governments of Europe.

McDowell. The McDowells of Rockbridge enjoy the distinction not only of being the first family to settle in the Borden grant, and probably the first in the county, but to have furnished a governor of Virginia and a number of other more or less eminent names of county, state, or national importance. Ephraim McDowell, the progenitor, had been at the famous siege of Londonderry in 1689, and was an elderly man when he came to Rockbridge. Yet he lived many years thereafter, and was sufficiently active to make for himself a place in the annals of the pioneer epoch. So far as we know, he was accompanied to America only by two sons and two daughters. The sons were John and James, but it is only the posterity of the former who appears to figure in Rockbridge history. John McDowell is said to have come here as a widower, but this is probably incorrect. However, it was not long after his arrival that he was married to Magdalena Woods, by whom he had a daughter, Martha. She married George Moffett, of Augusta. The children of his first wife were Samuel and James. John McDowell was a practical surveyor and assisted in laying off the Borden Tract. As a leader in the new settlement he was made captain of the first local militia company but fell in the battle with the Iroquois Indians at the mouth of North River. His gravestone in the family burial ground bears this legend:

> Hier Lyes The body of
> John Mack Dowell
> Deced Decembe 1743

The year is incorrectly marked, since the true time was 1742 and not 1743. But as the stone could not have been set up until some time in 1743, the error is easily accounted for.

Samuel, the oldest child of Captain McDowell, was almost exactly two years old when his father came to Timber Ridge in the fall of 1737. His wife was Mary McClung, to whom he was married in 1754. When only ten or eleven years old he carried a chain in the surveying parties, and thus became very familiar with the Borden lands. After coming to maturity he was very active in public affairs. Like his cousin, John Greenlee, he waived his rights under the British law of entail, and gave his brother and sister shares equal to his own in the parental estate. On his return from the House of Burgesses in 1775, he erected a liberty pole in his yard. Next May he and his colleague, Thomas Lewis, bore to the state capital the first official expression touching the matter of the independence of the colony. In the military movements of the Revolution he took a part, and he commanded a body of militia in the battle of Guilford. At Point Pleasant, in November, 1777, Colonel McDowell rendered an important service. General Hand had come from Pittsburg and was joined by 700 militia, who were expecting to be led against the Indian towns on the Scioto. Hand concluded that it was too late in the fall to set out. While at Fort Randolph he ordered the rations cut down on the ground that the men were living too well. The militia at once went on a strike. They buckled on their haversacks and shouldered their guns. McDowell acted as mediator and restored a semblance of harmony. Also, by order of the general, he rode before the line and announced the surrender of Burgoyne at Saratoga. The profession of Colonel McDowell was that of the law, and after his removal to Kentucky in 1783 he was a judge. He lived to old age and his depositions in the Borden suit are of much interest. His daughter Magdalene married Andrew Reid, the first clerk of Rockbridge. His son Ephriam, born 1771, died 1830, received the degree of Doctor of Medicine from the University of Edinburgh. He settled at Danville, Kentucky as a physician and surgeon, and has the distinction of being the first man to perform a successful operation in ovariotomy.

James, brother to Samuel, was two years younger, but died when only thirty-three years of age. James' wife, to whom he was married in 1793 was Sarah Preston, granddaughter to General William Campbell, one of the heroes of King's Mountain. James, Jr., the only son, was six feet two inches tall, but this commanding stature was not at all uncommon in the pioneer days. He was a man of "vigorous mind, strong common sense, and unflinching integrity." His decision of character and his patriotism are shown by his record in the 1812 war. He reported at Lexington, November 14, 1812, with a regiment of 1200 men, and the services of himself and his command were accepted. They were on duty more than two years, and although never in action, their aid was very important. The regiment acted as a flying-guard along the coast of the Chesapeake to keep parties of British marines from landing. Large quantities of brandy were distilled on Colonel McDowell's plantation of Cherry Grove, but when the temperance reform appeared on the horizon, he ceased the manufacture at once and absolutely. He went a step further. On a visit to Greenbrier he picked up a tract on the tobacco habit, and convincing himself that its arguments were sound, he immediately gave up using the weed, although he had been chewing or smoking for fifty years. The wife of Colonel McDowell, to whom he was married in 1793, was Sarah Preston, a granddaughter to General William Campbell, one of the heroes of King's Mountain. His children were Susan, James, and Elizabeth. The first daughter became the wife of William Taylor, who died while a member of the lower house of Congress. The second daughter wedded Thomas H. Benton, a statesman of national renown. A daughter of Benton became the wife of General John C. Fremont, whose chief title to fame rests upon his explorations in the Far West and his share in bringing California under the American flag. Fremont was the standard-bearer of the Republican party in the campaign of 1856, and was an unsuccessful leader of Federal armies in 1861-62.

James, the only son of Colonel James McDowell, was born at Cherry Grove, October 12, 1796, and was graduated from Princeton College in 1817. The same college gave him in 1846 the degree of Doctor of Laws. He read law but never practiced it. His vocational career was that of a planter, first in Kentucky and later in Rockbridge. Colonel McDowell was a model gentleman, very prepossessing in manner, and he made all visitors feel at ease in his presence. Yet he had very pronounced views with respect to personal conduct, and was not afraid of being called a Puritan. No liquors might appear at his dinners, and no amusement was permitted in his home which did not meet his approval. Being a polished orator and having an aptitude for statescraft, he gravitated into public life. Politically he was a Democrat. He served in the General Assembly, was governor of his state, 1843-46, and then succeeded his brother-in-law as a member of Congress. As a statesman, McDowell possessed unusual judgment and foresight, and in several important matters was ahead of his age. His state papers are able documents. He believed that emancipation of the slaves was inevitable, and the Nat Turner tragedy did not shake his advocacy of a progressive freeing of the negroes. During his administration as governor he gave his hearty support to a measure that nearly resulted in a system of free schools. His friendship for popular education is expressed in these words "I know not who was the originator of the school system of Massachusetts, but I would rather have been that man than wear the proudest diadem of Europe." McDowell's lack of ultra-partisanship appears in a brilliant speech against nullification in 1833, and in a speech in Congress in favor of the admission of California as a free state. Eight of the ten children of Governor McDowell arrived at the age of maturity and married. He died at Colalto, August 24, 1851.

McNutt. Alexander McNutt was granted lands in Nova Scotia after the expulsion of the Arcadians, visited England on a colonization errand, and returned with over 200 settlers and some supplies. He was complained of for parcelling out land without due authority. On the advent of the Revolution he joined the American "rebels" and although the lands appear to have been confiscated, he attempted to convey 100,000 acres to Liberty Hall Academy. In his later years he became a religious enthusiast. He died in 1811, and was buried at Falling Springs. His gold-mounted sword was long preserved in the family. While a lieutenant in the French and Indian war, he kept a diary, but unfortunately for the interests of Rockbridge he gave it to Governor Fauquier.

John, a brother to Alexander, married Catherine Anderson. A daughter married John McCorkle, who lost his life at Cowpens. A son, Alexander, was the father of Alexander G. McNutt and grandfather to two generals of the Confederate army; Albert G. Jenkins and Frank Paxton.

Alexander G. McNutt, son of Alexander and Rachael (Grigsby) McNutt, was born on North River one mile below Buena Vista. He was educated at Washington College, and at the age of twenty-one was settled as a lawyer at Jackson, Mississippi. Isaac McNutt, his uncle, had already migrated in this direction. The young man was well read and an easy writer. He was a fine stump speaker, but was pitted against Sergeant S. Prentiss, whose oratory was on a par with that of Patrick Henry or Daniel Webster. After 1838 McNutt declined to meet his antagonist on the platform. McNutt's intemperance and slovenly attire were made a target by Prentiss, but the future governor had the moral courage and strength of character to reform and his law practice became very renumerative. In 1829 he was Speaker of the House of Representatives for Mississippi, and as a Democrat was elected governor, his term covering the period 1838-42. McNutt died in 1848, in the midst of a presidential campaign. He was unmarried, and the four brothers who followed him to the Gulf country also died without issue.

A pioneer McNutt was Robert, who died on a voyage to Ireland, and his wife, whose maiden name was Rosanna Dunn, married Patrick McFarland. Still another was George, who came here with his brother William as advance agents for some kinspeople. Tradition has it that both brothers were in the battle of King's Mountain. William went to the Northwest, and George, who was three times married and had a numerous family, settled near Knoxville, Tennessee.

Montgomery.. Humphrey Montgomery, who settled on Buffalo Creek, was a son of Humphrey Montgomery, of Pennslyvania, and served under Captain Samuel Lapsley in 1777-79.

Moore. Andrew Moore, a son of David, was born at "Cannicello," in this county in 1752. In his youth he was shipwrecked while on a voyage to the West Indies. In consequence, he and several companions were marooned several weeks on an island, doubtless one of the Bahamas, and the lizards on which they subsisted must have been iguanas. This vegetable-eating reptile is considered a great delicacy. He was admitted to the bar in 1774 and was very a successful lawyer. In 1776 he was commissioned a lieutenant, and enlisted 100 men. securing nineteen at a single log-rolling. During the next three years he was a captain of riflemen under Daniel Morgan. In 1779 he resigned and from 1781 to 1789 was in the state legislature. In 1788 he was a member of the state convention that ratified the Federal Constitution. Ratification had been made a distinct issue in the campaign which resulted in sending Andrew Moore and William McKee to the Convention. But Patrick Henry wielded a great influence in that body, and because of his opposition, a large public meeting at Lexington instructed the delegates to vote against ratification. Both Moore and McKee decided that they were justified in disregarding these instructions and voted accordingly. A change of only five votes would have defeated ratification. Moore was re-elected when he again ran for office. He was defeated only once in twenty-nine candidacies, and then then only by one vote. Throughout Washington's administration he was in the House of Representatives. After again returning to the General Assembly, he was once more a Congressman and then a member of the

Federal Senate. In 1809 he was commissioned a major-general, and the next year was appointed a United States Marshall, holding this office until 1821, the year of his death. His wife was Sally, a daughter of Andrew Reid.

Samuel McDowell Moore, a son of General Andrew Moore, was born in 1796 and died in 1875. He was a man of powerful build, strongly marked countenance, and commanding force. He thought and acted for himself, called a spade a spade, and was not a person to be improperly interfered with. In any arena he was a dangerous antagonist. He was a leader in the Rockbridge bar and was a Congressman in 1833-35. Mr. Moore was a Whig in politics, of anti-slavery feeling, and in the state convention of 1861 he vigorously combatted the arguments of the secession leaders. He was married to Evalina, a daughter of Andrew Alexander. His only child was a daughter, who married John H. Moore.

William, the elder brother of General Andrew Moore, married Nancy McClung and lived near Fairfield. He was a merchant, and sheriff, and had a furnace on South River. His children were Samuel, David, John, Eliab, Jane, Isabella, Elizabeth and Nancy. William Moore was a man of most unusual physical strength. In the battle of Point Pleasant, John Steele was wounded and about to be scalped. Moore shot the Indian, knocked another down with his gun, and although Steele was heavy, he took him up and bore him to a place of safety. Perhaps this feat undermined Moore's constitution, for he only reached the age of about ninety-three years.

Morrison. James D. Morrison, a son of William, was a graduate of Washington College, and in the civil war was a captain in the 58th Virginia Infantry. He was sent to the Assembly in 1872, and five years later he founded the *Rockbridge Citizen.* He died in 1902, aged about seventy years. Captain Morrison married Laura Chapin, and his children were William, Kenneth, and Irene.

Nelson. Alexander L. Nelson, a native of Augusta, was graduated from Washington College in 1846 and succeeded General D. H. Hill in the chair of mathematics. Professor Nelson, who was a great grandson of Sampson Mathews, died in 1910 at the age of eighty-three. His wife was Elizabeth H. Moore.

Nichols. General Edward Nichols was born at Petersburg, 1858. He was graduated with high honors from the Virginia Military Institute in 1878, and took a post-graduate course in engineering. He entered the legal profession but left it to take the chair in engineering at the Institute in 1882. From 1890 until 1908 he held the chair of mathematics. In this interval he became the author of an "Analytical Geometry," and "A Differential and Integral Calculus." He is the present Superintendent of the Institute. The first wife of General Nichols was Edmonia L., a daughter of Doctor Livingston Waddell; the second is Mary E., the oldest daughter of the late William F. Junkin. Her first husband was Lawrence Rust, LL. D., of Loudoun county.

Parsons. Colonel Henry C. Parsons, several years owner of the Natural Bridge, was a native of Vermont. He was the author of "The Reaper," a volume of poems. Colonel Parsons was murdered at Clifton Forge, June 29, 1894, by a railroad man.

Paul. Captain Audley Paul was a son of Hugh Paul, a Presbyterian minister, who migrated from county Armagh, Ulster, to Chester county, Pennsylvania. He was a very useful officer, and was in military service nearly all the time from 1754 until the close of the Revolution. He led his company several times against the Indians. He was under Washington in the battle known as Braddock's Defeat, and he endured the hardships of the Big Sandy expedition. His son relates in 1839 that his father received no compensation for these services. Captain Paul lived near the line of Botetourt. His brother John became a Roman Catholic priest in Maryland.

Paxtons. The Paxtons, a very numerous connection in this county, fall into two groups, the progeny of two brothers. One of these settled on South River, the other south of Lexington. The Paxtons have been a prosperous folk and have stood high in the community. Several of the earlier generations were wealthy, aristocratic planters, and unusually heavy growers of hemp. Not a few of the descendants have attained prominence in literary, professional, and business circles.

Major James Paxton, a son of William and his wife Elenor Hays, was from 1818 until 1828 commandant of the arsenal at Lexington. He then retired to an estate at the mouth of the Cowpasture owned by his father-in-law, John Jordan. Here he died in 1866 at the age of eighty-five. Major Paxton was a great leader and scholar. A shadow came over his life through his killing of a Captain Dade in a duel.

Colonel James H., a son of Colonel William Paxton, was a graduate of Washington College in the class of 1833. He delighted in the classics and was the foremost Latin scholar in Rockbridge. At his home, "Mountain View," he maintained for twelve years a classical school, and was a friend of public schools. Colonel Paxton served a term in the Senate of Virginia. He died in 1902 at the great age of ninety years. His wife was Kate Glasgow, and his children were Nellie, Kate G., Archibald H., Robert (a captain in the United States army), William T., Professor James H., and J. Gordan.

John D. Paxton, who died in 1868 at the age of eighty-four, was also a graduate of Washington College. For some years he was a missionary in Europe. His sermons number 5769. He was a most vehement opponent to slavery, and in 1833 he published a volume against it. He also published a volume on his travels in the Eastern continent. A memoir of Mr. Paxton was written by his widow. His nephew, John W., a son of James H. Paxton, was an eminent physician.

Elisha F. Paxton, the one brigadier directly contributed by Rockbridge to the Confederate army, was a nephew to Governor McNutt, of Mississippi, and was born in 1828. He graduated from Washington College in 1845, from Yale College in 1847, and completed a law course at the University of Virginia in 1849. General Paxton was an original seccessionist, and at the outset of the war was a lieutenant in the Rockbridge Rifles. After serving as aide-de-camp to Stonewall Jackson, he took command of the Stonewall Brigade, November 2, 1862. He was killed at the head of his troops in the battle of Chancellorsville, May 2, 1862, just one day before his commander was disabled. Indifferent eyesight had caused him to abandon the law and turn to farming. The wife of General Paxton was E—— H. White. His children are Matthew W., the present editor of the *Rockbridge County News,* and the present dean of Rockbridge journalism, John G., an attorney of Kansas City, and Frank of San Saba county, Texas. James G., an elder brother of General Paxton, was killed August 6, 1870, in the train wreck at Jerry's Run on the Chesapeake and Ohio Railroad.

Alexander S., a son of Thomas P. Paxton, was the author of *Memory Days,* a delightful sketch of antebellum times in Rockbridge. The story centers about an old field school near the entrance to Arnold's Valley.

Poague. William T., son of John B., and Elizabeth (Stuart) Poague, came out of Washington College in the class of 1857, and entered the practice of law in St. Louis. In the Confederate army he rose from the rank of private to that of lieutenant-colonel. He was with General Lee in his Greenbrier campaign, and was in all of Stonewall Jackson's battles. In 1885 he became treasurer of the Virginia Military Institute. Other positions of honor and trust were held by him.

Preston. The Preston group-family is noteworthy for the exceptional number of eminent persons it includes. Colonel William Preston, a soldier and surgeon of the Dunmore and Revolutionary wars, was the only son of John, the immigrant and his wife, a sister to Colonel James Patton. Thomas L., tenth child of Colonel William, was an alumnus of Liberty Hall Academy, a lawyer and died in military service in the war of 1812. Colonel John T. L. Preston, son of Captain Thomas L., began active life as a lawyer, but for forty-three years was professor of language and literature in the Virginia Military Institute, a school that he helped in no small degree to establish. During forty years he was known as the "town speaker," yet he was somewhat unsocial and did not always choose to be on the popular side. All his seven sons were educated at Washington College. His first wife was Sally L. Caruthers, his second was Margaret, the eldest daughter of President Junkin, of the same institution. The children who reached adult age were Thomas L., Franklin, William C., John A., Elizabeth, George J., and Herbert R. Thomas L., and John A., became ministers.

Franklin and William C., were killed in the war, the first at New Market, the second at Second Manassas. Franklin, the best linguist of his age in the state, was assistant professor of Greek in Wahington College. George J., and Herbert R., were the children of the second wife. Both settled in Baltimore, the first as a physician, the second as a lawyer.

Reid. Andrew Reid, of Mulberry Hill, married Magdalene, daughter of Samuel McDowell, and had three sons and eight daughters. He was the first clerk of Rockbridge. Samuel McDowell Reid, one of the three sons, was born in 1790, and was an adjutant under his cousin, Colonel James McDowell, in the war of 1812. He succeeded his father as county clerk, after serving a time as deputy. He was a founder of the Franklin Society, more than fifty years trustee of Washington College and Ann Smith Academy, a chief organizer of the Rockbridge County Fair, and was mainly instrumental in opening the North River to Lexington. He died in 1869. From his marriage to Sarah E. Hare, only two children, Mary L., and Agnes, grew to maturity. The former married Professor James J. White.

Robinson. John Robinson came from Ireland to Rockbridge in 1770, when seventeen years of age. He learned the trade of weaver, but by turning horse-trader and speculating in soldiers' certificates, he became able to purchase Hart's Bottom in 1779. He enlarged his landed property to 800 acres, exclusive of his holdings on the Cowpasture. He was not highly successful as a planter, although he became owner of sixty slaves. It was mainly by the distilling of whiskey that he accumulated his fortune. Mr. Robinson was without an heir, and decided to devote his entire estate to educational uses. In 1820 he rescued the Ann Smith Academy from a sheriff's sale by taking up a judgment against it of about $3,000. His will begins by saying that "John Robinson, a native of the county of Armagh in the north of Ireland, but now a resident of Hart's Bottom, in the county of Rockbridge and the state of Virginia, having migrated to America just in time to participate in its Revolutionary struggle (which I did in various situations) and having since that period by a long, peaceful, and prosperous intercourse with my fellow citizens amassed a considerable estate which I am desirous of rendering back to them, upon terms most likely to conduce to their essential and permanent interests, do therefore will and ordain ————." He endowed a chair of geology and biology, and a clause in the will provides that two medals shall be given yearly. With the exception of General Washington he was the first considerable benefactor of the college. Mr. Robinson died in 1826, and in 1855 a monument to his memory was erected on the college campus.

Ruffner. Henry Ruffner, son of Colonel David Ruffner of Page county, and grandson of Peter Ruffner, a German immigrant, was born in Page in 1789.

He was educated at Washington College from which he was graduated in 1817. Two years later he entered the same college as a professor, and also was licensed to the Presbyterian ministry. From 1836 to 1848 he was the college president. He then retired to a farm on the Kanawha and ceased preaching a year before his death, which took place in 1861. Princeton gave him the degree of Doctor of Divinity. Doctor Ruffner was an occasional contributor to the religious press. His wife was Sarah, daughter of William Lyle of "Oakley" on Mill Creek.

William Henry Ruffner, son of Henry Ruffner, was born at Lexington in 1824, and was graduated from Washington College in 1842. He likewise entered the Presbyterian ministry, but his only pastorate was in Philadelphia in 1849-51. His leanings were very much in the direction of educational affort and scientific study. He devised the free school system adopted by Virginia in 1870, drafted the organization of the school that became the Virginia Polytechnic Institute, and organized the Farmville State Normal School, of which he was president three years. Doctor Ruffner twice declined to be made a college president, and in 1887 retired to "Tribrook," one mile from Lexington. He now gave his attention to geologic research and reports on mineral properties. Several volumes, inclusive of *Charity and the Clergy,* came from his pen, and he was a contributor to scientific periodicals. He died in 1908. His wife was Harriet G. Gray, of Harrisonburg.

Salling. A mist of romance attaches itself to the name of John Peter Salling. That individual lived in the heroic age of American history, and therefore it is not strange that some embellishment has crept into the narrative contained in the volumes written on border history. It is represented that Salling explored the Valley of Virginia as early as 1726, had a long and most eventful captivity among the red men, and after his restoration was the pathfinder who drew the attention of John Lewis and others to the "New Virginia" beyond the Blue Ridge. Accepting the family tradition as being more trustworthy than the rhetorical tales we have alluded to, we arrive at the following as the most probable statement of the whole matter.

John Peter Salling was a weaver by trade, and was one of the few Germans who settled in Tuckahoe. Hearing of the new country beyond the mountains, and being of a venturesome turn, Salling went on a journey of exploration. He was so well pleased with the beautiful bottom just above Balcony Falls that he did not think it worth his while to go further. He returned to his home at or near Williamsburg and took steps to secure a morsel of this choice land. This was probably in 1741. It could scarcely have antedated the coming of the McDowells, since it would have been imprudent to make a solitary settlement forty miles from other people. Salling's earliest patent was not issued till 1746. A transfer of a portion of his land names 1741 as the date of patent, but no such deed appears to be on record. It would seem that the year of settlement rather than the year of patent is the one mentioned in the conveyance. We know that Salling was living here at the time of the McDowell battle in December, 1742. And since this incidental mention indicates that he was then at home, it would not seem that he was captured earlier than the following spring. While Salling and a companion were prospecting on the Roanoke, the former was taken by the Cherokees and remained a prisoner until 1745. He was being sent to France as a spy, the struggle known in America as King George's war not yet having come to a conclusion. The French vessel was captured by a British cruiser, and Salling was put ashore at Charleston, South Carolina. He now made his way back to Virginia, perfected his title to his land, went to live on it, and was not again disturbed.

Traditions agree that during his captivity, Salling was carried as far as the Mississippi and in some way fell into the hands of the French. The more florid occount adds that a squaw of Kaskaskia adopted him as a son; that he several times journeyed down the Father of Waters, and was purchased by the Spaniards as an interpreter; that he was taken to Canada, redeemed by the French governor, and turned over to the Hollanders, of New York.

Henry Ruffner states that John Salling had a brother, Peter Adam Salling. This may have been the case, but Doctor Ruffner is incorrect in saying John was a single man. He had a wife named Ann, and at least five children. If there were two Sallings, it was the other who was a bachelor. John Salling, the only pioneer named in the records, had business dealings with the McDowells. That he was a man of force and consequence is manifest from his being commissioned an officer of militia. His will is dated Christmas day, 1754, and his death occurred shortly afterward, while he was still in the prime of life. He appears to have had no near neighbor of his own nationality. He spoke broken English, and his two daughters married Henry Fuller and Richard Burton. His sons, John and George Adam, had removed to North Carolina by 1760, probably because of the new Indian war, and only the third son, Henry, remained at Balcony Falls. The will, however, mentions an infant grandson of the name of John Salling. It also speaks of one Peter Crotingale as a tenant on one of his farms. The personality was appraised at $194.64, and it included four horses, four sheep, and twenty-two hogs. The last of the Sallings in Rockbridge was Peter A., who died without issue in 1856.

Saville. Abraham and Robert, sons of Samuel Saville, an immigrant from England, came to this country about 1770. The latter went with his family to Ohio. The former, who settled on the South Fork of Buffalo, is the ancestor of the Savilles of Rockbridge, although several of his own sons went to Ohio. The resident connection have generally been farmers or millwrights.

Smith. General Francis H. Smith was born at Norfolk, October 18, 1812, and was graduated with distinction from West Point in 1833. He was then placed in the artillery service, but soon resigned to accept the chair of mathematics in Hampden-Sidney College. The position was congenial and it was with some reluctance that he accepted a unanimous call to the superintendency of the newly organized Virginia Military Institute. His subsequent career is a part of the history of the institution over which he presided the extraordinarily long period of fifty years. The school was in the nature of an experiment when he became its head. He lived to witness an almost continuous growth, and to see it develop into the most famous military school in the United States with the single exception of West Point. General Smith died March 21, 1890, only three months after his retirement.

Stuart. Archibald Stuart left Ulster in 1731, and came to the Borden Tract in 1738, an amnesty having permitted him to send for his family. His wife, Janet, was a sister to the Reverend John Brown. Two sons were Thomas and Alexander, the latter born in 1735. Alexander was very tall and strong, and wielded a ponderous broadsword in the battle of Guilford, where he was wounded and taken prisoner. His son Archibald, who died in 1831 at the age of seventy-four, removed to Staunton in 1785. He was the father of Alexander H. H. Stuart, Secretary of the Interior in the Cabinet of President Fillmore. Robert Stuart of Rockbridge and Judge Alexander Stuart of Missouri were brothers to Archibald, a grandson of whom was the dashing Confederate cavalry leader, General J. E. B. Stuart.

Taylor. Five brothers of the name of Taylor,—George, James, William, John, and Caufield—came from county Armagh, Ireland, and settled in Rockbridge, 1760, investing their money in lands and slaves. John was killed in battle, April 25, 1778. Caufield was taken prisoner, but liberated after the surrender of Cornwallis. The four surviving brothers lived in a fine valley at the head of Cedar and are buried there. The wife of William was Janet Paul, said to have been a sister to the famous John Paul Jones of the Revolution. Admiral Jones was a Paul and added the name of his foster parent to his surname by birth. George and James married daughters of Captain Audley Paul. The Pauls were conscientiously opposed to slavery, and imparted their scruples to the families of these two brothers. Stuart, one of the youngest of the fourteen children of James, freed the last of the negroes in that branch of the family. In doing so he gave each freedman $50.

Hugh P. Taylor, a bachelor son of James, was an attorney and surveyor, and is buried at Rockbridge Baths. A love affair inspired him to write a beautiful poem. He also wrote "Hugh Paul Taylor's Sketches," a historical work covering the period, 1740-1781. Much of the material was derived from his maternal grandfather, Captain Audley Paul.

Stuart Taylor, who lived on the brow of Hogback Mountain, a few miles from Rockbridge Baths, was a tanner and currier by trade and a mechanical genius as well. Like his distinguished son, he was tall, large in frame, and fearless. Several of his hunting exploits have been related to us. Once he was attacked by wildcats, and another time he had to get upon a fallen tree the better to defend himself against some half-wild hogs. In each instance he was in much danger. He did not hesitate to go into a bear's den in the winter season, knowing that if the animal were not molested while in its lair, it would rush out after getting awake. His colored man, Joe, was left near the entrance to shoot the bear as it ran out. But on one occasion the bear slipped down a hillside in Goshen Pass, Taylor and his dogs clinging to the animal's shaggy back. Man, bear, and dogs slid out some distance on the ice which then covered North River, and the hunter dispatched the brute with his hunting-knife. Stuart Taylor was not a man of education, yet was a forceful local preacher of the Methodist communion. His wife, Martha E. Hickman, to whom he was married in 1819, was a most useful woman in her neighborhood and highly respected.

William, the oldest son of Stuart Taylor, was born May 2, 1821. He grew to manhood, a giant in size and strength, and could win people to his side by his feats at a log-rolling. At the age of nineteen he was converted at Shaw's campground, and he joined the Methodist Church at the Lambert meeting house on the Lexington circuit. A year later he was attending school in Lexington. A year later yet he taught the Rapp school on the South Branch of Buffalo. Already he had been licensed as a local preacher and occasionally conducted divine service. When admitted to the Baltimore Conference in 1845, his presiding elder announced to the assemblage that "here is a young man whom the sun never finds in bed." His first field was in Highland county. After six years of circuit work, he was assigned to mission effort in Baltimore and Washington. Already he was very successful as an evangelist, and his unusual gift of song was a wonderful help to him. In 1851 the young minister was sent to California. The three years preceeding had made that state cosmopolitan and a scene of almost unprecedented lawlessness. The Sabbath was a carnival of crime and immorality. San Francisco, a city of tents and shacks, was perhaps the most corrupt spot on earth. The choice proved very wise. Taylor's powerful physique, his abounding faith, his tactfulness, and his rare gifts as singer and preacher made him the man for the task. The Mission Board did not adequately understand the actual conditions in that land of high prices, but although Taylor's salary of $700 a year was entirely too low, he never complained, nor did he ask his friends in the East for a single dollar. He labored seven years in California, making a nationwide reputation as an evangelist. He could accomplish in a few hours what others were months in performing. Taylor next preached in every quarter of the United States and Canada, and made tours in Britain and other parts of Europe. He then visited South America, Africa, Malaysia, Australia, China, Ceylon, and India, two new conferences being the result in the country last named. In 1884 he was a delegate from India to the General Conference of the Methodist Episcopal Church, and was elected Bishop of Africa. This field he relinquished only because of advancing years. Bishop Taylor had preached more widely than any man of the Christian Church in any age. His leading road to influence among the heathen was through the children. But he was very successful in winning over the chiefs, and it was his design to span the Dark Continent with a chain of mission stations. His habits were simple. He use dalways a hard pillow, and his bedroom window was open, even in zero weather. At a late period in his life Bishop Taylor visited his native county and preached in crowded houses. His brother Archibald and Andrew also entered the ministry, the former going to California. Bishop Taylor died in that state in 1902 at the age of enghty-one.

Tucker. John Randolph Tucker, son of Henry St. George Tucker, was born at Winchester, December 24, 1823. He was graduated from the University of Virginia in 1844, and was admitted to the bar the following year. He settled in his native town for the practice of his profession and it remained his home until 1870, except that he was Attorney-General of Virginia in 1857-65. In 1870 he came to Lexington as professor of law and equity in Washington College. After four years of service in this field he was elected to Congress. He was re-elected for six successive terms. In the Forty-Eighth and Forty-Ninth congresses he was Chairman of the Judiciary Committee, and he was eight years on the Committee of Ways and Means. In 1887 Mr. Tucker returned to his professorship in Washington and Lee University, holding it until his death, February 13, 1897. Tucker Hall, one of the most imposing of the University buildings, is named in his honor. Mr. Tucker was a genial, thoroughly trained gentleman, an orator of great power and was regarded as one of the very ablest men of the South. To him the law was a science and in constitutional law he was a recognized authority. He was honored with the degree of Doctor of Laws by Harvard and Yale Universities and by the College of William and Mary. In 1844 Mr. Tucker was married to Laura H. Powell, of Loudoun county. The children of the couple were these: Powell, who died in youth; Evelyn, wife of Wilmer Shields, of Mississippi; Anne H., wife of William P. McGuire of Winchester; Virginia B., wife of John Carmichael; Henry St. G., of Lexington; Gertrude P., wife of Judge —— Logan; Laura P., wife of E. —. M. Pendleton.

Henry St. George Tucker, born 1853, took the degree of Master of Arts from Washington and Lee University in 1875. Two years later he settled as an attorney at Staunton, but in 1897 returned to Lexington, and resides on his estate of "Colalto." In 1889 Mr. Tucker went to Congress and remained four terms. Upon the death of his father he succeeded him as professor of Constitutional and International Law and Equity. In 1905 he was President of the Jamestown Exposition. Mr. Tucker has written a treatise on the treaty-making power of the Federal Government, and has edited his father's *Tucker on the Constitution.*

Vethake. Henry Vethake was a native of British Guiana who was graduated from Columbia College in 1808. He practiced law and also engaged in educational work. In 1835-36 he was president of Washington College, and until 1859 he held the chair of mental and moral philosophy. He died in 1866 at the age of seventy-four.

Wallace. William A. Wallace, known in American history as "Big Foot" Wallace, was born one mile south of Lexington, April 12, 1816. In the fall of 1837 he heard of the death of a brother at the hands of the Mexicans in the Fannin massacre. Leaving his plow and team in the field, he started at once for Texas on a mission of vengeance. He was accompanied by James Paxton and J. Frank Shields, the former dying in Texas. In the Texan army, Wallace was a lieutenant of rangers. He accompanied the Mier expedition and was captured, but by good fortune he drew a white bean, and thus escaped military execution. His captors called him the "Big Foot Gringo," and he was made to work a long while on the streets of the City of Mexico. Some time after his release he killed "Big Foot," a Lipan warrior, in single combat. Wallace made his home near San Antonio, but at length the region became too thickly settled to please him, and he went farther west. He visited Rockbridge in 1850 and again about 1872. He never married, and he died in Texas, January 8, 1899. Big Foot Wallace did not really have feet of unusual size, considering his stature, yet was conspicuous for immense shoulders and a very large head. He was a grandson of Colonel Samuel Wallace of the Revolutionary period.

White. Robert White was born in Ireland in 1775, and came to Lexington in 1800, going into the mercantile business. He was a lieutenant in the war of 1812, a justice and sheriff, and in politics was a Whig. In 1802 he was married to Margaret, daughter of Zachariah Johnston. His sons were Zachariah J. and Robert L. Mr. White died in 1851.

Woods. Richard Woods settled on Woods Creek in 1738 and gave it its name. It is thought that he was a son of Michael Woods, of Albemarle, who came to America with nine boys, three brothers and their families, and a widowed sister, Mrs. Elizabeth Wallace. Richard Woods was a sheriff and otherwise very prominent settler. He seems to have had a brother, Charles, who died in 1761, and three sisters, of whom Martha married Peter Wallace, and Sarah married Joseph Lapsley. Magdalena was successively the wife of Captain John McDowell, Benjamin Borden, Jr., and General John Bowyer. The name Woods was represented in Rockbridge until after the opening of the nineteenth cetury.

XXXV

THE MacCORKLE FAMILY

The Pioneer MacCorkles—The Rockbridge Branch—The Name in Britain—Line of John MacCorkle—Biographical Notes

In the history of the MacCorkles* of Augusta and Rockbridge are shown several interesting facts, true also of some other pioneer families. We find at the outset a number of individuals with the same surname. Some of these are soon lost to view. This fact is significant of the ceaseless emigration that set in from Old Augusta, even in the first decade of its settlement. For a long while this outflow was almost wholly to the westward and southward. But during the present industrial era, it is in part directed to the commercial centers of the Atlantic seaboard.

The MacCorkles that clung to the Forks of the James have been very large landholders in the most favored portion of that district. They are an industrious, forceful, intellectual, and religious people. These traits, coupled with a tenacity in holding on to a good choice in extensive landed possessions, could not but be reflected by prominence in public and professional life. That the men of this stock should be prompt in responding to a conviction of patriotic duty follows as a matter of course.

Even before Augusta set up a county government at the close of 1745, one James MacCorkle was living on a survey in Beverly Manor, apparently a few miles northeast of Staunton, and between Lewis and Christian's creeks. It would appear that in many instances the newcomer did not at once perfect a purchase, but held his land for a while on a rental basis. From an ejectment suit brought against him by the proprietor of the Manor, he came out victorious. In 1747 William Beverly gave him a deed for 370 acres, the price being $54.15. But in 1753 James MacCorkle and Jane, his wife, sold this tract, and we find no mention of another purchase. In 1751 the immigrant was a constable, and in the same year he and Robert Bratton were the guardians of Archibald Crockett of the Calfpasture. Ten years later he was one of the appraisers of the valuable estate of Adam Dickenson, the leading pioneer of the lower Cowpasture. And as both Dickenson and Bratton were men of wealth and position, it follows that only a man of proved character and known ability would have been appointed to these trusts. No will is on record in Augusta, and it is not clear that he is again named in the records. It is probable that he died before the Revolution.

---

*Within Rockbridge itself the name has usually been spelled with the prefix abbreviated—McCorkle. During the colonial period the orthography was less uniform than it is now. Thus we find in the public records the forms McCorkal, McCorkell, McChorkle, McKocle, etc.

In 1770 another James came from Ulster and was a merchant at Staunton. A few years later he removed to Montgomery, of which county he was sheriff in 1778. He died there in 1794. It was this James who was a trustee of Liberty Hall Academy in 1783. He had a brother William, whose daughters were Margaret, Martha, and Rebecca.

We are told that the first James was the parent pioneer, and that his sons were Alexander, William, and John. We are further told that Alexander, born 1722, died 1800, married Agnes, a daughter of John Montgomery, of Harris's Ferry—now Harrisburg, Pennsylvania—and that in 1752 he removed to North Carolina, settling fifteen miles west of Salisbury. A great grandson is Joseph W. McCorkle, Member of Congress from California.

But there was a Robert MacCorkle, who purchased of Beverly 269 acres, his tract appearing to be contiguous with that of the elder James. In 1752 he sold this land and went away, perhaps accompanying Alexander to North Carolina. There was also a Samuel, who in 1749 was a close neighbor to James and Robert. He may have been the Samuel who died in Augusta in 1785. The name of his wife was Sarah, and his children, at least two of whom were then married, were John, Mary, Martha, Samuel, Robert, Sarah, and Elizabeth. Samuel, Jr., seems to have left Augusta by 1796. Still another of the early McCorkles was Patrick, who in 1759 witnessed a deed given by Samuel Steele to Robert Steele, and in 1762 a deed by Benjamin Bennett to John McNutt. It was probably the same Patrick who helped to build a road in the south of the Rockbridge area in 1753, and who sold a parcel of land to Samuel Lyle in 1778.

Among the above mentioned MacCorkles we meet the same given names as occur in the Rockbridge line that we shall presently trace. Several of them were near neighbors to one William McNutt, and a McNutt became the wife of John MacCorkle. It was characteristic of the Scotch-Irish pioneers to come to America in bodies and not as isolated individuals. It is highly probable that the younger MacCorkles we first encounter in this region were the sons of two brothers, James and William, one or both of whom accompanied the sons.

The Alexander MacCorkle who settled in the Forks of James may therefore have been a cousin to the one already named. One or the other is mentioned in the appraisement of the estate of Andrew Boyd in 1750. Boyd appears to have lived near Old Providence Church. The first certain mention is in 1753, when he and Patrick worked on the road already spoken of. In 1757 he was an administrator of the estate of Robert Renick, who had been killed by the Indians. In 1761 he purchased 300 acres in the Borden Tract, and in 1766 conveyed one-half of this to Patrick MacCorkle. In 1768 he was given a bounty certificate for growing 1712 pounds of hemp, a quantity above the average for the colonial planter. No will is on record, and his name does not appear among the taxpayers for 1778. The inference is that he died near the beginning of the Revolution, and when he was in the prime of life.

The wife of Alexander, ancestor of the MacCorkles of Rockbridge, was Mary Steele. The children of the pair were James, John, William, and Nancy, and perhaps also a Samuel, since there was a tithable by this name in Rockbridge in 1778. James married Margaret McCollom. John married Rebecca, a daughter of John McNutt and aunt to Governor Alexander G. McNutt, of Mississippi. William, who lived on Elliott's Hill and died in 1818, is described as a recluse of eccentric disposition. His first wife, the mother of his children, was a McCluer. The second, whom he married in 1802, was Ann, a daughter of Captain Audley Paul and widow of the grandfather of Bishop William Taylor.

The children of James were six. William, born 1762, died 1847, was married to Nancy Welch in 1799. Patrick married Margaret Weeks, 1804. John went to Ohio. Elizabeth married Samuel Hamilton, 1811. The others of the family were James and Alexander, the latter of whom lived in Collierstown. The nine children of William were the only representatives of the next generation within this county. Of these, Eliza and Jane were unmarried. Nancy, Benjamin, Margaret, Samuel, Thomas, Sally, and William H. married, in the order of their mention, Samuel Adair, Mary Adair, William Morrison, Mary Simonds, Susan A. Harper, John Patterson, and Virginia Wilson. The sons of Benjamin were William A., John, Henry C., and Oliver C. John and Oliver C. are unmarried. William A. and Henry married, respectively, Jennie McMasters and Ida Coffey. The daughters were Sallie and Anna. Sallie was the first and Anna the second wife of Alexander Harrison. The children of Samuel were William A., Samuel B., Sallie, Margaret, Nancy, and Manie. The third, fourth, and fifth married in the order of their names, William H. Sale, John Dixon, and Samuel Mackey. Samuel B. resides in Staunton. William A. married a Davidson. His children, who are the only grandchildren of Samuel to remain in Rockbridge, are Carrie, William A., Gold, Stuart, and Daniel. Carrie married Ward Whitmer, and Gold married Mattie Swink. The first wife of William A., Jr., was a Davidson. The second was Agnes Gold. The children of Thomas, who died in 1879 at the age of seventy-five, went to Ohio. The descendants of William H. are hereinafter named.

The children of John, son of Alexander, the pioneer, were Alexander, Samuel, and Catharine. The daughter married Joseph Walker, 1804, and went West with him. Samuel married Catharine McCluer, 1804, and died 1833, leaving three children, John, Alexander, and Agnes. The daughter was then married to a McCluer. Alexander went West. It was not then known what had become

Wm. A. MacCorkle
Governor of West Virginia 1893 to 1897

Raphine Hall, Raphine, Virginia, Home of James E. A. Gibbs

of John. The names and the dates of birth of the children of Alexander and his wife, Mildred Welch, appear later in this chapter. Mildred was a sister to Nancy. Of the ten children, Sally married James Wilson, 1814; John was married to Elizabeth Mackey, 1820, and later to a Cunningham; Samuel, to a Douglass, and afterward to a Perry; Thomas, to Susan Alexander; Alexander B. to Lucilla Gamble; Patsy, to James W. Wilson; Jane, to James West; William, to Mary H. Morrison; Rebecca to Baxter Braford. Samuel, who had a large family, removed to Lynchburg. Two sons of John lost their lives in military service: Alexander C. at Monterey, Mexico, and James T. at First Manassas. The other children—George B., W. D., and Nannie—married, respectively, Mary McCullough, Aurelia Sterrett, and Moffett McClung. The children of George B. are Lelia, wife of a Doctor Burks, and Emma, Julia, and George, whose consorts are a Walker, a Smylie, and a Humphreys. The children of W. D. are Aurelia and Douglass. Thomas, third son of John, had six children: Thomas E., S. W., Alfred, Jennie, Mildred, and Margaret. All these married, their companions being, in order, an Anderson, Lula Strain, Mary V. Hutton, William Sterrett, Rice McNutt, and James Montgomery. The children of S. W. are Margaret, wife of Thomas Morrison, of Bluefield, West Virginia; Susie, wife of Samuel Dunlap, of Lexington, Virginia; Baxter, husband of Essie Kerr, Eldred, husband of Jennie Watson, and living at Red Ash, West Virginia; Morton, married to Nina Paxton and living near Lexington, Virginia; Samuel, married to Susanna Franc and living at Lewisburg, West Virginia; Thomas, serving in the United States Navy; and Lula, wife of H. E. Moore, of Rockbridge. Sadie, daughter of Thomas E., married C. C. Boppell, and died in Africa, where she was laboring as a missionary. A. C., son of Doctor Alfred McCorkle, married Grace Montgomery, and his only grandson in Rockbridge is A. C., Jr., of Collierstown. The children of Alexander B., who became a Presbyterian minister about 1836, were Gamble, William P., and Sallie. William P. is a Presbyterian minister.

William, third son of Alexander the pioneer, had four sons and four daughters. The sons were Alexander, John, Abner, and Henry. John, who was born 1777 and died 1846, was married to Polly Montgomery in 1800, but was without issue. Three of the daughters were Phœbe, Patsy, and Nancy. The first married James Elliott in 1809. Patsy appears to have married James Taylor in 1805, and Nancy to have married Archibald Taylor in 1812. William P., a son of Henry, was graduated from Washington College in 1847. He was editor of the *Valley Star* and of the Lynchburg *Republican*.

With respect to the following marriages of MacCorkles, we are unable to tell what may be the point of contact with the descendants of Alexander.

Alexander to Sally Peters, 1822; Esther to William Porter, 1799; Jean to

James Donald, 1805; James to Polly McClain, 1821; John to Sally Cunningham, 1821; Nancy to Samuel Paxton, 1825; Polly to John Adair, 1808; Polly to William Hamilton, 1800.

In the early records of Augusta there are these three MacCorkle marriages: John to Lydia Forrest, 1790; Mary of John to John McWhorter, 1791; Robert to Elizabeth Forrest, 1785.

There are few families in the United States, and in the Old Countries, whose history can be traced back as far as the history of the MacCorkles. We find branches of this old family in Canada and all over the United States, especially in the middle and Eastern States, and in Virginia. We find other branches in England, Scotland, Ireland, Germany, and Denmark. All these families use a coat of arms that shows, although differing slightly, the same main features, i. e.,

Crest: A stag, standing at gaze, attired gules;

Arms: A demi-stag, gules, naissant out of a fesse tortille;

Motto: Vivat Rex!

The difference between the arms is so slight that there is no doubt that these families belong together. Only the Danish branch of the family uses another coat of arms, but here are the complete historical evidences that it is the same family. The name is spelled in many different ways, but etymologically it is the same name. The following shows the development and the changes of the family name. The oldest form that could be traced is Thorgisl, in the Thorgisl Saga, about 700 A. D. This name changes in Thurkell, Thurkill, Thorkill, Thorquil, (Thurgesius, in the Latin text), Torquil, Thorquil-dale, Mac Torquil-dale, Mac Korkill-dale, McCorkindale, McCorquindall, McCorkuodell, McCorquedill, McCorkell, McCorkel, MacCorkle.

All these names appear in the old manuscripts, books, and inscriptions, and we find the different names in all the countries where members of the family live. The different branches did not keep a certain spelling. They are scattered all over the civilized world, using different spellings of their name, but all tracing back to the same family. The name that is mostly used by the branches in the United States is McCorkle, MacCorkle, or McCorkell.

Anderson's *History of the Scottish Nation* says:

MacCorquodale, otherwise Mac Toruil (the son of Torquill), Mac Corkle, or Corkindale, the surname of a Highland sept, the founder of which was Torquil, a prince of Denmark, who is traditionally stated to have been in the army of Kenneth the Great, on his coming over from Ireland to the assistance of Alpin, king of the Scots, against the Picts. Previous to Kenneth's arrival, King Alpin, in a battle with the Pictish king, was killed, and his head fixed on an iron spike in the midst of the Pictish city, situated where the Carron ironworks now stand. King Kenneth offered to any one in his army who would pass the Pictish sentinels and remove the head, a grant of all the land on Loch Awe side. Torquil, the Dane, undertook the hazardous enterprise, and brought the head to the king, for which act of bravery, he was rewarded by a charter of the lands promised. This charter was for a long time preserved in the family, though the greater part of the lands had passed to other hands. Shortly before the Revolution it was lent to Sir Alexander Muir MacKenzie, for his inspection, and was lost. At least, it disappeared from that time. The name, which is, in some places of the Highlands, still called Mac Torquil, is perhaps one of the most ancient in the county of Argyle. Donald McCorjuodale of Kinna-Drochag, on Loch Awe side, who died towards the end of the eighteenth century, was the lineal descendant of Torjuil and the chief of the clan; his grandson and representative, John McCorjuodale, at one period, resided at Row, Dungartonshire. The heirs of John McCorquodale afterwards lived in Row. The last lineal descendant afterwards moved to London, where he died a few years ago.

In the great Scottish invasion of North Ireland the family moved to County Derry, where a great many of them have resided ever since.

In about 1730 William MacCorkle came to America. He landed at Philadelphia and moved down to the Valley of Virginia and Southern Ohio. He was engaged in the Indian wars in what is now western Virginia. He had a son, Alexander, who purchased from Archibald Alexander, executor of Benjamin Borden, the tract of land known as the "MacCorkle Farm" on North River. Alexander MacCorkle conveyed one half of this farm to his son John. This deed was partially proved at Finncastle and docketed. A month afterwards Alexander McNutt appeared at Court at Finncastle and completed the proof. This was just before the marriage of John MacCorkle to Rebecca McNutt.

Governor Patrick Henry appointed John MacCorkle an ensign, and the records of Rockbridge County Court show:
State of Virginia,

At a Court held for Rockbridge County the 7th day of July, 1778.

John MacCorkle, produced a commission from his Excellency the Governor, appointing him Ensign in a Company of the Militia for this County, who took the oath required by the law.

In October, 1780, he made his will providing for his wife and three children, Alexander, the oldest, and for one not yet born. Then he joined the army in Carolina under General Morgan. Hon. William A. Anderson quotes an interesting incident arising from his going into the army:

Nov. 28, 1903.

Hon. W. A. MacCorkle:
Charleston, W. Va.
My dear Sir:

It was a pleasure to me to receive your kind letter of the 17th inst., and I gladly give you all the information I have about the interesting subject to which it refers. All that I know about it was learned from my father and uncles.

My grandfather, Colonel William Anderson, died several years before I was born. When a mere youth, he volunteered in a company from Botetourt County, was in the battle of Cowpens and other engagements, under Generals Morgan and Greene, and served through that Southern campaign in 1780-1. He was a first cousin of your great grandfather,

Lieutenant John MacCorkle's wife your great grandmother, but some years his junior. Both Lieutenant MacCorkle and his brother-in-law and my father's first cousin, Lieutenant or Ensign McNutt, spent the night at my great grandfather's (their uncle's) home, as their company from Rockbridge was passing through that portion of Botetourt County on their way to join the army of the South, some time in the year 1780. My grandfather, who was his father's oldest son, was exceedingly anxious to join his cousins and go with them to the war. He was only about seventeen years of age, and, as his father was frequently called from home to meet the Indian raids, (Botetourt County being then almost upon the frontier), his parents felt that they could not safely allow this stalwart son (he was over six feet in height) to leave them; and they considered that he was too young (vigorous and enured to hardships as he was) to encounter the exposure to which the Continental troops were necessarily subjected. They earnestly opposed his request, but he was so importunate that, two days after the Rockbridge Company had continued its march across the Blue Ridge mountains, towards North Carolina, they finally yielded to his importunity, and he struck out alone, through what was then largely a wilderness, and in due time joined his relatives and afterwards the Botetourt Company under the command, I think, of Captain Bowyer, some time before the battle of Cowpens, and was in that battle, as also was the Rockbridge Company. In that battle, Lieutenant MacCorkle was wounded in the foot, was carried, with those of Morgan's troops who afterwards participated in the battle of Guilford, to that vicinity, and there died of lock jaw, and was buried at or near Guilford, whether before or after that battle, I am unable to say. My grandfather was, of course, present at his funeral.

Many years afterwards, perhaps as many as forty, a man, whom my grandfather did not at the time recognize and who I think was named Lemon, came to him and asked him to certify to the fact that he (Lemon) had served with the Botetourt Company in that fight, so that he might obtain a pension. My grandfather could not recall him, but Lemon told him he could mention certain incidents that would satisfy him that he (Lemon) was with the army of General Greene, and was at the battle of Cowpens and at Guilford. One of the incidents Lemon mentioned to him was that, at the battle of Cowpens, General Morgan commanded his troops not to fire until he gave the order, and then to aim at the knee buckles, which were conspicuous upon the knees of the British soldiers. A young man in the Botetourt Company, before General Morgan gave the order to fire, had leveled his rifle and was taking aim at the British, who were then rapidly approaching General Morgan's lines, and were then in point blank range. General Morgan cursed this young soldier, asking him "what in hell" he meant by violating his orders; and the young soldier, with tears running down his cheeks, said, "General, I'm not going to fire; I'm just taking good aim." This man Lemon told my grandfather that he (Lemon) was this young soldier. My grandfather remembered the incident distinctly, and perhaps, then recalled that the man's name was Lemon.

Mr. Lemon told my grandfather that, afterwards, at or near Guilford, he (Lemon) was present at the funeral of Lieutenant MacCorkle, and that, when the body was being let down into the grave, the coffin caught upon a root, or some other obstruction, so that the coffin could not be properly lowered into position. My grandfather remembered the occurrence distinctly; and upon these and other statements made to him by Mr. Lemon, was so convinced that he must have been at Cowpens and in the Botetourt Company that he felt justified in signing, and did sign, his certificate.

I received the history of these occurrences more than once from my father, and from my uncle, John T. Anderson, and I think also from my uncle, Joseph R. Anderson; and I have no doubt that my cousins, William Glasgow, Miss Rebecca Glasgow, Mrs. Kate

Paxton, Miss Margaret Glasgow, and Colonel Archer Anderson, or some of them, have repeatedly heard the same account from my uncles, or from my aunt, Mrs. Catherine Glasgow. Cousin Rebecca and her brothers and sisters were double kin to Lieutenant MacCorkle, and probably learned other incidents as to his history and heroic services, which were not communicated to me. He was one of the immortal band, who, under General Morgan, achieved the great victory at Cowpens—an event which contributed as much to break the force of the invasion of the Southern States as any other, except King's Mountain.

Cordially yours,
(Signed) WILLIAM A. ANDERSON.

A letter from John MacCorkle, from Charlotte, N. C., is interesting:

Charlotte, N. C., Nov. 8th day, 1780.

My dear Wife:

I have long for an opportunity to write to you, but have never yet been so fortunate as to have any way to send the letter. I have written letters and left them at different places. Perhaps you may get some of them. I am well at present, thanks be to *God* for his mercies to me, and I hope these few lines may find you and all my near and dear connections in the same state of health.

On the 7th day of November we arrived at headquarters, about ten miles below Charlotte, where Major General Smallwoods regiment was in camp; but we are to join Colonel Morgan's light infantry, and we cannot tell how soon we must march from here, we expect to do most of the fighting.

The enemy have left Charlotte. Part of them went to Camden, and crossed the Catawba River. Some think they are on their way to Charleston.

We got to Hillsborough the 4th day of October, about ten o'clock; and that day we marched six miles on our way to Gilford. I did not then have time to write you. At Guilford I had the opportunity of seeing Colonel William Campbell, who informs me that he defeated Ferguson, and out of 1,125, he killed and took 1,105 English and Tories. The loss on our side was not great—only 28 killed and wounded.

Nathaniel Dryden was killed and three of the Edmundsons.

Being at such a distance, I almost think myeslf buried to you, not having many opportunities to write. If yau can write to me, you must do so. Write in care of Captain James Gilmore's company of militia, under General Morgan. Remember me to all my friends and neighbors. You may inform my neighbors that their sons, Alexander and Robert McNutt, Trimble, Moore, and Alexander Stuart, are well.

I add no more at present, but remain

Your loving husband,
JOHN MACCORKLE.

In 1781, John MacCorkle was severely wounded at the battle of Cowpens, and died. He was buried with military honors. Colonel William Anderson referred to it as the first burial he ever witnessed with military honors. Colonel Anderson was a first cousin of Rebecca, John MacCorkle's wife. His father and Rebecca MacCorkle were brother and sister.

John MacCorkle married Rebecca McNutt in 1771. Rebecca McNutt's father, John McNutt, married Catharine Anderson in Ireland and moved to

America, settling in Rockbridge County, then Augusta County, on North River. He owned the farm afterwards owned by Thomas Edmundson near Ben Salem.

John MacCorkle was the father of three children, Alexander MacCorkle, Samuel MacCorkle, and Katherine MacCorkle, (Walker).

Alexander MacCorkle, son of John MacCorkle, was born August 7, 1773. His wife was Mildred Welch, of Fancy Hill. Mildred Welch was a daughter of Thomas Welch, who married Sarah Grigsby, who was a daughter of John Grigsby.

John Grigsby was born in 1720, and accompanied Lawrence Washington with Admiral Vernon in the expedition against Carthagenia. This was one of the events of Governor Gooch's administration, and as taken in connection with the other colonies, it was part of the ultimate union.

John Grigsby's ancestors came to this country in 1660, which seems to be the most reliable date. They lived in Stafford County, Virginia, but Grigsby, in the autumn of 1779, moved to Rockbridge County, then Augusta, and settled on Fruit Hill place, where John Grigsby died on April 7, 1794.

The children of Alexander MacCorkle and Mildred Welch MacCorkle, were:

Sally McCorkle, born January 1, 1795, died 1842.
Jno. MacCorkle, born February 14, 1797.
Sam'l MacCorkle, born August 30, 1800.
Thos. MacCorkle, born May 21, 1804.
Alex. MacCorkle, born October 15, 1806.
Martha MacCorkle, born April 4, 1809.
Jane MacCorkle, born February 22, 1812.
Mildred MacCorkle, born March 6, 1815.
William MacCorkle, born October 25, 1815, (1817?), died February 28, 1864.
Rebecca E. MacCorkle, born April 3, 1820.

Alexander MacCorkle was for more than forty years an elder in the Presbyterian Church at Lexington, Virginia. He was a captain in the War of 1812, and was one of the most respected men in the Valley of Virginia.

William MacCorkle, son of Alxeander MacCorkle, married Mary Hester Morrison, of Rockbridge County, Virginia. The issue of this marriage were three children:

William Alexander MacCorkle, born May 7, 1857; Alvin Davidson MacCorkle, born February 10, 1862, and Willie May MacCorkle, born May 7, 1864.

William MacCorkle was a major in the Confederate army in service under General Price. He was president of the North River Navigation Company, and constructed much of the canal work in the county on the North River, and he was one of the directors of the James River and Kanawha River Canal Company. In that early day he was engaged in developing the Valley of Virginia.

Mary Hester Morrison, the wife of William MacCorkle, was a daughter of William Morrison, of Kerr's Creek. Her mother, Margaret Morrison, was a daughter of William MacCorkle. Mary Hester Morrison was a woman of vast determination and great energy and sweetness of character. At the death of her husband, in the last year of the war of 1861, she was left penniless among strangers. She never ceased for one minute giving her full energies to the raising and education of her children, and devoted her life to this object. The farm given by Alexander MacCorkle to his son John, remained in the MacCorkle family until about the time of the War of 1860.

William Alexander MacCorkle, the son of William MacCorkle, married Belle Farrier Goshorn September 19, 1881. From that union there were six children: William Goshorn MacCorkle, born July 18, 1882; Eliza Daggett MacCorkle, born November 10, 1884; a daughter, (died in early infancy), born December 20, 1885; Kenneth MacCorkle, born December 20, 1886, (died in infancy); Isabelle Brooks MacCorkle, born February 20, 1890; an infant, born February 22, 1891. Of these children, William MacCorkle and Isabelle Brooks MacCorkle are alive.

William Alexander MacCorkle was Prosecuting Attorney of Charleston, West Virginia, from 1881 to 1886; Governor of West Virginia from 1892 to 1898; State Senator from 1908 to 1912. He has held many other places of trust, has published a number of books, and is and has been for many years the head of many operations for the development of West Virginia.

William Goshorn MacCorkle, son of William Alexander MacCorkle, now a lieutenant in the U. S. army, in the world war, married Margaret Lyle, of Timber Ridge, Virginia. From this union there are four children, Eliza Daggett MacCorkle, born December 16, 1906; Margaret Lyle MacCorkle, born March 28, 1908; Hester Morrison MacCorkle, born October 13, 1909; William Alexander MacCorkle, born June 12, 1913; Samuel Lyle MacCorkle, born June 23, 1914; Torquil MacCorkle, born January 31, 1916, and William MacCorkle, born January 19, 1918, who are living, and William Alexander MacCorkle, and Hester Morrison MacCorkle, who are dead.

The MacCorkle family was for a hundred years about the largest family in Rockbridge County. It is connected with a great number of prominent families in the Valley of Virginia and the Piedmont section. In the Confederate army there were more than two hundred of the name and relation of the MacCorkle family, and the MacCorkle family has furnished the largest connected family who are alumni of Washington and Lee University at Lexington, Virginia. They have produced many distinguished preachers and developers of the country, and have wrought manfully for Virginia. It is probably one of the largest connected families in the United States, and everywhere they have shown about the same characteristics of energy, determination, and patriotism.

Alexander MacCorkle and his sons acquired a fine agricultural domain a little distance southeast of Lexington. The original tract is drained by Borden's Run and skirts North River several miles. The ancestral homes of the family are five. On a hill was a brick mansion with a double porch facing the rising sun and commanding a magnificent view of the Blue Ridge. A second lay to the northward on the old road to Lexington. A third lay just below the aforesaid hill and on the road to North River. In 1838 it was the tavern of John McCorkle, and in that year was made a polling place. This John was sheriff in 1840-41. A fourth was where Oliver C. McCorkle and his sister, Mrs. Anna Harrison, now reside. The fifth comes next on the road to Lexington, and was occupied by William McCorkle and his son, William H. In each instance, the original house was of logs, and in each instance except the fourth was followed by a brick dwelling. All these were the homes of Bible-reading, church-going people, who were intelligent, fond of reading, interested in the general weal, and given to the kindest hospitality.

William H., youngest of the nine children of William and Nancy McCorkle, sprang on the maternal side from the Welch and Grigsby families. Thomas Welch, his mother's father, established at Fancy Hill a wayside inn that was sometimes a meeting point for the Lexington presbytery. The early education of William H. was gained through the primitive yet thorough methods of the old field school. Some special branches were followed still further by private study, his fund of knowledge making him a safe adviser and interesting talker. He inherited Highlands, the family homestead, and cared tenderly for his aged mother, two years a helpless cripple in consequence of a fall, and for two sisters, one of them also an invalid. He was unfit for regular field service in the civil war, but gave generously of his time, means, and labor to the cause of the Confederacy. He hauled ammunition to Huntersville in 1861, sent men to work on the fortifications around Richmond, and took part in the tours of the Home Guards. Mr. McCorkle was of quiet manner, and was reserved in demonstrations of affection. He was a man of fine judgment, strict integrity, and untiring energy. He was neighborly, and was one of the most widely known and most highly esteemed citizens of his county. In the antebellum days he was a Whig. For near thirty years he was an elder of the Ben Salem church. He and his wife held lofty ideals before their children, and spared no pains to give them an education. Mr. McCorkle died in 1892 at the age of seventy-two years.

If the history of the family were extended into the female lines of descent, the accession of conspicuous names would be interesting. Lack of space forbids more than casual mention. Virginia, the eleventh of the thirteen children of James and Sallie (McCorkle) Wilson, married William H. McCorkle, September 11, 1850. Her affability, consideration for the welfare of others, and her knowl-

Rev. E. W. McCorkle, D. D., and Son
The only members of the immediate family now resident in the county.

Natural Bridge, in Rockbridge County

edge of past events pleased both the young and the old. She was a remarkable woman, a faithful wife, and devoted mother, who lived for her home and her children, as well as her church and community. Robert, a son of her sister Julia, who married Andrew Morrison, is the present sheriff of Rockbridge. Mary, another sister, married James Poague, and one of her daughters is Mrs. Sallie Lane, wife of a missionary to Brazil.

Eliza, a sister to William H., died New Year's day, 1882, aged seventy-four. Her memory was stored with interesting facts pertaining to pioneer manners and customs. A reminiscence of her grandfather's inn was the visit by a German duke and his retinue in the fall of 1825. The foreigner was on his way to the Natural Bridge, and afterward wrote a two-volume work on his observations in America. Miss MacCorkle was a faithful member of the Ben Salem church from its organization in 1845. She was cheerful, affectionate, unselfish, reverent, and industrious.

The children of William H. McCorkle, in addition to two boys who died in infancy, were Charles E., Walter L., Emmett W., Alice W., William H., and Henry H.

Charles E. McCorkle, born August 22, 1852, entered Washington College as a student. At the time of the funeral of General Lee he was recovering from an attack of typhoid fever, but insisted on marching with the students in the procession. An attack of meningitis supervened, and a long and severe illness left him a paralytic from the hips downward. It was felt by some of his friends that his struggle for life was little better than a drawn battle. But though he could now move only in his wheel-chair or in a carriage, it was not in this young man to accept his crippled situation as a total defeat and pass the rest of his days in bitterness of spirit and useless repining. He continued to be cheerful and pleasant. He had the more time for reading and study, and this time was diligently improved. He became a very well-informed man. In public and political matters he took a keen interest, and was known as one of the staunchest Democrats in his part of the state. Mr. McCorkle wrote much for the newspapers and magazines, and in the local history and genealogy of Rockbridge he was a recognized authority. His letter in behalf of a monument to the Confederate dead of Botetourt is not only beautifully written, but is eloquent and is pervaded by an intense earnestness. Yet he was no mere bookworm. He was a practical man, and managed the paternal homestead with much success.

In 1898 S. H. Letcher resigned as State Senator to become Judge of the Thirteenth Judicial Circuit. Mr. McCorkle entered the contest and secured the Democratic nomination for the vacant place. His active canvass enabled him to carry every county in his district except Highland. His majority was 322 in his home county and 530 in the district. The opposition party refrained from putting forward a direct nominee. But the fears of some of his friends that the excitement of a session of the Legislature would prove too much for his physical condition turned out to be well founded. The journey to the capital was itself a considerable tax on his strength, and he answered only two rollcalls. After a short illness he died at Richmond, December 14, 1899, closing a life that was useful and well spent and a blessing to his community.

In 1879 Walter L. McCorkle took the degree of LL. B. from the Law School of Washington and Lee University. He at once began the practice of his profession at Maysville, Kentucky, but in 1881 he sought a wider opportunity in the city of New York. He was first associated with the firm of Miller and Peckham, and later with Elliott F. Shepard. In 1886 he opened an office for himself, his present business address being 100 Broadway. During his long residence in the American metropolis, Mr. McCorkle has been concerned in much important litigation. He soon won a reputation as a trial lawyer, but for some years has given his attention to corporation, financial, and equity matters. As an organizer and counselor his industry, shrewdness, business foresight, and genial personality have made him highly successful. He has been counsel, ever since its beginning, of the Produce Building and Loan Association. During four years he was president of the New York Southern Society. This is one of the most influential of the city's social organizations. He is also a member of the New York State Bar Association. Mr. McCorkle was married in 1888 to Miss Margaret Chesebrough. Their son, Robert C., is a graduate of Lafayette College, and during the present war has been a junior lieutenant in the United States Navy. He married Gertrude Schmidt, and has one child, Robert C., Jr.

Emmett W. McCorkle was born August 28, 1855. He was graduated from Washington and Lee University in 1873, and from Union Theological Seminary in 1878, his licensure as a Presbyterian minister taking place the same year. In 1880 he was called to Clifton Forge, then a mission field with neither church organization nor house of worship. When he left in 1902 there were more than 300 members, a church building free of debt, and a manse. There were also organizations and church buildings at Lowmoor, Longdale, Iron Gate, and Sharon. During the next eight years he was pastor at Nicholasville, Kentucky. Since 1911 he has been pastor of Bethesda Church in his native county. Doctor McCorkle is a very busy man, and his vacations are usually given to missions for his church. He has visited Europe three times, once in 1888, as a delegate to the Centenary of Foreign Missions in London, and twice as a representative to the Pan-Presbyterian Council. On the last occasion he traveled as far as Egypt and Palestine, touring the Holy Land on horseback. He has served as chairman of important foreign missionary committees in both presbytery and synod, and has been president of the Rockbridge County Sunday School Convention, bringing that organization to a high state of efficiency. He has done much evangelistic work, and has written *The Scotch-Irish in Virginia, The Spirit of Progress in the Presbyterian Symbols,* and much else in church literature. In 1899, he was married to Miss Mary L. Bryant, an accomplished teacher and one of the founders of the Clifton Forge Seminary. To them have been born one son, Emmett, W., Jr.

Alice W. McCorkle married John T. Dunlop, a Maryland soldier who settled on a farm near Buena Vista and represented this country in the General Assembly. Soon after his death, Mrs. Dunlop took charge of the Orphan's Home of the American Inland Mission at Clay City, Kentucky. Since leaving this position she has been doing very efficient work as pastor's assistant in the First Presbyterian Church of Asheville, North Carolina.

William Howard McCorkle, born May 9, 1861, studied two years in Washington College, and in 1883 settled as a farmer and stockman in Fayette county, Kentucky. At length he removed to Lexington, where he followed several years the wholesale and retail mercantile business. A political career began in 1892. He was then elecetd a member of the General Council of Lexington under the administration of Mayor Henry T. Duncan, father of General George B. Duncan of the present war. During this term he was chairman of the Ways and Means Committee. Since then he has been almost continuously in public life, serving as president of the Board of Aldermen, president of the Lexington Chamber of Commerce, and a member of the Lexington Board of Education. He was also a chairman of the County Board of Equalization. He was very instrumental in inducing the American Tobacco Company to locate its first warehouse in Lexington. This step has resulted in Lexington becoming the largest loose-leaf tobacco market in the world. Under Mayor Skain, Mr. McCorkle became superintendent of Public Works, and when Lexington adopted the commission form of government in 1912, he was at once assigned to the Department of Public Works, and this position he is still filling. He is also Vice-Mayor. His popularity and efficiency are evidenced by the fact that whenever he has stood for the office of city commissioner he has run ahead of his ticket. During his six years as Commissioner of Public Works, he has built twenty-eight miles of improved streets, two large viaducts, and completed the city's sewerage system. He has also constructed a modern sewage disposal plant at a cost of more than $200,000. The city owns and operates its own streetcleaning equipment, and is one of the first in the South to use a motor-driven sweeper. The first wife of Mr. McCorkle was Sarah McMichael. In 1902 he was married to Mrs. Jean T. Miller, of Canton, Ohio.

Henry H. McCorkle was educated at Washington and Lee University. After being admitted to the bar he went to New York, and since then has been associated in the practice of law with his brother, Walter L. His wife was Bessie Glasgow, of this county.

The MacCorkles have made a very honorable record in the American wars.

At least two of the three sons of Alexander the pioneer served under General Morgan in th campaign of 1780-81, one as a lieuetnant and one as an ensign. The American loss in the brilliant victory of the Cowpens was but eleven killed and sixty-one wounded, although the British casualties were 784. James was killed in that battle and John died of his hurt. Several of the next generation served in the war of 1812. Alexander C. volunteered for the war with Mexico and died in service at Monterey. In the war of 1861 five representatives of the families were in the Rockbridge Battery alone. These were Baxter, Tazewell, Thomas E., William Alexander, and William Adair. In the navy was Lafayette Adair, Captain George B., of the Rockbridge Cavalry, was a brother to William D., who was wounded in the lungs, yet lived to become a sheriff of Rockbridge. Lieutenant Baxter McCorkle and William Adair McCorkle were killed in battle, as was also James T., brother to George B. and William D. Several of the MacCorkles were in the war with Spain, and Henry, son of William S., of Tennessee, fell at San Juan Hill. George, a son of Captain George B., was also in that war. A number of the great grandsons of Alexander have taken part in the late World War. One of these is Major Rice McN. Youell, of General Pershing's staff, and he gave the order for American troops to cross the German frontier. Others are Edward Lane, a chaplain, Captain W. M. McClung, of Alabama, Ensign Thomas of the Navy, and Robert B. Morrison of the ambulance unit of Washington and Lee University.

In the ministry are at least ten descendants of Alexander in the male line. These are A. B., of Talladega, Alabama; Daniel, of Pueblo, Colorado; Emmett W., of Rockbridge; Frederick, of Oxford, Mississippi; S. V., of Ocala, Florida; Samuel, of Thyatira, North Carolina, another Samuel, of Indianapolis, Indiana, still another Samuel, of Detroit, Michigan, Tazewell, of Lynchburg, Virginia, and William P., of Martinsville, Virginia.

From the foregoing survey of the MacCorkles of Rockbridge, it will appear that they are distinguished for energy, intellectuality, and public spirit. As wealthy and influential planters they have stood second to no other family. They have been greatly drawn to the professions, particularly law and the ministry. But industrial and commercial pursuits have been preferred by some of the connection. The Samuel McCorkle who went to Lynchburg was a very wealthy and conspicuous citizen of that city. In their home county it is not too much to say that they have been a backbone element in all important public enterprises. Those who have left Rockbridge to carve a career elsewhere seem generally to have been very successful in that undertaking. And last, but by no means least, the MacCorkles as a family have been staunch Presbyterians, often filling official positions in the church of their preference.

It remains for us to add that the MacCorkles of Ulster display the same characteristics as their cousins in America. One of the name was a recent mayor of Londonderry, the city that endured a notable siege in 1689.

XXXVI

ROCKBRIDGE IN THE WORLD WAR

Preliminary Stage—Activities Within the County

Until the summer of 1914 the opinion was widely accepted that military invention had made warfare so terrible that never again was it likely to occur among civilized nations. The events of the August of that year came as a rude shock to the neutral world.

For a while the American people were particularly interested in the money that was flowing across the Atlantic for the purchase of military supplies. They were slow to realize that from the very first the nations of the Entente were fighting a battle that belonged to us quite as much as to them. It at length penetrated the American consciousness that Germany was an outlaw by her own deliberate choice, and that until this criminal could be brought under control, civilization itself was in peril and the world could not be a fit place to live in. Yet there was a natural reluctance to believe the German government could be so lost to truth, honor, and decency as to act the hypocrite and the villain in the negotiations relating to its persistent disregard of American rights on the high seas. For almost three years America was a spectator, hoping against hope that it would not be drawn into the whirlpool, yet growing more and more indignant at the diabolic manner in which Germany was carrying on the war.

In February, 1915, the *Lexington Gazette* quoted an Englishman as saying that "the wrestling match between paganism and Christianity has continued nineteen hundred years, and we are now at the last and final grip. The umpire is America. America faces a far greater task than creating a republic or freeing her slaves; that of imparting to all the nations a spirit of political freedom and spiritual progress." In the same month the Rockbridge people noticed that Doctor Latané explained a submarine blockade of Britain as almost certain to bring America into the war.

Even after the dastardly sinking of the Lusitania, the diplomatic correspondence with Germany was accompanied by a considerable measure of confidence on the part of the American people, that war would not result. In October, General Nichols spoke in Richmond on the subject of preparedness. He favored preparedness as a necessary means of enforcing peace. He urged an adequate navy and standing army, a reserve corps of officers and enlisted men, and a more generous action on the part of the national government in supporting the militia of the several states.

But until the United States entered the war in April, 1917, the Rockbridge newspapers gave little space to the conflict, except as to the telegraphic news on the front page. As in 1861, the people of this county were not precipitant. Yet they were quick to rise to the situation when the crisis did arrive.

Two months before the war definitely came to the United States, Doctor Latané used these words in addressing the Democratic Club of Baltimore: "We must fight. No self-respecting nation can sit still while its ships are being kept in port by a submarine blockade of a foreign power." Next month Congressman Flood spoke to the same effect in Washington. In 1915 he had said that "neither the President nor the United States are afraid of war when the honor of the country is at stake."

A meeting was held in the courthouse at Lexington, March 26th, to discuss the relations between our country and Germany. William A. Anderson called the assemblage to order. E. L. Graham was made permanent chairman, and J. W. McClung secretary. Doctor D. B. Easter spoke on the nature of the government of Germany, Colonel R. T. Kerlin on the issues of the war, Doctor F. L. Riley on the failure of diplomacy, and General E. W. Nichols on what the United States can and ought to do. The meeting was also addressed by Colonel Hunter Pendleton, M. W. Paxton, and others. Numerous flags appeared on the courthouse, and the anti-German spirit of the audience was very pronounced. The following resolutions were adopted by a unanimous vote:

Resolved: That we urge Congress and the President of the United States to put an end to the present state of armed neutrality, assumed by this country towards the European conflict, by declaring war, or that a state of war exists between this country and Germany, and we furthermore urge the prosecution of such war with the utmost vigor, and with all our national resources.

At Fairfield, April 11th, a national flag, eight by twelve feet in size, was raised on a flagstaff sixty-five feet high. A week later Congress declared war, although the military aristocrats of Germany told their deluded countrymen that the action of America could not have the slightest effect on the outcome. These arrogant taskmasters were to learn to their cost that Americans learn war with speed and prosecute it with unequalled efficiency.

The war activities of Rockbridge were in the hands of efficient men and were well organized. Particularly was this true of the filling in of the questionaires required of the men called out by the selective draft. Whenever the situation required it, the professional and busienss men of the county gave their whole time to these new duties.

Very speedily after the declaration of war a military camp was opened by Washington and Lee University. Enthusiasm ran high, nearly every student signifying his desire to take two years of training. Before the close of April drilling was carried on every day. A committee of the faculty began enlisting the talents and capacity of both faculty and students for such special services as they might be called on to perform. The first unit to begin training was a volunteer ambulance corps. In June, 1918, it was given the croix de guerre for gallantry in the removal of wounded from the battle front. Had the war continued into 1919, military training would have been still further emphasized at Washington and Lee. It was the purpose of its authorities to enroll every student who was not physically disqualified. After October 1, 1918, all the students of military age who were detailed by the War Department for instruction in the army training schools were placed under military control and discipline. Already, the Doremus gymnasium and Castle Hill had been offered as a base hospital. Of the alumni of the university, 17.7 per cent. entered the military service of their country.

At the Virginia Military Institute, as a matter of course, the military feature was even more pronounced. The attendance was record-breaking. This school sent out in all about 2,000 soldiers. Its parade ground was a scene of great activity in drill. By April 25, sixty tents had been set up in front of the barracks. Nearly 100 men were already in its training camp, and applications were coming in daily. At a meeting held in May by the Virginia Council of Defense, General Nichols counseled putting a stop to the further distillation of alcoholic liquor from foodstuffs.

May 16, 1917, was Patriotic Day, and was fittingly celebrated in Lexington. Over 1,000 men marched in the morning procession, which was followed at one o'clock by a parade of 100 automobiles. At eleven o'clock in the morning there were stirring addresses at the courthouse by President Smith and William A. Anderson. A resolution introduced by Colonel Shields declared for conservation and economy and an increase in production. The following Sunday, Henry St. George Tucker gave an address on patriotism in the Methodist Church of Lexington. At the end of the month, Miss Elizabeth McCullough, of Missouri, arrived at Lexington to assume the duties of Woman Demonstrator for Rockbridge.

The first registration day was June 5th, and was conducted by Sheriff R. L. Morrison, Colonel A. T. Shields, and Doctor C. H. Davidson. The number embraced in the first draft, as estimated by the War Department, was 1650. The actual number was 1283 whites and 236 negroes. In the same month, B. E. Vaughan, president of the First National Bank of Lexington, accepted a call to represent the Tenth Congressional District on a committee of the American Bankers' Association for Virginia. The following citizens organized themselves into a committee of solicitation for the placing of the first Liberty Loan:

Town of Lexington ....Major J. W. McClung, Chairman
Lexington District ....L. G. Sheridan, B. P. Ainsworth
Natural Bridge District ....E. T. Robinson, S. O. Campbell

Buffalo District .... Benjamin Huger, P. M. Penick
Kerr's Creek District .... Frank Moore, S. M. Dunlap
Walker's Creek District .... D. E. Strain, A. P. Wade
South River District .... Dr. F. W. McCluer, F. L. McClung, J. McD. Adair

To the first Liberty Loan the subscription of the county was $207,666, the trustees of Washington and Lee deciding to invest $20,000.

As early as July the Lexington Branch of the National League for Woman's Service, working in a room on Washington street, sent off their fourth box, containing bandages worth $100.

The first contribution from Rockbridge by the selective draft left Lexington for Camp Lee, September 9th. It was made up of Charles P. Bragg, Howard E. Giles, Clem L. Irvine, Stokes K. Reid, Henry Rooklin, Martin B. Shafer, Thomas R. Simpson, Walter W. Thomas, and Samuel M. Wood. A second group of sixty-eight men went off September 20th. A third, of sixty, went out October 9th, after being banqueted at the Hotel Lexington by the business men of the town. A delegation of thirty colored men left October 27th, accompanied to the station by a colored band and by hundreds of other persons both white and colored.

Already, there was a suggestion to perpetuate the name of the Rockbridge Artillery of the war of 1861. The plan struck a very responsive chord. Organization was effected at the courthouse, July 7, in a meeting presided over by W. A. Anderson and P. M. Penick, and addressed by General Nichols. So far as possible, the membership of the battery was to be limited to the sons of Confederate veterans. The company, 140 strong and commanded by Captain Greenlee D. Letcher, was mustered into service August 4, as a part of the First Regiment of the Virginia Artillery. It drilled at Camp McClellan, Anniston, Alabama, and in October subscribed $12,750 to the Liberty Loan. The command reached France the next July, and was to have taken a position on the firing line, November 15. The armistice was signed four days too soon for this expectation to be realized.

Earle K. Paxton, county chairman on the conservation of food, appointed as local committee, William R. Kennedy, and Misses Elizabeth McCullough, Evelyn Davis, and Elizabeth Barclay.

A large audience assembled in the auditorium of the Lexington High School to hear addresses on the war savings drive by the Honorable D. P. Halsey, of Lynchburg, and Judge M. P. Burks, of the Supreme Court of Virginia.

For the first week of 1918, the three letter carriers in Lexington reported selling Thrift Stamps to the amount of $1560.16. The purchases by the white pupils of Lexington amounted to more than $1,000. The same month the Red Cross Chapter for Lexington sent out as hospital supplies, fifty-two bedsocks, seventeen pajamas, fifty-five tray covers, eighty-nine washcloths, fifty-eight comfort pillows, fifteen knitted squares, nine fracture pillows, eighty-four handkerchiefs, 5,900 wipers, and a box of linen. 171 sweaters were also sent out the same month. In February the membership of the Red Cross for Rockbridge was 1,705, distributed as follows: Lexington, 944; Brownsburg, 143; Fairfield, forty-one; Goshen, fifty-eight; Glasgow, sixty-six; New Monmouth, ninety-three; Natural Bridge, seventy; Murat, forty-eight; Raphine, 137; Vesuvius, sixty-nine; Timber Ridge, thirty-six. About this time several lady teachers were at work in the courthouse to assist in the draft registration.

In March the subscription for Camp Community Service was $932.73, the mark being $1,000. At the end of the thrift drive for April, a large meeting was addressed by the Honorable George E. Allen, Secretary of the American Bankers' Association. Sales of $2,063.69 were reported from the three booths. The ladies attending these were Dora Witt, Helen Campbell, Marion L. Beeton, Harriet Edwards, Lucy Patton, Leslie L. Weaver, Nell Carrington, and Elizabeth McCullough. John L. Campbell was the presiding officer.

April 6 was an ideal day for the Liberty Loan parade which then took place. The chief marshal was Major M. F. Shields, of the Virginia Military Institute, and he had fifty assistants. The number of visitors in Lexington was 5,000. The drive of the Third Liberty Loan closed May 4, Rockbridge being allotted $246,200, and subscribing $326,700. In one week in April the Lexington High School sold Thrift Stamps to the amount of $475.95. The county's quota was thus distributed:

Lexington Town	$123,300	Natural Bridge District	$35,800
Buena Vista	79,300	Kerr's Creek District	4,200
Lexington District	5,600	Walker's Creek District	41,650
Buffalo District	6,050	South River District	31,300

In the summer of 1918 service flags were presented to New Providence Presbyterian Church and to Trinity Methodist Church of Lexington, the stars thereon numbering twenty-five and twenty-one, respectively. In the registration of September 9, 2302 white and 305 colored men registered. October 1, the Students' Army Training Corps began work with six tactical officers.

The ministers of Rockbridge agreed to preach sermons on the thrift drive, March 24, 1918. The county has but a small representation among the non-resistant religious organizations. Consequently the "conscientious objector" was little in evidence. Neither were slackers conspicuously numerous, in comparison with other counties. As was the case elsewhere, selfishness and money-getting were at the bottom of some of the claims for exemption from the draft; more so than a deficient sense of patriotic duty. In July, 1918, several men were reported hiding in the Blue Ridge and in the Short Hills. The following October six deserters skulking in the Blue Ridge were brought in from Irish Creek.

Another died from the gunshot wound inflicted by a constable, the officer being exonerated.

Throughout the war period it was never possible not to observe at Lexington that the United States was in the throes of a mighty struggle. The injunctions to conserve food, fuel, and clothing were well observed, although in the winter of 1917-18 wood was scarce and high at Lexington. Among the young men who first went to the training camps, there was somewhat of a feeling that they were destined for the shambles. This was due to an exaggerated idea of the mortality on the European battle line, and it wore off considerably as the contest advanced. The epidemic of influenza, which appeared in the county before the signing of the armistice, claimed a greater death toll among the people at home than among the Rockbridge soldiers who faced German bullets and gas bombs. The granting of furloughs had a salutary effect. It could not but be noticed that the young men in khaki were improving in carriage, physique, and ease of deportment.

As a center of military activity, Lexington had a number of visitors during the war period. In September, 1917, Lieutenant J. J. Champenois, of the French army, visited the Virginia Military Institute as an adviser of the United States Army. He spoke English fluently. Next May two crippled Canadian soldiers gave very realistic lectures at Washington and Lee University. The same month Lieutenant T. McP. Glasgow related his experiences in Europe to a very large audience at the High School. At the end of August Thomas A. Edison and Henry Ford were guests at Castle Hill.

The commendation of Company G, Second Battalion, at the Officers' Training Camp, Plattsburg, New York, was of especial interest. All but six of the 146 members were from the Virginia Military Institute. Out of 219 Virginians present, only eighteen were not considered good material for commissioned officers.

XXXVII

SUPPLEMENTARY ITEMS

MATERIAL RECEIVED TOO LATE FOR INSERTION IN OTHER CHAPTERS*

At the court of Orange for October 27, 1737, Benjamin Borden presented by certificate thirteen wolf-heads, supplied by John McDowell, George Robinson and Robert McCoy.

The following, all heads of families, were presented by the Orange court, May 24, 1739, for failing to give in on time their lists of tithables: Robert Morphet, George Morphet, James Greenlee, John McDuel, Ephriam McDuel, Richard Wood, William Wood.

John McDowell proved, February 28, 1740, the importation of himself, Magdalene (wife), Samuel McDowell, and John Rutter, stating he came to America in 1737, and that "this is the first time of proving his and their rights to land." The proof for Ephraim, James, and Margaret McDowell was given in by John, the parent being too infirm to travel to court.

William Sawyer, was appointed constable in Borden Tract, May 23, 1740.

Benjamin Borden made oath, 1741, he was in fear of his life from George Moffett. Moffett was bound in twenty pounds.

Gilbert Campbell and Joseph Lapsley were constables in Borden Tract, 1743.

Peter Wallice, John Collier, and George Birdwell each bound in twenty pounds to go to Williamsburg as witnesses of the killing of Andrew Hemphill by Matthew Young,—1745.

Prices (taken from chancery suits), 1741-43: handkerchiefs, 30c; muslin, per yard, $1.00; one pair knitting needles, 5c; one fine comb, 41c; sickle, $1.50; frying pan, 83c; broadaxe, $1.08; weeding hoe, $2.33; felt hat, 66c; one ounce thread, 4c; one ounce cinnamon, 25c; Kendale cotton per yard, 18c; calico per yard, 72c; brimstone per pound, 12c; 500 feet plank, $7.50; lead, 11c; two sows, seven shoats, $5.67.

In Donoho v. Borden, Charles Donoho says Benjamin Borden had an order of council to take up 100,000 acres on several conditions, one of which was that Borden should have a patent for the same when he could prove 100 settlements had been made thereon; this in lieu of paying his majesty's rights for the land. Immediately after obtaining the order, Borden set up several advertisements, and continued to do so for upward of two years. To any person who would build

---

*NOTE: This appendix is largely from material supplied by Mr. Boutwell Dunlap, of San Francisco.

a little log house, or make other small improvements, so that he might be accounted one of the 100 settlers, Borden promised to give 100 acres adjacent to such improvement, and to sell as much more land as he would buy at the rates of three pounds for each 100 acres. Such improvements were to be made by April 1, 1738. The settler was to pay for drawing and recording the deed, and was also to pay eight shillings for laying off each tract. If any person were to settle on different parts of the grant he was to have a right to 100 acres for each separate improvement. Donoho made three such settlements, but Borden entirely refused to carry out his obligations.

Magdalena McDowell gave bond March 24, 1743, as administratrix of John McDowell. The appraisement of 112 entries totals 216 pounds, four shillings, three and one-half pence, of which forty-nine pounds, sixteen shillings, ten pence is cash. There are fourteen horses, eighteen cattle, seven sheep, a still, and thirty gallons rye brandy valued at $12.50. There were two slaves and one servant. The fall crop of wheat and rye was appraised at $10, the flax at $15.

The road by Stuart's Draft was the old pioneer route for people going southwest, and at certain seasons there was an almost endless procession of wagons. A part of the travel, however, went by Goshen. It was customary for statesmen and politicians to make speeches in the towns they passed through. Many of them must have paused at Lexington. This circumstance, and also the schools, probably made Rockbridge less provincial than most counties of the antebellum South.

Of the twenty-four commissioners to report on the proposed University of Virginia, all but three met in Rockfish Gap, August 1, 1818. Thomas Jefferson, the chairman, presented a model of the state in cardboard and a long list of octogenarians to prove that Charlottesville was more centrally located than either Staunton or Lexington, and also very healthful. All the fifteen commissioners from east of the Blue Ridge voted for Charlottesville. Of the other nine, three voted for Lexington, two for Staunton, and only one for Central College, at Charlottesville. Washington Academy was the most dangerous rival, its property being worth $25,000, and the Robinson estate believed to be worth $100,000. The Cincinnati Society was at first hostile to Charlottesville.

According to a phamplet by Harman and Mayo, published in 1868, a hunting party of Cherokees was ordered out of the Little Calfpasture by the Shawnees, who claimed an exclusive right to it. The Cherokees refused, and in the battle that followed the Shawnees were defeated. But as the victors were fewer in number, they threw up fortifications still visible and were besieged several days. They then retreated in the dark, were pursued, and were driven through Goshen Pass. The fighting was renewed on a more sanguinary scale on Walker's Creek. Far above the yells of the warriors could be heard a wild shriek from the summit of Jump Mountain. An apparition with streaming hair and outstretched arms was seen falling through the air and disappearing at the foot of the precipice. The superstitious fears of the combatants were aroused. Both parties believed the Great Spirit was angry and had hid his face under a cloud. A council was called, the pipe of peace was smoked, and the tomahawk was buried. Both the Cherokees and Shawnees buried their dead in a single mound. Before the fight the Cherokees sent their females some distance to the rear, except a pretty maiden, whose interests in a young chief induced her to climb the mountain and watch the battle. She beheld her lover fall at the hands of a Shawnee, and then leaped to her death, the mountain henceforward being given the name of the Jump.

We have given the substance of the above account for what it is worth, which is very little.

The paternal grandfather of Joseph G. Baldwin was a native of Connecticut, who set up in Rockbridge the first woolen and cotton mill in the Valley of Virginia. He wrote "Flush Times of Alabama and Mississippi," dedicating it to "the old folks at home in the valley of the Shenandoah."

W. A. Caruthers was well known in Savannah, Georgia, for his congenial ways and his skill as a physician. He was an antiquarian and hoarded an old tale or tradition as a treasure. He wrote "Cavaliers of Virginia," a story of Bacon's rebellion, "The Kentuckian in New York (1834)" a humorous and sociologically valuable narrative of early days, and "Knights of the Horseshoe." (1845.)

Archibald Alexander was perhaps the most influential man of his day in moulding religious thought.

James C. Ballagh, a son of the Rev. James H. Ballagh, was born at Brownsburg, October 10, 1868. His studies were completed at the Johns Hopkins University where he specialized in history, economics, and jurisprudence, won prizes and took the degree of Doctor of Philosophy. In 1895 he was made assistant professor of history. He has travelled over the greater part of the world, and is the author of numerous works, such as "The Scotch-Irish in Virginia" (1896,) "North and South in National Expansion" (1899), and "A History of Slavery in Virginia." (1902).

John Lyle Campbell, a native of this county, died at Lexington, February 2, 1886, aged sixty-seven. He wrote "Mineral Resources of the James River Valley" (1882), "Campbell's Agriculture," and was many years professor of chemistry and geology in Washington and Lee.

Joseph Hamilton Daviess, born in Rockbridge March 4, 1774, was killed in 1811 at the battle of Tippecanoe. His wife was a sister to John Marshall, chief justice of the United States. In being chosen to prosecute Aaron Burr, he became temporarily unpopular. Hence he published "A View of the President's Conduct Concerning the Conspiracy of 1806."

John Finlay, a poet, was born in Rockbridge January 11, 1797, and died in Richmond, Indiana, at the age of sixty-nine. He was the author of "The Hoosier's Nest and Other Poems."

John Leyburn, D. D., was born in this county April 25, 1814. He was editor of *The Presbyterian,* and was twenty years a pastor at Baltimore. He wrote "The Soldier of the Cross," "Hints to Young Men on the Parable of the Prodigal Son," and "Lectures on the Journeyings of the Children of Isreal."

John G. Paxton edited an interesting collection of letters written in camp and field by his father, General E. F. Paxton. The work is prefaced by a memoir.

Givens B. Strickler was a son of Joseph and Mary (Brown) Strickler, and was born at Wilson's Springs, April 25, 1840. After serving in the Stonewall Brigade, he completed his academic and theologic studies. After being thirteen years pastor at Tinkling Springs and the same length of time in Atlanta, he took the chair of systematic theology in Union Theological Seminary, from which he was graduated. Doctor Strickler was one of the ripest scholars and profoundest thinkers in the Presbyterian Church.

The leading works of Bishop William Taylor are "Seven Years Street Preaching in San Francisco," "The Model Preacher," "Reconciliation: or How to Be Saved," "The Story of My Life," "Infancy and Manhood of Christian Life," "Christian Adventure in South Africa," "Four Years Campaign in India," "Pauline Methods of Missionary Work," and "The Flaming Sword in Darkest Africa."

George A. Wauchope, a son of Joseph W. and Jane (Armstrong) Walkup, studied in Harvard University and in Germany, made literary pilgrimages in England and Scotland, and is a ripe scholar with critical powers of analysis. He has lectured on the great English and American poets, and since 1910 has been professor of English literature in the University of Virginia. Doctor Wauchope has furnished numerous poems, essays, and short stories to the high class periodicals.

Charles McG. Hepburn, born in Rockbridge, August 19, 1858, has been professor of law in Indiana University since 1903. He organized the American Institute of Law at the city of New York, and is the author of several books relating to his profession. His father, Andrew D. Hepburn, LL. D., was born in Pennslyvania in 1830. After being pastor at New Providence he was president (1871-73) of Miami University and of Davidson College (1877-85.)

Charles Campbell, one of the historians of Virginia, was a son of John W. Campbell of this county. The son was a bookseller at Petersburg.

Alexander Campbell, born 1750, died 1808, lived on Timber Ridge. He was a trustee of Washington College, county surveyor, and owned a half interest in the Rockbridge Alum. He was the father of Harvey D. Campbell, Ph. D., professor in Washington and Lee, and grandfather of Prof. John L. Campbell.

The Rev. Adam Rankin went from this county to Kentucky, and the first book published in that state was his volume, "A Process in the Transylvania Presbytery." (1793.)

Before Rockbridge Alum was developed, people were allowed to camp there and at Cold Sulphur Spring to use the waters. Cold Sulphur burned, and the ground is now owned by the Alleghany Inn.

Two United States senators were elected November 5, 1918, from the Gay and McCormick families. John H. Gay was the pioneer of the Gays in Missouri. He was the father of William T., and grandfather of John B., the millionaire. E. J. Gay, born in 1816, was worth $12,000,000.

"Jimmy" Blair was born in Augusta in 1761, and went to the Waxhaw settlement in South Carolina. When nineteen years old he rode back as far as Fort Defiance to arouse the patriots to meet Ferguson. His father was Colbert Blair, a Quaker, who left Pennsylvania about 1750 to get away from military influence. After 1771 the family moved south, but the four sons were in the Continental army. Colonel James Blair was known in verse and story as the "Rebel Rider." He settled in Habersham county, Georgia, and married a sister to Colonel Benjamin Cleaveland.

The father of Davy Crockett kept a drover's stand on the road from Abingdon, Virginia, to Knoxville, Tennessee. Jacob Siler, a German, was moving to Rockbridge with a drove of cattle, and hired Davy, then a boy and very poor, to help drive the cattle to the new home, three miles from the Natural Bridge. Davy was treated well and paid five or six dollars. Siler coaxed the boy to stay, and he remained about five weeks, although distressed at being put in the position of disobeying his father. Then three wagons, belonging to Dunn, who knew the Crocketts, came along. The drivers promised to take Davy home if he would join them at daybreak at a tavern seven miles ahead, and also promised to protect him if he were pursued. The boy got up at three o'clock in the morning and walked in eight inches of snow to the tavern, arriving in time.

Jesse B., daughter of Senator Thomas H. Benton, was born at Cherry Grove, in 1824, and married General John C. Fremont. She wrote "Souvenirs of My Time," "The Story of the Guard," "A Year of American Travel," and "The Way and The Will."

Hugh Campbell Wallace, ambassador to France, is a scion of the Wallace family of Rockbridge.

Richard G. Dunlap, a brother to William C. Dunlap, was minister to the United States from the Republic of Texas. He was of the Calfpasture Dunlaps.

Catherine Givens, who married James E. A. Gibbs, was a daughter of Samuel Givens, born 1793, and twenty years clerk of Nicholas county, of which he was also a sheriff. Robert, the father of Samuel, was born in Bath county, 1765, and was a member of the House of Delegates. He married Margaret, a daughter of Archibald and Sarah (Clark) Elliott, and was a son of William Givens, born 1740, and his wife, Agnes Bratton. William was the youngest son of Samuel the immigrant, who settled on Middle River.

John R. S. Sterrett was born at Rockbridge Baths, March 4, 1851, which is also the place of his burial. He was a son of Robert D., and Nancy S., (Sitlington) Sterrett, and his education was completed in Germany where he took the degree of Doctor of Philosophy at the University of Munich, 1880. He was professor of Greek at Miami University, the University of Texas, Amherst College, and Cornell University. He conducted various archæological tours to Asia Minor and Greece, and was one year at the head of the American School of Classical Studies at Athens, Greece. Doctor Sterrett was a member of several learned societies and wrote much on archæological subjects.

William McC. Morrison, D. D., was born near Lexington, November 10, 1867, and was graduated from Washington and Lee and from the Presbyterian Theological Seminary, of Louisville, Kentucky. In 1896 he was ordained and went as a missionary to the Congo Free State. He there exposed the atrocities perpetrated on the natives by order of the king of the Belgians, and was very instrumental in having the Free State placed under the direct control of the Belgian government. In this cause he appeared before the British Parliament. On his return to America in 1906 he edited a paper and further exposed the atrocities. He was sued for libel but acquitted. Doctor Morrison traveled extensively in Africa, and was the first man to reduce the Baluba language to a written form. Of this tongue he published a grammar and a dictionary. His wife died in Africa in 1910.

ALEXANDER MacNUTT GLASGOW*

Squire Glasgow, as he was generally known, was born on South River, five miles east of Lexington, on October 24, 1820, at the home of his father, where he was brought up and lived all his life, as a planter, and died August 4, 1894.

His father, John Glasgow, son of Arthur Glasgow—both of whom were prominent citizens of Rockbridge—on March 9, 1815, married Martha MacNutt, daughter of Alexander and Rachel Grigsby MacNutt.

---

*The remainder of this chapter is contributed by his daughter, Elizabeth Glasgow MacCorkle.

Arthur Glasgow was born in 1750, a descendant of Earl Glasgow, of Scotland, from which country Arthur emigrated to this country.

Governor A. Gallatin MacNutt, whose two administrations as Governor of Mississippi were marked by their efficient progressiveness, was an uncle on his maternal side.

The old Glasgow home, "Tuscan Villa," has been in the family since the original grant and is one of the few in the county—if, indeed, there be any—which remains in the possession of the heirs of the original grantee.

This is a part of a tract which was granted by the Commonwealth of Virginia to his ancestor, John MacNutt, in 1768.

His grandfather, Arthur Glasgow, fought in the battle of Cowpens as a Revolutionary soldier.

His grandmother, Rachael Grigsby MacNutt, was a woman of unusual character and ability. She was left a widow at about forty years of age with thirteen children, all of whom she reared and educated. Her sons reflected credit upon her and upon their country. Her daughters married prominent men and as wives and mothers reflected the sterling character of their mother.

His great uncle, Colonel Alexander MacNutt, was a gentleman of liberal education, fine mind and sterling character.

King George II received Colonel MacNutt, who carried letters from Governor Dinwiddie, of Virginia, and for his service and gallantry in the face of the enemy, in the battle of Sandy Creek with the Indians, knighted him and presented him with a dress sword. He was later Governor of Nova Scotia.

This sword is today retained in the possession of heirs of the subject of this sketch.

When on his raid through the Valley and Lexington in 1864, General Hunter and his forces took much property—silver and other property—from the old Glasgow home, among which was this sword. Fortunately, years after the war, it was located and Mr. Glasgow was able to recover its possession.

Mr. Glasgow entered Washington College, from which he was graduated with the degrees of A. B. and B. L.

He was a gentleman of the old school, of unquestionable character, high ideals, all his life a planter, and public spirited. He was active in all public matters, a great reader, and well informed.

As one of the first judges of Rockbridge county, he served with his associates, with rare credit to his profession and his people. It is said of those first judges who composed the County Court that they were governed, in rendering their decisions by sound common sense, rather than by decided cases and technical rules of evidence.

Appeals from their decisions were rarely ever taken, and their decisions were usually affirmed if appealed from.

It was through this service that he came to be known as Squire Glasgow.

Being beyond an age for active service at the front in the Civil War, he joined the Home Guard, in which he was commissioned captain. In addition to his military service, he bent every effort in producing and supplying necessities for the forces in the field.

Among his private papers are orders from headquarters concerning the movements of the Home Guards, receipts for supplies furnished the Army of Northern Virginia, numerous reports and letters of historical interest—all evidencing his spirit of service and patriotism.

Of rare interest, among his private papers is a pardon granted him by President Andrew Johnson. The pardon is signed by President Johnson, dated July 19, 1865, and sealed with the Great Seal of the United States.

Squire Glasgow had been convicted by the local carpet-bag administration of an alleged violation of law in not giving freedom to a former slave. Upon a review of the facts, the President granted the above pardon.

After his mother's death, to whom his life was affectionately devoted, he lived many years as a bachelor, but late in life married Laura B. Mackey, of Rockbridge county, daughter of Henry Mackey, and Nancy Hamilton.

They had issue: Alexander MacNutt, Jr., John Henry, Elizabeth Vance, Lucy G., Mary Thompson, and Otelia MacNutt.

His death left the young widow and children to be reared and educated. Mrs. Glasgow possessed those talents of character and business which alone, in adversity, enabled her to rear and educate her children.

The boys were educated at Washington and Lee, the girls at Mary Baldwin Seminary in Staunton, Virginia, and the State Normal School at Farmville, Virginia.

Mr. Glasgow was a Presbyterian and an elder in that church at his death.

His life was an integral part of the history of Rockbridge, to whose people and interests he was devoted.

McCormick Homestead, Walnut Grove Farm, Rockbridge County, Virginia

XXXVIII

ROCKBRIDGE INVENTIONS

The McCormick Reaper—Gibbs and His Sewing Machine—Other Rockbridge Inventions

I. The McCormick Reaper.*

The first successful reaping machine and the prototype of all harvesting machines now in use the world over was invented and constructed by Cyrus Hall McCormick at the forge on his father's farm in Rockbridge County. The McCormick homestead, "Walnut Grove," is situated on the northern edge of the county near Steele's Tavern, and part of the farm extends over into the adjoining county of Augusta. In this remote community was invented the instrument which wrought the greatest change in agriculture that has ever taken place, and which has affected profoundly the economic life of the world. Rockbridge county has given birth to many distinguished men, but the one Rockbridge name that has gone around the world, that is known today in every civilized land, is that of Cyrus Hall McCormick, the inventor of the reaper. In every country of Europe, in Asiatic Russia, in Persia, in India, in Australia, in South Africa, and in South America, wherever the harvest is bountiful, the invention of this Rockbridge boy is used in gathering it in.

The McCormicks were of Scotch-Irish stock, and Cyrus was of the fourth generation in America. His great-grandfather came from Ulster to Pennsylvania during the second quarter of the eighteenth century, and his grandfather, who moved to the Valley of Virginia, fought for American independence at Guilford Courthouse. Cyrus's father, Robert McCormick, was a man of some education, fond of reading and of astronomy, and greatly interested in mechanical pursuits. He owned several farms, aggregating about 1,800 acres, two grist-mills, two sawmills, a distillery, and a blacksmith shop. He was a skilled worker in wood and iron, and invented among other things a hempbrake, a bellows, and a threshing machine.

Cyrus was born in 1809. He inherited his father's talents, and from his earliest youth was associated with him in his mechanical experiments. John Cash, a neighbor of the McCormick family, wrote in after years: "Cyrus was a natural mechanical genius, from a child, as I have heard; from the time I knew him he was working at mechanical things, and invented the best hillside plow ever used in this country." At the age of fifteen he began his efforts to solve

---

*This portion of the present chapter was written by Doctor John H. Latané, of Johns Hopkins University.

the problem of harvesting grain by making for himself a cradle which he could easily swing in the field. His attention was drawn to the problem of inventing a reaping machine by his father, who began his experiments on a horse reaper in 1816 when Cyrus was seven years of age.

The following description of the elder McCormick's experiments was published originally in the *Farmers' Advance,* a journal controlled by Cyrus, and was therefore probably written either by Cyrus or with his approval:

> The elder McCormick (Robert) was the inventor and patentee of several valuable machines, among which were those for threshing, hydraulic hemp-breaking, etc. In 1816 he devised a reaping machine with which he experimented in the harvest of that year, and when baffled and disappointed in his experiments, he laid it aside and did not take it up again until the summer of 1831. He then added some improvements to it, and again tested its operation in a field of grain on his farm, when he became so thoroughly convinced that the principle upon which it was constructed could never be practically successful in cutting any promiscuous crop of grain as it stands in the fields, that he at once determined to abandon all further efforts at making it a success. The radical defect in his machine was that it sought to cut the grain as it advanced upon it in a body, by a series of stationary hooks placed along the front edge of the frame work, having an equal number of perpindicular cylinders revolving over and against the edge of the hooks, with pins arranged on the periphery of the cylinders to force the stalks of grain across the edges of the hooks, and so carry the grain in that erect position to the stubble side of the machine, there to drop it in a continuous swath. These different separations of the grain at the different hooks along the front edge of the frame work, for such subsequent delivery in swath at the side of the machine, especially in a crop of tangled grain, were found to be impracticable."

In Cyrus's application of January 1, 1848, for an extension of his original patent, he refers to his father's machine and says: "By his experiment in the harvest of 1831 he became satisfied that it would not answer a valuable purpose notwithstanding it cut well in straight wheat. Very soon after my father abandoned his Machine I first conceived the idea of cutting upon the principle of mine, viz: with a vibrating blade operated by a crank and the grain supported at the edge while cutting by means of fixed pieces of wood or iron projections before it (I think these pieces were of *iron* in 1831, but if not, iron was used for them certainly in the harvest of 1832). A temporary experimental Machine was immediately constructed, and the *cutting* partially tried with success, in cutting without a reel, a little wheat left standing for the trial; whereupon, the Machine was improved, and the reel which I had in the meantime discovered—attached and soon afterwards (the same harvest) a very successful experiment was made with it in cutting oats in a field of Mr. John Steele, neighbor to my father. The Machine at the time of this experiment contained all the essential parts that were embraced in the patent of June 21, 1834. It had the *platform;* the *straight sickle* with a *vibrating action by a crank;* the *fingers,* or stationary supports to the cutting, at the edge of the blade, and projecting forward into the grain; the *reel;* and the general arrangement by which the machine was (about) *balanced* upon *two wheels,* perhaps (9/10) nine-tenths of the whole weight being thrown upon the one behind the draught, *thereby* attaching the horses in *front and at one side* without the use of a separate two-wheeled cart, for the purpose of controlling the running of the Machine; and at the same time causing the Machine (upon its two wheels) to *accommodate itself* to the *irregularities of the ground*—which construction *I claim,* (and which *Hussey adopted*)."

This statement of the connection between the labors of Robert and Cyrus is borne out by the statements of various contemporaries and by the general tradition in the community where the McCormicks lived. William T. Rush, an intelligent neighbor, wrote out his personal recollections and impressions in 1885 as follows: "I have heard repeatedly all about Robert McCormick building a reaper long before C. H. ever thought of it. The old gentleman was working on it for quite a time. I never saw one of these old machines designed by Mr. Rob't McCormick, but his son Wm. S. (a brother of Cyrus) has often showed me most of the main pieces and explained them to me so that I was quite familiar with its plan and general build and operation. In the first place, it was pushed forward by the horses harnessed behind it. It had a small platform to receive the grain, but no reel, as a reel did not seem necessary to its plan. His cutting apparatus was like this. He had a series of reaping sickles, half moon shape, fastened to be stationary on a wooden bar. These sickles were supposed to do the cutting and the grain was brought into contact with and pressed against them by a series of perpendicular cylinders with spikes on their surface. These cylinders got motion from the traveling wheel and when they revolved, the spikes on their surface, which were fourteen inches long and somewhat curved or bent, forced the standing grain against the edge of the stationary sickle hooks. I was thirteen years old in 1833.

"This machine did not work, and was by himself pronounced a failure. The old gentleman made successive attempts in vain, and William S. said he never made any models, but built full sized machines without calculation. At last Mr. Robert gave the matter up as impracticable. Cyrus then took it up, and then the old gentleman gave up doing any more with it and left it all to Cyrus. Cyrus first made a model on a small scale of the plan he designed, to see how it would work.

"One day, after Cyrus had got his machine in good working shape, and had begun to sell two or three of them, I was at the old Homestead and his father was fixing up some gears (harness) that we might go out to set it at work, for I acted as agent in selling and setting up the machines in the early days, and we were talking together about its success, when the father made this remark: 'Well, I am proud that I have a son who could accomplish what I failed to do.'

These were his words, and he really was proud of his son's success. There is no doubt that old Robert McCormick first conceived the idea of making a machine to cut grain by horse power, and that but for this, C. H. perhaps would never have thought of making a machine, and I am glad that in all that has been ever written on this subject, this much credit has been given to Mr. Robert McCormick. While this is true, it is also true that but for the ingenuity and perseverance of C. H. McCormick, there never would have been a McCormick reaper, for, as I have said, his father's machine was a total failure."

The above facts in regard to the connection between the work of Robert and of Cyrus have been stated at some length, because half a century later Leander J. McCormick, a brother of Cyrus, undertook to prove that the reaper which Cyrus patented was really invented by his father Robert, and certain members of Leander's family have continued even to the present day to make assertions to the same effect. No suggestion that Robert, and not Cyrus, was the inventor of the McCormick Reaper is to be found except in the statements solicited by Leander after the dissolution of his partnership with Cyrus and published after the death of Cyrus. Leander had developed a bitter and relentless animosity toward his brother. This is clearly shown in his *Memorial of Robert McCormick*, published in 1885, the year after Cyrus died. This so-called "memorial" is in reality an attack on the fame and character of Cyrus. It undertakes to show that there was nothing very new after all in the machine patented by Cyrus, that most of its parts were known before, and that Cyrus merely brought together in successful combination features from the inventions of others. The so-called affidavits collected by Leander from neighbors and contemporaries of Robert fifty years after the invention of the reaper may be explained by the well known fact that Robert worked on a reaper for years and did invent a machine that would cut straight grain on level ground under favorable conditions, but this machine was constructed on a principle totally different from that of Cyrus. It was not a difficult task fifty years afterwards for Leander to create a confusion in the minds of these old neighbors of Robert between his efforts and the successful effort of Cyrus, and to get them to sign statements to the effect that Robert invented the reaper patented by Cyrus. Furthermore, Robert superintended for several years the manufacture of reapers for Cyrus, and no doubt some of Leander's witnesses remembered seeing him at work on these reapers. Cyrus left the community as a young man and visited it only for short times and at rare intervals. He was more or less of a stranger in later years in his own county, while Leander frequently visited his old home and went about the county looking up his old friends and relatives. He reminded people of the years his father had devoted to efforts to invent a reaper, and convinced some of them that the father deserved the credit for whatever success the son had achieved.

Leander was unable to produce a shred of contemporary evidence to substantiate his case. If there were the slightest truth in the contention that Robert was the real inventor of the reaper, we would naturally expect to find some evidence of it in the contemporary newspaper references to the reaper, but no such evidence has been brought to light. On the contrary, the Lexington and Staunton papers contained frequent notices of the reaper and long accounts of field trials, and yet in none of these accounts do we find the slightest suggestion of a doubt in anybody's mind that the machine was the invention of Cyrus. In the various suits over the reaper the opponents of Cyrus denied the priority of his invention and attacked its originality, but no one ever claimed that he had fraudulently procured a patent for a machine invented by his father, when the mere suggestion of such a thing would have served their purpose so well.

One of the serious difficulties in the way of inventing a reaping machine was the shortness of the harvest season and the limited period of time during which experiments could be made. Defects developed in one harvest could not as a rule be remedied in time for the improvement or new device to be tested in the same harvest. According to all the testimony, however, Cyrus constructed and tested his machine in the same harvest in which his father's last machine was tried and abandoned. Cyrus had been working with his father from childhood, had aided in the construction of his machine, and had noted all its defects and witnessed its failure. The solution of the problem to which he had devoted so much time and attention probably came to him quickly, and he lost no time in putting it to the test. From his father's abandonment of his machine to the end of the oat harvest he probably had not more than a month. He did the work at his father's forge, though the cutting blade, one of the most important features of the new machine, was made according to Cyrus's design by a skilled blacksmith, John McCown, who lived on South River. In connection with the Patent Extension Case McCown made the following sworn statement December 31, 1847, in regard to his part in the construction of Cyrus's machine:

> I reside some twelve or thirteen miles from the residence of Wm. S. McCormick, son of Robt. McCormick, decd. During the harvest of Eighteen Hundred & Thirty-One, Cyrus H., son also of Robt. McCormick decd., applied to me to make him a cutting blade for a Reaping Machine, which he was then constructing to be operated by horse-power; and by his directions I did accordingly make one about four feet long with a straight serrated or sickle edge, with a hole in one end of it for the purpose of being attached—as I was told and afterwards found to be the case—to a crank, which gave it a vibratory action. The machine was accordingly put in operation that harvest as I was informed, but did not see it. The present residence of Wm. S. McCormick was then the residence of his father and family."

A small group of neighbors witnessed the first trial of the machine on the McCormick Homestead, and several of these testified later as to the success of the experiment. Among them was Dr. N. M. Hitt, who made the following sworn statement January 1, 1848:

> During the harvest of eighteen hundred and thirty-one, whilst boarding at the house of Mr. Jno. Steele, about one mile from the farm of Mr. Robt. McCormick, decd., father of Cyrus H., I had notice that a machine had been constructed by the latter to cut wheat (or other small grain) and that a trial of it could be seen on said farm on that day. I, accordingly, as well as Mr. and Mrs. Steele, went to Mr. McCormicks and did on that day witness probably one of the first experiments made of the operation of the "Virginia Reaper." This experiment was made in cutting a piece of wheat, without the "Reel." Otherwise, the principles of the Machine, though imperfect, were, I believe, the same as afterwards patented —that is, the cutting was done by a straight blade with a sickle edge, which received a vibratory motion from a crank, the grain being supported at the edge of the blade by stationary pieces or points of wood projecting before it. On one side of the Machine the gearing was attached by cog wheels which operated the crank, driven by one main wheel running upon the ground and supporting one side of the Machine—the crank being attached to the blade by a connecting piece.
>
> From the frame work that supported the wheels, a pair of shafts were extended forward to which a horse was attached that pulled it—and the side of the Machine extending into the grain was supported by a small wheel.
>
> The cutting was fully established, as I thought, by this experiment. This Machine was further improved and a reel attached to it, and as I believe, though not present, was exhibited the same season in cutting oats in a field of Mr. Jno. Steele.
>
> This Machine had (of course) a platform behind the sickle for receiving and holding the cut grain until a sufficient quantity was collected for a sheaf—more or less. The "stationary pieces" before mentioned are not by me distinctly recollected.

Such are the essential facts in regard to the invention of the McCormick reaper. Makers of rival machines claimed later that McCormick was not an original inventor, that the various features of his machine had been devised and employed by earlier inventors, and that he merely combined them in successful operation. The fact that there is a certain amount of truth in these claims does not detract from McCormick's reputation nor from the credit due him as an inventor of the first order. None of the earlier machines worked successfully, and none of McCormick's rivals ever undertook to copy them. It was his machine that they borrowed from, and his patent that they fought in the courts and on the floor of Congress. One who has made a careful study of earlier machines and compared their several parts with that of McCormick has summarized his conclusions as follows:

> In all the art prior to the McCormick machine there is not even a prototype which could have developed into his machine by any improvement short of absolutely rejecting its fundamental plan of construction and starting on one of which it gave no suggestion. It was a radical and most essential departure from all prior devices to mount the machine on the master-wheel from which the power was derived and on which the machinery was sustained, while a cutting blade and grain platform were carried between that wheel and a free grain wheel whose movement was independent of but parallel to the master-wheel; to

support a serrated cutting blade in the front edge of a platform between these two wheels and rciprocate it between stationary forward projecting fingers by means of a crank connection with the master-wheel; to combine with the blade and teeth between which it reciprocated a reel which swept over the blade, bending the grain across it and between its fingers, thence over the platform, and deposited the grain thereon, and the divider coöperating with this reel and with the reciprocating cutting knife to isolate the cut from the standing grain and guide the former to the cutting knife; and to provide a reaper with a blade having a serrated or sickle edge reciprocating between teeth in the front edge of a grain-carrying platform. No machine having these constituents preceded it, and no machine lacking them has survived. They are fundamental in the reaper of today, and have been in every successful reaper. It may be said that reciprocating blades were not, in themselves, new; front or side draft was not new; platforms were not new; reels were not new; driving wheels were not new; teeth were not new—and all this may be conceded without diminishing in the slightest degree the originality or the magnitude of the invention. All new machines are made up of elements which, individually considered, are old. Invention consists in conceiving of some new method of organizing elements so as to bring them into successful coöperation and work out a useful result which has not been accomplished by their coöperation before. None of these elements had ever been so constructed and combined as accomplish the result which they accomplished in this machine, nor had any combination of elements been before contrived which operated together in the same manner or so as to secure the same advantage.

It was a new machine in the broadest sense. As first constructed, it required many improvements and refinements in order to make it a commercial success, but its plan was such as to qualify it for such improvements and refinements and to demonstrate that it was worthy of them and that ultimate success was to be achieved by adhering to that plan and from that starting point, rather than along other paths. It went steadily on, unchanged in general character, but taking upon itself such subsequent improvements or adjuncts as the further experiments of its inventor indicated to be desirable in order to deal with the various conditions encountered in the field. Under the guidance of its author it matured into a world-conquering machine, vindicated its right to a permanent possession of the fields and the market, and has compelled those who were most eager to disparage it to pay it the significant tribute of adhering with remarkable exactitude to the plan of construction which it inaugurated.

In an article on reaping machines in Johnson's *Universal Encyclopædia*, prepared by the head of the Agricultural Department of Cornell University, the following concise statement in regard to the McCormick reaper occurs: "In 1831 the machine of Cyrus H. McCormick was invented and successfully operated. This machine for the first time was an organized instrument, containing practical devices that have been incorporated in every successful reaper made since. As built and tested in the fall of 1831 it contained the reciprocating knife moving through fixed fingers to sever the grain, the platform which received the grain, the reel to hold the grain for the knife, and to incline it upon the platform, and the divider projecting ahead of the knife to separate the grain to be cut from that left standing. The horses traveled ahead of the machine, and beside the standing grain. It was mounted upon two wheels, and the motion to move the operating parts was derived from the outer wheel."

It was nearly three years after the tests on the McCormick homestead and the Steele farm before Cyrus McCormick applied for a patent, which was granted June 21, 1834. A few months earlier Obed Hussey, of Baltimore, took out a patent for a reaping machine which embodied several of the most important features of McCormick's machine. The knife, fingers, and general arrangement of the cutting apparatus were similar. The system of granting patents at that time was very lax. The Patent Act of 1793 then in force merely provided, "That every inventor, before he can receive a patent, shall swear or affirm, that he does verily believe that he is the true inventor or discoverer of the art, machine, or improvement for which he solicits a patent." The act further provided that if upon a judicial investigation "it shall appear that the patentee was not the true inventor or discoverer, judgment shall be rendered by such court for the repeal of such patent." The act of 1836 was the first of the patent acts to require a preliminary examination of the Patent Office records for the purpose of determining whether the claims of an applicant for a patent conflicted with the claims of earlier patentees. The fact that a patent was granted to Hussey before McCormick secured his patent does not imply priority of invention on the part of Hussey. It did, however, lead to long and bitter litigation, which we shall refer to again.

As soon as McCormick learned of Hussey's machine he denounced it as an infringment of his rights in the following vigorous letter:

To the Editor of the Mechanics' Magazine:

Dear Sir.—Having seen in the April number of your Magazine a cut and description of the reaping machine said to have been invented by Obed Hussey, of Ohio, last summer, I would ask a favor of you to inform Mr. Hussey, and the public, through your columns, that the principle, namely, cutting grain by means of a toothed instrument, receiving the rotary motion from a crank, with the iron teeth projecting above the edge of the cutter, for the purpose of preventing the grain from partaking of its motion, is a part of the principle of my machine, and was invented by me, and operated on wheat and oats in July, 1831. This can be attested to the entire satisfaction of the public and Mr. Hussey, as it was witnessed by many persons. Consequently, I would warn all persons against the use of the aforesaid principle, as I regard and treat the use of it, in any way, as an infringment of my rights.

Since the first experiment was made of the performance of my machine, I have, for the mutual interests of the public and myself, been laboring to bring it to as much perfection as the principle admitted of before offering it to the public. I now expect to be able in a very short time to give such an account of its simplicity, utility, and durability as will give general, if not universal, satisfaction.

The revolving reel, as I conceive, constitutes a very important, in fact, indispensable, part of my machine, which has the effect, in all cases, whether the grain be tangled or leaning, unless below an angle of forty-five degrees to the ground, to bring it back to the cutter and deliver it on the apron when cut.

Very respectfully yours, etc.,

Cyrus H. McCormick.

Blacksmith Shop, Walnut Grove Farm

In this building Cyrus Hall McCormick built the first practically successful reaping machine in 1831.

At twenty-two Cyrus McCormick had forged the instrument which was to revolutionize the agricultural industry of the world, but the battle was yet to be fought. The revolution was to be accomplished only by a life-long struggle against prejudice, against mechanical difficulties, against adverse decisions of the patent office, and against rival manufacturers who unscrupulously embodied his ideas in their machines. But McCormick combined with his inventive genius what is very rare in his class—indomitable energy. Had he lacked this, or had he invented his reaper later in life, it is probable that he would have died poor and unknown and that some one else would have gathered the rewards of his genius. Most men encountering the difficulties and discouragements that beset him would have given up the fight, but he was a man of undaunted courage, of untiring energy, and of unswerving purpose.

Having invented what he believed to be a successful reaper, Cyrus's next task was to convince the farmers that it was a practical device and to persuade them to buy it. As a means to this end the field test was introduced. After the trial on the Steele farm the next public exhibition, the date of which is uncertain, was given near Lexington, and this time the whole countryside turned out to witness it. The machine was first taken to the farm of John Ruff, but as the wheat to be cut was on a hill-side, the machine did poor work and scattered the grain. Ruff, who is described as a plain-spoken, hot-headed man, interrupted the performance by declaring in a loud voice that he did not want his wheat cut and threshed at the same time, and "with considerable indignation, ordered the machine out of his field." Fortunately for young McCormick there were some men of greater vision present. Colonel William Taylor, who represented the district in Congress, promptly stepped forward and, according to the statement of J. W. Houghawout, many years afterwards mayor of Lexington, "offered to give Mr. McCormick all the opportunity he needed to continue his operations on his land. The machine was then taken into Colonel Taylor's field, only a little ways off, and here it worked much better, and part of the time did good work. I well remember how closely Mr. McCormick walked with the machine, watching it and doing whatever was necessary when anything went wrong. He was calm and quiet, indeed, said little, while most everyone had something to say, such as, 'Oh, it will do, perhaps,' 'It will have to work better than that,' 'It is a humbug,' 'Give me the old cradle yet, boys.' But as I said, Mr. McCormick himself had not much to say at the trial. There was no brag about him. He was a plain and unassuming young man. At the close of the trial he was complimented by the leading and influential men for what his machine had done."

This and other tests finally convinced the editor of the local newspaper that the invention was of sufficient importance to be heralded in his columns. The first newspaper mention of the McCormick reaper was the following editorial which appeared September 14, 1833, in *The Union,* a weekly paper published at Lexington:

> We have omitted until now to furnish our agricultural friends with an account of a machine for cutting grain, invented by one of our ingenious and respectable county-men, Mr. Cyrus H. McCormick, and which we witnessed operating in a field of grain during the last harvest in the neighbourhood of this place. A large crowd of citizens were present at the trial of it, and although the machine (it being the first) was not as perfectly made as the plan is susceptible of, yet we believe it gave general satisfaction. We have been furnished with some certificates from several of our intelligent farmers, which we have appended to the following description of the invention.

This editorial was followed by a detailed description of the machine, which proves conclusively that it embraced all of the basic principles of the later models. There were added to the description testimonials from Archibald Walker, James McDowell, afterwards governor of Virginia, who stated that he was so satisfied with the reaper that he had bought one, and John Weir, who said that he had seen it in operation for two seasons and that it would cut "about twelve acres per day, by being well attended."

The next year *The Union* published another editorial on the reaper in the issue of August 9, 1834:

> We have frequently heard of the grain cutting machine of Mr. Cyrus McCormick, highly spoken of, but we never had the pleasure gratification of an ocular demonstration of its utility*. We publish in today's paper two certificates from gentlemen of the highest respectability, to which we call the attention of our agricultural readers. It is presumable from the general character of the machine, that it will ere long supersede in a great measure, the use of the cradle and the sickle; for it appears to cut both faster and with less expense to the employer.

The certificates referred to were as follows:

> The undersigned having witnessed the operation of a "Horse Cradle" or machine, invented by Mr. Cyrus McCormick, a young man of Rockbridge county, for cutting grain by the application of horse power, cheerfully gave an assurance of their belief in its usefulness and value. The machine was tried, when they saw it, in the neighbourhood of Lexington, upon a field of oats, and although the field was hilly, quite rough with clods, and the grain in places thin and light, yet the cutting was rapid and extremely clear and scarcely a stalk of grain being left, and little, if any, being lost by shattering from the working of the machine. Some small quantity of grain was uncut where sudden turns of direction at sharp angles had to be made, but it was altogether inconsiderable. Upon trial made for that purpose, they ascertained that this machine, drawn by two horses, with a boy to drive and a man to collect the grain into sheaves for binding, cut, when moved at its ordinary speed, about the third of an acre in ten minutes, and cut it, as they think, much cleaner than it could have been done by hand. The forming of the sheaf, however, which has to be done by other hands, was more difficult and less perfect, than might be desired. The cutting itself is done by a steel blade having the edge of a sickle, fastened to the end of a double crank and most ingeniously contrived to work horizontally.

---

*The editorship of the paper had changed hands since the notice of September 14, 1833.

The experiment made in the presence of the undersigned, was not long enough to enable them to judge whether this machine, which can be used only where the ground is without stumps, is or is not liable from its structure, to occasional or to much disorder. They witnessed its operations for an hour or two with much satisfaction, and cannot but regard it as an invention of a most singular and ingenious kind, and one which is entitled to public favor, as promising to introduce much additional expedition and economy into one of the most expensive and critical operations of agriculture. As a *first thought* the machine is admirable, reflecting great credit on the mechanicle capacity of its youthful inventor, and when improved in detail as experience shall suggest, will, as they confidently expect, be an acquisition of value and importance to the general husbandry.

> WM. C. PRESTON, of S. C.
> J. McDOWELL, JUN.

The undersigned have seen in operation a reaping machine invented by Mr. Cyrus H. McCormick, of Rockbridge County, Virginia. It was drawn by two horses driven by a boy; cuts six feet wide, smooth and clean, and is attended by a man who with a rake delivers the grain in bunches ready for tying up. We were satisfied that the grain was cut cleaner and saved with less waste than in the ordinary way. From an estimate in cutting a piece of oats, we believe that it will cut an acre in half an hour over smooth ground. We consider it a valuable acquisition to the agricultural community, and recommend it to the patronage of the public.

> SAM'L McD. REID,
> HUGH BARCLAY,
> JOHN JORDAN,
> P. P. BURTON,
> J. ALEXANDER,
> W. H. CARRUTHERS,
> WM. TAYLOR,
> J. W. DOUGLAS, (except as to the "estimate," which he did not make.)

The signers of the first certificate given above were both men of national prominence. James McDowell was later a member of Congress and governor of Virginia, and William C. Preston was a United States Senator from South Carolina. The signers of the second certificate were the most prominent men in the community. Samuel McDowell Reid was clerk of the county court and probably the most popular and influential citizen of his day. William Taylor was a member of Congress, and John Alexander was a brother of the celebrated Dr. Archibald Alexander, of Princeton.

Cyrus secured his patent, as already stated, June 21, 1834, but there was as yet no demand for reapers, and it was five years before he began to manufacture them for sale. Meanwhile his father gave him a farm of 300 acres on South River near Midvale Station, where with two of the family servants he made his residence. His attention was soon diverted from farming to the deposits of iron ore in the neighboring mountains, and he and his father formed a partnership with John S. Black for the purpose of erecting a smelting furnace for the manufacture of pig iron. Having acquired some mineral lands, they erected a furnace four miles north of Vesuvius and named the plant "The Cotopaxi Iron Works," after the great volcano in South America. The price of pig iron was then about $50.00 a ton, and so eager was Cyrus to get the enterprise started that he helped in laying the stone to build the stack. The furnace had been in operation about four years when the company failed. The financial panic which began in the great commercial centers in 1837 was not immediately felt in this remote section, but the price of iron finally fell. The furnace had been built and the preparatory work begun while the country was in a state of prosperity and prices high. The company had scarcely begun turning out its full output of pig iron when the price fell fifty per cent. and the supply of ore from the mines on which they relied began to fail. Debts began to accumulate, and under these conditions the enterprise collapsed in 1839. Black had previously transferred his property to a relative for the benefit of his personal creditors, so that the entire indebtedness of the company fell on the McCormicks. Cyrus relinquished his farm on South River to pay his debts, and his father had a hard struggle for several years to save the old homestead, "Walnut Grove." Every cent of the indebtedness was finally paid. Later in life Cyrus said with reference to this failure: "All this I have since felt to be one of the best lessons of my business experience. If I had succeeded in the iron enterprise, I would perhaps never have had sufficient determination and perseverance in the pursuit of my reaper enterprise to have brought it to the present stage of success."

Meanwhile Cyrus was still working on the reaper and endeavoring to improve its several parts so as to be able to turn out a perfect machine. Improved castings were made under his personal supervision in the foundry at Cotopaxi. When the iron business failed father and son began the building of reapers at the old forge at "Walnut Grove," and in order to promote the sale field trials were again given, the first near Staunton, as appears from the following advertisement in the *Spectator* of July 18, 1839:

At the request of Mr. Joseph Smith and others the Subscriber will exhibit his patent reaping machine cutting oats on the Scott Farm of Mr. Smith on the Lexington Road three miles south of Staunton, on Tuesday the 23rd instant, at which time (say 10 or 11 o'clock) and place, Persons to whom it may be convenient and who may be desirous of seeing the machine operate, can have an opportunity to do so. The Subscriber in consequence of other engagements and a failure in the crop of grain has done nothing with the machine for several years, until recently, since which he has made some important improvements upon it. He has cut with it during the present harvest about 75 acres of wheat and rye and thinks its performance now unexceptional. It will cut one and a half or two acres an hour with two horses and two hands leaving the grain in sheaves ready for tying and will cut and save the grain much cleaner than the ordinary mode of cradling, whether it be tangle or straight. The machine is not complicated or liable to get out of order, but is entirely durable and will cost about $50.

C. H. McCormick.

A week later *The Spectator* published the following editorial account of the field test, which shows that the machine worked much more smoothly than at the earlier tests in the neighborhood of Lexington. General Kenton Harper, editor of the paper, was one of those who witnessed the test. He wrote:

> We have just returned from the exhibition of Mr. McCormick's Reaping Machine and to say we were pleased with its operation would but poorly express the gratification we experienced. It is certainly an admirable invention. It moves through the grain with speed at a brisk walk, cutting a swath of about six feet without leaving a head. The machine is fixed on truck wheels with a knife in front to which the grain is brought in by arms fixed on a light wheel above and thrown on an apron behind from which it is raked off by a person who walks along the side. The machine is quite simple and cheap, costing not more than $50. A large number of gentlemen (farmers and others) were present, and as far as we heard, all were delighted with its operation.

The exhibition on the Smith farm was witnessed not only by the farmers of the community, but by many of the most prominent professional and business men of Staunton. In *The Spectator* of August 1 there was published a long account of the test, which begins: "The undersigned having witnessed the operation of Mr. Cyrus H. McCormick's improved patent Reaping Machine, in cutting oats, on the farm of Mr. Joseph Smith, take pleasure in bearing testimony to its admirable and satisfactory performance, and in recommending it to the attention of all large farmers." This statement was signed by twelve of the most widely known citizens of Augusta County—Abraham Smith, George Eskridge, Joseph Bell, Joseph Smith, Wm. W. Donaghe, Silas H. Smith, Nicholas C. Kinney, Edward Valentine, Kenton Harper, James Points, Benjamin Crawford, and Solomon D. Coiner. This testimonial was published by Cyrus H. McCormick as an advertisement in the Richmond *Enquirer* of December 12, 14, and 17, 1839, and January 25 and 28, 1840.

All of Cyrus's energies were now devoted to the manufacture and sale of reapers. The following advertisement inserted by him in the Staunton *Spectator* September 23, 1841, shows that his years of patient labor had not been without results:

> The Undersigned now offers his PATENT REAPING MACHINE to the public, upon terms that cannot be unsafe to them, having now satisfied himself that after several years' labor and attention in improving and completing the machine, he has triumphantly succeeded in effecting his object with as much perfection as the principle admits of, or is now desirable; performing all that could be expected, viz: the cutting of all kinds of small grain, in almost all the various situations in which it may be found; whether level or (moderately) hilly lands; whether long or short, heavy or light, straight, tangled, or leaning, in the best possible manner, by a machine operated by horse power, with little friction or strain upon any of its parts, and without complication, and therefore not subject to get out of order, but strong and durable—that operates with great saving of labor and grain.

The same issue of *The Spectator* contains an interesting account of a field test at Bridgewater, Rockingham county, the county adjoining Augusta on the north, and the success of the experiment was testified to by a number of the leading citizens. One of the witnesses, Colonel Edward Smith, wrote an account of this test for the *Southern Planter,* the leading agricultural journal of the South, published at Richmond, and it appeared in the November issue, 1841. By 1842 the reaper had attracted the attention of farmers in all sections of the state, and numerous notices and advertisements appeared in the daily papers and agricultural journals.

Meanwhile McCormick's principal rival, Obed Hussey, began selling some of his machines in Virginia, and in the harvest of 1843 McCormick accepted a challenge from Hussey for a competitive test near Richmond. This was the first of a series of contests which became a favorite method of promoting the sale of reapers and afforded rare amusement to the farmers. Field contests between different types of machines became especially popular in the West and were carried to great extremes. In some instances machines were drawn by four horses at a gallop through weeds, briars, brush, and saplings to see which could stand the most abuse. The following notice of the first competitive field test appeared in the Richmond *Enquirer* of June 27, 1843:

Farmers, ATTEND!

From the following challenge, we may look out for some "rare fun"—not on the "battle" but on the "wheat" field. We had expected some such trial of skill between the two master spirits of reaping, Messrs. McCormick and Hussey; and for the sake of the true farmer, as well as the amateur, we are glad that the sport is likely to come off so soon. The present contest, will, in all probability, decide the merits of one or the other of these labor saving machines; and we, therefore, invite a full attendance of the "Krights of the Plow-share." Much good always follows such a struggle for superiority, conducted, as it will be, in the most friendly spirit. It will be a beautiful thing, to see these two grand and powerful machines moving at a quick pace, and in their course, mowing down oceans of wheat. Should we, unfortunately, not be able to attend, we hope some of our farmer friends will send us a sketch.

An account of the contest with the report of the committee appears in the *Enquirer,* July 4, 1843:

On Friday last, according to the challenge given and accepted, the contest came off between McCormick's and Hussey's Reaping Machines. The *Champ de Mars* was a wheat field of Mr. Ambrose Hutcheson's, near 4 miles from Richmond, under an equal sky and a burning sun. The spectators numbered from forty to fifty; and principally consisted of farmers, who took a deep interest in the events of the day. A committee of five were appointed Judges of the Lists—and after the action was over, they made up the following report, which we have been requested to publish. We are also advised, that the two machines will again be run together on the wheat fields of Tree Hill, the beautiful farm of William H. Roan, Esq., where those who feel any curiosity on this interesting subject, will have a fair opportunity of testing and comparing the operations of the rival Machines. We are requested by the Proprietor to give a general invitation to farmers and others, to attend this experiment on Wednesday, (tomorrow).

MECHANICS' MAGAZINE,

AND

REGISTER OF INVENTIONS AND IMPROVEMENTS.

VOLUME IV.]   FOR THE WEEK ENDING OCTOBER 15, 1836.   [NUMBER 4.

"It is a strange thing to behold what gross errors and extreme absurdities men do commit for want of a friend to tell them of them. The help of good counsel is that which setteth businesses straight."—BACON.

CYRUS H. M'CORMICK'S IMPROVED REAPING MACHINE.

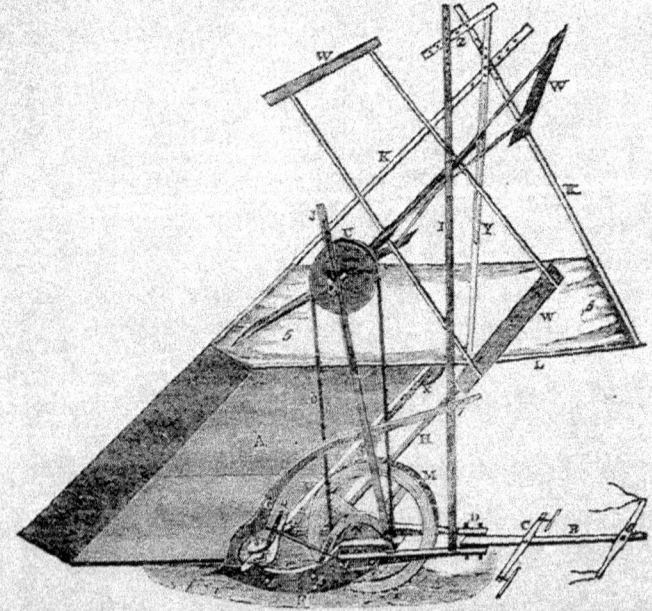

To the Editor of the Mechanics' Magazine.

DEAR SIR,—I send you a drawing and description of my Reaping Machine, agreeably to your request.

References—A, the platform; B, tongue; C, cross-bar; D, hinder end of the tongue; e e, projections in front; F, broad piece on each side; G, circular brace; H, diagonal brace; I, upright post; J, upright reel post; K, braces to upright; L, projection to regulate the width of swarth; M, main wheel roughened; N, band and cog wheel of 30 teeth; O, band; p, small bevel wheel of 9 teeth; Q, do. of 27 teeth; r, do. of 9 teeth; s, double crank; T, cutter; V, vibrating bar of wood, with bent teeth; U, reel pulley; W, reel; X, wheel of 12 inches diameter; Y, reel post.

The platform A is of plank, made fast to a frame of wood, for receiving the grain when cut, and holding it until enough has been collected for a sheaf, or more. The projections in front, e e, are two pieces of the platform frame, extending about 1½ feet in front, and one or more feet apart. On each outside of these pieces is to be secured a broad piece of wood, as at F, by screw bolts, as at I I, passing through them and the pro-

VOL. IV.—   14.

REPORT

The undersigned were called upon, at the farm of Mr. A. Hutcheson, to witness the performance of the wheat reaping machines, invented by Cyrus H. McCormick and Obed Hussey, and to decide upon the merits of the same. We are unanimously of opinion, that both of them are valuable inventions, and richly merit the encouragement of the farming community. They both performed most admirably. The committee feel great reluctance in deciding between them. But, upon the whole, prefer McCormick's.

C. W. Gooch,
W. H. Roane,
James Pae,
Curtis Carter,
Francis Staples.

From 1839 to 1844 McCormick was engaged in the manufacture and sale of machines at his father's farm. The sales were at first slow and discouraging. The record of sales during the life of the original patent, which expired in 1848, is as follows: 1841, two; 1842, seven; 1843, twenty-nine; 1844, fifty; 1845, fifty; 1846, 190; 1847, 450; making in the aggregate 778 machines, on which he received an average of $20.00 for his patent right.

In 1844 seven orders had come for "Virginia Reapers'" from the West, two from Tennessee, and one each from Missouri, Iowa, Wisconsin, Illinois, and Ohio. These machines had to be hauled in wagons over the mountains to Scottsville in Albemarle County, then sent by canal to Richmond, then down the James to Norfolk, then shipped to New Orleans, then sent up the Mississippi by river boat to various points, from which they finally reached the farmers who had ordered them. Four of them arrived too late for the harvest of 1844 and two of them were not paid for. Cyrus finally decided to go West where the land was level and labor scarce. Setting out with $300.00 in his belt he went up through Pennsylvania to Western New York, then to Michigan, Wisconsin, Illinois, Missouri, and Ohio. On this trip he gave public exhibitions in the harvest field of the machines he had sold, and on his return by way of Cincinnati he made a contract for the manufacture of 150 machines in that city for the harvest of 1845. From Cincinnati he went to Brockport, New York, where he contracted for the manufacture of 200 machines, most of which were to be shipped to the West through the Erie Canal. He also arranged for the construction of 100 machines at Chicago for the harvest of 1846, and for 100 more at points west of Chicago. This trip through the West revealed a new world to McCormick. He quickly realized that while the reaper was a luxury in Virginia, it was a necessity on the great plains of the West. After a brief visit to Virginia he returned to the West to superintend personally the construction of machines, first at Cincinnati, and then at Brockport, both of which were convenient points for the distribution of reapers. But with unerring judgment or intuition he soon concluded that Chicago was the strategic point for the creation of a great industry. So in 1848 he went to Chicago, then a village of 10,000 people, with muddy streets, stretching along the Lake front. Here he formed a partnership with William B. Ogden, the first mayor of the town, who gave $25,000 for a half interest in the business. The next year he bought out Ogden's interest for $30,000 and sent for his brother Leander to come out and supervise the machine shops. In 1850 his other brother, William, was persuaded to come out to manage the financial side of the business. He gave each of them an interest in the enterprise. McCormick's choice of Chicago was most fortunate for him, and an event of great significance in the history of the West. The reaper industry and the city grew up together.

In 1848 Cyrus McCormick applied for an extension of his original patent, which was about to expire. The patent law at that time limited the term of a patent to fourteen years, but provided that under certain circumstances the inventor might make application for an extension of the patent for seven more years. The law required that when such application was made the Commissioner of Patents should cause to be published in one or more of the newspapers of Washington and in such other paper or papers as he deemed proper, published in the section of the country interested most adversely against the issue of the patent, notice of such application and the time and place where it would be considered, and that any person might appear and show cause why the extension should not be granted. The Secretary of State, the Solicitor of the Treasury, and the Commissioner of Patents constituted the board to hear the evidence and to decide for or against the extension. The patentee was required to submit under oath a statement of all receipts and expenditures so as to show fully the profits accruing to him from his invention. The law further provided that, "if, upon a hearing of the matter, it shall appear to full and entire satisfaction of said board, having due regard to the public interest therein, that it is just and proper that the term of the patent shall be extended by reason of the patentee, without neglect or fault on his part, having failed to obtain in the use and sale of his invention a reasonable remuneration for the time, ingenuity, and expense bestowed upon the same and introduction thereof into use, it shall be the duty of the Commissioner to renew and extend the patent."

McCormick, acting in person and without the assistance of counsel, made application for an extension of his patent, and Hussey appeared to represent the opposition thereto. Hussey's patent, it will be remembered, had been issued a few months prior to McCormick's, and it expired the latter part of December, 1847. Ten or twelve days before the expiration of Hussey's patent he applied to the Commissioner of Patents for an extension, but as the rules of the Board required that notice of an application for extension should be published at least three weeks prior to the hearing, his application was not received. Hussey, therefore, decided to make a fight against the extension of McCormick's patent, arguing that McCormick had been abundantly rewarded by sales of his patent rights and by extensive sales of his machines, that the extension of the McCormick patent would injure him, and that certain elements of the invention were to be found in earlier foreign publications. As McCormick claimed that several features of the Hussey machine had been invented and employed by him two years before the issuance of Hussey's patent, the Commissioner granted McCormick's request for a continuation of the hearing until he could take testimony in substantiation of his claims. McCormick secured affidavits from Dr. N. M. Hitt, John Steele, Jr., and from his mother and two brothers to the effect that his machine was invented and used in cutting wheat and oats in the harvest of 1831. The statement of his mother and brothers was as follows:

Walnut Grove, Feby. 17, 1848.

The undersigned, mother and brothers of Cyrus H. McCormick, do hereby state, each for himself, (and herself) that during the harvest of Eighteen Hundred and thirty-one said C. H. McCormick did have constructed and put into operation in cutting wheat on this farm, and oats on the farm of Mr. Jno. Steele, (a near neighbor), a Reaping Machine for which a patent was granted to him on the 21st day of June, 1834. When used in cutting the oats at Mr. Steele's as aforesaid this machine we believe was essentially the same in principle as when patented, as above. * * * The undersigned do further state that said C. H. McCormick did make great efforts from time to time to introduce said machine into general use, but found many difficulties to contend with, which caused much delay in accomplishing the same. And they further state that they have no interest in the patent of said Reaping Machine.

WM. S. McCORMICK,
L. J. McCORMICK,
MARY McCORMICK.

These affidavits were submitted to the Board at its hearing February 24, 1848. As this testimony was *ex parte*, the Board ordered, "That the further hearing of this application be postponed to Wednesday, the twenty-ninth day of March next, and that the said McCormick be directed to furnish satisfactory testimony that the invention of his machine was prior to the invention of a similar machine by Obed Hussey, and that he be directed to give due notice to the said Hussey of the time and place of taking said testimony."

McCormick then gave due notice to Hussey, and the latter appeared at Steele's Tavern, where the signers of the affidavits above referred to were cross-qustioned for two days by McCormick and Hussey, March 17 and 18, 1848. When the Board met again March 29th, they refused to grant the extension, and the following entry was made on the record:

March 29, 1848—Board met agreeable to adjournment. Present: James Buchanan, Secretary of State; Edmund Burke, Commissioner of Patents; and R. H. Gillet, Solicitor of the Treasury, and having examined the evidence adduced in the case, decided that said patent ought not to be extended.

> JAMES BUCHANAN, Secretary of State.
> EDMUND BURKE, Commissioner of Patents.
> R. H. GILLET, Solicitor of the Treasury.

Edmund Burke, the Commissioner of Patents, stated later to a committee of the Senate that the decision of the Board was not based on the merits of the case, but on the fact that the testimony had been "informally taken." The only redress open to McCormick was an appeal to Congress for an extension of his patent, and this he promptly made. Such appeals were frequently made at that time. But opposition to the extension of McCormick's patent was not confined to Hussey. Rival manufacturers of reapers and their paid attorneys urged the farmers of the country to oppose the extension of McCormick's patent, and Congress was flooded with petitions from farmers, protests of manufacturers, and even resolutions from State legislatures. McCormick's fight for the protection of his patent rights was continued in Congress and in the United States courts for fifteen years. It became, in fact, a *cause célèbre,* and many of the ablest lawyers of that period were engaged on one side or the other. Among them were Harding, Watson, Dickerson, Reverdy Johnson, Douglas, Seward, Staunton, and Lincoln. Toward the end of the fight in Congress the anti-McCormick lobby became so active that Senator Brown, of Mississippi, made the following protest on the floor of the Senate:

> Why, Mr. President, if it were not for the parties out of doors—parties without inventive genius—parties without the genius to invent a mouse trap or a fly killer, who are pirating on this great invention of McCormick's—speaking through their attorneys to the Senate, there would never have been an hour's delay in granting all that McCormick asks in the bill. I know, and state here, in the face of the American Senate and the world, that these men have beset me at every corner of the streets with their papers and their affidavits—men who have no claim to the ear of the country—men who have rendered it no service, but who have invested their paltry dollars in the production of a manufacture which sprang from the mind of another man, and now, for their own gain, employ lawyers to draw cunning affidavits, to devise cunning schemes, and put on foot all sorts of machinery to defeat this application.

The wide-spread and persistent opposition to the extension of McCormick's patent is the most convincing evidence of the recognized value of the invention and of the fact that experience demonstrated it to be essential to the successful reaper.

Committees appointed by the Senate and the House, respectively, after examining the matter, reported in favor of a special act authorizing the extension. The report of the Committee on Patents of the Senate, March 30, 1852, which was afterwards adopted by the corresponding committee of the House, February 23, 1855, stated that Hussey having appeared before the Patent Board to oppose

McCormick's application for extension, an order had been made that McCormick should go into proof of priority of invention as between him and Obed Hussey." The report further stated:

> That such order of the board was based upon the fact that the patent of the said Hussey bore date previous to the date of the petitioner's first patent, and thus, prima facie, said Hussey appeared to be the first inventor.
>
> That testimony was thereupon taken, in compliance with the order of the board; and by the proof submitted on the part of said McCormick, it appeared conclusively that he invented his machine, and first practically and publicly tested its operation, in the harvest of 1831. That no proof on the part of the said Hussey appears to have geen submitted to the said board, as to the date of his said invention; but from the exhibits referred to your committee, it appears that his machine was first constructed and operated in 1833.

The report of the Senate committee also contained the following statement from Edmund Burke, Commissioner of Patents at the time that McCormick made his application for an extension:

> I will now give my views with regard to the merits of the invention itself. I do not hesitate to say that it is one of very great merit. In agriculture, it is in my view as important, as a labor-saving device, as the spinning-jenny and power-loom in manufacture. It is one of those great and valuable inventions which commence a new era in the progress of improvement, and whose beneficial influence is felt in all coming time; and, I do not hesitate to say, that the man whose genius produces a machine of so much value, should make a large fortune out of it. It is not possible for him to obtain during the whole existence of the term of his patent, a tenth part of the value of the labor saved to the community by it in a single year. Therefore I was in favor of its extension.
>
> There were, however, other reasons which induced me to favor its extension. One was the fact that the machine was one which could be used only a few weeks in each year. Therefore, for want of an opportunity to test it, its perfections must be a work of time and tediousness. It is not like the steam-engine and other machines in common use, upon which improvements may be at any time tested. Therefore, the invention and perfection of a reaping machine must be a work of slow progress. And such was the case with McCormick's machine. He was many years experimenting upon it before he succeeded in making a machine that would operate, as the testimony before the board (although informal) clearly proved. In the next place it is a machine which was difficult to introduce into public use. It was imperfect in its operation at first. It had to encounter the prejudice and the doubts and fears of agriculturists. And it appeared in proof, that Mr. McCormick was not able to sell but very few machines, until two or three years before the expiration of his first patent, which covered the leading original principles of his invention. Under that patent he never received anything like an adequate compensation for the really great invention which he had produced. And I now repeat what I have always said, that his patent should be extended. With regard to the conflicts of rights and interest between him and Mr. Hussey, it is proper for me to remark, that when both of these patents were granted, the Patent Office made no examination upon the points of originality and priority of invention, but granted all patents applied for, as a matter of course. Therefore, it is no certain evidence that, because an alleged inventor procured a patent before his rival, he was the first and original inventor. It, in fact, was a circumstance of very little weight in its bearing upon the question of priority between the parties. Besides, the testimony of

Mr. McCormick presented to the board of extension clearly proved that he invented and put in operation his machine in 1831, two years before the date of Hussey's patent.

The Senate committee went fully into the question of the amount of profits derived from the patent and found that the whole amount was less than twenty-three thousand dollars. The report concluded with the following sentence: "It would seem that, having done something for himself, while doing much for the country, his claims to the extension of the first patent, under which he failed to realize adequate remnueration, in accordance with the provisions of the law, should not be less than if he had done nothing for either."

Not only was McCormick denied an extension of his original patent, but he was unable to secure an extension of his subsidiary patents of 1845 and 1847 for improvements on the machine. An extensive organization was formed throughout the country to resist the extension and to bring to bear pressure upon Congress for that purpose by petitions, by letters to their representatives, and by resolutions of State legislatures. Circular letters were issued representing that the effect of such extension of the monopoly would be to compel all manufacturers and farmers to pay tribute to McCormick. The applications were denied, it would appear, on grounds of alleged public policy, in reality as the result of political pressure. The Commissioners of Patents could not refrain, however, from paying their tribute to McCormick. Although denying the application for an extension of the patent of 1845, Joseph Holt said (1859) of the applicant: "He has been so fortunate as to link his name indisolubly with a machine which, unless outstripped in the race of progress, may endure as a proud memorial, so long as the ripening grain shall wave over the boundless plains of the West, or the songs of the reaper shall be heard in its harvest fields." In denying the application for the extension of the patent of 1847, D. P. Holloway, Commissioner of Patents, paid the following tribute to McCormick (October 20, 1861): "Cyrus Hall McCormick is an inventor, whose fame, while he is yet living, has spread throughout the world. His genius has done honor to his own country, and has been the admiration of foreign nations, and he will live in the grateful recollection of mankind as long as the reaping machine is employed in gathering the harvest."

In the suit of *McCormick* v. *Seymour,* in the United States Circuit Court for the Northern District of New York, involving the question of validity and infringment of the McCormick patent of 1845, the defendants, in order to disparage McCormick's invention, introduced a large amount of evidence, including the Hussey patent and the testimony of Hussey, other devices before experimented with in this country, and evidence concerning a machine allgeed to have been invented by Patrick Bell, described in Loudon's *Encyclopædia,* published in London in 1831, and there represented to have been built and experimented with in 1828 and 1829. The charge to the jury in this case was delivered by Justice Nelson, of the United States Supreme Court. After speaking of the early Bell machine as an experiment which had not been successful, Justice Nelson said (3 Blatch. 216):

> In point of fact, therefore, it would seem, for aught that appears from the testimony in this case, that notwithstanding there have been seven attempts, and six of those American, to construct a successful reaping machine, but two out of the seven have ultimately become beneficial and useful instruments for the purposes for which they were constructed—that is, the machine of Hussey and the machine of McCormick. It appears, from the evidence in the case, that Hussey and McCormick turned their attention to the construction of a reaping machine very nearly at the same period—McCormick two or three years the earlier. They have persevered from that time down to the present, and they have each of them, it is conceded, brought out a successful reaping machine. All the others failed, failed early, gave up the pursuit, and abandoned their machines.

In this case there was a verdict of the jury for the complainant awarding $7,750.00 as damages, and judgment was entered in favor of complainant for over $10,000.00. The case was carried to the Supreme Court of the United States as *Seymour* v. *McCormick*, (19 How. 96). That court affirmed the judgment below except with respect to the taxation of costs, and gave McCormick the full amount of damages awarded.

In the subsequent suit of *McCormick* v. *Manny* and others for the infringement of the patents of 1845 and 1847, Justice McClean, of the United States Supreme Court, after finding that no infringment was shown, concluded his opinion as follows (6 McClean 557):

> Having arrived at the result, that there is no infringment of the plaintiff's patent by the defendant, as charged in the bill, it is announced with greater satisfaction, as it in no respect impairs the right of the plaintiff. He is left in full possession of his invention, which has so justly secured to him, at home and in foreign countries, a renown honorable to him and to his country—a renown which can never fade from the memory, so long as the harvest home shall be gathered."

Although as the result of widespread opposition stirred up by rival manufacturers, neither the Patent Office nor Congress would grant McCormick an extension of either his original or subsidiary patents, he succeeded, nevertheless, by sheer force of ability, in keeping ahead of all competitors. He did this by continually improving his reaper through the adoption of new devices and by the creation of business methods which carried his machine into every section of his own country and into all the great harvest fields of the world. He sold his machines on credit, and he made it a rule never to sue a farmer for the price of a reaper.

It was shortly after the expiration of his first patent that his triumphs in the way of formal recognition of the value of his invention began. In 1851 he was awarded the silver medal of the Michigan State Agricultural Society, the gold medal of the Mechanics' Institute of Chicago, the first premium of the Franklin Institute of Philadelphia, and the first premium of the State Agricultural Society of Wisconsin; in 1852 he was awarded the first premium of the Pennsylvania State Agricultural Society and the gold medal of the New York State Agricultural Society. But his greatest triumph was the Council Medal of the World's Fair at London, 1851, the first great international exposition. Here the reaper created a veritable sensation. The London *Times* of September 27, 1851, said:

"It will be remembered that the American department was at first regarded as the poorest and least interesting of all foreign countries. Of late it has justly assumed a position of the first importance, as having brought to the aid of our distressed agriculturists a machine, which, if it realizes the anticipations of competent judges, will amply remunerate England for all her outlay connected with the great exhibition. The reaping machine from the United States is the most valuable contribution from abroad to the stock of our previous knowledge that we have yet discovered, and several facts in connection with it are not a little remarkable." Mr. Pusey, a member of Parliament, and one of the committee of award, said in a letter to the Journal of the Royal Agricultural Society: "It's novelty of action reminded one of seeing the first engine run on the Liverpool and Manchester Railway in 1830. * * * It is certainly strange that we should not have had it over before, nor indeed, should we have it now, but for the great Exhibition, to whose royal originator the English farmer is clearly indebted for the introduction of the most important addition to farming machinery that has been invented since the threshing machine first took the place of the flail."

Referring to the sensation created by McCormick's reaper at the London Exhibition, William H. Seward, in an argument before the Circuit Court of the United States in 1854, said: "The reaper of 1834, as improved in '45, achieved for its inventor a triumph which all then felt and acknowledged was not more a personal one than it was a National one. It was justly so regarded. No General or Consul drawn in a chariot through the streets of Rome by order of the Senate, ever conferred upon mankind benefits so great as he who thus vindicated the genius of our country at the World's Exhibition of Art in the Metropolis of the British Empire."

This was merely the first of a series of European triumphs achieved by McCormick. A few years later he received the cross of the Legion of Honor at the hands of the Emperor Louis Napoleon, and a similar decoration from the Emperor of Austria. He was elected corresponding member of the French Academy of Sciences "as having done more for the cause of agriculture than any other living man."

Reverdy Johnson said in 1859 in an argument before the Commissioner of

ROCKBRIDGE COUNTY COURT HOUSE

JAMES E. A. GIBBS
Inventor of the Wilcox and Gibbs Sewing Machine

Patents: "He (McCormick) has contributed an annual income to the whole country of fifty millions of dollars at least, which must increase through all time."

Some idea as to the tremendous significance of the reaper as an economic factor in the life of the nation may be formed from the following expressions. Edwin M. Stanton said: "The reaper is to the North what slavery is to the South. By taking the place of regiments of young men in the Western harvest fields, it releases them to do battle for the Union at the front, and at the same time keeps up the supply of bread for the nation and the nation's armies. Thus, without McCormick's invention I fear the North could not win, and the Union would be dismembered." In the same address Stanton, pointing to a map to prove his statement, said that "McCormick's invention in Virginia, thirty years before, had carried permanent civilization westward more than fifty miles a year." Seward once made substantially the same statement as to the effect of the reaper in carrying the frontier westward at a rapid rate.

The reaper has made life easier for the toiling millions and enabled the production of food to keep pace with the vast increase of population. The name of Cyrus Hall McCormick is one that Rockbridge County may well hold in proud remembrance.

JAMES E. A. GIBBS AND HIS SEWING MACHINE

In the latter half of the eighteenth century the more civilized nations were slowly yet surely feeling their way toward an abandonment of the well-nigh exclusive absence of labor-saving machinery which had been true of the world's history since time immemorial. The movement has been marked by a constant gain in momentum, and by the middle of the nineteenth century the ultimate dominance of machinery was an assured fact. This tendency of the age had first to obtain a mastery over the stubborn conservatism which even yet influences the greater portion of mankind. Thus the first practical sewing-machine, the device of a French tailor, excited the rage of a furious Parisian crowd in 1841. The little factory was wrecked and the inventor was nearly murdered.

Yet the French machine aroused very little attention in Europe. It was in America that mechanical sewing was perfected. About 1834, Walter Hunt, of the state of New York, elaborated a machine with a vibrating arm, a curved, eye-pointed needle, an oscillating shuttle, and a lockstitch action. But no patent was sought, and no serious attempt was made to exploit the invention. An Englishman saw his opportunity and patented the needle in 1841. The first patent for a lock-stitch machine was taken out by Elias Howe, of Massachusetts, in 1846, and yet the essential features in his device were present in Hunt's. Allen B. Wilson came forward in 1850 with a rotary hook and bobbin combination and a feed for making the cloth move after each stitch. Next year William O.

Grover, a Boston tailor, patented his double chain-stitch action, and a differing machine was patented by Isaac M. Singer. These four machines, the Howe, the Wheeler and Wilson, the Grover and Baker, and the Singer, were holding the field when James E. A. Gibbs appeared with his chain-stitch invention in 1856. All four were crude and noisy as compared with the artistic machines of the twentieth century. At first the apparatus was designed to lie on a table or other support, and to be turned by the right hand. The foot-working attachment came later.

Richard Gibbs, born in Connecticutt in 1788, became fatherless when only four years old, and was sent to Vermont to be reared by a Mr. Allen, a great uncle. The boy was a descendant in the male line of John Gibbs, an early settler of the Nutmeg State. On the maternal side he sprang from John Burr, John Talcot, one of the founders of Hartford, and Joseph Hawley, an ancestor of the late United States Senator of the same name. About 1815 Richard Gibbs came to Fairfax county in a wagon, bringing the first carding machinery yet seen in the Old Dominion. A carding mill on Bull Run proved unsuccessful because of the unfavorable influence of the slavery system. In quest of a more favorable location, he came to Rockbridge, and thus secured somewhat of the advantage which would have been his had he gone Westward rather than Southward. In this county he spent the rest of his days, his death taking place in 1858 at the age of seventy. In 1819 he was married to Isabella G. Poague, of the Raphine neighborhood. His health permanently failed, but he followed the carding business until his mill was destroyed by fire in 1845.

James Edward Allen Gibbs, son of Richard and Isabella, was born near Raphine, August 1, 1829. Until he was sixteen he carded in the summer season and went to school in the winter. After the burning of his father's mill he left home with no more than his mother's blessing and the clothes he wore. For a while he continued to work at the carding trade. For a year or so he operated a carding mill at Lexington, leasing it from the owner, but the experience threw him into debt. About 1850 he went to Huntersville, then the county seat of Pocahontas, where he was taken into the carding business as a partner, but the mill was not financially successful and he sold out his interest. He perceived that carding was being absorbed by the large woolen factories that were springing up. It was in this village that Gibbs originated his first invention, which was an improvement in carding machinery. He was without the means to follow up his discovery, and the machine was not patented.

The next fifteen years in the career of the young man mark a period of vicissitude. He joined a surveying party in the woods of Randolph and cut his right knee. His comrades bandaged the wound as well as they could, left him on a flat rock with food, water, rifle, and ammunition, and went fifteen miles for help and a stretcher. He was in some danger from the wolves, panthers, and bears that haunted the unbroken wilderness, but there was no other harm than the delay in a proper treatment of his hurt. Gibbs was taken to the house of Alexander Logan at Mingo Flat, where he lay six months, crippled with a white swelling. He had nothing with which to pay his kind entertainers, and nothing was exacted from him. But when his circumstances had become easy, he remembered William Logan, the young man who was his principal nurse, and set him up in business at Midway.

After his recovery, Gibbs went to Nicholas county, and in the winter of 1851-52 built a saw and gristmill for Colonel Samuel Given. It was in this household that he found a wife. He was married to Catharine Given, August 25, 1852. The father-in-law offered 500 acres of land and the other essential help for a start in farming. Preferring to see what was going on in the world, Gibbs went back to Pocahontas, where he worked three years as a carpenter. The new trade was one he had never learned in any formal manner, yet he worked on a new courthouse at Huntersville, and was the architect of several buildings considered fine at that time.

It was during this episode at the carpenter's bench that the attention of Gibbs was first drawn to the sewing machine. As yet he had never seen a sewing machine of any description, and his only knowledge was derived from a woodcut of a Grover and Baker machine. He studied the picture very much as the men of his day used to study the rebuses which were a feature of the newspapers. Yet Gibbs had the inventive insight to devise a successful revolving looper. This feat appeased his curiosity for the time and he thought little more about the matter. But several months later he saw a Singer machine and read the Patent Office description of the Grover and Baker machine. He perceived that his idea was new and patentable, but before securing his right, he took out two patents on other features. Gibbs was still too poor to indulge personally in the luxury of paying fees to the Patent Office, and to get himself "grub-staked," he sold a half interest to John H. Ruckman.

The year 1857 was eventful. He visited Philadelphia to sell one of his early inventions, and there met James Wilcox, finding in him not only a business partner, but a lifetime friend. It was arranged that Gibbs should go to the shop of Wilcox and construct a model of his machine. In October, the two men entered into an agreement. The early patents were lost, but in June Gibbs had been granted a patent on the revolving looper which is the distinguishing feature of the Wilcox and Gibbs machine. Yet when the trial machine was nearly ready, the Patent Office announced what is known in patent law as an interference. A Boston man instituted a lawsuit, and the priority of the Gibbs invention was so bitterly contested that it was not decided in his favor for thirty-three years. The Wilcox and Gibbs machine was placed on the market in November, 1859, the factory being located at Providence, Rhode Island. Wilcox put $25,000 into the business, but this did not prove enough. T. S. Arthur, then a noted publisher of Philadelphia, came to the rescue with a loan which enabled the enterprise to be pulled forward into comparatively smooth water.

There had hitherto been many attempts to perfect a machine using a single thread, but none had proved successful. Contrary to the belief of the sewing machine experts of that day, Gibbs was able to demonstrate that a single thread would make the stronger and more durable stitch. But the four companies already in the field were fighting one another in a short-sighted manner. Each company controlled at least one feature that was needed by all the others. Rufus Choate, a famous attorney, induced the several companies to live and let live. Each company was to use the patents of the others, so far as necessary, paying a royalty on them, and reserving the control of its own patent or patents. The invention of Gibbs was original, but as some of the features of the older machines had to be used in the new one, it was necessary to enter the combine. Several of the good points of the improved Wilcox and Gibbs machines are due to Charles Wilcox, the son of James. Silent work, one of the newer features, was a mania with the younger man.

Gibbs spent two years at Philadelphia and Providence, giving his time to the successful launching of the new enterprise. Immediately after the news of the firing on Fort Sumter, in April, 1861, he left Providence to live on the farm he had purchased in Pocahontas. Matters political had a keen interest for Gibbs. He was a Democrat, and in the state campaign of 1855 he had made speeches in Pocahontas in favor of Henry A. Wise as a candidate for governor. For the Lewisburg *Chronicle* he wrote a parody in ridicule of the American, or Know Nothing, party. In the present crisis his sympathies were with the extreme Southern program. He went on the stump in advocacy of secession, and went to Richmond to get arms and uniforms for the first company of cavalry. These uniforms were sewed on two of his machines. Old guns and pistols were repaired in his shop. He went out with the Pocahontas cavalry, but his constitution was never strong, and in three weeks he was sent home, ill with typhoid-pneumonia. The advance of a Federal army caused Gibbs to return as a refugee to his native county and neighborhood. He bought the farm near Raphine which became the nucleus of an extensive possession. In Rockbridge he was assigned to the ordnance service to superintend the making of saltpeter. When General Hunter approached, he was ordered out with his twenty men, and they fought in the battle of Piedmont.

The return of peace found Gibbs in such financial straits that he was very desirous of knowing about his interest in the sewing machine business. His wife thought it unsafe for him to go North, yet he set out in June, 1865, after borrowing a broadcloth suit from a brother-in-law. After leaving Virginia he was shadowed all the way to the door of the sewing machine office by a detective who thought he was Gibbs of Louisiana, a man whose name was associated with mortar guns. But when Gibbs entered the office of Wilcox, the detective recognized that he had been trailing a man who was not known to have been particularly harmful to the Federal cause. Wilcox received his partner with open arms, and politics stood "adjourned." The conversation scarcely ranged outside the sewing machine industry. The books of the company showed a credit to Gibbs of $10,000. The inventor was now, at the age of thirty-six, and for the first time in his life, a dweller on Easy Street.

In 1866 the partnership between Wilcox and Gibbs gave place to a stock company. Of this, Mr. Gibbs was secretary and treasurer, and for some years it was necessary to spend a large share of his time in the North. But in the years immediately following the war he traveled extensively in the South, demonstrating his machine and establishing local agencies. In 1869 and again in 1870, he was called to the British Isles to defend his company in suits for infringment of patent. He continued to work for the company until 1886, a considerable share of his time being given to developing improvements in the machine. In all he took out twelve patents. The company is still in business, and more than one million of the Wilcox and Gibbs machines have been sold. The earlier patents have expired, but there is an income from the stock owned by the heirs.

By 1874 Mr. Gibbs was in independent circumstances. After having seen much of the United States and considerable of Europe, he became settled in the opinion that no locality suited him so well as the one where he was born and had spent his boyhood. In 1866 he spent $6,000 in improving his estate, which he called Raphine. This word is derived from the Greek word raphis, which means a needle. He had seen it used in "My Raphine," the title of a sewing machine advertisement story. During the latter half of his life, Mr. Gibbs lived very contentedly in the comfortable brown country house on the border of the town of Raphine which is still occupied by his widow. When the Valley Railroad came along, he donated to it a right of way through his lands, the distance being one mile and a fourth. The only condition he imposed was that he should name the station and determine its site.

The only schooldays known to James E. A. Gibbs were those of the old field school, and they came to a close when he was only sixteen years of age. But there remained the impulse to intellectual improvement. He was not one of those who are content if they never outgrow the world of their boyhood. So he read and observed, and pondered on what he read and observed. He ended his second visit to Europe by making a considerable tour of the Continent. After he came to enjoy a comfortable income, he gradually provided himself a good library, and was recognized as a cultured, well-informed gentleman, interested in lines of study quite outside the field of invention that gave him his wealth. His versatility was in thorough accord with his Connecticut ancestry. He could survey a new road or build a house of complex design. He could superintend a mill and unriddle many a mechanical problem. In 1861 he took out a Confederate patent on a breech-loading firearm. His last invention was a bicycle which he did not patent. Yet Mr. Gibbs was a man of very rural tastes, and he was at home in the management of his farm. His memory was very strong, and his power of concentrating his mind on a mechanical or other question was very unusual. In his opinions he was very positive, yet he was affable and tolerant. With the young he was popular, and he was an upholder of innocent amusements. He was a member of the Presbyterian communion, and was prominent in Sunday school work. Only once was Mr. Gibbs a candidate for an elective office. In 1879 he was a nominee of the Funder wing of the Democratic party for a seat in the House of Delegates. But the Readjuster wing was in the lead in this county, and he was defeated by a majority of about 200 votes.

The first wife of Mr. Gibbs was the mother of his four children. She died in 1887, and six years later he was married to Miss Margaret Craig, of Augusta county. Florence V., the eldest of the family, married Benjamin C. Rawlings, of Spottsylvania county; Cornelia A. married Robert G. Davis, and moved with him to Hot Springs, Arkansas; Ellabel B. married John C. Moore; Ethel R. married first George E. Wade, and second, Lancelot C. Lockridge. The last named lives near Raphine on a portion of the paternal estate. Captain B. C. Rawlings, a native of Spottsylvania, was the first Virginian to volunteer for the Confederate army, and the youngest all-the-war soldier. He joined the First South Carolina Regiment the first week in January, 1861, and surrendered with General Lee at Appomattox when twenty years and three months old. Before he was eighteen he was a lieutenant and commanded his company in the battle of Fredericksburg. He came to Rockbridge in 1874 and died on his farm near Raphine in 1908. His son, Doctor James E., of Florida, joined the British Expeditionary Army in the present war.

* * * * * * * * * * * *

Few other inventions seem to have originated in this county. Samuel Houston, a progressive farmer, as well as a divine of long service, patented a threshing machine. Doctor William Graham, a nephew to the William Graham who figures so largely in the founding of Liberty Hall Academy, invented a fire extinguisher, the principle of which is the same as that of the Babcock and other well known extinguishers. In recognition of the fact that Graham was first in this field, a patent was issued long after his death, and to his administrator. Charles H. Locher is the inventor of an aerial dump used in excavation work. Probably the most striking of the inventive discoveries named in this paragraph are those by Michael Miley on color photography. They were peffected by himself alone.

A HISTORY OF ROCKBRIDGE COUNTY, VIRGINIA

PART II

INTRODUCTION

In three of the author's earlier works on local history lines of descent were traced from the original settlers,—so far as this could be ascertained,—and carried far enough forward to include the adult living posterity. This was possible only by reason of a small population and a comparatively small number of group-families.

But family names in Rockbridge are exceedingly numerous. To trace the lines of ancestry on the scale practicable in the other counties would have caused an expense prohibitive to the getter-up of the book, and would have placed on the book itself a price prohibitive to many prospective purchasers.

This department of the History of Rockbridge does not purport to be anything more than a source-book. While collecting his material, the compiler put down all the surnames he came upon, together with the accompanying fact in each instance. In Sections II to XIII, inclusive, the names are classified according to the source from which they are derived. Miscellaneous facts, such as dates of birth, marriage, and death, lists of children, and sundry other particulars, are given in Section XIV. A complete index of names is not given, for the reason that all lists in Part Two are constructed in alphabetic order. The genealogic index that does appear is in the nature of a cross-index, wherever a cross-index is indicated. It also includes the genealogic particulars scattered through the other divisions of the book.

The authorities are as follows: For Section II, the deed-books of Orange and Augusta, and the chancery papers in the suit of Peck v. Borden; for Section III, the books of the Virginia Land Office; for Section IV, the deed-books of Orange, and Augusta, and Botetourt; for Section V, the first will-book, Rockbridge county; for Section VI, the personal property book on file in the Virginia State Library; for Section VII, order-book, Rockbridge county; for Section VIII, the tax-list for 1917; for Section IX, the deed-books and will-books for the years, 1778-1816, inclusive; for Section X, chiefly the order-books for the period prior to 1860, but the McDowell roster is quoted from Waddell's *Annals of Augusta;* for Section XI, the roster on file in the office of county clerk; for Section XII, the return of the selective draft of 1917-18 for Rockbridge county; for Section XIII, Orange order-book for 1739-41, Rockbridge order-books to 1886, Augusta order-books to 1778, a petition to the General Assembly, a pamphlet history of New Monmouth Church, Foote's *Sketches of Virginia*, and Chalkley's *Digest of the Augusta Records;* for Section XIV, chiefly the marriage-bonds and lists of marriages for Rockbridge, Augusta and Botetourt, the various record-books of the aforesaid counties, and the newspaper files in the office of the county clerk of Rockbridge.

It is hoped that the gleanings presented in this department may prove serviceable to the investigator who wishes to trace out some given family line in an exhaustive manner. It is easy to fill a book with a history of the descendants of one pioneer. It is utterly impossible to do this in hundreds of such instances, and still expect the results to be marshaled within the covers of a single volume.

By "group-family" is meant all the descendants of some particular pioneer.

SECTION I

Given Names and Surnames

The pioneers of this county did not use much variety in given names. The favorite ones for each sex were not more than twenty. Perhaps not more than one-twelfth of the population bore names outside of such a list. Almost innumerable were the men named Alexander, Andrew, Archibald, Charles, David, George, Henry, Hugh, James, John, Joseph, Michael, Nathaniel, Patrick, Richard, Robert, Samuel, Thomas, or William, and the women named Agnes, Catharine, Eleanor, Elizabeth, Esther, Hannah, Isabella, Jean, Magdalene, Margaret, Martha, Mary, Phœbe, Rachael, Rebecca, Sarah, or Susanna.

The larger share of the above names are taken from the Bible, bearing witto the influence exerted by the Reformation upon the Ulster people. Those applied to the female sex are almost entirely scriptural. But Charles, George, Henry, Hugh, Richard, Robert, and William are Norman-French. Alexander and Archibald, names of Greek and Teutonic origin, respectively, have been great favorites among the Scotch.

The various pioneer families had each their favorite names, and these were handed down from generation to generation. This circumstance is of much help to the genealogist.

Until little more than a century ago, middle names were infrequent. In a group-family we are therefore likely to find a number of Samuel Wilsons, Thomas Paxtons, or William Moores. And yet the woman named Mary in one place is very probably the Jean of whom we find mention somewhere else. In such instances, both the given and the middle name were not ordinarily used at the same time.

A middle name was more common among the German people than among the British. But since a German family might include a John Adams, a John George, and a John Michael, it was then the middle name which was in common use.

Our forbears were unacquainted with our modern hurry, and abbreviated names were rather less in use than among ourselves. They took time to say Susanna and Lucinda, instead of Susan and Lucy. So it is rarely that Henry Kirkham becomes Hen Kirkham, or that Patrick O'Brian becomes Pat O'Brian. But Mary, Martha, Elizabeth, and Sarah very often assume the forms Polly, Patsy, Betsy, and Sally, the styles prevailing to such an extent that oftentimes the nickname was used to the exclusion of the proper term. In like manner Agnes was often turned into Nancy. In some families, Martha was regularly pronounced Marthew, and Susanna was clipped to Susann with the accent on the last syllable.

Middle names came into vogue after the establishment of the Federal government in 1789. The practice of giving two names grew with such rapidity that within fifty years a single name had become the exception. The new fashion was largely political in its origin. Partisan feeling and a new-born Americanism ran high in those days, and we often find the initials G. W., T. J., and B. F., standing for George Washington, Thomas Jefferson, and Benjamin Franklin. It was but a step further to name a boy for some respected minister or some other man of local prominence. And the custom once established, middle names were given to girls as well as boys.

Since the war of 1861, and particularly during the latter half of this period, the American people have been living in a new era. In nothing is this more evident than in the changed usage with respect to given names. The number in fashion has very greatly increased, and it is not thought to matter very much if a name does happen to be unusual or peculiar. Much less often is a once favorite name perpetuated in a family. Nathaniel and Susanna, and all other long Biblical names are now rare, but such names as James and Mary, also taken from the Bible, continue very much in use.

As to surnames, the number in the Rockbridge area is surprisingly large. Not less than 1,500 come to light in a gleaning of documentary local history, while the actual number is as a matter of course somewhat larger yet. About three-fourths of this total are now extinct, so far as this county is concerned. In many an instance, it is true, the occurrence of a name is like a visit by a bird of passage. A single family, or perhaps only an unmarried person, lived here a few years and then passed on. In not a few instances, however, a family connection remained here two or three generations, yet disappearing so long ago as to leave but a faint memory behind. Others of the extinct families, like the Grigsbys and the Edmondsons, have figured very largely in the local annals. But the tendency ceases only with the supply, and with each decade the old names become fewer.

The heavy emigration from Rockbridge is the leading cause of the disappearance of names. A subsidiary cause lies in the fact that posterity in the female line tends to grow in a more rapid ratio than in the male line. If a certain John Smith has two sons and two daughters, all of whom marry and have each two sons and two daughters, and if the same average rule holds for later generations, no cousin-marriages taking place within the connection, then out of the 256 great-great-grandchildren, only sixteen would be Smiths. The other 249 would be Browns, Whites, Joneses, etc.

An inspection of the vast array of names occuring in the first century of settlement shows an overwhelming predominance of the Scotch-Irish element. But as was explained in an early chapter of this book, the Scotch-Irish is a composite stock, its own elements being Scotch, English, Irish, French, and Welch. Names originating in the Scottish Highlands are Celtic, and therefore are peculiarly Scotch. But a dialect of English has been the speech of the Lowlands for more than ten centuries. Ulster was colonized mainly from the south of Scotland and the north of England. Many surnames are common to both districts. Hence it is not always evident whether an Ulster surname has a Scottish or an English source. Could all doubt be removed, it would unquestionably show that the percentage of the English strain in the Ulster population is commonly underrated.

The Borden Tract was primarily settled by Ulstermen and by occasional families from east of the Blue Ridge. Other Ulster people were as a rule the original settlers of the remainder of the Rockbridge area. Yet in several instances, notably in the conspicuous one of the Sallings, German families were on the ground at a very early day. The German representation has increased, relatively as well as absolutely, and is a considerable infusion in the present population. The German has been less dispersive than the Ulsterman and more inclined to hold fast to good land. In Rockbridge he has been in the minority and has lived in close social relations with his neighbors of British stock. The fusion has therefore been quite complete. The clannishness seen in various counties of Pennsylvania is fortunately absent, as is also the persistent clinging to a broken down German dialect that serves no legitimate purpose whatever. Henry Ruffner, himself the grandson of a German immigrant, said of the "Valley Dutch" that, "without an efficient school system in Virginia another century will pass away before they become an intelligent people or adopt fully the language and manners of our general population."

Among the German names in the list we have mentioned are the following: Albright, Almonrode, Altizer, Armentrout, Bosserman, Counts, Crist, Entsminger, Fulwider, Ginger, Harnsbargar, Heizer, Hickman, Hite, Hostetter, Hoylman, Isenhower, Mohler, Muterspaw, Ornbaum, Rader, Rapp, Replogle, Ruffner, Salling, Shultz, Snider, Standoff, Stoner, Swisher, Swoope, Troxal, Unroe, Wence, Wilhelm, Windle, and Zollman.

The Irish, French, and Welch names are few and appear with the Ulster immigration. Among the Irish names are Bogan, Donoho, Dougherty, Flannagan, Ford, Kelly, McCafferty, McFadden, McMannama, Milligan, Murphy, O'Brien, O'Friel, Ryan, Shaner, Shaw, Sloan, and Sprowl. French names are Coursey, Defries, Dehart, Demasters, Estell, Flournoy, Larew, Lyle, Maupin, and Saville. Welsh names are Davis, Doak (Doag), Evans, Guin, Hughes, Owens, Pritchard, and Rogers.

The only Holland names we have noticed are Hull (Hohl), Sly, and Vansandt.

Names that are clearly English are Abbott, Adams, Bagby, Baxter, Bennington, Borden, Carter, Chandler, Chittum, Dryden, Fulton, Goodwin, Grigsby, Hadley, Harper, Nelson, Patton, Paxton, Taylor, Turpin, Ward, Watson, and Youell.

For many years the spelling of proper names has become nearly "standardized." But in the colonial time spelling was by sound, and surnames not infrequently appeared in a guise more or less unlike the prevalent usage of today. Notable instances are the following:

Baggs—Beggs, Beiggs.
Braford—Brafford, Brawford.
Bunton—Buntin, Buntain.
Dale—Deal, Dial.
Dryden—Dredin, Dreadden.
Eakin—Akin.
Edmondson—Edmiston.
Galbraith—Galbreath.
Houston—Huston.
Hutchinson—Hutcheson.
Kennedy—Kenady.
Logan—Loggan.
Poague—Poage.
Salling—Salley.
Sawyer—Siars, Sayers.
Summers—Sommers.
Telford—Talford, Tedford.
Walkup—Vahub, Vachob, Waughub.
Weir—Ware.

SECTION II

CONVEYANCES IN BORDEN TRACT, 1741-1780

The name of purchaser is followed in consecutive order by the acreage, the price, the year of sale, the description,—when definitely given,—and the first transfer prior to the organization of Rockbridge. When it is not quite clearly certain that the transfer is of the actual tract in question, a question mark is put down. The original sales recorded in Orange are indicated by a star attached to the date of purchase. All other sales are recorded in Augusta. P, s, and d are abbreviations for pounds, shillings, and pence in the old Virginia currency. To reduce pounds to dollars, add one cipher and divide by three. The shilling is 16 2-3 cents, and the penny is 1 7-18 cents. The name of a consort is in parentheses.

Adams, William—360—4p—1758—Moffett Cr.

Alexander, Archibald—987—29p—1747—near Punchbowl—sold (?): to Samuel Cummins of Chester County, Penn., 250 acres for 20p, 1763; to Joseph Alexander, 1765, 256 acres for 30p; to William Alexander, 1769, 208 acres for 8p.

Alexander, Ebenezer—312—100p—1748—corner George Jemison.

Allison, John (Jean)—291—8p 10s—1748—SW side North River, corner to Gilbert Campbell and John Moore—sold to Joseph Walker, 1765, for 100p.

Allison, John—290—30p—1768—near mill of Andrew Hays.

Allison, Robert—279 39-40—8p 5s—1747—North River near Halbert McClure.

Allison, Robert—200—30p—1771—North River.

Anderson, Jacob—350—10p—1750—sold to Isaac Anderson, 1756, for 9p.

Baxter, Andrew—200—6p—1742—near patent line—sold by Andrew (Sarah) Stevenson, 1766, to John (Mary) Paul for 50p. Stevenson was grandson to Baxter.

Beard, Thomas—605 39-80—33p, 5s—1753—Moffett Cr. near John Roseman—sold to William Beard, 1760 for 100p.

Beaty, John—118—5s—1750.

Beaty, Francis—265—17p 18s—1751—sold to Joseph Alexander for 50p in 1768, when land cornered on John Kerr's "old place." Beaty was then deputy collector of Mecklenburg county, N. C.

Berry, William—145—5s—1746—Moffett Cr.

Berry, William—130—5p 10s—1752.

Berry, Charles—326—12p—1752—140 acres sold to Robert Gamewell, 1753, for 20p 5s.

Bowyer, Michael—226—1p—1758.

Boyle, Mary (widow)—200—20p—1768—bank of North River.

Boyle, Charles—180—10p—1770—corner to Low Todd.

Brown, Abraham—482—14p 8s 9d—1754—W side North River.

Buchanan, John (Margaret)—634—19p—1742—North River—sold to William Young, 1756, 100 acres for 20p; to James Anderson, 1757, 200 acres for 75p; to Jacob Anderson, 1757, 232 acres for 40p; to Robert Allison, 1757, 83 acres for 25p.

Buchanan, John—293¾—8p 18s—1743.

Buchanan, John—100—3p—1750.

Buchanan, John—370—10p—1753.
Buchanan, Andrew—250—7p 10s—1756—corner to Andrew McCoskey.
Buchanan, Andrew—200—25p—1770—corner to Robert Kirkpatrick.
Buchanan, James—415—10p—1757—corner to Francis McCown.
Buchanan, William—280—10p—1758—corner to James Miles on North River.
Buchanan, Archibald—406—5p—1762—McCown's Run.
Buchanan, Samuel—240—37p—1770—corner to Robert Steele on Buffalo Draft.
Campbell, Gilbert—389—11p 13s 4d—1742—Woods Cr.
Campbell, James—434—6 p 10s—1756—adjoining James Young.
Campbell, James—115—30p—1768—Woods Cr.
Carr, John—280—7p—1743—Kerr's Cr.
Carr, David—368—30p—1750.
Caruthers, William—340—20p—1753—near Gray's 650-acre tract.
Caruthers, William—96—3p—1754.
Clements, Ezekiel—400—5s—1746—South River.
Coalter, John—212—6p—1753—Hays Cr.—sold, 1766, by James Coalter to Michael Coalter for 40p.
Cooper, James—112—5p—1768—adjoining Joseph Kennedy.
Cousart, Richard—333—10p—1742—corner Samuel Eakins—sold, 1752, to John Cunningham and Hugh Wier for 30p, and in 1736 Cunningham sold his interest to Weir for 100p.
Crowden, William—200 7-40—6p 2d—1742—corner to William Smith.
Craighead, Alexander—533—220p—1753—in 1765, ¡Craighead, then in Mecklenburg County, N. C., gave Archibald Alexander a power of attorney to sell.
Culton, Robert—368 133-160—3 p 11s—Moffett Cr.
Culton, Joseph—553 1-2—17p 10s.—1742—Moffatts Cr.—100 acres—sold 1752, to John Walker for 20s 6d.
Cunningham, Hugh (Sarah)—281—5s—1748—sold to John McKee, 1770, for 300p Cunningham was then in Botetourt.
Davis, James—626—18p 15s 7½d—1746.
Davis, James—436—165p—1762—corner to William Todd.
Davis, Samuel (Mary)—200—5s—1761—corner to James Anderson—sold to Samuel Lyle, 1764, for 55p.
Davis, William—100 5s—1761—corner Francis Rennolds.
Davison, John—353½—11p—1747—Mill Cr., cornering on John Houston and John Gray.
Donahy, Charles—231 9-20—2p 6s 11d—1742—Moffett's Cr.
Dryden, David, tailor—130 47-80—3p 16s—1747—corner to William Baskins. Baskins went to the Carolinas.
Dunlap, Robert (Elizabeth)—188 17-20—5p 15s 3d—1742—sold to John Wardlaw, 1757, for 20p.
Dunlap, Samuel—559½—16p 15s 9d—1742—corner to John Houston; 170 acres sold, 1750, to David Dunlap for 23p; 389½ acres sold, 1753, to Thomas Beard, for 140p.
Dunlap, Samuel (Margaret)—150—2p—1756—E bank North River opposite island at mouth of Hays—sold to Patrick Woods, 1769, for 10p.
Dunlap, John (Jennet)—150—11p—1766—SW side Hays Cr.—sold to Joseph Woods, 1769, for 10p.
Eakin, James—522¾—15s—13s 8d—1742.
Edmiston, Matthew—238—10p—1751—sold by John (Margaret) Edmondson to Samuel Patterson, 1764, for 55p.

Edmiston, John (Margaret)—448 and 609—55p—1753—sold, 1765 to Samuel Steele for 140p.
Edmiston, Robert—244—7p 11s 8d—1746—corner to Matthew Lyle.
Erwin, Robert—205—5s—1748.
Erwin, Robert—100—6p—1757—Kerr's Cr.
Evans, William—249—7p 9s 5d—1742—patent line, corner to Thomas Wilson—sold by Nathaniel Evans to William Ward, 1762, for 90p, and by Ward, 1769, to John McClung, for 55p 10s.
Finley, William (Mary)—500—5s—1742—part of 3143-acre tract.
Fitzpatrick, Andrew—150—20p—1765—corner to Moran and to John Fitzpatrick.
Fulton, John—200—6p—1752—Moffett Cr., adjoining Thomas Beard—sold to Thomas Fulton, 1758, for 40p.
Gay, Robert—100—10s—1765.
Gay, Samuel—175—5s—1747—Timber Ridge, corner to John Mathews and John Houston.
Gilmer, John—250—5s—1748.
Gilmer, James (Martha)—328—5s—1748—sold to Andrew McCampbell, 1764, for 111p.
Glasgow, John—427—15p 16s—1748—sold to William Parris, 1753, for 66p.
Gray, Benjamin—260—25p—1767—corner to William Taylor.
Gray, David—100—5s—1761—corner to John Davidson.
Gray, David (Ruth)—100—5s—1761—corner to James Greenlee—sold to James McCroskey, 1768, for 18p.
Gray, Isaac (Mary)—270—12p—1751—Mill Cr.—sold to Isaac (Jr.?) and Jacob Gray, 1752, for 18p.
Gray, Jacob—450—15p 10s—corner to John Brown.
Gray, John—203½—6p 2s 1d—1742—NW side Timber Ridge.
Gray, Robert—100—10s—1765—Moffett Cr.
Gray, Samuel—650—2p—1754—at William Caruther's old corner.
Gray, William—300—9p—1754—cornering on Beverly Manor line.
Greenlee, James—200—5s—1747—cornering on John McDowell—sold to Samuel Greenlee, 1763, for 50p.
Guin, William, yeoman—132 119-160—4p—1743.
Hall, William—353 11-40—10p 10s—1743—James River.
Hall, William (Janet)—150—?—1761—corner to Halbert McClure—sold to William Hall (son), 1766, for 5p.
Hall, William—346—26p—1763—adjoining homestead—sold to Nathaniel Hall, 1766, for 40p.
Hamilton, James—250—7p 10s—1751—sold to Robert Christian, 1753, for 70p.
Handly, John (Grosel)—257—15p—1751—adjoining Joseph Kennedy—sold to William Rhea, 1764, for 50p.
Harris, James—200—14p—1767—Hays Cr., near Francis Wilson.
Hays, Andrew—717 (3 tracts)—13p—1754—adjoining homestead.
Hays, Andrew—200—120p—1763—on hill above mill.
Hays, Andrew—100—20p—1766—Back Cr., adjoining Isaac Anderson.
Hays, Charles—189 9-16—6p—1742.
Hays, Charles—165—4p—1766—Hays Cr.
Hays, Charles—200—6p—1766—Hays Cr.
Hays, David—124—3p 15s—1749.
Hays, David—124—3p 5s—1749.

Hays, John (Rebecca)—318 59-80—?—1746—Hays Cr.—sold by widow: 50 acres to Charles (son), 1752, for 5p; 258 acres to John (son), 1752, for 50p; each son given a half interest in the mill and the 10 acres around it.

Hays, Patrick (Frank)—254—7p 12s 5d—1742—Beverly line—sold to William Hays, 1759, for 100p—deed says this tract is part of 854 acres held by Borden and Beverly.

Hazard, Samuel, gentleman—220—5p—1756—Beverly line.

Henderson, George, yeoman—320—9p—12s.

Henderson, George—282—6p—1750—Moffett Cr., corner to John Roseman—sold to Hugh Wardlaw, 1762, for 60p.

Henry, James (Mary), blacksmith—408—3p—1757—surveyed by Robert Henry—corner to Andrew Steele—200 acres sold, 1759, to Robert Telford, joiner, for 50p; 508 (?) sold, 1762, to Robert Buchanan for 32p.

Hill, Thomas—50—2p—1754—corner to Thomas Beard.

Houston, Robert—306 51-80—9p 3s 10d—N side Timber Ridge—1742.

Houston, Robert—200—6p—1748—Timber Ridge.

Houston, John—228—7p 10s—1748—corner to James Eakin.

Hunter, Elizabeth—124—3p 14s 5d—1743—Moffett Cr.

Kennedy, Joseph—414—30p—1752—corner to Andrew Steele—sold to William Kennedy, 1760, for 100p.

Kennedy, Andrew and John—341—20p—1762—Mill Cr., corner to Andrew Steele—sold to James Wardlaw, 1765, for 100p.

Kinner, Andrew—252—40p—1773—corner to David Hays.

Kirkham, Henry (Margaret)—198 73-160—5p 19s 4d—Woods Cr.—sold to John Paxton, 1750, for 100p.

Kirkpatrick, Robert—612—37p—1750.

Lackey, James—200—30p—1767—near Matthew Robertson.

Lam, Conrad—212—10p—1757—part of 800 acres.

Lapsley, Joseph—383—10p 2s 10d—1742—Woods Cr.

Lapsley, Joseph—1—2s 6d—1754—patent line adjoining homestead.

Little, Joseph—380—72p 10s—1774—corner to John Alphin and James McKee.

Lockridge, William (Agnes)—265 71-160—7p 19s 4d—1742—sold to John Weir, 1765, for 131p.

Lockridge, William—250—4p—1755—Halfway Cr., corner to Thomas Hill—6 acres sold, 1752, to Thomas Hill for 5s 1½d; 244 acres sold, 1762, to David Steele for 100p.

Logan, John—262—15p—1753—Kennedy's Mill Cr.—sold (?) to Alexander Logan (son), 1755, 237 acres for 10p.

Logan, John—195—6p 15s—1755—adjoining Thomas Beard.

Lowry, John, yeoman—344¼—10p—1742—Moffett Cr.

Lowry, John—200—6p—1748.

Lowry, John—170—3p—1757—adjoining Steele and Henry Dunlap.

Lowry, Robert—412—15p 16s—1753—sold (?) to William Edmondson, 1759, 130 acres for 34p 10s 4d.

Lusk, James—170—5p—1749—adjoining patent line and Samuel McCutcheon—sold by James (Eleanor) Lusk, 1754, to James Trotter for 40p.

Lusk, James—257—12p—1768—corner to Robert Lusk and Hugh McFadden.

Lusk, Robert—241—10p—1768—corner to Hugh McFadden.

Lusk, William—200—5s—1765—Mill Cr.

Lyle, Daniel—257—7p 14s 6d—1743—corner to Robert Houston.

Lyle, John—734—22p 5s—1746—corner to Matthew Lyle.

Lyle, Matthew—300—9p—1742—SE side Timber Ridge.
Lyle, Matthew—451 47-160—13p 10s—1746—adjacent to Thomas McSpadden, John Mathews, John Gray.
Lyle, Samuel—235—10p—1751.
Lyle, Samuel—100—11p—1767—adjoining homestead.
Martin, James—752—22p 11s 3d—1742—Moffett Cr.
Martin, Henry—674—16p 6s—1747—corner to James McDowell—sold (?) to Benjamin Borden, 1749, 624 4-5 acres for 80p.
Martin, Hugh—500—12p 10s—1748—Back Cr.—sold (?): to Charles Hays, 1752, 250 acres for 55p; 250 acres to Andrew Hays, 1754, for 30p 5s.
Mathews, John—295 9-20—8p 18s 5d—near Timber Ridge, corner to John Gray.
McCallister, James—150—?—1754—patent line on Kerr's Cr., adjacent to Robert Erwin—sold to Patrick McConnell, 1766, for 47p.
McCampbell, Andrew—73—6p—1765—adjoining Samuel Norwood.
McCanless, William—296—8p 17s 6d—1742—corner to John Moore—sold (?), 1768, to Andrew Moore, 150 acres for 60p.
McCanless, William—37—2p—1753.
McCaskery, John—440—5p—1749.
McCaskery, Alexander—200—20p—1750.
McChesney, Walter—100—10p—1775—corner to Henry Campbell.
McClenachan, John—359—28p 12s—1750.
McClary, Alexander—147 1-20—1p 8s 3d—1742.
McClung, William—314 29-32—30p 7s—1746—corner to Andrew Baxter.
McClung, William—165—5p—1754—adjoining homestead.
McClung, James—200—6p—1754—corner to John Mackey.
McClung, Henry—70—11p—1764—corner to Samuel Lyle.
McClung, John, Jr.—40—1p 15s—1775—adjoining homestead.
McClure, Alexander—266—7p 11s—1747—Mill Cr., corner to Isaac Taylor.
McClure, Arthur—153½—10p—1749.
McClure, Halbert—203—6p 1s 6d—1747.
McClure, Halbert—300—25p—1765—corner to Moses Trimble.
McClure, John (Catharine)—205—8p—1749—sold (?), 1751, 4½ acres to Nathan McClure for 2p.
McClure, Nathaniel (or Nathan)—180—5p 6s 6d—1747—Worm Run, a branch of Mill Cr.
McClure, Moses—380—2p—1748—"Warar Run," a branch of Mill Cr.
McClure, Moses—219—30p—1771—on the river.
McClure, Moses—110—3p 6s—1755—corner to Whiteside.
McClure, Samuel (Mary)—282—10p 10s—1752—50 acres sold, 1752, to John Paxton for 25p; 232 to James Campbell, 1760, for 160p.
McColerath, Robert—230—40p—1768.
McConnell, Francis—328—3p—1746.
McCorkle, Alexander, by power of attorney, to John Bowyer—300—3p—west side North River, corner to Abraham Brown—1761—150 acres sold, 1756, to Patrick McCorkle for 25p.
McCown, John—437—12p 18s—1750—Kerr's Cr.
McCown, Francis—328—3p—1746—corner to Joseph Kennedy; barrens on S side of creek.
McCroskey, John—306—9p 2s—1747—adjacent to Isaac Anderson.
McCroskey, John—284—10p—1748—corner to James Glasgow.

McCutchen, Samuel (Frances)—600—18p—1742—Beverly line—300 acres divided equally, 1768, between Samuel McCutchen, Jr., and John McCutchen; consideration, good will.

McDowell, Ephraim—300—5s—1747—sold to James McDowell, 1755, for 5p; by the latter, 1755, to John Bowyer for 175p; by Bowyer, 1763, to James McDowell for 200p.

McDowell, Samuel—1359—1s—1755—400 acres of this (the John McDowell homestead) conveyed to John Paul.

McElheny, Robert—280—11p 12s—1750.

McElheny, Robert—100—15p—1768—Kerr's Cr.

McElwrath, Robert—230—40p—1768—Walker's Cr.

McGavock, Alexander—100—3p—1763—Walker's Cr.

McKay, John—390—19p—1747—N side Mill Cr. corner to Baptist McNabb.

McKee, James (Lydia)—310—5p—1757—corner to Samuel Norwood—sold to Thomas Kirkpatrick, 1765, for 68p 10s.

McKee, James—301—50p—1766—corner to John Lyle.

McMurray, Thomas—250—35p—1750—former to John Patton—sold to the Rev. John Brown, 1755.

McNutt, Alexander—301—9p—1753.

McNutt, James—185—10p—1753.

McMurtry, Samuel and John—290—3p—1759—corner to Hall.

McPharrin, John—319—14p 11s 6d—1749.

McSpaden, Thomas—106—3p 3s 3d—1744.

Miller, Alexander, blacksmith—248—8p—1744—adjoining James McDowell—sold to Alexander Telford, 1763, for 120p.

Montgomery, James—654—3p—1746.

Montgomery, John—247½—7p 6s—1747—corner to John Houston and Samuel Dunlap.

Montgomery, John—150—4p 10s—1754—cornering on Beverly line.

Moore, James—327—10p—Hays Cr.—1743.

Moore, John—30¾—9p 2s 5d—1743

Moore, John—5043⁄8—12p—1748—corner to William Moore and Joseph Lapsley—sold to Robert Alexander, 1760, for 95p 10s.

Moore, Alexander—200—6p—1750.

Moore, Alexander—120—10p—1764—corner to McClung.

Moore, Alexander of Andrew—250—7p 10s—1754—part of 700-acre tract.

Moore, Andrew, only son of Samuel—250—4p—10s—1754—part of 700.

Moore, David of Andrew—250—6p—1754—part of 700.

Moran, Dominick—150—10p—1763—corner to Samuel Davis.

Morehead, Matthew—32—5p—1771—adjoining old survey.

Nesbitt, Samuel—100—17p—1770—adjoining John Berry.

Norwood, Samuel (Elizabeth)—243—5s—1750—Kerr's Cr.

Norwood, Samuel—400—6d—1760—sold, 1765, to Robert McElhany, blacksmith, for 150p.

Patterson, John, yeoman—380⅛—11p 12s 6d—1741—Moffett Cr.

Patterson, John—420—12p 12s—1741—Mill Cr., adjoining Isaac Taylor, John Henderson, Israel Pickens, Robert Poage.

Patterson, James—95—12p 10s—1776—adjoining James Cowden.

Patterson, Samuel—95—30p—1776—adjoining James Patterson.

Patton, John—200—20p 1750.

Paul, John—400—12p—1754—near Borden's home (Woods Cr.)

Paxton, Thomas, Sr. (Rebecca)—500—30p—1748—near Punchbowl on patent line—sold, 1764, to Samuel Paxton for 200p.

CONVEYANCES IN BORDEN TRACT, 1741-1780   349

Paxton, Thomas—774—52p—1769.
Paxton, Thomas, Jr.—673—18p—1748.
Paxton, Thomas, joiner—410—12p—1748.
Paxton, John—32—3p—1764—corner to Joseph Lapsley.
Poage, Robert—378—11p 10s—1742—Poage's Run.
Pollock, William—190—30p—1765—adjoining Thomas Beard and John Montgomery.
Porter, William—395½—12p—1743.
Porter, William—112—4p—1750.
Porter, William—200—16p—1754—W side of North River.
Porter, William—110—3p—1754—adjoining homestead.
Quin, David—210—?—1768—mouth of Rock Cr.
Randles (Reynolds), James—2000—1p—North River and Mill Cr.—sold, 1767, by Richard (Elizabeth) Reynolds to William Ramsay for 130p.
Randolph, James—200—6p—1749.
Reagh, William—230—7p—1750—sold to Archibald Reagh, 1769, for 100p.
Reagh, Archibald—200—8p—1753.
Reagh, Archibald, Jr.—33—5p—1771—Walker's Cr.
Reagh, Robert, carpenter and joiner—118—3p 10s 9d—1754—N side of Hays Cr.
Reynolds, Francis—100—5s—1761—corner to James Anderson.
Robinson, James (Hannah)—200—8p—1743—Hays Cr.—sold to Arthur Graham, 1765, for 76p.
Robinson, James—216—5p—1760—Hays Cr.—sold to James Wallace, 1767, for 137p.
Robinson, John—300—24p—1753.
Robinson, Matthew—400—32p—1753—sold to Henry Campbell and James Culton, 1763, 200 acres for 40p.
Robinson, William (Isabel?)—124—6d—1760—Hays Cr.—sold by Isabel Robinson and John Robinson (son), 1768, to Alexander Hindman for 60p.
Russell, David—200—45p—1777—corner to Robert Cooper.
Scott, John—100—5s—1761—corner to James Anderson and Francis Reynolds.
Shields, John—320—9p 12s—1742—sold to John Davis, 1756, for 9p.
Smiley, John—440—5p—1763—W bank of North River.
Smiley, Walter, Jr.—211—7p—1775—forks of Hays Cr.
Smith, William—999 99-160—9p—1742—sold (?), by William (Jean) Smith 711 acres to Joseph Kennedy, 1749, for 60p.
Sprowl, John (Margaret)—250—10p—1768—corner to Andrew Steele and William Alexander—sold to Alexander Wilson, 1769, for 40p.
Steele, Andrew—463½—?—1750.
Steele, Andrew—40—1p 10s—1755.
Stephenson, John (Jane)—290—12p—1751—Mill Cr.—sold to William Ramsay, 1753, for 58p 13s.
Stephenson, Thomas—248—130p—1780.
Stevenson, John—149—5p—1750.
Stevenson, John—199 141-160—6p—6p—1743—Falling Spring Br.
Stevenson, George—200—6p—1750—sold (?) to Samuel Henderson, 1762, for 4p.
Stuart, Robert—200—6p—1750.
Summers, John—440—40p—1768—corner to William McKee.
Tate, John—255—20p—1779—Beverly line.
Taylor, Isaac, Jr.—600—18p—1746—Mill Cr. "by a scallopy hill"—sold: to George

Taylor, 1762, 200 acres for 5p; to Andrew Taylor, 1765, 250 acres for 40p; to William Taylor, 1765, 150 acres for 5p.
    Taylor, William—200—12p—1762—corner to Isaac Taylor.
    Telford, Robert—250—40p—1768—North River.
    Telford, Alexander—40—7p—1770—corner to William Berry.
    Thompson, John and James—100—7p—1769—adjoining Robert Allison.
    Trimble, James—402—12p 1s 2d—1742—Moffett Cr.—sold, 1754, to Joseph Kennedy for 33p 10s.
    Trimble, Moses—570—8p—1750.
    Vance, Thomas—800—64p—1765—North River.
    Walker, Alexander—161—4p 16s 7d—1743—Hays Cr.
    Walker, Alexander—170—6p—1755—corner to John Robinson on Walker's Cr.
    Walker, James—321—11p 10s—1743—corner to Alexander Walker.
    Walker, John—213—6p 10s—1743—corner to James Walker.
    Walker, John (Ann)—190—5p 14s—1755—Walker's Cr.—sold, 1765, to George Duncan for 100p; by Duncan, 1760, to Samuel Lindsay for 102p 10s.
    Walker, John, Jr.—302—27p 5s—1753.
    Wallace, John—645 and 250—27p—1755—Walker's Cr.—322½ acres sold to James Rutherford, 1755, for 20p.
    Wallace, David—200—3p—1757—corner to James McNabb—sold, 1765, to Henry Black for 40p; by Black to Nathan Peoples, 1769, for 40p.
    Wardlaw, William—343—11p 2s—1752.
    Wardlaw, Robert—375—20p—1774—corner to James Moore.
    Weir, Robert—240—?—1754—Halfway Cr.
    Weir, Joseph—190—35p—1765—adjoining John Weir.
    Weir, John—201—35p—1765.
    Whiteside, Moses—570—8p—1750.
    Whiteside, Moses—145—4p 6s—1754—adjoining homestead and Samuel McCroskey.
    Wiley, John—200—11p 10s—1750.
    Wiley, John—236—30p—1770—Kerr's Cr.
    Wilson, Samuel—400—10p—1751.
    Wilson, James—382—5p—1760—Kennedy's Mill Cr.
    Wilson, William—377—5p—?—Kennedy's Mill Cr.
    Woods, Richard—570—17p 2s—1742—Woods Cr.
    Woods, William—382—11p 9s 2d—1742—Woods Cr., cornering on patent line and Joseph Lapsley.
    Woods, John—504 33-80—12p—1747.
    Young, James (Sarah)—401½—12p 10s—1742—Whistle Cr.—251 acres sold to Low Todd, 1750, for 12p; 150½ acres sold, 1750, to Matthew Young for 12p. Todd sold to Hugh Cunningham, 1760, for 78p.
    Young, James—440—15p—1747—mouth of Whistle cornering on John Allison—sold, 1753, to Patrick Young for 100p.

SECTION III

EARLY PATENTS OUTSIDE BORDEN TRACT

The following list of patents on the waters of the upper James between the Blue Ridge and the North Mountain, and is carried forward to the year when Botetourt county was organized. No attempt has been made to eliminate those lying within the present border of Augusta or within the present limits of Botetourt. With occasional abbreviation the descriptions are those of the records in The Virginia Land Office. "Forks" is a shortened expression for "Forks of the James," the district between the North River and the main stream. The acreage is followed by the date of the patent.

Allen, Malcom: (1) 200—1762—north side James nigh Half-Moon Bottom; (2) 285—1762—small branch of James (3) 80—1765—south side of James; (4) 90—1769—Grassy Bottom on James.

Allison, Robert: 285—1746—southwest side James opposite the Narrows.

Allison, Hugh: 110—1767—Forks.

Anderson, William: 100—1760—James.

Armstrong, Robert: (1) 200—1756—south Broad Creek; (2) 80—1765—Forks.

Arnold, Stephen: 355—1752—Taylor's Branch of Buffalo.

Bailey, James: 175—1759—Forks adjoining Samuel McDowell.

Bell, Robert: 380—1756—head of Hays.

Beiggs, Alexander: 150—1765—Mill Cr.

Berryford, John (1) 200—1760—Forks; (2) 350—1760—both sides North Branch.

Borden, Benjamin: (1) 92,100—Nov. 11, 1739—on the north and southeast branches of James between the Blue Ridge and the North Mtn; (2) 3553—1740—west side of Blue Ridge; (3) 400—1740—near Spreading Spring Branch; (4) 400—1740—in the fork made by the North Branch and Buffalo; (5) 400—1740—under the foot of the Blue Ridge and on a branch of James called the Mary (South River.)

Bowen, John: 100—1755—Forks.

Brush, Blakely: (1) 234—1769—adjoining his homestead in Forks; (2) 150—1769—Brush Run.

Buchanan, John: 320—1767—north side of James.

Buchanan, John, and William Thompson: 100—1765—Forks.

Burton, Richard: 400—1748—Buffalo adjoining Borden grant.

Carr, James: 235—1749—Broad Creek of Buffalo.

Caruthers, Hugh: 86—1755—branch of James

Cleek, Mathias: 50—1769—North Branch.

Clements, John: 80—1764—South River.

Collier, John: (1) 400—1746—Buffalo; (2) 277—1756—Buffalo.

Cunningham, James: (1) 400—1745—Tee's Creek (Kerr's); (2) 62—1755—branch of James between House Mountain and North Mountain.

Davis, William: (1) 100—1762—adjoining the widow Davis' in Forks; (2) 160—1756.

Davis, Nathaniel: 115—1763—Buffalo.

Davison, John: 350—1746—both sides North Branch.

Dale, Alexander: (1) 80—1755—branch of Carr's; (2) 110—1760—branch of Carr's.
Dennis, Joseph: (1) 70—1769—Forks, near homestead; (2) 60—1769—gap on Short Hill on Hutcheson's Branch.
Doak, John: 400—1746—James.
Donoho: 380—1763—head of Buffalo and Dever's Lick.
Dougherty, Charles: 80—1756—Cunningham Creek between House Mountain and North Mountain.
Evans, Nathaniel: (1) 100—1750—"on the South River alias the River Mary between the South Mountain and a high ridge on the west side of the river"; (2)—1756— west side of Mary; (3) 30—1769—Forks.
Evans, William: 150—1756—adjoining Borden's large tract on the south.
Finney, Michael: (1) 106—1756—Forks; (2) 650—1764—James.
Gibson, Samuel: 90—1763—Buffalo adjoining homestead.
Greenlee, John: 140—1769—Elk Creek, south side James.
Gilmore, William: 67—1767—branch of Tee's.
Greenlee, James: 100—1769—south side James opposite George Salling.
Hall, William: (1) 115—1760—Todd's Spring in Forks; (2) 390—1765—branches of James; (3) 500—1765—Cedar Creek.
Hamilton, Robert: 120—1768—Forks.
Hannah, John: (1) 230—1756—Buffalo; (2) 45—1763—adjoining homestead in Forks.
Hargar, John: 225—1768—Short Hill.
Harrison, John: 241—1746—west end of Short Hill.
Hays, Andrew: 337—1760—branches of James.
Holman, William: 320—1759—Forks.
Houston, James: 120—1761—Forks.
Hutton, James: 84—1755—branch of Buffalo adjoining William Todd.
Kemp, Francis: 92—1757—Harrison's Branch in Forks.
Long, Joseph: 400—1746—Buffalo, north side of Short Mountain.
Long, Samuel: 400—1746—Buffalo, north side of Short Mountain.
Lugar, James: 180—1765—Forks, adjoining John Gilmore.
Lusk, William: (1) 220—1759—north side Buffalo; (2) 400—1761—main branch of James.
Mathews, John: (1) 296—1749—northwest side North Branch opposite Philip Weaver's Bottom; (2) 350—1755—Borden Creek.
Mathews, Sampson: 18—1760—Borden Creek.
Mathews, Richard: 100—1767—adjoining homestead in Forks.
McClung, James: 50—1760—Mary.
McClure, Moses: 165—1750—Spreading Spring, south side North Branch.
McClure, Samuel: (1) 190—1759—Cedar; (2) 60—1769—adjoining homestead in Forks.
McClure, John: (1) 233—1756—southwest side John Allison's land on long "bent" of Buffalo; (2) 140—1759—adjoining Borden tract.
McCorkle, Alexander: 80—1768—Forks.
McCown, (McCune), Francis: (1) 360—1743—Tee's; (2) 368—1743—Tee's.
McDowell, John: (1) 400—1740—Big Spring Branch running into North Branch; (2) 400—1747—branches of Cedar.
McDowell, Alexander: 350—1745—Mary.
McDowell, James: (1) 400—1750—Forks; (2) 150—1768—adjoining homestead.
McDowell, Samuel: (1) 340—1751—Forks; (2) 170—1767—James.

McKemy, (McKemmy), William: 90—1757—branch of Kerr's.
McMachon, William: 400—1746—head of a north branch of Buffalo.
McMurray, William: 85—1769—Mary.
McNab, Andrew: 138—1749—Back Creek of Tee's.
McNair (McEnere), Daniel: 400—1743—Borden Creek.
Mills, John: (1) 400—1744—Persimmon Branch of James; (2) 300—1748—Buffalo.
Mitchell, David: (1) 220—1744—Persimmon Branch; (2) 220—1744—Persimmon Branch.
Mitchell, John: (1) 400—1744—Broad Spring Branch; (2) 400—1746—branch of Buffalo; (3) 386—1756—Buffalo.
Moore, James: (1) 325—1748—northeast side North Branch below mouth of South River; (2) 400—1746—branch of Buffalo; (3) 400—1756—north branch of Buffalo.
Moore, William: 80—1764—Buffalo.
Moore, David: 95—1768—Mary.
Morris (Mores), Hugh: 300—1765—Forks.
Neely, John: 125—1769—James.
Patton, James: (1) 70—1746—branches of James; (2) 150—1748—branches of James; (3) 337—1749—James; (4) 400—1749—James; (5) 60—1749—James; (6) 61—1750—Buffalo adjoining Whitley's land; (7) 50—1750—Buffalo; (8) 140—1750—branch of Buffalo; (9) 104—1750—Cedar; (10) 280—1750—head of Buffalo; (11) 230—1750—Broad Spring of James; (12) 100—1750—Poplar Bottom; (13) 120—1750—McDowell's Meadow Run in Forks; (14) 120—1750—head of Cedar; (15) 185—1740—Broad Creek in Forks; (16) 170—1750—head branch of Mill Creek; (17) 197—1750—branch of James; (18) 400—1750—adjoining Samuel Walker in Forks; (19) 220—1750—Poage's Draft; (20) 207—1750—branch of Cedar; (21) 220—1750—Forks; (22) 115—1750—north side James; (23) 100—1750—branch of Buffalo.
Poage, John: 214—1749—Poage's farm on west branch of Cedar.
Poage, Robert: (1) 950—1750—Mill Creek; (2) 218—1761—Cedar.
Poage, William: 100—1763—branch of Cedar.
Porter, Samuel: 300—1748—below the forks of Buffalo.
Porter, William: 107—1755—south side North Branch where it runs through the mountains from the Calfpasture.
Preston, William: 32—1761—north side James.
Rhea (Rea), Elizabeth: 98—1766—North Branch.
Stuart, David: 50—1764—Halfway Creek.
Renick, Robert: (1) 300—1749—Timber Plain on a head branch of Cedar; (2) 90—1756—Purgatory Creek.
Reynolds, Richard: 300—1765—east side North Branch.
Robinson, Isabella: 280—1769—Forks.
Rowland, Robert: (1) 241—1755—James; (2) 113—1755—James.
Rusk, John: 100—1751—northwest side Borden's big survey.
Salling, John P. (1) 400—1746 (1741?)—east side North Branch; (2) 170—1748—east side North Branch.
Sayers, James: 100—1760—east side Buffalo.
Sharp, Edward: 335—1760—Cedar.
Smiley, Walter: 104—1769—James.
Steele, Samuel: 150—1768—Halfway Creek.
Stephenson, John: (1) 262—1748—branch of Buffalo; (2) 180—1759—Borden Creek.
Stuart, David: 50—1764—Halfway Creek.

Stuart, Thomas: 145—1760—Forks.
Tarr, George Peter: 150—1760—North Branch.
Taylor, Isaac: 181—1756—James.
Taylor, John: (1) 124—1766—south side James; (2) 75—1766—south side James; (3) 4—1769—north side James.
Thimble, James: (1) 400—1760—Forks; (2) 95—1766—west side Camp Mountain; (3) 230—1766—Forks; (4) 188—1769—Buffalo.
Trimble, David: 399—1765—Forks.
Walker, James: 130—1765—adjoining Borden tract on west side.
Walker, Alexander: 154—1769—Broad Creek of James.
Whitley, Paul: (1) 400—1746—branch of James; (2) 34—1763—Buffalo.
Whitley, Solomon: 100—1759—branch of Buffalo.
Wiley, (Willey), John: (1) 170—1760—branch of Buffalo; (2) 70—1765—Buffalo.
Williams, Thomas: (1) 400—1749—Forks; (2) 65—1749—opposite Anne Salling's hill; (3) 128—1749—Poplar Spring, a branch of North River.
Williamson, David: 348—1754—Halfway Creek on southeast side Borden tract and adjoining David Mitchell.
Wilson, George, and Matthew Reed: 50—1769—Forks, adjoining Edward McGee's survey.
Wood, James: 400—1746—both sides Buffalo.
Woods, Richard: 200—1756—north branch of Collier.
Young, Robert: (1) 400—1740—on a branch of Buffalo; (2) 112—1749—Forks.

SECTION IV

SECONDARY LAND CONVEYANCES PRIOR TO 1778

LIST A

(RECORDED IN AUGUSTA COUNTY)

In the record of each transaction, the following particulars are given in consecutive order: name of grantor, name of grantee, acreage, price, year of sale, and description. For an explanation of Virginia currency, see Section II.

Allison, Robert—to Joseph Paxton—285—30p—1748—opposite Narrows.

Allison, John (Janet)—to Charles Allison—195—25p—1765—Mill Cr., corner to John Gilmore.

Anderson, Samuel of West Nottingham, Chester County, Penn.—to John Moore—304 27-32—75p—1753—(formerly sold by Moore to Anderson).

Anderson, William (Elizabeth)—to John Dealy—400—200p—1765—North River.

Armstrong, John and Robert, of Greenville county, S. C.,—to John Moore—180—770—1767—Broad Cr.

Arnold, Stephen (Jane)—to John Poage—335—5p—1755—Taylor's Br. of Buffalo.

Arnold, Stephen (Jane)—to George Campbell—120—40—1766—"at the Cove," James River.

Bailey, James—to Benjamin Bennett, blacksmith—175—40p—1761—adjoining Samuel McDowell.

Bennett, Benjamin—to John McNutt—175—43p—1762.

Bennett, Benjamin—to Isaac Ward—320—48p—1767—adjoining William Fowler.

Berrisford, John (Mary)—to James Edmondson—416—15p—1755—adjoining Samuel McDowell.

Berry, Thomas (Esther)—to James Berry (son)—168—25p—1763—Kennedy's Mill Cr.

Berry, William—to Thomas Berry—65—10p 5s—1753—Moffett Cr.

Berry, William (Jane)—to John Trotter—210—?—1764—Moffett Cr., adjoining William Clark.

Berry, John—to William Berry—427—100p—1764.

Breckenridge, Robert—to James Simpson—242—35p—1758—Buffalo, opposite "long bent."

Brown, William and Robert—to Robert Campbell—220—30p—1751—corner to John Anderson.

Buchanan, Matthew (Martha)—to James Wilson—711—161p 5s—1764.

Buchanan, Robert (Mary)—to William Alexander—208—100p—1765.

Burton, Richard (Ann), gentleman—to James Davis—400—40p—Buffalo adjacent to Borden line.

Burton, Richard—to Sampson Mathews—400—47p—1762—James River.

Campbell, William (Sarah) and Robert (Margaret) Gay—to Thomas Gillom—200 of Campbell and Gay homestead—20p—1751—Calfpasture.

Campbell, James (Elizabeth)—to James Crawford—181—18p—1756—North River adjoining Robert McElheny.

Campbell, George (Agnes)—to Arthur McClure—190—130p—Woods Cr.

Campbell, Robert—to Charles Campbell—220—20p—1765—corner to Robert Erwin.

Campbell, John (Mary)—to John Carlile—202 of where Jacob Clements lived—75p—1768.

Campbell, James (Elizabeth)—to James Crawford—181—18p—1756—North River corner to Robert McElheny.
Campbell, James (Elizabeth)—to Charles Kirkpatrick—250—92p—1768—corner to Patrick Young.
Campbell, James (Lettice)—to Moses Bennett—64—28p—1769—North River.
Campbell, Charles—to Joseph Walker—188—135p—1769—Woods Cr.
Campbell, Samuel—to William Lockridge—208 of 308—114p—1769—Calfpasture.
Carlile, James—to James Callison—275—30p—1750—Little Calfpasture.
Carlile, John (Mary)—to Thomas Adams—200—117p—10s—1766—Calfpasture.
Carmichael, John (by Richard Buchanan)—to William Burks—100—?—1756—between Thomas Lewis and Richard Burton. Carmichael in Roane County, N. C.
Carr, James—to John Beaty—235—28p—1751—Broad Cr. of Buffalo.
Carr, John (Ann)—to Francis Beaty—336—60p—1753—near head of Kennedy's Mill Cr., and adjancent to David Kerr and Robert Gray.
Caruthers, William—to John White—187—30p—1753—adjoining John Gray, deceased.
Caruthers, William—to Nathan Peoples—187½—30p—1753.
Caruthers, William—to John White—10—1p—1755.
Caruthers, William (Margaret)—to John Mackey—361—115p—1756—corner to John White.
Chamberlain, Jeremiah of York County, Penn.—to John Neely—400—26p—1751—James River.
Clements, Jacob (Mary)—to John Campbell—202 of homestead—20p—1751—Calfpasture.
Cloyd, David (Margaret)—to James Cloyd—400—20p—1760—head of north branch of James.
Cloyd, David, Sr.—to David Cloyd, Jr.—400—20p—1761—south branch of Cedar.
Cloyd, David—to Michael Cloyd—400 and 262—15p—1761—Persimmon Br.
Cochran, Peter (Margaret)—to James McAfee—32—40p—1765—N side James.
Collier, John (Sisly) :—(1) to William Hall—212—6p—1750—on a branch of Buffalo; (2) to John Summers—44 (of patent for 277 acres, 1756)—8p—1759; (3) to Robert Huston—95 of above patent—25p—1760—Collier's Cr. (4) to Moses Collier—106—5p—1764.
Cunningham, James—to Jacob Cunningham—100 (patent of 1745)—5p—1753—Kerr's Cr.
Cunningham, William (Gennet)—to Charles Kirkpatrick—90—14p—1755—head of Moffett.
Cunningham, James, yeoman—to Isaac Cunningham—128 of 400, patented 1745—10p—1756—Kerr's Cr., corner to William Gilmore.
Cunningham, John and Robert Weir—to Hugh Weir—333—100p—1763—adjoining James Eakin and William McCanless.
Cunningham, Hugh—to Jonathan Cunningham—281—5p—Kerr's Cr., adjoining John Carr.
Cunningham, Patrick—to Edward Erwin—230—80p—1766—Thorny Br.
Cunningham, Hugh (Sarah) of Botetourt—to John McKee—281—300p—1770—"Kerr's formerly called Teaze's Creek, where Jonathan, deceased son of Hugh, formerly lived."
Davis, John (Judith)—to George Berry—198—135p—1762—corner to John McPheeters and on line of James Young, deceased.
Davis, John of Roane County, N. C.—to James Davis—436—62p—1769—Borden line, adjoining William McKee (formerly land of William Todd and Robert Young).

SECONDARY LAND CONVEYANCES PRIOR TO 1778

Davis, James (Jean), gentleman—to John Davis—350—5p—1762—Borden line at head of Buffalo.

Davis, John and Sarah (relict of Nathaniel)—to Moses Cavet—115, patented 1763—35p—1765—Buffalo Cr. „

Davis, William of Mecklenburg County, N. C.—to Morris O'Friel—160, patented 1756—5s—1768—Bell's Spring Run.

Davis, John—to Joseph Davis—350—10p—1769—head of branch of Buffalo.

Davis, John—to Samuel Davis—400—10p—1769—Buffalo adjoining Borden line.

Davison, John (Jean)—to William Henderson—350—30p—1747—mouth of Buffalo.

Dickenson, John (Martha)—to William Thompson—168—60p—1767—Calfpasture and Davis' Mill Cr. adjoining William Jameson.

Doughat (Douthat), Mary—to John Mackee—170—40p—1750.

Dryden, James—to David Dryden—144—50p—1765—below fork in Buffalo.

Dunlap, David—to Hugh Beard—170—29p—1757—adjoining John Cunningham and William Lockridge.

Dunlap, John—to Robert—295 of 625—100p—1761—Calfpasture.

Eakin, John—to James—261—120p—1768.

Edmondson, John (Margaret): (1) to John Stewart—132—50p—1765; (2) to John Berry—170—5p—1765.

Edmondson, James (Agnes)—to James Welch—140 of homestead—53p 15s—1764.

Elliott, Archibald—to Archibald Armstrong—213—55p—1755—Little Calfpasture.

Evans, Nathaniel—to James Hay—100—4p—1765—South River.

Evans, Nathaniel (Mary): (1) to John Hays—161, patented 1759—15p—1761—"South River alias river Mary"; (2) to Thomas Paxton—190—100p—North River.

Finney, Michael (Catharine): (1) to John Collier—106—5p—1759; (2) to Samuel Moore—335 of 700, homestead—38p—1761; (3) to William Foster—365—20p—1764—corner to Samuel Moore and Samuel McClure; (4) to James Bailey—330—31p—1764; (5) to John Taylor—320—35p—1764.

Fuller, Francis (Elenor)—to Alexander Hamilton—271—90p 10s—1766—Little Calfpasture.

Gabbart, Jacob (Barbara)—to Frederick Hanger—255, bought of McNabb—60p—1769.

Gay, James—to David Martin—354—116p 10s—1763—Little Calfpasture, adjoining William Gay and William Elliott.

Gay, Henry (Martha)—to James Frazier—100—10p—1769—Calfpasture, adjoining Francis Donally.

Gibson, George (Isabella)—to James Gilmore, Jr.—200—150p—1768—north branch of Collier.

Gilmore, James—to James Todd—185—77p—1756.

Gilmore, John, Sr.—to William Gilmore—250 of 500—10p—1758—Kerr's.

Gilmore, John, oldest son of John, deceased—to Thomas Gilmore—200—5p—1760—"Tees alias Carr's Creek."

Graham, Robert—to John Graham—307—20p—1754—Little Calfpasture.

Graham, Jane, executor of Robert—to Lancelot Graham—307—82p—1763—Little Calfpasture.

Graham, John: (1) to James Graham (son) 150 of 696—5p—1763—Calfpasture; (2) to Robert (son)—128 of 696—5p—1763—Calfpasture; |3) to John (son)—28 of 696—5p—1763—Calfpasture.

Gray, Samuel (Agnes)—to Joseph Reed—241—20p—1765—adjoining William Caruthers.

Greenlee, John, eldest son of James, deceased: (1) to James Greenlee, Jr.—250, patented 1745—25p—1763; (2) to David Greenlee—400, patented by Thomas Williams, 1749—10p—1763; (3) to Samuel Greenlee—200—50p—1763—adjoining James and Ephraim McDowell.

Gwin, Robert, Jr.—to Joseph (brother)—120 of 544—5p—1762—Calfpasture.

Hadley, Jeremiah, of Orange County, N. C.—to John Reed—215, patented by James Patton—42p 10s—1762—N. side James.

Hall, William (Jean): (1) to Andrew Hall—280—100p—1758; (2) to Andrew Hall—110 and mill—50p—Whistle Cr., where James Young formerly lived.

Hall, William (Margaret) of N. C.—to James Davis—212—40p—1759—Buffalo adjoining John Collier.

Hall, William, Sr.—to William Hall(son)—175 of 500 and 390, patented 1765—20p—1766—Cedar.

Hall, William—to William Logan—300—50p—1768.

Hall, William (Jenny)—to John Hall—415—10p—1768—Cedar.

Hall, James (Agnes)—to John Lusk—100—90p—1767—South River.

Hamilton, John, of Newcastle, County, Penn.—to John Lowry—300—35p—1749—North River.

Hamilton, William (Elsie)—to Alexander Hamilton—107—100p—1767—Calfpasture.

Hamilton, Alexander (Margaret)—to John Stephenson—271—90p—1766—Little Calfpasture.

Hays, Andrew: (1) to Henry Miller—231—5p—1762—Moffett Cr. (2) to William Miller—337—30p—1765.

Hays, Andrew (Margaret)—to John Miscampbell (McCampbell)—250—50p—1765.

Hays, Charles (Barbara)—(1) to John Hays—160—20p—1765; (2) to Andrew Hays—90—10p—1765—adjoining James Anderson; (3) to John Hays—160—20p—1765.

Hays, Patrick (Frances)—to Hugh Hays—400—100p—1765—corner to Robert Alexander.

Henderson, George—to Hugh Wardlow—284—60p—1762—Moffett Cr., corner to John Roseman.

Henderson, William (Susanna)—to Nathaniel Evans—350—?—1761—North River.

Henry, James (Mary)—to Robert Buchanan—508—32p—1762—corner to Robert Telford.

Hodge, Samuel (Elizabeth)—to William Kinkead—350 of 700, patented by William Beverly, 1743—20p—1765—Calfpasture.

Houston, William—to Samuel Houston—283—30p—1749.

Houston, John—to William Robinson—198—46p—1752—corner to Robert Kirkpatrick.

Houston, Robert—to Samuel McDowell, John McClung, John Lyle, William Alexander, John Tomson, trustees of Timber Ridge meeting-house—1 9-160—5s—Nov. 21, 1759.

Houston, James (Agnes)—to Henry Larkin—120—30p—1765.

Hutson, William and John Cloyd, of Chester County, Penn., by David Henderson—to William Henderson—350—60p—1753—Buffalo.

Hutton, James (Ally)—to David Wallace—84, formerly William Todd's—65p 10s—1765—Buffalo.

Johnston, John (Mary)—to Archibald Elliott—213—5p—1765—Little Calfpasture.

Jones, John (Elizabeth)—to Daniel Young—260—11p 5s—1764—Snodon's Spring.

Kelly, William—to Anthony Kelly—95—5p—1765—corner to James Moore.

Kelly, John—to William Hill—105—27p—1767—Hays Cr.

Kennedy, Joseph—(1) to John Roseman—230⅛—45p 10s—1752—Moffett Cr. (2) to trustees New Providence meeting house—3 59-80—good will—Aug. 21, 1754; (3) to Matthew Buchanan—711—80p—1755—adjoining Samuel Houston; (4) to James Wardlaw—236—100p—1761; (5) to James Wardlaw—231—100p—1765—corner to Hugh Wardlaw.

Kennedy, Arthur (Jane)—to Thomas Berry—168, purchased of David Kerr—6p 12½s—1755—Kennedy's Mill Cr., adjoining Robert Gray.

Kennedy, William—to William Clark—402—120p—1761.

Kennedy, James—to James McNutt—118½—20p—1763—Nut Cr.

Kerr, David (Katrine)—to Robert Gray—200 of 368—5s—1753—McNutt Mill Cr. adjoining John Kerr and Joseph Kennedy.

Kinkead, Robert (Leona)—to Andrew Lockridge—159½ of 334—30p—1767.

Kinkead, John of Penn.—to Samuel Griffin—230½—250p—1769—Calfpasture adjoining James Campbell and Andrew Hamilton.

Kirkham, Jean and Elizabeth (by Joseph Lapsley, guardian)—to William Cleghorn—30—5s—1757—S side James.

Lewis, Thomas—to William Crawford—370, patented 1753—48p—1761—between first and second runs in Forks.

Lockridge, James (Isabella)—to Moses McElvain—260—50p—1763—Calfpasture.

Lockridge, James—to Andrew (son)—283—20p—1764—Calfpasture.

Lockridge, James of Greenville County, S. C., by John Poage—to John Dickenson—168—50p—1767—Calfpasture.

Lockridge, Robert (Rebecca)—to David and John Kinkead of Albemarle—520—90p—1764—Calfpasture.

Logan, Alexander (Rachael)—to James Kennedy—237—35p—1763—Kennedy's Mill Cr.

Long, Joseph—to Samuel Gibson—50—?—1755—Buffalo.

Long, Samuel—(1) to John Long—15—100p—1764; (2) to Henry Long—200—100p—1764; to James Long—185—5s—1764.

Lusk, William—to Hugh Lusk—220, patented 1759—5s—1761—Buffalo.

Lusk, William (Elizabeth)—to Robert Breckenridge—400—100p—1762—James River.

Lyle, John's executors—to James Greenlee—203—94p—1757—NW side of Timber Ridge.

Lyle, John—to James McKee—210—35p—1758—corner to James Gray.

Mackey, John—to James McClung—390—120p—1762—Mill Cr.

Martin, Hugh—(1) to Francis McCown—227—60p—1751—Kerr's Cr. (2) to Charles Hays—250—55p—1752—Back Cr. (3) to Andrew Hays—250—30p 10s—1754—Back Cr.

Martin, William (Jenet)—to John Davis—198—110p—1760—adjoining James McPheeters (formerly James Young's place) and Robert Campbell.

Mathews, John, yeoman—to William Caruthers, yeoman—297 9-16—65p—1748—Timber Ridge.

Mathews, John (Ann)—(1) to John Berrisford—296—25p—1750—NW side North River, opposite Philip Weaver's Bottom; (2) to Richard Mathews—300—10p—1756—Mill Cr. (3) to George Mathews—300—10p—1765—Mill Cr.

Mathews, John's executors—to William McBride—306—?—1767—corner to John Mathews.

Mathews, Sampson—(1) to John Mathews—180—5p—1754—E side North River corner to Henry Fuller; (2) to John Bowen—400—47p—1762—James River; (3) to Patrick McCollum—350—130p—1763—Borden Cr. near patent line.

Mathews, George—to James Wilson—300 of 1600, patented by John Mathews—130p—1766—Mill Cr.

Mathews, Archer—to William Mathews—299, willed to Archer—100p—1768—Mill Cr.

Maxwell, John (Mary)—to John Mathews, Jr.—381—100p—1753—Mill Cr.

McBride, William (Martha)—to Edward Erwin—352, part of larger tract—50p—1769.

McCarroll, James—to John Jones—260—12p—1761—Snodon's Spring.

McClenachan, Robert—to Robert Breckenridge—242—5p—1753—S side Buffalo at "Whiskey Hill opposite long bent."

McClung, William—to John McClung—260—10p—1759.

McClung, James (Mary)—(1) to Henry McClung—150 of 393 (homestead)—60p—1765; (2) to William McClung—212—50p—1765—Mill Cr.

McClure, John (Catharine)—to Nathan McClure—4½ of homestead—2p—1751—E side North River.

McClure, John (Mary)—(1) to Moses McClure—325—250p—1764—South River; (2) to Alexander McClure—11—10p—1764—James River; (3) to John Davis—100, formerly Robert Armstrong's deceased—43p—1766.

McClure, John—to Samuel McClure—90—80p—1769.

McClure, Samuel (Mary) (1) to John Paxton—50—25p—1752; (2) to James Campbell—232—160p—1760; (3) to James Gilmore—190—100p—1760; (4) to William McClure—274—100p—1769.

McClure, Moses (Isabel)—to Samuel Paxton—165—30p—1753—Spreading Springs.

McClure, Nathan—to Alexander—166½—38p—1756—corner to Francis Allison, North River.

McClure, Alexander (Susanna)—to Thomas Dryden—163—38p—1756—North River.

McClure, Alexander—to John Allison—370—130p—1761—North River.

McColgan, Edward (Marian)—to Hugh McFadden—300—68p—1765.

McColm (McCollom), Patrick—to John McCollom—168 of homestead—20p—1767.

McCown, Francis, yeoman—(1) to Hugh Martin—227 of 728—15p—1746—Kerr's Cr. (2) to Robert Erwin—200 of 728—12p—1746—Kerr's Cr. (3) to Samuel Norwood, yeoman—300 of 728—90p—1746—Kerr's Cr. (4) to Andrew Steele—10 59-80—3p—1749; (5) to Robert Hamilton, late of this county—237 of 728—112p—1753—Kerr's Cr.

McCown, Francis (Margaret)—(1) to John Maxwell—250—65p—1755—Timber Plain on Cedar Cr. (2) to Andrew Duncan—317—140p—1757—Moffett Cr.

McCown, James—to Francis McCown—400—100p—1752—on a timber ridge, S side of North River.

McCown, James (Margaret)—to William Buchanan—370—90p—1759.

McCown, Malcolm, Jr.—to Samuel Wilson—150½—100p—1769—Whistle Cr.

McCroskey, John, Sr. (1) to Samuel McCroskey—440—50p—1754—corner to David Lyle; (2) to David—300—50p—1754.

McCutchen, Samuel (Frances)—to James Shields, cordwinder—298½—18p 5s—1746—Moffett Cr.

McCutchen, William—(1) to Thomas Meek—310 of 895—40p—1755—Little Calfpasture; (2) to Joans Henderson—314 of 585, patented by Beverly—80p—1761—Smith's Cr. of Little Calfpasture; (3) to Francis Fulton—271 of 585—62p 10s—1761.

McDowell, Rev. Alexander, of Newcastle County, Penn.—to William McRorey—350—10p—1751—South River.

McDowell, James—to Joseph Lapsley—400—35p—1752.

McDowell, James (Elizabeth)—to John Bowyer—400—300p—1762; (2) to James Templeton—300—250p—1767—Big Spring, a branch of James.

McDowell, James (Frances)—to Thomas Paxton—400, patented 1743—250p.

McDowell, James of James City County—to John Berry—120—52p 10s—1768—S side James opposite mouth of Cedar.

McDowell, Samuel (Mary)—(1) to James McGavock—400, patented 1747—60p—1757—Cedar Cr. (2) to James McDowell—400—100p—1757; Big Spring, a branch of North

River; (3) to James McDowell—400—100p—1757; (4) to Walter Smiley—200—5s—1761 —South River; (5) to Samuel McClure—400, patented 1741—45p—1762; (6) to James Welch—200, patented 1741—10p—1761—Poke Bill Run, a branch of South River; (7) to Christian Vineyard—300, patented, 1742, by John McDowell—60p—1765; (8) to James Edmondson—178—10p—1768.

McDowell, Samuel—to John and Robert Moffett—340, patented 1751—20p—1764—corner Lawrence Morren.

McGee (McKee?), William (Jane)—to William McDowell—158—60p—1769—on Borden line between Timber Ridge and Smith Cr.

McKorey (McCrory?), William (Margaret)—to Andrew Reed—175 of 350, patented, 1745, by Alexander McDowell—34p—1752.

McMachan, John—to John Berry—427—105p—1762—bought by McMachan of William Davis (1).

McNabb, John—(1) to Baptist McNabb—218—70p 5s 16d—1750—Mill Cr., (2) to Samuel Lyle—101—5p—1751.

McNabb, Andrew to John Gilmore—138—5s—1751—Back Cr., a branch of Kerr's and adjoining Borden's line.

McNair (or McEnaire), Daniel, gentleman—to James Trimble—400—22p 10s—1746—Borden's Cr.

McNair, Daniel—to James Sayers—147 of 400, patented 1750—80p—1756—adjoining Thomas Gardner and Alexander Gibson.

McPheeters, John—to William Martin—190 of homestead—25p—1754—adjoining James Young and James Berry.

Meek, Thomas—to James Risk—200—10p—1760.

Miles, James—to William Morrow—201 sold by Robert Renick—26p 3s—1753—Buffalo.

Mills, John—to David Cloyd—400—20p—1748—Persimmon Br.

Miller, Henry (Elener)—to Andrew Hays—231—550—1765—forks of Walker's Cr.

Millican, Charles of Orange County, N. C., John Buchanan—to John McClelon—297 —?—1761—James River.

Millican, Charles—to John McClelon—60, bought of James Patton—65p—1761.

Milliron, Christian Godfrey (Mary)—(1) to James Bailey—16 of homestead—5p 10s—1767; (2) to Joseph Cooper—124—50p—1768—North River.

Mitchell, John—to William (Margaret) Mitchell—400—40p—1746—Borden line.

Mitchell, John—to John McCollom—119—10p—1764—Buffalo.

Mitchell, William (Margaret)—(1) to James McClung—200—16p—1748—South River (2) to Thomas Wilson—400, patented 1744—135p—1752—Broad Spring Br. on Borden line.

Mitchell, David, yeoman—to Thomas McFerran, son of John—200—15p—1753—Persimmon Br.

Montgomery, John: (1) to Samuel Houston—2 43-160—1p 10s—1758; (2) to James Houston—?—40p—1761—adjoining Matthew Houston; (3) to Matthew Houston—1 107-160—10p—1768.

Moore, James (Jean)—(1) to Alexander McClure—163 (Morris homestead)—38p—1751 —E side North River, "where Francis Allison now liveth"; (2) to John Moore—136—50p—1762—Hays Cr.

Moore, William—to Francis Smith—275—30p—1763—James River.

Moore, John—to Charles Campbell—230—60p—1764.

Neely, James—to Alexander Ingram—245—60p—1752.

Nichols, John of Frederick County, Va., by John Hardin—to Robert Alexander and David Telford—500—30p—1757.
Norwood, Samuel—to John Gilmore—300 of 728—?—1746.
Norwood, Samuel (Elizabeth)—to Robert McElhany, blacksmith—400—150p—1765—Kerr's Cr.
Park, John (Rebecca)—to William Kennedy—143—100p—1764—South River.
Patrick, William (Mary Chittum)—to William McElhany—214—53p—1761—adjoining Robert Penick.
Patterson, Erwin—to John Maxwell—381—35p—1750—between Mill Cr., and Ann Sally's Hill.
Patton, James—(1) to John Poage—283—30p—1750—branches of James (2) to Edward McDonald—140—7p—1753—Buffalo; (3) to Maurice O'Freel—400, patented 1750—10p—1753—adjoining Samuel Walker.
Paxton, Thomas, Jr.—to John Robinson—160—4p—1751.
Paxton, Thomas (Rebecca)—(1) to Matthew Robinson—210—40p—1763—South River; corner Moses McClure (2) to James and Samuel McDowell and James Cowden—378—52p—1769; (3) to James McCampbell—396—80p—1767.
Paxton, Thomas (Elizabeth)—to John Paxton—230—100p—1768—S side James.
Paxton, Samuel's executors—to John Allison—165—52p—1763—North River at Spreading Spring.
Parris, William, weaver—to John McMachan, of Frederick county, Va.—427—86p—1753.
Poage, John (Mary)—to William Cleghorn, blacksmith—214—17p—1752—1753.
Poage, John (Elizabeth)—to James Gilmore—285—30p—1755—head of Mill Cr.
Poage, John—(1) to Robert—190—100p—1765—Buffalo; (2) to John, Jr.—270—100p—1765—Buffalo.
Poage, Robert (Elizabeth)—(1) to Robert, Jr.—104—5p—1753—Cedar; (2) to John Allison—195—50p—1754—Mill Cr., a branch of James; (3) to John Poage—200—25p—1754—Mill Cr., corner to John Mathews; (4) to John Mathews—194—30p—1755—Mill Cr.
Poage, Robert—to John Bailey—250, patented 1760—50p—1761—Cedar Run, a branch of North River.
Poage, Robert (Jean)—to William—104—60p—1762—Cedar Cr.
Porter, Samuel, schoolmaster, of Lancaster County, Penn., by John Mitchell—to James Dryden—300—25p—1765—below forks of Buffalo.
Pritchard, James (Abigail) of Orange County, N. C.—to Joseph Borden—1000—90p—1761.
Ramsey, John (Mary)—to John Gilmore, Jr.—220 of 400—145p—1767—James River; (2) to John White—180—100p—1768—corner to James Gilmore, James River.
Ramsay, William (Jane)—to Moses Moore—582—210p—1767—Little Calfpasture.
Renick, Robert, yeoman—(1) to James Miles—201 of homestead—10p—1747—Buffalo; (2) to Francis McCown—300—5s—1751—Timber Plain at head of Cedar.
Reas, Elizabeth—to Henry Larkin—98—30p—1768—North River, corner to John Harger and Alexander Baggs.
Reigh, William—to Archibald Reigh—230—100p—1769.
Robinson, George—to David Robinson—400, patented 1746—80p—1749—Buffalo.
Robinson, William—to Patrick Denny—80—51p—1765—Cunningham's Br. between North Mountain and House Mountain.
Robinson, John (Margery)—to William Caruthers—160, sold by Thomas Paxton—43p 1756.
Roseman, John (Sarah)—to Robert Gay—380—100p—1765—Moffett Cr.
Russell, William—to John Ramsay—400—55p—1749.

Salling, John Peter (Ann)—to Henry (Catharine) Fulton—130—20p—1751—E side North River; (2) to Sampson Mathews—180—24p—1754—adjoining Fulton.

Salling, John Peter—to Joseph (Mary Elizabeth) Burton—200—100p—1754—adjoining Fulton.

Salling, George Adam, of Cumberland County, N. C.. and John Salling of Orange County, N. C.—to John Paxton—200 of 400, patented, 1741 (?) by John P. Salling, deceased—120p—1760—"first fork of James."

Salling, George Adam, of Orange County, N. C.—to George Salling, of Augusta—200—170p—1762.

Salling, George Adam Salling and Joseph (Mary E.) Burton—to Thomas Paxton, millwright—200—180p—1764—E side North River.

Scott, John (Catharine) and William (Mary) Davis—to William McCutchen—200—105p—1765—corner to Hays.

Sharp, Edward—to Robert Whitly—335, patented 1761—5p—1768—Cedar.

Shields, John—to John Davis—320—9p—1756.

Smith, John (Mary)—to Andrew Lockridge—200—80p—1768—Calfpasture.

Smith, William—to Samuel Houston—283—?—1749.

Steele, Andrew—to Samuel Steele (son)—240—60p—1757—**corner to Robert** Henry.

Steele, Samuel (Mary)—to Robert Steele—34—17p—1765.

Stephenson, John—to Henry Kirkham—262—30p—1749.

Stevenson, George (Rebecca)—to Alexander Brown—220, bought of James Patton—35p—1755—Poage's Draft on Borden line.

Stewart, Thomas—to Thomas Jones—145—2p—1761—corner to John Mathews.

Stewart, John (Mary)—to Samuel Steele—148—50p—1765.

Taylor, Isaac, Sr.—to Isaac Taylor, Jr.—70—10p—1765—Purgatory Cr.

Taylor, John (Mary)—to Benjamin Bennett—320—45p—1765.

Todd, Low, of Bedford County—to Hugh Cunningham—251—78p—1768—Whistle Cr. corner to Matthew Young.

Todd, James—(1) to Joseph McBride—185—5p—1761—Buffalo; (2) to James McBride—185—80p—1768—Buffalo.

Todd, William—to Samuel Todd—400—40p—1761—head of north branch of Buffalo.

Todd, Samuel (Jane)—to William and John McKee—400—170p—north branch of Buffalo on Borden line.

Trimble, James (Sarah)—Alexander Beggs—250—25p—1750—Buffalo.

Trimble, James—to Joseph Kennedy—402—133p 10s—1754—Moffett.

Walker, Alexander, planter—to Alexander Walker, wheelwright—7 19-32—3p 15s—1752—Hays Cr.

Walker, James (Mary)—to Hugh Kelso—74 43-160—5p—1763.

Wallace, Peter (Martha)—to Francis McCown—150½—56p—1757—Whistle Cr. corner to Low Todd.

Ward, John—to Joseph Walkup—276—?—1761—head of Grassy Lick Run, Calfpasture.

Ward, Joseph (Jenet)—to John Hay and Elizabeth Ray—220, sold by Andrew Brown, 1753—37p—1766—Poage's Draft on Borden line.

Welch, James (Agnes)—to James Richey—200—100p—1765—"river Mary now known as South River."

White, John, yeoman—to William Caruthers—10—21½s—1755.

White, John (Katherine)—to William Peoples—187½—28p—1761—adjoining Nathaniel Peoples, William Caruthers, James Greenlee.

Whiteside, Moses (Margaret)—to David Gray—109—10p—1762.

Wiley (Willey), John—(1) to Thomas Wilson—70—25p—1766—Buffalo; (2) to Thomas Wilson—170, patented 1760—100p—1765.

Williams, Thomas and Jane—to James Greenlee—400—109p—1752.
Williams, Thomas—to John Mathews, Jr.—65—26p—1753—W side North River opposite Ann Salling's place.
Wilson, George—to Benjamin Watson—173—50p—1754—Broad Cr.
Wilson, John—to William Rhea—600—245p—1767—Elk Cr.
Wilson, Thomas (Elizabeth)—to Nathaniel Wilson—200 of 400—100p—1769—North River.
Wood, James, of Frederick County, Va.—to James Gilmore—400, patented 1746—20p—1752—Buffalo (1).
Woods, Richard (Elizabeth)—to Richard Woods (son-in-law)—195—25p—1757—corner to Borden patent line: (2) to George Gibson—200—?—1758—north branch of Collier.
Woods, Samuel and William—to Benjamin Borden, Jr.—263—100p—1753—Woods Cr.
Woods, Richard—to Peter Wallace—195—60p—1760—Borden line.
Young, Robert—to William Todd—400—32p—1750—north branch of Buffalo.
Young, Robert (Mary)—to John Young—112—5s—1767.
Young, James (Sarah) and Patrick (Isabella) Young—to Andrew Hall—110 with mill—50p—1756—Whistle Cr.
Young, Daniel—to Samuel Beard—260—12p—1764—Snodon's Spring.

LIST B
(Recorded in Botetourt)

Allison, James (Elizabeth)—to Samuel McCorkle—165—95p—1770—North River at Spreading Springs.
Berry, John—to George Dougherty—120—?—1775—opposite mouth of Cedar.
Buchanan, John—to John Sommers—100, patented 1765—15p—1770.
Christian, William (Annie)—to Patrick Henry of Hanover—1000—1000p—1773—both sides James.
Cowarden, John (Margaret)—to William Taylor—200—90p—1772—North River.
Davis, James (Agnes)—(1) to Smith Williams—188—120p—1770—Buffalo adjoining John Collier; (2) to John Collier—24—27p 10s—1770—Buffalo.
Gibson, Samuel—to William Bates—50—50p—?—Buffalo.
Gibson, Samuel (Ruth)—to Joseph Gibson (son)—70—30p—1773.
Little, David—to Joseph Snodgrass—260—150p—1770.
Long, Joseph, Jr.—to Michael Kirkham—94 of 400—80p—1770—Buffalo—willed by Joseph Long, Sr., to Joseph Long, Jr., and John Long.
McAdams (McEdams), Joseph (Mary)—to John Ward—96—27p 12s—1777—Elk Cr.
McBride, William (Martha)—to John (Margaret) Cowarden—154—100p—1771.
McClenachan, William (Sarah)—to Hugh Barclay—204—500p—conveyed to McClenachan by William Poage.
McCorkle. Alexander—to Elizabeth McIntosh—80—10p—1770.
Patton, James's executors—to James Lawrence, Jr.—150—76p 5s 6d—1770.
Renick, William (Sarah) (1) to James Gilmore—173—75p—1771—sold to Renick by Benjamin Watson; (2) to Henry Cartmill—90—40p—1771—Purgatory; (3) to Henry Cartmill—210—60p—1772.
Sharp, Edward's executors—to Joseph Jenkins—144—72p—18s—1770—Big Meadows.
Summers, John (Isabel)—to Mathias Cleek—100—30p—1774.
Walker, Alexander—to William Crawford—154—12p—1765—Broad Cr.
Wallace, Peter (Martha)—to Andrew Wallace—170—150p—1775.
Watson, Benjamin—to William Renick—173—75p—1770—sold to Watson by George Wilson, 1754.
Wiley, John (Elizabeth)—to Samuel Davis—280—110p—?—head of Buffalo.

SECTION V

TITHABLES OF 1778

When there is more than one tithable in a home the number follows the name.

Abit, Thomas
Alexander, Archibald
Alexander, Joseph—2
Alexander, Samuel
Alexander, Thomas
Alexander, William—5
Alexander, William
Allen, Benjamin—2
Allen, Hugh—3
Allen, James—2
Allen, John—2
Allen, Thomas
Allet, James—2
Allet, William
Allison, John—2
Altizer, Emorick
Anderson, Isaac—5
Angelly, Peter
Arnold, James
Arnold, Stephen
Bagg, Alexander—2
Bailey, James
Bambridge, James
Barclay, Hugh—2
Barclay, Hugh
Barclay, John
Barty, James
Beach, Waldring
Beard, Hugh
Beard, David—2
Beaty, William
Bell, George
Bennett, Benjamin
Berry, William—4
Berryhill, John
Black, Henry
Black, Mary
Black, Robert
Blackburn, Benjamin—4
Blackburn—2
Blair, Daniel
Blair, James
Bogle, Barnabas

Bowen, James
Bowyer, John—9
Boyd, John
Boyl, James
Bradford, Samuel
Brown, Rev. John—5
Brown, Patrick
Brownlow, James
Brush, Bleakly
Buchanan, James—2
Buchanan, James
Buntin, Moses
Buntin, William
Caldwell, George
Caldwell, George—2
Caldwell, Henry—3
Caldwell, Isaac—3
Caldwell, John—4
Caldwell, Joseph
Caldwell, Joseph
Caldwell, Thomas
Caldwell, William—3
Campbell, Charles—2
Campbell, Charles
Campbell, George—2
Carr, Thomas
Carson, John
Caruthers, John
Caruthers, Robert—2
Caruthers, Samuel—4
Caruthers, William
Casady, James
Christian, Israel
Christian, Sampson
Clark, Michael
Cleek, Jacob
Cleek, Mathias
Cleek, Palsor
Cloyd, David—2
Colbrath, Andrew
Collier, Aaron
Collier, Alexander
Collier, Moses

Connor, Dinnis
Cooper, James
Cooper, John
Cooper, William
Cope, Adam
Corbit, James
Coulter, James—2
Coulter, Michael—3
Cowan, Andrew
Cowan, Samuel
Cowan, William
Craig, John
Crawford, James
Crawford, William—3
Crawford, William
Crawford, William
Crocket, Alexander
Crocket, James
Cross, Samuel
Crump, Edmund
Culton, Alexander
Culton, James, Sr.—2
Culton, James, Jr.
Culton, Joseph—4
Culton, Robert, Sr.—3
Cummins, John—2
Cunningham, James—2
Cunningham, Moses
Davidson, Samuel
Davidson, William—2
Davis, Philip
Davison, John
Deal, Alexander
Dever, John
Dick, Abraham
Dick, David
Dillon, James
Dixon, James—2
Donnald, Henry
Donnald, Matthew
Donnald, William
Donally, Henry

Donally, John
Donally, Sarah
Dougherty, George
Dougherty, James
Dougherty, William—2
Dryden, James—2
Dryden, Nathaniel
Dryden, William
Dunlap, John—3
Dunlap, Robert—3
Eakin, Andrew—2
Eakin, James
Eakin, John
Eakin, William
East, Josiah—2
Edminson, David
Edminson, James
Elder, Andrew
Elder, Matthew—2
Elliot, Capt. George
Elliot, Robert
Ewin, Edward
Ewin, Robert—3
Ewin, Robert
Evans, Henry
Evans, John
Evans, Nathaniel
Faris, Robert (constable)
Faris, William
Fletcher, Robert
Foster, William
Francisco, Michael
Frazer, John
Fuller, Daniel
Fuller, Francis—2
Galbrath, Hugh
Gay, Henry—2
Gay, James
Gay, John—4
Gay, John
Gay, Margaret—2
Gay, Robert—2
Gill Pressley
Gill, Richard
Gilmore, James
Gilmore, John, Sr.—2
Gilmore John, Jr.
Gilmore, John
Gilmore, John (colonel)—4

Gilmore, Sarah—2
Goodbar, Joseph
Gooding, Abraham
Goul, George—2
Gordon, James
Gordon, John
Graham, Arthur—2
Graham, Michael
Graham, Rev. William—3
Gray, David (captain)
Green, Joshua
Greenlee, John—3
Greenlee, Mary
Greenlee, Samuel
Greenlee, William
Greer, Alexander
Grigsby, James—6
Guffey, Alexander
Guttery, John
Haddon, Thomas—2
Hair, Henry
Hall, Andrew—2
Hall, James (captain)
Hall, Nathaniel
Hamilton, Archibald
Hamilton, John
Hamilton, Robert
Hamilton, Samuel
Hamilton, William—2
Hamilton, William
Hammon, Thomas
Hannah, Alexander
Hannah, John, Sr.
Hannah, John, Jr.
Harkins, Edward
Harris, James
Harriston, Thomas
Harvey, Daniel
Hays, Andrew—6
Hays, Charles—4
Hays, Charles
Hays, James—3
Hays, John (captain)—2
Hickman, Adam
Hickman, John—2
Hill, Climuel
Hill, John
Hill, Thomas
Hill, Thomas

Hindman, Alexander
Higgens, Peter
Hiram, Frederic
Hodge, James—2
Holdman, William
Houston, Henry
Houston, James—2
Houston, John—3
Houston, John
Houston, Samuel
Houston, William
Howell, Thomas—3
Hoylman, Christopher
Hudson, Thomas
Huphman, Henry
Jack, Alexander
Jack, Samuel
Jack, William
Jamison, George
Jamison, William
Johnson, James
Johnson, Joseph
Johnson, Michael
Johnston, James
Jones, John
Jones, John
Kelly, Anthony
Kelly, George
Kelly, Samuel
Kelso, David
Kelso, Hugh—3
Kelso, Moses
Kelso, Samuel
Kennedy, Ezekiel
Kennedy, James—2
Kennedy, John
Keys, Benjamin
Keys, Roger
Keys, Samuel
Kilpatrick, Charles—3
Kilpatrick, James
Kilpatrick, John
Kilpatrick, John
Kilpatrick, Thomas
Kilpart, Charles—2
Kilpart, John
Kindred, Peter
Kingery, Jacob
Kingery, Peter

TITHABLES OF 1778   367

Kingery, Tobias
Kirkham, Michael
Kirkpatrick, Patrick
Kirkpatrick, Samuel
Koontz, Henry
Lackey, Thomas
Lackey, Thomas
Lackland, Joseph
Laird, David
Laird, William
Lane, James
Lanthron, Reuben
Lapsley, James
Lapsley, Joseph—6
Larkin, John—2
Lawrence, Samuel—2
Lehy, William
Letcher, John—3
Liggett, Alexander—2
Linneen, Cornelius
Little, David
Little, Joseph—2
Lockridge, Robert—2
Logan, David—2
Logan, James—2
Logan, James
Logan, Thomas
Logan, William
Love, James
Lowry, Robert
Lusk, John, Sr.
Lusk, John
Lusk, Samuel
Lusk, William
Lyle, Daniel
Lyle, David—6
Lyle, James, Sr.—3
Lyle, James (D. S.)
Lyle, John (captain)
Lyle, John (skinner)
Lyle, John
Lyle, Robert
Lyle, Samuel—6
Lyle, William
Lyle, Stephen
Mackey, Mary—2
Mackey, Robert
Martin, Jane—2
Mathews, John

Mathews, Richard—2
Maxfield, John
Maxfield, William
Maxwell, James
McBride, Joseph
McCallister, John—2
McCallister, John
McCampbell, Andrew—2
McCampbell, James—3
McCampbell, James
McCampbell, John—2
McCampbell, William, Sr.
McCampbell, William
McCappen, John
McCappen, Robert
McCartney, John
McCaskey, Alexander
McCaskey, David
McCaskey, John, Jr.
McCaskey, Samuel
McChesney, Samuel
McChesney, Walter
McClain, John
McClung, Henry—2
McClung, James, Sr.
McClung, James—2
McClung, James
McClung, John—2
McClung, William, Sr.
McClung, William
McClure, Alexander—3
McClure, Alexander, Jr.
McClure, Arthur—3
McClure, Daniel
McClure, Halbert
McClure, James—2
McClure, John
McClure, John
McClure, John
McClure, Moses
McClure, Samuel—3
McClure, William—2
McCollum, John—2
McCollum, Patrick—4
McConnell, John
McConnell, Patrick
McCorkle, John
McCorkle, Samuel
McCorkle, William

McCowan, James
McCowan, Joseph
McCown, James
McCown, James
McCown, John, Sr.—2
McCown, John, Jr.
McCown, John
McCown, Malcolm
McCrary, James—2
McCrary, James
McCrary, Joseph
McCurdy, Archibald
McCurdy, Henry
McDowell, Elizabeth
McDowell, Samuel (colonel)
McElhany, William—2
McElroy, William
McEntosh, John
McFaddin, Hugh
McGavock, William
McGee, Richard
McKee, James
McKee, John—3
McKee, John—3
McKee, Robert
McKee, William—2
McKee, William
McKeharry, Robert—3
McKemy, Alexander
McKemy, James
McKemy, John
McKemy, Robert—2
McKemy, Samuel
McKemy, William
McKemy, William, Jr.
McKinney, John
McMath, James
McMath, William
McMullen, John
McNab, Samuel
McNight, John—2
McNight, Timothy
McNutt, Alexander
McNutt, John—2
McSpaden, John
McSpaden, Moses—4
McSpaden, Samuel
McTeer, Samuel
Meath, Christopher

Miller, Henry—2
Miller, Samuel
Milligan, John, Sr.—2
Milligan, John, Jr.
Milligan, William
Mitchell, John—3
Mitchell, John, Jr.
Montgomery, William
Moore, Alexander
Moore, Andrew (captain)
Moore, David
Moore, David
Moore, Hugh
Moore, James
Moore, James
Moore, John, Sr.—3
Moore, John—2
Moore, John, Jr.
Moore, John
Moore, Joseph, Esq.
Moore, Robert—2
Moore, Samuel—2
Moore, Samuel
Moore, William—3
Moore, William—3
Moore, William
Morris, Thomas
Morter, William
Muckleroy, James
Muckleroy, William
Murphy, John
Neely, John
Neely, William
Nesbitt, Samuel
Nevil, Henry
Nowling, John
O'Brian, James—2
O'Diddle, James
Park, John
Parks, James
Patterson, Samuel
Patterson, William—3
Patton, James
Patton, William
Paul, John
Paul, John, Jr.
Paxton, John—2
Paxton, John—6
Paxton, John (captain)—2

Paxton, Samuel—2
Paxton, Samuel
Paxton, Thomas—7
Paxton, Thomas
Paxton, William, Sr.—5
Paxton, William
Peoples, John—3
Peoples, Nathan
Peoples, William
Perkins, John
Pickens, James
Pine, James
Poage, James
Poage, John (captain)—6
Poage, John
Poage, Robert
Pollock, Samuel
Porter, John
Porter, William, Sr.
Porter, William, Jr.—2
Pressley, William, Sr.—2
Pressley, William, Jr.
Ramsay, Samuel
Ramsay, William
Ratliff, Thomas—2
Read, Patrick—2
Reagh, Archibald—2
Reagh, William
Reah, John
Reid, Adam
Reid, Andrew, Esq.—2
Reid, Daniel
Reid, Joseph
Reid, Thomas, Sr.
Reid, Thomas
Reid, William
Right, John
Riley, Barnabas
Riley, John
Richey, David
Richey, James
Richey, John
Roads, Christian
Roberts, Leonard
Robinson, Alexander
Robinson, James
Robinson, John
Robinson, John
Robinson, Matthew

Robinson, Robert—2
Robinson, Thomas
Robinson, William
Rowan, William
Rush, John—2
Russell, William
Saianter (?), William
Sally, George—2
Sea, John
Sea, Martin
Scott, Andrew—2
Scott, David
Scott, James
Scott, John
Scott, Samuel—3
Shaw, Robert—3
Shields, Patrick
Shields, Robert
Skeen, Henry
Skeen, Joseph
Skeen, Robert—3
Skillern, William—2
Smiley, Alexander
Smiley, Alexander
Smiley, Andrew
Smiley, John, Sr.
Smiley, John, Jr.
Smiley, Walter
Smith, James
Smithers, Andrew
Snodgrass, James
Snodgrass, Joseph—2
Something, John
Spear, John
Spence, John
Spencer, Ninian
Sprague, Thomas
Staton, Thomas
Steele, Robert
Steele, Samuel (captain)—2
Steele, Thomas
Stephenson, James
Stephenson, Joseph—2
Stephenson, Robert
Sterrett, Robert—3
Stuart, Alexander
Stuart, John—3
Stuart, Robert (miller)
Tagart, James

Tate, James
Taylor, Andrew
Taylor, David
Taylor, Elizabeth
Taylor, Isaac
Taylor, Isaac
Taylor, James
Taylor, William
Tedford, James, Sr.
Tedford, James
Telford, Alexander, Sr.—2
Telford, Alexander
Telford, David
Telford, George
Telford, Robert, Sr.—2
Telford, Robert
Telford, William
Templeton, James
Templin, Terah
Terry, Stephen
Thompson, Edward
Thompson, John—4
Thompson, John
Thompson, Joseph
Thompson, William
Thornham, Thomas
Todd, James
Todd, John
Todd, Samuel
Todd, William
Tolly, Christian
Townley, James
Trafford, Charles
Trimble, Isaac
Trimble, John—5
Trimble, Moses

Trimble, Moses, Jr.
Vernor, John
Vickers, Riley
Vickery, John
Vineyard, Christian
Walker, Alexander—4
Walker, Alexander
Walker, James, Sr.
Walker, James
Walker, James
Walker, John, Jr.,—2
Walker, John—2
Walker, John—2
Walker, Joseph—
Walker, Samuel
Walker, William
Wallace, James—3
Wallace, John—2
Wallace, John
Wallace, Joseph
Wallace, Peter—3
Wallace, Samuel—3
Wardlaw, James—2
Wardlaw, Robert
Wardlaw, William—3
Welch, James
Welch, John
Whiteside, Moses—2
Whitesto, Stephen
Whitley, James
Whitley, Jonathan—5
Whitley, Solomon—2
Wickenson, Benjamin
Wickenson, Peter
Wiley, Alexander
Wiley, John, Sr.—7

Wilkenson, John
Wilkenson, John
Williams, Richard
Williams, Smith—3
Williamson, Benjamin
Williamson, David
Wilson, Alexander
Wilson, David
Wilson, Ephraim
Wilson, George
Wilson, Hugh
Wilson, James—2
Wilson, John—3
Wilson, John
Wilson, John
Wilson, Nathaniel
Wilson, Samuel—2
Wilson, Samuel
Wilson, Samuel
Wilson, Seth
Wilson, Thomas—4
Wilson, William
Weir, George—2
Weir, Hugh—2
Weir, Hugh
Weir, John
Weir, John
Weir, Joseph
Weir, Samuel
Woods, Jass
Woods, David—2
Woods, Elizabeth—4
Woods, Patrick
Young, Benjamin—3
Young, William
Total—997.

SECTION VI

Taxpayers of 1782

The names which follow are those of the householders of Rockbridge in 1782. T stands for tithable, S for slave, h for horse, and c for cattle. Where there is no mention of tithables there was no more than one in the home. The names of women are those of widows. The personal property lists for the various counties of Virginia were used as a state census in 1782.

Abbot, Thomas—4h—6c
Adair, James—6h—14c
Adair—Sarah—1h
Adair, Thomas—3h—3c
Alexander, Jane—1S—8h—20c
Alexander, Joseph—3S—6h—23c
Alexander, Morris—1S—6h—10c
Alexander, William—11S—10h—38c
Allen, Hugh—5S—11h—3c
Allen, John—6h—26c
Allison, John—2h—6c
Anderson, Isaac—7S—13h—31c
Anderson, James—5S—7h—18c
Anderson, William—no mention
Archibald, Samuel—3h—6c
Bailey, James—6h—14c
Bambridge, James—1h
Barclay, Hugh, Sr.—7S—11h—19c
Barclay, Hugh, Jr.—4S—9h—15c
Barclay, James—3h—5c
Barclay, William—3h—5c
Barnes, George—1h—1c
Beach, Walden—4h—9c
Bean, Robert—6h—10c
Beard, David—4S—9h—18c
Beard, Hugh—1S—8h—23c
Beaty, Arthur—3h—12c
Bennet, Benjamin—5h—9c
Berry, James—1h
Berry, William—2T—2S—8h—25c
Berryhill, John—1S—6h—16c
Black, Henry—4h—15c
Black, Robert—2h—8c
Black, Thomas—5h—11c
Blair, James (1)—2h—4c
Blair, James (2)—1h
Boggs, Alexander—2T—5h—28c
Bogle, James—1h—2c

Bogle, Joseph—2T—3h—11c
Botorpp, Philip—1h—3c
Bousman, Henry—5c
Bowen, James—1h—5c
Bowen, William—4h—4c
Bowyer, John—21S—17h—47c
Boyles, Charles—4h—9c
Bradford, Hugh—6S—7h—11c
Bradford, Samuel—4h—12c
Bradley, William—returned prisoner of war.
Brads, Daniel—1h—2c
Brown, Esther—3h—6c
Brown, George—3h—7c
Brown, Patrick—4h—4c
Brown, William—2S—6h—8c
Bryan, James—2h—5c
Buchanan, Alexander—1h—3c
Buchanan, James—7h—19c
Buchanan, James—4h—6c
Budinot, Ebenezer—1h
Bunton, Moses—5h—6c
Bunton, William—3h—5c
Burgess, Thomas—3h—10c
Byers, William—9S—4h—9c
Caddell, Samuel—1h
Caldwell, George—2S—8h—13c
Caldwell, Joseph—8h—19c
Campbell, Alexander—3T—1S—8h—21c
Campbell, Charles, Esq.—2T—9h—30c
Campbell, George—7h—12c
Campbell, George—6h—17c
Campbell, Henry—2T—4h—15c
Campbell, John—no mention
Campbell, John—4c
Campbell, Joseph, Sr.—2h—4c
Campbell, Joseph, Jr.—3h—11c
Carlock, Caroline—6c

TAXPAYERS OF 1782

Carlock, Catharine—6c
Carson, John—1S
Carson, Robert—2h—3c
Caruthers, Anne—2S—6h—15c
Caruthers, James—1h
Caruthers, John—2S—9h—22c
Caruthers, William—5h—10c
Cashady, James—3h
Cashady, Michael—3h—8c
Cashady, Peter—1h
Chambers, John—2h—9c
Chanby (?), John—2S
Clark, Nicholas—1h
Clark, ——— —4h—18c
Cleek, Jacob—5h—18c
Cleek, Mathias—9h—18c
Cleek, Michael—5h—12c
Cleek, Palser—2h—8c
Cloyd, David—2S—9h—13c
Collier, Aaron—4h—13c
Collier, Moses—4h—6c
Colter, James—3S—8h—15c
Coontz, Henry—4h—12c
Cooper, Elizabeth—1S—4h—9c
Cooper, Jean—4h—10c
Cooper, John—5h—14c
Cooper, Thomas—2h—5c
Cornet, John—2h
Coster, William—no mention
Cowan, Andrew and James—7h—8c
Cowan, Israel—5h
Cowan, Samuel—4h—9c
Cowan, William—3h—8c
Craig, John—4h—10c
Crawford, James—6h—20c
Crawford, William—2h—11c
Crawford, William—5h—8c
Crocker, George—3h—9c
Crocket, James—1S—13h—50c
Crocket, Mary—3S—9h—17c
Croddy, John—3h—11c
Cross, Samuel—8h—15c
Culton, Alexander—2T—15h—26c
Culton, James—6h—13c
Culton, John—2h—7c
Cummings, George—3c
Cummings, John—8h—9c
Cunningham, James—1S—5h—17c
Cunningham, Moses—4h—11c

Cunningham, Thomas—3h—2c
Dalbridge, Robert—1h—4c
Dale, Alexander—2T—10h—17c
Dale, Peter—2h—3c
Davidson, Elizabeth—2T—10h—17c
Davidson, John (Smith)—1h
Davidson, John (Collierstown)—6h—23c
Davidson, Samuel—6h—11c
Davidson, William, Sr.—5h—5c
Davidson, William, Jr.—1h
Davies, Hugh, Sr.—2T—10h—18c
Davies, James—2h—4c
Decker, Isaac—3h—1c
Defries, James—3h—9c
Dickson, James—2T—2h—12c
Dillon, James—2h—7c
Donald, Matthew—7h—14c
Dooley, Valentine—1h
Dougherty, Anthony—3c
Dougherty, James—5h—11c
Dougherty, Thomas—2T—2h—4c
Dougherty, William—4h—9c
Drain, John—3h—1c
Draper, Aaron—1h—3c
Dryden, Agnes—5h—7c
Dryden, James—6h—15c
Dudding, Valentine—1h
Duff, Roger—3h—6c
Dunlap, John—3S—20h—50c
Dunlap, Mary—4S—19h—43c
Eakin, John—1h
Eakin, Samuel—2h—8c
Eakin, William—1h
East, Josiah—2h—4c
Eastham, Robert—9S—4h—9c
Edmundson, David—1S—5h—16c
Edmundson, Joseph—7S—6h—18c
Edmundson, Robert—3h—6c
Elliott, George—2S—6h—12c
Elliott, James—2S—6h—20c
Elliott, Robert—6h—17c
English, Robert—5h—4c
Erwin, Edward—3h—10c
Erwin, Henry—no mention.
Erwin, Robert, Sr.—2T—3S—8h—19c
Erwin, Robert—2h—6c
Erwin, Robert—3h—5c
Ferguson, Peter—4c
Fields, John—2h—3c

Fiemster, John—1h
Finley, John—5h—7c
Fleming, George—1h—4c
Fletcher, Joab—2h—32c
Fletcher, Robert—8h—29c
Frame, John—3h—7c
Frame, William—4h—21c
Frazier, George—3c
Frazier, James—2h—6c
Frazier, John—5h—8c
Fuller, Henry—4h—6c
Fulling, Francis—6h—13c
Gabbart, George—2h—5c
Gabbart, Mathias—8h—18c
Gadberry, John—2h—4c
Galbraith, Agnes—4h—7c
Galbraith, John—3h—4c
Galbraith, James—1h
Garner, John—2h—3c
Gay, Elizabeth—4h—9c
Gay, Henry—2h
Gay, John, Esq.—7S—10h—26c
Gay, John, Jr.—3h—10c
Gay, Martha—1S—2h—9c
Gay, Robert—1S—3h—13c
Gay, Robert—4h—15c
Gay, William—1h
Gayler, Edward—4c
Gibson, James, Esq.—4S—9h—23c
Gibson, William—6h—14c
Gilbert, John—1h—1c
Gill, Pressley—1h
Gill, Richard—2h—3c
Gilmer, James—2T—8S—17h—36c
Gilmer, John, Esq.—3S—9h—19c
Gilmer, John, Jr.—1h
Gilmer, John—4h—7c
Gittens, Evan—no mention
Givens, Thomas—3h—5c
Goodbar, Joseph—3h—12c
Gordon, John—8h—8c
Glasgow, Arthur—3h—7c
Glasgow, Joseph—3h—7c
Glasgow, Robert—2h—5c
Gotted, William—1h—4c
Goul, George—5h—18c
Graham, Arthur—2h—15c
Graham, Rev. William—4S—6h—15c
Grant, John—1h

Gray, David, Esq.—6h—13c
Gray, John—no mention
Gray, William—3h—3c
Gray, William—2h
Greenlee, David—3S—16h—7c
Greenlee, John—8S—10h—36c
Grier, Alexander—1S—5h—16c
Grigsby, James—3T—8S—4h—12c
Grigsby, John—9S—7h—20c
Groves, William—9S—7h—20c
Groves, William—1S—3h—6c
Guffey, Alexander—3h—5c
Guffey, James—7h—3c
Gwin, Morris—1h
Haddon, Dorothy—1h—2c
Haddon, William—4h—13c
Hall, Andrew—1S—8h—13c
Hall, James—1S—5h—12c
Hall, Nathaniel—7h—14c
Hamil, Robert—2h—4c
Hamilton, Agnes—1h—9c
Hamilton, Archibald—1h
Hamilton, James—3h—8c
Hamilton, Robert—3T—4h—24c
Hamilton, William—8h—18c
Hannah, Alexander—6h—9c
Harkins, Edward—3h—9c
Harris, James—4h—6c
Harrison, Thomas—3h—14c
Harvey, Daniel—3h—9c
Hay, David—2h—7c
Hays, Andrew—11S—9h—27c
Hays, Charles—4S—3h—10c
Hays, James—2S—10h—4c
Hays, James—2h—7c
Hays, John—6S—6h—18c—1 two-wheeled carriage
Henderson, Alexander—2T—8h—20c
Henderson, Alexander, Jr.—4h
Henderson, Archibald—3h
Henderson, Joseph—6h—1c
Henderson, William—2h
Hickman, John—2T—3S—8h—22c
Hiers, Henry—5h—4c
Hill, John—2h—8c
Hindman, Alexander—5h—13c
Hodge, Eliner—2h
Hodge, James—6h—27c
Holdman, William—4h—9c

TAXPAYERS OF 1782

Holmes, Gabriel—4h—13c
Houston, James—1S—6h—12c
Houston, John, Esq.—5h—18c
Houston, John—2T—12h—18c
Houston, Mary—1S—3h—9c
Houston, Samuel—1S—4h—4c
Houston, William—3h—12c
How, Edward—2c
Howell, Thomas—5h—16c
Hoylman, Stophel—3h—6c
Hudson, Thomas—4h—5c
Hughes, James—4h—6c
Jameson, Robert—2h
Jameson, William—7h—39c
Jemson, John—2h
Jarcht (?), Samuel—4h—7c
Jarcht, William—1h—2c
Johnston, James—3h—5c
Johnston, James—no mention
Jones, John—2h—7c
Jones, John—1h—4c
Jones, Richard—no mention
Jones, William—2h—2c
Kelly, George—2h—6c
Kelso, Hugh—2S—8h—4c
Kelso, John—2h—4c
Kennedy, Andrew—2S—5h—12c
Kennedy, James—4h—9c
Kerkham Rosana—2h—3c
Keys, Samuel—4h—6c
Keys, Sarah—2h—4c
Killavane, John—1h—6c
Kincade, Robert—3T—7h—11c
Kincade, Thomas—3h—5c
Kinder, Peter—7h—23c
Kingery, Peter—3h—10c
Kirkpatrick, Charles—3T—11h—32c
Kirkpatrick, Charles—3h
Kirkpatrick, John—7h—16c
Kirkpatrick, John—2h—1c
Kirkpatrick, John—6h—16c
Kirkpatrick, Robert—1S
Kirkpatrick, Samuel—2h—13c
Kirkpatrick, Thomas—3h—12c
Kirkpatrick, Thomas—1h
Kingery, Jacob—4h—8c
Kingery, Tobias—3c
Lackey, Thomas—2T—8h—13c
Lackey, Thomas—2h—6c

Lackland, John—2h—2c
Lackland, Joseph, Sr.—2h—6c
Lackland, Joseph, Jr.—1h—4c
Laid, Morris—no mention
Lain, John—no mention
Laird, David—6h—10c
Lander, Reuben—2h—2c
Lane, James—4h—13c
Lane, James—1h—5c
Lapsley, Joseph, Sr.—5S—9h—27c
Lapsley, Joseph, Jr.—4h
Lapsley, Samuel—6h
Laremore, John—4h—5c
Law Michael—3h—5c
Lawrence Samuel—9h—21c
Lawson, Isaac—1h—4c
Leck, John—4h—13c
Letcher, John—5S—6h—7c
Lewis, Daniel—no mention
Lewis, Joseph—4h—6c
Ligget, Alexander—1h—11c
Ligget, James—3h
Ligget, John—1h
Liptrap, Isaac—4h
Little, Joseph—5h—13c
Little, Thomas—3h—6c
Lockhart, Thomas—1h—3c
Lockridge, Robert—10h—32c
Logan, David—2S
Logan, James—1S—4h—8c
Logan, James (Gilmore's company)—5h—17c
Logan, Thomas—4h
Logan, William—2T—3S
Lowry, Melvin—4c
Lusk, Hugh—2h—1c
Lusk, John, Sr.—4h—8c
Lusk, John, Jr.—1h—7c
Lusk, Samuel—1h
Lusk, William—3h
Lyle, Agnes—6h—11c
Lyle, Daniel and James—4h—14c
Lyle, James—4S—12h—27c
Lyle, John (skinner)—2h
Lyle, John—6h—9c
Lyle, Robert—1h
Lyle, Samuel and Jame(son)—8S—10h—41c
Lyle, James (same as above)—3h

Lyle, William—1S—2h—3c
Lyon, Stephen—6h—16c
Martin, William—5h—15c
Marton, Joel—8h—23c
Mason, John, Jr.—1S—4h—8c
Mason, Robert—2T—2S—9h—24c
Masters, Thomas—1h
Mathews, Frances—3S—6h—11c
Maxwell, John—2S—10h—23c
McCallister, George—2h—4c
McCampbell, Andrew—1S—4h—6c
McCampbell, Andrew—1S—7h—22c
McCampbell, James—4S—5h—18c
McCampbell, James and Andrew (son)—5h
—14c
McCampbell, John—6h—13c
McCampbell, Robert—1S—7h—15c
McCampbell, Solomon—3h
McCampbell, William—2S—5h—15c
McCappin, Robert—4h—7c
McCappin, Robert—3h—6c
McCartney, James—1h
McChesney, Isabella—4h—5c
McChesney, James—5S—11h—17c
McChesney, Samuel—6S—12h—14c
McClain, John—2h—6c
McClenachan, Alexander—1S—5h—14c
McClenachan, Reuben—4h—6c
McClung, Henry—1S—5h—20c
McClung, James—2T—9h—16c
McClung, James—4h—13c
McClung, John and William—5S—9h—17c
McClung, William—5h—12c
McClung, William—no mention
McClure, Alexander—5h—10c
McClure, Alexander—2S—7h—16c
McClure, Arthur—8h—21c
McClure, David—1S—5h——8c
McClure, Halbert—6h—11c
McClure, Isabel—1S—4h—12c
McClure, John—6h—20c
McClure, Samuel—11h—15c
McClure, William—1S—9h—16c
McClure, William—2h—6c
McCollam, John—1h—3c
McCollam, Patrick—2T—2S—6h—8c
McCollister, Benjamin—3h—5c
McCollister, Joseph—2h—2c
McColloch, John, Sr.—4h—11c

McColloch, John—1h
McConnell, James—5h—15c
McConnell, Patrick—2h—8c
McCorkle, Samuel—5h—10c
McCorkle, William—3h—8c
McCoskey, Samuel—4h—11c
McCormick, Robert—1S—4h—10c
McCown, Alexander—4h—3c
McCown, James—4h—12c
McCown, James—3h—4c
McCown, John, Sr.—2T—1S—5h—21c
McCown, John, Jr.—1h
McCown, Joseph—3h—6c
McCoy, Archibald—1h
McCray, James—3h—10c
McCray, Joseph—4h—5c
McCrory, James—1S—10h—20c
McCroskey, David—4h—14c
McCroskey, John—2T—5h—15c
McCroskey, John—3h—2c
McCroskey, —————1h
McDonnell, Randolph—4h—7c
McDowell, Elizabeth—10S—10h—13c
McDowell, James—1S—5h
McDowell, Samuel—2T—4S—16h—30c
McElhany, John—2h
McElhany, Robert—8S—5h—17c
McElhany, Robert—1h
McElhany, William—5h—12c
McElroy, William—2T—3h—6c
McElroy, William—1h
McEntosh, John—4h—9c
McGee, John—1h—3c
McGee, Richard—5h—11c
McGlaughland, Edward—1h—7c
McFadden, Hugh—7h—13c
McFall, John—1h—2c
McFarlin, Robert—1S—7h—12c
McFarlin, Thomas—no mention
McFarlin, William—1h—2c
McKee, Esther—1S—4h—9c
McKee, James—6h—5c
McKee, John—3T—5S—6h—24c
McKee, Lydia—3S—4h—8c
McKee, Mary—5S—6h—31c
McKee, Robert—1h
McKee, William—1S—8h—28c
McKemy, James—2h
McKemy, John—4h—6c

TAXPAYERS OF 1782 375

McKemy, Samuel—1h—1c
McKemy, William, William, Jr., and Alexander—3T—4h—11c
McKenny, John—2h—4c
McKinny, Daniel—1h
McMath, James—5h—17c
McMullen, John—3h—18c
McNabb, Samuel—2T—7h—12c
McNeely, James—2h—3c
McNight—Timothy—1S—7h—18c
McNut, Thomas—1h—4c
McNutt, Alexander—2h
McNutt, John—6h—19c
McWilliams, David—4h—12c
Metcer, Samuel—8h—23c
Miller, Daniel—3h—9c
Miller, Henry—2T—11h—24c
Miller, Samuel—2h—8c
Millikan, John—2h—7c
Millikan, John—4c
Millikan, William—4h—8c
Mitchell, John—2h—13c
Mitchell, William—4h—6c
Mogotion (?), Benjamin—no mention
Montgomery, Alexander—3h—6c
Montgomery, James—1h
Montgomery, Robert—1S—7h—10c
Montgomery, Robert—1h
Montgomery, William (tanner)—1h
Month, Christopher—1h—4c
Moor, Alexander—2T—1S—9h—18c
Moor, Andrew, Esq.—1S—6h—13c
Moor, Andrew, Jr.—2h
Moor, David—3h—8c
Moor, Hugh—4h—3c
Moor, James—5h—9c
Moor, John, Sr.—2T—1S—15h—27c
Moor, John—2S—10h—15c
Moor, John—2h—2c
Moor, Joseph, Esq.—4S—12h—20c
Moor, Samuel—2h
Moor, Samuel, Jr.—5h
Moor, Samuel (merchant)—4S
Moor, William, Sr.—3S—7h—16c
Moore, Andrew (attorney)—3S—3h—4c
Moore, Samuel—3T—12h
Moore, William—3T—12h—17c
Morris, Mark—2h—1c
Morris, Thomas—7h—19c

Morris, Thomas—4h—18c
Murphy, John—4h—12c
Neely, James—2h—4c
Neely, John—2h—3c
Nelson, John—2h—4c
Nesbit, Samuel—4h—16c
Nesbit, William—2h—6c
Newells, Henry—3h—6c
Oldhauser, Emorty—2h—3c
Pagan, Nicholas—3h
Parks, John—1S—7h—13c
Patterson, James—1S—4h—11c
Patterson, Samuel—1S—5h—22c
Patton, John—3h—7c
Patton, William—7h—19c
Paul, John, Sr.—1S—8h—17c
Paul, John, Jr.—3h—2c
Paxton, John—1S—5h—22c
Paxton, John—1S—7h—18c
Paxton, John, Sr.—5S—10h—26c
Paxton, Samuel—4h—11c
Paxton, Samuel—3h—11c
Paxton, Thomas—7S—12h—19c
Paxton, Thomas—5h—9c
Paxton, William—9S—9h—32c
Paxton, William—3S—9h—10c
Peel, James—2h—3c
Peoples, John—2S—5h—8c
Peoples, Nathan—4h—8c
Petries, John—2h
Pickens, John—2h
Pickens, John—1h
Poage, James—4h—11c
Poage, John—2T—1S—4h—12c
Poage, Jonathan—2h
Pollock, James—5h—7c
Pollock, Samuel—1h—6c
Porter, John—7h—20c
Porter, William—1S—10h—41c
Pressly, William—2T—4h—12c
Pressly, William—1h—3c
Pusy (Posey), Robert—5h—4c
Ramsay, James—1S—2h
Ramsay, Samuel—6h—6c
Ramsay, William—7S—15h—18c
Randon (Reardon), John—no mention
Ratliff, Thomas—1S—6h—11c
Reah, Archibald—10h—16c
Reah, William—1S—4h—16c

Reid, Adam—5h—16c
Reid, Andrew—1S—7h—12c
Reid, Daniel—2h—4c
Reid, Elizabeth—2h—1c
Reid, Joseph—7h—14c
Reid, Michael—2h—7c
Reid, Patrick—1h
Reid, Thomas—1h
Rhodes, Robert—1h
Riley, Barney—4h—11c
Ritchey, James—2T—5h—7c
Robertson, James—2T—5h—11c
Robertson, Matthew and James—2T—3h —3c
Robertson, Thomas—2h—4c
Robinson, David—3h—5c
Robinson, Britton—2c
Robinson, John—3h—7c
Robinson, John (jockey)—5h
Robinson, William—5h—11c
Rondoun, James—3h—5c
Rowan, William—4h—4c
Rush, John—1S—6h—1c
Russel, Thomas—3h—6c
Ruth, Joseph—5h
Salley, George—14h—30c
Scott, Andrew—2S—5h—14c
Scott, David—5h—11c
Sea, John—4h—13c
Sea, Martin—6h—23c
Sensibah, John—5h—13c
Shaw, John—2h
Shaw, Robert—1S—7h—18c
Shick, Andrew—1h—4c
Simpson, Robert—2h—3c
Sisson, Caleb—5S—11h—5c
Skean, Henry—5h—12c
Skean, Jonathan—2h—3c
Skean, Joseph—3h—4c
Skean, Robert—5h—10c
Slaton, Thomas, Sr.—3h—5c
Slaton, Thomas—2h—7c
Slaton, William—1h—4c
Smiley, Alexander—4h—11c
Smiley, Andrew—3h—9c
Smiley, James—2h—5c
Smiley, John—3h—2c
Smiley, Walter, Jr.—7h—20c
Smith, Isabella—3h—10c

Smith, James—1h
Smithers, Sarah—5h—8c
Snodgrass, Joseph—3T—8h—16c
Snodgrass, Robert—3h—8c
Spear, John—5h—6c
Spence, John—2h—7c
Spence, William—2h
Sprowl, William—2h—18c
Steel, David—5h—13c
Steel, Peter—2S—7h—32c
Steele, Samuel—2T—1S—12h—21c
Steele, Thomas—7h—12c
Sterret, Jonathan—no mention
Stephen, John—2h
Stephenson, James—2S—7h—23c
Stephenson, Joseph—1h
Stoop, Robert—2h—8c
Strahan, Robert—2h—5c
Strickler, Joseph—4h—17c
Stuart, Alexander, Esq.—1S—10h—26c
Stuart, Alexander—2h—6c
Stuart, James—2h
Stuart, John—3S—13h—17c
Stuart, William—2h—14c
Tade, James—1c
Tate, Joseph—3h—6c
Taylor, Elizabeth—7h—19c
Taylor, George—1S—5h—7c
Taylor, James—6h—12c
Taylor, James—1h—2c
Taylor, Robert—1S—5h—12c
Taylor, William—5h—9c
Tedford, Alexander, Alexander, Jr., and Daniel—3T—8h—20c
Tedford, David—6h—14c
Tedford, George—1h
Tedford, James—2h
Tedford, James, Jr.—1h
Tedford, John—1S—2h—8c
Tedford, John—3h—11c
Tedford, Robert, Sr.—4h—11c
Tedford, Robert—6h—9c
Tedford, William—5h—7c
Templeton, James—3S—6h—14c
Templeton, ———— —3S—2h—11c
Terry, Stephen—1h
Thompson, James—1h
Thompson, James—1h—2c
Thompson, John—1S—7h—17c

TAXPAYERS OF 1782

Thompson, John—8S—8h—24c
Thompson, Joseph—5h—8c—1 tavern license
Thompson, William—9h—15c
Tolley, Christian—3h—15c
Trimble, Moses—2T—3S—10h—19c
Trimble, Isaac—3h
Trimble, John, Esq.—1S—4h—8c
Vance, John—5h—19c
Vance, Joseph—3h—4c
Vance, Patrick—2h—13c
Vernor, John—1h—4c
Walker, Alexander, Sr.—4h—6c
Walker, Alexander, Jr.—6S—5h—21c
Walker, Alexander—8h—18c
Walker, James—3S—4h—11c
Walker, James (farmer)—5h—14c
Walker, James (smith)—5h—9c
Walker, John, Sr.—2T—1S—7h—14c
Walker, John (smith)—7h—24c
Walker, John—5h—5c
Walker, John—2h
Walker, John—7h—10c
Walker, Joseph, Esq.—7S—7h—17c
Walker, Joseph, Sr.—5h—22c
Walker, Joseph, Jr.—1h
Walker, Samuel—4h—15c
Walker, Samuel, Jr.—4h—26c
Walker, Samuel—no mention
Walker, William—5S—5h—27c
Walker, William—5h—8c
Wallace, James—11h—13c
Wallace, John—no mention
Wallace, Peter—1S—4h—12c
Wallace, Robert—1S—9h—15c
Wallace, Samuel—2S—7h—20c
Wallace, William—1S—3h—12c
Wardlaw, James—1S—15h—32c
Wardlaw, Robert—4h—16c
Wardlaw, William—3S—13h—36c
Wason, John—4h—6c
Wason, Robert—7h—8c
Watters, Jonathan—2h—3c
Weir, Abraham—1S—7h—16c

Weir, Hugh—7h—20c
Weir, James—3h—12c
Weir, Jeane—2S—5h—9c
Weir, John—1h—3c
Weir, Joseph—no mention.
Welch, James—2h—11c
Welch, Patrick—3c
Welch, Samuel—2h—3c
Welch, Thomas—2h—10c
Whiteside, Moses—7h—20c
Whitly, Jonathan—4S—6h—25c
Whittemore, Nathaniel—2h—2c
Wiley, Alexander—5h—6c
Wiley, John, Joseph, Andrew—3T—9h—20c
Wiley, Peter—2h—7c
Williamson, Benjamin—1c
Williamson, David—3h—3c
Williamson, Richard—2h—8c
Williamson, Smith—3h—11c
Williamson, Thomas—1h—3c
Wilson, Abraham—2h—8c
Wilson, Alexander—6h—17c
Wilson, Daniel—2T—9h—20c
Wilson, Hugh—3h—11c
Wilson, James—7h—12c
Wilson, John—3S—7h—14c
Wilson, John—4h—10c
Wilson, John—3T—7h—17c
Wilson, John—4h—7c
Wilson, John (farmer)—2h—2c
Wilson, Nathaniel—4h—8c
Wilson, Samuel—1S—7h—23c
Wilson, Samuel, Jr.—1S—5h—16c
Wilson, Samuel—5h—3c
Wilson, Thomas—4S—6h—25c
Wilson, William (Timber Ridge)—no mention
Wilson, William—5h—11c
Winegar, John—3h—8c
Woods, Patrick—3h—9c
Woolf, Michael—3h—4c
Yard, William—4h—14c

Whites—771—poll tax, 385 pounds, 10 shillings
Horses—3250—tax, 325 pounds
Negroes—503—poll tax, 251 pounds, 10 shillings
Cattle—1—tax, 10 shillings
Cart—1—tax, 10 shillings
Tavern license—1—tax, 5 pounds
Total tax, 1,060 pounds, 6 shillings, 9 pence—($5,534.56.)

SECTION VII

Taxpayers of 1841

The figures refer to the road precincts in which the persons lived. For a description of the precincts, see Appendix D.

Ackerley: Peter—18; John P.—20; William—21; Stephen—29.
Adair: John and Samuel—56; James and William—68.
Adams: Hugh—62; Captain James—68.
Agnor: William—33; George, Jacob, Sr., Jacob, Little Jake, John, and John H.—43; James—56; Andrew—63.
Ailstock: James—93.
Albright: John—68; Frederick—73.
Alexander: Robert—48; John—57; Andrew, Archibald F., and Reid—75.
Alphin: William—36.
Amole: Henry and Jacob—48.
Anderson: Thomas—23; William H.—31; John—44; Stephen—50; Robert—51; James and Robert B.—61; Thomas M.—72; Samuel B.—81.
Archibald: Henry C. and Zachariah—20.
Armentrout: John—38.
Armstrong: Quinton—68; William J.—70.
Atkins: Richard—48.
Ayers: Henry C.—57.
Baggs: James—15.
Bailey: David, William (1), and William (2)—49; Samuel—56.
Baldwin: Cornelius C.—14; Oliver P.—63; Peter—92.
Barclay: Alexander T.—24.
Barger: George, John, and Peter—1.
Bartlett: George—55.
Barton: Robert R.—23.
Beale, John (free negro)—51.
Bear: Jacob and Joseph—93.
Beard: Archibald D.—24; Philip—27; James M.—56; David S., William, Sr., and William—70; David—80.
Beaty: George and James—85.
Beers: William J.—44.
Beeson: John—92.
Bell: John—12; Elizabeth—22; John M.—89; Joseph and William H.—92.
Bennington: Job—5.
Bethel: Samuel—92.
Black, James, John, and William B.—23; Benjamin and William—40; Joseph—64.
Blessinger: Michael—65.
Bobbitt: Oregon—58.
Borden: Henry—33.
Bousserman: Isaac—94.
Brads: James (1), James (2), Jacob, Francis, and George—36.
Brooks: William—21.

Brown: Nelson—22; John W.—45; Jacob—62; John of Jacob—69; William of South River, William J., and William S.—74; William—83.
Brownlee: James—78.
Bryan: Mrs. Mary—63; Matthew—71.
Buchanan: William—68; John—85; George—92.
Bunch: John—51.
Burgess: George W.—25.
Burks: Charles S.—8; William L. and William T.—23.
Byers: Fleming—22.
Cahoon: John, Mark, and William—18.
Caldwell: Thomas Y.—3; Smith—5.
Camden: Jesse—15; James, John, and Washington—75.
Cameron: Andrew W.—58.
Campbell: Rev. Samuel D.—1; Alexander—64; John—55; James T.—70.
Capper: Dennis—47.
Carskaddon: Richard H.—25.
Carter: John—44; David—52.
Caruthers: William H.—58.
Cash: Benjamin and William M.—20.
Caskey: Joseph—7; Mrs. Grizzy—11; Thomas—23.
Chandler: John and Samuel T.—46.
Charlton: Soborn—24.
Childers: Andrew—76.
Chittum: William J.—44.
Christian: James—1.
Clark: Robert (stonemason)—13; Daniel and John—34; James—38; James, Joseph, and Nelson—96.
Clarkson: John—27.
Clemer: Francis—68.
Cloyd: Joseph—1
Clyburn: John—62.
Cochran: Jamison—62.
Collins: Columbus—61.
Conaway: Lawrence—61.
Cooper: William—96; William (free negro)—58.
Cornelius: George W.—49.
Cotter: John, Sr.—74
Cowan: Samuel—96.
Cowman: William—73.
Cox: Spottswood A.—9; Philip—80; George—95.
Craig: James—12
Crawford: Robert—81.
Crist: David—63.
Croddy: John, Jr., and William—9; John and Christopher—10.
Cross: John A.—63.
Crossley: James—4
Crouse: Abraham—68; heirs of John—85.
Culton: heirs of Alexander—88.
Cumings: John A.—42.

Cummings: John S.—48; Samuel—73.
Cunningham: Jacob (millwright) and Thomas, Jr.—45.
Currier: Jonathan—68.
Curry: Peter—30.
Daniel: James—6.
Darst: Samuel—14.
Davidson: Andrew B.—24; James, James, Jr., and Madison—54.
Davis: David, Richard, and Samuel W.—55; David and William—89.
Day: William—76; John and Solomon—82.
Deakins: William—31.
Decker: Samuel—57
Demasters: James—27; Cornelius—65.
Dempsey: William A. W.—43
Dickey: William—58; Robert—75
Dietrick: Michael—67
Dikel: George—24
Dixon: James and William—49; James and William—56; Samuel—61; Thomas—65.
Doak: Alexander F.—80.
Donald: Mrs. Nancy—73
Douglass: James and Robert M.—8; William—22.
Drain: James and William—38.
Drawbone: Matthew—69
Dryden: James and Thomas—23
Dunlap: Robert—58; Thomas—76
Ebbard: Samuel—91
Echols: Edward—24
Edes: Jonathan W.—13
Edmondson: Thomas—50
Elliott: Hugh—24; William—36; John—55
Engleman: David—70
Entsminger: Alexander, David, and Lewis—37; David—43
Eskew: Clarence—74
Ewing: Daniel—3; Rev. John D.—12
Eyres: John—33
Falls: William—62
Ferguson: William—58
Figgat: William—58
Finley: John M.—15; William—26
Firebaugh: John—68; Henry—85; Benjamin F.—88
Fisher: Martin—33; William—44
Fitzpatrick: Ford—34; Alexander—61
Fix: Adam—57; Christian and John—61.
Forbes, William, Sr.—93
Ford: Jacob—33; Allison—34; John—38
Foster: Isaac N. and Joseph—11; William R.—74
Frazier: Henry and Samuel—91
Fry: Matthew—10; George—93
Fulwider: John—1; Jacob, Jr.—33
Galbraith: John—2

Garrett: Albert—23; John—51
Gaylor: Dennis and Nathaniel—52.
Gibson: John—64
Gilbert: Leroy—20
Gilliat: Albert—43
Gilmore: Paxton—9; Addison—34; Robert—52
Ginger: Samuel—10
Glasgow: Joseph—15; Robert—60
Glass: George W.—1
Glover: John—70
Gold: James and Robert H.—33; Samuel—64
Goodbar: John M. and Joseph—36
Gordon: Alexander and John H.—61
Gore: Samuel—20
Goul: Mrs. Nancy—57
Gouyne: Spencer—58
Graham: Andrew—92
Grant, Alexander—13
Green: Joseph and Samuel—36; Thomas—70; Lawrence—76; John—86
Griffin, Archibald—68
Grigsby: James S.—16; Elisha—22
Gue: Addison, Johnston, and Rosemary—2
Guffey: David—83
Gutridge: John—24
Hall: Joshua—31; John F., John, Jr., and William—32; James, Jr.—33
Hamilton: Alexander—12; William—31; Robert—32; John, Sr.—47; Galbraith and William G.—49; John W.—51; James—57; John—65
Hanger: William: William—93
Hardy: Henry and Wesley—18
Harper: Hugh—42; John, John M., and William—56
Harris: Nathan—58
Harris: James (1), James (2) and William—63; Frederick and Samuel—78; Robert—90
Harrison: John—14; Abner—95
Harshbarger: William—32
Hart: Benjamin A. and Rebecca—4; James, Matthew—44
Hartigan: David C. and James H.—31
Hartsook: James—50; John—81
Haslip: Thomas—72
Hatcher: Henry M.—21; Jonathan C.—23
Hayslett: Andrew, Ezekiel, George, John, and John of Zachariah—35; Ezekiel, Jr., Henry, Robert, and William—45.
Heck: Daniel—1
Henderson: William—32
Henry: Williamson—49; Jason, (free negro)—58
Hepler: John and Samuel—91
Herrin: Walter—61
Hickman: Jacob—12
Hicks: John and William—60

Hileman: Daniel—69
Hill: George, Samuel (1), and Samuel (2)—1; George, James, and Samuel—8; Henry—16; James H., Jonas, Madison, and William—32
Hinkle: Henry and John—45
Hite: Samuel—2
Hodge: Benjamin, James, John H., and Renix—91
Hoffman: David S., and George, Jr.—15
Hogue: John—29
Holmes: Benjamin A. and Joseph—5; Alexander, Benjamin, and John—13
Hopkins: William—19
Hostetter: Andrew—45
Houston: David G.—1; John D.—6; Matthew and William—21; William—86
Hughes: Abner—7; Eli—23; Samuel—40
Hull: Philip—33; Peter and William—54
Hunt: Bernard and Elisha—9
Hutcheson, Robert—86
Hutton: James—33
Hyman: Samuel—95
Ingles: William—58
Ingram: Alexander, Hezekiah, John, Jonathan, and William—91
Ireland: George and John M.—65
Irvine: Robert—24; Isaac—28
James: George—91
Jarvis: Jeremiah—91; William—96
Joe: George—91
Johnston: Nathaniel—1; Clifton O.—7; Samuel—22; James, Samuel, Thomas, William G., and Zachariah—24; Damascus and John—64
Jones: Ambrose—11; Lane, Sr.,—27; John W. Lane, and William—49; William—50; Richard F.—67.
Jordan: John W.—11; Prier—15; Benjamin J. and John—53
Judy: Jacob—85; Henry—1
Kagan: John—15
Kahle: Mrs. Rebecca—1
Keffer: Henry—6
Keizer: Jacob—31
Keller: Peter, Jr.—57; George, and Peter, Sr.—69—John—61
Kelso: Ewen, Joseph, and Walker—89
Kennedy: Hugh—83
Kerr: John—24; Charles M.—42; Thomas—44; David—61
King: William—5; George W.—42
Kinkaid: William—40
Kinny: Madison—28
Kirkpatrick: William—26; Joseph—86
Kirkwood: William—4
Kurtz: Frederick—24
Lackey: John G. and Thomas, Sr.—4; James—52; James, Jr. and Thomas—57; Nathan and William—65
Lair: Peter—91
Laird: John—3; David—51

Lam: John—57; Matthias—64
Lambert: Daniel—19
Larew: Benjamin, John, and Reuben F.—56; Jacob—61
Lawhorn: Pleasant—1
Lawson: John—24
Lawton: Robert—18; Lindsay—56
Layman: John—65
Layne: Henry A.—15
Leech: James and John—21; Adam, James, and John—31; David, David, Jr., and William—33; Henry—40
Lessley: Samuel—33
Lewis: Joel—1; William C.—24; Elias B. and John—61; Abraham—63
Lindsay: James, James W., and Thomas—56
Liggens: William—50
Link: Daniel—18; Catharine and John—47
Littich: Cyrus J.—19
Little: David and William—92
Lowman: David—44; David—51
Luckess: William—3
Lusk: Michael—66
Lyle: Archibald, Major James, and Matthew—65
Mackey: James S.—25; Andrew—27; Hugh W.—40; William K.—64
Martin: James T.—15; Hudson and James—65; Charles—76; William—90
Masterson: John—24
Mateer: Martha and William—23
Matheny: James—24
Mathews: Mrs. Mary—11
May: Joseph—1
Mayse: Henry—95
McAllison: Halbert—60
McCalpin: Joseph—12; John—13; Samuel—49
McCampbell: David—41
McCauley: James—94
McClain: John and William—64; Samuel—65
McCleland: John—22; John—41
McClintic: Shanklin—40
McClung: William A.—3; James—49
McClure: Arthur and Robert C.—3
McCluer: John and Robert—6; Nathan—22; Moses, Nicholas J., and William—75.
McCown: Alexander—24; James G. and Moses—55; John H.—56; John—75
McCorkle: Samuel—47; Alexander, Sr., Alexander (little), Benjamin, John, Thomas, and William—51; Samuel R.—68
McCormick: Henry A.—61; John B.—62; Henry—67; James and John T.—68
McCoy: James—68
McCray: Henry B.—52
McCue: John—24
McCully: Peter—2
McCutchen: Albert—67; Samuel—89
McDaniel: Matthew—15; Matthew, Sr.—20; James—29; William H.—44

McDowell: Robert—24; James—47
McFarland: John—44
McGinnis: Nancy—52
McHenry: Edward—45
McKee: John T.—44; Samuel W.—56
McKemy: John (1), John (2), and William—61
McKenly: David—24
McKerny: Nathan and Samuel—20
McKinsey: William—78
McLaughlin: Andrew S. and Edward S.—92
McNeal: George—55
McNutt: Elizabeth—13
Miller: Samuel, Sr., and Samuel, Jr.—5; Sarah—15; James—17; Thomas L.—18; Andrew, George, and Samuel—45; Joseph—70; Jacob—80; Jacob—93
Mitchel: Henry—15
Moffett: John—3; William—6
Moler: George and Philip—56
Mohler: John and William K.—57
Montgomery: Alexander and James—40
Moore: Garland and Nathan G.—3; Samuel R.—23; Jordan—34; Thomas S.—41; James C. and James C. C.—44; Abner W. and Preadam—45; John—51; Samuel McD. Mrs. Sarah—76
Morgan: Henry C.—82; John D.—85
Morris: Henry E.—82; John D.—85
Morris: John and Urias—35; John, Sr.—36; Thomas—42; John (free negro)—68; Mack—45
Morrison: Robert A.—2; Robert, Jr.—44; Robert, Sr.—57
Nash: William—13
Nesbit: Andrew and John—92
Nevius: John—78
Newcomer: William—27
Nicely: Samuel—16; David—19
Nicholson: Archibald (free negro)—16
Nick: Adam and John—37
Norcross: William—61
Northern: William—3
O'Brian: Peter—44
Ocheltree: David—5
Odell: John—1
Ornbaum: Michael—79
Ott: Frederick—65
Oyler: Alexander—20
Painter: Frederick—12
Palmer: John—4 3
Parker: Caleb—44
Patterson: James and Morris—3; Jameston, Jr.—88
Patton: David and John—61; Joseph—64; David—80
Paul: John—73
Paxton: Peter—12; James—14; James—18; Samuel—21; James H. and William—50;

Captain William—68; Alexander, John of James, and John of Samuel—74; David—75; Samuel—79; John L.—96
    Penn: Richeson—10
    Peters: Samuel—46
    Pettigrew: William—1; Eli J.—18
    Pinkney: Edmund O.—8
    Plott: Abraham—52
    Poage: Eli and John—2; James M.—6; John B.—11; John and William F.—12; James A.—33
    Porter: Benjamin F.—30
    Potter: David and John—61; Jacob—70
    Powers: Larkin—53
    Ptomy: John M.—90
    Pullen: William—31
    Ramsay: Anderson and Lewis—56
    Randal: Isham (free negro)—16
    Rapp: Anthony—63
    Ray: Hugh—21
    Reany: William—87
    Reid: Frederick—68; Samuel McD.—76; John—86
    Replogle: Jacob and John, Jr.—25; John—39
    Reynolds: John A.—8
    Rhodes: Benjamin—8
    Riddle: George and John—18—Stephen—89
    Risk: Harvey and James—68
    Ristine: John C.—24
    Roach: William B.—6
    Roadcap: Chrisley and George—92
    Robertson: John H.—61; William—68; Anderson—78
    Robinson: Joseph—39
    Rodes: Aaron D.—56
    Rolison: Lang and heirs of Nathaniel—19; Sylvanus—20
    Ruff, John—24
    Ruley: William T.—43
    Runnels: William—82
    Sale: John, Jr.—6
    Sallis: George W.—82
    Sanford: James—31
    Scott: Thomas, Sr., Thomas, Jr., John, Sr., and John, Jr.—33
    Selph: Benjamin—19; Thomas—20
    Shalter: Frederick—85
    Shaver: Jacob—20; John—40
    Shaw: Daniel, James, Matthew, and William—61; James—73
    Sheltmas: Jacob G.—25; Mrs. Dorcas—58
    Shewey: David—78
    Shields: William—18; William—70; John—75
    Short: James and Robert—19
    Shieldtz: Jackson—94
    Siler: Jacob and Philip—23

Sizer: Fielding—1
Smiley: Alexander of Daniel, Daniel, and John—73; Robert—87
Smith: Thomas (blacksmith)—2; John C.—6; James—25; John—28; Jacob B.—61; Robert—65; George W.—86; John, William (stiller), and William P.—93; Abraham—95
Snider: David—83
Snyder: Daniel—72
Somewell: William—63
Spitler: Daniel—91
Sprowl: Alexander—61
Staton: Daniel—62
Steele: Dr. John M.—3; Robert C.—86
Steiner: Alexander and William—4
Sterrett: William B.—3
Stewart: Andrew—61
Stoner: Jacob—95
Strain: David—70
Strickler: Daniel M.—67
Stuart: Alexander B.—62; James, Jr.—64; Captain John—81; Henry—84
Surfer: heirs of Christian—70
Sweet: Alexander and William—83
Swink: John—57; Enos—80
Swinney: John P.—6; Robert—22; James—23
Swisher: Jacob, Jr.—86
Swoope: George—87
Syron: Nathaniel—20
Tardy: Nathan C.—9; James—21
Taylor: Samuel—19; John H.—61; Mrs. Ann—64; David and James—77; Matthew—89
Temple: John—81
Templeton: John, Jr., and Robert—68
Thomas: Archibald and Camp—90
Thompson: William—11; John—49; George—58; Horatio—64
Tinsley: John H.—15
Tolly: Christopher, Jr., and Samuel—8; Andrew, Joseph, William (1), and William (2)—37; Alexander—38
Tuck: Edmund—81
Turpin: Josiah—8
Tygret: John W.—8
Tyler: John—61
Unroe: Adam and George—39
Vance: Philip—5; Thomas—14
Varner: Charles—24
Vess: Eli, George, Hiram, John, Samuel, Samuel H., and William—36; Levi—60
Walker: Joseph C.—22; Captain Alexander and Alexander, Jr.—81; William—83; Archibald B.—88
Walkup: Samuel—41; James W. G.—45
Wallace: John—2; James S.—24; Andrew—46; John—68; Jesse D.—73
Ward: John—24
Waskey, John, Sr., and John, Jr.—1; William—5
Watkins: William A.—3

Watts: Caleb—9; James—11
Weathers: George—15; Vincent—65; George, Sr., James, and William E.—77
Weaver: William—16
Webb, Michael—49
Weir: William E.—42
Welch: Benjamin (cooper)—1; Thomas—2; Benjamin and John—3; Robert—28; John—58; Samuel—82
Welchance: William—60
West: James, Sr.—61
Wheat: William D.—68
White: James, John, and Thomas—55
Whitmer: John—72; Peter—80
Whitsel: Samuel—65
Whitzel: Eli and Jacob—76
Wilhelm: Jacob A.—3; Lewis—18; William—68
Wilmore: John H.—22
Wilson: Thomas—7; Hugh L.—9; Deborah and William—11; James, James, Jr., Thomas, and John—16; Hugh, Jr., James J., Joseph, and Thomas—29; Hugh and William—39; James, James, of Walker's Creek, and Robert—42; Edward—49; David and James P.—64; William M.—67; James—76; John—80; William—96
Winn: Joseph—59
Wiseman: Peter—81
Withrow: John, Jr., (free negro)—68; Samuel—70
Wood: John J.—88
Worth: Spencer—19
Wright: Cary, Charles, and Harden—11; William—73; Thompson A.—4; Robert—68
Youel: James G. W.—90
Zink: Samuel—24
Zollman: Henry and William—28

SECTION VIII

PRESENT SURNAMES

As shown in the tax list for the three years ending May 5, 1917.

Abbreviations: B—Buffalo; K—Kerr's Creek; L—Lexington; N—Natural Bridge; W—Walker's Creek; S—South River.

NOTE: When there is more than one person to a name in a given district, the number follows the initial letter. Thus, Adison—L, means there is one Adison on the tax list in Lexington District, and as no other initial letter is given, it consequently follows that there is but one such Adison in the county. Austin—N, 8 means there are eight Austins on the voting list in Natural Bridge District.

Ackerly—L—N, 2—B, 3
Adair—L, 4—N—K
Adams—K
Adison—L
Agnor—L, 9—B, 3—K, 2—W—S, 5
Ailstock—B, 2
Ainsworth—L
Albertoli—N, 2
Alexander—L—S, 2
Alger—S
Allen—N—W, 2—S, 4
Alphin—N—B, 2—K, 2—W—L
Alvis—W
Alwin—N
Anderson—L—B, 2—K—W, 3
Arehart—W—S, 9
Armentrout—B, 2—K, 2—W, 2
Armstrong—B, 9—S, 4
Arndt—N
Arthur—L
Ashburne—L
Austin—N, 8
Ayres—L—N—B, 4—K, 2—W—S
Bailey—B
Baldwin—N
Ballard—B, 2
Balser—W, 4
Bane—B, 8—K
Barclay—L—S—N
Bare—L, 4—N, 3—W, 2
Barger—N, 7—B, 2
Barnett—S
Bartly—S
Batman—K
Bayne—W—S, 3
Bazzanella—K
Bear—L—N

Beard—L—N—B—W, 9
Beasley—L
Beatty—K
Bechtel—N
Beckner—W, 3—S
Beeton—L, 2
Bell—N—W, 6—S, 2
Bender—N
Bennington—K, 3
Benson—W
Berry—K, 4—W, 3—S
Besenfelder—L
Birmingham—N
Black—L—B, 2—N, 2—K, 3
Blackburn—N, 3
Blackwell—K, 3—W, 4
Bogan—B
Bolen—W, 3
Boley—L, 2—N
Booth—L
Bosserman—L, 2—W
Bosworth—W, 2
Bowlin—B
Bowyer—B—S, 2
Bradley—S
Brads—N, 3—B
Brady—N
Braford—N, 6
Branch—N
Breeden—N
Breedlove—L
Britton—W
Brockenbrough—N
Brogan—W, 4
Broughman—B
Brown—L, 8—N, 2—B, 3—W, 6—S, 4
Bruce—L, 2

PRESENT SURNAMES

Bryan—K—S, 2
Bryant—N, 4—K
Buchanan—K—W, 6
Buckley—S
Burch—N
Burgess—L
Burke—S
Burger—N, 2
Burks—L—N, 3—W, 3
Burwell—L
Byers—W
Byrd—B—S
Bywaters—S, 2
Cale—W, 2
Camden—L—N, 7—S, 3
Camper—W, 3
Campbell—L, 8—N, 6—K—S, 16
Carroll—W, 2
Carter—L, 2—N, 2—B, 6—K, 2—W, 2
Cash—N, 4—K, 2—S, 7
Catlett—L
Champ—L
Chaplin—N—K, 3
Chapman—N, 5
Charleton—L
Childress—L
Chiles—N, 2
Chittum—L—N—B—K, 5—S, 5
Clark—L—N, 5—B, 12—S, 12
Clatterbaugh—N
Claytor—N, 5
Clemmer—B, 4
Cleveland—N
Cline—S
Clinebell—L
Cobb—L—W
Coe—L, 3
Coffey—S, 5
Coleman—N—B
Collins—N
Condon—W
Connor—L, 6—N—K, 4—W—S, 2
Cook—K
Cooper—L
Copper—K, 2—W, 2—S, 2
Cornelius—L, 2
Corse—L
Cowherd—K
Cox—L, 2—S, 6

Craft—W—K—L
Craig—S
Crawford—L, 3
Crigler—L
Crist—L—B—K—S
Critcher—W
Crutchfield—B
Culton—W—S
Cummings—L—B, 13—K, 2—W
Cummins—N, 6—S, 2
Cunningham—K, 3
Cupp—N—W
Curtis—W
Dale—L—N, 2—K, 3
Damron—W
Daniel—B, 2
Davidson—L, 4—N—K—W, 2—S, 3
Davis—L, 7—W, 8—S, 10
Day—L—N, 2
Deacon—L, 2—B, 11
Deaver—L, 8
Decker—N—S, 4
Deihl—S
Denison—S, 2
Derbyshire—L
Dice—W, 3
Dickenson—N
Dickey—L
Didawick—L
Dill—W
Dillon—L
Divine—L
Dixon—N—B, 2—K, 6—W, 3—S, 2
Dodd—N
Dold—L, 2
Donald—L, 3—N, 7
Douglas—W
Downey—N—B—K, 2
Doyle—W
Drain—N—B, 2
Drawbond—S, 3
Dudley—B—K—W
Duff—S
Dunaway—W
Duncan—N
Dunlap—L, 4—B, 4—K, 5—S
Dunn—L
Durham—W
Eads—N, 2

Eakin—S
Earhart—S
Earman—L
East—W, 8
Easter—L
Ebeling—L, 2
Echols—N
Edwards—L
Effinger—N
Eichelberger—L
Ellinger—W
Elliott—N—B
Emore—L—K—S
Engleman—L—K, 6—S
Ervine—W
Eton—L—N
Ettinger—L
Ewing—B
Fahrenback—N
Fainter—N, 2
Falls—W—S
Falwell—N
Farmer—S
Farror—L—N—S
Farrow—L
Fauber—W—S, 3
Ferguson—N, 13
Finney—N, 2
Firebaugh—L—N, 2—K—W
Fitch—L
Fitzhgerald—N—S, 5
Fitzpatrick—K, 3
Fix—L, 6—N—B, 6—K—S, 2
Flint—N, 3
Flippo—S
Floyd—S, 3
Foltz—L
Forbes—W
Ford—L, 2—N, 2—B, 2—K
Foster—N—B, 2
Foutz—K
Fox—L, 2—N—S
Frame—W
Frazier—B
Fridley—W
Fry—N—S
Fultz—N—S, 6
Fulwider—W—S, 4
Funkhouser—L, 2

Furr—L
Garrett—N, 2
Garrison—N
Gassman—L, 2
Gaylor—K, 4—W—S
Gibson—K, 2—W—S
Gilbert—N
Gilkerson—S
Gillespie—L
Gillock—L, 5
Gilmore—L, 2—N
Ginger—N, 2
Glasgow—L, 3—S
Glass—N
Glendy—K—W, 2
Glenn—N—B
Glover—L
Goodbar—B, 12
Goodloe—W
Goodman—S, 3
Goodwin—B
Gordon—W—S
Gorrell—L
Goulsby—N, 3—S, 3
Gound—N
Gough—W
Graham—L, 4—W, 2
Granger—L
Grant—E, 15
Graves—S
Greaver—L—B, 3—K—W, 2
Green—N, 2—S, 13
Grim—N, 3
Grogg—W, 2
Grove—W
Grow—L—N—S, 2
Guffey—K—W
Guinn—W, 4
Gunter—N
Haislip—S
Hall—N, 2—B, 4—K, 10
Halterman—S
Hamilton—N—B—K, 3—S. 2
Hancock—L
Hannah—N, 2—B
Hardin—N, 2
Harlow—L—K—W
Harman—L, 3—W
Harold—N

Harper—L, 2—K
Harrah—B, 2
Harris—L, 3—N, 5, K, 2—S, 9
Harrison—L, 3—N, 3
Hart—K, 4—W
Hartbarger—K, 6
Hartigan—L, 4—N, 3
Hartless—S, 2
Hartley—L
Hatcher—N, 3
Hatter—S
Hatton—K
Hawkins—L—N
Hawpe—L
Hays—B
Hayslett—L—N, 3—B
Heck—L
Heizer—S, 2
Helmick—W
Hemp—W, 2
Henderson—N—B, 2
Henkle—K—W
Henry—S, 4
Herring—N, 2
Hess—L, 2—S
Hickman—L—N, 6—B—W, 2
Higgenbotham—S
Higgens—L, 3—B—K, 2
Hileman—L—S, 4
Hill—N—W
Hilmore—S
Hinton—S
Hinty—L—N, 3
Hite—K, 2—W—S, 5
Hobson—N
Hockman—S, 2
Hodge—W
Hogan—N, 4
Hogue—B, 2
Holmes—W, 2
Hook—L
Hopkins—L
Horn—K
Hostetter—L—N—B, 9—K, 5
Hotinger—B, 3—K
Houser—L—S, 3
Howe—L
Howerton—L
Houston—L, 2—S

Hoyt—L
Huffman—N, 14—B, 3—W, 2—S, 3
Huger—L
Hughes—N—B—K, 3—W
Hull—B—K—W
Humphries—L, 2—W, 2—S, 4
Hunley—L
Hunt—N—S, 2
Hunter—K—S
Huske—K
Hutchens—W
Hutcheson—K, 2—W, 2
Hutton—L, 4—B
Illig—L
Ingram—W
Irvin—L, 4—B, 6—K
Irwin—L
Jackson—L, 2
Jarvis—W—S, 2
Jeffress—S
Jenkins—N
Jennings—L
Jeter—L
Johenning—L
Johnson—L—N, 6—B, 7—K, 2
Johnston—L, 3—N
Jones—L, 2—W, 3—S, 2
Judy—W, 2
Kahle—L
Kayton—K, 2
Keffer—L, 2
Kelso—W
Kendall—L
Kennedy—L
Kent—L
Kerlin—L
Kern—L
Kerr—L—K, 2
Kesler—K
Kesterson—S
Kidd—L, 2
Kincaid—K
King—L, 2—S
Kinnear—L—S
Kirby—L, 3—K
Kirkpatrick—K, 10—W, 3
Kneighton—L
Knick—B, 14—K, 6
Koogler—S

Kramer—L
Krause—L
Krebbs—L
Kyger—L
Kyle—S
Lackey—L, 2—N, 4—B, 2—K, 2—S, 7
Lady—L
Lair—N—W
Laird—K
Lam—K, 8—S
Lambert—N
Landers—S
Larew—S, 2
Largen—S
Larrick—L
Lavelle—N, 2
Lawhorn—S, 5
Lawson—B, 2
Layne—L
Lee—L, 2—S, 2
Leech—L, 2—N, 6—B, 4—W, 3
Leighton—N
Leslie—B
Letcher—L
Letiro—W
Lewis—N, 2—S, 4
Lilley—S
Lilley—N
Lincoln—N, 2
Lindsay—L, 4—K, 3
Link—N, 3
Linkswiler—K, 2
Liptrap—W
Little—K, 2—W, 2
Lloyd—N
Loan—W
Locher—N, 2
Locke—L
Lockridge—W
Logan—K—W
Logwood—S
Long—L
Lotts—L—N, 7—W, 2
Lovegrove—S
Lowman—K, 3
Lowe—S
Loyall—L
Lucas—L—W, 6—S, 6
Lusk—W

Ludwick—S, 2
Lunsford—N—W, 2—S, 2
Lyle—W, 3—S
Lyons—L, 4
Lytle—B
Mabray—S
Mackay—N, 2—S, 6
Maddox—W, 2
Mahood—N
Major—N
Mallory—L
Mangus—S, 2
Manley—L
Manspile—N, 2—B, 6
Maphis—S, 2
Marks—S
Marshall—N
Martin—L, 3—W—N, 4
Masters—L, 2
Mason—S
Mateer—N
Mathews—N, 2—S—L
May—N, 2
Mayo—N, 2
Mays—N—S, 3
McAlphin—N
McCabe—S
McCauley—S
McClain—L
McClelland—N
McCluer—L
McClung—L, 3—W, 5—S, 3
McClure—N—S, 2
McCorkle—N, 3—B, 5—K
McCormick—L, 4—N, 6—W, 2—S, 6
McCown—K, 12
McCoy—L, 5
McCray—W, 2
McCrowry—S, 2
McCrum—L
McCullough—N, 6—K
McCurdy—K, 3
McCutchen—S
McDaniel—N, 9
McDonald—W
McDowell—L
McElroy—N, 2
McElwee—L
McFadden—L—N—W

McGuffin—K—S, 4
McKeever—W
McKemy—L—K, 3
McKenry—N, 2—B
McKinney—N
McLaughlin—W
McManama—N, 2
McMillen—N
McMullen—W
McNair—N
McNamara—N
McNeal—L
McNeil—N
McNutt—N
Meeks—L—W, 2
Miley—L, 5—S, 2
Miller—L, 7—N, 4—K, 11—W, 5
Milner—L—N, 2
Mitchell—L, 2—N, 5
Mohler—N, 4—K, 4—W
Moneyham—S
Monroe—N, 3
Montgomery—L—B, 10—K, 4—S, 2
Moore—L, 10—N, 14—B, 4—W—S, 11
Moose—N, 3
Moran—N—W, 2
Moreland—L
Morris—N—B, 4—K, 3—S
Morrison—B, 8—K, 5—S, 5
Morter—W, 2
Moses—L, 4
Moxley—N, 2
Mundy—N
Murray—B
Muse—S
Muterspaw—L, 2—K, 6
Myers—B, 3
Mynes—W
Newcomer—K, 3—W
Nicely—L, 3—B, 11—K—S
Nichols—L
Nickel—N, 2
Noel—L—W
Norcross—W
Nuckols—L
Nutty—K
Oakey—W, 2
Obenchain—K, 3
O'Conner—N

Ogawie—W
Ogden—N—S
Osborne—L, 2
Ott—S
Overby—W
Padgett—N, 7
Page—L
Painter—N, 2—B—S, 6
Palmer—L—S
Pappert—L
Parker—B, 2—S, 2
Parks—N, 2
Parrent—L, 2—S, 3
Parsons—L, 5
Patterson—N—B, 2—K, 5—W, 5—S
Patton—L, 3
Paul—S
Paxton—L, 4—N, 4—W—S, 6—W
Pearce—N, 4
Peck—L—N
Peery—N, 4
Pence—K—W
Pendleton—L, 2
Penick—L, 2
Pennington—S
Pettigrew—L
Phillips—K, 3—W, 3
Pierce—N
Pleasants—S, 2
Plott—K—W, 2
Poague—L—S
Poindexter—N
Pole—L
Pollard—L
Potter—B, 10—K, 5—W, 4
Powell—N, 6—K—W—S
Preston—L
Price—N, 3—K, 4—W, 4
Pryor—N
Puckett—N
Pugh—N
Pultz—L, 4—S, 11—N
Quate—N
Quintin—W
Quisenberry—L, 6
Rader—B, 2
Radford—N
Ralston—W, 2
Ramsay—W—S, 3

Randolph—L
Rapp—B
Ratliffe—W
Rawlings—S
Reece—W, 3
Reed—N, 5—W, 7—S, 2
Rees—N, 3—W, 6
Reid—L—B, 8—K—S, 2
Remsburg—L
Reverley—L
Reynolds—N, 2—B, 2—K, 5
Rhea—B
Rhodes—L—N, 3—B, 2—S
Rice—L, 2—N, 9
Richie—W—S, 3
Riley—L, 2—N—K, 8—S
Rinker—K
Roadcap—W, 4
Roberts—N
Robertson—W, 3—S—2
Robinson—L, 2—B, 5—K, 2
Roche—W
Rodenizer—B
Rogers—L, 2
Roop—L
Root—L
Rose—L
Rosen—W—S
Ross—L, 2
Rosser—N
Rowan—S
Rowe—W
Rowsey—B—S
Ruble—L
Rucker—K
Rudasil—S
Ruff—L, 3—N, 2
Ruffner—L
Ruley—K, 3
Runkle—W, 2
Sale—S, 3
Sandridge—W
Sanford—W
Sarver—B, 3
Saunders—S
Saville—B, 7
Scott—N—B, 7—S
Seal—L
Seale—L
Seay—B—2
Secrist—S
Seebert—K, 2
Selph—S

Sensabaugh—K, 11—W, 11
Serrett—W, 2
Seymour—N
Shafer—N, 7—B
Shaner—N, 4
Shaw—K—S—W, 5
Sheltman—S
Shelton—S
Sheppard—S, 2
Sheridan—L,
Shewey—K, 2—S
Shields—L, 3—S, 3
Shifflett—L
Shipp—L
Shoemaker—L, 2—S, 2—K
Short—B, 2—N, 4—B
Shoulder—N—K
Showalter—L, 2
Shuey—K
Siler—B—N
Simbrew—W
Simpson—L
Siron—B, 2
Slough—N, 6
Slusser—L
Smallwood—W
Smedley—L
Smiley—W, 4—S, 2
Smith—L, 8—N, 7—B, 2—K, 6—W—S, 5
Smithson—L
Snead—W
Snider—L, 4—K, 5—W, 2—S, 6
Snow—L
Snyder—N—W, 2
Sorrells—L, 2—N—S, 2
Southerland—W
Spicer—N
Spillman—L
Spitler—K
Starke—N, 2
Staton—N—K—S, 3
Steele—L, 2—S, 2—N—K
Sterrett—N—K—S, 3
Stevens—L—N
Stone—W
Stoner—N, 2—K—W—S
Strain—W
Straub—L, 6—S, 3
Strausburg—K
Stryker—S
Stuart—W, 3
Sullivan—L—N
Supinger—N—W

Suthers—S, 5
Swann—W
Swanson—N
Swartz—N, 2
Sweet—S—W
Swink—L, 2—N—B, 5—W—S
Swisher—L—N—K, 3—W, 10—S, 2
Switzer—L
Swope—L—S
Tankersly—L, 2
Tardy—N, 3—B, 2—K
Taylor—N—B, 2—K—W, 2—S, 4
Teaford—K, 5
Templeton—L—S
Terrell—W
Thomas—B, 2—L—N—W
Thompson—L, 3—N, 3—B, 3—K—W, 2
Thornhill—N
Tolley—L, 9—N, 3—B—K, 5—W, 3
Toman—S, 2—W, 2
Topping—S, 3
Trevey—N, 2
Tribbett—B, 5
Troxell—W, 4—K—S
Trolan—L
Truslow—L, 2
Trussell—K
Tucker—L, 2
Turnbull—L
Turpin—B, 3
Tutwiler—W
Tyler—S
Tyree—S, 3—L, 2—K—W
Vaden—S
VanDevaner—K
Van Devaner—B
Van Derveer—K, 3—W
Van Leer—W
Vanness—B, 5
Varner—L, 2
Vaughan—L
Vess—B, 6
Vest—N, 2—K, 4—W, 2
Waddell—L
Wade—W, 11—S, 3—L, 2—B—K
Walker—L, 5—N, 2—W, 9
Wallace—N, 4—L—S
Walters—W, 2
Walton—S
Ward—W—S
Warfield—L
Warren—N, 2

Wash—K,
Watkins—N,
Watts—N, 12—W, 3—L
Wayland—L
Weade—B
Weaver—L, 2—W
Webb—B—W
Weeks—K, 2—S, 3
Weinberg—L
Weiss—S
Wells—N
Welsh—L, 2—S, 2—K, 3
West—B, 2
Wheeler—W
Whipple—W, 2
White—L, 6—B—W
Whitesell—N, 2—W, 2—S, 4
Whitmore—L, 3—N—K, 2—W—S, 3
Whitney—S
Whiteside—K
Wilfong—W
Wilhelm—B, 6—K, 8
Wilkenson—L
Wilkerson—L
Williamson—S, 2
Wills—L,
Wilmer—N—S, 2
Wilsher—N
Wilson—L, 2—N, 5—B, 3—K, 8—W, 2—S, 5
Wines—L—N
Wise—S
Wiseman—W, 2—S, 4
Withers—S
Withrow—L, 2—W, 5—K
Witt—L
Womelsdorff—L, 3—W
Wood—B—3
Woods—K
Woodson—N
Woodward—L, 2
Woolfolk—N
Worley—N, 2
Worth—B—N
Wray—L
Yancey—S
Yarbro—K
Yost—N
Young—L, 2
Yowell—S, 3
Zimmerman—W, 4
Zollman—L, 3—N, 3—B

SECTION IX

MILITIA OFFICERS, PRIOR TO 1816

Note: D—deceased; res—resigned; ref.—refused; v.—in place of. A star following a date indicates the year of commission. A date without a star indicates nomination only, no record of subsequent qualification appearing in the order-books. But nomination was usually followed by qualification.

Adams, James—captain v. John McCown, 1815.
Adams, Robert—ensign, 1807.
Alexander, Andrew—lieutenant of cavalry under Alexander Shields, v. William Caruthers, 1803.
Alexander, James—captain in First Battalion, 1794.
Alexander, James of John—lieutenant under Campbell, 1809.
Alexander, John—lieutenant, 1799.
Alexander, Joseph—lieutenant colonel, 1793.
Alexander, William—captain in First Battalion v. James Finley, 1805.
Allen, James—lieutenant in First Battalion v. John Bratton, 1800.
Allen, Joseph—major v. David Templeton, 1811.
Anderson, Robert—captain v. Samuel Houston, 1803—res. 1807.
Bailey, William L.—captain v. William Wilson, 1795—res. 1801.
Barclay, Elihu—captain v. Hugh Barclay, 1796—D, 1802.
Blair, Joseph—lieutenant v. John McMullen, 1807
Bradford, Hugh—captain of new company in Second Battalion, 1794—res. 1806.
Bratton, John—captain in Second Battalion, 1793.
Bratton, John—lieutenant in First Battalion, 1794.
Bratton, Robert—lieutenant v. William Elliott, 1812.
Brown, Preston—captain of rifle company, 1797.
Brownlee, Isaac—lieutenant, 1806.
Brownlee, William—major in First Battalion, 1794—res. 1796.
Buchanan, James—captain, 1784.
Burks, Landon—ensign v. Joseph Paxton, 1815.
Burks, Samuel—Ensign under John Croddy, 1812.
Burks, Samuel C.—lieutenant under Henry Salling, 1815.
Cail, David—ensign, 1812.
Campbell, Alexander—captain in Second Battalion, 1793.
Campbell, Alexander—lieutenant v. William Alexander, 1805.
Campbell, Alexander—lieutenant—res. 1796.
Campbell, Charles—captain—1784.
Campbell, Hugh—lieutenant v. Samuel Wilson, 1795.
Campbell, Robert—ensign under John Dixon, 1809.
Carrick, Samuel—lieutenant under Thomas Ocheltree, 1809.
Caruthers, James—captain, 1794—res. as major, 1805.
Caruthers, James—second lieutenant, 1815.
Caruthers, John—captain in Second Battalion, 1794.
Caruthers, Joseph—lieutenant in Second Battalion v. James Cunningham, —res. 1797 (1800).

Caruthers, William—lieutenant of cavalry, 1795—res. 1803.
Caruthers, William, Jr.—ensign v. Matthew White, 1815.
Chandler, John—lieutenant v. John Alexander, 1801.
Cloyd, Andrew—ensign in First Battalion, 1793.
Chandler, Samuel—cornet v. Joseph Grigsby, 1803.
Cloyd, David—lieutenant—1802.
Cloyd, Joseph—ensign under Thomas Ocheltree, 1805.
Crawford, Thomas—ensign in Second Battalion v. James Wilson, 1797.
Croddy, John—ensign under Henry Salling, 1811.
Culton, Joseph—lieutenant under John Stuart, 1805—res. 1815.
Culton, Patrick—lieutenant v. Henry Stuart, 1803.
Culton, Robert—ensign in Second Battalion, 1793.
Cummins, Samuel—ensign v. James McKnight, 1800.
Cunningham, Andrew—ensign v. Thomas Welch, 1797.
Cunningham, James—lieutenant in Second Battalion, 1794—res. 1797.
Cunningham, John—ensign v. Robert McCampbell, 1803.
Cunningham, William—captain, 1813.
Davidson, John—lieutenant, 1813—res. 1815.
Davidson, Robert G.—captain v. Hugh Wilson, 1808.
Davidson, Robert G.—lieutenant v. William Logan, 1815.
Davidson, William—lieutenant, 1787.
Dixon, John—captain v. James McKnight, 1805.
Donald, Blair—ensign, 1805.
Donald, William B.—lieutenant under Dixon, 1806.
Dorman, Cornelius—captain—1806.
Douglass, William—ensign, 1812.
Dryden, Samuel—lieutenant v. William Gilmore, 1802.
Dunlap, William—captain in First Battalion v. John Gay, 1801.
Edmondson, David—major in First Battalion, 1793.
Edmondson, David—captain in Second Battalion, 1794.
Edmondson, David—lieutenant in new company, 1812.
Elliott, James—captain, 1784.
Elliott, James—lieutenant v. James Allen, 1803.
Elliott, William—ensign under William Dunlap, 1806.
Finley, James—captain, 1803—res. 1805.
Gay, Archibald—ensign, 1792.
Gay, John—major—res. 1803.
Gilkeson, Henry—ensign v. Andrew Hodge, 1803.
Gilmore, James—captain v. Thomas Ocheltree, 1809—res 1815.
Gilmore, John—lieutenant colonel, 1778.
Gilmore, John—captain, 1784.
Gilmore, William—captain v. William Hutton, 1811—res. 1815.
Gray, David—captain, 1784.
Greenlee, James—ensign in Second Battalion, 1794.
Greenlee, Samuel—ensign—res. 1802.
Grigsby, Elisha—cornet under Lyle, 1811—res. 1815.
Grigsby, Joseph—cornet—res. 1803.
Grigsby, Reuben—captain of cavalry, Third Regiment, 1815.
Hall, James—captain, 1785.

Hall, Nathaniel—ensign—1786.
Hall, William—lieutenant v. James Allen, 1801.
Hamilton, Archibald—ensign, 1787.
Hamilton, William—captain, 1787.
Hanna, Alexander—lieutenant v. Isaiah McBride, 1805.
Harkins, Samuel—captain v. David Lusk, 1805.
Harper, Samuel—lieutenant of new company in Second Battalion, 1798.
Hays, Charles C.—third lieutenant, 1815.
Hickman, Jacob—captain—res. 1811.
Hodge, Andrew—ensign in Second Battalion v. Hugh Campbell, 1797.
Hoffman, Daniel—ensign v. Isaiah Kincaid, 1805.
Hoffman, ———— —captain, res. 1815.
Hopkins, David—ensign in Light Infantry, 1815.
Hostetter, John—ensign—res. 1815.
Houston, James—lieutenant in First Battalion, 1794.
Houston, John—ensign, 1805.
Houston, Robert—captain of Flying Artillery, 1815.
Houston, Robert—ensign, 1812—ref.
Houston, Samuel—major, 1803—res. 1805.
Houston, William—lieutenant v. James Leech, 1805.
Hutchinson, David—ensign—res. 1815.
Hutchinson, Robert—ensign v. Hugh Stuart, 1800.
Hutton, William—captain—res. 1811.
Irvine, John—lieutenant v. Andrew Wallace, 1815—ref.
Jameson, John—captain v. William Hamilton, 1878.
Jameson, Robert—ensign under William Dunlap, 1805.
Jenkins, William—lieutenant under John Davidson, 1815.
Johnston, James—lieutenant v. William Wilson, 1811.
Johnston, Zachariah—ensign—res. 1797.
Jordan, James—second lieutenant v. John McCampbell, 1811.
Jordan, John—first lieutenant v. Reuben Grigsby, 1815.
Kennedy, James—ensign in First Battalion, 1794.
Keys, Samuel—lieutenant in Second Battalion, 1793.
Kincaid, Isaiah—captain v. Samuel Harkins, 1806—res. 1811.
Kirkpatrick, Charles—captain v. Hugh Weir, 1795.
Lapsley, Joseph—lieutenant v. Alexander Shields, 1788.
Leech, James—lieutenant of new company, 1797—res. 1805.
Leech, John—ensign v. John Hostetter, 1813.
Leech, John, Jr.—lieutenant under Hugh Wilson v. Robert Davidson, 1806.
Letcher, John—ensign v. Sylvanus Rollison, 1815.
Leyburn, John—captain of artillery—1806.
Lindsay, Robert—lieutenant v. William Hall, 1802.
Lindsay, James—captain v. John Gilmore, 1815.
Lusk, David—lieutenant in Second Battalion v. Andrew Weir, 1797.
Lyle, Archibald—second lieutenant v. Andrew Alexander, 1797.
Lyle, James—major—1813.
Lyle, William—ensign, 1803.
Mackey, James—second lieutenant of Light Artillery—res. 1815.
Mackey, William—lieutenant in Second Battalion, 1793.

Maxwell, Audley—lieutenant in Second Battalion, 1794.
McAllister, Charles—captain in First Battalion v. Preston Brown, 1797.
McBride, Isaiah—lieutenant v. Samuel Patterson, 1800.
McCalpin, Robert—captain v. Jacob Hickman, 1811.
McCampbell, James—captain in First Battalion, 1794—res. 1797.
McCampbell, John—second lieutenant in Lyle's cavalry, 1806—res. 1811.
McCampbell, Robert—lieutenant v. William Hutton, 1803.
McCampbell, Samuel—ensign in Second Battalion, 1794.
McClung, Benjamin—ensign v. James Paxton, 1813.
McClung, Henry—captain of artillery v. Thomas L. Preston, 1812.
McClung, James—captain, 1798—res. 1803.
McClung, Joseph—lieutenant v. James Lyle, 1800.
McClung, William—lieutenant—1788.
McClure, John of John—lieutenant v. William Walker, 1815.
McCorkle, Alexander—captain v. James Templeton, 1811.
McCorkle, Samuel—lieutenant v. William Paxton, 1812.
McCown, John—captain v. Robert Anderson, 1807—res. 1815.
McCrory, William—lieutenant, 1798.
McCue, Cyrus—ensign v. Robert Houston, 1812.
McDowell, James—colonel commandant, 1796
McDowell, Samuel—colonel, 1778
McElheny, John—major, 1785.
McKee, John—captain in First Battalion, 1793.
McKee, John—lieutenant of Rifles, 1794.
McKee, John T.—lieutenant, 1808.
McKee, William—colonel commandant—res. 1796.
McKnight, James—captain v. James McClung, 1803—res. 1805.
McMullen, John—captain of light infantry v. William Wallace, 1807.
McNabb, Samuel—lieutenant, 1787.
McNabb, William—lieutenant in Second Battalion, 1794.
Miller, Henry—captain v. James Gilmore, 1815.
Miller, Samuel—ensign v. William Gilmore, 1811.
Montgomery, John—lieutenant v. Robert Bratton, 1815.
Montgomery, Robert—lieutenant in First Battalion, 1793.
Montgomery, Robert—ensign in Second Battalion, 1794.
Montgomery, Samuel—second lieutenant of light artillery v. James Mackey, 1815.
Moore, Alexander—lieutenant in Lyle's rifle company, 1801—res. 1813.
Moore, Andrew—lieutenant colonel, 1787.
Moore, David—lieutenant—1786.
Moore, Hugh—ensign, 1805.
Moore, John—ensign under Hugh Wilson, 1806.
Moore, Joseph—captain, 1785.
Moore, Samuel—captain, 1795—res. 1797.
Moore, Samuel McD.—ensign v. James Taylor, 1815.
Moore, William—captain, 1784.
Moore, William—ensign v. John Hostetter, 1815.
Moorhead, John—ensign v. William Wallace, 1806.
Ocheltree, Thomas—captain v. Elihu Barclay, 1803—res. 1809.
Patterson, Samuel—lieutenant v. Alexander Wardlaw, 1797.

Patton, Alexander—ensign v. William Alexander, 1803.
Paxton, Alexander—second lieutenant, 1815.
Paxton, James—captain of rifle company v. James Lyle, 1813.
Paxton, James—ensign—res. 1815.
Paxton, John—captain, 1784—D, 1787.
Paxton, Jonathan—ensign v. John Letcher, 1815.
Paxton, Joseph—captain, 1812—res. 1815.
Paxton, Joseph—ensign v. Samuel C. Burks, 1815.
Paxton, Joseph, Jr.—lieutenant v. Joseph Walker, 1806.
Paxton, Thomas—lieutenant v. Alexander Campbell, 1796.
Paxton, William—major in Second Battalion, 1794.
Paxton, William—captain in new company, 1812.
Poage, Jonathan—captain in First Battalion, 1793.
Poague, Jonathan—lieutenant in Second Battalion, 1794.
Porter, William—lieutenant, 1803.
Preston, Thomas L.—captain of artillery v. John Leyburn, 1806.
Reid, Samuel McD—captain v. Daniel Hoffman, 1815.
Rhea, James—ensign, 1815.
Robinson, William—captain v. Hugh Bradford, 1805.
Rogers, Allery—lieutenant v. Samuel Wilson, 1812.
Rogers, Andrew—ensign v. Allery Rogers, 1812.
Rollison, Sylvanus—ensign, 1811—res. 1813.
Ruff, John—ensign, 1809—ref.
Salling, Henry—captain v. Joseph Paxton, 1815.
Salling, Hugh—ensign v. Hugh Paxton, Jr., 1806.
Scott, Andrew—lieutenant in Second Battalion, 1794.
Scott, Jesse—ensign v. William B. Donald, 1806.
Seacott, Charles—captain in Second Battalion v. Elihu Barclay, 1802.
Shields, Alexander—captain of cavalry, 1795.
Shields, David—lieutenant v. John McKee, 1798.
Shields, William—cornet v. Elihu Grigsby, 1815.
Simons, John—lieutenant, 1797.
Sissons, James—lieutenant under Thomas Ocheltree, 1803.
Sloan, John—ensign v. Joseph Blair, 1807—res. 1815.
Smiley, Daniel—lieutenant v. Alexander Moore, 1813.
Steele, William—colonel, 1788.
Stuart, Hugh—lieutenant v. Alexander Walker, 1800.
Stuart, John—captain in First Battalion, 1794—res. 1800.
Stuart, John—ensign v. William Walker, 1796.
Stuart, John, Jr.—lieutenant in Second Battalion, 1793.
Stuart, Walker—lieutenant v. Joseph Culton, 1815.
Tate, John—ensign v. John Taylor, 1809.
Taylor James—ensign—res. 1815.
Taylor, William—lieutenant, 1815.
Tedford, James—captain in First Battalion v James McCampbell, 1797—res. 1803.
Tedford, John—captain, 1784.
Tedford, Robert—lieutenant in Second Battalion, 1793.
Templeton, David—major v. James Caruthers, 1805—res. 1811.
Templeton, James—captain v. David Templeton, 1805—res. 1811.

Walker, Alexander—captain v. John Stuart, 1800.
Walker, John—ensign, 1809—ref.
Walker, John C—ensign v. Walker Stuart, 1815.
Walker, John M.—lieutenant under Jacob Hickman, 1806.
Walker, Joseph—ensign under Jacob Hickman, 1809.
Walker, William, Jr.—lieutenant v. John McCown, 1807—res. 1815.
Wallace, Andrew—lieutenant v. Daniel Hoffman, 1811—res. 1815.
Wallace, William—lieutenant under Samuel Harkins v. Isaiah Kincaid, 1806—D, 1807.
Wardlaw, Andrew—lieutenant in First Battalion, 1794—res. 1797.
Weir, Andrew—lieutenant under Windle, 1795—res. 1797.
Weir, Hugh—captain in Second Battalion—res. 1795.
Welch, Benjamin—ensign, 1815.
Welch, John—ensign, 1802.
Welch, Thomas—ensign in Second Battalion, 1794—res. 1797.
White, Matthew—ensign v. David Hutchinson, 1815—ref.
White, Nathaniel—first lieutenant, 1815.
White, Robert—first lieutenant v. Henry McClung, 1812.
Wiley, Joseph—ensign v. Samuel McCampbell, 1797—res. 1801.
Wilson, David—major v. Samuel Houston, 1805—res. 1813.
Wilson, David—ensign in First Battalion—res. 1795.
Wilson, Hugh—captain of new company, 1797—res. 1805.
Wilson, Hugh of Thomas—lieutenant v. William McNabb, 1795.
Wilson, James—captain in First Battalion, 1793.
Wilson, James—ensign in Second Battalion, 1794—res. 1797.
Wilson, John—major in First Battalion v. William Brownlee, 1796.
Wilson, John—ensign v. Thomas Wilson, 1812.
Wilson, Joseph—ensign, 1813—res. 1815.
Wilson, Samuel—lieutenant, 1786—res. 1795.
Wilson, Samuel—lieutenant v. Alexander Hanna, 1811.
Wilson, Thomas—ensign v. Joseph Wilson, 1815—res. 1815.
Wilson, William—captain in Second Battalion, 1794—res. 1803.
Wilson, William—captain v. James Allen, 1811.
Wilson, William—ensign, 1815.
Windle, ——— —captain—1795.
Withrow, John—ensign in Grenadier Company, 1794.
Woods, James—lieutenant v. John Dixon, 1805.
Woods, James—ensign under Thomas Ocheltree, 1809.
Young, Andrew—ensign v. Alexander Hanna, 1805.
Young, James—lieutenant v. John Dixon, 1805.

SECTION X

SOLDIERS OF THE REVOLUTION

Backhouse, Joseph—died in service, 1777—Thomas Steele, executor.
Beattie, John—killed at King's Mountain, 1780.
Berry, Thomas—in expedition against the Cherokees, 1778.
Borden, James—Judith, widow, had pension of 10 pounds, 1796.
Bradley, William—born, 1759—sergeant in Seventh Virginia under Buford—had 13 wounds in the Waxhaw massacre—pension of $60 a year, 1788—many signers to his application for increase, 1815.
Bunton, Alexander—given pension, 1787—living in Ohio, 1812.
Caldwell, John—disabled and drawing pension of $40, 1788.
Campbell, James.
Carr, Richard—Margaret, widow, was drawing $40 a year, 1792—petitions Assembly for increase—children: David (born 1775), Margaret (born 1777), Robert (born 1779).
Caruthers, John—lieutenant.
Cuddy, James—in Cherokee expedition, 1778.
Davidson, John.
Dryden, Nathaniel—killed at King's Mountain.
Dunn, James—married Martha Long—came to Rockbridge about 1762—in Clarke's expedition, 1778.
Dunn, Samuel—son of above—captain.
Edmondson—three of this name killed at King's Mountain.
Erwin (or Ervine), John—born about 1755—in Fourth Virginia under Colonel Haws—in Yorktown campaign—served against the Indians, 1781-3—in 1818 asks a balance due him.
Fenter (or Finder), Frederick—born 1760—served under Buford—wounded at Guilford—asks Assembly for pension, 1816.
Forehand, John—died 1838—wife, Rebecca, whom he married 1785, was born 1756.
Fulton, Andrew—13 wounds at Guilford, but lived to old age and served in Assembly.
Fulton, Hugh—major—in battle of Guilford.
Gilmore, James—captain.
Gray, ————Captain.
Graham, William—captain.
Greiner, John—captain in Cherokee expedition, 1778.
Grigsby, William—wounded at Guilford.
Hall, James—captain.
Hays, John—captain.
Henderson, Samuel—under Greiner in Cherokee expedition, 1778.
Hosteter, Ulrich—born 1749—pensioner, 1832.
Houston, Samuel, Sr.—major.
Houston, Samuel—in battle of Guilford.
Hughes, John—pensioner—died 1851—children: Cynthia (Giles county, Tenn.), Hannah (Floyd county), Edward (Ohio), Polly, Rebecca, Susan, and Wildey in Rockbridge. Cynthia and Hannah married Tankersleys, Susan, a McCrory.
King, John—born 1765—thigh broken at Yorktown, where he was serving under Captain Charles Calloway—asks for pension, 1818.

Kirkpatrick, Samuel—born about 1759—wounded at Guilford.
Logan, James—three years in Twelfth Virginia under Colonel Wood.
Lyle, William—lieutenant.
Lyons, William—killed in service—wife, Mary—children: William (born 1776), John (born 1778), Peter and Paul (born 1781), Ephraim (born 1783).
Malcolm, James—servant to Andrew Alexander.
Mathews, Sampson—colonel.
Mathews, George—colonel.
McClure, Robert—in Cherokee expedition, 1778.
McCorkle, James—ensign—killed at Cowpens.
McCorkle, John—ensign—died of wounds received at Cowpens.
McCown, Joseph—served against the Indians, 1777-8, and in Yorktown campaign—asks for pension, 1818.
McDowell, Samuel, Sr.—colonel.
McGier, Samuel—in Cherokee expedition, 1778.
McKee, William.
McLaughlin, James—in Cherokee expedition, 1778.
McNutt, Robert—mortally wounded at Cowpens.
McNutt, Alexander.
McNutt, William.
McNutt, George—said to have been in battle of King's Mountain.
Moody, William—born about 1743—in Eighth Virginia Continentals—wounded near Amboy and at Brandywine, captured at Charleston—asks Assembly for relief, 1812, Dr. Campbell saying he is "a good deal cut and hacked"—General James Wood says he is entitled to land bounty.
Moore, William.
Paul, Audley, Sr.—in military service from 1745 to the close of the Revolution and received no pay—Audley, Jr., his youngest son, asks for pension, 1839.
Plunkett, Thomas—came out of the Revolution with his constitution impaired—keeping a small shop, 1816, and through ignorance of the law, fined for selling liquor—quit selling it, but cannot pay his fines without selling his house in Lexington—petition to Assembly has many signers—granted $60 a year pension, 1817—wife Polly—died 1831.
Reardon—under Captain Adam Wallace in Seventh Virginia—six wounds at Waxhaw—six children and asks,—about 1815,—for an increase in pension above his present allowance of $40.
Ritchy, William—in Cherokee expedition, 1778.
Robinson, John.
Russell, Samuel—died 1832—wife Hannah, born 1787.
Stuart, Alexander—wounded at Guilford.
Taylor, John—killed in service.
Taylor, Caufield—taken prisoner.
Thomas, James—clerk to Captain Greiner in Cherokee expedition, 1778.
Valentine, James—in Cherokee expedition, 1778.
Vineyard, George.
Wallace, Adam—captain in Buford's Continentals—killed at Waxhaw.
Wallace, Andrew—captain—killed at Guilford.
Wallace, ———died of smallpox in service.
Ward, William.

Watkins, William—served under Captain William Armistead—asks for pension, 1828.

Watkins, John—died 1838—children: Harriet, Poly, Paulina, Eliza, married, respectively, Isaac Thomas, John Wilcher, Lewis Collins, James Withrow. Harriet lives on the Kanawha, Paulina in East Tennessee.

Wier (or Wear), Samuel—born about 1750—married Mary Thompson—at King's Mountain.

Wilhelm, Michael—came from Germany about 1764, at the age of seven—witnesses in pension claim: Adam Unroe, Richard Morris, William Wintz.

Wilson, James—right arm nearly stiff from wound received from the Mohawks in 1763—volunteered in 1777—had 10 pounds pension a year under colonial rule, but lost it after independence came—petitions Assembly, 1811.

SECTION XI

ROCKBRIDGE ARTILLERY

The following officers and men were mustered into the service of the Confederate States at Staunton, Va., on the 11th day of May, 1861:

Capt. W. N. Pendleton, Brigadier General, Chief Artillery A. N. V., paroled at Appomattox.

1st Lieut. J. B. Brockenbrough, wounded 1st Manassas, Capt. Baltimore Artillery A. N. V.

2nd Lieut. Wm. McLaughlin, Capt. Lieut.-Col. Artillery.

2nd Lieut. W. T. Poague, Capt., Lieut.-Col. Artillery A. N. V., wounded at 2nd Cold Harbor, paroled at Appomattox.

1st Serg. J. McD. Alexander, Lieut. Rockbridge Artillery, entered Cavalry.

2nd Serg. J. Cole Davis, Lieut. Rockbridge Artillery, wounded Port Republic, paroled at Appomattox.

3rd Serg. Arch. Graham, Lieut and Capt. Rockbridge Artillery, paroled at Appomattox.

PRIVATES

Agner, Jos. S., killed at Fredericksburg, Dec. 13, 1862.

Ayres, Jas., discharged for physical disability, Aug., 1861.

Ayres, N. B., deserted, went into Federal Army.

Anderson, S. D., killed at Kernstown, March 23, 1862.

Beard, John E., killed at Fredericksburg, Dec. 13, 1862.

Beard, W. B., died from effects of measles, summer of 1861.

Bain, Sam'l.

Brockenbrough, W. N., Corp., transferred to Baltimore Light Artillery.

Brown, W. M., Corp., Serg., Lieut., wounded and captured at Gettysburg.

Bumpus, W. N., Corporal, paroled at Appomattox.

Conner, Geo., arm broken by stallion, absent after winter of 1861-2.

Conner, Jas. A., wounded at Sharpsburg and Gettysburg, took the oath in prison—joined Federal Army and fought in northwest.

Conner, John C., paroled at Appomattox.

Coffee, A. W.

Craig, John B., paroled at Appomattox.

Crosen, W.

Curran, Caniel, died of disease in summer 1862.

Davis, Mark, deserted.

Davis, R. G., died from disease in 1861.

Doran, John, wounded at Malvern Hill 1862, disabled.

Dudley, R. M.

Ford, Henry, discharged after one year.

Ford, Jas. A., wounded.

Gibbs, J. T., Jr., wounded at Port Republic, June 22, 1862, died from disease.

Gold, J. M., captured at Gettysburg and died in prison.

Gordon, W. C.

Harris, Alex., captured at Gettysburg, died in prison.

Harris, Bowlin, captured at Gettysburg, kept in prison.
Hetterick, Ferdinand, discharged after one year.
Henry, N. S., Corporal, Serg., paroled at Appomattox.
Hughes, Wm., discharged.
Hostetter, G. W., transferred to Infantry.
Johnson, Lawson, died in summer of 1861.
Johnston, W. F., Corporal, Q. M. Serg., paroled at Appomattox.
Jordan, J. W., wounded at 1st Manassas, Corp., Serg., Lieut., paroled at Appomattox.
Leopard, Jas., transferred to Carpenter's Battery.
Lewis, Henry P., transferred to Cavalry in spring of 1862.
Leyburn, John, Lieut. Rock. Arty., Surgeon on Privateer.
Martin, Thomas, wounded, captured at Gettysburg.
McCampbell, D. A., died from disease at J. Poague Lackey's, Oak Bank, Rock. Co., Va., Dec. 11, 1864.
McCampbell, W. H., paroled at Appomattox.
McCluer, Jno. G., Corporal Rock. Arty., transferred to Cavalry.
McCorkle, J. Baxter, Corp., Serg., Lieut., Rock. Arty., killed at Fredericksburg.
Montgomery, W. G., killed at 1st Fredericksburg.
Moore, D. E., Corp., Serg., w'd Winchester and Malvern Hill, paroled Appomattox.
Moore, Jno. D., Q. M. Serg., captured after Gettysburg, prsnr. till close war.
Moore, Sam R., mortally wounded at Sharpsburg.
Morgan, G. W., sick and absent most of time.
O'Rourke, Frank, wounded at Malvern Hill, deserted.
Paxton, J. Lewis, Serg., lost leg at Kernstown.
Phillips, James.
Preston, Frank, lost an arm at Winchester, May 25, 1863, Capt. V. M. I. Co.
Raynes, A. G., detailed as miller.
Rader, D. P., wounded at Fredericksburg, Dec. 13, 1862.
Rhodes, J. N., discharged over age.
Smith, Jos. S., transferred to cavalry, killed in battle.
Smith, S. C., Corporal, Serg., paroled at Appomattox.
Smith, Adam, discharged after one year.
Strickler, Jas.
Strickler, W. L., Corporal, Serg., paroled at Appomattox.
Silvey, James, paroled at Appomattox.
Tharp, Benj. F., transferred to Cavalry in spring of 1862.
Thompson, Jno. A., paroled at Appomattox.
Thompson, S. G.
Thompkins, J. F., Corporal, detailed in Ordnance Department.
Trevy, Jacob, wounded at Gettysburg, paroled at Appomattox.
Wallace, John, killed at Kernstown, March 23, 1862.
Wilson, S. A., discharged for physical disability, Aug., '61, joined cavalry.

The following joined the battery after May 11, 1861, dates of enlistment being given as far as known.

Adams, Thos. T., enlisted 1863, discharged, afterwards killed in battle.
Adkins, Blackburn, paroled at Appomattox.
Agner, Oscar W., paroled at Appomattox.
Agner, John, enlisted July 21, 1861.
Agner, Jonathan, En. July 29, 1861, killed at 1st Winchester, May 25, 1862.

Agner, Sam. S., En. Fall of 1862.
Alexander, Edgar S., En. Sept. 2, 1861, lost an arm at Fredericksburg, 1862.
Alexander, Eugene, Enl. Aug. 23, 1861, w'd at 2nd Manassas, transf'd to Cavalry.
Armistead, Chas. J., paroled at Appomattox.
Arnold, A. E., En. Sept. 1, 1861, Corporal, Asst. Surgeon.
Bacon, Edloe P., paroled at Appomattox.
Bacon, Edloe P., Jr., paroled at Appomattox.
Baldwin, Wm. Ludlow, paroled at Appomattox.
Barger, Wm. G., paroled at Appomattox.
Barton, Dav. R., Enl. June 27, '61, Lieut. in Carpenter's Battery, killed.
Barton, Robert T., Enl. March 7, '62.
Bedinger, G. R., July 9, '61, transferred to Inf. Kld. at Gettysburg, Capt.
Bealle, Jerry T., Enl. Nov. 21, 1861.
Bell, Robert S., Enl. Nov. 19, 1861, killed at Rappahannock Station.
Black, Benj. F., paroled at Appomattox.
Blain, Daniel, Enl., May 27, '61, detailed in Ord. Dept., paroled Appomattox.
Blackford, L. M., enl. Sept. 2, '61. Adjt. 24th Va. Inf.
Bolling, W. H., enl. March 10, '62, Corporal
Boteler, A. R., Jr., enl. March 1, '62, wounded May 25, '62.
Boteler, Chas. P., enl. Oct. 23, '61, transferred to Cavalry.
Boteler, Henry, enl. Oct. 10, '61, Corporal, paroled at Appomattox.
Boyd, E. Holmes, enl. June 28, '61. Transferred to Ord. Dept.
Brooke, Pendleton, enl. Oct. 28, '61, discharged for physical disability.
Brown, H. C., enl. 1862, detailed in Signal Corps.
Brown, Jno. L., enl. July 23, '61. killed at Malvern Hill.
Brown, Jno. M., enl. Mar. 11, '62. w'd Malvern Hill, paroled Appomattox.
Bryan, Edward, enl. Nov. 22, '61.
Burwell, Lewis P., enl. Sept. 21, '61, transferred.
Byers, G. Newton, enl. Aug. 23, '61, Corporal, paroled at Appomattox.
Byrd, W. H., enl. Aug. 15, '61, killed at Kernstown, Mar. 23, '62.
Carson, Wm., enl. July 23, '61, Corporal, paroled at Appomattox.
Caruthers, Thornton, enl. Dec. 21, '62.
Chapin, W. T.
Clark, Jas. G., June 15, '62., transferred.
Clark, J. Gregory, enl. July 16, '62, transferred.
Cook, Richard D., paroled at Appomattox.
Compton, Robert K., enl. July 25, '61., paroled at Appomattox.
Conner, Alex., enl. July 23, '61, wnd. May 25, '62 at Winchester, par. Appomattox.
Conner Daniel enl. July 27th, '62.
Conner, Fitz. G.
Conner, Henry G., paroled at Appomattox.
Cox, W. H., enl. July 23, '61.
Craig, Joseph E., enl. March 2, '63.
Crocken, Francis J., enl. March 21, '61.
Dandridge, A. Stephen, enl. 1862, paroled at Appomattox.
Darnell, Andrew M., captured at Deep Bottom.
Darnall, Henry T., enl. July 23, '61, paroled at Appomattox.
Davis, Chas. W., paroled at Appomattox.
Davis M. M., paroled at Appomattox.

Davis, John E., died from disease June 1864.
Dixon, W. H. H., enl. July 23, '61, wnd. Dec. 13, '62, paroled at Appomattox.
Dold, C. M., enl. March 3, '62, wnd at Newtown. Paroled at Appomattox.
Effinger, W. H., wdn. at Sharpsburg. Transferred to Engineers.
Emmett, Michael J., enl. June 15, '61. Wnd. and captured at Gettysburg.
Eppes, W. H., wnd. Sept. '62.
Estill, W. C., paroled at Appomattox.
Fairfax, Randolph, enl. Aug. 10, '61, wnd. at Malvern Hill, killed 1st Fredkbg.
Friend, Ben. C. M., paroled at Appomattox.
Fuller, Jno., enl. July 23, '61. wnd. at Mal. Hill, killed at 1st Fredkbg.
Garnett, Jas. M., enl. July 17, '61, Lieut. on Staff.
Gerardi, Edward.
Gibson, Henry B., enl. May 13, '62.
Gibson, Jno. T., enl. Aug. 14, '61.
Gibson, Robert A., paroled at Appomattox.
Gilliam, Wm. T.
Gilmer, James M., paroled at Appomattox.
Gilmore, J. Harvey, enl. March 7, '62, chaplin.
Ginger, Geo. A., enl. March 6, '62, wnd. at Newtown, paroled at Appomattox.
Ginger, W. L., enl. March 6, '62, wnd. and captured at Gettysburg, prs. till end war.
Gold, Alfred, enl. July 23, '61. wnd. at 2nd Fredkbg.
Gooch, Jas. T., transferred from Engineers 1863, paroled Appomattox.
Goul, Jno. M., enl. June 14, '61. Chaplin A. N. Va., died of fever in service.
Gray, O. P., enl. Mar. 21, '62, killed at Kernstown Mar. 23, '62.
Gregory, Jno. M., enl. Sept. 7, '61, wnd. May 25, '62, Capt. in Ord. Dept.
Green, Thos., enl. 1862, transferred
Green, Zach, enl. 1862, transferred.
Gross, Chas., enl. July 27, '62.
Hall, Jno. F., enl. July 23, '61. Died near Richmond, '62.
Heiskell, J. Campbell, enl. Feb. 9, '62, wnd. in 64 paroled at Appomattox.
Herndon, Francis T., enl. Mar. 21, '62, killed at Mal. Hill.
Hither, Jno K., enl. Mar. 17, '62, wnd.
Holmes, Jno. A., enl. March 11, '62.
Houston, Jas. Rutherford, enl. July 23, '61.
Houston, M. W., enl. Aug. 10, '61, Chaplin A. N. V.
Hughes, Wm., enl. July 23, '61.
Hummerickhouse, John R., enl. Mar. 28, '62.
Hyde, Edward H., enl. Mar. 28, '62, paroled at Appomattox.
Johnson, Thos. E.
Jones, Beverly R., enl. July 3, '61.
Kean, Otho G., enl. after capture at Vicksburg, paroled at Appomattox.
Kean, Wm. C., enl. fall '61, transferred
Knick, Wm., enl. Aug. 11, '62, mortally wnd. at 2nd Fredkbg.
Lacy, Richard B.
Lacy, Wm. S., enl. Mar. 17, '62, detailed Sig. Service, Chaplin.
Lawson, Joseph, enl. July 20, '63.
Lawson, Wm., enl. July 20, '63.
Leathers, John P., paroled at Appomattox.
Lackey, Jno. H., enl. July 23, '61, transferred to Cavalry.

Lee, Robert E., Jr., enl. Mar. 28, '62, Lieut. on Staff and Capt.
Lee, Jas. M., paroled at Appomattox.
Letcher, Sam. H., paroled at Appomattox.
Lewis, Jas. P., enl. July 23, '61, wnd.
Lewis, Nicholas H., enl. June 17, '61.
Link, David, transferred from Rice's Battery.
Luke, Williamson, enlisted Oct. 7, '61, soon transferred to Cavalry.
McAlpine, Jos., enlisted March 3, '62, mortally wounded at 1st Fredericksburg.
McCauley, Jno. E., enlisted July 23, '61, Serg., paroled Appomattox.
McCauley, Wm. H., transferred from Infantry. Corp., killed April 7, '65.
McClintic, W. S., enlisted October 4, '61, wounded, paroled at Appomatox.
McCorkle, Tazewell E.. enlisted in Hampden-Sidney Co. '61, captured at Rich Mountain, joined Battalion '64.
McCorkle, Thos. E., enlisted March 9, '62, paroled at Appomattox.
McCorkle, Wm. A., enlisted July 23, '61, paroled at Appomattox.
McCrum, R. Barton, paroled at Appomattox.
McGuire, Hugh H., Jr., enlisted March 10, '62, transferred to Cavalry, Capt.
McKim, Robert B., enlisted July 6, '61, killed at Winchester May 25, '62.
Macon, Lyttleton S., enlisted June 27, '61, Corp., Serg., discharged.
Magruder, Horatio E., paroled at Appomattox.
Marshall, Jno. J., paroled at Appomattox.
Marshall, Oscar M., enlisted March 6, '62.
Massie, John Livingston, enlisted May 15, '61. Capt. Artillery, killed.
Mateer, Sam. L., enlisted January 11, '63, paroled at Appomattox.
Maury, Magruder, enlisted in fall of '61, transferred to Cavalry.
Maury, Thos. B., enlisted in fall of '61, detailed in Signal Service.
Meade, Francis A., enlisted November, '62, paroled at Appomattox.
Merrick, Alfred D., enlisted December 30, '61.
Minor, Chas., enlisted November 16, '61, transferred to Engineers.
Minor, Carter, N. B. Enlisted July 27, '61.
Minor, Launcelot, wounded Cum. Church.
Moore, Edward A., enlisted March 3, '62, wounded at Sharpsburg, twice at 2nd Cold Harbor, paroled at Appomattox.
Moore, Jno. H., transferred from Rockbridge Rifles in spring of '61, paroled at Appomatox.
Moore, Jno. L., enlisted July 23, '61, wounded.
Mooterspaugh, Wm., enlisted '62, paroled at Appomattox.
Montgomery, Ben. T., transferred from another Battalion. paroled at Appomattox.
Myers, Jno. M., paroled at Appomattox.
Nelson, Francis K., enlisted May 17, '61, transferred to Albemarle Light Horse.
Nelson, Kinlock, transferred from Albemarle Light Horse. Disabled by caisson turning over on him.
Nelson, Phillip, enlisted July 27, '61, discharged by furnishing substitute.
Nicely, Geo. H., enlisted March 7, '62, died from disease, '64.
Nicely, Jas. W., enlisted March 7, '62, deserted.
Nicely, Jno. F., enlisted July 23, '61, wounded at Port Republic.
Otey, Wm. M., enlisted '62, transferred soon after.
Packard, Jos., enlisted July 7, '61, Corp., Lieut. Ordnance Dept.
Packard, Walter J., enlisted October 23, '61, died summer of '62.

Page, Richard C. M., enlisted July 14, '61, transferred, Capt., Major, Artillery.
Page, R. Powell, enlisted May 1, '64, detailed to Col. Carter.
Paine, Henry M.
Paine, Henry R., enlisted July 23, '61, Corp., Serg., killed at 2nd Manassas.
Paine, Jas. A.
Paxton, Sam. A., enlisted March 7, '62.
Pendleton, Dudley D., enlisted June 19, '61, Capt. and A. A. Gen. Artillery A. N. Va.
Pleasants, Robert A., enlisted March 3, '62.
Pollard, Jas. G., Jr., enlisted July 27, '64, paroled at Appomattox.
Porter, Mouina G., enlisted September 24, '61, detailed courier.
Phillips, Chas., detailed in Signal Service.
Pugh, Geo. W., enlisted March 6, '62, paroled at Appomattox.
Pugh, Jno. A., paroled at Appomattox.
Rawlings, Jas. M.
Rentzell, Geo. W., enlisted July 23, '61, wounded at Kernstown and disabled.
Robertson, Jno. W., paroled at Appomattox.
Robinson, Authur, enlisted March 28, '62, mortally wounded at 1st Fredericksburg.
Root, Erastus C., paroled at Appomattox.
Ruffin, Jefferson, transferred from another Battalion, paroled at Appomattox.
Rutledge, Chas. A., enlisted November 3, '61, transferred.
Sanford, Jas., paroled at Appomatox.
Saville, Jno., enlisted July 23, '61. Transferred to Cavalry, died in service.
Shaner, Jos., enlisted July 23, '61, wounded 1st Fredericksburg, paroled at Appomattox.
Shaw, Campbell A., paroled at Appomattox.
Shoulder, Jacob M., paroled at Appomattox.
Singleton, Wm. F., enlisted June 3, '61, wounded and captured at Fort Republic.
Schammerhorn, Jno. G.
Smith, J. Howard, enlisted September 2, '61, Lieut. Ordnance Dept.
Smith, Jas. P., enlisted July 9, '61, Lieut. and Capt. on Staff of Gen. Jackson.
Smith. Jas. Morrison.
Smith, Summerfield, enlisted September 2, '61, died from disease.
Stuart, J. W. C., enlisted May 13, '62, wounded May 25, '62, killed 2nd Fredericksburg.
Strickler, Jas., paroled at Appomattox.
Stuart, W. C., wounded 2nd Cold Harbor, paroled at Appomattox.
Swan, Minor W., enlisted August 15, '63, paroled at Appomattox.
Swan, Robert W.
Swisher, Sam S., paroled at Appomattox.
Swisher, Geo. W., enlisted March 3, '62, wounded May 25, '62, paroled at Appomattox.
Swisher, Sam. S., paroled at Appomattox.
Tate, Jas. F., paroled at Appomattox.
Taylor, Chas. F.
Taylor, Stephens M., paroled at Appomattox.
Thompson, Ambrose, died July, '64.
Thompson, Lucas P., enlisted August 15, '61, paroled at Appomattox
Tidball, Thos. H., enlisted March 3, '62, paroled at Appomattox.
Timberlake, Francis H.
Tomlinson, Jas. W., enlisted July 23, '61.
Trice, Leroy F., paroled at Appomattox.
Truehart, Chas. W., enlisted October 24, '61, Corp., Asst. Surgeon.

Tyler, D. Gardner, paroled at Appomattox.
Tyler, Jno. Alex., enlisted April, '65, paroled at Appomattox.
Van Pelt, Robert, enlisted July 23, '61.
Veers, Chas. O., enlisted September 10, '61, transferred to Cavalry soon after.
Vest, Andrew J., enlisted July 23, '61. Discharged.
Wade, Thos. M., enlisted March 7, '62, paroled at Appomattox.
Walker, Geo. A., enlisted July 23, '61, transferred to Carpenter's Battery
Walker, Jas. S., enlisted July 23, '61, transferred to Carpenter's Battery.
Walker, Jno. W., enlisted July 23, '61, transferred to Carpenter's Battery.
Whitt, Algernon S., enlisted August 8, '61, Corp., paroled at Appomattox.
White, Wm. H., paroled at Appomattox.
Williams, Jno. J., enl. July 15, '61, transferred to Chew's Battery.
Williamson, Thos., wnd. at Gettysburg, escaped at Appomattox with cavalry.
Williamson, Wm. G., enl. July 5, '61, Capt. Engineers.
Wilson, Calvin.
Wilson, Jno., enl. July 22, '61, prisoner after Gettysburg, took the oath.
Wilson, Sam. A., enl. Mar. 3, '62, wdn. at Gettysburg, '62, captured, died in prison.
Wilson, Wm. M., enl. Aug 12, '61, Corporal
Winston, Robert B, enl. Aug. 25, '61.
Wiseman, Wm., enl. March 10, '62.
Withrow, Jno., paroled at Appomattox.
Woody, Henry, transferred from Infantry, '64, deserted.
Wright, Jno. W., enl. '64, wdn. and disabled at Spottsylvania Court House.
Young, Chas. E., enl. Mar 17, '62.

SECOND ROCKBRIDGE ARTILLERY

The company was organized at Fairfield, July 10, '61, with Rev. John Miller, captain, Samuel Wallace, J. A. M. Lusk, and J. C. Dickinson as Lieuts., in the order named. At the reorganization of the army, May 1, '62, J. A. M. Lusk was made captain and W. K. Donald, Samuel Wallace, and A. J. Hayslett, Lieuts., in the order named. Captain Lusk resigned June. '63, on account of ill health. W. K. Donald was made captain and served as such until the end of the war. A. J. Hayslett prior to May 1, '62, served as company surgeon, and in 1863 was made surgeon of the Battalion, and Wm. T. Wilson, then a member of the Danville Blues of the Eighteenth Virginia Infantry, was selected lieutenant and served as such till the surrender. After the promotions in consequence of Capt. Lusk's resignation, Daniel Paxton was elected Lieutenant and continued as such till close of the war. The battery did much hard service and ranked inferior to none in the faithful discharge of duty. Owing to capture of a large number of the members of the company on the morning of April 2, '65, where the Confederate line was first broken, near the P. & W. R. R., there were only about forty of the company who surrendered at Appomattox.

The following members served as non-commissioned officers.

Sergeants

Wilson, S. W.	Bowman, Jno.	Wallace, Ed.
McCormick, Thos. R.	Paxton, J. L.	Wilson, Jno. A.
Paxton, Jas. P.	Strickler, Arch W.	

CORPORALS

Campbell, M. B.
Coffey, P. J.
Campbell, Nimrod M.
Hinty, Wm. H.

Clemmer, Wm. L.
Jarvis, J. E.
Heslep, Jos. E.
Humphries, Jas. H.

Miller, Richard S.
White, Robert
Hughes, E. M.
Patterson, Wm. D.

LIST OF MEMBERS

Alexander, W. P.
Allen, Wm.
Allen, Jas. G.
Barnett, B. F.
Beard, Hugh S.
Bartley, Wm.
Bowman, John
Campbell, M. B.
Campbell, Jas. A.
Campbell, W. A., Jr.
Campbell, N. M.
Cash, W. H.
Cash, Wm.
Coffey, Wm. M.
Crist, Wm. M.
Culton, Z. J.
Culton, Jas. B.
Cupp, J. W.
Decker, H. W.
Doyle, Jno. F.
Drayton, J. E.
Drawbond, J. L.
Durham, Eugene
Eakin, J. M.
Drain, L. C.
Ford, Jno. T.
Ford, Wm. A.
Ford, Jas. P.
Gaylor, — —
Cash, J. W.
Cash, John
Cash, B. D.
Cash, Joseph
Cash, Jas. P.
Carver, Valentine
Cave, John
Chandler, Wm.
Clemmer, W. L.
Cline, Dewitt
Cochran, A. A.
Coffey, P. J.

Coffey, Marvel
Lawhorn, Wm.
Long, Wm. M.
Lovegrove, Wm.
Ludwick, J.
Lynn, J. C.
Moore, ———
Mann, J. A.
Moran, Nat.
Morris, Dudley
Miller, S. S.
Miller, D. L.
Miller, John
Miller, R. S.
Meeks, J. P.
McCormick, Thos. M.
McCrory, Ed. H.
Goolsby, Wm. C.
Goolsby, Jas.
Gordon, Thos.
Griffin, A. J.
Hamilton, W. L.
Hamilton, Harvey
Hamilton, Jno. F.
Hamilton, J. J.
Hamilton, Henry
Hamilton, Geo. J.
Heslep, Joseph
Heider, Ed. N.
Hite, Jno. M.
Hite, Samuel
Hite, W. N.
Hite, W. P.
Hinty, W. H.
Holyman, John B.
Holler, Jacob B.
Humphries, Jas. H.
Hoylman, George
Hughes, J. P.
Houchen, ———
Hughes, E. M.

Hughes, Calvin
Jarvis, Jas. E.
Johnston, R. W.
Keffer, Henry
Kerr, L. D.
Kerr, W. D.
Jenkins, Churchville
Leech, L. T.
Leech, J. C.
Sly, Alfred F.
Sly, Adolphus
Smiley, Wm. A.
Lawhorn, Preston
Smiley, Jno. B.
Sorrels, Jos.
Sorrels, Geo.
Steele, Jas. E.
Strickler, Arch W.
Taylor, J. Ed.
Taylor, Jos.
Taylor, Geo. W.
Templeton, Wm. P.
Templeton, Benj.
Thorn, Job.
McCown, Jas. H.
McDowell, Thos. P.
McGuffin, Wm. W.
McGuffin, S. R.
McManama, Thos. P.
McNutt, Robert
Ott, D. A.
O'Brien, L.
McCrory, Wm. T.
Orenbaum, Wm.
Painter, Jas. H.
Paul, A. J.
Patterson, Wm. D.
Patterson, Wm. A.
Patterson, John
Paxton, S. D.
Paxton, Jas. T.

Paxton, Jas. P.	Shewey, Franklin	Whitesel, J. W.
Paxton, Jno.	Shields, Wm. C.	Whitesel, Z. T.
Paxton, Wm. H.	Shover, Franklin	Wiseman, E. M.
Paxton, Jas. H.	Sloan, Cooke	Wine, Jas. A.
Paxton, Thos.	Tribbett, R. R.	Wilson, Jno. A.
Potter, Samuel	Tribbett, F. M.	Wilson, S. W.
Pearl, John	Wallace, Allbright	Wilson, Jos. M.
Pugh, Wm.	Wallace, J. W.	Vess, Mathew
Pugh, Jas. H.	Wallace, Ed.	Vess, C. D.
Risk, John W.	White, Geo.	Womeldorf, J.
Risk, Jas. P.	White, Robert	Wood, Geo.
Ramsey, Dabney	White, L. M.	Withers, Cyrus.
Selvy, Wm. H.	White, John	

LIST OF CASUALTIES

Killed—J. H. McCown, Alleghany Mountain, Dec. 12, '61; W. P. Templeton, J. Ludwick, Cross Keys, June 8, '62; Adolphus Sly, Chancellorsville, May 3, '63; Preston Lawhorn, Robert Coffey, Bristow Station, Oct. 14, '63; Geo. Holyman, Wm. J. Bartley, Geo. White, Gettysburg July 3, '63; Cyrus Goolsby, Petersburg, July 30, '64; Thos. N. McCormick, and John T. Ford, Petersburg, date unknown; John L. Drawbond (the time and place cannot be recalled); James T. Paxton, Franklin Shover and Lieut. Samuel Wallace, Petersburg, April 2, '65.

Died from wounds—W. H. Paxton, wounded at Strasburg, June 1, '62; ——— Houchens and ——— Gaylor, wounded at Cross Keys, June 8, '62; Jas. P. Risk and Jas. B. Culton, wounded at Petersburg, Va., Oct. 14, '63; A. J. Griffin, wounded at Alleghany Mountain, Dec. 12, '61.

Died from disease—Wm. Allen, Jos. Cash, John Cash, Wm. Cash, Marvel Coffey, Sam Hite, W. N. Hite, Cooke Sloan, and Benj. Templeton, at Staunton, in '61; Eugene Durham, '64; Jas. Goolsby, '61; Thos. Gordon, '61; W. L. Hamilton, at Petersburg, in '65; Ed. N. Heizer, at Charlottesville, June, '65; Wm. Lawhorn, at Staunton, '62; S. S. Miller, Thos. P. McDowell, at Gordonsville, '62; Wm. Orenbaum, '61; James P. Paxton, in prison in '63; John Paxton, at Richmond in '62; Jas Steele, at Point Lookout, April, '65; Jno. White; Cyrus, at Richmond, '62; J. Womeldorf, '61.

Wounded and recovered—Hugh S. Beard, Chancellorsville, May 3, '62; Cooke Sloan, Alleghany Mountain; Jas. P. Cash and Wm. H. Cash, Fredericksburg, Dec. 13, '62; Wm. M. Crist, Petersburg, April 2, '65, (lost leg); H. W. Decker, '62 Jas. P. Ford, Petersburg, July 30, '64; Geo. J. Hamilton, Petersburg, April 2, '65; Robert W. Johnston, Petersburg, '64; Robert McNutt, Spottsylvania, May, '64; D. A. Ott, Strasburg, June 1, '62, (lost arm); Thos. Paxton, Strasburg, June 1, '62; Franklin Shewey, Bristow Station, Oct. 14, '63; C. D. Vess, Cross Keys, June 8, '62, (lost leg); Allbright Wallace, Alleghany Mountain, Dec. 12, '62; Robert White, F. M. Wiseman (lost foot), W. P. Alexander, Valentine Carver, J. F. Doyle, J. J. Hamilton, John M. Hite, J B. Holler, L. D. Kerr, L T. Leech, S. S. Miller, Arch Strickler, Lieut. W. T. Wilson, Lieut. W. K. Donald, Chancellorsville, May 3, '63.

ROCKBRIDGE 1ST DRAGOONS, COMPANY "C" 1ST VA. CAVALRY

The following is a list of the dead and living who at any time during the war served in the company:

Captains.—Matthew X. White, Charles F. Jordan.

414   A HISTORY OF ROCKBRIDGE COUNTY, VIRGINIA

Lieuts.—John S. Cummings, C. H. Burks, Chas. J. Cameron, L. C. Davidson, John W. Moore.

Serg.—James P. Goul, W. D. McCorkle, John W. Moore, Samuel C. Mackey, James M. Lackey, Wm. B. Poindexter, S. F. Patterson.

Corporals.—Charles Q. Michie, D. H. Ford, R. K. Estill, N. H. Lackey, James Compton, Isaac Bare, John M. Dunlap, Robert Barton

PRIVATES

Adair, Wm. H.
Agnor, Samuel
Alexander, Jno. McD.
Armentrout, Cornelius
Armentrout, Henry
Armentrout, John
Arnold, Harry
Barger, Wm.
Barclay, Elihu H.
Bare, Adam
Bare, George
Buckner, E. P.
Bowlin, John P.
Bowlin, Wm. H.
Brockenbrough, Wm. S.
Chandler, Norborne E.
Chandler, S. T.
Cameron, John H.
Cameron, Geo. H.
Campbell, William
Cooper, Robert
Crigler, Daniel
Cummings, Frank
Davidson, Givens B.
Davidson, Robert G.
Davidson, Wm.
Dixon, Geo. D.
Dixon, Jno. J.
Effinger, Geo. Wm.
Elhart, Adolph
Figgatt, James S.
Figatt, Chas. M.
Fisher, Jno. A.
Floyd, Robert K.
Ford, Robert
Fuller, Sam. B.
Gilbert, Ezekiel
Gilbert, John

Glover, Andrew Y.
Gold, John W.
Gold, S. McD.
Goul, Sam.
Graham, E. L.
Greenlee, R. B.
Greenlee, James S.
Greenlee, Marshall
Greenlee, Wm. Wood
Grigsby, Lucian P.
Gilmore, A. J.
Gold, Jas.
Hanger, Augustus T.
Hamilton, John G.
Hamilton, W. W.
Harlan, G. Boyd.
Harlan, Hunter.
Harlan, Silas
Harlan, J. Scott
Harlan, Wilkie H.
Harris, Jas. F.
Hartingan, Wm. P.
Hanger, James R.
Hanger, Michael
Harper, Calvin
Hill, John
Holden, John S.
Holden, Sam. M.
Holden, Thos. W.
Johnston, Thos. C.
Johnston, W. J.
Johnston, J. Montgomery
Jordan, Frank
Jordan, John J.
Kelly, Jeremiah
Kelly, Jos.
Lam, A. C.
Lackey, Isaac Caruthers

Lackey, James T.
Laird, D. E.
Laird, John Ewing
Laird, Henry Ruffner
Laird, Sam. McKee
Lavelle, Abraham
Leake, Robert Sharp
Leyburn, Alfred
Mackey, Philander
Martin, A. J.
Martin, Geo.
Marks, W. H.
McClintic, John H.
McCorkle, W. P.
McCown, R. McD.
Meade, W. T.
Miller, Benj. F.
Moore, Sam. R.
Moore, Harry E.
Moore, Richard L
Montgomery, Thos. L.
Montgomery, John
Montgomery, B. S.
Montgomery, J. G.
Morrison, R. Culton
Morrison, Robert H.
Morrison, Henry Ruffner
McClung, J. McD.
McFaddin, W. H. C.
McGravy, Dennis
McGovern, Thos.
McNutt, Jas. M.
Myres, Henry H.
Myres, John D.
Nicely, Hezekiah
Parry, John McK.
Patton, John A.
Poague, James E.

NOTE: This list is given without rearrangement or other change from the original in the office of county clerk at Lexington.

Poague, Jas. W.
Powers, Oliver B.
Pulse, Chas,
Pulse, Jacob
Pulse, Levi
Rader, Zebulon
Rhodes, Jacob N.
Robertson, John W.
Root, Iverson S.
Ruff, Jas. W.
Ruff, John A.
Robinson, Andrew
Sale, Wm. H.
Supinger, Jacob A.

Shafer, Sam. J.
Supinger, Robert
Schindel, Charles
St. Clair, Wm. C.
Scott, T. Lackey
Taliaferro, Peachy R.
Taylor, Wm. H.
Thompson, A. A.
Trevy, A. S.
Trevy, Cyrus A.
Trevy, David A.
Tribbett, W. W.
Turpin, Jas.
Turpin, Nash

Unroe, Adam
Wash, Wm. Jas.
Welch, Wm. Luckess
White, Thos. S.
West, John
Wilson, Robert K.
Wilson, Sam. A.
Wilson, Sam. L.
Wilson, Jos. S.
Wilmore, Jacob H.
Withrow, Jas. M.
Witt, David H.
Wright, John W.
Zollman, John W.

CASUALTIES

Killed—Wm. H. Adair, at Gettysburg, Pa., July, '63; Wm Barger, at High Bridge, April, '65; John P. Bowlin, at Gettysburg, July 3, '63; John M. Dunlap, at Gettysburg, July 3, '63; Jas. S. Figgatt, at Mt. Jackson, Nov. 22, '64; Ezekiel Gilbert at Cannons Farm, '64; Samuel McKee Laird, at Hawes Shop, '64; Jas. W. Ruff, at Columbia Furnace, '64; Thos. McGovern, at Buckland, Va., '63; Peachy R. Taliaferro, at Hawes Shop, '64.

Wounded—Wm. H. Bowlin, at 1st Manassas, July 21, '61; Adam Bare, at Hanover, Pa., June 30, '63; Geo. H. Cameron, at Mt. Jackson, Nov. 22, '64; Norborne E. Chandler, at 1st Manassas, July 21, '61; Givens B. Davidson, Wm. Davidson, Geo. D. Dixon, at Mt. Jackson, March 7, '65; D. Houston Ford, Hartwood Church, March '63; S. McD. Gold, Tom's Brook, '64; Lucian P. Grigsby, at 1st Manassas, July 21, '64; J. Scott Harlan; J. M. Johnston, at Spottslyvania C. H., May '64; Isaac C. Lackey, at Chancellorsville, May '63; N. Harvey Lackey, at Spottsylvania C. H., May, '64; John W. Gold, at Mt. Jackson, March 7, '65; Joseph Kelly, at Kelly's Ford, '63; Robert Sharpe Leake, at Shepherdstown, '63; Samuel R. Moore, at Front Royal, Aug. 16, '64; W. H. C. McFaddin, near Salem, Fauquier Co., '62; John H. McClintic, at Five Forks, Va., April '65; A. J. Martin, at Flint Hill, Va., '62; Harry E. Moore (twice) at Todd's Tavern, '64 and Mt. Jackson, '64; Jas. W. Poague, (mortally) Spottsylvania C. H., May 7, '64; A. S. Trevy (mortally) at Yellow Farm, '64; Robert K. Wilson, at Spottsylvania C. H., March '64; Jacob H. Willmer, at Front Royal, Va., Aug. 16, '64; Robert K. Estill, at Hawes Shop, '64; Lieut. Jno. S. Cummings, at Mt. Jackson, Nov. 22, '64; Lieut. Jno. W. Moore, at Tom's Brook, '64; Capt. C. F. Jordan (twice) at Kelly's Ford, '62; and Tom's Brook, '64; Wm. D. McCorkle, at Spottslyvania C. H., '64; Wm. B. Poindexter, at Munson's Hill, Fairfax Co., '61; Sam. F. Patterson at Front Royal, Aug. 16, '64; and Robert Barton, at Tom's Brook, '64.

Captured—Jno. McD. Alexander, at Gettysburg; Robert G. Davidson, at Tom's Brook, '64; John A. Ruff, at Tom's Brook, '64; Geo. Wm. Effinger, Rockbridge Co., Va., '64; Jeremiah Kelly, John Ewing Laird, Flint Hill; Robert Floyd, Mt. Holly, Pa., Dr. E. L. Graham, at Spottslyvania C. H.; Jno. W. Robertson, at Gettysburg; A. J. Martin, at Flint Hill; H. H. Myres, at Chancellorsville; Isaac Bare, at Hanover, Va.

Died of disease—John Armentrout, '61; John Gilbert, James F. Harris; John Hill, at home; Sam Goul, near Louisa C. H., '62; Jas. Gold, at Staunton, '61; Philander Mackey, at home, '62; Hezekiah Nicely, at home; John McKee Parry, at home, '65; Zebulon Rader, at home, '62; W. P. McCorkle, at Manassas, July, '61; Nash Turpin, at Richmond, '62; Jos. F. Wilson, Sept., '62; Wm. Wash, at Charlottesville, '62; and Jas. P. Goul, at Lexington, Va.

ROCKBRIDGE 2ND DRAGOONS—COMPANY H., 14TH VA. CAVALRY

This company was organized in the lower end of Rockbridge, principally in the vicinity of Brownsburg, previous to the war, and was mustered into service, April 21, '61. The officers at that time were: John R. McNutt, Capt.; Robt. McChesney, 1st Lieut.; John A. Gibson, 2nd Lieut.; Dr. Z. J. Walker, 3rd Lieut. They were ordered to West Virginia, (then Va.), where Lieut. McChesney was killed, probably the first Virginian killed on Virginia soil. His tragic death occured near St. George, Tucker County. Lieutenants Gibson and Walker were promoted to 1st and 2nd Lieuts. by the vacancy, and John Y. Anderson, was made 3rd. Lieut.

At the reorganization in '62, after the first year's service, John A. Gibson was made Capt.; James A. Strain, 1st Lieut; James Archibald Lyle, 2nd Lieut., and James Lindsay, 3rd Lieut. The company was then doing service in Major William L. Jackson's battalion, composed of the following companies: Churchville Cavalry, from Augusta County, Charlotte Cavalry from Charlotte County, and Rockbridge 2nd Dragoons, from Rockbridge County.

The 14th Va. Cavalry was organized in January, '63, at Salem, Va., and these three companies were assigned to it, the Dragoons becoming Company "H." Capt. John A. Gibson was made Lieut. Col. and promotions were made in the Dragoons as follows: James A. Strain, Capt.; James Lindsay, 1st Lieut.; William M. Sterrett, 2nd Lieut.; Z. J. Culton, 3rd Lieut., who died in Salem while the regiment was in winter quarters near that town, the winter of '62-'63. A. B. Mackey was elected to fill Lieut. Culton's place. Lieut. Lackey was killed near Moorefield, Hardy County, on the retreat from the burning of Chambersburg, in '64. Wm. N. Wilson was elected to supply the vacancy caused by Lieut. Mackey's death. At the surrender the company officers were as follows: Capt. A. Strain; 1st Lieut. James Lindsay; 2nd Lieut. Wm. M. Sterrett; 3rd Lieut. Wm. N. Wilson.

This company holds undisputed the unique position of having had probably the first and the last Virginian killed on Virginia soil. Lieut. Robert McChesney was the first, being bush-whacked in West Va., and James Wilson, and Samuel A. Walker were killed at Appomattox on the 9th of April, '65. In the last charge where the last two named members of the company "H" were killed, the Federal line was broken and a part of a battery of Federal artillery captured.

LIST OF MEMBERS

Adams, William
Anderson, W. A. L.
Anderson, Jas. Y.
Anderson, John Y.
Anderson, Jacob H.
Anderson, Robert
Bagley, H. W.
Balser, John
Black, D. S.
Blackwell, William
Brown, A. M.
Buchanan, Charles B.
Brownlee, William
Breedlove, James

Chittum, Wm. T.
Chittum, John J.
Culton, Z. J.
Culton, Jos. A.
Campbell, John
Davis, Archibald
Davis, J. Wm.
Davis, L. P.
Dice, David
Dice, George W.
Dice, John
Ervin, Andrew
Firebaugh, Henry
Firebaugh, James B.

Firebaugh, James W.
Ford, Taylor
Ford, Alexander
Fox, James B.
Friend, Isaac
Fulwiler, Robert
Gibson, J. W.
Gibson, John A.
Gibson, J. Sam.
Glendy, James L.
Green, Henry A.
Green, C. P.
Griener, John H.
Griener, C. C.

Griener, Granville
Hanger, John
Hill, Lorenzo
Houston, W. Howard
Hull, N. B.
Huffman, James H.
Huffman, John
Irvine, Chas. W.
Johnston, John
Kennedy, Joseph
Kennedy, Hugh
Kennedy, David
Kinnear, Joseph P.
Kirkpatrick, John M.
Lackey, W. R.
Lackey, H. A.
Leech, W. B. F.
Lindsay, James
Lindsay, H. T.
Lowman, John
Lyle, Jas. A.
Lyle, Wm. A.
Lyle, John A.
Lockbridge, James
Lotts, Isaac
Ludwick, Jacob J.
Mackey, A. B.
Mackey, John W.
Mackey, Geo. A.
Mackey, Henry (little)
Mackey, John Henry
Marks, Gideon
Mines, Sam. S.
Morter, John L.
Miller, Ananias J.
Moore, John K.
Moore, A. H.
Moore, A. A.
Morrison, H. Rudd
McBride, J. J.
McClung, B. F.
McClung, D. B.
McClung, James A.
McClung, John T.
McClung, A. A.
McChesney, Robert

McCluer, N. B.
McCutchen, Wm. A.
McCray, David H.
McKensey, John
McMasters, Samuel C.
McNutt, John R.
Newlon, Chas.
Norcross, Geo.
Norcross, Willoughby N.
Ott, James W.
Ott, Frank A.
Palmer, Chris.
Patterson, Cyrus
Parrent, Marion
Patterson, H. W.
Patterson, John
Patterson, Nimrod
Patton, Franklin
Parrent, Wm. H.
Patterson, W. L.
Pettigrew, Sam. G.
Fultz, David
Paxton, Wesley
Paxton, Abner
Paxton, John A.
Pinkerton, Brainard
Pinkerton, Tay
Payne, Harvey
Runnels, W. W.
Runnels, James
Reed, John H.
Rhea, Sam. T.
Strain, Jas. A.
Strain, Sam. P.
Sandridge, William A.
Shaner, Jacob H.
Stoner, John N.
Stoner, D. H.
Sale, Wm. M.
Sale, P. B.
Short, Sam. W.
Sheridan, John
Snider, John N.
Snider, James H.
Sensabaugh, Thos.
Smallwood, Wm. W.

Smiley, James
Smiley, Andrew
Stuart, Alexander
Stuart, S. W.
Stuart, J. G.
Sterrett, Robert
Sterrett, Wm. M.
Sterrett, Sam. W.
Swisher, Daniel
Swisher, James
Taylor, Arch
Taylor, Wm.
Templeton, F. H.
Terrill, H. L.
Terrill, Jas.
Thompson, H. H.
Tribett, John F.
Trevy, Jos.
Vines, Wm.
Wilson, G. E.
Weir, A. H.
Wilson, Wm. N.
Wilson, Thos. M.
Wilson, M. D.
Wilson, Sam. N.
Wilson, John Edgar
Wheat, John W.
Withers, James
Withers, H. A.
Whitemore, John H.
Wright, Wm.
Wright, John R.
Wilson, J. Alpheus
Wilson, H. Robert
Welch, John
White, Matthew X.
Walker, William A.
Walker, Cyrus
Walker, Dr. Z. J.
Walker, Alexander Stuart
Walker, Sam. A.
Weir, Sam. H.
Withrow, Arch.
Wilson, Jas.
Wilson, J. Howard

Killed—A. A. Moore; Robert McChesney, bush-whacked, near St. George, Tucker County, in '61; Andrew Ervin, at Bratton's Farm; W. Howard Houston, at Cedarville, Va., in '64; Wm. W. Smallwood, at Rich Mountain, W. Va.; James Lockridge, near Williamsport, in '63; Lieut. A. B. Mackey, at Moorefield, W. Va., in '64; Sam. A. Walker and James Wilson, April 9, '65, at Appomattox C. H.; M. X. White, shot by Hunter's command near Lexington, while a prisoner, in '64.

Died of disease—William Adams, Samuel B. Anderson, Robert Anderson, Chas. B. Buchanan, Lieut. Z. J. Culton, (in Salem, Va.); J. Wm. Davis, at Monterey, Va.; Wm. B. Firebaugh, Henry Firebaugh, Jos. P. Kinnear, Robert Sterret, Alexander Stuart. The following died in prison: H. W. Patterson, Cyrus Patterson, John Henry Mackey, Gideon Marks, Wm. Brownlee, Franklin Patton, Wm. Blackwell, and John Campbell. Wesley Paxton, was drowned in the Kanawha River, in '62.

Wounded—Lieut. Wm. N. Wilson, John J. Chittum and Chas. W. Irvine, at Brandy Station; Lt. Col. John A. Gibson, at Monacacy in '64; S. H. Weir, Racine, Ohio; Lieut. Jas. Lindsay, Lieut. Wm. M. Sterrett, Wm. L. Patterson, L. P. Davis, at Cedarville, Va.; D. B. McClung, near Gordonsville, Va., Dec. 22, '64; Abner Paxton and Isaac Friend, near St. George, Tucker Co., W. Va.; Geo. W. Dice, Jas. Withers and John N. Snider, storming fort at North Mt. Depot, W. Va.; B. F. McClung, at Shepherdstown, W. Va.

COMPANY "C" 14TH VA. CAVALRY

This company was formed in '62 and was made up largely of enlisted men who had seen service in West Va., as members of the Rockbridge 2nd Dragoons and the Churchville Cavalry, of Augusta County. These companies exceeded in number army regulations and it was deemed to form another company of the surplus. This will account for the fact that some names will appear on the roll of Company "C" and also on that of Company "H." The Churchville Cavalry was raised in West Augusta and in Highland County.

The following is a list of the dead and living, who at any time during the war served in the company:

COMMISSIONED OFFICERS

Captain William A. Lackey, Rockbridge.
1st Lieut. L. H. Stephenson, of Highland.
2nd Lieuts. Samuel Cochran, of Augusta, and Granville Regar, of Barbour Co., W. Va.
3rd Lieuts. William Allen, of Augusta Co., and Andrew W. Cameron, of Rockbridge.
Orderly Sergeant, Arthur J. Shafer, of Rockbridge.
Second Sergeant, S. Brown Allen, of Augusta.
Third Sergeant, J. E. Stuart, of Highland.
Fourth Sergeant, J. R. McCutchen, of Rockbridge.
First Corporal, Abe Hoover, of Augusta.
Second Corporal, Jos. M. Runkle, of Augusta.
Third Corporal, Jas. W. Spitler, of Augusta.
Fourth Corporal, Irvine W. Runkle, of Augusta.

PRIVATES FROM ROCKBRIDGE

Anderson, Wm.	Baltimore, John H.	Campbell, William
Ackerly, David	Campbell, R. Granville	Dryden, Phil E.
Ackerly, Shanklin	Clark, John	Fitzpatrick, John
Balser, John	Campbell, Sam.	Flint, Jos.

ROCKBRIDGE ARTILLERY 419

Glover, Andrew
Green, Sam.
Gatcher, W. L.
Hite, John
Houston, William
Irvine, James
Irvine, Maslin
Irvine, John
Irvine, T.
Knick, Alexander
Knick, Richard M.
Kirkpatrick, G. McD.
Kirkpatrick, Jas. L.
Kirkpatrick, Sam L.
Kennedy, Jos.
Kirkpatrick, John A.
Lawhorn, Mat.

Lackey, H. A.
Lackey, Robert
Lackey, J. W.
Lackey, Thos.
Lackey, T. S.
McChesney, Jas. Z.
McHenry, Sam. A.
McMasters, Sam. C.
Marks, Gideon
Nicely, Chas.
Nicely, Marion
Reynolds, John
Ramsey, Thos.
Snider, John Jack
Snider, Andrew
Snider, Jas.
Snider, John D.

Snider, Jos.
Snider, David
Sheridan, John
Teaford, Daniel
Tribbett, John F.
Tribett, Mat.
Vest, Sam.
Vest, John
Wilson, J. Howard
Wilson, Thos.
Wilson, Frank
Wilson, Jas.
Wilmore, Jas.
Wilmore, Andrew
Wilson, Alfred
West, James
Zollman, Alex.

PRIVATES FROM AUGUSTA

Anderson, Perry
Anderson, Edward
Anderson, Wm.
Albright, Andrew
Burton, W.
Cline, Sam.
Echard, Wm.
Fishborne, Geo. W.
Horn, Jas.

Jones, John H.
Spitler, Jas.
Spitler, B.
Spitler, P.
Spider, S.
Long, Jas. C.
Landes, David
McCutchen, Robert
McCutchen, Wm.

Mann, John
Mann, Chas.
Newlin, Chas.
Newman, Lot
Sillings, Dick
Stover, John
Stewart, John
Sillings, John
Van Lear, John

PRIVATES FROM HIGHLAND

Arbogast, Dr. J. E.
Arbogast, John W.
Beverage, Wesley
Cruikshank, John
Cruikshank, Sam.
Floyd, Wm. H.
Floyd, Edward
Fox, Chas. H.
Goff, Levi.
Gum, John E.

Gwyn, William
Grog, Ami
Hidy, Jacob H.
Kericoft, — —
McClung, Silas B.
McClung, Louis M.
Murphy, John
Newman, Andrew T.
Newman, Salsberry
Newman, J. S.

Pool, John
Selver, John A.
Sipe, John E.
Stephenson, E. Tyler
Stephenson, Oscar A.
Wilmer, Andrew
Wymer, Cornelius
Waybright, Andrew J.

FROM OTHER COUNTIES

Faris, Robert, Pendleton Co., W. Va.
Faris, Jacob, Pendleton Co., W. Va.
Goff, John, West Virginia.
Long, John, West Virginia.
Parsons, ———, West Virginia.

CASUALTIES

Killed—John F. Tribett and Jas. Wilmore, at Monocacy, Maryland, in '64; Lieut. Allen, of Augusta, at Gettysburg; Maslin Irvine, killed or lost near Washington, D. C.

Wounded—Thos. Ramsey, at Charleston, W. Va.; Jas. L. Kirkpatrick, at Monocacy, Md.; Jas. C. Long, at Georgetown, D. C., Louis M. McClung, at Winchester, (lost leg); ——— Parsons, at Greenbrier River, W. Va.; John Long, at Meadow Bluff, W. Va.; Irvine W. Runkle, at Pond Gap, Va.

Died of disease—Lieut. Sam. Cochran, of Augusta Co., John Balser, died in prison; Jos. Flint, Chas. Nicely, and Jas. Wilson; Gideon Marks, while a prisoner at Alton, Ill.

COMPANY "G" 14TH VIRGINIA CAVALRY

This company was largely composed of men already in the service who had re-enlisted before the passage of the "Conscript Law" in April, '62. It was organized some time that summer. Its membership was drawn from the "Stonewall Brigade," principally from the 4th regiment. Nineteen were from Rockbridge, fourteen of whom were members of the Rockbridge Grays.

COMMISSIONED OFFICERS

Captains—Walter R. Preston, of Montgomery Co., was the first Capt., and resigned and was succeeded by Alexander M. Peck, of Montgomery Co., who held the office until the surrender.

Lieutenants—1st, Chas. Norvell, of Lynchburg; 2nd, Chas. Keiffer, of Pulaski Co., (who never did much service with the company, being aide to Gen. Jenkins); 3rd, William W. Cornett, of Grayson Co., who acted in that capacity until the close of hostilities.

Sergeants—1st, John P. Tribett, of Rockbridge; 2nd, John Jameison Bunch, of Rockbridge; 3rd, John A. Bourn, of Grayson; 4th, John S. Perkins, of Grayson; 5th, David B. Davis, of Montgomery.

Corporals—1st, John W. Small, of Rockbridge; 2nd, Geo. W. Barnett, of Montgomery; 3rd, Byrd Anderson, of Montgomery.

NAMES OF MEN FROM ROCKBRIDGE COUNTY

Ayres, J. W.	Johnson, Jas.	Slough, B. Augustus
Agner, Sa. McD.	Miller, John W.	Sullivan, John
Armentrout, C. H.	Moore, J. Scott	Tribett, G. G.
Barger, John J.	Moore, Wm. W.	Vest, P. G.
Donald, Jas. C.	Northern, R. L.	Webb, Wm. D
Hensley, John G.	Pritchard, John F.	

NAMES OF MEN FROM MONTGOMERY, ROANOKE, AND PULASKI COUNTIES

Austin, Isaac	Dudley, Thos.	Gordon, Chas. H.
Barnett, Jas. D.	Dooley, A. M.	Graige, Giles
Barnett, Sam. G.	Deyerle, T. Jefferson	Hammers, Jos.
Brown, Henry	Deaton, Griffith	Hatcher, R. E.
Brown, John	Deaton, Chas	Heslip, G. W.
Bones, Jas.	Early, J	Heslip, G. W. R.
Davis, S. H.	Fulwiler, R. W.	Layne, R. P.
Deyerle, Abe.	Gillespie, W. E.	McConkey, Jas.

Moses, Jas.	Preston, J. P.	Thomas, Montgomery
Milholland, A. J.	Smith, J. H.	Waskey, James
Murray, John F.	Stoner, B. E.	Watterson, Sam
Peck, Jas.	Taylor, Jos.	Waskey, W. C.
Phillips, Sam.	Thomas, William H.	Wills, W. G.
Preston, Jas.	Thomas, Jas.	Womack, Allen

NAMES OF MEN FROM GRAYSON COUNTY

Cornett, Foy	Jones, Ceph.	Rhudy, Jas.
Cornett, K. C.	McLean, Joe'	Stone, William E.
Cornett, Wint.	Perkins, Rufus	Wright, George
Hale, Maslin	Rhudy, Floyd	Wright, Jeff.
Hale, H.	Rhudy, Fred	Wyatt, Arche

Casualties—The survivors of Company "C" are so widely separated by distance, and their post offices unknown, that it is impossible to get an accurate list of the killed and wounded.

One of the most disastrous fights in which the company participated was when Milroy was driven out of Winchester, in '63. The company was doing picket duty on the Valley pike between Middletown and Cedar Creek. When the order came to advance the picket line, Company "G" and Captain Raison's Company of the First Maryland Cavalry slowly moved down the pike. They had gone about a mile when a battery of the Federals opposed further progress. A charge to capture the battery, was made. On each side concealed behind rock fences were two regiments of Pennsylvanians (infantry) who rose up when the Confederates were in thirty feet of them, and delivered a deadly fire. Agreeably to Harry Gilmore's book, *Four Years in the Saddle*, five men were killed dead, nine wounded, and twenty-three captured. Of Company "G," Lt. Norvell, J. Scott Moore, Sam. H. Davis, Sergeant Bunch, Griffith Deaton, and William Taylor were wounded, some slightly, and some badly. Sergeant Bunch was shot in the throat and twenty years afterwards expelled the bullet in a paroxysm of coughing. The captured were Lt. Norvell, Sam. H. Davis, J. Scott Moore, W. W. Moore, R. E. Hatcher, Sam C. Barnett, and James Waskey.

Chas. Deaton was killed near Charleston, Va.; Lt. Chas Keiffer, Serg. John Brown, Abe Deyerle, Griffith Deaton, James McConkey, Serg. John Perkins, and John J. Barger, were wounded in the Valley—(unable to give places and dates.) J. Scott Moore was again wounded at Brandy Station, Va. Byrd Anderson and Sam C. Barnett and Serg. John P. Tribbett, were captured near Petersburg, in April '65. R. L. Northern was wounded in the forehead.

THE ROCKBRIDGE RANGERS

This company as now recalled is as follows:

L. C. Davidson, Captain; Geo. Hordan, 1st Lieut.; John H. Cameron, 2nd Lieut.; Rev. W. F. Junkin, 3rd Lieut.; Albert Davidson, Orderly Serg.; J. W. Haughawout, 2nd Serg.; Ed. L. Graham, 3rd Serg.; Cornelius Armentrout, 4th Serg.; Robert Bradford, Corporal.

PRIVATES

Anderson, Wm. L	Craig, Robert S. (Aug. Co.)	Harris, Jas. H.
Bell, J. C.	Campbell, Wm.	Hamilton, A. J.
Branham, Dr. H. M.	Dodd, Robert	Hartsook, M. M.
Bowyer, John H.	Figgatt, Jas.	Johnson (son of Douglass)
Brafford, James E.	Glendy, Jas. L.	Jenkins, Philip
Copper, T. J.	Hall, Jas. C.	Lackey, Wm. A.

Lackey, Jas. M.
Leech, Miller
Leech, W. C.
Leech, W. B. F.
Luckess, Wm.
Wilson, R. L.
Wilson, J. C.
Wilson, John B.
Wilson, Wm. S.
Williams, Rev.
Miller, Ben. F.
Mackey, Jas. S.
Mann, William A.

Mann, George
McCorkle, W. Philander
Moore, Wm. T.
McMaster, Sam. C.
Moore, Richard
Newcome, ———
Patterson, John M.
Poague, J. Wilson
Rhea, Sam
Shafer, Arthur J.
Shafer, Sam.
Sandford, Jas.
Steele, Wm.

Tribbett, W. W.
Turnin, Nash
Tindall, Thos. A.
Thomas, Jas.
Trevy, David
Trevy, Cyrus
Vess, John A.
Wilson, Jas.
Wilson, John
Wilson, Jas. Brown
Young, Jacob

LIBERTY HALL VOLUNTEERS, COMPANY I, 4TH VA. INFANTRY

This company was composed almost exclusively of those then connected with the Washington College and recent graduates, more than one-half of whom were professors of religion and about one-fourth candidates for the ministry.

The roll as called on the College campus June 8th was as follows:

Capt. Jas. J. White.
1st Lieut. John N. Lyle.
2nd Lieut. Joseph L. Sherrard.
1st Serg. Wm. A. Anderson; 2nd Serg. D. E. Ruff; 3rd Serg. E. A. Mitchell; 4th Serg. Chas. W. Bell; 5th Serg. Chas. F. Nelson.
1st Corporal G. B. Strickler; 2nd Corp. Frank T. Brooke; 3rd Corp. Wm. L. Paxton; 4th Corp. Wm. F. Meade.

PRIVATES

Anderson, J. M.
Arnold, Jacob W.
Amole, J. P.
Arnold, J. Harry
Barclay, A. Tedford
Bird, John A.
Brooks, Andrew
Bell, Wm. J.
Bradley, Ben. J.
Brooks, Wm.
Davidson, Givens K.
Goodwin, Thos. J.
Gwynn, Bronson B.
Hallett, Robert J.
Jones, John H. B.
Johnston, S. A.
Jordan, Harry
Kanle, Matthew S.
Paxton, Alex. S.
Paxton, Horace A.
Ramsey, Alex. B.
Raymond, Jos. S.

Reiley, John W.
Reed, Thomas H.
Roberts, Thos. H.
Richardson, Wm. E.
Rollins, Thos. S.
Redwood, J. T.
Strickler, Cyrus D.
Suddarth, Jas. L.
Thompson, Wm. J.
Turner, Thos. M.
Utz, Calvin
Varner, John A. R.
Watson, John G.
Williams, Chas.
Wilson, Wm. N.
Wilson, John T.
White, Hugh A.
Wilson, H. L.
Woods, J. Watson
Laird, H. R.
Lam, C. M.
Lyle, Sam. H.

Logan, N. B.
Lightner, John P.
Lightner, Sam. M.
Lackey, Geo. W.
Mackey, Jas. S.
Meade, Everard
Moore, J. Julius
Morrison, H. R.
Moore, Sam. R.
Myers, Henry H.
McKee, John T.
McCoughtry, Jack W.
Neel, Cyrus F.
Ott, W. B.
Page, Copeland R.

Anderson, John R.
Amole, T. F.
Anderson, Robert M.
Almond, R. R.
Baine, George
Bare, George

Brooks, Moffett
Bacon, A. S.
Bartley, H. A.
Benson, H. M.
Brooks, Chas.
Brown, Wm. L.
Buchanan, J. W.
Bryan, J. H.

Burke, T. N.
Bushong, Abraham
Cash, G. R.
Culton, J. B.
Chapin, Geo.
Coffman, J. H.

Chester, Jos. T.
Crist, G.
Copper, J. M.
Clyce, G. A. E.
Carr, E.
Clifton, Robert
Day, W. E.
Dunlap, R. K.

RECRUITS

The following names were added to the original at different times during the war, to-wit:

Adair, Alex.
Day, Sam. M.
Dunlap, S. M.
Dunlap John
Echard, W. K.
Ervine, John H.
Gaylor, Jas.
Glasgow, A. M.
Green, Thos.
Gross, John
Gordon, F.
Guy, John R.
Gwynn, Worth O.
Hodge, J.
Hall, A. H.
Holt, P. W.
Helmick, Wm.
Hutton, Gardner P.
Irvine, J. C.
Johnson, R. J.
Johnson, Wm. M.
Jackson, J.
Lackey, Nathan A.
Lam, M. H.
Lackey, J. T.
Link, A. T.
Lewis, Edward
Larew, M. F.

Lackey, Wm. H.
Lackey, Thos. T.
Lunsford, Wm.
Miley, John W.
Myers, John D.
McCray, J. C.
McCalpin, R.
McClung, A. A.
Moore, Wm.
McCurdy, Wm. T.
McClung, Chas. B.
McNutt, Benj. F.
McClelland, Wm. A.
McFaddin, Joseph
McCraw, J. W.
Moore, W. Dorman
Moore, John F.
Moore, John P.
Ott, Henry
O'Brien, Dennis
Patterson, W. L.
Paxton, J. Mc.
Preston, W. C.
Pettigrew, J. M.
Pettigrew, Sam.
Roadcap, D. L.
Rollins, W. R.
Rozen, D. H.

Rowsey, Lafayette
Shields, Geo. W.
Sheckle, Danl.
Shelton, ———
Smiley, W. S.
Snyder, D.
Snyder, A.
Steele, Wm.
Sterrett, J. D.
Spohr, James W.
Stoner, G. H.
Stoner, W.
Stratton, Thos.
Taylor, I. M.
Trevy, David
Welsh, John H.
White, Thos. S.
Wilbourn, Wm. R.
Whitmore, G. W.
Whitmore, David
Wilhelm, Sam. H.
Wilson, J. Edgar
Withers, Marion H.
Youell, Wm. A.
Zollman, Madison
Williams, S. P.

The following is a list of the officers of the Company during the war, in the order in which they succeeded each other:

Captains:—James J. White; Henry Ruffner Morrison; Hugh A. White, and G. B. Strickler.
    1st Lieuts.:—John N. Lyle, G. B. Strickler, and Sam H. Lyle.
    2nd Lieuts.:—Joseph L. Sherrard, and J. H. B. Jones.
    3rd Lieuts.:—James B. Culton.
    1st Sergs.:—William A. Anderson, and J. S. Raymond.
    2nd Sergs.:—D. E. Ruff, and Alexander S. Paxton.

3rd Sergs:—E. A. Mitchell, Joseph T. Chester, and J. J. Moore.
4th Sergs.:—Chas. J. Bell, J. W. Arnold, and S. A. Johnson.
5th Serg.:—Chas. F. Nelson.
1st Corp.:—H. H. Myers, and Worth O. Gwynn.
2nd Corp.:—Wm. T. Meade, G. K. Davidson, and J. Mc. Paxton.
3rd Corp.:—Wm. L. Paxton, Thos. J. Godwin, C. R. Page, and J. T. McKee.
4th Corp.—F. T. Brooke, S. R. Moore, and Geo. W. Lackey.

A. Tedford Barclay, a member of the company served as ensign of the regiment, with honors.

CASUALTIES

1. 1st Manassas.
   Killed: Serg. Chas. W. Bell, Corp. W. L. Paxton, Benj. A. Bradley, W. B. Ott, Calvin Utz, H. L. Wilson, and Cyrus D. Strickler.
   Wounded: Serg. W. A. Anderson, Corp. G. B. Strickler, Sam H. Lightner, H. A. Paxton (left hand), C. F. Neel, and Bronson B. Gwynn.
2. —Kernstown.
   Killed: Serg. Chas. F. Nelson.
   Wounded: W. J. Bell.
   Captured: Capt. H. R. Morrison, Andrew Brooks, John N. Lyle, Corp. John T. McKee Horace A. Paxton, John A. R. Varner, J. Watson Woods, and A. B. Ramsey.
3. 1st Winchester.
   Captured: Worth O. Gwynn.
4. 2nd Manassas.
   Killed: Capt. Hugh A. White, Jack W. McCoughtry, W. C. Preston.
   Wounded: Chas. Brooks, Robert K. Dunlap, Everard Meade, J. Mc. Paxton, David E. Ruff, Lieut. G. B. Strickler, and John T. Wilson.
   Captured: James L. Suddarth.
5. Sharpsburg.
   Wounded: Corp. S. R. Moore.
6. Kearneysville.
   Killed: W. Dorman Moore.
   Wounded: Serg. J. S. Raymond, Corp. S. A. Johnson, Corp. Givens K. Davidson.
7. Chancellorsville.
   Killed: Nathan A. Lackey, Sam Day, and Andrew Brooks.
   Wounded: J. P. Amole, H. M. Benson, Geo. Chapin, R. K. Dunlap, Bronson B. Gywnn, Corp. T. J. Godwin, Lieut. S. H. Lyle, John P. Moore, Alex. S. Paxton, (left leg), Alex. B. Ramsey, W. D. Gywnn, Geo. H. Stoner, Isaac M. Taylor, H. A. Bartley, and John T. Wilson.
8. Gettysburg.
   Killed: Alex. Adair.
   Wounded: T. F. Amole, Thos. J. Goodwin, Wm. H. Lackey, Corp. J. M. Paxton, and H. A. Paxton (right foot.)
   Captured: Sam. M. Dunlap, Thos. J. Godwin, W. D. Gwynn, R. J. Johnson, Wm. H. Lackey, John F. Moore, J. Julius Moore, John T. McKee, J. Mc. Paxton, Serg. J. S. Raymond, Capt. G. B. Strickler, W. S. Smiley, Jas. L. Suddarth, Isaac M. Taylor, Thos. M. Turner, and John A. R. Varner.
9. Bealton Station.
   Wounded: H. A. Bartley, Alex. B. Ramsey, and Serg. J. S. Raymond.
10. Mine Run.

Killed: Geo. Chapin.
Wounded: Lieut. S. H. Lyle, J. P. Amole, A. B. Ramsey, and A. S. Paxton.
11 Wilderness.
Wounded: Lieut. J. H. B. Jones, S. A. Johnston, John M. Miley (died), Jas. S. Mackey, Horace A. Paxton (left hip broken), A. B. Ramsey, and Ensign A. T. Barclay.
12. Spottsylvania C. H.
Killed: Serg. Joseph T. Chester, and William Steele.
Wounded: John P. Moore, Wm. E. Day, and Wm. A. McClelland.
Captured: J. P. Amole, Ensign A. T. Barclay, W. M. Johnson, Lieut. S. H. Lyle, Wm. A. McClelland, Thos. H. Roberts, J. S. Raymond, Thos. S. Rollins, Jas. S. Mackey, and Geo. W. Whitmore.
13. Monocacy.
Wounded and captured: T. F. Amole.
14. 2nd Winchester.
Wounded: Geo. W. Lackey, and A. T. Link.
Captured: A. T. Link.
15. Bell Grove.
Wounded: J. H. Coffman, Jas. W. Spohr.
Captured: A. B. Ramsay.
16. Fort Steadman.
Killed: Robert Anderson, N. B. Logan, Geo. H. Stoner, and Marion H. Withers.
Wounded: John H. Ervine, J. Hodge, Wm. L. Patterson, and John H. Welsh.
Captured: Abraham Bushong, ——— Shelton, Wm. R. Wilbourn, Wm. L. Patterson, and J. H. Coffman.
17. Petersburg.
Killed: John P. Moore.
Wounded: Serg. A. S. Paxton, and J. Edgar Wilson.
18. Hatcher's Run.
Killed: Wm. A. Youell, and Madison Zollman.
Wounded: M. H. Lam, and Wm. L. Patterson.

DIED OF DISEASE

Anderson, Jos. M.
Anderson, John
Brooks, Wm.
Brooks, Moffett
Clifton, Robert
Jordan, Harry

Lightner, S. M.
Larew, Milton F.
Lightner, John P.
Mitchell, Edward A.

McCraw, J. W.
Reed, Thos. H.
Richardson, W. E.
Smiley, Wm. S.
Thompson, Wm. J.
Wilhelm, Sam H.

ROCKBRIDGE GRAYS, COMPANY "H" 4TH VA INFANTRY
STONEWALL BRIGADE

This company when organized had as Captain, Jas. P. Updike; First Lieut. Alex. M. Hamilton; Second Lieut. William Patton; Third Lieut. Clifton C. Burks.
Sergs.—First, A. J. Hamilton; Second, A. H. Cummings; Third, John W. Small; Fourth, John S. Moffett; Fifth, George Baxter McCorkle.
Corporals.—First, Hugh N. Burks, Second, John D. Cox, Third, Wm. J. Garrett; Fourth, LaClaire A. Marstella.
With these officers it was mustered into service, but there were quite a number of

changes in a short time. The death of Second Lieut. Wm. Patton, at Winchester, July 16, '61, created a vacancy, Third Lieut. Clifton C. Burks was on July 27, made Second Lieut. On June 3rd, Andrew Jackson Hamilton, First Serg., was discharged on Surgeon's certificate on account of disability and promotions followed among the non-commissioned officers, Andrew H. Cummings being made Orderly Serg.

March 20, '62, Capt. Jas. G. Updike tendered his resignation on account of continued bad health, which was accepted April 20th. By order of General Winder, commanding the Brigade, the company was reorganized and the following officers were elected:

Captain, Alexander M. Hamilton; A. H. Cummings, 1st Lieut.; Geo. B. McCorkle, 2nd Lieut.; Robert A. Glasgow, Jr., 3rd Lieut.

Capt. Hamilton resigned in '63, owing to bad health, and Lieut. McCorkle was made Captain. The Lieuts. were: 1st C. C. Burks; 2nd Patrick Hogan; 3rd Wm. A. Sterrett; First Lieut. Andrew Cummings was killed and 3rd Lieut. Robert A. Glasgow died in '62. With these exceptions the above named officers surrendered at Appomattox, April '65.

The following is a list of those who served at any time in the Company, not repeating the names of officers:

Ackerly, J. P.
Ailstock, C. P.
Anderson, J. B.
Anderson, T. A.
Ailstock, T. P.
Barger, D. W.
Barger, J. J.
Berry, W. C.
Black, J. T.
Brownlee, J. A.
Bryant, A. W.
Bunch, J. J.
Bunch, W. H.
Burks, H. N.
Camden, Oscar
Camden, W., Jr.
Clark, R. G
Cox, J. J.
Cox, S. J.
Denton, W.
Donald, J. C.
Davis, Jno. D.
Eads, J. M.
Eads, R. H.
Edmondson, David T.
Elliot, S. P.
Elliot, J. M.
Farrow, Wm.
Fainter, Jas. A.
Fisher, Henry
Fisher, Wm. R.
Fitzgerald, J. C.

Ford, A. D.
Garrett, W. J.
Glasgow, Robert A.
Goolsby, J. M.
Hartsook, Newton B.
Hall, R. H.
Hicks, J.
Hite, R. E.
Hensley, Jas. G.
Helms, Jas. W.
Hogan, Patrick
Hayes, B. H.
Hall, J.
Harris, Peter
Henderson, R. D.
Hensley, John D.
Hill, B. F.
Heffron, Edward
Imboden, Sam. W.
Johnston, Edwin
Johnston, Jas.
Kennedy, E. F.
Lawson, J. E.
Lackey, Wm. A.
Leech, J. A.
Lilly, Miller M.
Lewis, G. S.
Lewis, J. D.
La Bree, Jos.
Lauck, C. E.
Lilly, John A.
Leech, F. A.

Marstella, L. A.
McLain, G. W.
McCorkle, Jas. T.
Moxley, Benj. P.
Major, Joshua B.
McDaniel, M. T.
McClure, W. G.
McManama, J. A.
Miller, John W.
Moore, Wm. W.
Mullen, Jas. B.
Moffett, Wm. B.
Northern, R. L.
Nicely, Dudley
Paxton, Jos. M.
Pugh, Jas. H.
Pritchard, John F.
Pleasants, J. J.
Rapp, Benj. F.
Rogers, Wm. H.
Reynolds, L. F. C.
Ricketts, Jas.
Rapp, Sam. C.
Reynolds, J. F.
Rogers, G. M.
Selby, W. A.
Slough, B. A.
Spence, Jos.
Sterrett, Wm. A.
Selby, J. F.
Shewey, Wm.
Slough, Jas. W.

Sullivan, John S.	Thompson, W. H.	Wilson, S. P.
Small, John W.	Tomlinson, R.	Withers, Jas. E.
Slough, Baxter	Tharp, Hiram	Wilmuth, Wm. A.
Tribbett, John P.	Vest, Philip G.	Withrow, J. R.
Turner, J. J.	Vest, T. R.	Wills, Elisha
Tomlinson, M.	Wallace, A. A.	Witt, William E.
Tribbett, J. F.	Webb, Wm. D.	Webb, J. A.
Tribbett, Wm. M.	Wilson, Thos. J.	Webb, Jas. H.

CASUALTIES

The battle of Manassas, July 21, '61, was the first time the company was under fire. They were commanded by Capt. Updike and from a company report made August 30th of the same year it is noted that sixty-four went into action and out of this number five were killed and fourteen were wounded, nearly one-third of the whole number engaged. The killed were: Serg. John S. Moffett (shot through the brain), Jas. T. McCorkle, Jas. McManama, John M. Goolsby, Sam. R. Wilson.

Wounded—Lieut. C. C. Burks, J. D. Cox, L. A. Marstella, Thos. Anderson, W. C. Berry, David T. Edmondson, John Fitzgerald, B. E. Hite, John W. Miller, William Selby, Alexander A. Wallace, J. B. Wilson, J. E. Withers, and Benj. Moxly.

Lieut. Andrew H. Cummins, and W. H. Selby, killed at second battle of Manassas, Capt. Hamilton and fifteen wo....ded; Jos. La Bree, W. F. Fisher, Edwin Johnston, William W. Lackey, and Jas. W. Slough, were killed and W. E. Witt, wounded at Gettysburg; Thos. J. Wilson, killed at Sharpsburg; Sam. G. Rapp, killed at Malvern Hill, '62; Sam. J. Cox, killed in battle at Payne's Farm, in '64; Reuben D. Henderson, killed at Chancellorsville, May 2, '63; Benj. F. Rapp, wounded in '63; Jos. Spence, wounded in '62; J. F. Tribbett, wounded and died.

DIED DURING THE WAR

Mason Tomlinson, died on the way home from prison in '65; Lieut. Robert A. Glasgow, died at the residence of Jas. Bumgardner, Augusta County, May 11, '62, of typhoid fever; John M. Elliot, and George S. Lewis, in '63; Lieut. Wm. Patton, died in Winchester, July 16, '61; Jas. Ricketts, died at Mt. Jackson, March 24, '62; Jas. H. Pugh, died at Point Lookout prison in '64; Benj. Hite, died in hospital at Winchester; R. G. Clark, died at Swift Run Gap in 63; J. J. Pleasants, died in hospital; Wm. H. Rogers, died in '63; Baxter Slough, died at Fort Delaware.

THE VALLEY REGULATORS
COMPANY "K" 11TH VIRGINIA INFANTRY

The following are the officers and men from Rockbridge:
Captains—Andrew M. Houston, and Thos. D. Houston.
1st Lieuts.—Andrew M. Houston, and Thos. D. Houston.
2nd Lieuts.—Thos. R. Gilmore, and Thos. D. Houston.
3rd Lieuts.—Robert Campbell, Edward T. Dixon, Jas. T. Hardy, E. H. Walker, and Wm. M. Walkup.

PRIVATES

Agner, Geo. W.	Black, J. L.	Brown, Jas. N.
Agner, David	Boggs, Daniel	Brown, Richard
Austin, John	Bradford, M.	Carr, John
Austin, Jos.	Brafford, Philander S.	Cash, J.

428 A HISTORY OF ROCKBRIDGE COUNTY, VIRGINIA

Crawford, Bill Dick	Isaacs, John	Ray, John
Campbell, Wm.	Johnston, Luther	Kayton, John W.
Campbell, Sam	Johnston, J.	Ray, Jas. H.
Campbell, Jas.	Jones, Wm.	Rice, Benj.
Coyle, Peter	Kerr, John	Rice, William
Ferguson, Eli	Kidd, John W.	Reed, Stuart
Ferguson, Jas.	McClelland, Alfred	Reed, Wm.
Ferguson, Wm.	McClelland, Wm.	Reed, Jas.
Fitzgerald, J.	McClelland, Jos.	Shorter, Wm. H.
Fortune, John	McClelland, George	Shindle, John
Gorman, John	McCullough, Jos. C.	Shindle, Sam.
Grady, Wm.	McCullough, Wm.	Walker, J. M.
Hardy, Wm.	McCullough, John S.	Watkins, J. K.
Houston, E. M.	Oyler, Jno. M..	Wilcher, Jas. T.
Hutson, Thos.	Painter, Jas. M.	Walkup, Sam Houston
Hutson, Robert	Parks, Chas.	Walkup, Jas. D.
Hunt, Barney	Parker, Hezekiah	Walkup, Matthew
Hughes, Jonathan	Powers, John	
Isaacs, George	Powers, Jas.	

KILLED AND WOUNDED FROM ROCKBRIDGE

Killed—J. Cash and Thos. Hutson, at Frazier's Farm; Lieut. Robert Campbell, 2nd Manassas; Lieut. Jas. T. Hardy, at Drury's Bluff; Lieut. Edward T. Dix, at Malvern Hill; Wm. Hardy, at Gettysburg; Wm. McCullough, at Drainsville; Chas. Parks and Barney Hunt, at Gettysburg; Jas. M. Walker and Wm. Hutson, at Williamsburg; and Wm. Hardy.

Wounded—Jas. H. Ray, 1st Manassas; J. L. Black, Drainsville; John Shindle and John S. McCullough, at Drury's Bluff; Capt. Thos. D. Houston, and Capt. Andrew M. Houston, at Gettysburg; Bill Dick Crawford and James Walkup, First Manassas; James Ferguson, at Gettysburg; John Isaacs, at Yorktown, Va.

Died of disease—Hezekiah Parker, at Manassas Junction, soon after the first battle of Manassas.

ROCKBRIDGE GUARDS, COMPANY "H" 25TH VA. INFANTRY
LIST OF OFFICERS AND MEN

Captains

Curry, David P., wounded and taken prisoner at Rich Mount., July 11, '61.
Whitmore, Jacob J., killed at battle of McDowell, May 8, '62.
Stuart, R. E. A., wounded at battle of McDowell, May 8, '62. Captured at Spottsylvanin, May 12, 64.

Lieutenants

Buchanan, Jno. R., wounded and captured at Wilderness.
Culton, Jas. B., honorably discharged, June 7, '61.
Hamilton, Geo. J., captured at Rich Mount, July 11, '61.
Hoover, Henry L., captured at Rich Mount, July 11, '61. Returned June, '63. Captured at Wilderness and imprisoned.
Stuart, Wm. M., mortally wounded at McDowell, May 8, '62.
Wilson, J. Alpheus, transferred to cavalry in '62.
McKemy, Jas. L., captured in Wilderness, May 5, '64. Died since the war.
Massie, Edwin B., joined late '62, went to artillery fall, '63.

ROCKBRIDGE ARTILLERY

First Sergeants

Perry, Erasmus L., captured at Rich Mountain, July 11, '61. Captured a second time at Wilderness, May 5, '64. Died since the war.

Anderson, Jas. D., wounded at battle of McDowell, May 8, '62.

McKemy, Robert A., wounded at Alleghany Mountain. Captured at Wilderness, May 5, '64. Died since the war.

Alexander, Tzvelle, captured at Aldie, wounded at Fredericksburg, Dec. 13, '62. Captured at Spottsylvania, May 12, '64.

Sergeants

Rice, John, killed at battle of McDowell, May 8, '62.

Mainwaring, George, captured May 12, '64. Died since the war.

Dixon, J. Wm., captured at Spottsylvania, May 12, '64. Died in Illinois, '90.

Bryan, Jas. E., wounded at Rich Mount. Died since the war.

Wilson, J. Howard, transferred to cavalry.

Corporals

Campbell, John A., captured at Wilderness, May 5, '64.

McCutchan, John F., captured at Alleghany Mountain, Dec. 13, '61, and captured at Wilderness, May 5, '64.

Teaford, Jacob P. S., captured at Wilderness, May 5, '64.

Thompson, John W., died since the war.

Via, Wesley T., wounded at McDowell, May 8, '62, captured at Wilderness, May 5, '64.

Privates

Adams, Hugh, wounded at Rich Mountain, died since the war.

Allen, Leroy, wounded and captured at Petersburg. Died since the war, '99.

Anderson, John Y., surrendered at Appomattox.

Beaty, William, captured at Rich Mountain, May 5, '64. Exchanged and died in camp at Monterey.

Bosserman, William, captured at Rich Mount., and exchanged. Died in '94.

Bosserman, Henry B., captured at Rich Mount., and exchanged.

Benson, Jacob, wounded with a spent ball at McDowell, May 8, 62.

Benson, John G., captured at Wilderness, May 5, 64. Imprisoned at Point L.

Benson, John W., sent to hospital sick, and never returned.

Benson, Preston, wounded at battle of McDowell, May 5, '62.

Balser, Benj., left the army May 1, '64, and never returned.

Balser, Sam., wounded at battle of Fredericksburg. Died since the war, April 13, 1900.

Brownlee, Wm. J., captured at Rich Mount., wounded and captured at Gettysburg, died in '86.

Brownlee, H. H., captured at Rich Mount., again at Petersburg. Died since the war, March 8, '96.

Brownlee, R. A., captured at Rich Mount, again at Petersburg, March 25, '65. Wounded at Wilderness May 5, '63.

Blackwell, Meredith, discharged soon after the McDowell Battle. Died since the war, May 10, '77.

Bare, John, belonged to Mt. Crawford Company and assigned to this company after Battle of Rich Mount.

Childress, D. D., captured at Spottsylvania May 12, '64. Died since war.

Conner, George, captured at Rich Mount, exchanged. Still living in 1900 in State of Ohio.

Clifton, John M., captured at Rich Mount, exchanged. Captured again at Wilderness May 5, '64, sent to Point Lookout.

Campbell, R. Granville, wounded and captured at Petersburg. Died since the war, '94.

Craver, John, died since the war.

Decker, Wm. C., wounded at McDowell May 8, '62.

Decker, Samuel, wounded at McDowell May 8, '62, and captured at Wilderness.

Day, Columbus C., wounded and captured at Wilderness. Died since the war.

Dixon, Tobert A., captured at Wilderness May 5, '64. Still living in Missouri.

Deaver, Thos. A., died since the war.

Dickey, W. Telf., mortally wounded at battle of McDowell May 8, '62.

Forbes, Jasper, left the company in '62 and never returned.

Forbes, Sam, killed at battle of McDowell May 8, '62.

Fulwiler, Robert D., transferred to Cavalry and wounded.

Fix, Jas., captured at Rich Mountain, exchanged. Captured at Wilderness May 5, '64.

Firebaugh, Robert D., captured at Rich Mount, exchanged and afterwards enlisted in Co. "I" 62nd Infantry.

Gordon, Jas., captured at Wilderness May 5, '63. Imprisoned at Point Lookout and afterwards at Elmira, N. Y.

Glee, Isaiah, captured at Wilderness and died at Point Lookout Prison Aug., '64.

Graham, D. E., captured and died at Elmira, N. Y., April 11, '62.

Hodge, Henry, killed at battle of McDowell May 5, '62.

Hite, Geo. W., died during the war in the hospital.

Jarvis, John, captured at Spottsylvania May 12, '64.

Jarvis, William, died since the war, '99.

Kelly, Wm. H., wounded at Fredericksburg, '63.

Kelly, Sam M., killed at Rich Mountain in '61.

Kennedy, Moses W., wounded at McDowell and Fredericksburg. Died since the war.

Kerr, Sam. A., died since the war.

Kerr, J. McD., wounded and captured at Gettysburg. Died in prison at Point Lookout.

Kelly, John, sent home sick from Greenbrier River, never recovered sufficiently to return.

Kirkpatrick, R. D., survived the war and died in Ray County, Mo., 1902.

Kirkpatrick, C. W., captured at Wilderness May 5, '64, and imprisoned at Point Lookout, Md., and Elmira, N. Y.

Kirkpatrick, W. H., crippled in feet and discharged during the war.

Kirkpatrick, Jno. A., wounded at Hatcher's Run, died since the war.

Lowman, Wm. H., wounded at Fredericksburg and Alleghany Mt. and captured at Wilderness May 5, '64.

Lowman, John F., killed in battle of McDowell May 8, '62.

Lucas, Jno. F., captured at Wilderness and imprisoned at Elmira, N. Y.

Lucas, Andrew, died in camp at Greenbrier River.

Lucas, Peter, died since the war at Greenville, Augusta Co., Va., '99.

Lucas, Andrew, ———————

Lucas, David, died since the war, '90.

Marks, Jas., died in Lynchburg since the war.

Moneymaker, John C., captured at Wilderness, sent to Elmira. Died in prison at Elmira,

N. Y., Dec. 10, '64.

Moneymaker, Arch, captured at Wilderness and sent to Elmira, N. Y.

Muck, Jos., ——————

Matheny, John, captured at Wilderness, took oath and sent to fight Indians.

Matheny, Arch, ——————

Matthews, Jos., died in camp at Greenbrier River.

Moneymaker, Daniel, died during the war at Monterey, '62.

Myers, J. H., captured at Spottsylvania May 12, '64. Died in prison at Point Lookout June 23, '64.

Myers, A. J., captured at Spottsylvania May 12, '64. Died at Point Lookout.

Mackey, Henry, mortally wounded at 2nd battle of Manassas and died in Aldie Hospital.

Mays, Jos., died since the war.

McCown, Wm. M., captured at Wilderness, imprisoned at Elmira, N. Y.

McLaughlin, J. M., transferred to Confederate Navy. Died since the war.

McCauley, Wm. H., transferred to Artillery and killed at High Ridge a day or two before the surrender.

McCutchan, Jas. H., captured at Wilderness May 12, '64, and imprisoned at Point Lookout and Elmira; slightly wounded six times; now in Los Angeles.

McKemy, Wm. D., wounded May 10, '64, at Spottsylvania C. H. Captured at Spottsylvania C. H. May 12, '64, and imprisoned at Point Lookout and Elmira.

McMullen, George, accidentally wounded in camp at Greenbrier River.

McCurdy, Alfred A., wounded at Hatcher's Run, Feb. 6, '65.

Norcross, Thos. J., captured at Gettysburg July, '63.

Nicely, Salome, wounded in left leg in battle of Alleghany Mt. Dec. 13, '61.

Nicely, John A., died during the war.

Nuckols, John, died since the war.

Nicely, Marion, wounded at Alleghany Mountain.

Patterson, Jas. A. ——————

Perry, W. W., wounded at Hatcher's Run. Sick in Richmond Hospital when the army surrendered. Died since the war.

Ramsey, Jas. A., captured at Wilderness May 5, '64, and imprisoned at Elmira.

Ramsey, Wm. G., captured at Wilderness May 5, '64, and imprisoned at Elmira.

Rapp, Wm. A., wounded at Gettysburg.

Rosen, D. H., ——————

Rosen, W. T., wounded at the battle of McDowell May 8, '62.

Reid, F. S., died during the war Sept. 21, '63.

Reid, Jas. W., died during the war at Brandy Station Nov. 31, '63.

Rippetoe, Adam, ——————

Sensabaugh, Sam., captured at Spottsylvania (Horse Shoe Bend) May 12, '63, imprisoned at Point Lookout, knocked down with shell at Gettysburg 2nd day's fight.

Sensabaugh, Jacob, died since the war, '65.

Sensabaugh, John, captured at Wilderness May 5, '64, and imprisoned at Elmira.

Sensabaugh, David., ——————

Snider, John Mack, wounded at the battle of Gettysburg. Died since the war.

Snider, John Joe, captured at Wilderness May 5, '64. Died in prison at Point Lookout Aug. 3, '64.

Snider, Jacob S., mortally wounded at the battle of McDowell May 6, '62.

Snider, Abram, killed in battle at Rich Mount, July 11, '61.

Snieder, John Jack, wounded in the battle of Alleghany Dec. 13, '61.
Snider, Jas., ———————
Snider, Jas. C., wounded at Hatcher's Run Feb. 6, '65.
Snider, David, ———————
Snider, Daniel, captured at Hatcher's Run Feb. 6, '65.
Strickler, Jas., captured at Petersburg and imprisoned at Point Lookout. Died since the war.
Strickler, Jacob, died since the war, '97.
Strickler, Sam, killed in battle at Rich Mount July 11, '61.
Strickler, David, wounded and captured at Gettysburg.
Selby, Wm. H., died in camp at Monterey, '61.
Sweet, John W., captured at Wilderness and took oath and sent to the frontier to fight the Indians.
Sherman, Geo. F. ———————
Shipplett, John., ———————
Taylor, J. Ballard., ———————
Taylor, H. H., ———————
Teaford, John H., captured at Wilderness and died in prison at Elmira Sept. 24, '64.
Thomas, William, wounded at McDowell May 8, '62.
Tooman, Wm. H., captured at Wilderness, took the oath, and sent to fight the Indians.
Via, C. C., ———————
Walker, John F., captured at Wilderness. Died in prison at Elmira, N. Y., Oct. 8, '64.
Wilson, John T., survived the war and died at Wilson Springs Oct. 9, 1901.
Welsh, R. Alex., captured at the Wilderness Battle, imprisoned at Point Lookout and then taken to Elmira, N. Y.
Wiseman, G. W., captured at Wilderness. Died in Harrisonburg, Va., '63, returning from prison.
Whitmore, David H., captured at Battle of Wilderness and died in prison at Elmira Dec. 12, '64.
Whitmore, John B., captured at Wilderness and imprisoned at Elmira, N. Y. Died since the war.
Withrow, J. W., captured at Wilderness May 5, '63. Died in prison at Elmira, N. Y.
Withrow, H. J. V., captured at Petersburg March 28, '65, and imprisoned at Point Lookout and released June 19, '65.
West, Robert D., killed in battle at Rich Mountain.
Wilson, Thos. M., transferred to cavalry.
Lucas, Andrew ———————

ROCKBRIDGE RIFLES. COMPANY "H" 27TH VA. INFANTRY STONEWALL BRIGADE

List of the Rockbridge men, as heyt left Lexington April 18, '61.
Captain—S. H. Letcher, afterward Colonel 58th Va. Infantry.
First Lieut.—E. F. Paxton, afterward Brigadier—General Stonewall Brigade, killed at Chancellorsville, May 3, '63.
Second Lieut.—J. K. Edmondson, afterwards Colonel 27th Va. Infantry, lost arm at Chancellorsville.
Third Lieut.—W. W. Lewis, afterward Adjutant 27th Va. Infantry.
Quartermaster—R. C. Turpin, D. L. Hopkins, clerk.

ROCKBRIDGE ARTILLERY — 433

First Serg.—J. C. Boude, afterward captain of the company, and lost a leg at Chancellorsville.
Second Serg.—John H. Reeton.
Third Serg.—Geo. W. Chapin.
Fourth Serg.—J. J. Hileman.
First Corporal—A. S. Wade.
Second Corporal—Frederick Davidson.
Third Corporal—R. H. Campbell.
Fourth Corporal—Jos. H. Marston.

PRIVATES

Breedlove, J. W.
Bailey, G. W.
Bowyer, D. G.
Boogher, E. N.
Charlton, Sam C.
Charlton, John A.
Campbell, Jas. M.
Criser, J. H.
Campbell, Sam J.
Donald. Benj.
Davidson, P. A.
Donald, John A.
Edmondson, John M.
Fuller, S. B.
Fonshill, J. H.
Gaither, G. W.
Gillock, Jas. W.
  (afterward Lt.)
Gordon, S. A.
Green, Wm. L.
Hanger, M. R.
Hite, Caleb V. M.
Houston, W. H.
Heilbroner, Henry

Hutcheson, J. H.
Helm, M. E.
Haney, J. R.
Jessup, Edward
Jordan, R. A.
Kahle, W. H.
Kelly, Thos.
Kelly, Jerry
Laird, D. E.
Lokey, W. R.
Lynch, Ed.
Middleton, J. W.
Mullen, T. B.
Moore, J. H.
Miller, Adam
Moody, W. T.
McCluer, A. D.
McCown, R. McD.
McCampbell, S. J. N.
McCluer, A. C.
McCullough, Sam S.
McNamara, Lawrence
McAleer, Robert E.
Norgrove, E. W.

Northern, E. Y.
Neff, Joel
Parrent, F. M.
Paine, Robert
Ruff, J. W.
Reilley, C. A.
Rollins, C. A.
Rickett, R. M.
Spears, J. W.
Smith, Henry D.
Sizer, Chas.
Snider, John
Smith, Jas. S.
Tanquary, J. S.
Thomas, J. S.
Thompson, J. S.
Varner, A. W.
  (afterward Lt.)
Webb, P. M.
Wallace, J. W.
Wallace, H. H.
Wright, W. G.

Volunteers in the Rockbridge Rifles after the company left Lexington April 18, '61.

Adams, Chas.
Agnor, Thos. B.
Ayers, Matthew
Ayres, A. G.
Bell, Robert
Barger, Jno. A.
Camden, Jos.
Charlton, W. C.
Campbell, R. G.
Claireborne, Alfred
Conner, David
Crawford, Henry

Dickenson, J. C.
Drumheller, John
Drumheller, Wm.
East, Jas.
East, John
Eskew, Wyatt
Evans, Jas. S.
Garrison, Newton M.
Gordon, Thos.
Greiner, Erastus
Hayslett, Andrew
Harrison, W. H.

Hite, John
Halk, A. G.
Hartigan, John W.
Higgans, Jos.
Hileman, Daniel
Hook, N. D.
Hartman, Henry
Kramer, John
Kirkpatrick, Thos. M.
Marks, Wyatt L.
Mitchell, Wm.
Miller, Alfred

Miller, Geo. W.
Moore, J. Scott
Mullen, Jack
McGowan, Robert
Parks, Joshua, Jr.
Patterson, Alex.
Patterson, John
Patton, Wm.
Radford, Calvin

Robinson, Levi.
Siders, Wm.
Shields, Jas. H.
Shields, Wm.
Seal, Morgan
Shelton, M. H.
Shoemaker, N. M.
Slough, A. A. P.
Slough, Jas. M.

Senseny, Jas. M.
Smith, Alphonso
Smith, Jacob
Standoff, Henry
Trayson, Wm.
Vanpelt, Jesse
Varner, C. V.
Wash, Thos. H.
Wilhelm, John

CASUALTIES

Falling Waters—Wounded, Arthur D. McCluer and Lawrence McNamara.

1st Manassas—Killed, Frederick Davidson and A. C. McCluer; wounded—David G. Brower, skull broken, wounded badly in the leg and shot in the right side; P. A Davidson, W. H. Kahle, W. T. Moody, Adam Miller, D. M. Reilly, Chas. Rollins, J. W. Ruff, Wm. J. Speers, J. J. Hileman, Joel Neff, E. Y. Northern, Joshua Parks, Jr.

Kernstown—Mortally wounded, John Drumheller, died in Staunton; wounded, J. W Hartigan.

Honeywood Mill, or Dam No. 5—Killed, Joshua Parks, Jr.

Port Republic—Mortally wounded, Alfonso Smith, died July, '62; wounded, Henry Heilbroner and Wm. Mitchell.

Malvern Hill—Killed, Arthur D. McCluer.

2nd Manassas—Wounded, Serg. J. C. Boude and Robert Gowan.

Chancellorsville—Killed, General E. F. Paxton and E. W. Norgrove; wounded, Col. J. K. Edmondson, lost arm; Capt. J. C. Boude, lost leg; Joseph Higgans, badly; S. J. H. McCampbell, wounded in mouth and throat.

Gettysburg—Killed, W. H. Kahle, Joseph Camden, J. S. Thomas, and Jack Mullen; wounded, Lieut. Andrew W. Varner, who commanded company, lost arm and captured; J. Hileman, shot in thigh.

Spottsylvania C. H.—Killed, Alfred Claiborne and John M. Edmondson, J. W. Wallace.
Mine Run—Wounded, T. B. Mullen and Geo. W. Miller.
Near Richmond—Wounded, S. C. Charlton.
Fort Steadman—Wounded and captured, R. G. Campbell.
Slaughter Mountain—Killed, David Conner.
Duffield Depot—Wounded, J. S. Thomas.
In front of Petersburg—Killed, Levi Robinson, Harris Hill; wounded, W. H. Harrison.

COMPANY "E" 52ND VIRGINIA INFANTRY 4TH BRIGADE

Roll of the company:

Capt. Thos. H. Watkins; Lieut. Jos. S. Paxton, Lieut. Wm. V. Knick, Lieut. M. B. Campbell; S. W. Paxton, First Serg.; ————————— Second Serg; G. W. Ackerly. Third Serg; J. A. Fisher, Fourth Serg.; W. S. Newcomer; First Corporal; J. H. Shafer, Second Corporal; ————————— Third Corporal; ————————— Fourth Corporal.

PRIVATES

Arthur, Jos. D.
Barger, Joel
Beard, W. S.
Black, John
Black, Jas.

Black, A. H.
Black, A. D.
Byers, W. C.
Camden, Layne
Camden, John

Cash, Jos.
Drain, David
Dixon, W. A.
Entsminger. J.
Fisher, Jos. S.

ROCKBRIDGE ARTILLERY 435

Ford, W. A.
Glenn, Jos.
Gilbert, A. J.
Gilbert, J. M.
Gilmore, A. J.
Gilmore, Sam. C.
Glenn, Jas.
Griffith, Wm.
Grossly, S. W.
Hall, H. L.
Hall, W. T.
Hamilton, A. C.
Harris, John
Hayslett, B. F.
Hayslett, R. M.
Hayslett, Wm.
Hayslett, S. McD.
Hicks, W. H.
Hostetter, L. J. M.
Hostetter, Henry
Hogue, Wm. M.
Hughes, Lewis
Hughes, D. E.

Hughes, J. Frank
Irwin, Geo.
Jenkins, J. A. J.
Jones, Oliver
Knick, Jas. C.
Kidd, J. P.
Lackey, W. H.
Lawhorn, J. K.
Lawhorn, Sam.
Long, J. M.
Long, W. P.
McManamy, W. C.
Muterspaw, Daniel J.
Miller, J. P.
Miller, Jas. H.
Miller, Jos.
Moore, B. F.
Ochiltree, D. L.
Patterson, J.
Parsons, W. A.
Phillips, J. S.
Reed, W. H.
Robinson, A. D.

Ruly, J. F.
Scott, C. A.
Self, B. D.
Scott, T. F.
Shafer, R. P. G.
Shepherdson, A.
Simpson, J. J.
Simpson, W. D.
Smith, Ananias
Smith, J. W.
Smith, Josephus
Syron, Simon
Tinsley, Geo.
Tygret, Robert
Wallace, J. M.
West, Wm.
White, J. M.
White, W. W.
Whitten, J. W.
Wilhelm, Wm.
Woody, H.
Zollman, A.
Zollman, J. W.

RECRUITS

Ayres, ———
Bradshaw, A. K.
Camden, Jas.
Clark, J. A.
Clark, J. D.
Hayslett, B.
Hughes, R. H.
Johnston, R. M.

Lacy or Lang, Robert
Lam, Jos.
Miller, B. F.
Ochiltree, T. A.
Paxton, M. L.
Reese, J. A.
Reed, J. A.
Selph, W. J.

Smith, J. A.
Shafer, S. J.
Silvey, Jas.
Simpson, C. A.
Tucker, G. L.
Wiseman, J. A.
Wood, J. A.

CASUALTIES

At McDowell—May 8, '62.—Killed, W. H. Hicks and Alfred Shepherdson; wounded, John A. J. Jenkins.

At Cross Keys—Wounded—R. M. Hayslett, Ananias Smith and John W. Zollman.

At Port Republic—Wounded, Jos. Knick and Wm. Hayslett.

At Gaines' Mill—Wounded, Sylvester W. Grossly (lost leg), S. D. Gilmore, Wm. B. Beard, John W. Zollman, W. L. Paxton, B. F. Miller, W. S. Newcomer and J. A. Wiseman.

At Slaughter's Mountain—Killed, Lieut. Wm. Knick, John Black, and Jos. Smith; wounded, Serg. J. A. Fisher, (lost arm), R. P. D. Shafer.

At Winchester, J. Y. W.—Killed, W. C. McManamy and Jas. W. Smith.

At Winchester, Sept. 19, '64—Killed, W. L. Paxton.

At Sharpsburg—Killed, A. H. Black; wounded, Joseph Phillips.

At Cold Harbor—May 30, '64—Killed, Lieut. Col. Thos. H. Watkins, Jas. S. Fisher, B. F. Self and Wm. Wilhelm; wounded, Jos. S. Paxton.

At Spottsylvania—Killed, Jas. Black, W. A. Parsons, Geo. Tinsley; wounded, Capt. S. W. Paxton, Wm. M. Hogue.
At Gettysburg—Killed, J. M. Gilbert.
At Middletown—Wounded, J. A. J. Jenkins, J. P. Miller, and J. A. Reese.
At the Wilderness—Killed, A. D. Black.
At Fort Steadman—Wounded, Capt. S. W. Paxton.

DIED OF DISEASE

Layne Camden, John Camden, David Drain, W. T. Hall, Lewis Hughes, Oliver Jones, John Muterspaw, David L. Ochiltree, T. A. Ochiltree, T. F. Scott, and John W. Whitten.

KERR'S CREEK CONFEDERATES—COMPANY "G" 58TH VA. INFANTRY

The original organization was as follows:

Officers—James D. Morrison, Captain; John Chaplin, 1st Lieut. J. Preston Moore, 2nd Lieut. Geo. W. Teaford, 1st Serg.; Perry Farrow, 2nd Serg.; John S. Lam, 3rd Serg.; Jas. W. Montgomery, 4th Serg.; Jas. W. Lam, 3rd Corporal; Joseph C. Deacon, 4th Corporal.

PRIVATES

Alexander, John F.
Archer, John T.
Ailstock, Absalom
Agnor, John
Ailstock, Geo.
Bennington, Nelson
Blackburn, Richard
Blackwell, Richard
Brown, Sam A.
Bennington, John L.
Crist, Hector C.
Campbell, John A. J.
Conner, Fitzallen
Crist, Richard A.
Echard, William
Ford, Joseph
Fitzgerald, Sam.
Hayslett, Jas. M.
Fisher, John A.
Gaylor, Jas. M.
Graham, Andrew J.

Grant, Andrew J.
Grant, Seaton L.
Hamilton, Robert S.
Hardbarger, Frederick
Harris, Daniel W.
Hattan, Mark
Hayslett, Andrew J.
Hayslett, Andrew
Hayslett, Ezekiel
Higgans, Chas.
Hinkle, Adam
Irvine, John M.
Kelly, John H.
Layman, Henry
Linkswiler, Sam.
Linkswiler, Franklin
Lowman, Sam.
McDaniel, Jas. H.
Muterspaw, George W.
Miller, Andrew
Miller, Sam H.

Mohler, Jas. H.
Mohler, Wm.
Montgomery, John C.
Morris, Jas. D. W.
Morris, Mark
Nuckols, Silas H.
Plogger, Jas. M.
Ramsay, Nathaniel
Rowsey, Marion
Shaw, Sam B.
Shaw, Henry W.
Sheppard, Chas.
Smith, Benj. F.
Smith, Thos., Jr.
Smith, Thos., Sr.
Tolley, Chas. W.
Thomas, Levi.
Vess, Harvey
Wandless, Stephen H.
Wiseman, Andrew

RECRUITS

Ailstock, Joseph
Archer, Peter
Archer, Jos. B.
Brads, John A.
Bane, Sam
Carter, John A.
Donald, Robert A.
Hall, Sam E.
Hostetter, George
Hinkle, Preston D.

Hauber, Rufus
Miller, Henry M.
Morris, Elihu B.
Muterspaw, William C.
Mohler, Winston P.
McKemy, Sam.
Plott, Wm. M.
Plott, Joseph N.
Plott, John A.
Ruly, Robert

Stein, Nimrod
Smith, John H.
Stanley, Lewis
Sprouse, Joseph L.
Thompson, Alex.
Thompson, Thos.
Vess, Jackson
Wiseman, John A.
Wilhelm, John H.

The following were the officers of the company during the war:

Captains: Jas. D. Morrison from Aug. 1, '61, to May 1, '62; J. Preston Moore, from May 1, '62 to Aug., '64, (Capt. J. Preston Moore being permanently disabled by wounds received in battle, was retired from field service, with his rank and pay, under act of Congress, and assigned to duty as Commandant of the Military Post at Lexington, Va.); Mark Hatton, from Aug. '64 to close of war, April 9, '65.

First Lieuts.: John Chaplin, from Aug. 1, '61, to May 1, '62; George W. Teaford, from May 1, '62, to June 10, '62; H. R. Morrison from about April, '64, to about May 10, '64.

Second Lieuts.: J. Preston Moore from Aug. 1, '61 to May 1, '62; Jas. W. Montgomery from about Dec., '62, to ——————; Mark Hatton from about Dec., '63, to Aug., '64.

Third Lieuts.—Rev. J. C. Richardson, from about March, '62, to May 1, '62.

Chaplain: Rev. J. C. Richardson, from Aug. 1, '61, to March, '62

Note: Above are commissioned officers.

NON-COMMISSIONED OFFICERS

1st Serg.: Geo. W. Teaford and Perry Farrow.
2nd Serg.: Perry Farrow and J. C. Deacon.
3rd Serg. John S. Lam and Mark Hattan.
4th Serg.: Jas. W. Montgomery and John S. Lam.
5th Serg.: Wm. H. Mohler.
1st Corporals: Jas. W. Lam and F. Linkswiler.
2nd Corporal: J. C. Montgomery.
3rd Corporals: Michael C. Reynolds and Jas. M. Plogger.
4th Corporals: Jos. C. Deacon and Mark Morris.

KILLED AND WOUNDED

McDowell, May 8, '62: Wounded, J. A. J. Campbell (died), Franklin Linkswiler and Henry Miller.

Harrisonburg, June 6, '62: Killed, John A. Fisher and Marion Rowsey; wounded, Perry Farrow, J. C. Deacon, Jno. S. Lam, Jas. M. Gaylor, Fitzallen Conner, and Sam. A. Brown.

Port Republic, June 9, '62; Wounded, Captain J. Preston Moore, Lieut. Geo. W. Tedford (mortally.)

Seven days' battle around Richmond, June, '62; Killed, Sam Linkswiller; wounded, J. C. Montgomery, Jos. B. Archer, A. J. Grant, D. W. Harris, Jno. A. Brads, Geo. Ailstock, and Silas N. Nuckols.

Second Manassas, Aug. 27, '62; Killed Mark Morris; wounded, Geo. Ailstock (mortally) and Henry Miller.

Sharpsburg, Sept. 17, '62: Wounded, Jno. H. Smith (mortally.)

Fredericksburg, Dec. 13, 62: Killed, Jas. H. Mohler; wounded, Jno. F. Alexander, Winston P. Mohler, John A. Carter, and Richard A. Crist.

Chancellorsville, May, '63: Wounded, John Agnor and Robert Ruly.

Wilderness, May 6, '64: Wounded, Jas. H. McDaniel, Jas. M. Plogger, and Jos. Ailstock.

Spottsylvania C. H.: Killed, A. J. Grant.

Second Cold Harbor, June 27, '64: Wounded, Henry Layman, Sam, Lowman (mortally.)

Winchester: Wounded, Mark Hattan and Wm. Muterspaw.

Lynchburg: Killed, Jos. Ailstock.

Near Winchester: Killed, Andrew J. Wiseman, Wm. Echard and John A. Wiseman (last named supposed to have been killed—was never heard of afterwards.) Near New Market: Wounded, Alexander Thompson. Hatcher's Run, Feb. 6, '65: Wounded, Capt. Mark Hattan.

DIED OF DISEASE

Lieut, H. R. Morrison, Jas. W. Lam, Jas. M. Hayslett, Ezekiel Hayslett, Levi Thomas, Stephen H. Wandless, Thos. Smith, Sr., S. L. Grant, Chas. W. Tolley, Thomas Smith, Jr., John H. Kelly, Jno M. Irvine, Rufus Hauber, and Henry W. Shaw.

"THE BOY COMPANY" (JUNIOR RESERVES) IN THE CONFEDERATE ARMY FROM ROCKBRIDGE COUNTY

Chas. W. Freeman, Captain; Ducan C. Lyle, First Lieut.; Alexander F. Laird, Second Lieut.; John C. Paxton, Orderly Serg.; Jas. Daly, Serg.; Nathan Strickler, Serg.; David Black, Serg.; Milton Swink, Corporal; H. T. Wilson, Corporal.

PRIVATES

Baldwin, Jos.
Bell, Jas. B.
Black, Calvin
Campbell, Isaac N.
Campbell, John T.
Cash, John R.
Cash, Schuyler B.
Childress, J. Sam.
Coffman, Taylor
Dixon, John
Drain, Jas. C.
Drawbond, Wm. H.
Dunlap, Wm. M.
Dixon, Sam.
Edwards, Thos.
Figgat, Robert H.
Firebaugh, John

Ford, Jas. A.
Garland, Wm.
Gold, John W.
Hensley, George
Jessup, Henry
Johnston, Thos.
Kahle, Jacob P.
Kirkpatrick, Sam. L.
Lam, J. Calvin
Leech, Isaac
Long, Amos
McClung, J. Moffett
McCown, Robert E.
McCown, Sam.
McCullough, John
McCutchen, Frank
Nutty, John W.

Parsons, John Steele
Paxton, Adolphus
Poague, Wm. Gordon
Pring, J. Calvin
Robertson, Alfred
Robertson, John A.
Ruff, A. Wallace
Swartz, Jos. G.
Short, Jas. M. M.
Smith, John P.
Stuart, J. Gerard
Tyler, D. Gardiner
Wilson, H. T.
Wilson, Jas. A.
White, Wm. H.

In May preceding the organization of the foregoing company, the Reserves of Rockbridge, both senior and junior, were called in service to aid in checking the advance up the valley of the Federal army under Major-General David Hunter, and the name of the following boys are recalled as having rendered service at that time:

Black, David S.
Barger, Alexander
Coffman, Taylor
Drawbond, Wm. H.
Daniels, W. C.
Freeman, Chas. W.
Gold, John W.
Hensley, George

Laird, A. F.
Montgomery, J. C.
Moore, Warren
Moore, Sam P.
Presser, (a student)
Paxton, John C.
Smith, John P.
Swink, Milton

Strider, John P.
Sanderfer, J. C.
Smith, Mac.
Tyler, Gardiner
Wright, Sam.
Watts, Thos.
Wilson, Horatio T.
Wright, Schuyler B.

The following named senior reserves were in service in May '64:

Bacon, Capt. A. S.	Miller, Andrew	Templeton, Capt. John M.
Boone, Abram	Montgomery, Robert	Turpin, R. C.
Boone, Lewis W.	Moore, W. T.	Wilson, William
Hill, George	Moore, Abner W.	Wright, Wm. G.
Hostetler, George	Ramsey, Calvin	Wallace, Charlton
Lackey, Andrew H.	Shaw, William	Wallace, Sam.
McCaleb, J. Wesley	Sweet, Jacob	Webb, Jas. M.

MISCELLANEOUS

The following named persons from Rockbridge County, Va., were soldiers in the Confederate Army, but did not serve in companies from the county, to wit:

Lieut-General Thomas J. Jackson (Stonewall), wounded at Chancellorsville, Va., May 2, '63, died May 10, '63.

Francis H. Smith, Colonel 9th Virginia Volunteers Provisional Army.

William Gilham, Colonel 21st Virginia Infantry.

R. E. Colston, Colonel 16th Virginia Volunteers—afterward Brigadier General C. S. A.

J. T. L. Preston, Lieut-Colonel 9th Virginia Volunteers, Provisional Army—afterward on Stonewall Jackson's staff.

S. Crutchfield, Lieut-Colonel 9th Virginia Volunteers, Provisional Army, succeeded Col. Preston and afterward Colonel and Chief of Artillery Stonewall Jackson's Corps, killed at Sailor's Creek.

John D. H. Ross, 1st Lieut. of Engineers on Gen. Loring's Staff, afterward Lieut. Colonel of 52nd Va. Infantry, twice wounded at Cross Keys, Va.

Jas. W. Massie, Lieut. Colonel 51st Virginia Volunteers.

R. H. Catlett, Lieut. Colonel Gen. Echol's Staff.

Thomas H. Williamson, Lieut. Colonel and Chief Engineer Staff of Gen. Holmes.

A. S. Pendleton, Lieut. Colonel and Adjutant General of General Thos. J. Jackson's Corps—afterward of Early's Corps.

Scott Shipp, Captain Provisional Army, Adjutant General Camp of Instruction at Richmond, Major 21st Virginia Infantry and afterward Lieut. Colonel C. S. A.

Daniel Truehart, C. S. A., Major Artillery.

M. B. Hardin, Major 9th Virginia Volunteers (provisional Army), afterward Major C. S. Artillery.

Jas. C. Paxton, Major and Quarter-Master C. S. A.

Major Jas. B. Dorman, Quarter-Master C. S. A.

Capt. William C. Williamson, Engineer Corps, C. S. A.

Marshall McDonald, Captain and Ordnance officer at Vicksburg.

John McCausland, Brigadier General, C. S. A., Cavalry Brigade.

John P. Welsh, Captain Co. B., 27th Va. Infantry.

Chas. A. Davidson, Captain Co. E. 1st Va. Infantry Batallion.

Greenlee Davidson, Captain Letcher Artillery, killed at Chancellorsville.

Otho Alexander, Captain 20th Va. Cavalry.

William, Walker, Captain in Wright's Brigade.

Frank C. Wilson, Captain Monroe Guards, 27th Va. Infantry.

Capt. Robert L. McCullough, Danville Grays.

Robert McFarland, Captain in General Morgan's Cavalry.

O. C. Henderson, Captain 1st Va. (Irish) Battalion Army Northern Va.

W. H. Morgan, Captain 21st Va. Infantry, killed at Cedar Mountain.
J. H. Morrison, Lieut. Pemberton's Staff.
T. M. Semmes, Lieut. and Adjutant Rust's Arkansas Regiment.
John H. Lackey, Lieut. in 26th Va. Cavalry.
Wm. H. Norgrove, Lieut. in Botetourt Artillery, died from wounds received at Port Gibson, Miss., in '63.
Albert Davidson, Lieut. Staff of General Robert Preston.
Robert L. Brokenbrough, Surgeon of 58th Va. Infantry, afterward Chief Surg. of Early's Division.
Dr. Sam. Temple Chandler, Assistant Surgeon in hospital at Farmville, Lynchburg and Culpeper C. H.
Dr. Henry G. Davidson, Surgeon of 3rd and 5th Va. Infantry, and afterward in hospitals at Danville, Richmond, Va., and Corinth, Miss.
Dr. Sam. M. Dodd, Asst. Surgeon in hospital in Richmond and Lexington, Va., and Wilmington, N. C.
Dr. John Alexander Graham, Surgeon 5th and 42nd Va. Infantry and Medical Director of the Artillery of the Army of Northern Va.
Dr. R. L. Madison, Surgeon in hospital at Orange C. H.
Dr. Eusebius H. Strain.
Anderson, W. L., Co. F, 27th Va. Infantry, captured May 12, '64, exchanged and captured again at Hare's Hill, a few days before the fall of Petersburg, Va.
Agner, W., 11th Va. Cavalry.
Agner, Oscar, Co. E., 11th Va. Cavalry.
Anderson, Francis T., Jr., Cadet in service around Richmond, was not at New Market.
Arehart, ———, Co. ———, 11th Va. Cavalry.
Ackerly, Wm., Co. E., 27th Va. Infantry.
Byrd, Rowland, Co. E., 11th Va. Cavalry.
Bell, A. D., Co. K., 14th Va. Cavalry.
Bowyer, John, Co. E., 11th Va. Cavalry.
Bell, A. N., Co. K., 14th Va. Cavalry (afterward in Bryan's Battery.)
Beard, John E., Co. E., 11th Va. Cavalry.
Brown, A. G., 27th Va. Infantry (Shriver's Co.)
Bennington, Frank, Petersburg Artillery.
Brooks, Jas., Co. E., 3rd Engineer Regiment, C. S. A.
Black, Rice, Co. E., 27th Va. Infantry.
Black, W. L., Co. E., 27th Va. Infantry.
Black, J. L., Co. E., 27th Va. Infantry.
Brooks, John F., Co. F., 14th Va. Cavalry.
Bell, Robert B., Co. E., 27th Va. Infantry.
Black, R. T., Co. —— 27th Va. Infantry.
Bare, N. M., Co. E., 5th Va. Infantry.
Bumpis, Jas. J., Capt. Kurtz Co., 5th Va. Infantry.
Bird, John, Co. F., 27th Va. Infantry (killed.)
Banker, Van, Carpenter's Battery.
Barger, Chas. F., Co. D., 15th Va. Cavalry.
Carter, Jas. M., Co. E., 27th Va. Infantry.
Copper, John D., Co. E., 20th Va. Infantry.
Conner Fitzallen.
Cooly, J. F., Co. E., 27th Va. Infantry.

Cummings, Jas., Co. E., 27th Va. Infantry.
Campbell, A. D., 19th Va. Cavalry.
Charlton, Jas., Capt. Kurtz' Co., 5th Va. Infantry.
Cummings, Robert, Co. E., 20th Va. Infantry.
Chittum, Jas. A., Co. C., 6th Va. Cavalry.
Davidson, Jas. G., Co. F., 27th Va. Infantry (killed at Wilderness.)
Donald, Alex., Co. C., 20th Va. Infantry.
Daniel Robert, Co. F., 27th Va. Infantry (killed.)
Deacon, W. D., Co. E., 3rd Engineers Reg't, C. S. A.
Day, Wm. H., Co. L., (West Augusta Guards) 5th Va. Infantry (wounded).
Davidson, C. H., Co. K., 22nd Va. Infantry.
Davis, Chalkly, Co. B., 27th Va. Infantry.
Echard, John, Co. C., 20th Va. Infantry.
Ewing, John Mc., Co. F., 27th Va. Infantry.
Ewing, Jas. A., Co. F., 27th Va. Infantry.
Fulwider, Jas., 20th Va. Battalion.
Ford, Jas. Preston, Co. F., 1st Va. Cavalry.
Painter, William, Co. F., 27th Va. Infantry.
Figgat, Ford, Carpenter's Battery.
Green, Zack, Co. E., 11th Va. Cavalry.
Green, Jas., Co. E., 11th Va. Cavalry.
Gibbs, Chas. W., Courier to Gen. Forrest.
Goodbar, Harvey, Co. E., 27th Va. Infantry.
Goodbar, George, Co. E., 27th Va. Infantry.
Gibbs, Geo. S., Alabama Cadets.
Greever, Adam, Co. E., 5th Va. Infantry.
Gibbs, Major John T., Quarter-Master, C. S. A.
Gaylor, Thos. M., Co. C., 26th Va. Cavalry.
Hotinger, Abraham, Co. D., 27th Va. Infantry.
Higgans, Jas., Co. B., 27th Va. Infantry.
Harrison, Howard M., Co. E., 27th Va. Infantry.
Hardy, Geo. W., Co. D., 14th Va. Cavalry.
Hull, Wm. M., Co. K., 22nd Va. Infantry.
Hull, Jno. M., Co. K., 22nd Va. Infantry.
Hall, A. D., Co. F., 27th Va. Infantry.
Hall, J. C., Co. E., 27th Va. Infantry.
Hanger, Z. F., Orderly Serg., Co. F., 27th Va. Infantry.
Huffman, P. I., Co. G., 27th Va. Infantry.
Hanger, G. M., Co. C., 27th Va. Infantry, killed at Sharpsburg, Sept. 17, '62.
Hite, Robert, Co. E., 5th Va. Infantry.
Hileman, Philip C., Co. B., 27th Va. Infantry.
Hattan, Jacob, Co. E, 5th Va. Infantry.
Hart, John H., Co. B, 27th Va. Infantry, wounded at Gettysburg and captured at Williamsport, Md.
Irvine, Wm. H., Co. I, 27th Va. Infantry, and Co. I, 20th Va. Cavalry.
James, Sam, Co. E., 11th Va. Cavalry.
Jeffries, David, H., 17th Va. Cavalry.
Johnston, Chapman, Co. E., 27th Va. Infantry.
Johnson, George, Co. F., 27th Va. Infantry. (South Buffalo.)

Johnson, J. Henry, Co. E., 27th Va. Infantry.
Johnson, George, Co. E., or D., 27th Va. Infantry, (South River).
Johnson, Reuben A., Co. E., 27th Va. Infantry.
Leech, W. P., Co. K., 22nd Va. Infantry.
Leech, David, Co. E., 27th Va. Infantry.
Leech, Jas. M., 20th Va. Battalion.
Lockridge, E. F., 20th Va. Cavalry.
Leech. Wm. A., 27th Va. Infantry.
Leopard, Jas., Carpenter's Battery.
Lackey, John F., Co. D., 27th Va. Infantry.
Lotts, Frank, Carpenter's Battery.
Little, Jas. H., Co. B., 27th Va. Infantry, wounded and leg amputated.
Martin, Reuben, Carpenter's Battery.
Miley, A. J., Co. C., 5th Va. Infantry.
Myres, Allen, Co. E., 27th Va. Infantry.
Miley, Jacob, Co. D., 27th Va. Infantry.
Mortar, John J., Co. A., 11th Va. Cavalry.
Moore, John N., Co. C., 27th Va. Infantry.
Montgomery, Sam., Co. K., 22nd Va. Infantry.
Miley, Michael, Co. C., 27th Va. Infantry.
Miller, Sam., ——————— (Plank Road.)
Moffett, W. Legge, Co. D., 14th Va. Cavalry.
Moffett, John F., Co. D., 14th Va. Cavalry, (killed at Cedarville, Warren Co., Nov. 12, '64.)
Mackey, John M., Carpenter's Battery.
Miller, Alfred, Co. E., 27th Va. Infantry.
Martin, William, Co. I., 11th Va. Cavalry.
McClung, Chas. B., Co. A., 11th Va. Cavalry.
McCown, Jas. L., Kurtz Co., 5th Va. Infantry.
McCoy, M. H., Co. B., 4th Va. Cavalry.
McDaniel, Matthew W., Co. F., 27th Va. Infantry.
McChesney, Jas. Z., Co. F., (Bath Squadron) 17th Va. Battalion, afterward became 11th Va. Regiment.
McFaddin, Abraham, Co. E., 27th Va. Infantry.
Nuckols, William, Co. F, 27th Va. Infantry. (Killed).
Ochiltree, Sam, Co. D, 14th Va. Cavalry, (killed at Cedarville, Warren Co., Nov. 12, '64).
Pierce, Daniel E., Co. A., 11th Va. Cavalry.
Poague, Wm., Co. C., 27th Va. Infantry.
Poague, Sam., Co. C., 27th Va. Infantry.
Poague, John E., Co. K., 22nd Va. Infantry.
Patterson, John M., Co. K., 22nd Va. Infantry.
Paxton, Wm. Henry, Hays La. Brigade.
Parmer, Josiah H., 11th Va. Cavalry, Rosser's Brigade, wounded at battle of the Wilderness.
Rhodes, J. J., Co. K., 5th Va. Infantry.
Robinson, John H. H., 27th Va. Infantry.
Reid, Sam., Co. E., 27th Va. Infantry.
Reid, John A., Co. E., 27th Va. Infantry.

Robinson, W. F., Co. K., 22nd Va. Infantry.
Reynolds, O. B., Co. E., 27th Va. Infantry.
Ruly, B. W., Co. E., 3rd Engineer Regiment, C. S. A.
Reed, Alexander, Co. I., 52nd Va. Infantry.
Risque, John W., 1st Serg., Charlottesville Artillery.
Reece, Jas. G., Co. G., 27th Va. Infantry, Stonewall Brigade.
Reed, Jas. F., Co. H., 5th Va. Infantry.
Smith, John, Co. E., 11th Va. Cavalry.
Showalter, Sam., Co. E., 27th Va. Infantry.
Saville, John, Co. B., 27th Va. Cavalry.
Smiley, Jacob, Co. D., 27th Va. Infantry.
Short, Telford, Co. A., 11th Va. Infantry.
Shortee, Jas. F., Co. E., 3rd Engineer Regiment, C. S. A.
Sterrett, Jas. R., Capt. Avis Co. of Provost Guards, at Staunton, Va., serving the greater part of the time as Clerk in the Provost Marshall's Office.
Scott, T. L., Co. K., 22nd Va. Infantry.
Sorrels, T. J., Co. E., 27th Va. Infantry.
Shafer, S. J., Co. E., 27th Va. Infantry.
Smith, Hezekiah, Lynchburg Guards.
Siler, P. M., Co. ————, 27th Va. Infantry.
Sanford, Henderson, Co. E., 27th Va. Infantry.
Seebert, Jacob F., Co. K., 22nd Va. Infantry.
Wilson, Jas. C., 10th Va. Cavalry.
Wilson, John B., Co. E., 27th Va. Infantry.
Wilson, Jas. W., Co. E., 27th Va. Infantry.
Wilson, John M., Co. E., 27th Va. Infantry.
Webb, Chas. W., Co. E., 27th Va. Infantry.
Walker, Sam. S., Carpenter's Battery.
Walker, John, Carpenter's Battery.
Walker, Geo. M., Carpenter's Battery.
Wade, J. B., Co. E., 27th Va. Infantry.
Welsh, Joseph, Co. E., 11th Va. Cavalry.
Welsh, Sa., Co. E., 11th Va. Cavalry.
Wade, Benj. F., Co. C., 19th Va. Infantry.
Winn, Wm. J., Carpenter's Battery.
White, John S., Cadet Battalion, New Market.
Watkins, G. W., Co. F., 27th Va. Infantry.
White, Joseph, Cadet Battalion, New Market.
Zollman, Jas. M., Capt. Dabney's C. Heavy Field Artillery.

The following named persons from Rockbridge County, Va., served in the Confederate States Navy: Dr. John Leyburn, Surgeon on the Privateer Tallahassee. Jas. N. Brown, Marine on Albemarle. J. L. Adair, Marine on Tallahassee.

SECTION XII

SOLDIERS OF THE WORLD WAR

NOTE: This list is corrected to October, 1919. Names followed by a star are those of the volunteers. The addresses in the margin at the right are for Virginia unless otherwise specified. In the correction of this list, Captain Greenlee D. Letcher and other citizens of Lexington have given very valuable assistance.

WHITE

Ackerly, John ....Lexington
Ackerly, Otto C. ....Rapp's Mill
Ackerly, William* ....Lexington
Adair, Edwin G. ....Lexington
Adair, J. M.—dentist—1st Lieut. Lexington
Addison, William M. ....Lexington
Agnor, Blair M. ....Covington
Agnor, Charles W. ....Lexington
Agnor, Emmett M.—115 Prav. Co.
        Kerr's Creek
Agnor, George G.—U. S. Navy
        Kerr's Creek
Agnor, Gilmore L. ....?
Agnor, John W.—Co. A, 39th
    Infantry ....Kerr's Creek
Agnor, Owen M. ....Murat
Agnor, Robert L. ....Murat
Agnor, Robert R. ....Lexington
Agnor, Thomas ....Lexington
Allen, Frank L. ....Aqua
Allen, John L. ....Aqua
Amick, Eldon A. ....Lexington
Anderson, Charles B. ....Lexington
Anderson, Chastain McC.
        Rockbridge Baths
Anderson, J. Kyle*—Lieut. ....Murat
Anderson, Stewart W.*—Lieut of
    Engineers ....Murat
Anderson, W. B. A.—Lieut. Col.
Armentrout, Ira L. ....Kerr's Creek
Armstrong, Hampton ....Lexington
Arnold, Lester D.* ....Lexington
Artz, Charles R. ....Buena Vista
Austin, Edwin C. ....Greenlee
Austin, James L. ....Greenlee
Austin, John L. ....Greenlee
Austin, Sherman L. ....Greenlee

Ayers, Calvin ....Rapp's Mill
Ayers, Edgar ....**Rapp's Mil**
Ayers, George H. ....Aqua
Ayers, James H.—24th Co., 6th
    Training Bn. ....Kerr's Creek
Ayers, John G.* ....Collierstown
Ayers, Percy C.* ....Lexington
Ayers, Peter R. ....Collierstown
Ayers, Wilmer ....Collierstown
Balser, Albert E. ....Buena Vista
Balser, David E. ....Rockbridge Baths
Bane, James F.—U. S. Engineers—
    died at Camp Humphreys ....Lexington
Barclay, W. Houston* ....Lexington
Bare, Eugene W.* ....Lexington
Bare, James E. ....Lexington
Barger, Charles W. ....Lexington
Barkley, Robert P. ....Buena Vista
Bartlett, Roy ....Buena Vista
Bartow, Fred P. ....Lexington
Beard, Admiral D. ....Raphine
Beard, Chas. C. ....Raphine
Beard, T. R. ....Raphine
Beckner, Albert M. ....Rockbridge Baths
Beeton, Robert B. L. ....Lexington
Bell, Albert S. ....Lexington
Bell, Edward P. ....Goshen
Bell, Henry L. ....Goshen
Bennington, Albert S. ....Lexington
Bennington, Harry S. ....Lexington
Berry, Ollie G. ....Kerr's Creek
Bibb, William H.* ....Glasgow
Blackwell, Ray D. ....Fairfield
Blackwell, Roy L. ....Brownsburg
Bletcher, Frank O. ....Lexington
Bolen, Hugh R. W. ....Lexington
Bolling, Robert W. ....Lexington

SOLDIERS OF THE WORLD WAR 445

Bock, Paul L. .... Lexington
Bond, Robert H. .... Lexington
Booth, Ray P. .... Lexington
Bowyer, Ertel V. .... Lexington
Boykin, H. P.—Lieut. V. M. I., Lexington
Bradds, J. Albert .... Collierstown
Bradds, John B. .... Fancy Hill
Bradds, Richard L. .... Cornwall
Bragg, Chas. P. .... Marlbrook
Bragg, Emmet H. .... Marlbrook
Branch, Alpheus .... Lexington
Branch, William R. .... Greenlee
Britton, John N. .... Walker's Creek
Brogan, Herbert H. .... Lexington
Brooks, George M.*—Lieut. Col.,
                                            Lexington
Brooks, William N. .... Greenlee
Brown, Ambrose McC.* .... Buena Vista
Brown, Briscoe B.—Lieut. ...... Goshen
Brown, Coray S. .... Lexington
Brown, Leonard I. .... Murat
Brown, Nelson L. .... Lexington
Brown, Percy .... Lexington
Brown, Robert C. .... Buena Vista
Brown, William P. .... Buena Vista
Bruce. Richard B. .... Lexington
Bryant, Ashby G. .... Glasgow
Bryant, Herbert .... Buena Vista
Bryant, Homer S. .... Lexington
Bryant, Percy A. ...... Rockbridge Alum
Bryant, Rufus .... Buena Vista
Buchanan, Clyde .... Buena Vista
Buchanan, Cyrus H. .... Aqua
Buchanan, Guy H. .... Brownsburg
Buchanan, James O. .... Brownsburg
Buchanan, James W.—U. S. Infantry—
  died at Camp Lee, Oct. 16, 1918
                                        Brownsburg
Burger, Henry I. .... Natural Bridge
Burger, Luther J. .... Buena Vista
Burgess, George G. .... Buena Vista
Burks, Clifton—U. S. Infantry—killed in
  action, Oct. 13, 1918 ...... Fancy Hill
Camden, Abb—38th Infantry, Regulars—
  killed in action, July 18, 1918 .. Glasgow
Camden, Ashby D. .... Glasgow
Camden, Clarence .... Glasgow
Camden, James .... Glasgow
Camden, Willie H. .... Buena Vista

Campbell, A. C.—U. S. Regulars
                                          Lexington
Camden, Edwin D. .... Lexington
Campbell, Herman H. ...... Irish Creek
Campbell, John H., Jr. ...... Lexington
Campbell, Paul .... Goshen
Campbell, William E. .... Raphine
Carter, Herman W. .... Goshen
Carter, William .... Collierstown
Cash, Charles W. .... Lexington
Cash, James .... Rockbridge Baths
Cash, James H. .... Aqua
Cash, John E. .... Buena Vista
Cash, Lewis E. .... Greenlee
Cash, William D. ...... Rockbridge Baths
Cephas, Samuel ...... Rockbridge Baths
Cephas, William ...... Rockbridge Baths
Chaplin, Charles P.—U. S. Navy—died in
  Norfolk, Oct. 14, 1918 ...... Lexington
Chaplin, Emmett H. ... Rockbridge Baths
Chaplin, Malcolm ..... Rockbridge Baths
Chaplin, Robert C. .... Buena Vista
Campbell, C. F. .... Glasgow
Chandler, Stuart A. .... Lexington
Chapman, John W. ...... Natural Bridge
Chaplin, H. H. ...... Rockbridge Baths
Cheatham, Edward W. ..... Buena Vista
Chayne, William E. .... Lexington
Chittum, Elmer W. .... Fairfield
Chittum, Emmett W. .... Fairfield
Chittum, Graham .... Glasgow
Chittum, Harrell—2nd Lieut.
                                        Timber Ridge
Chittum, Otho H. .... Buena Vista
Clark, A. L. .... Irish Creek
Clark, Benjamin H. .... Alto
Clark, Bligh N. .... Collierstown
Clark, Emmett M. .... Collierstown
Clark, Erskine E. .... Natural Bridge
Clark, James P. .... Cornwall
Clark, John H. .... Collierstown
Clark, Leonard L. .... Collierstown
Clark, Milton .... Irish Creek
Clark, Ollie A. .... Cornwall
Claytor, Fountain C. .... Glasgow
Clements, Aubrey W. .... Cornwall
Clemmer, Herman L.—U. S. Infantry—
  killed in action, July 22, 1918,
                                        Brownsburg

A HISTORY OF ROCKBRIDGE COUNTY, VIRGINIA

Clifton, Russell R. ....Fairfield
Clinebell, Charles M. ......Buena Vista
Clinebell, Roy L. ....East Lexington
Coe, Frank D., Jr.,—Lieut. ....Lexington
Coffey, Walter L. ....Buena Vista
Coffey, William H. ....Buena Vista
Collins, James W. J. ....Natural Bridge
Connor, Bolivar—died at Washington, D. C., Jan. 25, 1917 ..Rockbridge Baths
Connor, Charles W. ....Rockbridge Baths
Connor, Frank B. ....Lexington
Conway, Eustice R. ....Lexington
Coorman, M. D.—Capt. ......Lexington
Copenhaver, Marcus L. ...Natural Bridge
Cooper, Benjamin F. ....Buena Vista
Cooper, Hugh C. ....Buena Vista
Cooper, John D. ....Buena Vista
Cooper, Montry J. ....Buena Vista
Cornelius, Percy ....Lexington
Cox, Frank B. ....Raphine
Cox, Lewis B.—Lieut. ....Lexington
Cox, R. T. ....Lexington
Crabill, H. M. ....Buena Vista
Crist, Charles S. ....Lexington
Cruthirds, Archie B. ....Lexington
Cummings, Addison G. ....Lexington
Cummings, John W. ....Buena Vista
Cummings, George L. ....Natural Bridge
Cushman, Lawrence C. ....Lexington
Darden, Avery H. ....Gilmore's Mill
Dale, Walter ....Lexington
Dameron, Wickam D. ....Goshen
Davidson, Elbert L. — 317th Artillery—died of wounds in France, Oct. 8, 1918, Buena Vista
Davidson, Herman P.—Lieut. Lexington
Davidson, Howard D. ......Buena Vista
Davidson, James M. ....Buena Vista
Davis, Albert W. ....Buena Vista
Davis, Emory F. ....Buena Vista
Davis, Edward P.—Lieut. ....Lexington
Davis, Franklin E. ....Goshen
Davis, Franklin L. ....Goshen
Davis, John L. ....Goshen
Davis, John L. ....Lexington
Davis, Noranda ....Lexington
Davis, Samuel ....Lexington
Davis, Samuel C. ....Goshen
Davis, William P. ....Buena Vista

Deacon, Claude B. ....Murat
Devine, Charles J.—Lieut. Surgeon Lexington
Dixon, Floyd C. ....Lexington
Dixon, Irvin B. ....Lexington
Dixon, James E. ....Lexington
Dixon, Percy G. ....Midvale
Dodd, Ashton T. ....Buena Vista
Donald, Lyle B. ....Glasgow
Drain, Napoleon* ....Collierstown
Drenner, C. T. ....Lexington
Driscoll, John W. ....Buena Vista
Dudley, Thomas J. ....Rapp's Mill
Dudley, Willie L. ....Brownsburg
Duff, George W. ...Natural Bridge Sta.
Duff, Mitchell ....Midvale
Dunaway, Frank S. ....Brownsburg
Duncan, Stanley ....Lexington
Dunlap, Charles W. R. ....Lexington
Dunlap, W. Algie ....Collierstown
Dunlap, Wallace E. ....Fairfield
Dunlap, Walter*— Lieut.—Gilmore's Mill
Eads, William F. ....Glasgow
Ebeling, Andrew A. ....Lexington
Echols, Frank ....Glasgow
Echols, Ralph ....Lexington
Eggleston, Rolley A. ....Buena Vista
Ellis, Emmett ....Natural Bridge
Engleman, Russell C.—C. O. C., 317th Infantry—transferred to S. A. T. C., Baltimore, Md. ....Kerr's Creek
Entsminger, Fremont M. ....Collierstown
Entsminger, Marion F. ....Lexington
Eubanks, Palmer* ....Lexington
Falls, Raymond H. ....Buena Vista
Farmer, Emmett O. ....Lexington
Ferguson, Joseph C. ....Natural Bridge
Fitzgerald, Harry N. ....Vesuvius
Fitzgerald, James E. ....Murat
Fitzgerald, Willie H. ....Vesuvius
Fitzpatrick, John H. ....Lexington
Fitzpatrick, Willie E.* ....Lexington
Fix, Adam D. ....Lexington
Fix, Decker R. ....Lexington
Fix, Howard A. ....Lexington
Fix, Samuel G. ....Lexington
Fix, William M. ....?
Flint, Jesse ....Glasgow
Floyd, Charles R.* ....Buena Vista

SOLDIERS OF THE WORLD WAR 447

Floyd, James I. ....Buena Vista
Ford, Charles F. ....Lexington
Ford, James H.—Supply Co., 317th
   Infantry ....Kerr's Creek
Ford, William A. ....Natural Bridge
Fox, Harry ....Buena Vista
Fox, J. M. ....Buena Vista
Fox, John H. ....Rockbridge Baths
Fultz, Isaac ....Fairfield
Fulwider, Carl C. ......Rockbridge Baths
Gallo, Vincenzo ....Natural Bridge
Garing, Robert*—Lieut. ....Lexington
Garrett, Ashby C. ....Buena Vista
Gaultieri, Francisco .....Natural Bridge
Gibson, Samuel F.* ....Cornwall
Gilbert, Elmer E. ....Natural Bridge
Gilbert, John L. ....Natural Bridge
Gilbert, William C. ......Natural Bridge
Giles, Howard E. ....Buena Vista
Ginger, Warren ....Natural Bridge
Glasgow, Charles ....Lexington
Glasgow, Thomas McP.—Lieut. Lexington
Glenn, Guy B. ....Murat
Glickstein, J. M. ....Lexington
Glover, Emmett B. ....Bell's Valley
Goldsby, Robert G.—38th Infantry, Regulars—killed in action, July 15, 1918 ....Buena Vista
Goodall, Yancy H. ....Lexington
Goodbar, Howard W. ......Collierstown
Graham, Edward L., Jr., Capt., Lexington
Graham, John A.*—Lieut. ....Lexington
Graham, Mercer—Lieut. ......Lexington
Graham, Samuel M. ....Lexington
Grant, Alexander C. ....Irish Creek
Graves, Hugh R. ....Aqua
Gray, John H. ....Goshen
Green, Eillie F. ....Greenlee
Green, Homer G. ....Cornwall
Green, Edward E. ....Midvale
Gridley, Webster G. ....Lexington
Groah, Robert ....Vesuvius
Grogg, Harry W. ....Goshen
Groome, Grover* ....Aqua
Grover, Paul ....Lexington
Grow, Aubrey L. ....Buena Vista
Grow, Hansford McC.—officially reported as died of wounds in France ——— 24, 1917 ....Buena Vista

Grow, John H. ....Buena Vista
Guffey, Lester* ....Lexington
Hall, Harry H. ....Lexington
Hall, Roy F. ....Rockbridge Baths
Hall, William R.* ....Kerr's Creek
Hallman, E. B.* ....Lexington
Hamilton, Mack D. ....Buena Vista
Hamilton, Robert E.* .....Kerr's Creek
Harlow, Hampton ....Lexington
Harper, Andrew F. ....Buena Vista
Harper, John E. ....Lexington
Harper, John S. ....Lexington
Hall, L. K. ....Kerr's Creek
Harris, Emmett E.—Co. D., 110th
   Infantry ....Kerr's Creek
Harris, Floyd W. ....Lexington
Harris, Harry G.—Co. D, 305th Motor Supply Train ....Kerrs Creek
Harris, Oliver E.—Co. C, 18th
   Infantry ....Kerr's Creek
Harris, Willis G. ....Fancy Hill
Harrison, Arthur F. ....Lexington
Harrison, Gordon P. ....Lexington
Harrison, John G. ....Buena Vista
Harrison, Lee* ....Buena Vista
Hart, Freeman H. ....Lexington
Hart, John McC.* .....Rockbridge Baths
Hart, Surry C.—Corporal, Battery D, 57th Heavy Artillery, C. A. C., 31st Brigade ....Kerr's Creek
Hartigan, James S. ....Lexington
Hartless, Harry A.* ....Lexington
Hartless, Hite ....Buena Vista
Hartless, Howard P.* ....Lexington
Hartless, John A. ....Lexington
Hartless, William D. E. ....Buena Vista
Hatton, Jacob H.—Battery F, 111 F. A. 29th Division ....Kerr's Creek
Hawkins, Ira S. ....Lexington
Hayslett, Andrew J. ......Natural Bridge
Hayslett, Clarence E. ....Glasgow
Hayslett, James A. ......Natural Bridge
Hayslett, James W. ....Lexington
Heck, Preston L. ....Fancy Hill
Henkle, Andrew ....Collierstown
Henkle, Clem ....Collierstown
Henkle, Homer S. ....Brownsburg
Henson, Jack H. ....Buena Vista
Hartwell, Benjamin W.

Hepner, John F. ....Lexington
Herndon, Robert G. ....Greenlee
Herrington, Stuart McC.—38th Infantry,
  Regular—killed in action, July 15,
  1918 ....Oakdale
Heslip, Graham C. ....Fairfield
Heslip, Hunter L. ....Fairfield
Hess, Robert—Corporal ....Lexington
Hick, Preston L. ....Fancy Hill
Hickman, Charles ....Lexington
Hickman, Henry S. ....Timber Ridge
Hickman, Lacy ....Glasgow
Hickman, Nathan A.* ....Glasgow
Hiezer, Boyd ....Lexington
Higgens, Charles ....Lexington
Higgens, G. W. ....Lexington
Higgens, Robert H. ....Lexington
Hileman, Ernest N.* ......Timber Ridge
Hileman, Samuel P. ...Rockbridge Baths
Hill, Cecil C. ....Buena Vista
Hinty, Cecil ....Lexington
Hite, Ellet B. ....Vesuvius
Hite, Daniel H. ....Montebello
Hockman, Oscar L. ....Fairfield
Holt, Lawrence G. ....Buena Vista
Holtz, Henry C. ....Raphine
Holtz, William R.—Died at Camp Grant,
  Oct. 11, 1918 ....Collierstown
Hopkins, William S.* ....Lexington
Hostetter, Clarence A. ....Lexington
Hostetter, James M.—U. S. Engineers—
  died at Camp Humphreys, Oct.
  12, 1918 ....Collierstown
Hostetter, John A. ....Collierstown
Hostetter, Mays* ....Lexington
Hostetter, Milton*—Corporal ..Lexington
Hostetter, Randolph C. ......Lexington
Huffman, Herbert ......Natural Bridge
Huffman, Thomas R.* ......Buena Vista
Humphreys, Ewing S.*—Lieut., Lexington
Humphreys, Robert L. ......Buena Vista
Humphris, Curtis L. ....East Lexington
Hunklee, Elmer ....Rockbridge Baths
Hunkle, R. R. ....Rockbridge Baths
Hutcheson, Robert S.*—Lieut.
                      Rockbridge Baths
Hutton, Alfred C.—Lieut., Veterinary
  Corps, ...Lexington
Ingram, Albert B. ....Goshen

Ingram, Andrew P. ....Goshen
Ingram, Preston ....Bell's Valley
Irvine, Brownie E. ....Lexington
Irvine, Bud R. ....Lexington
Irvine, Clem L. ....Collierstown
Irvine, Eldride C. ....Glasgow
Irvine, Lawrence ....Lexington
Irvine, T. M. ....Lexington
Irvine, William D.—317th Infantry—died
  at Camp Lee ....Lexington
Irwin, George* ....Lexington
Jackson, Holland H.* ....Goshen
Jackson, Houston L. ....Goshen
Jackson, John L. ....Goshen
Jarvis, Harry L. ....Timber Ridge
Jarvis, John J. ....Brownsburg
Jarvis, Levi H. ....Brownsburg
Jenkins, James T. ....Buena Vista
Jennings, Elmer L. ....Buena Vista
Jennings, William L. ....Lexington
Johnson, Benjamin W.* ......Lexington
Johnson, Clide E. ....Buena Vista
Johnson, Earl ....Lexington
Johnson, Horace E. ....Buena Vista
Johnson, James C. ....Greenlee
Johnson, James T. ....Greenlee
Johnson, Tulley H.* ....Buena Vista
Jones, John W. ....Lexington
Jones, Lemon S.* ....Natural Bridge
Jones, Sidney ....Brownsburg
Junkin, Edward L.—Lieut. ....Lexington
Junkin, William McC.* ......Lexington
Kane, Frederick C. ....Lexington
Keife, Leland G. ....Lexington
Kelley, Emmett ....Buena Vista
Kendall, George W. ....Buena Vista
Kesler, Archie A. ....Lexington
Kesler, William W.* ....Lexington
Kester, Walden* ....Lexington
Key, James E. ....Buena Vista
Kicklighter, Ebenezer C.* ....Lexington
Kiefe, Leland G.* ....Natural Bridge
Kinnear, John A. ....Lexington
Kinner, Leckey McC.—Captain..Lexington
Kinnear, William A. ....Lexington
Knapp, Fred D. ....Lexington
Knick, Amos S.—Co. F., 4th Regiment
                              Kerr's Creek
Knick, Calvin ....Collierstown

Knick, Jesse M.—Aviation Section
  Kerr's Creek
Krebs, Robert H.* ....Buena Vista
Kennedy, W. T. ....Lexington
Lackey, William K. ....Buena Vista
Lair, Hugh M. ....Goshen
Lam, Edgar* ....Rockbridge Baths
Lam, George H.* ....Lexington
Lam, William B.—U. S. Infantry—died of wounds, Oct. 7, 1918..Rockbridge Baths
Lane, Ide R.* ....Buena Vista
Lane, William ....Gilmore's Mill
Lannum, Joseph A.* ....Buena Vista
Lawhorn, Arthur T. ....Buena Vista
Lawhorn, Charles Z. ....Buena Vista
Lawhorn, J. M. ....Riverside
Lawhorn, Lester W. ....Midvale
Lee, P. H. ....Fairfield
Lee, You Chu ....Lexington
Leech, Frank McC. ....Murat
Leech, Harry T. ....Lexington
Leech, Loyd L.*—Captain of Marines
  Lexington
Leighton, Christopher ....Greenlee
Leighton, Cecil H. ....Greenlee
Leighton, ———
Letcher, Christopher .... Greenlee
Letcher, Greenlee D.*—Captain, Battery F, 111 F. A. (Rockbridge Artillery)
  Lexington
Lair, Hugh M. ....Goshen
Lilley, James .... Cornwall
Lindsay, Paul C. ....Lexington
Lipscomb, William ....Glasgow
Liptrap, James H. ....Bell's Valley
Little, Jesse F. ....Rockbridge Baths
Locher, Bailey J.* ....Glasgow
Locher, Charles L.—Regular Army— accidentally killed in France, Nov. 12, 1918. .... Glasgow
Logan, Earl L. ....Goshen
Lotta, William A. ....Brownsburg
Lowman, John* ......Rockbridge Baths
Lunsford, Walter I. ....Raphine
Lycias, Robert L. ....Raphine
Lyons, Harry .... Lexington
Mack, James C.* ....Lexington
Magann, Ernest T. ....Buena Vista
Major, Floyd H.* ....Buena Vista

Manspile, Albert L. ....Rapp's Mill
Manspile, Leo. S. ....Rapp's Mill
Marchann, Bernard W. ...... Lexington
Marcum, Alonzo ....Natural Bridge
Marks, Eston S. ....Timber Ridge
Marks, Henry T. ....Fairfield
Marshall, Amos A. ......Natural Bridge
Martin, Earl D. ....Goshen
Martin, Emmett B. ......Natural Bridge
Martin, Frank ....Lexington
Martin, Oriel B. ....Lexington
Mason, Frank ....Lexington
Massie, Roy E. ....Buena Vista
Mattingly, Earl S. ....Lexington
Mays, Earl B. ....Midvale
Mays, Edward F.—20th Prov. Co.
  Kerr's Creek
Mazingo, William E. ....Buena Vista
McAlphin, Charles M.* ....Glasgow
McBride, Stuart*—Lieut. ......Lexington
McCabe, Charles R. ....Buena Vista
McCabe, Daniel S. ....Buena Vista
McCabe, John W. ....Buena Vista
McClain, James ....Lexington
McCorkle, Thomas A.* ....Lexington
McCormick, Edgar L. ....Lexington
McCormick, Emmett W. ......Lexington
McCormick, Marion L. ....Lexington
McCormick, Wallace ....Fairfield
McCown, Albert S.*—Lieut. ...Lexington
McCoy, Kenton H. ....Lexington
McCoy, M. S. ....Lexington
McCoy, Richard H. ....Lexington
McDaniel, James L.* ....Natural Bridge
McDaniel, John L. ....Buena Vista
McDaniel, John W. ....Fancy Hill
McDaniel, William W. ...Natural Bridge
McGuffin, Charles N. ....Fairfield
McKeever, William ....Lexington
McKinney, Sydney S.* ......Lexington
McKinon, Angus*—1st Lieut. ..Lexington
McNair, John W.* ....Lexington
McNair, Stuart H.* ....Greenlee
Meeks, William L. ....Goshen
Metz, Charles R. ....Lexington
McClain, James .... Lexington
McCown, Samuel W. ....Lexington
McDaniel, John L. ....Buena Vista
McKeever, Burnett H. ....Lexington

McKemy, Harry S. ....Kerr's Creek
McNair, John W. ....Natural Bridge
Miller, Alonzo C.* ....Lexington
Miller, Eldered G. ....Brownsburg
Miller, Herbert G. .....Rockbridge Baths
Miller, Luther R. ....Lexington
Miller, Walter D. ....Brownsburg
Miller, Houston L. ....Timber Ridge
Millner, Samuel M.*—Lieut. ...Lexington
Mitchell, Samuel A.* ......Natural Bridge
Moncure, James A. ....Lexington
Monroe, Robert M. ....Lexington
Montgomery, Joseph B. ....Lexington
Montgomery, Melven R. ....Lexington
Moomaw, Clovis*—1st Lieut. ..Lexington
Moore, A. Marshall*—Lieut. ..Lexington
Moore, C. D. ....Buena Vista
Moore, Carl C. ....Raphine
Moore, Earl* ....Collierstown
Moore, George U. ....Natural Bridge
Moore, Harry* ....Raphine
Moore, Harry C. ....Lexington
Moore, John A. ....Raphine
Moore, John E.* ....Fairfield
Moore, John S. ....Lexington
Moore, John W.*—Captain ...Lexington
Moore, Paul M. ....Lexingotn
Moore, Stuart ....Lexington
Moore, William G. ....Lexington
Moore, William R. ....Raphine
Moran, Nubie W. ....Brownsburg
Morris, D. E.—U. S. Inf.—died at
  Camp Lee Sept. 28, 1918 ..Collierstown
Morris, Fred S. ....Lexington
Morris, J. Leon* ....Lexington
Morris, O. M. ....Collierstown
Morris, Robert G.* ....Lexington
Morrison, George E. ....Lexington
Morrison, R. B.* ....Murat
Moses, Jesse H. ....Lexington
Moses, Noah D. ....Lexington
Moxley, Hiderburks ....Glasgow
Musgrove, Lewis S. ....Buena Vista
Muterspaw, Clarence E.—33d Infantry ....Kerr's Creek
Muterspaw, Jack ....Lexington
Muterspaw, Raphael E.—29th Engineers, 19th Division ......Kerr's Creek
Myers, Graham H. ....Murat

Myers, Harry G. ....Murat
Newcomer, John W. ...Rockbridge Baths
Newland, Preston S.* ......Buena Vista
Nicely, Guy C. ....Murat
Nichols, E. H.* ....Lexington
Nichols, E. W.—General, V. M. I.
  Training Camp ....Lexington
Niswander, Carl D ....Lexington
O'Connell, Stuart A. ....Buena Vista
Ogden, Hamilton McK. ......Buena Vista
Ogden, John M. ....Buena Vista
Ordeman, George F.* ....Lexington
Ott, William A.* ....:....Fairfield
Padgett, George T. ......Natural Bridge
Page, J. Alexander* ....Glasgow
Page, Roy* ....East Lexington
Painter, J. Henry ....Lexington
Painter, Samuel W. ....Vesuvius
Painter, William T.—U. S. Army
  —died at Camp Lee, Jan. 16,
  1918 ....Rapp's Mill
Palmer, Frank H. ....Lexington
Parker, Carah E.* ....Greenlee
Parker, George D. ....Glasgow
Parker, William F. ....Lexington
Parsons, Lewis R. ....Natural Bridge
Patterson, Stuart* ....Brownsburg
Patton, John M., Jr. ....Lexington
Paxton, Frank L. ....Lexington
Paxton, H. M. ....Fairfield
Paxton, Matthew W.—Lieut. ..Lexington
Paxton, P. L. ....Lexington
Paxton, William A. ....Fairfield
Paxton, William McC. ....Fairfield
Pearce, Charles C.* ....Glasgow
Pendleton, E. Morgan* ....Lexington
Pendleton, R. Tucker*—Captain,
  Regular Army ....Lexington
Phillips, J. Henry ....Collierstown
Phillips, Robert L.—Infantry—officially reported as killed in action, Nov. 23(?), 1918 ....Goshen
Phillips, Tobias C.—Lieut .....Lexington
Phillips, W. Martin ....Collierstown
Pickens, Paul* ....Lexington
Pierce, Charles C. ....Glasgow
Plogger, Alexander J.—Co. A—reported killed in action July 15, 1918 ....Collierstown

SOLDIERS OF THE WORLD WAR 451

Plogger, Edward W. .... Kerr's Creek
Plogger, Frederick—Regular Army—
   first Rockbridge soldier reported
   as killed in action; July 15,
   1918 .... Kerr's Creek
Plogger, William H. ... Rockbridge Baths
Plott, Wallace M.—317th Infantry .. Goshen
Plott, William L. .... Goshen
Poague, Henry G.*—Captain ... Lexington
Poague, W. Thomas—Captain ... Lexington
Poe, Arthur .... Buena Vista
Poindexter, Emmett W. .... Lexington
Pole, Gwyan* .... Lexington
Pollard, J. W. H.—Lieut.—sur-
   geon .... Lexington
Pooley, William S. .... Lexington
Poston, William C. .... Buena Vista
Potter, George L. .... Collierstown
Potter, L. Letcher—National Army
   —died at Camp Greene, Jan. 21,
   1918 .... Collierstown
Powell, Charles M. ...... Natural Bridge
Preston, N. W. .... Lexington
Pruthirds, Ardie E.* .... Lexington
Pugh, Horace .... Buena Vista
Pugh, Morris J. .... Buena Vista
Pultz, Leslie W. .... Lexington
Purcell, John A. .... Lexington
Quigley, E. M. .... Lexington
Quisenberry, John E.*—1st
   Lieut. .... Lexington
Ramsey, Lomonie .... Buena Vista
Ree, Rodney C. .... Rockbridge Baths
Reece, C. B. .... Lexington
Reece, W. E. .... Brownsburg
Randolph, D. W.—Major ...... Lexington
Reed, Stokes N. .... Lexington
Rees, Robert H. .... Lexington
Reid, H. Money .... Lexington
Reid, Rodney C.* ...... Rockbridge Baths
Reid, Wallace W. .... Murat
Reynolds, Joseph R. .... Glasgow
Reynolds, Willie G. .... Collierstown
Rhineholt, John R.* .... Buena Vista
Rice, William M. .... Greenlee
Riley, Franklin* .... Lexington
Riley, Herbert A. .... Lexington
Riley, Herbert L. .... Fairfield
Riley, Robert C. ...... Rockbridge Baths
Riley, Walter H.* .... Lexington

Roadcap, Walter S. .... Goshen
Roberdeau, Horace L. .... Lexington
Roberts, E. F. .... Lexington
Roberts, William T .... Lexington
Robertson, Absalom W.* Major
                              Buena Vista
Robinson, James K. .... Lexington
Robey, Harry R.* .... Buena Vista
Rodenizer, C. H. .... Murat
Roderick, C. Garland* .... Lexington
Rogers, John D.*—Captain .... Lexington
Rogers, Loyd R. .... Buena Vista
Robinson, H. E.—U. S. Engineers—
   accidentally killed at Aberdeen, Md.,
   Aug. 15, 1918 .... Collierstown
Rocklin, Harry .... Buena Vista
Root, Philip W. .... Lexington
Root, Philip* .... Lexington
Rose, Benjamin R. .... Lexington
Rosser, Loyd H. .... Glasgow
Rowsey, Charles L.* .... Lexington
Rowsey, Grover L.—Naval Reserves—
   died in Norfolk, Feb. 25,1917
                              House Mountain
Rowsey, Harry E. .... Buena Vista
Ruff, Will O. L.*—Rockbridge Artil-
   lery—died at Camp McClellan, April
   22, 1918 .... Natural Bridge
Ruffin, Thomas E. .... Lexington
Ruffner, David F.—Captain, Field
   Army .... Lexington
Ruffner, Richard* .... Lexington
Ruffner, Percy* .... Lexington
Runkle, Elmer .... Rockbridge Baths
Runkle, Robert R. .... Rockbridge Baths
Ryman, Ernest W.* .... Buena Vista
Sales, William E.* .... Fairfield
Sandridge, Charles W. .... Raphine
Satterfield, Frederick M. ..... Lexington
Saville, Charles S. .... Murat
Saville, Harry L. .... Murat
Saville, William O. .... Lexington
Scott, Charles H. .... Natural Bridge
Scott, Roy* .... Natural Bridge
Seal, Elwood H.* .... Lexington
Searson, Walter C. .... Raphine
Seay, George B.—U. S. Army—officially
   reported killed in action, Dec. 15, 1917
                              Natural Bridge
Secrist, Otho H. .... Buena Vista

Sedwick, J. H. ....Lexington
Seebert, Joseph E.*—Lieut.—surgeon
    Lexington
Seebert, Walter D.* ....Lexington
Sensabaugh, Elmer C. ..Rockbridge Baths
Sensabaugh, Frank ....Rockbridge Baths
Sensabaugh, John W. ....Brownsburg
Serpell, Robert ....Lexington
Shafer, Jerry B. ....Natural Bridge
Shafer, Martin B. ....Natural Bridge
Shaner, Joseph C.* ....Lexington
Shaw, Harry H. ......Rockbridge Baths
Shaw, Homer L. ....Lexington
Shaw, James T. ....Buena Vista
Shepherd, Harvey T. ....Buena Vista
Shields, Lewis C. ....Fairfield
Shields, William R.*Lieut. ....Lexington
Shipley, Howard V. ....Lexington
Shipp, Arthur M.*—Lieut. ....Lexington
Shirey, Hugh M. ....Buena Vista
Shirey, Walter H.* ....Buena Vista
Shoemaker, Edward O. ..East Lexington
Shorter, Claude M. ....Rapp's Mill
Silven, Richard H. ......Natural Bridge
Simpson, Thomas R. ....Buena Vista
Slough, Edgar S. ....Glasgow
Smiley, Henry C. ....Fairfield
Smiley, James D. ....Moffatts Creek
Smith, Edgar*—Corporal .....Lexington
Smith, Emmett E. ....Fancy Hill
Smith, Frank M. ....Buena Vista
Smith, J. Henry—died at Camp Zachary
    Taylor, Dec. 6, 1918 ....Lexington
Smith, John T. ....Lexington
Smith, Lige ....Cornwall
Smith, Marcus L. ....East Lexington
Smith, Mark H. ....Kerr's Creek
Smith, Ott ....Natural Bridge
Smith, Porter H. ....East Lexington
Smith, Reid H. ....Buena Vista
Smith, Robert G. ....Lexington
Smith, Sidney A.* ....Buena Vista
Smith, Walter J. ....Lexington
Smith, Will A. ....Lexington
Smith, William O. ....Lexington
Sorrells, Clarence J. ....Midvale
Sorrells, Henry H. ....Riverside
Sorrels, Robert W.—Lieut.-Col. Lexington
Souder, Mack E. ....Buena Vista

Staton, Baron O. ....Buena Vista
Staton, Brown H. ......Rockbridge Baths
Staton, Chester A. ....Vesuvius
Steele, Frank C. ....Fairfield
Sterrett, William R.* ..Rockbridge Baths
Stoner, John ....Natural Bridge
Stoner, John B. ....Lexington
Story, David C. ....Lexington
Stratton, Charles* ....Buena Vista
Straub, Lurty F ....Lexington
Straub, Robert* ....East Lexington
Supinger, Bolivar* ....Raphine
Superinger, Clyde C. ....Raphine
Surber, Francis F.* ....Buena Vista
Surber, Thomas F. ....Buena Vista
Swisher, M. B. ....Moffatts Creek
Swisher, Thomas G. ..Rockbridge Baths
Tardy, Houston ....Murat
Tardy, Jackson*—38th Regular Inf.—
    killed in action, July 15, 1918
Taylor, Charles A. ....Raphine
Taylor, Oliver P. ....Lexington
Taylor, Samuel* ....Aqua
Taylor, Walter W. ....Fairfield
Taylor, William ....Aqua
Teague, C. C.* ....Lexington
Terry, Calvin ....Cornwall
Thomas, Walter W.—Headquarters
    Troop, 3rd Division ......Collierstown
Thompson, Frank ....Lexington
Thompson, Joseph D. ....Fairfield
Thompson, Harry L.* ....Murat
Thompson, Laird ....Lexington
Thompson, Prentiss A.—Corporal,
    Headquarters Troop, 3rd Divi-
    sion, U. S. Infantry—died in
    France, Dec. 3, 1918 ....Goshen
Thompson, W. F. ....Lexington
Thompson, William ....Murat
Tindle, Bird ....Goshen
Tolley, Emory W.* ....Lexington
Tolley, James R. ....Buena Vista
Tolley, Joseph H. ....Natural Bridge
Tolley, Oscar L. ....Riverside
Tomlin, Emmett B. ....Buena Vista
Trolan, William A. ....Lexington
Truslow, George L. ....Buena Vista
Tucker, A. S. J.—Major,
    Regular Army ....Lexington

SOLDIERS OF THE WORLD WAR

Tucker, Harry St. G.* ....Lexington
Tucker, Herbert S. ....Lexington
Turner, Herbert S. ......Natural Bridge
Tucker, Hunington M. ....Lexington
Tyree, Houston S. ....Buena Vista
Tyree, Leo H. ....Buena Vista
Tyree, Philander L. ....Cornwall
Tyree, Warren B.* ....Buena Vista
Updike, Andrew R. ....Buena Vista
Van Devender, Letchard*
                        Rockbridge Baths
Vaughan, Fort F. ....Lexington
Vest, Benjamin F. ....Buena Vista
Vest, George A. ....Buena Vista
Vest, Harry A.—Cor. Co., 116th Inf.
                          Kerr's Creek
Vest, Herbert M.—killed in action at
   Chateau Thierry, June 6, 1918
                           Buena Vista
Vest, Houston L. ....Buena Vista
Vest, Mackson ....Buena Vista
Vest, Obie ....Buena Vista
Viar, Clarence H. ....Buena Vista
Viar, Joseph E. ....Buena Vista
Viar, Roland ....Glasgow
Wade, Frank H. ....Lexington
Wade, Roy B. ....Brownsburg
Wagner, George W. ....Glasgow
Wagner, George M.* ....Glasgow
Walker, Douglass* ....Buena Vista
Walker, James E. ....Jump
Walker, Floyd A.* ....Jump
Walker, Samuel F. ....Lexington
Walton, Jesse I.* ....Lexington
Warren, Howard L. ....Fancy Hill
Warren, James R. ....Lexington
Ward, Carroll R. ....Lexington
Watts, Ernest J. ....Buena Vista
Watts, William J. ....Natural Bridge
Weeks, Joseph T.* ....Lexington
Weever, R. C. ....Lexington
West, Harrington K.* ....Lexington
White, George W.*—Captain ..Lexington
White, Graham A. ....Lexington
White, James ....Lexington
White, Thomas P.* ....Lexington
Whiteside, Clarence G. .....Buena Vista
Whiteside, Glossie O. ......Buena Vista

Whiteside, John H.* ....Buena Vista
Whitesell, Robert L. ......Buena Vista
Whitmer, Raymond* ....Raphine
Whitmer, William H. ....Lexington
Widdifield, Barnum M. ....Lexington
Wilbourn, Raymond A. ....Raphine
Wilbourn, Arthur* ....Lexington
Wilhelm, Herbie C.—486th Motor
   Truck Co. ....Kerr's Creek
Wilhelm, Homer M. ....Collierstown
Wilhelm, O. McK. ....Collierstown
Williams, Harry B. ....Lexington
Williams, W. T. ....Lexington
Willis, Walter B. ....Buena Vista
Wilson, Estill ....Collierstown
Wilson, George W.—Headquarters Co.,
   135th, Field Army ......Kerr's Creek
Wilson, James H. ....Raphine
Wilson, M. Lorenzo* ....Lexington
Wilson, Samuel B.—317th Inf.—died of
   wounds received at Buzancy, Nov.
   4, 1918 ....Raphine
Wilson, Walter S. ....Raphine
Wilson, William O. ....Kerr's Creek
Wise, David C. ....Buena Vista
Winston, William A. ....Lexington
Wise, David C. ....Buena Vista
Withers, Martin B.* ....Lexington
Withrow, Ernest L. ....Lexington
Witt, Robert R.*.............Lexington
Womelsdorf, Bruce D.* ......Lexington
Womelsdorf, Joshua C. ....Lexington
Womelsdorf, Raymond* ......Lexington
Wood, George W. ....Cornwall
Wood, Joseph D. ....Cornwall
Wood, Reas W. ....Cornwall
Wood, Samuel M. ....Goshen
Wood, Will H. ....Cornwall
Woodson, Gille N. ....Buena Vista
Woodson, Herman J. ......Buena Vista
Worth, C. E. ....Lexington
Worth, J. Estill ....Natural Bridge
Worth, Owen A. ....Natural Bridge
Wright, James* ....Buena Vista
Youell, Rice* ....Lexington
Youell, William A.* ....Lexington
Young, Danzel R. ....Glasgow

COLORED

Ailstock, Howard ....Raphine
Ailstock, Scott ....Raphine
Alexander, Robert ....Raphine
Anderson, Leo G. ....Glasgow
Anthony, Hickerson ....Glasgow
Baker, Will O. ....Buena Vista
Banister, Lucian ....Collierstown
Barber, Ernest J. ....Lexington
Beal, Forrest W. ....Murat
Bolen, Lewis ....Lexington
Booker, James M. ....Buena Vista
Borgas, Brown C. ....Lexington
Bowyer, William L. ....Lexington
Brown, Douglass—reported to have died of disease in France, Dec. 19, 1917 .... Brownsburg
Brown, William F. ....Brownsburg
Brown, William L. ....Brownsburg
Carter, Samuel G. ....Buena Vista
Carter, Frank ....Lexington
Chambers, Acres ....Timber Ridge
Chandler, John D. ....Natural Bridge
Chandler, Stuart A. ....Lexington
Clark, Nelson ....Lexington
Clark, Robert L. ....Lexington
Clark, Walter ....Lexington
Cobbs, James H. ....Buena Vista
Cosby, John ....Lexington
Craney, Glasgow ....Brownsburg
Cuff, Purcell E. ....Lexington
Dandridge, Frank ....Buena Vista
Dandridge, William P. ......Buena Vista
Davis, Allen B. ....Goshen
Dickenson, Wade A. ....Fairfield
Diggs, Clarence ....Lexington
Dillard, Malcolm A. ....Glasgow
Dixon, James O. ....Natural Bridge
Dixon, Robert H. ....Natural Bridge
Ellis, Emmett ....Natural Bridge
Ellis, Richard ....Natural Bridge
Evans, William R. ....Lexington
Fields, Robert ....Buena Vista
Franklin, Andrew M. ....Glasgow
Franklin, Nelson ....Lexington
Gilmore, Walter L. ......Natural Bridge
Ginger, Warrent ....Natural Bridge
Gooch, Mitchell D.—U. S. Army—died at Camp Greene, N. C., Oct. 11, 1918
....Lexington
Green, George L. ....Buena Vista
Green, Henry L. ....Buena Vista
Green, Robert J. ....Buena Vista
Hale, Jackson ....Lexington
Haliburton, Howard ....Brownsburg
Harris, James A. ....Lexington
Harris, Isaiah ....Lexington
Hawkins, Ira J. S. ....Lexington
Hawkins, Nathaniel S. ....Lexington
Henderson, John C. ....Rockbridge Baths
Hinton, Preston ....Lexington
Hinton, William ....Lexington
Holtz, Harry C. ....Raphine
Holtz, Henning ....Jump
Holtz, William R.—died at Camp Grant, Oct. 17, 1918 ....Collierstown
Hughes, Samuel ....Lexington
Hunt, Guy A. ....Natural Bridge
Hunt, Morris ....Natural Bridge
Irving, Boyd P. ....Buena Vista
Jackson, Lance ....Lexington
Jackson, Percy A. ....Buena Vista
Johnson, Lacy E. ....Lexington
Johnson, Robert* ....Buena Vista
Jones, Elmer* ....Lexington
Jones, Ferdinand ....Lexington
Jones, Preston C. ....Lexington
Jones, Sidney ....Brownsburg
Jordan, John ....Glasgow
Keir, Harry H. ....Rockbridge Baths
Kiley, Silas G. ....Goshen
Kings, John ....Goshen
Kinney, Sherman O. ....Lexington
Lee, Benjamin ....Brownsburg
Lewis, Frederick H. ....Raphine
Logan, Lester P. ....Lexington
Logan, Nathaniel ....Lexington
Lyle, John L. ....Fairfield
Lyle, Walter W. ....Lexington
Madison, Nickerson ....Glasgow
Madison, Sylvester A. ....Lexington
Massie, Roy C. ....Fairfield
Massie, William A. ....Fairfield
Mathews, John ....Lexington
Merchant, Garrett M. ....Collierstown

Miller, James M. ....Goshen
Miller, Rufus O. ....Lexington
Minor, Alonza ....Goshen
Minor, Harris T. ....Goshen
Nichols, Walter L. ....Goshen
Nowlen, Frank ....Buena Vista
Nowlen, Joseph J. ....Buena Vista
Payton, Bruce ....Lexington
Peters, Fred F. D. ....Brownsburg
Pettigrew, Wonderful P. .....Lexington
Pleasants, Glasgow ....Brownsburg
Pleasants, Oscar ....Lexington
Powell, David ....Buena Vista
Pryor, John ....Lexington
Randolph, Thomas ....Lexington
Rhoades, Lacy E. ....Raphine
Richardson, Reid ....Buena Vista
Robinson, Colonel ....Buena Vista
Ross, Robert ....Buena Vista
Rowland, Alvie ....Lexington
Rowland, Fenton H. ....Lexington
Sadler, Harry ....Natural Bridge
Sanderson, Sidney ....Buena Vista
Sanderson, Thomas P. ......Buena Vista
Sanderson, Walter L. ......Buena Vista
Scott, Charles H.—U. S. Army—died in
  N. Y., Aug. 5, 1918 ....Natural Bridge

Scott, Jacob R. ....Raphine
Scudder, George ....Natural Bridge
Sholtz, Albert ....Lexington
Sholtz, Charles W. ....Brownsburg
Sholtz, Robert S. ....Brownsburg
Stuart, Roy ....Brownsburg
Swinley, Lorenzo ....Buena Vista
Thomas, Jesse J. ....Goshen
Thomas, John E. ....Goshen
Thompson, Isaac ....Buena Vista
Tindle, Bud ....Goshen
Tindle, John ....Goshen
Tinsley, Listras ....Lexington
Toles, Robert N. ....Goshen
Turner, Ferdinand ....Lexington
Twitty, James C. ....Buena Vista
Walker, Cyrus A. ....Brownsburg
Walker, Early ....Buena Vista
Warrick, James E. ....Glasgow
Washington, Andrew ....Lexington
Watts, Robert L. ....Natural Bridge
Waugh, Fulton ....Baltimore, Md.
White, Preston A. ....Lexington
Williams, Harry B. ....Lexington
Wilson, James A. ....Buena Vista
Winfield, Douglas ....Lexington
Woods, Horace ....Glasgow

SECTION XIII

VARIOUS LISTS

IMPORTATIONS, 1739-1740—NATURALIZATIONS PRIOR TO 1886—ROAD WORKERS, 1752-53—COMMUNICANTS AT TIMBER RIDGE, 1753—SETTLERS OF KERR'S CREEK AND VICINITY—HEMP CERTIFICATES—NEW MONMOUTH MEMBERSHIP, 1790—RESIDENTS OF LEXINGTON, 1790—TAVERN-KEEPERS—LOCATIONS AND ARRIVALS—REPORTS OF PROCESSIONERS

"IMPORTATIONS," 1739-1740

A list of Augusta settlers who "proved their importation from Great Britain at their own expense," in order to become entitled to enter public land. These proceedings were before the county court of Orange.

The name of the wife is not always explicitly stated. In such instances it is presumably the first female name in the household.

FEBRUARY 28, 1739

Patrick McCaddan; for himself and Samuel Givens.
William Ledgerwood; for himself and Agnes, Martha, Jane, Elener, William, James.
Robert McDowell; for himself and Martha, Jane, Margaret, William.
John McDowell; also for Magdalene (wife), Samuel (son), and John Rutter.

JUNE 26, 1740

Robert Young; for himself and Agada, Julia, Samuel, James.
John Smith; also for Margaret (wife) and Abraham, Henry, Daniel, John, Joseph; and for Robert McDowell.
James Bell; for himself and John, Margaret, and Elizabeth Bell, John Mulhollen, Jane McAlegant, Agnes Reed, William and Elizabeth McCanlos.
John Trimble; for himself and Ann, Margret, Mary.
John Hay; for himself and Rebecca, Charles, Andrew, Barbara, Jane, Robert.
Morris O'Friel; for himself and Catharine (wife.)
Patrick Hays; for himself and Frances, Jean, William, Margaret, Catharine, Ruth.
Patrick Campbell; for himself and Elizabeth, Charles, William, Patrick, Jr., John, Mary, Elizabeth, Gennet.
Robert Patterson; also for Mary (wife), and Thomas, Mary, Elizabeth.
David Logan; also for Mary (wife) and William.
Robert Poague; also for Elizabeth (wife) and Margret, John, Martha, Sarah, George, Mary Elizabeth, William, Robert.
John Anderson; for himself and Elizabeth (wife) and William, Margret, John, Frances.

JULY 24-25, 1740

John Wilson: for himself and Martha, Matthew, William, John, Sarah, Elizabeth.
James McClure; also for Agnes, John, Eleanor, Andrew, Jane, James, Jr.
John Davison; also for James, George, Thomas, William, Samuel.
William Hutcheson; also for John, Sr., John, Jr., Margret, Mary.
Moses Thompson; also for Jane, William, Robert, John, and for Jane Cox.
John Maxwell: for himself and Margaret, John, Jr., Thomas, Mary, Alexander.

VARIOUS LISTS   457

James Davis; also for Mary, Henry, William, Samuel.
Patrick Crawford; also for Ann, James, George, Margaret, Mary.
Francis McCowen; for himself and Mary (wife) and Markham and Elizabeth.
David Edmiston; for himself and Isabella, Jesse, John, William, Rachael, David, Moses; and for Jesse and James Daley.
James Robinson; for himself and Jean, William, George.
George Hutcheson; for himself and Eleanor (wife) and Jennet; also for Joseph Carr.
William Johnston; also for Ann, Elizabeth, John; and for Samuel Brawford.
John Carr; also for Lucey (wife), and Margaret and Matthew Glaspey, her children. This entry is dated April 27, 1740.

NATURALIZATIONS PRIOR TO 1866

When the year of naturalization is not followed by a star final papers were taken, otherwise only first papers. The year of birth is indicated by b. When such date is only approximately known, it is followed by a c.

James Caskey—1807.
James McCroskey—1808.
Hugh Laughlin—from Ireland—b. 1774c—1815.
Samuel Henderson—from Scotland—b.1755c—1815.
James Farley—from Scotland—b.1781—1815.
Michael McAleer—from Ireland—b.1815—1841*.
Edward Really—1844*.
Josiah Day—1844*.
Daniel Phalby—1844*.
John R. Maben—1845*.
John Breen—1844*.
Patrick Kaine—1851*.
Seligman Schwartz—from Bavaria—1851*.
Francis Jenks—from England—1851*.
Henry Rice—from Ireland—1851*.
John B. Ricardi—from Sardinia—1851*.
Patrick McAndrew—from Ireland—b. 1829—1852*.
John Callaghan—b.1830—1852*.
Michael Godfrey—b.1822c—from Ireland—1852*.
Dennis Cronan—from Ireland—b.1812c—1852*.
John Masterson—from Ireland—b.1801c—1852*.
Dennis Lary—from Ireland—b. 1821c—1852*.
Daniel Brion—from Ireland—b.1819c—1852*.
John Cadagan—from Ireland—b.1824c—1852*.
John Doil—from Ireland—b.1831c—1854*.
Patrick Minitor—from Ireland—b.1828c—1852.
William Hagan—from Ireland—b.1828c—1852*.
Thomas Martin—from Ireland—b.1827—1852*.
Patrick Hayley—from Ireland—b.1818—1852*.
Jerry McCarty—from Ireland—1852*.
David Shutterley—from Baden—b.1825c—1852*.
John Chapin—from England—1852*.
George Chapin—from England—1852*.
Samuel Kahn—from Germany—1852*.

James McCool—from Ireland—b.1811—1853*.
William Welch—from Ireland—b.1825—1853*.
Thomas Jones—from England—b.1831—1853*.
Thomas Caset—from Ireland—b.1830—1853*.
Martin Casey—from Ireland—b.1832—1853*.
Max Schwartz—from Bavaria—b.1822—1854*.
John Kremer—from Prussia—b.1828—1859.
Michael McNamara—from Ireland—b.1825—1857.
Maleck Fearney—from Ireland—b.1830—1855*.
John Fitzgerald—from Ireland—b.1813—1855.
Andrew Cunningham—b.1834—1855*—from Ireland.
John McNamar—from Ireland—b.1820—1855*.
Patrick O'Brian—b.1812—from Ireland—1857.
Patrick Cusack—from Ireland—b.1816—1855*.
Michael Cusack—from Ireland—b.1816—1855*.
Joseph Labree—from Canada—b.1818—1858.
William Mason—from England—1855*.
Francis Jenks—from England—1855*.
John Reid—from Ireland—b.1795—1855.
Patrick Gregory—from Ireland—b.1832—1856*.
Michael Murphy—from Ireland—b.1833—1856*.
James Martin—from Ireland—b.1828—1856*.
John Chapman, Jr.—from England—1858.
Carl M. Stephani—from Prussia—b.1831—1860*.
Daniel Cruden—1865*.

ROAD WORKERS, 1752-3

Tithables required to turn out to build a road ordered September 27, 1752, from James Young's mill to John Buchanan's mill:

William Akry
John Bartley
John Berry
John Brigham
John Buchanan
John Campbell
James Clark
Andrew Cowan
Robert Davis
Cornelius Donaho
Samuel Downing
Francis Dunn
James Gilmer
Thomas Kirkpatrick
William Ledgerwood
Patrick Martin
William Martin
William McClintock
John Black
John Jameson

Robert McClenon
James McCorkle
Alexander McFeeters
William McFeeters
James Moody
William McNab
Maurice O'Friel
George Peary
Thomas Peary
James Phillips
Thomas Reid
Josias Richards
Robert Scott
Major Scott
Adam Thompson
John Trimble
John Vance
Samuel Wallace
Hugh Young
James Young

Tithables to build a road from Joseph Long's mill to James Young's mill, thence to the great road on James Thompson's plantation. Order given in 1753. Overseers, Joseph Long and James Young.

James Boils
William Brown
Thomas Barton
James Campbell
John Carr
John Collier
Gilbert Crawford
George Gibson
Samuel Gibson
William Hall

John Hanna
James Huston
James Moore
John Ruckman
James Todd
William Todd
William Wadington
Solomon Whitley
James Young
Patrick Young
Robert Young

COMMUNICANTS AT TIMBER RIDGE, 1753

The names in this list are those who signed a call for the Reverend John Brown:

Alexander, Archibald
Allison, Francis
Allison, Robert
Beaty, Francis
Berry, Charles
Berry, Thomas
Berry, William
Borden, Magdalena
Buchanan, Samuel
Caruthers, William
Coulter, James
Davis, Samuel
Davis, William
Davison, John
Douglass, John
Dryden, David
Dryden, Thomas
Dunlap, Samuel
Eakin, James
Eakin, Walter
Edmiston, John
Fitzpatrick, Andrew
Gamble, Robert
Gaor, Edward
Gray, Jacob
Gray, Samuel
Gray, William
Greenlee, James
Hamilton, William

Hawely, John
Hay, Joseph
Hay, Samuel
Hearken, Edmund
Henderson, George
Henry, Robert
Hill, Thomas
Houston, John, Sr.
Houston, John, Jr.
Houston, Matthew
Houston, Robert
Houston, Samuel
Kennedy, Joseph
Kerr, John
Keys, John
Keys, Rodger
Kirkpatrick, Robert
Lockridge, William
Logan, John
Lowry, John
Lusk, James
Lusk, William
Lyle, Daniel
Lyle, John
Lyle, Matthew
Lyle, Samuel
Macky, John
Martin, Agnes
M'Anelly, Charles

460   A HISTORY OF ROCKBRIDGE COUNTY, VIRGINIA

M'Clung, James
M'Clung, James, Jr.
M'Clung, widow
M'Cluer, Alexander
M'Cluer, John
M'Cluer, Nathaniel
M'Cluer, Halbert
M'Crosky, John, Sr.
M'Crosky, John, Jr.
M'Crosky, Alexander
M'Cutchen, Samuel
M'Dowell, James
M'Dowell, Samuel
M'Glister, Neal
M'Murry, Thomas
M'Nabb, Baptist
M'Nabb, John
M'Speden, Thomas
Miller, Alexander
Mitchell, John
Montgomery, John
Moore, Alexander
Moore, John
Patton, John
Paxton, Samuel
Paxton, Thomas
Peoples, Nathan
Reagh, Robert

Reagh, William
Robertson, Robert
Robinson, James
Robinson, John
Robinson, Matthew
Robinson, William
Roseman, John
Sayer, David
Shields, John
Smiley, John
Smith, William
Sprowl, John
Steele, Andrew
Steele, Samuel
Stuart, John
Thompson, James
Trimble, James
Trimble, Moses
Walker, Alexander (1)
Walker, Alexander (2)
Walker, James
Walker, John
Wardlaw, William
Weir, Robert
Whiteside, Moses
Whiteside, William
Winiston, John

Other persons who contributed to the pastor's salary in the same year:
At New Providence, John Handly, Edward McColgan, and Patrick Porter; at Timber Ridge, John Bowyer and Thomas McSpaden.

SETTLERS OF KERR'S CREEK AND VICINITY

Mentioned, November 18, 1760, as debtors to the estate of Jacob Cunningham:

John Berry
Edward Bevill
James Brains
Richard Brush
John Coler
James Cunningham
William Dacis
James Davis
Alexander Deel (Dale)
John Dunlap
Edward Fearis

Samuel Gibson
John Gillmor
James Gilmor
William Hall
Robert Hamilton
Samuel Horad
James McCalester
Neaiell McClister
Halbert McClure
Francis McCown
Robert McHeney

Alexander Miller
Robert Moor
William Olley
Francis Randell
Daniel Lyle
Samuel Lyle

Matthew Lyle
John Scot
David Tallford
James Trimble
Patrick, Young
Robert Young

HEMP CERTIFICATES

The persons named below were among the leading hemp growers of Augusta for the years indicated. The figures following the names are for the pounds of dry, winter-rotted hemp, for which certificates were issued by the county court:

1766

Alexander, William—1400
Allison, John—1354
Anderson, James—164
Beaty, John—1328
Campbell, James—1528.
Crawford, Andrew—328
Cunningham, Jonathan—824
Evans, Nathaniel—2659
Finlay, John—124
Frazier, John—27
Frazier, Patrick—457
Frazier, Robert—362
Gilmore, William—994
Hutchinson, John—1157

McCampbell, Andrew—393
McClure, Moses—2392
McDowell, James—853
McDowell, Samuel—694
McElheny, Robert—1328
Paul, Audley—1179 (" 11 cwt, 3 quarters, 4 pounds")
Paxton, John—4442
Paxton, Thomas—5426
Ramsay, William—435
Smiley, Walter—546
Telford, James—785
Walker, Joseph—1340
Whitley, Paul—810

1767

Alexander, Joseph—2600
Alexander, William—1866
Allison, John—1700
Beaty, John—1905
Culton, James—490
Culton, Robert—866
Dryden, David—479
Dunlap, John—1300
Dunlap, William—462
Edmondson, James—390
Gay, James—1000
Gilmore, James—2548
Greenlee, James—2141
Hays, Charles—1972
Kerr, William—1814
Kirkpatrick, Thomas—1784
Lyle, Matthew—1884
Lyle, John—379
Maxwell, William—499
McClung, James—440
McClung, John—621
McClung, William—730

McClure, Andrew—1832
McCorkle, Alexander—1712
McCullough, Thomas—1540
McCown, James—400
McDowell, Matthew—162
McDowell, Samuel—2090
McElheny, Robert—967
McGavock, James—1740
McKee, William—631
McKemy, William—960
McNabb, Baptist—1330
Mitchell, John—463
O'Frield, Maurice—419
Paxton, John—8772
Paxton, Samuel—832
Robinson, Reed—250
Reah, William—1650
Simpson, James—420
Wallace, Peter—3039
Willey, John—1875
Woods, Richard—1402

NEW MONMOUTH MEMBERSHIP, 1790

Names of persons who had taken seats in the Old Monmouth meeting house, September 5, 1790:

- Blakely Brush
- John Cooper
- James Cunningham
- Elizabeth Dale
- Robert Erwin
- James Gilmore
- John Gilmore
- Joseph Goodbar
- Morris Gwin
- Andrew Hall
- John Hamilton
- Robert Kinkaid
- Charles Kirkpatrick, Sr.
- Charles Kirkpatrick, Jr.
- John Kirkpatrick
- Robert Lawson
- James Logan
- Samuel McCampbell
- Ann McCampbell
- Robert McCampbell
- Joseph McCown
- William McKee
- John McKee
- James McKee
- John McElheny
- Robert McElheny
- James McMath
- James Moore
- John Moore, Sr.
- John Moore, Jr.
- William Priestly
- Henry Skeen
- John Thompson
- George Townsley
- Robert Wason
- Hugh Weir
- Alexander Wiley
- John Wilson
- Samuel Wilson
- James Wilson

RESIDENTS OF LEXINGTON, 1796

- James Blair
- James Gold
- Jacob Fuller
- William Tidd
- James Hopkins
- Arthur Beaty
- Isaac Whitaker
- John Thompson
- Bernard Katon
- George Edgar
- Hugh McAllister
- Andw. Alexander
- John Dalton
- Nathan Shields
- Isaac Caruthers
- Wm. Gregory
- Jno. Shields
- Christian Varner
- William Hillis
- Dan. Armstrong
- Anthony Geiger
- James Williams
- Alexr. Stare
- James Gamble
- Samuel L. Campbell
- John Hopkins
- Thos. Margrave
- Daniel Windall
- M. Hanna
- Alexander Shields
- Jno. Galbraith
- Cornelius Dorman
- Robert Scott
- James Caruthers
- James Bailey
- John Caruthers
- Josias Anderson
- Henry Williams
- Benja. Darst
- Jno. M'Mullin
- William Caruthers
- George Mitchel
- Saml. Harkins
- Arthur Walkup
- David Shields
- Wm. Jones
- Robeart L. McDowell
- John Newcomer
- John Cox
- Smith Thompson, Jr.

HOLDERS OF TAVERN LICENSE, 1778—1864

When there are two dates the second is the latest one in which we find mention of the person as tavern-keeper.

Albright, John, at Fairfield—1840-1849
Alexander, William—1779, 1784
Anderson, Josiah—1792, 1793
Anderson, Robert B.—1845
Athon, Joseph—1805, 1807
Bacon, A. S. & Co., at Lexington 1850
Bailey, William S.—1802
Barclay, Hugh, Jr.—1784
Barton, Philip B.—1830
Bay, Jeremiah—1799
Beers, William—1795
Bell, Joseph—1826
Bell, Alexander N.—1836, 1851
Bett, Horatio—1817
Bow, Levi—1796, 1798
Brown, William, at Lexington—1779
Burk, Elizabeth—1818
Campbell, Isaac—1778, 1779
Campbell, James and Addison H. at Alum Springs—1837
Cress, George—1837
Cress, George—1797, 1800
Darst, Benjamin—1804
Darst, Samuel—"Blue Ridge Canal Inn"—1838
Daugherty, James—1787
Dietrick, Jacob at Fairfield—1826
Donaho, Thomas U.—1848
Douglass, William—1832
Douthat, William H.—1831
Eastham, James at Lexington—1785
Edgar, Thomas—1786
Eisenhower, Jacob B—1818
Ellis, Humphrey—1795
Evans, Abraham—1788
Ewing, Robert—1780
Falconer, Alexander—1851
Firebaugh, John—1864
Fultz, Uriah—1845
Gilmore, James—1780
Glyce, Christopher—1796, 1810
Grigsby, James—1779
Hanna, Matthew at Lexington—1796
Hartley, Peter—1800
Hatcher, Henry M.—1855

Hawthorn, James—1787
Hillis, William—1793
Houghton, Joseph—1795
Hutchinson, George W.—1835
Johnson, George W.—1861, 1863
Jordan, William—1849
Keily, Joseph, at Brownsburg—1852
Kerr, Andrew, at Brownsburg—1796
Kerr, Zachariah H.—1851
Keys, David—1798
Kirkpatrick, John—1778
Kirkwood, Robert—1801
Mackay, John—1796
Manson, Robert E.—1835
Maxwell, John—1788
McCaul, William—1850
McChesney, George W., at Brownsburg—1837
McConkey, Samuel—1793
McCorkle, John—1839
Miles, Francis—1801
Miller, Samuel—1825, 1845
Miller, John A.—1849, 1850
Mitchell, John B.—1821
Moffett, William—1835, 1849
Moore, Samuel—1798, 1803
Newcomer, John—1804
Niblack, William—1801
Northern, William—1849
Payne, Ambrose—1792, 1793
Porter, Edwin—1851
Roads, George—1803
Ruff, Jacob—1789, 1792
Russell, Samuel—1821
Scott, Andrew M.—1826
See, Charles P., at Natural Bridge—1850
Shaner, Mary—1861
Shaw, Matthew—1837
Shields, Alexander—1802, 1820
Siler, Jacob—1841, 1850
Sloan, Alexander T., the "Jefferson Hotel"—1841
Spriggs, Joseph—1841
Spring, Nicholas—1801, 1803
Steele, Samuel—1795

Stuart, Alexander—1778
Tedford, Jacob—1855, 1862
Templeton, John—1780
Trevy, Jacob—1809
Trevy, Joseph Y., at the "Red House"—1836
Varner, Christain, at Lexington—1796

Walkup, Andrew—1796, 1809
Wallace, Samuel, at Lexington—1778, 1785
Welch, Benjamin, at "Fancy Hill Tavern"—1835
West, James—1825, 1826
Whiteside, Thomas—1791, 1802
Windle, Daniel—1790, 1801

LOCATIONS AND ARRIVALS

The present list includes some facts relating chiefly to the arrival or location of various settled families. A date without comment means that there is documentary mention of the person in Rockbridge in the said year. A name in parentheses is that of a consort.

Allen, James (Mary)—sells on Kerr's Creek, 1780.
Allen, Benjamin (Margaret)—Buffalo, 1779.
Allison, Margaret (John)—near Stuart's Mill, 1780.
Anderson, William (Elizabeth)—1778.
Archer, Sampson—settled at Gilmore's Spring on James.
Archibald, Samuel (Catharine)—1784.
Bane, Robert, late of Augusta—buys, 1780, of James (Mary) Allen.
Beach, Waldron—Kerr's Creek, 1778.
Beats, James (Jane)—end of Short Hill, 1778.
Beaty, Arthur (Eleanor)—about 1780.
Bennett, Benjamin—North River, 1779.
Bennett, Moses—place on North River sold, 1778.
Blackburn, Benjamin (Mary)—1781.
Bradford, Samuel, Jr., of Augusta—buys of George (Agnes) Berry, 1777.
Brown, George (Margaret)—1782.
Brownlee, Alexander—came, 1739.
Bunton, William (Sarah)—about 1778.
Bunton, Moses and William—buy of James (Ann) Harris, 1778.
Cassady, James (Elizabeth)—Buffalo, 1786.
Cleghorn, Robert (Mary)—Lexington, 1785.
Corbett, James (Margaret)—1779.
Crawford, William (Margaret)—Collier's Creek, 1786.
Crawford, Robert, shoemaker—near Steele's mill, 1767.
Cunningham, Moses—Kerr's Creek, 1786.
Cunningham, Moses (Hannah)—Collier's Creek, 1777.
Dale, Robert (Sarah)—Kerr's Creek, 1779.
Davidson, William (Sarah)—1786.
Davidson, Robert G.—Kerr's Creek, 1822.
Davidson, John—buys on Collier's Creek, 1779.
Davis, Samuel (Jean)—1778.
Defries, James (Mary)—South River, 1783.
Dougherty, George (Agnes)—sells, 1779.
Dougherty, Henry, oldest son of Michael—Cedar, 1782.
Dryden, William (Mary)—Borden Tract, 1778.
Edmondson, Matthew (Margaret)—1755.
Erwin, Robert—Kerr's Creek, 1822.

Evans, Nathaniel (Mary)—1779.
Fulton, Hugh—came, 1739.
Gabbert, Matthew (Christina)—opposite mouth of Buffalo, 1781.
Gadberry—plantation on Buffalo mentioned, 1805.
Galbraith, John (Barbara)—Lexington, 1782.
Gibson, George—near House Mountain, 1768.
Gilmore, James (Martha)—1764.
Goodbar, Robert—buys on Kerr's Creek, 1779.
Graham, Arthur (Mary)—Walker's Creek, 1787.
Gray, David (Ruth)—1784.
Gray, Samuel (Agnes)—1764.
Grigsby, James (Franky)—buys on Mill, 1778, and on Buffalo, 1779.
Guthrie, Robert—Cedar, 1788.
Hall, Nathaniel (Elizabeth)—1786.
Hall, James—neighbor to William Murphy, Robert Skeen, Elijah Forsythe, Robert Clark, George Cress—Collier's Creek, 1780.
Hannah, Alexander (Isabel)—Buffalo, 1784.
Hannah, John—has mill license on Collier, 1768.
Harper, James—Collier's Creek, 1802.
Henderson, Samuel, Sr. (Mary McClure)—1780.
Hill, Thomas (Elizabeth)—1780.
Houston, John (Sarah)—Hay's Creek, 1788.
Houston, William (Jane)—1786.
Howell, Thomas (Ann)—Buffalo, 1784.
Hoylman, Stophel—buys of Isaac Taylor, Jr., 1777.
Jack, Samuel—north side North River, 1780.
Kelly, Samuel (Catharine)—Walker's Creek, 1779.
Kelly, Anthony (Elizabeth)—Walker's Creek, 1779.
Kelso, Moses (Jane)—Dry Run, 1779.
Kennedy, William—came, 1772.
Kidd, Daniel (Christina L.)—1785.
Kingery, Jacob—buys of Andrew Taylor, 1777.
Kirkpatrick, John—Buffalo, 1778.
Lackey, Thomas, wheelwright—1788.
Laird, James—South River, 1805.
Leech, John—from Cumberland county, Pa., 1778.
Liggett, Alexander (Jean)—1784.
Logan, David (Mary)—Buffalo, 1778.
Logan, James (Martha)—Collier's Creek, 1779.
Long, Joseph (Elizabeth)—Buffalo, 1778.
Lusk, John (Isabella)—South River, 1778.
Lusk, William—came 1744.
Lyle, John (Frances)—1780.
Magee, Richard (Sarah)—Buffalo, 1780.
Martin, William (Mary)—Collier's Creek, 1787.
Mathews, Richard (Eleanor)—Mill Creek, 1778.
McCallister, George (Sarah)—Buffalo, 1785.
McCallister, John—buys on James, 1779.
McCalpin, Robert—Buffalo, 1777.

McCampbell, Samuel (Martha)—Back Creek, 1783.
McCampbell, James—came about 1759.
McCampbell, William—came about 1753.
McChesney, James (Sarah)—Borden Tract, 1784.
McChesney, Samuel (Joanna,—Hays Creek, 1778.
McClung, John—came in fall of 1744.
McClure, Moses (Isabella)—South River, 1777.
McClure, Alexander, Sr. (Martha)—North River, 1778.
McConnell, Patrick (Judith)—Buffalo, 1780.
McCorkle, Patrick—sells to Samuel Lyle, 1778.
McCown, James (Jane)—came, 1747, sells on Cedar, 1779.
McCown, John—bought of Thomas Kindell on Kerr's Creek.
McCullough, Thomas—South River, 1805.
McFadden, Hugh (Elizabeth)—Kerr's Creek, 1785.
McKee, John and James—came in summer of 1754.
McKee, John—Buffalo, 1779.
McKemy, John (Mary)—Buffalo, 1784.
McNear, Robert (Margaret)—Collier's Creek, 1778.
McNeely, David (Martha)—Borden Tract, 1781.
McSpadin, Moses (Jean)—1780.
Milligan, William (Martha)—Broad Creek, 1778.
Mitchell, John—Buffalo, 1789.
Neely, John (Elizabeth)—Buffalo, 1786.
Nesbitt, Samuel (Mary)—1788.
Patterson, James (Isabella)—1787.
Patton, William—came 1750.
Paxton, Thomas—came 1744, but prospected two years earlier.
Pickens, James—Buffalo, 1788.
Pine, James—buys on Collier, 1779.
Poague, Robert (Margaret)—1779.
Pollock, James (Margaret)—Great River, 1786.
Porter, Samuel—improvements on Buffalo valued, 1751, at $378.29 by John Poage and James Davis.
Pullin, Joseph—buys on Buffalo, 1787.
Ramsay, Joseph—buys on Buffalo, 1787.
Ramsay, Samuel—opposite mouth of Whistle and just below Andrew Hall, 1800.
Robertson, John (Sarah)—Walker's Creek, 1786.
Robinson, Robert—bought of William Snodon, about 1747.
Robinson, Robert (Elizabeth)—Broad Creek, 1779.
Robinson, John (Mary)—1780.
Sawyers, David—lived with Solomon Moffett, 1762.
Siler, Philip—buys on Walker's Creek, 1781.
Smiley, John (Elizabeth)—North River, 1779.
Snodgrass, James (Jean)—1780.
Steele, Robert (Agnes)—1787.
Steele, Samuel—came 1739.
Stevenson, James (Margaret)—Little River, 1787.
Stuart, Archibald—Kerr's Creek, 1822.

Summers, John (Agnes)—1788.
Tate, Joseph—1781.
Telford, Hugh—settled at Falling Springs.
Todd, James (Susannah)—Buffalo, 1777.
Todd, Samuel—Whistle Creek, 1767.
Vance, Patrick (Mary)—1787.
Vanmaple, John (Jean)—1786.
Walker, John, blacksmith—1784.
Wallace, James (Elizabeth)—Walker's, "formerly Hays" Creek, 1785.
Ward, Isaac (Elizabeth)—Buffalo, 1781.
Ward, John (Mary)—Elk Creek of James, 1779.
Wardlaw, James—came 1745.
Wasson, Robert—Kerr's Creek, 1820.
Weir, Samuel (Margaret)—sells to Thomas Steele, 1780.
Whitley, Jonathan (Sarah)—Buffalo, 1784.
Whitley, Paul—settled on Cedar.
Williamson, Richard (Ann)—Collier's Creek, 1780.
Willson, Thomas—near House Mountain, 1805.
Wilson, Abraham (Catharine)—sells, 1778.
Wilson, James—Borden Tract, 1779.
Woods, Joseph (Mary)—Borden Tract, 1781.
Woods, Patrick (Margaret)—1782.
Woods, Samuel (Jane)—1783.
Woods, Stephen (Martha)—1783.

REPORTS OF PROCESSIONERS

In 1747, Joseph Long and Richard Woods were ordered to procession in the Forks of James; Alexander McClure and Robert Houston from the North Branch of James to Andrew Baxter's, thence, on a straight line to the mill of John Hays, "joining the North Mountain"; Francis McCown and John Montgomery from the North Branch of James on a straight line from the Hays mill to the upper end of Beverly Manor.

Houston and McClure reported for the following settlers, April, 1748:

Andrew Baxter (present, Nathaniel Evans), William Givins, John Gray, William Hall (present, Robert Allison), Charles Hays (present, Andrew Hays), Robert Huston, Matthew Lyle (present, John Lyle,) Alexander McCleary (present, Moses Whiteside), John McNab (present, Baptist McNab), John Paul (present, Roger Keys), John P. Paul (present, Michael Finney), John Stevenson (present, Andrew Stevenson.)

Montgomery and McCown reported for these:

James Archer, Samuel Anderson, Thomas Berry, William Berry, William Cowden, Joseph Coulton, Robert Coulton, Samuel Dunlap, Robert Dunlap, Patrick Hays, George Henderson, John Lowry, Nathan Lusk, William Lockridge, William McCanless, William Mitchell, Francis McCown (present, John Downey), James Moore, Samuel McCutchen, James Martin, James Robinson, James Shields, John Shields, James Trimble, Alexander Walker, John Walker.

In 1764, John Paxton and Abraham Brown processioned between North River and the Buffalo for the following:

James Allison, James Bailey, Andrew Brown, Abraham Brown, Edmund Crump, James Campbell, George Campbell, James Davis, James Edmiston, William Foster, William Hall, William Holeman, Joseph Lapsley, Robert Morre, John Moore, Samuel Moore,

Samuel McClure, John McKnight, John McCollom, Patrick McCollom, Christian Milliron, James McLang, William Paxton, John Paxton, John Sommers, John Taylor, James Trimble, Joseph Walker, Richard Woods, James Welch, Peter Wallace.

A part of the precinct of Paxton and Brown was processioned by Alexander Collier and Andrew Miscampbell (McCampbell) for the following:

John Beaty, Archibald Buchanan, James Campbell, Moses Cunningham, Hugh Cunningham, Margery Crawford, Alexander Deal (Dale), James Davis, Robert Erwin, Edward Fairies, George Gibson, John Gilmore, William Gilmore, William Hall, Robert Hamilton, John Hanna, John Huston, James Hutton, Henry Kirkham, William McCasney, John McKee, Robert McKee, John McMurtry, James McCalster, George McConne, (McCown), John McConne, Robert McKelhenny, Robert McHenry, William Moore, William Porter, John Somers, Robert Talford, David Talford, Solomon Whitley, John Wylie, John Wylie, Jr., James Young, Robert Young.

In the same year, Andrew Hall and James, son of William Buchanan, processioned for the precinct between North River and the Beverly line, and between North Mountain and the great road leading from Captain Bowyer's to the courthouse. The men they visited were these:

Robert Allison, John Allison, Isaac Anderson, James Anderson, Jacob Anderson, William Berry, Reverend John Brown, Andrew Buchanan, James Buchanan, Jasper Buntin, William Davies, Samuel Dunlap, Andrew Fitzpatrick, James Greenlee's heirs, Andrew Hays, John Lyle's heirs, William Lusk, James McLang, Henry McLang, Alexander McCroskey, David McCroskey, John McCroskey, Captain Samuel McDowell, James McKee, William Patton, Samuel Robinson, Edward Tarr, Alexander Telford, James Thompson, William Young.

In 1767, James Simpson and John Mitchell processioned for the following, between the Buffalo and the James:

Charles Allison, Alexander Baggs, William Crawford, John Davis, David Dreadden, James Dreaddin (Dryden), James Gilmore, John Gilmore, John Hickman, Richard Mathews, William Mathews, William McBride, Arthur McClure, James McGavock, Robert Miller, John Murray, John Paxton, John Poage, George Salling, John Thompson, John Walker, Benjamin Wattson, John White, Robert Whittle.

SECTION XIV

MISCELLANEOUS DATA

The material in this section is taken from will-books, deed-books, marriage lists, and other miscellaneous sources of information. The given names which are grouped under the various surnames are arranged alphabetically, and are numbered in consecutive order, except where all the given names belong to a single household. All statements following a given number and ending at the next higher number belong to the name following the first number. Surnames are ordinarily spelled according to the usage of the present time, but unusual or doubtful names follow the original spelling. In those instances where the documentary spelling differs from the present, the former is also given. The spelling of given names usually follows that which is found in the records. In certain instances, two or more persons named John or Mary may be one and the same individual, and probably are. But since the evidence in hand is not conclusive, we have thought it best to treat such names as those of distinct people.

The special abbreviations used in the present section are these:

admr—administrator
Aug.—Augusta county
b—born
bro.—brother
c—about or nearly
C—children
d—died
dau.—daughter
dy—died in youth
g'son—grandson

k—killed in battle
m—married
New P.—New Providence
n. c.—no children
unknown—whereabouts unknown
Rbg—Rockbridge county
s—unmarried
post.—unborn at death of father
w—wife

A date without special mention, as in "John—1775," means we have nothing more than the solitary fact that the John is incidentally spoken of in connection with the year 1775. A date followed by c, as "1816c," means that the date is approximate and not necessarily exact. A date preceded by by, as "by 1810," means that the occurrence preceded 1810, perhaps by a considerable number of years. The question mark is used in cases of uncertainty. Thus, "C(?)": means that the children whose names follow the semicoln appear to be of the couple just previously mentioned. "John(?)Smith" means that a man, known to be a Smith, is believed to have had the given name John. The word "others," coming just after a list of children, means that there were still other children in the family, but that their given names are unknown. Such a name as "Mary Kirk White," refers to a widow, whose first husband was a White.

Ackerly.—John P.—d. 1827—m. Sarah Miller—C: John P., William, Peter, Stephen, Mary (m. Daniel Carr, 1817), Peggy (m. ——— Almonrode), Elizabeth, Sarah, Barbara, Magdalene (m. Wiley H. Beckett, 1813), Ama.

Adair—1. Betty (m. James G. Paxton). 2. Elizabeth—m. Samuel Snodgrass, 1792. 3. George—m. Peggy Ramsay, 1808. 4. James—m. Jane ———. 5. Johnson of 4—b. in Pa., 1781, d. 1856. 6. John—m. Mary O'Donnell by 1773. 7. John—m. Polly McCorkle, 1808. 8. Martha—m. Daniel Lyle, 1801.

Adams.—1. Hugh—m. Nancy Ward, 1799, d. 1831—C: Williamson, Rebecca, John, James, Hugh, Rachel. 2. James—son of 4—C: Robert, John, Joseph, Hugh (b. 1820, d. 1880, m. Amanda J. McCormick, 1845), Patsy, Mary J., Nancy. 3. James—m. Eleanor Ewin, 1813. 4. John—d. 1837—m. (1) Jean Hutchinson, (2) Margaret McElheny, 1809—C: Robert H., Hugh(s), Pully, James (m. Sarah McCroskey), Patsy (m. Robert Rea), Betsy (m. David Rea), James (m. Joseph Trevy), John (b. 1802), Martha. 5. Rebecca—m. John H. Hoffman, 1817. 6. Thomas—1766.

Agnor.—1. James Agnew—m. Elizabeth Ocheltree, 1801. 2. John—d. 1833—C: Susanna (m. ——— Syders), George, Christina (m. ——— Muterspaw). 3. Margaret—dau. of G. and S——— —b. 1769, d. 1859—m. Jonathan Ingraham. 4. Mary—m. John Fordan, 1814.

Albright.—Frederick—m. Betsy Ornbom—C: John (m. Sarah Phillips, 1807), Hannah (m. George Griffin, 1813).

Alexander.—1. Andrew—m. Isabella Paxton, 1800.
2. Andrew—m. Nancy (or Anna D.) Aylett, 1803.
3. Archibald—m. (1) Margaret Parks, 1734, (2) Jane McClure, 1757—C: William, Phœbe; by 2d w.—Mary (b. 1760, m. John Trimble), Margaret (s), John (b. 1764, d. 1838), James (m. Martha Telford), Samuel (m. ——— McCoskie), Archibald (m. Isabel Patton,) Jane (b. 1773, m. John W. Doak).
    4. Elizabeth—d. 1756—m. John Paxton.
    5. Elizabeth—m. Samuel Tate, 1785.
    6. Elizabeth—m. Henry McClung, 1802.
    7. James—m. Martha Telford, 1794.
    8. James—m. Peggy Lyle, 1801.
    9. James—m. Mary Cowen, 1804.
    10. James—estate, $462, Botetourt, 1776.
    11. John—m. Jinny Ocheltree, 1803.
    12. John—m. Elizabeth Lyle.
    13. John—m. Betsy Reid, 1815.
    14. Margaret—m. Samuel W. Lyle.
    15. Margaret—m. William Scott, 1790.
    16. Martha—m. Benjamin H. Rice, 1814.
    17. Mary—dau. of John and Phœbe—b. 1787, d. 1859—m. William Preston.
    17x. Mary—m. William Carson, 1795.
    18. Mary C.—m. James G. McClung.
    19. Nancy—m. William Turner, 1806.
    20. Phœbe—dau. of 3—m. John Paxton by 1787.
    21. Thomas—1765.
    22. William—d. 1749c—C: Archibald (b. 1708), Robert (d. 1787), William (d. 1755, m. Martha ———), Elizabeth (m. John McClung, 1754c).
    23. William—son of 22—b. 1738, d. 1797, m. Agnes A. Reid—C: Margaret (m. Edward Graham, 1792), Archibald, Sarah (m. Samuel L. Campbell, 1794), John, Nancy, Phœbe, Elizabeth, Martha.

24. William—d. 1825—m. Elizabeth Campbell, 1805—C: Margaret, Sarah, Elizabeth.
25. ——— —m. Esther Beard by 1799.
26. ——— —m. Nancy McCluer by 1821.
27. ——— —m. Agnes Brewster.

Allen.—1. Cornelius—m. Jane Weir, 1785. 2. Hugh—d. 1744. 3. Hugh—d. 1796—m. Jane ——— —C: John, Joseph, William. 4. Jane—m. John Walkup, 1816. 5. Jean—m. William Murphy, 1796. 6. John—uncle to Elizabeth Steele. 7. John—d. 1830—m. Jean ——— —C: Robert, Polly (m. ——— Hanger), Betty, James, Benjamin, William, Martha (m. ——— Kelso), Jane (m. ———< Walkup), Montique, Thomas. 8. John—m. Margaret Moore, 1787. 9. John—m. Elizabeth Poague, 1801. 10. Joseph—m. Jenny Poague, 1808. 13. ——— —m. Elizabeth Logan by 1821. 14. ——— —m. Eleanor Steele.

Allison.—1. Charles—1765. 2. James—mill license, 1747. 3. John—d. by 1780—m. Margaret ———. 4. John—m. Janet ——— —here by 1755. 5. John—m. Sally Woods, 1815. 6. Lydia—m. Samuel Ginger, 1817. 7. Mary—m. Francis Nash, 1787. 8. Patsy—m. Henry Ginger, 1817. 9. Robert—m. Hannah McClure—C: James, Mary (m. ——— Davidson), Agnes, Robert, Francis, Halbert, Janet.

Alphin.—Richerson—d. 1839—m. Elizabeth ——— —C: William, George, Nancy, (m. ——— Hartigan), Frances (m. ——— Gifford), Elizabeth, Catharine, Palina, Lucius, Thomas, Julian, Mary F.

Anderson.—1. Betsy— m. James W. Steele, 1818. 2. Catharine—m. John McNutt. 3. David—m. Catharine Wence, 1808. 4. Esther—m. George Parsons, 1805. 5. Isaac—m. Martha ——— —d. 1749—C: John (k. by Indians before 1749), Isaac (b. 1730), William, James (m. Jane Allison), Jacob (m. Esther Baxter), Mary (m. James Bayless), Elizabeth (m. William Gilmore). 6. Isaac—son of 5—m. Margaret Evans—C: William (m. Nancy McCampbell, 1779), Martha (m. James McCampbell, 1774), Mary (m. Andrew McCampbell), Esther (m. John Edmondson, 1794), Jeanette (George McNutt), Margaret (m. James Harris), Rebecca. 7. James ("Deaf James")—d. 1798—C: James, Jacob, John, Isaac, Martha, Jean, Margaret, Robert. 8. James—son of 7—presented, 1802—C: John, James, Henry, Robert, Nancy. 9. Jane—m. Nathan Lackey, 1819. 10. Jean—m. James Ellis, 1799. 11. Jennet—m. James Baggs, 1787. 12. John—m. Mary McKinzie, 1819. 13. Joseph—m. Margaret Brown, 1792. 14. Josias—m. Margaret ——— by 1797. 15. Nancy —m. Alexander Jordan, 1814. 16. Nancy—m. Isaac Lawson, 1815. 17. Polly—m. Christopher Bradley, 1816. 18. Robert—m. Margaret Walker, 1791—C: Isaac, William. 19. ——— m. Patsy McCroskey by 1839.

Andrews.—1. Moses—d. 1784—C: James, Mary, Robert, Elizabeth, Dougald, Campbell. 2. Polly—m. Solomon Keys, 1795.

Armentrout.—1. Ann.—m. Andrew Miller, 1817. 2. Charles—b. 1770c—m. Elizabeth ———. 3. Charlotte —n. Solomon Syders, 1809. 4. George —b. 1775c —m. Margaret Standoff. 5. George S.—b. 1815, d. 1879—m. Elizabeth Bare. 6. Henry—d. 1877—C: Charles, Molly (m. ——— Haslet), George, Henry, Christiana (m— Unrow), John (has 5 children by 1826). 7. Henry—m. Nancy Moore, 1819. 8. Jacob—m. Margaret Stout, 1798. 9. Mary—m. Dennis Conner, Jr., 1819. 10. Molly—b. 1781, d. 1853, m. Andrew Haselet, 1802. 11. Polly—m. Mathias Circle, 1818.

Armstrong.—1. Archibald—Little River, 1755. 2. Benjamin—m. Pussy Evans, 1815. 3. James—m. Ann Forsythe, 1819. 4. John—m. Catharine McDonald by 1757. 5. John— m. Mary Kirkpatrick, 1791. 6. John—m. Elizabeth Nick, 1815. 7. John—m. Jane ——— —m. d. 1839—C: Quinter, Deborah (m. James McCray), Rebecca, Mary (m. Robert Smiley), Jane (m. William Reaney). 8. Mary—m. Joel Hampton, 1797. 9. Rachel—m. (William Nick, 1816). 10. Thomas—son of Robert—b. 1778, d. 1858, m. Betsy ——— Mc-

Campbell, 1792—C: Robert. 11. Thomas—m. Margaret Harris, 1809. 12. —————— —m. Peggy Jameson, by 1797.

Arnold.—James—m. Agnes —————— —by 1779. 2. Stephen—m. Jane —————— by 1755. 3. —————— —m. Sophia Welch by 1821.

Aston.—1. Ann—m. Joseph Black, 1808. 2. Esther—m. Asa Bennen, 1796. 3. Jane—b. 1726 c —m. Thomas Paxton.

Atkinson.—1. Catharine—m. Samuel Paxton, 1791. 2. Eliza—m. William Paxton (cousin). 3. George—m. Sally McCalpin, 1794. 4. Susan—m. 1800c—m. Samuel Paxton. 5. William H.—m. Elizabeth Wallace by 1836.

Auld.—1. John—m. Catharine Forsythe, 1807. 2. Nellie—m. William Forsythe, 1809.

Ayres.—1 Betsy—m. James Smith, 1817. 2. Catharine—m. William Gill, 1793. 3. Charles—m. Martha Skean, 1812. 4. Charles—m. Polly Riplogle, 1816. 5. Daniel Eyres—m. Hannah Riplogle, 1816. 6. Elizabeth Aires—m. David Morris, 1789. 7. Henry—m. Isabel Reid, 1788. 8. John—m. Rachael Gill, 1793. 9. John—m. Rachel Entsminger, 1817. 10. Nancy Eyres—m. William Fink, 1807. 11. Polly Eyres—m. William Campbell, 1812. 12. Rebecca —————— Eyres—m. Joshua Barcus, 1809. 13. Sally—m. John Brown, 1810. 14. Samuel Eyres—m. Elizabeth Hyman, 1798. 15. —————— —m. Elizabeth Jones, 1801.

Aylett.—1. Nancy—m. Andrew Alexander, 1803. 2. Rebecca—m. Joseph Lapsley, 1804.

Bagby.—1. Elvira—m. Joseph Paxton, 1815. 2. Martha—m. Nathan D. Terry, 1815.

Baggs.—1. Agnes—m. Joseph Hickman, 1786. 2. Alexander—d. 1786—m. Ann ——————
—C: Jean, Margaret, Martha (m. Jonathan Poague, 1794), Frances, Thomas (m. Ann Whitley, 1786), James (m. Jennet Anderson, 1787), Mary (b. 1770, d. 1860, m. John Hamilton, 1794). 3. David—m. Isabella Scott, 1790. 4. Elizabeth—m. Frederick Painter, 1815. 5. Fanny—m. Mordecai Cross, 1801. 6. Isabella—m. Andrew Reid, 1798. 7. Jane—m. John McClung, 1814. 8. Sarah—Samuel Whitley, 1787. 9. Thomas—m. Mary Santon, 1801. 10. —————— —m. Andrew Bailey, 1809.

Bailey.—1. Andrew—m. —————— Baggs 1809. 2. George—m. Peggy Elliott, 1819. 3. John—m. Peggy Cusack, 1819. 4. Martha—m. William Patton, 1803. 5. Mary—m. Samuel Montgomery, 1814. 6. Peggy—m. James Walker, 1815. 7. Sarah—m. Thomas Caskey, 1806. 8. William—m. Polly Greenlee, 1809. 9. William S.—m. (1) Elizabeth Mackey, 1788, (2) Jane Elliott, 1814.

Baker.—1. Catharine—m. Alexander McKemy, 1799. 2. Eliza—m. Robert T. Dickson, 1799. 3. Margaret—m. John Lyle, 1789. 4. Rebecca—m. William Sprowl, 1800.

Baldwin.—1. Clark—m. Rhodema ——————. 2. Cornelius C.—m. Margaret Paxton, 1837—C: John (b. 1838, d. 1881), Aurelia (m. Alexander M. Garber), Joseph S. (m. Nannie Bissell), Charles C. C. (dy). Cyrus B.—son of Clark—b. 1783, d. 1855. 3. Samuel—m. Mary With, 1778.

Bane.—1. Robert—m. Jane —————— —C: Prudence (b, 1775, d, 1853), William (m Mary Harper, 1804). 2. Susan (m. William Young, 1818).

Banning.—Asa—C (?): Abagail (m. Henry Rippy, 1797), Hannah (William Aston, 1800), Elizabeth Black, 1797), Thomas (Keziah Gallifee, 1801).

Barclay.—1. Alexander T.—son of 2—m. (1) Nancy Poague, 1819, (2) ——— ———, (3) Mary E. Paxton. 2. Elihu—d. 1803—m. Sarah Telford, 1796. 3. Elihu H.—son of 1—b. 1846, d. 1902. 4. Hannah—m. James Moore, 1791. 5. Hugh, Sr.—d. 1806—C: Polly, Peggy, Rachel, Hannah, Elihu. 6. Polly—m. Alexander Culbertson, 1799. 7. Rachel—m. John Crawford, 1790. 8. —————— —m. Sarah Edmondson, by 1796. 9. —————— —m. Jinny Walker by 1818. C: Alexander T., Hugh, Elihu.

Barger.—1. Caty—m. Moses Garrett, 1813. 2. Jacob—m. Polly Bowman, 1809. 3. Peter—m. Ann Pettigrew, 1816.

MISCELLANEOUS DATA

Barnett.—1. John—m. E———— ———— —C: Sally (b. 1782, d. 1858, m. J———— Smiley). 2. ———— —m. Ann Clemens by 1759.

Baxter.—1. Andrew—b. 1670, living 1747. 2. ———— —m. Mary Sare by 1788.

Beach.—Waldron—d. 1792c—C: Elizabeth (m. John Gilmore, 1791), Pheby (m. Robert Clark, 1795), Sarah (William Priestly, 1787), Samuel (Hannah Haslet, 1797).

Bear.—1. Jacob—m. Elizabeth Blosser—C: Esther (b. 1781, m. Daniel Hite), Joseph (b. 1783, m. Ann Hite), John (m. ———— Frazier), Barbara (s), Susanna (m. ———— Clyce), Elizabeth (b. 1791, m. James Dunlap, 1813), Jacob (b. 1793, m. Susan Clyce), Anna (m. Thomas O'Kane), Fronica (m.————Shank). 2. Elizabeth—b. 1837—m. George S. Armentrout. 3. Joseph—son of 1—C: John (s), Mary (s), Ann (b. 1811, m. Rev. James Hill), Joseph (m. Martha McCarthy), Rachel (s), Fannie (m. Samuel H. Decker), Noah (m. Frances Shank), Samuel, Elizabeth (m. Philip Ebberd).

Beard.—1. Dickey—m. Peggy Taylor, 1800. 2. Hugh—son of 5—d. 1807—m. Sarah ————, d. 1811—C: Robert (has Nancy and Sally by 1806), Ann, Jane, Alexander, Sarah (m. Andrew Kennedy, 1797), Esther (m. ———— Hoffman), Thomas. 3. Hugh —m. Esther McCoskey, 1797. 4. Jonathan—m. Betsy Whealiss, 1819. 5. Thomas—admr, Alexander Smiley, 1749—d. 1769—C: Jane, Hugh, Esther (m. Robert Alexander), William, Elizabeth (m. ———— Mitchell), Mary (m. ———— Dunlap), (Robert Ramsay),—the last four have each a Thomas. 6. Thomas—m. Sarah Jameson, 1785.

Beaty.—1. Elizabeth—m. Thomas Bowyer, 1806. 2. Isabella—m. David Campbell, 1782. 3. James—m. Isabella Paul, 1789. 4. John—on Kerr's Cr., 1750c to 1772c—C: David (b. 1752c), John (k. 1780), Agnes (m. James Dysart, 1775). 5. John—m. Elizabeth Morris, 1798. 6. Sarah—m. Edward Ballin, 1808. 7. Sarah—m. Joseph Little, 1788.

Beaver.—1. Abraham—m. Margaret Harnest, 1816. 2. David—m. Peggy Thomas, 1808. 3. John—m. Esther Thomas, 1810.

Beers.—1. Mary D.—m. Patrick Neil, 1800. 2. Mary—m. Dennis Connor, 1808.

Beets.—1. Adam—m. Mary Rowlinson, 1801. 2. Catharine—m. Christopher Wise (Weir?), 1813.

Bell. 1. David—m. ———— Henderson by 1770. 2. Elizabeth—m. Valentine Dooly, 1784. 3. James—m. Elizabeth Hindron, 1804. 4. John—d. 1792c—C: Martha Lettice, Betsy. 5. John—m. Mary Cloyd, 1787. 6. Joseph—m. ————Henderson by 1770. 7. Joseph—at Goshen, 1830. 8. Lettice—m. Joseph Walkup, 1803. 9. Margaret—ward of John Moore, 1751.

Bennett.—1. Benjamin—heirs, 1779: Mary (m. John Beresford), John (m. Mary Ward), Margaret (m. John Robinson), James (m. Agnes Arnold), Ezekiel (m. Jane Kenady), Lydia (Frances Beresford, and (probably) Benjamin, Jr. 2. Richard—fahter of 1—d. intestate, 1743, before getting deed to 300 acres in Beverly Manor—Martha, widow, later m. William McNabb—William Thompson, brother-in-law to Richard.

Bennington.—1. John—m. Elizabeth Morris, 1818. 2. Thomas—m. Rachel Watkins, 1812.

Berrisford.—John—d. by 1765—m. Mary ———— —C (?): see Bennett.

Berry.—1. Charles—on bond with John Pattison, 1746. 2. George—m. Agnes Hall by 1777. 3. James—d. 1751c—C: John (b. 1743), George, others. 4. James—guardian of children of 3. 5. Jean—m. John G. Ustick, 1804. 6. John—d. 1771c—Alexander Walker, wheelwright, and William Edmiston, admr.—C: James (has John), William (has John, Mary, Elizabeth), Francis, (has John), Charles (has Elizabeth), Mary, Rebecca. 7. Nancy—m. Solomon McCampbell, 1782. 8. Thomas—m. Elizabeth Walker, 1788. 9. William—d. 1793—m. Jane ———— —C: James, William, Jane Mary. 10. ———— ——m. Betsy B. Walkup by 1834.

Berryhill.—1. Agnes—m. James Patterson, 1794. 2. John—d. 1818—m. Rachel ———— —C:

John, James, Alexander, William, Rachel, Polly. 3. John—d. 1825—bro. to William Berryhill and Rachel Cassady, of Ohio, and to Polly Kincaid, who was James and Isaiah. 40 acres left to Amy Beverly, colored .

Biby.—Nancy, orphan of Thomas—1801.

Black.—1. Alexander—m. Susanna Garrison, 1797. 2. Benjamin—m. Jean Clark, 1804. 3. George—m. Jenny Standoff, 1802. 4. Henry—m. Martha ——— —C: John, James, William, Joseph, Benjamin, Elizabeth (m. John Banning, 1797), Jane R. 5. James —m. Margaret Moore, 1818. 6. Jean—m. William Ruth, 1801. 6.* John—m. Margaret Ford, 1793. 7. Joseph—m. Ann Acton, 1818. 8. Samuel—m. Polly Letcher, 1808. 9. William—m. Ruth Evans, 1798.

Blair.—1. Betsy—m. Joseph Ford, 1813. 2. Betsy—m. James Paxton, 1814. 3. James —m. Elizabeth Wilson, 1786. 4. Jane—m. Andrew Wallace, 1812. 5. Joseph—Elizabeth Paxton, 1812. 6. Mary—b. 1726, d. 1821, m. John Paxton. 7. Mary—in John Houston's household, 1748.

Bodkin. 1. James—R, 1807. 2. Mary—m. Edward Brown, 1806. 3. Thomas—m Catharine Bannington, 1817. 4. William—m. Jean Steele, 1808.

Bogan.—1. Andrew—m. Nancy Dickson, 1799—d. 1825—uncle to Jenny Wallace—bro. to Sally, Smith (Roanoke Co.), ——— (m. James Wallace). 2. Betsy—m. George Saville, 1808. 3. William Bogins—m. Elizabeth Pullin, 1801.

Boils.—1 Charles—m. Mrs. Rebecca Rollin by 1794—C: Mary. 2. Mary—m. John Poague, 1796. 3. ——— —m. Jain Ritchy by 1797c.

Borden.—1. Benjamin—m. Zeruiah ——— —d. 1742—C: Benjamin, Abegal (m. 1 ——— Worthington, 2. James Pritchard), Rebecca (m. ——— Branson), Debourah (m.— Henry), Hannah (m. Edward Rogers), Lidy (m. Jacob Peck, 1745), Elizabeth (m. ——— Nicholas—d. 1755c), Marcey (m. William Feamley), John, Joseph.

2. Benjamin—son of 1—m. Mrs. Magdalene Woods McDowell, 1744c—d. 1753—C: Martha, Hannah, one other.

3. Henry—stonemason—Collierstown, 1787 and later.

4. Joseph—son of 1—m. Jane ——— —d. 1803, Iredell Co., N. C.

5. Martha—dau. of 2—m. Robert Harvey, 1779c.

6. Mary—dau. of 3 (?)—m. John Brackley, 1789.

7. ——— —son of 3 (?)—m. Judith Miller, 1795.

Bosserman.—Sarah—servant to Joseph Weir, 1779.

Bowyer.—1. John—son of Michael—m. Mrs. Magdalene Borden—C: Frances (— George Poindexter). 2. John—d. 1806—bro. to Michael—uncle to Luke and to Polly Caldwell—m. Mary ———. 3. Phanny —m. William Bedford, 1797. 4. Polly—m. James Caldwell, 1797. 5. Thomas—m. Elizabeth Beaty, 1806.

Boyd.—1. Nancy—m. Charles Kirkpatrick, 1791. 2. Peggy—m. Joseph McNutt, 1807.

Boys.—1. Daniel—m. Sally Rynes, 1801. 2. John—m. Isabella Campbell, 1793.

Boils.—1. Charles—m. Mrs. Rebecca Rollin by 1794—C: Mary. 2. Mary—m. John Poague, 1796. 3. ——— —m. Jain Ritchy by 1797c.

Bradley.—1. Christopher—m. Polly Anderson, 1816. Hannah—m. Benjamin Eaton, 1794. 3. William—b. 1759—m. Mary Carlock, 1791—mentioned in will of John Jameson, 1790.

Bradds.—1. James—son of Daniel and Mary—b. 1774, d. 1860, m. Barbara Nicely, 1807. 2. James—m. Elizabeth Garrison. 3. John—son of 2—b. 1778, d. 1853, m. Mary Fowlyer, 1808. 4. Polly—m. John Clark, 1809.

Brady.—1. McCord Brady—m. Mary Trimble, 1795. 2. Nancy—m. John Kenny, 1808.

Braford.—1. Ann—m. Samuel Harper, 1801. 2. Elizabeth—m. Samuel Dryden, 1803.

3. Hugh—bro. to James—d. 1817—m. Polly ——— —C: Jane (m. James Staples, 1809), Spottswood, Belinda. 4. James—m. Sarah S. Davis, 1793. 5. James—m. Nancy Wilson, 1810. 6. James—b. 1784—boatman and tanner. 7. Polly—m. Joseph Dilliard, 1803. 8. Samuel —w. a Wallace?—C: William, James.

Bratton.—1. Robert—b. 1712, d. 1785, m. Ann McFarland Dunlap, 1745—C: James, John, George, Adam (m. Elizabeth Feamster), Agnes (m. William Given), Mary(s). 2. James—son of 1—b. 1746, d. 1823, m. Rebecca Hogshead, 1774—C: Robert, William, John (m. Polly G. Berry), David, Margaret (m. William Crawford), Rebecca (m. John McClung), ——— (m. John Porter), Andrew (m. Mary J. T. McKee, 1829), Lewis (m. Martha B. Dunlap). 3. Robert—son of 2.—m. Ann Dunlap, 1800.

Brice.—William—son of Elizabeth Close—d. at Lexington, 1818.

Brown.—1. Abraham—constable below Brushy Hills in Forks, 1755. 2. Alexander—m. Elizabeth Gay, 1784. 3. Alexander—m. ——— Coalter by 1818. 4. Ann—m. Joseph Patton, 1810. 5. Betsy—m. Henry McClelland, 1787. 2. Daniel—m. Betsy Caruthers, 1815c. 7. Edward—m. Mary Bodkin, 1806. 8. Jacob—m. Betsy Lewis, 1815. 9. Jacob J.—m. Jean McCaleb, 1803. 10. James—m. Isabella—d. by 1777—C: Rebecca. 11. James—m. Sarah Hinton, 1794. 12. John—m. Sally Ayers, 1810. 13. John—m. Rachel McKeever, 1818. 14. Margaret—m. Joseph Anderson, 1792. 15. Margaret—m. John Lawson, 1816. 16. Mary —m. Alexander Humphreys, 1788. 17. Mary—m. William Long, 1803. 18. Mary—m. Peter McKeever, 1794. 19. Nancy—m. John Hamilton, 1796. 20. Polly—orphan of William, 1797. 21. Samuel—d. 1749—bro. to Henry, Daniel, David—m. Mary ———. 22. Samuel—b. 1766, d. 1818, m. Mary Moore, 1798—minister—11 C. 23. Stephen—m. Mary Miles, 1804. 24. William—m. Peggy McBride by 1819. 25. William—m. ——— Walker by 1836.

Brownlee.—1. Alexander—m. Prudence Hays by 1786. 2. Mary—m. John McCleland, 1788. 3. Moffett Bronlee—m. Margaret Kirkpatrick, 1819. 4. William—left Rbg by 1798.

Brush.—1. Blakely—m. Janet ——— —C(?): John (m. Agnes Cowen, 1803), Rachel (m. William Riley, 1796), Elizabeth (m. Robert Wauson, 1790). 2. Richard—d. by 1763.

Bryan.—1. Cornelius—Buffalo, 1753. 2. Edward—m. Polly Parker, 1790. 3 Edward—d. 1838—m. Polly Shaw, 1819.

Buchanan.—1. David—m. Margaret Steele, 1789. 2. George—m. Nancy Casady. 1803. 3. James—m. Isabella ——— —d. 1797. 4. James—b. 1739, living 1806. 5. Jean—m. James Parks, 1786. 6. John—m. Margaret ———has mill, 1752. 7. John—m. Martha Wilson, 1789. 8. Peace W.—m. Samuel Petticrew, 1812. 9. Rubena—in suit, 1747. 10. William—d. 1836—bro to John (w. Rhoda). 11. ——— —m. Jane Walker by 1816. 12. ——— —m. Isable Hall by 1772. 13. ——— —m. Susanna Weir, by 1779. 14. ——— —m. Isabella Montgomery.

Buntin.—1. Alexander—in Ohio, 1812. 2. John—m. Elizabeth Reed, 1809. 3. John— m. Lavinia Jones, 1811. 4. Polly—m. Adam Cochran, 1809.

Burgess.—Thomas—m. Catrin—C(?): Elizabeth (m. Samuel Crosby, 1792), Samuel (m. Barbara Peters, 1800).

Burks.—1. John—m. Elizabeth ——— —C: Nathaniel D., Samuel C. (m. Pamelia Hunter, 1811), Arthur L., Elizabeth M. (m. Robert Irvine, 1815), Charles L., David J. 2. Sarah P.—m. William Paxton.

Burton.—1. Joseph—m. Mary E. Salling. 2. Richard—m. Ann ——— by 1748.

Butt.—1. Richard—m. Mary Dickey, 1797. 2. Sally—m. Joseph Lyle, 1791.

Byers.—1. Fleming—b. 1766, d. 1853, m. Fanny McClure, 1804. 2. Hyram—m. Elizabeth Camden, 1806.

Caldwell.—1. James—m. Polly Bowyer, 1797. 2. Joseph—m. Susanna Duff, 1797. Polly —m. Samuel Ogle, 1811. 4. Sarah—m. Alexander Fulton, 1787.

Callavan.—Hannah and Sarah, bound servants to Robert Hamilton, 1786.

Camden.—1. Elizabeth—m. Hiram Byers, 1800. 2. Jesse—b. 1780c—m. Jane, James. 3. John—m. —— Shields by 1825—C: Rachel.

Campbell—1. Abraham—m. Elizabeth McCormick, 1793.
2. Alexander—d. 1758—C: William, Alexander, Florence, Mary, James.
3. Alexander—m. Janet Smith, 1786—C: Samuel R. (doctor), William G. (b. 1799, d. 1881, had James and Addison).
4. Alexander—d. 1822—bro. to Elizabeth (William Alexander, 1805), Mary (m. David Doak, 1802).
5. Ambrose—m. Rhoda Chittum, 1817.
6. Andrew—orphan of Moses, 1800.
7. Ann—m. Solomon Hughes, 1817.
8. Charles—m. Margaret Buchanan—C: William.
9. Charles—b. 1741—d. 1826—son of 20—m. Mary A. Downey—C: Rachel (m. Anniel Rogers), John W., Samuel L., —— —(m. James McClung).
10. David—rendered a bill, 1759, for maintaining and burial of Martha, w. of Robert Cunningham, whom Robert had turned out.
11. David—m. Isabella Beaty, 1782.
12. Dougal—d. 1795—C: Joseph, Duncan, James, Alexander, Mary ——(m. James Finlay).
13. Duncan—d. 1813—m. Margaret —— —C: Alexander (see 4), Elizabeth, Mary.
14. Elenor—m. John Dudding, 1796.
15. Eliza—m. John Ramsay, 1792.
16. Elizabeth—m. William Alexander, 1805.
17. Elizabeth—m. Michael Kenear, 1786.
18. George—blacksmith—Big River, 1755.
19. Gilbert—levy-free, 1765.
20. Gilbert—d. 1750—C: Prudence (m. —— Hays, 1750c), Sarah, Elizabeth—(or Lettice)—(b. 1743—m. —— Woods), James, George, Charles—sons were minors, 1750—personalty, $176.42.
21. Gilbert—m. Mary Crawford, 1797.
22. Isaac—went from Lexington to Montgomery Co. before 1776.
22x. Isaac—m. Sarah Lapsley of Joseph, 1773.
23. Isabella—m. John Boys, 1793.
24. James—b. 1682c, d. 1753, m. Margaret —— —C: Daniel, John, ——(m. —— White), —— —(m. Samuel Steele).
25. James—admr Jacob Clements, 1759.
26. James—personalty, 1777, $1272.11.
27. James—m. Sarah Trotter, 1793.
28. James—m. Martha Patton, 1800.
29. Jean—m. James Lackey, 1808.
30. Jean—m. Nathan Patton, 1809.
31. Jenny—m. Henry Thompson, 1788.
32. Joel—m. Easther Shaw, 1809.
33. John—d. 1750c—C: John, James, Mary, Martha.
34. John—Mary Smith, 1788.
35. John—m. Elenor Ocle, 1797.
36. John—m. Nancy McCarty, 1815.
37. John—m. Catharine Woods, 1816.

38. John T.—m. Reubenia B. Paxton.
39. Magdalene—d. 1830—sister to Margaret Gray of Ky.
40. Malcolm—d. 1763—C: Archibald, William, Elizabeth, Mary, Jean, Rebecca.
41. Margaret—m. Robert Grier, 1786.
42. Mary—m. James Jones, 1787.
43. Mary—m. George Vineyard, 1790.
44. Mary J.—m. Abner W. Moore.
45. Nancy—m. Henry Winegar, 1815.
46. Patrick—d. 1778—bro. to Isaac and James—m. Anne Weir—C: James.
47. Peggy—m. John Kirkpatrick, 1808.
48. Robert—in Rbg, 1741—C: Hugh, John, Charles (see 9).
49. Robert—d. 1777—m. Sarah ———— —C: Sarah (m. Hugh Fulton), Mary (m. ——— Ritchie), Martha (m. William Kenady), Isabella (m. James Brown).
50. Robert—b. 1755c—m. Martha Paxton.
51. Robert S.—son of Alexander—m. Mary J. Paxton, 1814—C: Alexander P., John L., James D., Samuel B., William A.
52. Robert—m. ——— Donoho by 1789.
53. Robert— m. Polly Sylor, 1812.
54. Samuel L.—son of 9—b. 1766, d. 1840, m. Sarah Alexander, 1794—C: Charles F., William M., Samuel D., John A.
55. Sarah—m. Alexander Foster, 1795.
56. Seley—m. James Cash, 1811.
57. Sophia—m. Robert McCluer, 1816.
58. Thomas—m. Elizabeth Hardbarger, 1801.
59. William—son of 8—b. 1745, d. 1781—general—a daughter m. General Francis Preston of S. C.
60. William—m. Polly Eyers, 1812.
61. ——— —m. Richard Poston.
62. ——— - m. Thomas Tate.
63. ——— —m. Nathaniel C. Calhoun (minister).
64. ——— —m. ——— Taylor (captain).
65. ——— —m. John S. Wilson.
66. ——— —m. Agnes McClure by 1779.
67. ——— —m. Rebecca Wallace by 1782.
68. ——— —m. Elis Wilson by 1804—C: James.

Carlock.—Catharine—C: Barbara (m. John Jameson), Mary (m. William Bradley), 1791.

Cardiff.—Miles—d. 1794—C: Sarah.

Carper.—1. Adam—m. Susanna Knicely, 1799. 2. Catharine—m. Joseph McAlpin, 1815.

Carr.—1. Daniel—m. Mary Ackerly, 1817. 2. John—m. Rebecca Glasgow, 1814. 3. Richard—m. Margaret ———, d. after 1809. 4. Robert—m. Christina Hoylman, 1798.

Carson.—1. James—m. Isabella Gibson, 1789. 2. Jinny—m. William West, 1792. 3. Samuel—d. 1839—C: James, Jane, Isabella, Samuel, John, David, Andrew, Sally, Hannah. 4. William—m. Mary Alexander, 1795. 5. William P.—son of Robert—d. 1833—m. Betsy Rogers, 1810.

Carter.—1. Tiddy—m. George Sally, 1791. 2. William—m. Nancy Shaw, 1819.

Cartright.—1. Anthony—m. Hannah McCaleb, 1811. 2. Charles—m. Betsy Paxton, 1812. 3. Dicie Cartright—m. Thomas Paxton, 1818c.

Caruthers.—1. Esther—m. William McCrory, 1797. 2. Isaac—m. Ann Poague by 1760.

3. James—b. 1759, d. 1828, m. Hannah M. Paxton, 1793—C: John (m. Ann R. White), William H. (b. 1797, d. 1879), Franklin (s), Samuel (m. Ann Backus), James (s), Mary (m. Adolphus Ware), Margaret (m. James M. Woods), Betsy (m. Daniel Brown), Madison. 4. John—d. 1882—m. (2d w?) Sally McConkey, 1815—C: Isaac, William (has Julia and Ann E.), Phœbe (m. Alexander Shields, 1796). 6. Margaret—m. William McPheeters, 1789. 7. Nancy—dau. of William and Ann—b. 1799, d. 1857, m. ——— Wilson. 8. Peggy— m. William Wilson, 1811. 9. Robert—m. Ann ——— —C: William (only son), Margaret, Phily, Esther, Hannah, Nancy. 10. Sally—m. William Thompson, 1798. 11. Samuel—d. 1779—m. Rebecca ——— —C: James—bro. to Robert, John, James, Rachel. 12. William— m. Phebe Alexander, 1796. 13. William—m. Jinny Wilson, 1798. 14. William—m. Ann ——— —C: Nancy (b. 1779, d. 1857, m. ——— Wilson).

Cash.—1. James—m. Seley Campbell, 1811. 2. Thomas—b. in Amherst, 1766, d. 1856.

Caskey.—1. Archibald—m. Rhoda Thomas, 1819. 2. Elizabeth—orphan of Archibald, 1807. 3. John—m. Grizzy Greenlee, 1811. 4. Joseph—m. Elizabeth Wallace, 1819. 5. Thomas —m. Sarah Bailey, 1806.

Cassady.—1. James—m. Elizabeth ——— —C(?): Barbara (m. William McFadden, 1809), James (m. Mary McClung, 1812), Mary (m. Jacob Hostater, 1801), Nancy (m. George Buchanan, 1803)—James, Jr., has a James. 2. Peter—m. Mary McClung—C: Samuel, John, Alexander A. (b. 1800, d. 1880), George W., James, 1 other son and 6 dau. 3. Samuel—son of 2—b. 1795, d. 1876, m. Esther McFarland.

Casteel.—1. Elenor—m. Joseph McFaddin, 1795. 2. Elizabeth—m. William Walker, 1795.

Cawfell.—1. Catrine—m. George A. Bright, 1794. 2. Mary Cawful—m. Mathias Ruff, 1796.

Chambers.—1. Agnes—m. Andrew McCampbell, 1782. 2. Katty—named in will of Elizabeth Steele. 3. Robert—m. Elizabeth McKnight, 1797.

Chandler.—1. John—m. Polly Darst, 1802. 2. Polly—m. James Hopkins, 1817. 3. Richard W.—m. Catharine Shields, 1819. 4. Samuel—m. Salome Hoffman, 1793. 5. Samuel—m. Lucy Chandler, 1819.

Childress.—1. Elizabeth—m. John Paxton, 1818. 2. John—d. 1839—C: John A., Polly.

Chittum.—1. Nathaniel—b. 1798, d. 1894, m. (1) ——— Deason, (2) ——— Kepler—son of John (m. ———Sly), an English immigrant—C: 8 by 1st w, 4 by 2d. 2. Rhoda—m. Ambrose Campbell, 1811. 3. Sally—m. Joshua Householder, 1816. 4. Stephen G.—m. Betsy Green, 1819. 5. William—m. Matilda Green, 1813. The last is styled "Chillim," seemingly a slip of the pen.

Clark.—1. Charles—m. Nancy Dean, 1809. 2. James—m. Nancy Clark, 1809. 3. Jean—m. Benjamin Black, 1804. 4. John—m. Mary Harless, 1804. 5. John—m. Polly McCampbell, 1806. 6. John—m. Polly Bradds, 1809. 7. Nancy—m. Joseph Garven, 1808. 8. Polly—m. William Tharp, 1813. 9. Rebecca—m. George Elwood, 1806. 10. Robert—m. Pheby, 1795. 11. Robert—m. Jane ——— —b. 1796, d. 1873.

Cleek.—1. John—m. Elizabeth Jacobs, 1797. 2. ——— —m. Sophia ——— —C: Jacob (d. 1825), Elizabeth.

Cleghorn.—Robert—m. Mary ——— —Lexington, 1785.

Clements.—1. Jacob—d. 1759—Big River—C: Ann (m. ——— Barnett), Rachel (m. ——— Barnett), Mary (m. ——— McKnight), Sarah, Margaret, Elizabeth, Rebecca, Ruth, Isabel. 2. ——— m. Mary Campbell by 1754.

Cloyd.—1. Cynthia—b. 1780c, d. 1830—gives to foreign missions and other church work, $550 and 5 shares of stock in Bank of the Valley.

2. David—d. 1792—m. Margaret ——— —C: James, David, Michael, Elizabeth (m. James McDowell), Margaret (m. —— Templeton).
3. David—son of 2—m. Elizabeth ——— —d. 1789—C: David (d. 1808), Andrew, Joseph, James, Martha (m. Matthew Houston), Margaret (m. —— Houston), Mary (m. David McClung, 1803), Betsy (m. John Stephenson, 1808), Cynthia (see 1).
4. James—son of 2—m. Elizabeth ——— —d. 1797.
5. John—d. 1760c—C: Mary, John.
6. Mary—m. Joseph Bell, 1787.
7. Michael—son of 2—C: Betsy and 8 sons.

Clowney.—James L.—d. in Tenn. 1833—m. Delia Hannah, 1805—C: Samuel C., Martha M., Esther A., Mary A. E.

Clyce.—1. Adam—m. Eva Cooper, 1804. 2. Elizabeth—m. David Dryden, 1800. 3. Mary E.—m. Joseph Cool, 1811.

Coalter.—1. David—d. 1818—C: David, Isabel—Isabel or a sister is the w. of Alexander Brown. 2. Dorcas—m. George Hamilton, 1814. 3. George—m. Polly Paxton, 1809. 4. James—d. 1784—m. Margaret ——— —C: Michael, Elizabeth (m. ——— Wardlaw), Agnes (m. ——— Steele), Mary (m. ——Wardlaw), Sarah (m. Samuel Paxton), Jennet (m. —— Loggan). 5. Samuel—d. 1800c—C (minors): Nancy, Mary, Nelson.

Cochran.—1. Adam—m. Polly Buntain, 1809. 2. Charles—m. Nancy Tenant, 1799. 3. David—d. 1818—bro. to Charles.

Cohenour.—1. Catharine—m. William Ruly, 1813. 2. Polly—m. Hiram Vess, 1819. 3. —— —m. Margaret Dice by 1830—C: Isaiah.

Collier.—1. John—d. 1764—m. Sisely ——— —C: Alexander (m. Sarah ——), John, Jean, Moses, Aaron (m. Margaret ———), Margaret; admr: Frederick Armentrout, Augustine Price.

Collins.—1. James—m. Polly Wilson, 1804. 2. Lewis—m. Pauline Watkins, by 1838. 3. Peggy—m. Stoddard Neil, 1807.

Connor.—1. Dennis—m. Mary Beers, 1808. 2. Dennis, Jr.—m. Mary Armentrout, 1819. 3. Elenor—m. John Gaylor, 1800. 4. John—m. Catharine Standoff, 1810. 5. Patrick—m. Sarah Clark, 1796. 6. Thomas—m. Elizabeth Standoff, 1803.

Cook.—1. Elizabeth—m. Jacob Nicely, 1817. 2. John—m. Elizabeth Miller, 1811. 3. Joseph—m. Mary E. Clyce, 1811. 4. Patrick—d. 1784—C (minors): Mary, John.

Cooper.—1. Elizabeth—m. Conrad Kyme, 1793. 2. Eve—m. Adam Clyce, 1804. 3. James—d. 1781—personalty, $208.33—brother-in-law to John and James McKemy—m. Jean —— —C: Agnes, Thomas, James, John. 4. John—m. Margaret Wiley, 1809. 5. Joseph—b. in Aug., 1774, of Robert and S———, d. 1859—s. 6. Martha—m. Robert Wiley, 1794. 7. Mary—m. John Wiley, 1791. 8. Robert—m. Martha Steele, 1789. 10. William—d. 1782—personalty, $190.50—w. and C.

Coursey.—1. James—m. (1) Winifred Riddle, d. 1777, (2) Mary Gay Dunlap, 1785—C (by 1): James, Mary (m. Jacob Peck), William (S. C.), Elizabeth (b. 1768, m. William Dunlap, 1790), Lewis (S. C.), —— (m. Mr. —— Surber), Joanna (m. —— Eastham), Winifred (m. James Frazier), 2 others. 2. James—son of 1—b. 1761— m. Mary Frazier—C · William R., Julia F. (m. George A. Armentrout).

Cowan.—1. Agnes—m. John Brush, 1802. 2. Andrew—son of 9—d. 1836—m. Susan —— —C: Samuel, William A., David T., Esther, Eliza, Andrew H., James B., Joseph F. 3. Betsy—m. Joseph Defries, 1789. 4. George—m. Caty Epley, 1810. 5. James—m. Peggy Wright, 1806. 6. John—m. Margaret Weir, 1796. 7. John—m. Sally Paxton, 1815. 8. Mary —m. —— Buckridge, 1795. 9. Mary—m. James Alexander, 1805. 10. Samuel—m. Mary —— —C: Andrew (see 2), David, Mary, Isabella, Sarah M. (d. 1818), Elizabeth, Jenny, Rebecca (m. Thomas Wauson, 1803).

Cowden.—1. James—has stone house near Samuel McDowell's 2. William—d. 1748 —m. Jane ——— —will witnessed by Walter Eakin, Samuel and Alexander Moore—C (minors): John, William.

Cox.—1. Abraham—m. Mary Muterspaw, 1809. 2. George—m. Elizabeth ——— —in suit, 1764. 3. Nathaniel Cox—m. Mary Steele, 1812. 4. ——— m. Eve Stoner by 1826.

Craig.—1 Charles—m. Mary Graham, 1790. 2. James B.—m. Polly Tooly, 1815.

Craven.—1. Jane T.—m. Matthew Garvey, 1812. 2. Sarah—m. Barnet Rupe, 1789.

Crawford.—1. Alexander—d. 1768c—C: Rebecca (b. 1752), Alexander, Robert, Samuel (b. 1759). 2. Alexander—d. 1830—m. Mrs. Elizabeth McClure, 1796—C: Polly, Catharine, Betsy (m. William Logan), Robert, James. 3. Elizabeth—m. William Stainer, 1801. 4. James—d. 1803—m. Catharine ———, d. 1815—C: Mary A., Martha (m. ——— Montgomery), Elizabeth (m. Thomas Leech, 1792), Sarah (m. John Walker, 1797), Rachel (m. Thomas Mitchell, 1799), Margaret (m. Alexander Harris, 1790), Mary (m. William McNabb, 1787), Michael, Thomas—one son seems to have m. Patsy Leech, the other Eleanor ———. 5. James—1749. 6. Jane—b. 1781—m. Thomas Paxton. 7. Jean M.—m. John Coleman, 1808. 8. John—m. Margaret Holmes by 1819. 9. John—m. Sarah Rowlison, 1818. 10. John—m. Rachel Barclay, 1790. 11. Mary—m. Gilbert Campbell, 1797. 12. Robert—shoemaker near Steele's mill, 1767. 13. Robert (see 2)—C: Nancy. 14. Thomas —son of Michael and bro. to James—d. 1824. 15. Thomas—m. Jenny Todd, 1794. 16. William—d. 1783—m. Mary ——— —C: Elenor, Isabel, Mary, Elizabeth, William, George, John.

Cress (Cross?).—1. Betsy—m. William Flint, 1803. 2. Henry—m. Christianna Bay, 1794. 3. Jacob—m. Elizabeth Linn, 1802. 4. Margaret—m. George F. Moats, 1817. 5. Mary —m. John Upton, 1808. 6. Mordecai—m. Fanny Baggs, 1801.

Crockett.—1. Alexander—d. 1781—had mill—personalty (1784), $770.67—m. Mary ——— —C: Robert, John, Margaret, Elizabeth, Mary, Martha. 2. Robert—m. Ann ——— —C: Hannah (m. 1, ——— Irwin, 2 James Logan). 3. Robert—m. Mary Hodge, 1804. 4. ——— —m. Polly Dunlap, 1808.

Croddy.—1. Elizabeth—m. Charles Roach, 1804. 2. John—d. 1838—C: John (has John and George), Christopher, William (m. Polly ———), Ann (m. Samuel Ginger), Elizabeth (m. ——— Roach), Achilles, Margaret 3. Margaret—dau. of 2—d. by 1838—m. Garret Peck, 1810.

Culton.—1. Alexander—d. 1827—m. Rebecca Woods, 1782—C: Joseph, Nancy (m. Samuel Porter), Peggy (m. ——— Rodgers), Alexander. 2. James—d. 1824—C: James, Patrick, Priscilla (m. ——— Walker), Robert, Joseph W. 3. Nancy—m. Alexander Walker, 1797. 4. Patrick—m. Mary Hutchinson, 1807—Tenn. 5. Polly—m. David Porter, 1803. 6. Polly—m. John McCown. 7. Robert—m. Elizabeth Kelso, 1783. 8. Robert—d. 1806—C: Mary. 9. Robert—d. by 1824—son of 2—C: James. 10. Robert—d. 1781—personalty, $442.25—C: James, Alexander, Robert, 2 dau.

Cummins.—1. Elizabeth—m. Andrew McKnight, 1793. 2. Esther—m. John L. Paxton, 1812. 3. Gabriel—m. Jean Walker, 1787. 4. James—d. 1831—C: William, Samuel (has James), John A. 5. John A.—m. Ann C. Shields, 1818. 6. Martha—m. John Scott, 1814. 7. Polly—m. Charles Tooly, 1805. 8. Robert—m. Letty Ford, 1810. 9. Samuel—m. Sally Paxton, 1809. 10. William—m. Sally Cunningham, 1818.

Cunningham.—1. Hugh—m. Sarah ——— —d. in Botetourt, 1772—C: John (m. Mary McKee), Isibel, ——— (John Young)—estate, $1365.42—James Davis, stepson—witnesses to will: James McMath, Michael Johnson, Robert Hamilton.

2. Isaac—d. by 1760—m. Jean ——— —C: John.

3. Jacob—d. 1759—admr: Hugh and John—C: James.

4. James—m. Margaret ——— —C: Moses (m. Hannah ———), Jacob (see 3), James, Isaac, John, Mary, Elizabeth.

MISCELLANEOUS DATA   481

5. James—son of 4—m. Agnes Moore (?)—C: Agnes (b. 1776), William, Peggy, Taylor, 1807), Elizabeth (b. 1780, d. 1856, m. John Moore, 1801), John (b. 1782, m. Betsy Cunningham, 1801, Margaret Kirkpatrick, 1803), Nancy (m. John Taylor, 1806), Isabella (m. Isaac Lackey, 1807), Polly (m. William Hutton, 1807), Patsy (m. David Ford, 1813), James (m. Polly Leach, 1818), Jacob (m. in Botetourt).
6. James—d. 1807—C (minors): Isabella, Martha, Jacob.
8. James—m. Mary Weir, 1781.
9. Jane (widow)—d. 1819—C: Ollner (m. ——— Gilmore), Polly (m. ——— Hull).
10. Jane—m. Thomas Dougherty, 1811.
11. Jean—m. Samuel Smith, 1806.
12. John—C: Patrick, Robert (b. 1739, d. 1813), John, David, several dau.
13. John—d. 1765—C: Moses, Hugh, Elizabeth, James, Jacob, Mary, Anna.
14. John—m. Jane Garner, 1808.
15. Margaret—b, 1740, d. 1837, m. Robert Armstrong of S. C.,—her mother a McKemy.
16. Martha—b. 1730c—m. Matthew McClung.
17. Richard—m. Esther Mitchell, 1810.
18. Robert—guardian of Martha Campbell, 1747.
20. Robert—m. ——— Kilpatrick, by 1772.
21. Sally—m. William Cummins, 1818.
22. Samuel—d. 1746c—m. Mary ———, who m. Andrew Mitchell, 1747—C: Margaret.
23. Thomas—d. 1806—C: William, Isabella, Betsy, Jenny.
24. Walter—son of John and Sarah—1773.
25. William—m. Rosanna Welch, 1801.
26. William—m. Peggy Taylor, 1807.
27. ———m. Polly Welch by 1821—C: Jean, Nancy, Sally.

Curry.—1. George—m. Agnes Hamilton. 2. James—m. Hannah Archibald, 1798. 3. Jean—m. Andrew Harper, 1794.

Dale.—1. Isabella—m. James Lawson, 1791. 2. Hannah—m. David Lawson, 1793. 3. Rebecca—m. Andrew K. Lawson, 1817. 3. Samuel—1792.

Dalton.—1. Benjamin—d. 1802c—C: Polly. 2. Benjamin—m. Sally Payne by 1804. 3. Benjamin—m. Hannah B. ——— —d. 1835—C: Samuel, Benjamin—d. by 1835. 4. Benjamin—son of 3—C: John, Benjamin, Thomas. 5. Benjamin—m. Elizabeth Welch, 1810. 6. Samuel—son of 3—C: Lucy W. (m. ——— Jordan), Sarah (m. ——— Dunkum), Esther A., Benjamin F., Robert, Francis, Mildred, Selina. 7. Thomas W.—b. 1817, d. 1882— son of 5—m. (1) Margaret Miller, (2) Margaret Glendy—C (by first w.): Thomas C., 4 others.

Davidson.—1. Andrew—m. Susan Dorman, 1807. 2. Andrew B.—b. in Botetourt, 1780, d. 1861—minister. 3. Ann E.—m. John Wilson, 1796. 4. Anna—m. Robert Kirkpatrick, 1799. 5. Elizabeth—m. Henry McKay, 1795. 6. Elizabeth—m. William H. Letcher, 1810. 7. James—m. Polly Gilmore, 1808. 8. James—son of 20—C: Madison G. (b. 1817c, d. 1895, m. Martha McCutchen), C——— H. 9. James D.—son of 1—m. Hannah McD. Greenlee, 1836. 10. John—d. 1762—m. Elizabeth ———. 11. John—d. 1835, "far advanced in life"—C: John, William, Joseph, Phebe, Patsy (m. William H. Letcher, 1810), Mary (m. ——— Rogers). 12. John—m. Sally McCrea, 1801. 13. John—m. Elizabeth Erwin, 1807. 14. Joseph —m. Jinny Wilson, 1805. 15. Matthew—m. Elizabeth Gordivare, 1807. 16. Robert—m. Christina Fink, 1808. 17. Robert G.—m. Lucinda D. Hyde, 1819—Kerr's Cr. 18. Robert— d. 1751—m. Ann ——— —C: John, Mary (m. ——— Huston). 19. Sally—m. William— m. Elizabeth ——— —bro. to John, Ann (m. ——— McAmey). 22. William—m. Elizabeth Vance, 1790. 23. William—m. Elizabeth McCrea, 1792. 24. William—m. Jinny Davidson,

1799. 25. William—m. Martha Gilmore, 1811. 26. ——(m. Mary Willson by 1823). 27. ——(m. Mary McClure, 1740c). 28. ——(m. Martha Hutton).

Davis.—1. Benjamin—m. Catharine Thomas, 1808. 2. Bowling—d. by 1815—C (minors): Elizabeth, Maria, Bowling. 3. Daniel—m. Susannah Shaw, 1816. 4. David—m. Polly Willson, 1810. 5. Eleanor—1746—C: Samuel. 6. Elizabeth—m. Larkin Tungit, 1816. 7. Hugh—d. 1786—m. Frances ——— —C: Hugh, James, Janet (m. ——— Doak), Rosannah (m. ——— Thompson), Mary (m. ——— Rowan), Nancy, John, Nathaniel, Josiah. 8. Hugh—son of 7—d. 1786c—has land on Salt Lick, tributary of Ohio, surveyed for John Davis, Jr., July 20, 1773, and sold to Hugh. 9. James K.—merchant at Fancy Hill, 1839. 10. James—m. Mary ——— —Todd's Cr., 1788. 11. Jesse—m. Nancy Paton, 1806. 12. John—m. Mary Presly, 1788. 13. Joseph Daviess—m. Jean, sister to Mrs. Margaret McKee. 14. Judy—m. James Shaw, 1817. 15. Keziah—m. James Ramsay, 1798. 16. Leanna—m. John Dunfield, 1810. 17. Maria—m. Thomas Harris, 1815. 18. Mary—m. Edmund McCoy, 1817. 19. Nancy—m. Andrew Graham, 1819. 20. Peggy—m. Daniel Wright, 1799. 21. Polly—g'dau. of Mary Mackey, 1810. 22. Rebecca Daviess—m. John Scott, 1816. 23. Richard—m. Mary Wilson, 1803. 24. Robert—neighbor to Halbert McClure, 1787. 25. Sarah S.—m. James Braford, 1793. 26. William—m. Elizabeth Martin, 1795. 27. William—m. Priscilla Dawson, 1801. 28. William—Forks, 1768.

Dawson.—1. William—m. Dinah McCormick, 1795. 2. Priscilla—m. William Davis, 1801.

Deal (Dale).—1. George—m. Susanna Whiteman, 1809. 2. Samuel—m. Isabella Lawson, 1793.

Dean.—1. Charles—m. Rachel Smith, 1818. 2. ——— m. Elizabeth Letshaw, 1819. 3. John—b. 1759. 4. Samuel—m. Nancy McDonnel, 1803.

Dennison.— ——— m. Elizabeth Goodbar—b. 1775c.

Dial (Dale).—1. Catharine—m. John Riddle, 1909. 2. Catharine Dyal—m. Charles Walker, 1798. 3. Mary M.—m. Elijah Walker, 1800.

Dickey.—1. Adam—m. Hannah Dougherty, 1810. 2. Jenny—m. Peter Hull, 1805. 3. John—m. Mary Walker, 1801. 4. Joseph—m. Margaret Johnston, 1804. 5. Margaret—m. William Martin, 1801. 6. Mary—m. Richard Butt, 1797. 7. Nancy—m. William Duncan, 1801.

Dingledine.—1. Balsor—m. Susannah Hoilman, 1812. 2. Elizabeth—m. John Moore, 1817.

Dickson.—1. Agnes—b. in Pa., 1785c—m. James Moore. 2. David—m. Susanna McNutt, 1790. 3. James—d. 1797—C: Samuel, Patrick, Agnes (m. ——— Telford), James, Robert. 4. James—m. Martha ——— —d. 1811—C: Thomas, John, James, Martha, Nancy. 5. James —m. Nancy Douglass, 1804. 6. John—brother-in-law to James (Agnes) Paxton. 7. James —m. Nancy Douglass, 1800c. 8. Nancy—m. Andrew Bogan, 1799. 9. Patrick—son of 3— d. 1802. 10. Patsy—m. Robert Templeton, 1809. 11. Robert—m. Eliza Baker, 1799. 12. Robert—son of 3—C: Nancy. 13. Samuel—m. Mary Tedford, 1789. 14. Thomas—m. Sarah Paxton, 1809. Thomas.

Doak.—1. Ann—b. 1784, d. 1866, m. Hugh, M. Guffey. 2. James—m. Jane Dunn. 3. John W.—b. 1770c—m. Jane McClure. 4. Robert—immigrant—m. ——— Breckenridge, sister to Robert—C: James (see 2). 5. Samuel—brother to John—admr, David Steele, 1747. 6. Samuel—immigrant—m. (on voyage) Jane Mitchell.

Dods.—1. Alexander Dods—d. 1823—m. Peggy ——— —C: John, Alexander. 2. Christana—m. William Moore, 1812. 3. Jenny—m. Benjamin Beeson, 1812. 4. John—Lavina Rowlinson, 1816.

Dold.—Samuel M.—merchant, 1831.

Donnald.—1. James—Nancy Paxton, 1813. 2. John—Betty Paxton. 3. Margaret—m. William Keys, 1802.

Donaho.—1. Dennis—m. Anness Moody, 1787. 2. Hugh—in Ky(?), 1789—C: ———m. Robert Campbell of Aug. 3. John Donihoo—m. Martha M. Walker, 1811. 4. Nancy Donohoe—m. James Ky, 1811. 5. Susnna Donahow—m. Thomas Rowan, 1789. 6. William Donahy—m. Betsy Wine, 1808.

Dorman.—1. Charles P.—m. Amanda McCue. 2. James B.—son of 1—b. 1823, d. 1873, m. Mary J. White Newman, 1871. 3. Susan—m. Andrew Davidson, 1807.

Dougherty.—1. Ann—m. Jacob Leece, 1802. 2. Anthony—d. 1792—C: Rebecca, Jacob. 3. Charles—family k. by Indians, 1759. 4. Hannah—m. Adam Dickey, 1810. 5. John—m. Hannah Letcher. 6. Nathaniel Douherty—m. Sarah Wise, 1812. 7. Polly—m. James Whiteside, 1796.

Douglass.—1. Alfred—m. Agnes A. Paxton. 2. Elizabeth—m. John Jameson, 1807. 3. Elizabeth—m. Matthew Wilson, 1811. 4. James—d. 1811—m. Elizabeth—C: William (m. Agnes McClure, 1803), John (m. Sally Hickman, 1810), Agnes, or Nancy, (b. 1783, d. 1855, m. James Dickson, 1804), Elizabeth, James (m. Elizabeth Hamilton, 1819), George, Robert. 5. Joice A.—m. William Viers, 1818. 6. Patsy—m. Jacob Mathews, 1819.

Douthat.—1. Mary J.—m. Corbin Lackland, 1819. 2. William H.—Natural Bridge, 1830.

Drummond.—George—servant to Samuel McClure, 1779.

Dryden.—1. David—d. 1772—C: Thomas, James, David, Eliner, Jane, Elizabeth, Nathaniel, William. 2. David—d. 1787c—m. Dorothy McClure—C: Thomas, Nathaniel, William. 3. David—m. Esther Glasgow, 1792. 4. David—m. Elizabeth Clyce, 1804. 5. James—m. Catharine Windell, 1796. 6. Margaret—m. Thomas Reyburn, 1803. 7. Nathaniel—m. Mary McClure, 1785. 8. Polly—m. William McClung, 1810. 9. Samuel—m. Elizabeth Braford, 1803. 10. Thomas—m. Rebecca Poague, 1803. 11. Thomas—oldest son of 2—d. by 1787—C: Nathaniel.

Duff.—1. Mary—m. Isaac Thompson, 1786. 2. Roger—d. 1789—m. Mary ——— —C: Jean (b. 1786), Susanna, Isaiah. 3. Roger—d. by 1797—C: Susanna (m. Joseph Caldwell, 1797).

Dunlap.—1. Adam—m. ———, 1761.

2. Alexander—d. 1744—m. Ann McFarland—C: John, Robert, Alexander, Elizabeth (m. 1. William Warwick, 2. Andrew Sitlington).

3. Alexander—son of 2—b. 1743—m. Agnes Gay.

4. James—m. Agnes ——— by 1751—k. 1758—estate, $200.

5. John—son of 2—d. 1804—m. Ann Clark of James, 1761—C: Elizabeth (b. 1762, m. James Gay), Alexander (m. Jane Walkup), James (b. 1766, m. Elizabeth Bear, 1813), Ann (b. 1768, m. Robert Bratton, 1800), Mary (m. 1. Samuel Hodge, 2. Robert Crockett), John (b. 1770, m. Dorcas Dowell).

6. Madison—son of Robert, immigrant—b. 1808—m. Martha H. McKee—C: Robert K., John McK., Margaret J. (m. Dr. D. E. Strain), Bailey M., Samuel McK., William M., Walter W., Ophelia.

7. Preston—m. Jane Moore.

8. Robert—son of 2—b. 1740, k. 1781—m. Mary Gay of William, 1763—C: Anne (b. 1765, m. David McKee), William (b. 1767, m. Polly Coursey), Alexander (b. 1768, m. Jane Alexander), Margaret (m. William Deniston), Robert (b. 1772, m. Martha Graham), John (m. ——— Hickman, Bath Co.), Agnes (b. 1779, M. Samuel McCutchen).

9. William—son of 8—d. 1834—C: Elizabeth, Alexander, Robert (b. 1791), Winifred (m. J. Fulton Whitlock, 1810), James C., William, Mary G. (m Robert? Houston), Preston L. Elizabeth.

10. ——— m. Mary Beard.
Dunn.—James—came to Rbg, 1762c—m. Martha Long—C: Samuel (m. Eleanor Brewster.
Eakin.—1 James—d. 1785—C: Elizabeth (m. Thomas Paxton, 1758c), others. 2. Peggy m. George Ford, 1805). 3. Robert—m. Mary Martin, 1778. 4. Samuel—m. Mary Moore, 1787.
Eaton.—1. Benjamin—m. Hannah Bradley, 1794. 2. Valentine—servant of John Paxton, 1755.
Echols.—Edward—b. 1817, d. 1874, d. Susan H. ———.
Edington.—1. Ann—m. Evan Day, 1801. 2. Sarah—m. Charles Kirkpatrick, 1791.
Edley.—v. David—m. Elizabeth Lawrence, 1787. 2. Nancy—m. Robert Spence, 1816. 3. Polly—b. 1805c—m. Thomas Paxton. 4. Sally—m. Arthur McCoy, 1807.
Edmondson.—1. Abraham—m. Elizabeth Smith, 1818. 2. David—son of James and Agnes—d. 1821.
Elliott.—v. Archibald—m. Phebe Jemison, 1802. 2. Hannah—m. Andrew Johnston, 1808. 3. Hugh—m. Nancy West, 1808. 4. James—d. 1799—m. Martha Elliott—C: Mary, Jean, Hannah, Margaret (m. ——— Kennedy), Martha (m. ——— McClure), James, John, William. 5. James—m. Phebe McCorkle, 1809. 6. Jane—m. William S. Bailey, 1819. 7. John—m. Sally Taylor, 1798. 8. Jane—servant of Thomas Tate, 1756. 9. John—admr. William, 1771. 10. Martha—m. Alexander McClure, 1795. 11. Moses—m. Isabella Mackey, 1810. 12. Peggy—m. George Bailey, 1819. 13. Phebe—g'dau. of Mary Little Mackey, 1810. 14. William—d. 1771—m. Jane ——— —C: James, William, Archibald, Lancelot. 15. William—d. 1795—C: James (has William). 16. William—b. 1769, d. 1856—son of Archibald and Sarah of Pa. 17. William—m. Hanna Johnston, 1808. 18. ——— —m. Jean McClure by 1779. 19. ——— —m. Sarah Taylor by 1807. 20. ———. Phebe Taylor by 1818.
Elwood.—v. George—m. Rebecca Clark, 1806. 2. Robert—m. Anna Clark, 1806. 3. Sally—m. William Patton, 1802. 4. William—m. Ann Nichols, 1804.
Entsminger.—1. Andrew—m. Mary Plott, 1791. 2. Catharine—m. Henry Plott, 1791. 3. David—m. Mary Clark, 1790. 4. John—m. Elizabeth Haslet, 1798. 5. John—m. Sarah Knick, 1818. 6. John H.—blacksmith, Cowpasture River, 1768. 7. Jonathan—m. Elizabeth Gabbert, 1794. 8. Katrine—m. William Sutherland, 1789. 9. Philip—m. Mary Wauson, 1792. 10. Rachel—m. John Ayres, 1817. 11. Sally—m. James Morris, 1817.
Epley.—1. Caty—m. George Cowan, 1810. 2. Margaret—m. Alison Tapscote, 1812.
Erwin.—1. Edward, Sr., (immigrant)—C: John (m. Jane Williams), Robert (m. Ann Crockett), Andrew (m. Ann ———), Edward (m. Mary Curry), Francis (m. Jane Curry). 2. Edward—m. Rosanna ——— —d. 1796—C: Hannah, John, Jonah. 3. Elizabeth—M. John Davidson, 1807. 4. Robert—d. 1789—C: Robert, Hannah (m. ——— Logan), Benjamin, Jonas, Joseph. 5. ——— —m. Mary Hamilton by 1786.
Evans.—1. Agnes—niece of John Murphy, 1809. 2. Andrew—m. Mary Plott, 1791. 3 David—m. Mary Clark, 1790. 4. Isaac—d. 1786—C: John, Abraham, Elizabeth, Martin, Rebecca, Rachel. 5. John—m. Rebecca Parks, 1780c. 6. John—m. Elizabeth Haslet, 1798. 7. John—m. Sarah Nick, 1818. 8. Jonathan—m. Elizabeth Gabbert, 1794. 9. Catharine—b. 1715, d. 1818, m. John White. 10. Mark—d. 1748—estate, $99.75—Daniel, admr. 11. Mary—m. David Moore, by 1750. 12. Phillip—m. Mary Watson, 1792. 13. Pussy—m. Benjamin Armstrong, 1815. 14. Ruth—m. William Black, 1798. 15. ——— —m. Margaret Ritchey, by 1780.
Ewing.—1. Anne—m. David Moore, 1800. 2. Eleanor—m. James Adams, 1813. 3. Peggy m. Thomas Patton, 1805. 4. ——— —m. Drusilla Tate—b. 1783c.
Faris (Farris).—Edward—orphan of William, 1754—Francis McCown, guardian.

Fenter.—1. Frederick, Jr.,—m. Rachel Mappins, 1814. 2. Nancy—m. John Riddle.
Fink.—1. Christiana—dau. of Timothy—m. Robert Davidson, 1808. 2. William—m. Nancy Eyers, 1807.
Finley.—1. Andrew—m. Jane Lyle, 1812. 2. Betsy—m. Michael Ocheltree, 1798. 3. Eliza L. S.—b. 1808, d. 1876, m. James Johnston. 4. James—m. —+—— Campbell by 1790. 5. John—m. Anna Letcher, 1816. 6. John T.—m. Mary J. Greenlee by 1844. 7. Michael—d. 1821—C: Polly (m. Samuel Patterson, 1797), Elizabeth (m. —— Scott). 8. Polly—m. James Smiley, 1802. 9. Sarah—m. Hugh Wilson, 1793. 10. —— —m. Jane Lyle by 1815. 11. John (m. —— Doak by 1738.)
Fleming.—John—servant to John Paxton, 1756.
Firestone.—1. Madalene—m. John Renn, 1800. 2. Susanna—m. Philip Hoylman, 1800.
Fletcher.—Agnes—orphan of Job, 1802.
Flint.—1. James—m. Margaret E. Sylor, 1809. 2. John—orphan of John, 1815. 3. John—m. Elender Deen, 1817. 4. Thomas—m. Betsy Mitchell 1812. 5. Thomas—m. Elizabeth Deen, 1817. 6. William—m. Betsy Cross, 1808. 7. —— —m. Betsy McKinsey—C (1824) : Polly, John, Betsy, Daniel.
Ford.—1. Allison—m. Eliza Tate, 1803. 2. David—m. Patsy Cunningham, 1813—n. c. 3. David—d. 1825—bro. to Patrick (N. Y.), Robert (Ireland), James, George, Elizabeth (m. —— Darst). 4. Elizabeth—m. John Skeen, 1798. 5. George—m. Peggy Aken, 1805. 6. James—m. Ann Standoff, 1800. 7. James—d. 1826—C:' William, David, Jacob, Peggy, Betsy, Polly. 8. Jacob—m. Ann Scott, 1813. 9. Jacob—m. Betsy Blair, 1813. 10. Letty—m. Robert Cummins, 1810. 11. Margaret—m. Alexander Black, 1797. 12. Polly—m. Adam Hosteter, 1812. 13. William—m. Rachel Clark, 1801.
Forehand.—1. Elizabeth Foran—m. Thomas Thompson, 1807. 2. John—d. 1838—m. Rebecca ————, 1785, b. 1756—C: Polly (m. Stephen Brown), Rebecca (m. Francis Hatton, 1819), Peggy (m. John Smith), (Monroe Co.) 3. Margaret—m. Nathan Gaylor, 1801. 4. Polly—m. William Smith, 1814. 5. Sally—m. Zachariah Woods, 1814. 6. John—m. Mary Agnor, 1814.
Forsythe.—1. Ann—m. James Armstrong, 1819. 2. Catharine—m. John Auld, 1807. 3. Elijah—d. in Ohio, 1829c. 4. Samuel—m. Jinny Moore, 1802. 5. William—m. Nelly Auld, 1809.
Fortune (Forchan).—1. John m. Sarah Forchan, 1806. 2. Robert—m. Rachel Fuller, 1809. 3. Timothy—m. Jimmy Garvin, 1816.
Foster.—Alexander—m. Sarah Campbell, 1795. 2. Mary—m. James Pinkerton, 1788. 3. William—m. Mary Gilmore by 1780.
Foutz.—David—b. in Md. 1773, d. 1858—s.
Fowler.—1. Andrew—m. Hannah Lapsley, 1812. 2. Mary—b. 1782, d. 1858, m. John Bradds—dau. of Joseph and Betsy.
Frazier.—1. George—m. Margaret Johnston, 1788. 2. James Phrasher—m. Margaret Walker by 1786. 3. John—levy-free, 1765. 4. John Frasher—m. —— Gay by 1779. 5. Joseph Frazer alias McAdams—m. Polly Houston, 1811. 6. Thomas W. —b. in Rbg, 1780, d. in Tenn., 1847.
Frush.—1. Eleanor—m. Robert Wilson, 1815. 2. Henry—m. Polly Siders, 1818. 3. Prudence—m. Matthias Hillyard, 1815. 4. Rosanna—m. John Hillyard, 1810.
Fuller.—1. Betsy—m. Eli Parent, 1818. 2. Esther—m. William Whitley, 1770c. 3. Henry—m. Catrin Salling by 1755. 4. Margaret—m. Samuel R. Smith, 1818. 5. Polly m. William Young, 1805. 6. Rachel—m. Robert Foreman, 1809. 7. William—m. Jane McQueen, 1812.
Fulton.—1. Alexander—m. Sarah Caldwell, 1787. 2. Andrew—m. Elizabeth Hall, 1780c

3. Hugh—b. 1729 b. living, 1806. 4. Hugh—m. Mrs. John Tate, 1782c. 5. James—d. 1753—C: Hugh, James, William, David, Thomas, Elizabeth, Eleanor, Jane. 6. Jane—m —— Risk, 1813. 7. John—d. by 1764—C: Elizabeth, b. 1748. 8. John—d. 1804—m. Jean —+— —C: David, John, Robert, Mary, Sarah, Jean, Elizabeth (m. —— Reed), Martha (m. George Reid, 1792). 9. Robert—son of 8.—d. 1815.

*Gabbert.—Mathias—*d. 1798—m. Christena —— —C: Hannah, Michael (m. Rachel Reed, 1786), Rebecca (m. Benjamin Hart, 1787), Peter, Elizabeth (m. Jonathan Entsminger, 1794), John (m. Judith Tuley, 1792), Sarah, Christina (m. Peter Gabbert, 1803.

*Galbraith.—*1. Eleanor—m. Mark H. Goshen, 1810. 2. Elizabeth—m. Jacob Ware, 1817. 3. Jean—m. Thomas McCleland, 1795. 4. Jean—m. Daniel Hutcheson, 1807. 5. John —1746. 6. John—d. 1815—m. Barbara —— —C: George, John, Peggy (m. John Long, 1803), Ellen (see 1), Joseph, Nancy (m. Nathaniel Warren, 1815), Jane (see 3), William (d. by 1815) 7. Peggy—m. John Leech, 1800. 8. Polly—m. Anderson Wallace, 1809. 9. Sally—m. John Henry, 1818.

*Gamewell.—*William—merchant, 1800.

*Gardiner.—*1. Francis—m. Polly Hinkle, 1797. 2. James—m. Mary Shirley, 1788. 3. Nancy—m. James Lowther, 1803.

*Garner.—*1. Jane—m. John Cunningham, 1808. 2. Susanna—m. James Smiley, 1805.

*Garrison.—*1. Priscilla—m. Thomas Patterson, 1794. 2. Susanna—m. Alexander Black, 1797.

*Garvey.—*1. John—d. by 1809—C (minors): Matthew, John. 2. Matthew—m. Jane T. Craven, 1812.

*Garvin.—*1. Jinny—m. Timothy Forchan, 1816. 2. Joseph—m. Nancy Clark, 1808. 3. Mary—m. George Smith, 1803. 4. Thomas—d. 1803—m. Sarah —— —C: Joseph, David, John, Rebecca.

*Gay.—*1. Agnes—b. 1745—dau. of 6.—m. Alexander Dunlap. 2. Ann—m. Richard B. Paine, 1810. 3. Elizabeth—m. Alexander Brown, 1784. 4. Henry—d. 1760—m. Mary ——. 5. Henry—d. 1779—m. Marthew ——, d. 1785—C: Sarah, Ann, Marthew, Reckbkah, Sarah; 4 of whom m. John Gay, John Frasher, a Gillespie, a Moore.

6. James—son of 18—d. 1758—m. (1) Sarah Matton of Matthew, (2) Elizabeth Dunlap, (3) Mrs. Mary Kirtley Barnes—C: John, Agnes, Jane, James, Martha, Samuel, Robert.

7. Jane (widow)—sister to Hannah, Martha—C: Robert, Martha, Samuel.

8. Jean—dau. of 6.—m. Samuel Stevenson, 1771.

9. John—son of 18—d. 1776c—m. Jean Ramsay—C: John, Mary, Elizabeth, Jean (m. Humphrey Montgomery).

10. John—son of 9—m. Agnes McKee—Ind.

11. John—son of Henry—d. by 1759—C: Henry.

12. John—son of 6.—b. 1740—m. Sarah Lockridge.

13. Polly—m. John M. Cale, 1815.

14. Robert—m. Hannah Moore, 1793.

15. Robert (g'father to Agnes Reagh)—m. Mrs. Sarah Jameson, 1750c.

16. Robert—d. 1816—m. Sarah —— —C: Martha, Ann (see 1), Mary (m. —— Gilkeson).

17. Thomas—m. Mary Swearingen, 1791.

18. William (immigrant)—C: William, John, James, Robert, Samuel, Eleanor (m. William Kincaid).

19. William—son of 18—d. 1755—m. Margaret Walkup—C: Mary (m. Robert Dunlap, 1763), Agnes (m. Robert Clark), John (s), Robert (s).

MISCELLANEOUS DATA 487

20. William—m. Mary Craig, 1788.
21. William—orphan of William, 1767.
22. ――― —m. Jean Kirkpatrick by 1777.

Gaylor.—1. Catharine—m. Michael Pearman, 1792. 2. Edward Gealor—m. Barbara ――― —C: John (b. 1772, d. 1857, s). 3. Edward—m. Barbara Nicholas, 1739. 4. Esther —m. James Riley, 1791. 5. John—m. Eleanor Connor, 1800. 6. Nathan—m. Margaret Foran, 1801. 7. Nelly—m. John Smith, 1791.

Geerhart.—1. Catharine—m. Jacob Keller, 1803. 2. Elizabeth—m. Christian Trout, 1795. 3. Henry—m. Barbara Young, 1794. 4. Lewis—m. Pheby Jacob, 1807. 5. William—m. Sarah Morris, 1801.

Gibson.—1. Eleanor—m. George Guilenger, 1806. 2. Daniel—d—1751—C: Alexander. 3. George—m. Eleanor Lowry, 1798. 4. Mary—m. John McCrea, 1788. 5. Robert—d. 1760 —m. Isabella ――― —C: Robert, George, John. 6. Rosey—m. James Sweet, 1792. 7. William—m. Elizabeth McCormick, 1794. 8. William—d. 1820—m. Lettice ――― —C: John, Sarah, Alexander, Patrick. 9. Jane—m. Nathaniel Paxton.

Gilkeson.—Henry—d. by 1820—m. Mary Gay—C: Sally, James, Hugh, Mary H.

Gill.—1. Elizabeth—m. James Peel, 1800. 2. James—m. Sophia Kinging, 1810. 3. Presly—m. Sarah Butt, 1798. 4. Rachel—m. John Ayres, 1793. 5. Rachel—m. Theophilus Smith, 1797. 6. William—m. Catharine Ayres, 1793.

Gillespie.—1. James—d. 1769—bro. to John—C: John, James, William, Agnes, Elizabeth. 2. Martha—g'dau. of Martha Kilpatrick, 1823. 3. William—m. (1) Anne Houston, 1794, (2) Isabella Houston Henderson—C: Polly (m. S. ――― Bird), Betsy (m. Abram Bird), James (Peggy Houston), John (m. Patsie Houston), Robert, Nancy.

Gilmore.—1. Archibald—m. Jane ――― —C: Robert (b. 1780, d. 1855, m. Martha ―――) 2. James—d. 1782—C: Joseph, William, Samuel, John, Mary (m. William Foster), Margaret (m. ――― Anderson), Martha (m. ――― Hall), James.
3. James—m. Sarah Davidson by 1802.
4. James—m. Polly Grigsby, 1813.
5. Jane—m. Thomas Lackey, 1813.
6. John—d. 1759—admr, Thomas.
7. John d. 1838—w. already d. —C: Thomas, William, Sarah, Martha (James Lecky), Magdalene.
8. John—b. 1758—orphan of Thomas—John, guardian.
9. John—d. 1781—m. Elinor Cunningham—C: James, John.
10. John—m. Elizabeth Beach, 1791.
11. John—m. Polly Orbison, 1808.
12. John—m. Elizabeth Wallace by 1779—C: Martha.
13. Joseph—bro. to Thomas of Kerr's Cr.—m. Susanna Paxton, 1793—C: Madison (b. 1794, d. 1859, m. Janetta M. Houston), Paxton (m. Sarah P. Irvine), Mary, James P. (s), Eliza, Thomas, Joseph.
14. Martha—m. William Davidson, 1811.
15. Mary—m. Jesse Rowland, 1819—(see 13).
16. Mary—m. Joel Layne by 1828.
17. Nancy—m. Andrew McCampbell, 1817.
18. Polly—m. James Davidson, 1808.
19. Robert—d. 1779c.
20. Robert—m. Martha Paxton, 1818.
21. Thomas, Jr.—k. 1763—m. Jennie ――― —admr, James and John.
22. Thomas—m. Margaret Leech, 1815.

23. William—Kerr's Cr., 1822.
24. ———— —m. Sally Holbrook by 1826.
25. ———— —m. Polly Moore by 1838.

Ginger.—1. Henry—m. Patsy Alison, 1817. 2. Ludovick—d. 1812—m. Anne ———— —C: Henry, Samuel, and others, both sexes. 3. Samuel—m. Lydia Alison, 1817. 4. Samuel—m. Ann Croddy, by 1838.

Glasgow.—1. Arthur—d. 1822—m. Rebecca McNutt McCorkle, 1782c—C: Joseph, Robert, John, Peggy, Rebecca (m. John Carr, 1804), Nancy (m. ThomasMcCleland, 1804). 2. Esther—m. David Dryden, 1792. 3. Jenny—m. Thomas Patton, 1805. 4. John—son of 1—C: Arthur (b. by 1819). 5. John—m. Patsy McNutt, 1815. 6. Joseph—son of 1—C: Rebecca J. (b. by 1819). 7. Joseph—m. Nancy Glasgow, 1805.

Glass.—1. Robert—m. Jean Dalton, 1817. 2. ———— —m. Daniel Lyle by 1807.

Gold.—James—Lexington, 1796—C (?): Peggy (m. Adam Bickle, 1817), Robert (m. Margaret Hall, 1795).

Good.—Polly, orphan of John Good, 1801.

Goodbar.—1. Elizabeth—b. 1777, d. 1853, m. John Davidson—dau. of Joseph and Nancy. 2. Joseph, Sr.—d. 1807—m. Agnes ———— —C: John (Rachel Hosteter, 1809), Mary, Elizabeth (m. Robert Irvin, 1800), Joseph (m. Mary Irvin, 1806).

Goodwin.—1. Byrd—m. Polly Sally, 1804. 2. Cornelius—m. Hannah Paxton, 1796. 3. ———— —m. Mary Reed by 1816.

Gordon.—1. John—m. Mary Strange, 1813. 2. Sarah—m. Thomas Brown, 1786. 3. Sarah A.—m. William Jones, 1812. 4. Nancy—m. George Strickleather, 1807. 5. John, Sr. —d. 1825—C: Peggy (m. Joseph White), Nancy, Betsy, Sarah (see 3), William, Polly, James, Robert. 6. James—son of 5—d. by 1821—C: Jane, James, John, Samuel.

Gore.—1. James—m. Rebecca Ross, 1790. 2. Jane—m. William Lowe, 1811. 3. John —m. Nancy Taylor, 1790. 4. ———— —m. Priscilla Sare by 1788.

Goul.—1. Christian—d. 1839—C: Betsy A., William, John, James. 2. George—m. Elizabeth ———— —1782. 3. Margaret E.—m. Peter Nicholas, 1783. 4. ———— —d. 1841— m. Nancy McCown.

Graham.—1. Andrew—C: Andrew (b. 1782, d. 1855). 2. Andrew—m. Nancy Davis, 1819. 2x. Christopher—d. 1748c—C: ———— (m. Joseph Walkup), probably also Robert (m. Jean Hicklin). 3. Edward—m. Margaret Alexander, 1792. 5. George—m. Rebecca Patterson, 1803. 5. James—orphan of William Grimes, 1801. 6. James—m. Isabella Hartless by 1820. 7. James—m. Margaret Whiteman, 1815. 8. Jane—m. John McClenahan, 1812. 8x. John—C: Lancelot, John (b. 1726,m ———— Walkup), Robert (m. Elizabeth Lockridge), Florence (m. James Graham, 1762), Elizabeth (m. Robert Armstrong), Jane (m. Andrew Lockridge), Anne (m. John Kinkead), Rebecca. 9. Margaret—m. John Wallace, 1785. 10. Martha—d. 1796—C: Ann. 11. Mary—m. Isaac Trimble, 1787. 12. Michael—m. Elizabeth Lyle, 1786. 13. Nancy—m. Charles Craig, 1790. 14. Polly—m. Thomas Booz, 1817. 15. Sally—m. William S. Lacy, 1816. 16. Samuel—d. 1815—m. Betsy ———— — nephew to John of Montgomery Co. 17. Samuel B.—m. Sally Paxton, 1816. 18. William —d. 1748—m. Jane ———— —C: James, David—admr., John. 18. William—d. 1797—C: Jehab, Jenny, Polly, Susanna, Peggy, William, James. 19. William—bro. to 8x—m. Jane Armstrong—C: David (m. Jean Walkup), James (b. 1741, m. Florence Graham, 1762). 20. William—m. Polly Sample, 1811. 21. ———— —m. ———— Mackey by 1810—C: James, William. 22. ———— —m. Mary Walker by 1797.

Grant.—William—merchant near Reid Alexander's mill, 1835.

Gray.—1. Agnes—witness in suit, 1747. 2. Ann—m. James McClung, 1755c. 3. Jacob— witness for Borden, 1752. 4. John—d. 1752—m. Agnes ———— —C: Jacob, William, David,

Joseph, Benjamin, Ann. 5. Margaret—in Ky., 1824—sister to Magdalene Campbell. 6. Thomas—orphan of Joseph, 1784. 7. William—levy-free, 1764—guardian of Benjamin of John, b. 1745. 8. ———— —m. Agnes McClung, 1750c.

Green.—1. Betsy—m. Stephen G. Chittum, 1819. 2. Henry—m. Rebecca Taylor, 1799. 3. Matilda—m. William Chittum, 1819. 4. Milly—m. Samuel Biddle, 1800. 5. Samuel—m. Elizabeth Ciders, 1814.

Greenlee.—1. Griselda—m. John Caskey, 1811.
2. David—m. Hannah Grigsby, 1818.
3. James—d. 1762c.—m. Mary E. McDowell—C: John, Robert, James, Grace (m. Charles McDowell), Mary (b. 1745, m. Hugh Hays), David, Samuel, Margaret.
4. James—son of 3—d. 1813.
5. James—b. 1769, d. 1840, m. Mary Paxton, 1812—son of 9—C: Hannah McD. (m. James D. Davidson, 1836), Mary J. (John F. Finley), John F. (b. 1817, d. 1915, s), Sarah A. E. (m. James L. Watson), Martha T., William P. (m. Lizzie Foster, 1850), Frances. 6. James—m. Betsy Campbell.
6. James—m. Sarah Caskey, 1805.
7. James—m. Polly Paxton, 1798.
8. John—son of 3—b. 1734c—d. 1810c—m. Jane Grigsby—n. c.
9. John—son of 4—m. Sarah McClenahan.
10. John M.—m. Mary Greenlee, 1810.
11. Polly—m. William Bailey, 1809.
12. Robert—b. 1736—son of 3—Tenn., 1772.
13. Samuel—b. 1743—son of 3—m. Mary ———— —Ky. 1796.
14. ———— —g'dau. of 3—b. 1776—m. Ephraim McDowell.

Greer.—1. Alexander—d. 1815—m. Mary ———— —admr., Samuel Eakin. 2. Robert—d. 1828—m. Margaret ————. 3. Mary—m. Joseph Kennedy, 1793—C: Alexander.

Grigsby.—1. Betsy—m. David Templeton, 1818.
2. Hannah J.—m. David Greenlee, 1818.
3. James—C: Benjamin (b. 1770, d. 1810).
4. James—m. Mrs. Rebecca Wallace, 1785.
5. Hugh B.—son of Benjamin (see 3).
6. Jane—m. Robert Pettigrew, 1818.
7. John—b. 1720, d. 1794—m. Elizabeth ———— —C: John, Charles (m. Elizabeth Wallace, 190), William (m. Sally McClure, 1790), Sarah (m. ———— Welch), Jane (b. 1769, d. 1832, m. William Paxton, 1787), Rachel (m. Alexander McNutt, 1790), Martha (m. Alexander Trimble, 1793), Elizabeth, Frances (m. Thomas Beckham, 1800), Joseph, Elisha, Reuben.
8. John—m. Phebe Paxton, 1815.
10. Phoebe—m. Robert Trench, 1817.
11. Polly—m. James Gilmore, 1813.
12. Polly—m. Andrew Weis, 1793.
13. Reuben—b. 1780, d. 1863, m. Virlinda A. Porter.

Groves.—1. Elizabeth—m. Thomas Pullen, 1809. 2. Mary—m. Daniel Miller, 1785.

Guinn.—1. Anne—m. William Morris, 1799. 2. Daniel—m. Betsy Picket, 1819. 3. William Gywnne—d. 1772.

Gutherie.—1. Robert—d. 1789—m. Esther ———— —C: John, Phoebe (m. John Gadberry, 1791), Mary, Sarah, Richard (m. Elizabeth McEntosh, 1790), Robert—John King, g'son.

Hall.—1. Alexander—m. Mary Howard, 1786.

2. Alexander L.—m. Jane L. Paxton, 1818.
3. Andrew—d. 1798—m. a dau. of William ———, a Borden purchaser —C: (n. Samuel Houston), Jenny (m. John Houston, 1788), Margaret (m. Robert Gold, 1795), Nancy T. (m. James Steele, 1798).
4. Andrew—m. Isabella McClure, 1799.
5. Betsy—m. Thomas Houston, 1802.
6. Eliza—dau. of John—1804.
7. Edward—m. Eleanor Stuart—C: Elizabeth (m. Andrew Fulton, 1780c).
9. Elizabeth—John Raredon, 1797.
10. Elizabeth—m. Henry Leech, 1815.
11. Grace—d. 1823.
12. James—m. Patsy Leech, 1816.
13. James—d. 1816—C: William, Elizabeth (m. ——— Houston), Martha b. 1807, (m. James Montgomery), Nancy, Isabella, Peggy, Polly, Sally, James.
14. John—bro. to 11—C: George, Grace—1823.
15. John—m. Sally Wilson, 1790.
16. John—m. Rachel Hopkins, 1795.
17. John—m. Jean Smith, 1796.
18. Mary A.—m. Robert McCormick, 1808.
19. Nancy—m. James Robertson, 1804.
20. Nancy—m. James Kinkade, 1819.
21. Polly—m. John Leech, 1815.
22. Sally—m. Nathan Leech, 1817.
23. William—m. Jean—C: William (1766)—other C (?): Andrew (Margaret) Nathaniel.
24. William—same (?) as 23—d. 1772c—C: Andrew, Sr. (has William, Joseph) Agnes (m. —+— Berry), John, Sr., Isabel (m. ——— Buchanan), William, Nathaniel, James, George.
25. William—m. Isabella Hunter, 1792.
26. William—m. Sally Moore, 1799.
27. ——— —m. Margaret Thompson by 1798—C: Nancy.
28. ——— —m. Sarah Moore by 1821.

Hamilton.—1. Alexander—m. Eleanor Robinson, 1812.
2. Alexander—b. 1801, d. 1868.
3. Andrew—Isabella—1812.
4. Andrew—witnesses will of Jacob Clements, 1759.
5. Galbraith—son of James and Jain—b. in Berkely, 1781, d. 1857—m. Nancy ———.
6. George—m. Dorcas Coalter, 1814.
7. James—d. 1805—m. Margaret ——— —C: James, Robert.
8. James—m. Peggy Robinson, 1804.
9. John—miller, 1798.
10. John—b. 1765c—m. Mary Baggs.
11. Polly—g'dau. of Mary Mackey—1810.
12. Robert—d. 1788—m. Margaret ——— —C: William, Joseph, Jennet, Mary (m. ——— Erwin), Miriam, Magdalen; also 5 others who d. in massacre of 1759.
13. Robert—"late of this county"—1753.
14. Robert—1813.
14x. Robert—m. Sallie Letcher—C: Narcissa B., Mary H., John L. (m. Mary A. Hancock), Owen W. (dy), Cynthia A. (m. Robert T. Marshall), Isaacc M., James F.
15. Samuel—m. Elizabeth McCorkle, 1811.

MISCELLANEOUS DATA   491

16. William—d. 1839—m. Poll y———— —C: William, Jane (m. ——— McCown), ————
(m. William Lecky), Eliza (m. James Douglass, 1819), Julia, Nancy (m. ——— Mackey),
Mary, Alfred, John—bro. to John.
17. William—m. Elizabeth ——— by 1781.
18. William—m. Polly McCorkle, 1800.
19. William—m. Mary Thompson, 1815.
Hammond.—1. Enos—m. Margaret Keith, 1797. 2. Joel—m. Hanna Keith, 1800. 3. Thomas—m. ——— Keys, by 1781.
Hampton.—1. Joel—m. Mary Armstrong, 1797. 2. Mary—m. Stephen Yeats, 1803.
Hamil.—Robert—m. Jean ——— —1781.
Hanger.—1. Frederick—d. 1836c. 2. ——+—— —m. Polly Allen by 1825.
Hannah.—1. Elizabeth—m. James McCormick, 1784. 2. Elizabeth—m. James McIlvain, 1784. 3. Mary—m. Neal East, 1791. 4. Matthew—d. 1815—m. Martha ———, d. 1821—C: Agnes (m. John McKee, 1806), Elizabeth (m. ——— Wilson), Martha (m. John Parry, 1797), Delia (m. James L. Clowney, 1805), Polly (m. Daniel Blane, 1797).
Hardbarger.—1. Elizabeth—m. Thomas Campbell, 1801. 2. Mary—m. John Speer, 1792.
Hardy.—1. Dennis—m. Jemima ———, by 1788. 2. Harvey—m. Mary Defries, 1789.
Hartless.—1. Mary—m. John Clark, 1804. 2. Nancy—m. Joseph Jervis, 1804.
Harnest.—1. Anna—m. Samuel Downey, 1801. 2. Margaret—m. Abraham Beaver, 1816. 3. Susanna—m. John Williams, 1804.
Harnsbarger.—1. Abraham—m. Jane Vines—b. 1764c. 2. Elizabeth of Bath Co.—m. Stephen Hook, 1808
Harper.—1. Andrew—d. 1830—m. Jane Curry, 1794—C: George C., Jane, Eliza, Peggy, Hugh, James W., Andrew, William C. 2. Christina—m. Benjamin Holmes, 1796. 3. Hugh —m. Nancy McCampbell, 1807. 4. James—d. 1802—m. Elizabeth ——— —C: Mary (m. Dr. Andrew Morton), James, William. 5. James—nephew to 4. 6. James—son of 4—C: Elizabeth. 7. James—bro. to Andrew—d. 1806—m. Elizabeth ———+— —C (mostly minors): John, Martin, Sophia (m. ——— Parker), James, Mary, William. 8. James F.—merchant, 1838—m. Patsy Moore—C: Calvin M., James H., Eliza J. (m. ——— Rowan), Esteline M. (m. ——— Brown), Amanda C. (——— Oates). 9. Sally (widow)—m. William Ayres, 1818. 10. Samuel—m. Ann Brawford, 1801. 11. Thomas—m. Polly Stewart, 1817. 12. William m. Elizabeth Wilson, 1813.
Harris.—1. Alexander—m. Margaret Crawford, 1790. 2. James Hares—m. Margaret Anderson, 1790c. 3. Margaret—m. Thomas Armstrong, 1809. 4. Reuben—m. Betsy Welch, 1818. 5. Thomas—m. Maria Davis, 1815. 6. ——— —m. Deborah McCune by 1814—C: John, Mary.
Hart.—1. Betsy—m. Philip Potter, 1804. 2. Christiana—m. William Strickland, 1812. 3. James—m. Polly Null, 1801. 4. John B. (m. Julia Lyle). 5. Nancy—m. Richard Simmons, 1812. 6. Polly—m. Robert Skeen, 1817. 7. Valentine—d. 1792—C: Leonard, Moses, Benjamin (m. Rebecca Gabbert, 1787), Valentine (m. Polly Standoff, 1795), 8. William—d. 1760c.
Harvey.—1. Elizabeth—m. John Fletcher, 1791. 2. James—m. Agnes Pines, 1788. 3. James—m. Elizabeth Reed, 1789. 4. John—m. Abigail Taylor, 1789.
Hatton.—1. Elizabeth—m. Robert Young, 1795. 2. Francis—m. Rebecca Foran, 1819. 3. William—m. Rebecca Lawson, 1817.
Hays.—1. Andrew—admr, Isaac Anderson, 1747—d. 1786—miller—C: John, Charles James, Prudence (m. ——— Brownlee), Joseph, David, Mary.
2. Charles—m. Margaret ——— by 1778.

3. Charles—m. Barbara ——— —admr, William Paul, 1757.
4. George—d. 1747c—m. Sarah ——— —C: James (b. 1738).
5. Hugh—m. Mary Greenlee, 1760c.
6. James—son of 7—m. Agnes ——— —Colliers Cr., 1782—C: James.
7. John—pioneer—d. 1751—m. Rebecca ———, —C: Charles (see 2), Andrew (see 1), Barbara, Jenette (m. ——— Mills), Robert, James.
8. John—d. 1808—m. Anne ——— —C: Michael, John, Andrew, Campbell.
9. Mary—m. Robert Piper, 1795.
10. Patrick—pioneer, South River, 1747—d. 1761—m. Frances ——— —C: William.
11. John—m. Nancy McCampbell, 1789.
12. Robert—nephew to 7.
13. Samuel—admr, James Cuttland, 1759.
14. ——— —m. Prudence Campbell by 1750.

Hayslet.—1. Andrew—m. Molly Armentrout, 1802. 2. Elizabeth—m. John Entsminger, 1798. 3. Hannah—m. Samuel Beach, 1797 4. James—m. Nancy McCormick, 1798. 5. Jean —m. David Drain, 1801. 6. Mary—m. John McFarland, 1799. 7. Nancy—m. John McClenahan, 1800. 8. Nancy—m. Joseph Ford, 1813. 9. Robert—m. Ellen Henkle, 1799. 10. Thomas—m. Letty McFall, 1799.

Heizer.—Hezekiah—b. 1808, d. 1879, m. Lucy J. ———, b. 1830, d. 1893.

Henderson.—1. James—m. Prudence Campbell, 1786. 2. John (or George?)—m. Isabella Houston—C: William (m. Susan Gillespie), Jane (m. Matthew Russell), Susan (m. ——— McCullough). 3. William—improvements valued, 1751. 4. William—b. 1693c, d. 1770— C: William, David, John (has Susanna), Martha (has Finley), James; also dau. m. to David Bell, Joseph Bell, John Leeper. 5. ——— —m. Rebecca Wilson by 1804—C: James.

Henry.—1. John—m. Sally Galbraith, 1818. 2. Mary A.—m .James McClung. 3. Samuel—m. Sarah Thompson by 1786. 4. William—witness in suit, 1747. 5. William— m. Eleanor Morrison, 1787.

Hepler.—1. John—m. ——— Harness—C: Jacob, John, Polly (m. Peter Weaver), Kate (m. Samuel Ebberd), Samuel (b. 1785). 2. Samuel—son of 1—m. Kate Laird—C: Elizabeth (m. Alexander Dunlap), John (m. Margaret Miller), Isaac (m. Mary E. Williams), Priscilla (m. David Burger).

Herron.—1. Walter—b. 1768, d. 1845. 2. ——— m. ——— McCampbell by 1823.

Hickman.—1 Adam—b. 1752c—m. Peggy ———. 2. George—m. Sophia Walter, 1812. 3. Hugh—m. Rebecca McNutt, 1816. 4 Jacob—m. Agnes Baggs, 1786. 5. John—d. 1784— bro. to 1. 6 Nancy (widow)—b. 1759, d. 1826. 7 Sally—m. John Douglass, 1810.

Hicks.—1. Hannah—m. James Wilson, 1809. 2. Joseph—m. Polly Campden, 1812. 3. Mary—m. Robert Lawson, 1800. 4. Mary—m. David Hosteter, 1808.

Hiers.—Samuel—1800.

Hill.—1. Joseph—m. Margaret McMillen, 1799. 2. Thomas—m. Elizabeth—by 1780. 3. William—b in N. J. 1767, d. 1853—son of James and Sarah—m. Hannah ———. 4. William—d. 1749—m. Mary ——— —C: Sarah. James, Mary, John, Joseph, Hannah, Rachel, Elizabeth.

Hilliard.—1. John—d. 1813—m. Rosanna Frush—C: Amos. 2. Matthias—m. Prudence Frush, 1815.

Hillis.—1. Abigail—m. Jacob Houglemont, 1811. 2 Mary—m. Hugh Laughlin, 1805. 3. William—C: ——— (m. William Young by 1795).

Hinds.—1. Agnes—m. Thomas Dougherty, 1800. 2. Sally—m. John Lowe, 1811.

Hite.—1. Ann—b. 1782—dau. of Daniel (Appalonia Keller) of Shenandoah Co.—m. Joseph Bear. 1x. Daniel—bro. to 1—m. Esther Bear, 1802—C: Levi (m. ——— Alexander), Mary (m. William Dunlap), Susannah (m. ——— Wardlaw), Elizabeth (m. ——— Scott).

2. George—d. 1838—C: Joel, William P., Tillman (m. Elis Holmes, 1813). 3. John—m. Betsy Riley, 1815 4. John—m. Sally Mitchell, 1819. 5. Magalin—m. William Jones, 1816. 6. Peter—m. Catharine Fowlyon, 1815. 7. Samuel—m. Betsy Wilson, 1792.

Hodge.—1. Eleanor—m. John Robinson, 1786. 2. James—d. 1809—m. Mary ———, d. 1810—C: John, Moses (d. 1813), William, James (d. 1816), Renick, Betsy, Andrew, Martha (m. ——— Gilliam), Catharine. 3. Mary—m. Robert Crockett, 1804. 4. Samuel D.—son of ——— and Mary Dunlap—b. 1800c. 5. William—d. 1824—m. Drusilla ——— —C (minors): John, Martha, William F.

Hogshead.—1. John—m. ——— Kilpatrick by 1772. 2. Rebeckah Hogset—m. Thomas Paxton, 1790.

Holbrook.—Ezra—d. 1829—m. Judith ——— —C: Selah, Thomas E., John S., Sally (m. ——— Gilmore).

Holman.—1 Jean—m. John Leech, 1808. 2. Salley—m. Thomas McCoy, 1798.

Holmes.—1. Benjamin—m. Christina Harper, 1796. 2. Benjamin—m. Jenny Welch, 1806. 3. Christopher—d 1829—m. Elizabeth ——— —C: Mary, John. 4. Gabriel—d. 1810—C: Rebecca (m. Peter Salling, 1787), Benjamin (d. by 1799), Margaret (m. John Crawford). 5. Elis—m. Tilman Hite, 1813.

Hopkins.—1. Ann—m. John McFilton, 1807. 2. David—m. Ann Scott, 1818. 3. James—d. 1810—m. Nancy ———, who went to Ohio after 1810. 4. James—m. Polly Chandler, 1817. 5. Rachel—m. John Hall, 1795. 6. William—m. Betsy Patton, 1805.

Horn.—1. Betty—m. Solomon Letshaw, 1802. 2. Edward—m. Nancy Tolly, 1809. 3. H——— —m. Barbara Kahle—b. 1783c. 4. Jacob—b. 1786, d. 1874, m. Elizabeth ———, b. 1794, d. 1857.

Hostetter.—1. Adam—m. Polly Ford, 1812. David—m. Mary Hicks, 1808. 3. David—m. Margaret Standoff, 1816. 4. Elizabeth—m. Jacob Wilhelm, 1817. 5. Jacob—m. Mary Cassady, 1801. 6. Jacob—m. Peggy Plot, 1814. 7. Mary—m. Seth Smith, 1804. 8. Rachel—m. John Goodbar, 1807.

Houston.—1. John—b. 1689, d. 1755, m. Margaret ———, 1717c —C: James (dy) Robert (b. 1720c, m. Mary Davidson), Isabella (m. William Gillespie), Esther (m. John Montgomery), John, Mary (m. ——— Blair), Samuel, Matthew.

2. Robert—son of 1—C: John, Samuel, Bettie (m. James McClung), Margaret (m. James Hopkins), Esther (m. James McKee), Mary (m. John Letcher).

3. John—son of 2—m. Anne Logan, 1769—d. 1809—C: Robert, William, Elizabeth (m. Samuel Goodman, 1803), Esther (m. John Scott, 1795), Anne (m. William H. Scott, 1804), Mary (m. John Speer, 1797).

4. Samuel—son of 2—d. 1806—m. Elizabeth Paxton—C: Paxton (s), Robert (s), James, John, Samuel, William, Isabella (dy), Mary (m. 1. Matthew Wallace, 2. William Wallace), Eliza (m. ——— Moore).

5. John—son of 1—b. 1726, d. 1798, m. Sarah Todd—C: James, John, Samuel, William (unknown), Robert, Matthew, Alice (m. William Stephenson), Margaret (m. 1| Alexander McEwen, 2. Samuel Doak), Esther (m. Joel Wallace).

6. James—son of 5—b. 1754, d. 1810, m. Elizabeth Weir—C: Polly (b. 1779, m. Andrew Irvine), George (s), William, ,Hugh W., John (dy).

7. William—son of 6—b. 1786, d. 1868, m. (1) Elizabeth H. Finley, (2) Susan Weir —C: James (unknown), Ann E. (m. George White), George W. (m. Anetta L. Wilson), Elvira, Mary J., John F., William H. (m Elizabeth H. Irvine).

8. George W.—son of 7—C: Finley W. (m. Grace A. Alexander), Mary (m. G——— W. Row), William E., Ann E.

9. William H.—son of 7—C: Charles (k. 1864), Margaret C., William H., Susan.

10. Samuel—son of 5—b. 1768, d. 1839, m. (1) Elizabeth Hall, (2) Margaret Walker, 1794—C: Elizabeth S. (m. James Paxton), Maria T. (m. Samuel Walkup), Jannetta M. (m. Madison Gilmore), Matilda R. (m John H. Myers), Elvira M. K. (m. John J. Moorman), Samuel R., ,John D.

11. Samuel R.—son of 10—b. 1806—m. (1) Mary R. Rowland, (2) Margaret P. Paxton)—C: Rutherford R. (m. Maggie Steele of Ill.) William P., Samuel A., A. Coray, Mary M., Helen A., Elizabeth M., Janet H., James B., Hubert T.

12. William P.—son of 11—b. 1843, d. 1918, m. (1) Edith J. McClung, (2) Hannah M. Barclay.

13. John D.—son of—10—b. 1809, d. 1878, m. (1) Martha Wilson, (2) Lizzie Steele, Ill.—C: Samuel W., Margaret W., Mary R., Bettie S., Horace, Ella M., Janetta M., Jennie C., Martha H., Leroy D., Robert B., Anna L., Matilda P., John, Mabel.

14. Matthew—son of 5—b. 1762, d. 1847, m. Patsy Cloyd—C: Sophia C., Emily H., Andrew C., David G., Matthew H., Cynthia M.

15. Samuel—son of 1—b. 1728c, d. 1797, m. Elizabeth MsCroskie, 1753—C: John (m. Martha Jones), James (m. 1. Esther Houston, 1780, 2. Pollie Gillespie, 1791), Robert (m. Elizabeth Lockard, 2. Martha Blackburn), William (m. Mary Black), Matthew (b. 1772, m. Martha Lyle), Elizabeth (b. 1789 of 2d w).

16. William—son of 15—C: John (m. James McNeely), Polly (m. Nelson Wright), Rebecca (m. Jefferson Young), Hettie (m. John Nichols).

Other Names:—1. Alexander—d. 1836—C: John, William. 2. Anne—m. William Gillespie, 1794. 3. James—m. Phoebe McClung, 1790. 4. John—m. Margaret McClung. 5. James—1746. 6. John—m. Jennie Hall, 1788. 7. John—m. Nancy Snodgrass, 1815. 8. Polly—m. Joseph Frazier alias McAdams, 1811 9. Robert—1742. 10. Samuel—1749. 11. Thomas—m. Betsy Hall, 1812. 12. William—m. Polly Poage, 1805—d. 1814—C: 2. 13. ——— —m Mary D. Dunlap by 1834.

Howard.—1. Elizabeth—m. William Peel, 1797. 2. James—m. Sarah Myers, 1811. 3. John—m Sarah Lawless, 1797. 4. John T —m. Sarah Willson, 1799. 5. Nancy—m. Alexander Hall, 1786.

Hoylman.—1. Christina—m. Robert Carr, 1798. 2. Christopher, or Stophel—d. 1812 m. Christianna ——— —C: Philip, Christianna; a dau. m. Abraham Troxal. 3. Daniel —m. Diannah Trevy by 1825. 4. Philip—son of 2—d. 1811—m. Susanna Firestone, 1811 —C: Daniel, Betty, Sally. 5. Philip—m. ——— Mohler. 6. Simon—m. Polly Thompson, 1808. 7. Susanna—m. Balson Dingledine, 1812.

Huffman.—1. David—b. 1766, d. 1872. 2. John—d. 1817—m. Elizabeth—C: Elizabeth m. James Wallace, 1801), Mary (m. Hezekiah Jordan, 1807), John (m. Jean McQuilten, 1809), Joseph (m. Betsy Windle, 1811), David, Sally (m. Adam Shultz, 1815), Salome (m. Samuel Chandler, 1793), Daniel, Christopher (m. Mary Windle, 1804), Rachel (m. David Lusk, 1794), ——— dau. (m. ——— Shields). 3. John H.—m. Rebecca Adams, 1817. 4. ——— —m. Esther Beard by 1811.

Hull.—1. Daniel—m. Sarah Winegar, 1812. 1x. Peter—m. ——— Linkenfelter—C: John (m. Amy Strickland). 2. Peter—m Jenny Dickey, 1805. 3. Philip—m. Elizabeth Newcomer, 1816. 4. ——— —m. Polly Cunningham by 1818.

Humphreys.—1. Alexander—m. Mary Brown, 1788. 2. Meriwether A. Humphris—b. 1806, d. 1878. 3. Samuel—m. Peggy Moore, 1812.

Hunter.—1. Isabella—m. William Hall, 1792. 2. Jean—m. Abraham Care, 1790. Mary— m. David Kingea, 1792. 4. Pamelia—m. Samuel C. Burks, 1811. 5. Sarah—m. Samuel Steele, 1755c 6. William—d. 1741c—m. Elizabeth ——— —C: ——— dau. (m. ——— Green, 1750c).

MISCELLANEOUS DATA

Hutchinson.—1. Mary—m. Patrick Culton, 1807—dau. of Robert. 2. Robert—d. 1806—C: Martha (m. —— Stewart), Susanna, Nancy, Mary, Robert, Jean (m. John Adams). 3. Robert—b. 1776, d. 1842—New P. 4. S—— m. Margery Paxton.

Hutton.—1. Gardner P.—m. Mary Potter—11 C. 2. James C.—m. (1) Nancy Montgomery, (2) Martha Davidson—C: Gardner P. (see 1), Mary V. (m. —— McCorkle). 3. William—m. Polly Cunningham, 1807—C: James C. (see 2), others.

Hymes.—1. Andrew—m. Mary Hoff, 1806. 2. John—m. Mary Kisor, 1809.

Ingraham.—Jonathan—b. 1765c—m. Margaret Agnor.

Irvine.—1. Alexander—m. Sophia W. Houston, 1818. 2. John—merchant of Lexington, 1807-1815. 3. John M.—son of Hugh and Sarah—b. in Ireland, 1786, d. 1853—m. Elizabeth ——. 4. Mary—m. Joseph Goodbar, 1806. 5. Nancy—m. Isaac Groove, Sr., 1794. 6. Nancy—m. Robert Crawford, 1819 7. Robert—d. 1822c—m. Esther —— —C: Hugh (m. Sally Ripley, 1818), George, John (m. Ann Orendorf, 1813), Robert (m. Elizabeth M. Burks, 1815), Nancy (m. Samuel Darst, 1811), Sally (m. Robert Gilmore, 1807), Tina (m. —— Gilmore). 8. —— m. Polly Houston by 1806.

Isenhower.—1. Catharine—m. John Webb, 1807. 2. George—m. Jennet Walker, 1810. 3. Jacob—m. Ann Robinson, 1808.

Jackson.—1. James—m. Hannah Shaw, 1795. 2. Margaret—m. Daniel Lambert, 1803. 3. Nancy—m Henry Miller, 1810. 4. Thomas—cousin and admr, Joseph Paxton, 1756. 5. William—d. 1828—m. Agnes —— —C: William, Mary, Margaret (see 2), Jane (m. —— Tardy).

James.—Jane—b. 1780, d. 1853, m. Jesse Camden—dau. of Samuel and Elizabeth.

Jameson.—1. John—d. 1790—m. Barbara Carlock—C: John, Jean, Cathrin, John. 2. John—d. 1813—m. Martha McClure, 1800; widow m. James Hughart. 3. John—m. Elizabeth Douglass, 1807 4. Phœbe—m. Archibald Elliott, 1802. 5. Sarah—m. Thomas Beard, 1785. 6 William—d. 1797—m. Rachel —— —C: John, William, Robert, Peggy (m. —— Armstrong), Phese. 7. William—d. 1753c—C: George, Andrew, William. 8. —— m. Nancy Patton by 1822.

Johnson.—1. Jane—m. John Sharpe, 1812. 2. John—m. Sarah Worley, 1803. 3. Peggy—m. Samuel Wilson, 1804. 4. William—m. Nancy Montgomery, 1807.

Johnston.—1. Abraham—d. 1834—C: Douglass, Robert, Thomas (m. Adaline ——), Martha, Marget. 2. Anderson—m. Nancy Windell, 1810. 3. Andrew—m. Hannah Elliott, 1808. 4. Hannah—m. William Elliott, 1808. 5. Jackson—d. 1818—C: James, John, Elizabeth (m. —— McChesney), Zachariah, Ann (m. —— White), Thomas, Alexander, Margaret (m. Robert White, 1802), Jenny (m. —— Sharp). 6. James—b. 1780, d. 1835, m. Jean Montgomery, 1807—m. Sally Boyd—Samuel (m. Mildred Wilson), James (b. 1811, d. 1880, m. Eliza L. S. Finley, 1841), Alexander (m. Ellen Wilson), Polly M. (m. Samuel McHenry), Robert (b. 1818, m. Laura E. Criss), Margaret, Humphrey, Sally (b. 1826, m. Addison Rapp), Chapman, Jean (b. 1830, d. 1864, m. Lafayette Sehorn). 7. James—son of 6 —C: William F. (m. Margaret Campbell), Matilda J. (m. John M. Wilson), James M. (m. Martha E. Patterson), Mary E., Roberta A. 3. Margaret—m. George Fraiser, 1788. 9. Margaret—m. George Dickey, 1804. 10. Nancy—m. Joseph Wilson, 1802. 11. Nancy—m. David McCampbell, 1808. 12. Thomas—m. Susan McMath—b. 1774c. 13. Zachariah—b. 1743, d. 1800, m. Ann —— —C: Thomas, George, Zachariah, Alexander, John, Elizabeth (m. Robert McChesney, 1792), James.

Jones.—1. Elis—m. Moses McClure, 1812. 2. Blackburn—m. Sarah J. Windle, 1809. 3. Elizabeth—m. —— Eyers, 1801. 4. James—m. Mary Campbell, 1787. 5. John—m. Mrs. Mary Berry, 1752c. 6. Lavinia—m. John Bunton, 1811. 7. Mary—m. Lewis Minick, 1801. 8. Mary A.—m. William Kenny, 1815. 9. Michael—d. 1831—C: William, Nicholas, Sally (m. —— Martin), Nancy (m. —— McDaniel), Lavinia (see 6), Winston, Susan (m. —— McAlison).

Jordan.—1. Alexander—m. Nancy Anderson, 1814.
2. Catharine—b. 1780c—m. James Paxton.
3. Hezekiah—m. Polly Huffman, 1807.
4. James R.—b. 1800, d. 1862—doctor.
5. John—b. 1777, d. 1854, m. Lucy Winn, 1802—C: Edwin J. (m. Mary J. Paxton, 1827), Samuel F., John W. (m. Rachel Davis), William M., Mary W., Ira F. (Mary Skeen), Lucy A. (m. Evans Christian), Isaac L.(s), George W.(s), Charles, Hezekiah K. (m. 1. Mattie Skeen, 2. ——— Penn), Benjamin J. (m. Elizabeth A. Paxton), Jessee, Robert S.(s).
6. Lewis—m. Mary Trimble, 1785.
7. Samuel F.—b. 1805—m. (1) Hannah Davis, (2) Elizabeth Liebert of Philadelphia.
8. ——— —m. Lucy W. Darst by 1835.
Keith.—1. Daniel—d. 1821—m. Elizabeth Ruth. 2. Hanna—m. Joel Hammer, 1800. 3. Margaret—m. Enos Hamer, 1797. 4. ——— —m. Lisey McColpin by 1789.
Keller.—1. Joseph—m. Catharine Geerheart, 1803. 2. Peter—b. 1778, d. 1857—son of Lewis and Sarah of Rockingham—m. Mary ———.
Kelly.—1. Alexander—1761. 2. Patsy—m. George Waskey, 1811.
Kelso.—1. Betsy—m. Robert Culton, 1783. 2. Hugh—d. 1813—m. Mary Walker—C: Joseph, William, James, Charles, Hugh (m. Fanny Moore, 1794). 3. James— b. 1761—went to Bath. 4. Ketty—m. Joseph Walker, 1794. 5. Peggy—m. ——— Walker by 1809. 6. ——— —m. Jane Walker by 1816. 7. ——— —m. Martha Allen by 1825.
Kender.—1. Peter—d. 1749c—C: Sarah, Peter, Catharine. 2. ——— —m. Dolly See by 1806.
Kennedy.—1. Andrew—d. 1821—m. Margaret ——— —C: Janet (m. William McKee), Elizabeth (m. William Mackey, 1801), Ann (m. Michael Wardlow, 1802), Margaret (m. James Young, 1802), Joseph (m. Mary Greer, 1793), William, Hugh, Rachel. 2. Andrew—m. Sarah Beard, 1797. 3. Ezekiel—m. Jane Bennett by 1779. 4. Michael—m. Eleanor McCafferty, 1786. 5. William—m. Martha Campbell by 1787. 6. William—merchant, 1787. 7. ——— —m. Margaret Elliott by 1797.
Kerr.—1. Daniel—b. 1782c—m. Margaret Black. 2. Daniel—m. ——— Kilpatrick by 1823—C: Robert, William, Nancy, Elizabeth, James, Thomas. 3. John—neighbor to David, 1753. 4. Thomas—d. 1825—bro. to James of O. and Samuel (who has Thomas and Samuel in Bedford Co., Pa.) 5. ——— —m. Isabella Robinson by 1789.
Keys.—1. Andrew—m. Sarah Beard, 1797. 2. Anthony—1803. 3. Joseph—m. Mary Greer, 1793 (?). 4. Michael—m. Eleanor McCafferty, 1786. 5. Roger—d. 1791—m. Sarah ——— —C: Benjamin, ——— (m. Thomas Haman). 6. Samuel—d. 1803—blacksmith—m. Esther ——— —C: John, William, Samuel, Andrew R., Jane, Betsy, Polly.
Kidd.—Peggy—C: Betsy (b. 1800c).
Kiddy.—1. Jacob—m. Sarah Nicely, 1808. 2. Mary—m. Adam Summers, 1802.
Kiger.—1. Anthony—d. 1806c—C: Sally. 2. Eve—m. George Linn, 1807. 3. Henry—m. Elizabeth Smith, 1807. 4. Jacob—d. 1804c—C: Benjamin. 5. ——— —m. Rebecca Reed by 1816.
Kilpatrick.—1. Charles—d. 1772c—m. Elizabeth ——— —C: Roger, Alexander, Elizabeth; dau. are m. to John Hogshead and Robert Cunningham. 2. John—d. 1823—m. Katharine ——— —C: Betsy, Samuel, Margaret (m. ——— Reid), James, Andrew. 3. Martha—widow—d. 1823—C: Elizabeth (m. ——— McCutchen), James, Mary (m. John Armstrong, 1791), ——— (m. ——— Gillespie), ——— (m. Daniel Kerr).
Kincaid.—1. Isaiah—d. 1824—m. Dolly ——— —C: Joseph, Iseah, Samuel, Rachel (m. Thomas Patton, 1817), Jinny (m. William Skeene, 1822), William, James. 2. James—m.

Nancy Hall, 1819. 3. Jean—m. David Kelsey, 1791. 4. William—ward of Thomas Fulton, 1753.

King.—1. John—g'son of Robert Guthrie, 1788. 2. Robert—d. 1749—m. Catharine ———
—C: John, Sarah, Elizabeth, Katharine.

Kingen.—1. David—m. Mary Hunter, 1792. 2. James—m. Sophia Pullen, 1797.

Kinnear.—1. Andrew—d. 1813—m. Susanna ——— —C: Hannah (m. Andrew Stuart, 1794), Andrew. 2. Givens—merchant at Fancy Hill, 1838. 3. John—d. 1829—C: John, Nancy, Paulina, Givens, Margaret (m. ——— Wilson), Andrew, Susan, Hannah, Eliza, Martha. 4. Margaret—m. David Wilson, 1819. 5. Michael—m. Elizabeth Campbell, 1786. 6. Susanna—sister to Andrew—m. Michael Kirkpatrick, 1797.

Kinney.—1. John—m. Nancy Brady, 1808. 2. William—m. Mary A. Jones, 1815.

Kirk.—William—orphan of Thomas, 1799.

Kirkham.—1. Henry—d. 1765c—m. Mary (or Margaret) ——— —estate, $629.50—C: Robert, Samuel, Michael, John (b. 1749), Henry, Jane, Margaret, Elizabeth, post. 2. Michael—d. 1746c—Robert and Henry Kirkham and Richard Woods, admr. 3. Michael—son of 1—apprenticed to learn hatter's trade, 1763. 4. Robert—d. 1749—m. Sarah ——— —estate, $150.75—C: Henry, Nancy, Elizabeth, Margaret, Sarah.

Kirkpatrick.—1. Charles—d. 1795—m. Agnes ——— —C: John, Charles, Elizabeth. 2. Charles—son of 1—C: Mary. 3. Charles—m. Polly Patton, 1806. 4. Elizabeth—m. Alexander Wiley, 1806. 5. James—m. Elizabeth Cunningham, 1815. 6. John—m. Peggy Campbell, 1808. 7. Margaret—m. John Cunningham, 1803. 8. Mary—m. John Armstrong, 1791. 9. Mary—m. James Moore, 1797. 10. Isabella—b. 1800c—m. William Paxton. 11. Michael—d. 1825—m. Susan Kinnear—C: Nancy, Joseph, Peggy, James, Andrew, Margaret (m. Moffett Brownlee, 1819). 12. Nancy—m. John McTear, 1806. 13. Peggy—m. James Reid, 1818. 14. Peggy—m. Joseph Smith, 1818. 15. Robert—d. 1780—m. Margaret ———
—C: Jean (m. ——— Gay), Elizabeth (m. ——— Stevenson), Hannah (m. ——— Hilton). 16. Robert—m. Rebecca Thompson, 1816. 17. Samuel—m. Jean Kirkpatrick, 1803. 18. Samuel—m. Jean McLaughlin, 1812. 19. William—m. Betsy Kline, 1817.

Kirkwood.—1. Catharine—m. Standly Seisson, 1796. 2. Nancy—m. Charles Seacot, 1796.

Klemmer.—George—d. 1828—m. Modlena ——— —C: George L., Andrew, David, Mary (m. Jacob Brosius), John, Elizabeth (m. Reuben Lunceford), Peggy, Polly (m. William McCormick).

Lackey.—1. Eleanor—m. William Wilson, 1791. 2. Isaac—m. Isabella Cunningham, 1807. 3. James—C: Samuel, Thomas, Nathan, 1814. 4. James—m. Jean Campbell, 1808. 5. James—m. Martha Gilmore by 1838. 6. Jean—m. Matthew Walker, 1802. 7. Nathan—m. Jane Anderson, 1819. 8. Thomas—wheelwright—m. Agnes ——— —C: Thomas (see 3). 9. Thomas—m. Martha Leech, 1800. 10. Thomas—m. Jemima Taylor, 1801,—d. 1827—C: Thomas, James, ——— (m. Matthew Walker), Isaac, Nathan, William, Martha. 11. Thomas—m. Jane Gilmore, 1813.

Lair.—1. Andrew—m. Catharine Rhoads, 1803. 2. John—d. 1803—m. Barbara ———
C: David, John, Elizabeth (m. Christian Roadcap, 1802), Barbara, Mary, Ann, Catharine, Magdalene, Susan.

Laird.—1. Ann—dau. of H. H.—b. in Botetourt, 1778, d. 1854—m. Daniel Taylor. 2. David—b. 1797, d. 1869, m. Mary ———. 3. Elizabeth—m. Thomas Edmondson, 1814. 4. James—South River, 1805. 5. James—d. 1827—C: John, Sarah (m. ——— Hannah), Polly (m. John McNutt, 1807), Elizabeth (m. Thomas P. Edmondson, 1814), David. 5. John—b. 1778, d. 1854. 6. John C.—C: John H. (b. 1836), Samuel McK., Henry R. (m. Sarah H. McCluer), Agnes J. (m. J——— P. Moore), Alexander R. (m. ———
Moore), Mary E. (m. Samuel R. Moore), James M., William R.

Lambert.—1. Daniel—m. Margaret Jackson, 1803. 2. Rebecca—m. John Linkswiler, 1816. 3. Tobias—d. 1823—m. Magdaline ——— —C: Joseph.

Lance.—1. Nancy Lants—m. Richard Parsons, 1805. 2. Peter—m. Margaret Rowlinson by 1839.

Lapsley.—1. Hannah—m. Andrew Fowler, 1812. 2. John—levy-free, 1765. 3. Joseph d. 1788—m. Sarah Woods—C: Joseph, John, others. 4. Joseph—m. Rebecca Aylett, 1804—minister. 5. Martha—m. William McBride by 1782. 6. Samuel—m. Betsy Winegar, 1814. 7. William—1780.

Larew.—1. Benjamin—m. Jean Rea, 1808. 2. Jacob—b. 1793, d. 1875—m. Margaret Gay, d. 1904.

Larkin.—1. Henry—d. 1773—m. Jean ——— —C: James, Henry, John, Mary, Elizabeth, David, Thomas. 2. James—m. Mary Tudor, 1804.

Laughlin.—Hugh—b. in Scotland, 1774c—m. Mary Hillis, 1805.

Law.—Michael—d. 1784—m. Rebecca ——— —C: Rebecca (m. John Lincks, 1787), Mary (m. Simson Sturgen, 1793), Sarah (m. Henry Vance, 1803).

Lawrence.—1. Elizabeth—m. David Edley, 1787. 2. James—m. Grace Smith, 1811. 3. ——— —m. Mary Logan by 1791.

Lawson.—1. David—d. 1823—C: David, Ann, Jane, Susan A., Hannah, Alexander. 2. Isaac—d. 1821—m. Agnes ——— —C: Jane R., Robert (m. Mary McCampbell, 1792), Isabella (m. Samuel Deal, 1793), Elizabeth (m. John Murphy, 1799), David (m. Hannah Dale, 1793), Agnes, Isaac (m. Nancy Anderson, 1815), James (m. Mary Taylor, 1810), Rebekka (m. William Hutton, 1817), Andrew K. (m. Rebecca Dale, 1817), Jean R. 3. Nancy—m. Samuel Miller, 1808. 4. Susanna—; Justin McCarty, 1815.

Leech.—1. Ann—m. John Miller, 1812. 2. Eleanor—m. Michael Crawford, 1799. 3. James—d. 1822—m. Martha ——— —C: John, Patsy (m. ——— Crawford), Susannah, Nancy, Jane (m. ——— Steele), David (m. Margaret Miller, 1788), Thomas (m. Elizabeth Crawford, 1792), James (m. Isabella Steele, 1800), Henry (m. Isabella Hall, 1815), Willam, Adam (b. 1853, s). 4. John—m. ——— Montgomery. 5. John—m. Martha McComb—Buffalo—C: James (m. Isabella Steele, 1800). 6. John—m. Peggy Galbraith, 1803. 7. John—m. Jane Holman, 1808. 8. John—m. Elizabeth Sivell, 1814. 9. John—m. Polly Hall, 1816). 10. Margaret—m. Thomas Gilmore, 1815. 11. Martha—m. Thomas Lackey, 1800. 12. Nathan—m. Sally Hall, 1817. 13. Patsy—m. James Hall, 1816. 14. Polly —m. James Cunningham, 1819.

Leister.—James—d. 1769—Samuel McDowell witnesses will—C: John, Jean, Martha.

Letcher.—1. John—d. 1793c—m. Mary Houston, d. 1820—C: Hannah (m. John Dougherty, 1799), Sally (m. Robert Hamilton, 1808), William H. (m. Elizabeth Davidson, 1810), Isaac A. (m. Julia A. Babb), Polly (m. Samule Black), James, Giles.

2. John—son of 4—m. Mary S. Holt of Augusta Co.—C: William H., Elizabeth S., Ann H., Andrew T., John D., Mary K., Virginia L., Fannie P., Greenlee D. son of 4.

3. Isaac A.—son of 1—C: John, William H., Giles P., Robert F., Julia A, Jacob J.

4. William H.—C: John (see 2), Mary B. (m. John C. Blackwell), William M., Samuel H.

5. John—m. ——— Montgomery by 1827.

Letshaw.—1. Elizabeth—m. ——— Deen, 1819. 2. Polly—m. George Danner, 1818.

Lewis.—1. Betsy—m. Jacob Brown, 1815. 2. Elias—m. Mary Whiteside, 1795. 3. Ephraim—m. Phebe Whiteside, 1810. 4. Eleanor—m. William Jameson, 1818

Leyburn.—1. George—m. Jane Ocheltree, 1815. 2. George—d. 1810—bro. to William in Scotland—C: William, John. 3. John—d. 1831—C: Mary S. (m. William W. Watts, 1819), Alice M., George W., Jane, John, Alfred (doctor), Alice M. 4. John—b. 1815, d. 1893, m. Mary L. Mercer—n. c.—minister.

Liggett.—1. Stephen Leget—m. Margaret Newcomer, 1791. 2. William Leget—m. Hanna Scott, 1792. 3. William—son of James A. of Londonderry—to Ohio, 1806—C: John (m. Mary McCormick).

Lindsay.—1. Andrew—b. 1809, d. 1883—m. (1) Sallie Davidson, 1834, (2) Mary T. Gilmore—C (by 1st w.): William, James, Mary, Sally; (by 2nd w.), Marion, Charles, Warren, Bruce. 2. James—b. 1773—m. Agnes McCampbell, 1797—C: Jane (m. ——— Renwick), William(s?), Sophia (m. ——— Kirkpatrick), James W., Andrew (see 1), Agnes (m. ——— Lacky), Mary (m. ——— Mateer), Thomas M. 3. John—m. Betsy Willson, 1791. 4. Robert—estate, 1772, $112.50. 5. Robert—Sali Logan, 1797.

Linn.—1. Christina—m. Charles Wimer, 1806. 2. Jacob Lyn—d. 1818— m. Rheua ——— —C: Peter, Jacob, Betsy (m. Jacob Cress, 1802, d. by 1816), Susanna, George (m. Eve Kiger, 1807).

Little.—1. Abraham—m. Elizabeth McAlpin, 1801. 2. David—m. ——— McCalpin by 1789—levy-free, 1801. 3. David—m. Peggy McCalpin, 1801. 4. David—m. Ann McCalpin, 1811. 5. Joseph—m. Mrs. Mary Mackey, 1785—C (1782): Elizabeth, Margaret, Joseph. 6. Joseph—m. Sarah Beatty, 1788. 7. Margaret—m. Thomas Dougherty, 1791. 8. Peggy —m. ——— How, 1810. 9. William—m. Agnes McCalpin, 1787. 10. William—m. Rebecca Smith, 1805.

Lockhart.—1. Thomas—d. 1783—m. Margaret ——— —C: Charles. 2. Walter Lockard—m. Jane Otty, 1814.

Lockridge.—1. James—levy-free, 1748—m. Isabella ——— —C: Andrew (m. Jean Graham), Sarah (m. John Gay), Elizabeth (m. 1. Robert Graham. 2. Samuel Gwin.) 2. William—bro. to 1—m. Agnes ——— —C: Elizabeth (m. John Eakin), Eleanor (m. ——— Cunningham), Samuel, John, William. 3. ——— —m. Ann Rhea by 1777.

Logan.—1. Jane—k. 1763—m. John McKee, 1744. 2. James d. 1825—m. Hannah ——— —C: Ann (b. 1767, d. 1856, s), Benjamin, Erwin, John, Robert, Alexander (m. Jean McCampbell, 1796), James, Joseph, Peggy (m. James McCampbell, 1791), Elizabeth (m. ——— Allen), Mary (m. John Welch, 1809). 3. Sally—m. Robert Lindsay, 1797. 4. Stephen—m. Agnes ———, by 1785. 5. William—d. 1791—m. Elizabeth ——— —C: John (has Hugh), Thomas (has Hugh), Mary (m. ——— Lawrence), David, Ann (m. Houston, William. 6. William—son of 5—m. Sarah ——— —C: William (only child). 7. Elizabeth —m. John Paxton, 1789.

Long.—1. James—m. Sally Mackey, 1794. 2. John—m. Peggy Galbraith, 1803. 3. Mary —m. John Putnam, 1795. 4. William—m. Mary Brown, 1797

Love.—1. Alsa—m. John Marshall, 1790. 2. John—m. Sally Hinds, 1802. 3. Thomas —m. Rosanna McClure, 1789.

Lowry.—1. Eleanor—m. George Gibson, 1798. 2. John—d. 1759c. 3. Lydia—m. Samuel Wallace, 1804. 4. Peter—d. 1799—C: Nelly, Lydia, Mary, Peter (m. Peggy Taylor, 1806). 5. Polly—m. William McVey, 1805. 6. Robert—d. 1780—estate, $2,281.67.

Luckess.—William—b. 1773, d. 1859.

Lusk.—1. David—m. Rachel Hoffman, 1794. 2. Isabel—m. David M. Dougherty, 1803. 3. James—m. Eliner ——— —witnesses will of William Cowden, 1749. 4. John—b. 1672, living, 1744. 5. John—C: Robert (ward of Andrew Hays, 1751). 6. John—b. 1712, living, 1784. 7. Mary—m. William McCampbell, 1791. 8. Nancy—m. Richard Tankersly, 1800. 9. Nathan—d. 1748—m. Elizabeth ——— —C: John, James, Agnes (m. Matthew Young). 10. Robert—d. 1778—m. Elizabeth ——— —estate, $139.67. 11. Samuel—m. Sarah ——— — 1750. 12. William—m. Elizabeth ——— —d. 1771—C: John, William, Mary (m. ——— Phillips), Joseph, Elizabeth, Sarah, Margaret. 13. William—sponsor for Agnes Gray in suit, 1747. 14.—m. ——— Crawford—C (1815): James, Margaret, Martha, Mary

Lyle.—1. Daniel—m. Martha Adair, 1801.
2. Daniel—m. ——— Glass—in Dunmore war.
3. Daniel—m. ——— Paxton.
4. David—m. Margaret Scott, 1819.
5. Elizabeth—m. Michael Graham, 1786.
6. Esther—m. Joseph Paxton, 1787.
7. Esther—witness in suit, 1747.
8. Hannah—m. William McLean, 1819.
9. James—d. 1791—m. Hannah ——— —C: Joseph, Archibald, Jane, Matthew, Elizabeth, Peggy, John.
10. James—d. 1802c—C: William.
11. Jane—m. James Ramsay, 1786.
12. Jane— Andrew Finley, 1812.
13. Jenny—m. John McClung, 1797.
14. John—d. 1758—m. Jean ——— —C: John, William, Martha, Elizabeth, Sarah, Esther.
15. John—b. 1746, d. 1815—m. Flora Reid—C: John, Jane (see 12), Martha (m. ——— McCutchen), Joel R., William.
16. John—b. 1757.
17. John— d. at 86—C: Samuel W. (m. Margaret Alexander), James G. (m. Elvira McClung), William A. (s), John B. (s), Elizabeth (m. John Alexander), Sarah M. (m. Henry Ruffner, 1819, d. 1849), Martha A. (m. Archibald Graham), Elizabeth H. (m. B——M. Hobson).
17. John—m. Margaret Baker, 1789.
18. John—m. Frances ——— by 1780.
19. John—son of ——— —m. Isabella Paxton—b. 1742.
20. Joseph—m. Sally Butt, 1791.
21. Mary P.—son of 19—m. James McDowell.
22. Matthew—d. 1774—C: James, Elizabeth (m. William Lyle of William), Martha; a dau. m. Matthew Donald.
23. Matthew—m. Sarah Lyle, 1794—minister.
24. Peggy—m. James Alexander, 1801.
25. Samuel—d. 1796—m. Sarah McClung, 1751—C: William James (m. Margaret Baker), Mary (m. John Dalhouse), Jane (m. John Ramsay), Elizabeth (m. Michael Graham), Sally (m. Rev. Matthew Lyle, 1794).
26. Samuel—immigrant—C: James, Robert.
27. William—son of 25—b. 1752c—m. (1) Julia A. Stuart, (2) (Elizabeth Lyle, 1796), 9 C.
28. William—m. Susannah Walker, 1807.
29. William—d. 1782—estate, $2,240.47.

Lyon.—William—k. 1783c—m. Mary ——— —C: William (b. 1776), John (b). (1778), Peter and Paul (b. 1781), Ephraim (b. 1783).

Mackey.—1. Elizabeth—m. William S. Bailey, 1788. 2. Elizabeth—b. 1769, d. 1853. 3. Esther—m. Arthur Walkup, 1797. 4. Isabella—m. Moses Elliott, 1810. 5. James—m. Mary Macky 1801. 6. James S.—b. 1780c—m. Nancy McMath. 7. James L.—m. Sarah Wilson, 1807—C: Hugh W. 8. John—d. 1806—C: Isabel, Seragh, Mary, John, James, Jane, Betsy 9. John—m. Peggy Wilson, 1810. 10. Jean—m. William Willson, 1806. 11. Sally —m. James Long, 1794. 12. Samuel C.—1810. 13. William—m. Elizabeth Kennedy, 1797. 14. ——— —m. Mary Porter Little, 1785. 15. ——— —m. Nancy Hamilton.

Margrave.—Thomas—d. 1804c—C: Anne (m. Alexander McCorkle, 1805), Sally (m. John Pryor, 1812), Nancy, Elizabeth (Valentine M. Mason, 1804).

Martin.—1. Andrew—d. 1749c—estate, $218.79—admr, Patrick. 2. David—d. 1778—estate, $2,302.08—m. Jean ———, d. 1801—C: Ann, William, James, Jacob, David, Jean, Thomas, Elizabeth (m. William Davis, 1795), Margaret (m. ——— Perry). 3. Elizabeth—m. John Solomon, 1789. 4. Ephy—m. Peter Mines, 1783. 5. Hugh—levy-free, 1752—d. 1766. 6. Hugh—d. 1749c—admr, Patrick. 7. Isabella—m. Andrew Moore—d. 1777. 8. Jacob—admr, Moses Moore, 1758. 7. James—m. Ann McClung, 1791 8. John—m. Polly Troxel, 1815. 9. John O.—m. Sarah McNabb, 1789. 10. Joseph—m. Polly McCreery, 1813. 11. William—m. Margaret Dickey, 1801. 12. William—son of 5. 13. ——— —m. Sally Jones by 1831.

Mathews.—1. Archer—d. 1786—m. Letitia ———, who as widow m. Joseph Keyser and died 1815c.

2. Daniel—m. Esther Shaw, 1801.
3. Elizabeth—m. Isaac Otey, 1789.
4. George—b. 1739, d. 1812, m. Polly (or Ann) Paul.
5. Jacob—m. Patsy Douglass, 1819.
6. James W.—bro. to Joseph—d. 1834—m. Polly G. ——— —C (all in Greenbrier): Mason, Thomas, Nancy (m. ——— Weir), Elizabeth.
7. John—d. 1757—m. Betsy Ann Archer—C: Sampson (see 11), John (see 8), Joshua (see 9), George (see 4), Archer (see 1), William, Jane, Rachel, Elizabeth.
8. John—himself, wife, and 6 C. murdered, 1764c.
9. Joshua—d. 1767c—C: Anne, Elizabeth (b. 1753).
10. Ruth—m. Beverly Ligan, 1796.
11. Sampson—d. 1807—m. (1) Mary Lockhart, (2) Mary Warwick.
12. William—see 7—d. 1772—m. Frances ——— —estate, $669.04—C: Ann, Elizabeth, John, Joseph, James.

Maxwell.—1. Audley—1761. 2. John—d. 1788—estate, $367.72.

Mays.—1. Ann—widow———; Jacob Bailor, 1818. 2. Samuel—m. Polly Russell, 1811.

McAdams.—Thomas—shoemaker, 1789.

McAllister.—1. Benjamin—m. Hannah McDonald, 1789. 2. Patsy—m. David Kyler, 1812.

McBride.—1. John—b. 1745, d. 1821—C: Isaiah (b. 1777, d. 1830), Jane (m. Andrew Young, 1799), Peggy (m. William Brown). 2. Thomas—d. 1765c—C: Joseph. 3. William—m. Martha Lapsley—k. (?) at Blue Lick, 1782.

McCaleb.—Enos—d. 1803c—C: Enos, Jean (m. Jacob J. Brown, 1803), Joseph, Samuel, Hannah (m. Anthony Cartright, 1811), Eli.

McCalpin.—1. Elizabeth—m. Abraham Little, 1795. 2. Isabel—m. John Shaw, 1816. 3. Mary—m. William Smith, 1799. 4. Robert—d 1791c—m. Elizabeth ——— —C: Robert, Joseph (b. 1778, d. 1855), —m. Catharine Carper, 1815), James John. 5. Robert—d. 1790—C: Robert, William, Peggy (m. David Little, 1801), Nancy, ——— (m. William Robinson). 6. Robert—m. Grizzy Spence, 1811. 7. Sally—m. George Atkinson, 1794. 8. William—d. 1802—C: William, Robert, Mary, Esabella. 9. William—m. Sarah Wear, 1807.

McCampbell.—1. Andrew—Kerr's Cr.—d. 1786.

2. Andrew—d. 1799—m. Nancy ——— —C: John, Polly, Rachel, Nancy, Betsy.
3. Andrew—m. Agnes Chambers, 1782.
4. Andrew—m. Nancy Gilmore, 1817.
5. Ann—m. John Scott, 1812.
6. David—d. 1778—estate, $878.58.

7. David—m. Nancy Johnston, 1808.
8. David—m. Jane McElheny, 1817—C: Elinor.
9. Elizabeth—m. Thomas Armstrong, 1792.
10. James—m. Margaret Logan, 1791.
11. James—m. Mary McCampbell, 1797.
12. Jean (widow)—d. 1827—C: Mary (m. —— Wiley), Agnes (m. James Lindsay, 1797), Hannah (m. John McKemy, 1803), Jane (m. James Lackey, 1808), —— (m. —— Heron).
13. Jean—m. Alexander Logan, 1796.
14. John—m. Martha Bennett, 1786.
15. John—m. Susanna Weir, 1789.
16. John—m. Mary Pinkerton, 1797—d. 1811—C: a dau.
17. John—m. Polly Reid, 1806.
18. John—m. Mildred Moore, 1806.
19. Mary—m. Alexander Tadford, 1787.
20. Mary—m. Robert Lawson, 1792.
21. Nancy—m. William Anderson, 1777.
22. Nancy—m. John Hais, 1789.
23. Polly—m. John Clark, 1806.
24. Robert—d. 1815—C: James, Betsy, Andrew, Judy, Sally, Nancy (m. Hugh Harper, 1807).
25. Samuel—Back Cr. 1783—m. Martha ——.
26. Sarah—m. Robert Weir, 1791.
27. Solomon—m. Nancy Berry, 1782.
28. William—d. 1822—m. Jane —— —C: John, William, Mary (m. Joseph Wiley, 1791), Agnes (m. James Lindsay, 1797), Hannah (m. John McKamy, 1803), Jenny (m. James Lecky, 1808).
29. William—m. Mary Lusk, 1791.
30. William—m. Elizabeth Porter, 1804.
31. William—m. Elizabeth Orbison, 1807.
32. ———— —m. Thomas Orbison by 1827.

McCandless.—William—b. 1713—m. Elizabeth —— —surety for Ann Rogers as admr, 1760.

McCarty.—1. Betsy—m. Robert Simpkins, 1798. 2. Justin—m. Susanna Lawson, 1815. 3. Nancy—m. John McCampbell, 1815.

McCaskey.—1. Andrew—servant to Robert Caruthers. 2. David—m. Grizzle —— by 1785.

McChesney.—1. James—b. 1795, d. 1846, m. Frances A. ——. 2. J—— E.—m. Thomas W. D. Steele, 1818 3 Mary—m. James B. McClung—b. 1785c. 4. Mary—m. William Archer, 1782. 5. Robert—m. Elizabeth Johnston, 1792. 6. —— —C: James (m. Sarah Patterson), Hugh (m. Joanna Hanan), Robert (m. Jane Hall), Martha (s).

McClain.— —— —m. Isabella Wasson by 1832.

McCleary.—Alexander—d. 1852—m. Margaret —— —C: Rachel.

McClelland.—1. Anna—m. William Wilson, 1805. 2. Henry—m. Betsy Brown, 1787. 3. Jean—m. Nathaniel Steele, 1802. 4. John—son of Stanhope—b. in Pa. 1769, d. 1855. 5. John—m. Mary Brownlee, 1788. 6. Polly—m. William Jones, 1791. 7. Polly—Jesse Jarrett, 1812. 8. Thomas—m. Jean Galbraith, 1795. 9. Thomas—m. Nancy Glasgow, 1804. 10. William—m. Polly Wilson, 1809.

McClenachan.—1. Hannah—dau. of Elijah—m. John Greenlee. 2. John—m. Nancy Hayslet, 1800. 3. John—m. Jane Graham, 1812. 4. Polly—m. Thomas Poague.

MISCELLANEOUS DATA

McClintic.—1. Elizabeth—m. John Moore, 1793. 2. William—m. Rosanna Sloan, 1796.

McClung.—1. ——— —C: John (b. 1731, d. 1817), Matthew (Del.), James, ——— (Del.), dau. (m. ——— Alexander), Mary (m. Samuel McDowell).
2. David—m. Mary Cloyd, 1803.
3. Elizabeth—b. 1724, d. 1773, m. Thomas Paxton, 1746.
4. Elizabeth—m. Alexander Telford, 1797.
5. Elvira—m. James G. Lyle.
6. Henry—b. 1739, d. 1784, m. Esther Caruthers—C: William, James, Samuel, Margaret, Easther, Henry.
7. Henry—m. Elizabeth Alexander, 1802.
8. James—C: James (m. Mary ———), William (d. 1784), Hugh (m. Frances ———), Charles (Pa.), Mary (Pa.), Matthew (Pa.), John (m. Sarah Laughlin), Margaret (m. John Houston).
9. James (see 8)—C: Henry (see 6), William (d. 1793, m. Jane ———), James (m. Bettie Houston), Agnes (m. ——— Gray).
10. James—son of 9—d. 1813—C: Mary (m. Peter Cassady, 1812), Agnes (m. ——— Snodgrass), Jane (m. Samuel Patton, 1784), Anne (m. James Martin), Easther (m. John McColloch, 1802), James (m. Mary A. Henry), Samuel, Margaret (s), John (m. Jane Baggs, 1814).
11. James—d. 1798—m. Ann ——— —C: Rebecca, William, Elizabeth, Samuel, James.
12. James—bro.-in-law to William Patton, 1824.
13. James W.—m. Phœbe A. Paxton—n. c.
14. Janet—m. David Moore, 1782.
15. John—son of 1—m. Elizabeth Alexander, 1755c—C: Margaret (m. Robert Tate), William (b. 1758, m. Susan Marshall), John (m. Mary Stuart), Archibald (s, d. at 84), Elizabeth (m. Robert Stuart), Phœbe (m. James Paxton), Rebecca (m. William Steele), James (doctor), Joseph (b. 1775, d. 1867), Esther (s), Polly (s).
16. John—son of 15—d. 1830—C: Elizabeth, Benjamin. Isabalah. Synes, Mary, Joseph, Archable, James.
17. John—d. 1836—C: James, Sarah, Samuel, John Elihu, William.
18. John—m. Jenny Lyle, 1797.
19. Joseph—m. Hettie McClung, 1814.
20. Mary—in suit, 1747.
21. Nancy—m. William Moore, 1770c.
22. Phœbe—m. James Houston, 1790.
23. Rebecca—m. William Telford, 1798.
24. Sarah—m. Samuel Lyle, 1751c.
25. William—d. 1784—C: Sarah (see 24), James, John.
26. William—son of 8—C: Elizabeth (see 3), Matthew (m. Martha Cunningham), William (Del.), Sarah (see 24), Mary (m. Samuel McDowell), James (m. Ann Gray).
27. William—b. 1761, d. 1837, m. Euphemia Cunningham—C: Phœbe (see 22), Rebecca, Elizabeth (see 4), Matthew (m. Betsy Curry), John (see 18), Samuel, David (see 2), Mary (m. ——— Hamilton), James G. (m. Mary C. Alexander).
28. ——— —m. Jean Paul, d. 1826—C: James A. J.

McClure.—1. Agnes—m. William Douglass, 1803.
2. Alexander—d. 1790—m. Martha ——— —C: Halbert, Nathaniel, Alexander, Samuel, John, Martha, Susanna (all minors but Halbert).
3. Alexander—m. Martha Elliott, 1795.
4. Alexander T.—m. Betsy Paxton, 1808.

5. Alexander, Sr.—m. Martha ——— —1751.
6. Arthur—Nancy Edmondson, 1798.
7. Arthur—m. Frances McNabb?—C: Arthur (b. 1752c, m. Isabella McCorkle).
8. Catharine—m. James Taylor, 1808.
9. David—m. Rhoda Jones, 1819.
10. David—m. Eleanor Steele—had Halbert, David.
11. Elizabeth—m. Jacob Morgan, 1807.
12. Halbert—d. 1754—m. Agnes ——— —C: Alexander, Nathaniel, Moses.
13. Halbert—b. 1737c.
14. Halbert—b. 1754—d. 1830c—m. ——— Steele.
15. Isabella—m. Andrew Hall, 1799.
16. James—pioneer—b. 1690c—m. Agnes ——— —C: John, Jane (m. Archibald Alexander, 1757), others.
17. John—d. 1822—m. Agnes ——— —C: Arthur, John J., Nathan, Robert, Catharine (m. Samuel McCorkle, 1804), Nancy (m. ——— Alexander), Fanny (m. Flemin Byers, 1804), Jane (d. by 1821, m. John McClure, 1808).
18. John—m. Nancy L., sister to Sally (John McCorkle)—d. 1835—C: Eglantine (m. Addison J. Henderson by 1836), John T. (d. 1835).
19. John—m. Jane ——— —C: Jenny J. (b. 1786, d. 1855, m. James Lackey).
20. John—d. 1778, C (minors): Samuel, Alexander, Mary, Agnes, Jennet, Malcolm, Hannah, Rebeckah, John, Halbert, Moses, Nathaniel.
21. John—b. 1750c, d. 1822—m. Nancy Steele, 1775c—C: Arthur (see 6), Paxton(s), David (s, doctor), Sally (m. William McClure, Jr.), Robert C. (d. 1881, m. Mary Parry).
2. John—m. Isabella Hall, 1799.
23. John—m. Ann McFall, 1801.
24. John—m. Jenny McClure, 1808.
25. Malcolm—m. Elizabeth McClure, 1787—C: John, Mary (m. Walker Stuart)—d. 1791—widow m. Alexander Crawford, 1796.
26. Martha—m. John Jameson, 1800.
27. Matthew—in Mecklenburg, N. C., 1751.
28. Mary—m. David Templeton, 1791.
29. Mary—m. Nathaniel Dryden, 1785.
30. Mary—m. ——— Henderson by 1782.
31. Moses—son of 12—d. 1778—m. Isabella Steele—C: Halbert (see 13) David (m. Eleanor Steele), Moses, Alexander H. (see 3).
32. Moses—son of 14—d. 1829, m. Elizabeth Jones—C: Alexander, Nicholas J., Mary S., Moses F., David K., William P.
33. Nancy (widow)—d. 1837—C: Thomas.
34. Nathan—same as Nathaniel?—1746.
35. Nathaniel—d. 1761—estate, $800.31—Mary, admr. d. 1767—C: Halbert (b. 1740c, d. 1771, m. Mary Henderson), Mary (m. Joseph Reed), James, Nathaniel, Dorothy (m? David Dryden), Hannah (m. John Smiley), Thomas (b. 1753), Margaret (b. 1756, m. ——— Lee), Moses (b. 1759).
36. Nathaniel—m. Jean Porter.
37. Phœbe—dau. of Alexander T.—b. 1805c—m. Thomas P. Paxton.
38. Robert—m. Sophia Campbell, 1816.
39. Sally—m. William Grigsby, 1790.
40. Sally—m. John McCorkle by 1836—sister to Nancy L.
41. Samuel—d. 1779—m. Mary ——— —C: Samuel, Alexander, William, Elizabeth,

MISCELLANEOUS DATA   505

Anna, Agnes (m. ——— Campbell), Hannah, Mary (m. ——— Ratliff), Jean (m. ——— Elliott).
42. Susanna—m. Joseph Stephenson, 1794.
43. William—son of 41—d. 1785—m. Jean Trimble—C: Samuel, Agnes, James(s), William (m. Mary Shields, 1790), Samuel, John (d. 1834), m. Jane ———, 2. Nancy ———), Sarah, Mary, Alexander.
44. ——— —m. Catharine McColm by 1784.
45. ——— —m. Jane Porter by 1803.
46. ——— —m. Elizabeth Stuart by 1823.
47. ——— —m. Agnes McCorkle by 1833.
48. ——— —m. William McCorkle.

McCollem.—1. Catharine—m. ——— McClure by 1784. 2. John—m. Jane McNabb, 1785. 3. Margaret—m. Isaac Fencher, 1785. 4. Patrick—d. 1784—C: James, Margaret (m. ——— McCorkle), John, Catharine (see 1).

McComb.—1. Martha—m. John Leech, 1775c. 2. William—d. 1808—m. Martha ——— —C: Mary (m. James Price, 1808), Sarah (m. James Cosby, 1819), Elizabeth, Samuel, Jane, Hugh, William (m. Martha Parks, 1806).

McConkey.—1. John—d. 1813—m. Sarah ———, bro. to Jacob, Samuel, Anah, Marthew, Mary (m. ——— Ramsay). Margaret—m. Aaron Robinson, 1793. 3. Sally—m. John Caruthers, 1815.

McCormick.—1. Ann—m. Philip Stoops, 1789.
1x. Cyrus H.—son of 14—C: Cyrus H., Mary V., Robert, Anita, Alice F., Stanley R.
2. Dinah—m. William Dawson, 1795.
3. Elizabeth—m. John Watt, 1790.
4. Elizabeth—m. Abraham Campbell, 1793.
5. Henry A.—b. 1796, d. 1877.
6. Isabella—m. John Spence, 1786.
7. James—d. 1789—bro. to Hugh and William of Ireland—C: Peggy.
8. James—m. Elizabeth Hannah, 1784.
9. Lydia—m. William McManamy, 1802.
10. Margaret—m. John Thompson, 1798.
11. Nancy—m. James Hayslet, 1798.
12. Nancy—m. William Tate, 1809.
13. Robert—b. 1737, d. 1818, m. Martha Sanderson—C: George (m. Jane Steele), James (m. Irene Rodgers), William (m. Mary Steele), Elizabeth (m. William Gibson), 1794), Martha (m. Richard Briant), Robert (see 14).
14. Robert—b. 1780, d. 1846, m. Mary A. Hall, 1808—C: Cyrus H. (b. 1809, d. 1884, m. Nettie Fowler, 1858), Robert (dy), Susan J. (dy), William S. (b. 1815, d. 1865, m. Mary A. Grigsby, 1848), Mary C. (b. 1817, d. 1888, m. James Shields, 1847), Leander J. (b. 1819, m. Henrietta M. Hamilton, 1845), John P. (. 1820, d. 1849), Amanda J. (b. 1822, d. 1891, m. Hugh Adams, 1845).
15. Robert—m. Hannah Paxton, 1817.
16. Samuel—d. 1802—C: Lydia, Esther.
17. William—m. Polly Klemmer by 1819.

McCroskey.—1. Alexander—son of 9—d. 1812. 2. Andrew—servant to Robert Caruthers. 3. Ann—Searight Woods, 1797. 4. David—son of 9—C (1797): John, Maty, Ann, Easther, Nancy. 5. Esther—m. Hugh Beard, 1797. 6. George—m. Eleanor Harkins, 1796. 7. James—m. Jean Price, 1808. 8. Jane—m. James Tedford, 1789 9. John—d. 1758—m. Elizabeth ——— —C: Samuel, David, Alexander, James, William, John, Elizabeth; also the wives of William Caruthers, Samuel Houston, James Hope—estate, $55.95. 10. John—son of 9—d. 1810—C: Joseph and others. 11. John—b. 1715, living 1805. 12. Joseph—d. 1839—m. Martha ——— —C: Sally (m. ——— Adams), Betsy (m. ——— Wilson), Patsy (m. ——— Anderson, Polly, Jane, Hugh, David. 13. Mary (or Jean)—m. James Tedford, 1785. 14. Polly—m. Hugh Weir, 1811. 15. ——— —m. Ann Montgomery. 16. ——— —m. Samuel Alexander, 1790c.

McCoy.—1. Arthur—m. Sally Edley, 1807. 2. Daniel—m. Sarah Slaughter, 1814. 3. Edmund—m. Mary Davis, 1817. 4. Thomas—m. Sally Holman, 1798. 5. ——— —m. Eleanor Walkup by 1828.

McCrory.—1. James—d. 1817—C: James (m. Esther Caruthers, 1797), John, Samuel 2. James—son of 1—C: James. 3. ——— —m. Susan Hughes by 1851.

McCullough.—1. George—m. Jane Paxton. 2. John—m. Rachel Shields by 1808. 3. John—m. Elizabeth Teal, 1791. 4. John—m. Mary McClung, 1794. 5. John—h. Esther McClung, 1802. 6. Robert—d. 1804—bro. to Abel and John. 7. Thomas—d. —C: John W——— (m. William Murphy), dau. (m. ——— Campbell), 8. Thomas—m. Jean McClung, 1800. 9. ——— —. Susan Henderson.

McCutchen.—1. Eleanor—1824.
2. James—m. Elizabeth Hunter, 1786.
3. James—b. 1775, d. 1852, m. Elizabeth ———, by 1780, d. 1822.
4. Jane—m. Thompson Edmondson, 1810c

4x. John—son of 16—C: Samuel (b. 1773), Margaret (m. Robert Jameson), Robert, Eleanor (b. 1780, m. John McClung), Joseph (m. Nancy Youell, John (m. Elizabeth Youell, 1810). William (m. Rebecca McKnight), Elizabeth L. (b. 1792, m. William Wilson), James (b. 1795, m. Ellen Benson).

5. John—m. Elizabeth Youell, 1810.
6. John—m. Agnes Porter, 1789.
7. John, Jr.—m. Betsy Robinson, 1824.
8. John—M. Isabella Patrick, 1797.
9. Joseph—m. Nancy ——— by 1824.
10. Joseph—m. Jane Searight, 1785.
11. Margaret—m. James McClung, 1800c.
12. Margaret—m. Robert Jemison, 1795.
13. Martha—m. Madison G. Davidson—b. 1820c.
14. Priscilla—John Stuart, 1823c.
15. Rebecca—m. John Black, 1788.
16. Robert.1805—C: John (b. 1750, m. Elizabeth Hodge of Samuel), Joseph, Jonas, Robert, (m. Mary McKnight), James. Margaret (m. ——— Moore), Samuel, Hannah (m. Joseph Henderson), Mary, William.
17. Samuel—son of John and Betty—b. 1772, d. 1857.
18. Samuel—m. Mary Patrick, 1792.
19. Samuel—m. Catharine Almonrode, 1818.
20. Sarah—m. Isaac Morris, 1787.
21. William—m. Jane Finley, 1794.
22. William—d. 1789—m. Janet ——— —bro. to James, Robert, Samuel, John, each except John having a William.
23. ——— —m. Elizabeth Weir by 1779.
24. ——— —m. Martha Lyle by 1815.
25. ——— —m. Elizabeth Kilpatrick by 1823.
26. ——— —m. Nancy Youell by 1829.

27. William—k. by tree, 1757.

McDonald.—1. Bryan—d. 1757—m. Catharine ——— —C: Catharine (m. John Armstrong), Prisla, Richard, James, Edward, Joseph, Rebecca (m. ——— Bean), Mary (m. ——— Smith). 2. James—m. Jean McCorkle, 1805. 3. John—d. 1764—C: Mary (b. 1748), John (b. 1750), Francis, Hugh, Rebecca, William, Elizabeth, Samuel. 4. Mary—m. William Millirons, 1787. 5. Nancy—m. Samuel Deal, 1803. 6. Randal—d. 1810—C: John (m? Hannah Caskey, 1805), Samuel (m ?Ann Wise, 1812), William (m? Hannah Whiteman, 1799), Matthew (m? Elizabeth Whiteman, 1802), Hannah (m. Benjamin McCallister, 1789), Jenny (m. Philip Walker, 1795).

McCune.—1. John—d. 1820—bro. to Deborah Harris. 2. ——— —m. Elizabeth Paxton, 1775c.

McDowell.—1. Charles—m. Grace Greenlee, 1760c.

2. Ephraim—b. 1672—C: Mary, John, James (m. Mary McClung).

3. James—son of 7—b. 1738, d. 1771—m. Elizabeth Cloyd—C: Sarah (m. John McDowell), Elizabeth (m. David McGavick), James.

4. James—son of 3—b. 1770, d. 1835, m. Sarah Preston, 1793—C: Susan (m. William Taylor), Elizabeth (m. Thomas H. Benton, 1821), James.

5. James—son of 4—b. 1796, d. 1851, m. Elizabeth ——— —C: Sally C. (m. John Miller), Mary B. (m. ——— Ross, Md.), Frances (dy), Sophonisba (m. James W. Massie) Lewis M. (dy), Susan P. (m. Charles W. Carrington), Margaret C. (m. Charles S. Venable), Thomas P. (m. Constance Warwick), Eliza P. (m. Bernard Wolf).

6. James—m. Sarah Withrow, 1788.

7. John—son of 2—k. 1742—m. (1) ——— ———, (2) Magdalene Woods—C: Samuel, James, Martha—or Sarah (b. 1742, m. George Moffett).

8. John—m. Isabella Lyle, 1798.

9. Joseph—m. Margaret Moffett, 1786.

10. Magdalene—b. 1770c—m. Andrew Reid.

11. Mary E.—dau of 2—b. Nov. 17, 1707, d. March 14, 1809—m. James Greenlee.

12. Robert—m. Margaret Moore, 1792.

13. Robert—m. Patsy Dold, 1798.

14. Samuel—son of 7—b. Oct. 27, 1735, d. 1817—m. Mary McClung, 1754.

15. Thomas—d. 1822c—m. Sarah Patton—C: William, Margaret.

16. Ephraim—m. ——— Greenlee.

17. ——— —m. Elizabeth Paxton, 1775c.

McElheny.—v. Elizabeth—m. Christian Good, 1820. 2. John—m. Barbara Walkup, 1807. 3. Peggy—m. John Adams, 1809. 4. Robert—d. 1799—m. Mary ———, d. 1812—C: Robert, Ann (m. Robert Moore, 1787), Jenny (m. ——— Harrison), Mary, Eleanor, Peggy, Isabel. 5. Robert—m. Mary McKnight, 1794. 6. Strother L. —m. Jane Stoops, 1817—C: John. 7. William—1761. 8. James—1755. 9 ——— C: Ellinor (d 1831), Isabella, Polly, Peggy, Jane (m. David McCampbell, 1817), Strother L. (see 6), ——— (m. Thomas Armstrong), John (d. by 1828: C: Polly), Robert.

McElroy.—James—went from Rbg. to Ky. 1788.

McElwee.—Michael—m. Piddie De Mott—C: Nellie (m. Robert P. Toomey), Michael (m. Mary Payne of Lekis), William, George (m. Elizabeth Dunlap), John (m. Betsy Payne of Lewis), Sallie (s).

McFadden.—1. Elizabeth—m. Samuel Dold, 1820. 2. Jacob—m. Betsy Dice, 1823. 3. John—bro.-in-law to James Young, 1828. 4. Joseph—m. Elenor Casteel, 1795. 5. William —b. 1745c. 6. William—m. Barbara Casady, 1809.

McFarland.—1. John—m. Mary Hayslet, 1799. 2. Margaret—dau. of Robert—m.

Nathaniel White, 1780c. 3. Peggy—m. Isaiah Kincaid, 1820. 4. Robert—d. 1798—m. Esther ——— —C: Thomas, Rachel, William, Rebecca. 5. Rebecca (m. Robert Roach, 1787).

McGee.—James—d. 1759—Erwin Patterson, admr.

McGuffin.—1. Polly—m. Joseph McLaughlin, 1821. 2. Richard—b. 1769, d. 1841, m. Jane ———, b. 1784, d. 1843.

McHenry.—1. Barnabas—b. 1715, k. at Great Meadows, 1754. 2. James—m. Deborah Crasley, 1793. 3. John—m. Jean Wilson, 1801. 4. John—son of 1—b. 1740—m. Susanna Viney—bro. to Robert, Samuel.

McIlvain.—Moses—m. Margaret Hodge of Samuel, d. 1773—C: William (m. Sarah Gay of John).

McKamin.—1. Daniel—m. Isabella Lemon, 1801. 2. John—m. Ann Thomas, 1801. 3. Polly—m. ——— Thomas, 1810.

McKay.—Henry—m. Elizabeth Davidson, 1795. 2. Robert and Moses—sworn to as being Quakers, 1752. 3. Robert—d. 1746—bro. to Zachariah, James.

McKee.—1. Robert—b. 1692, d. 1774, m. Agnes ———, b. 1700, d. 1780—C: William, John.

2. William—son of 1—b. 1732, d. 1816, m. Miriam McKee, 1766—C: John (b. 1767, m. Polly Patton, 1797), Nancy (m. James Wilson, 1788), William (m. Mrs. ——— Davis, a relative), Samuel (b. 1774, d. 1826, m. Martha Robertson), Mary W. (m. John A Lapsley). David L. (m. Betsy B. Letcher), Hugh W. (m ——— ———), James (b. 1790, d. 1866, m. Mary C. Lapsley, 1818)

3. John—son of 1—m. Esther Houston—C: John (s). Robert (s), William, Nancy (m. John Gay)—d. 1788.

4. John—bro. to 1—b. 1707, d. 1792, m. (1) Jane Logan, 1744, (2) Rosanna Cunningham, 1765—C: Mary (b. 1746, m. Hugh Weir), Miriam (b. 1747, d. 1796, m. William McKee, 1766), James L., Robert (m. Margaret Hamilton), William (m. Jane Kenady, 1790). David (m. Ann Dunlap, 1788), John.

5. James L.—son of 4—b. 1752, d. 1832, m. (1) Jane Tedford, 1782, (2) Mrs. Nancy Scott, 1807),—C: John T., Jane T. (b. 1807, m. Matthew H. Parry), Samuel W. (m. Mary A. Davidson), Martha H. (b. 1811, m. Madison Dunlap), Mary S. (m. John C. Laird).

6. John—son of 4—b. 1771—m Susanna Simonds, 1798, n. c.

7. William—son of 4—C: James (m. Rachel W. Moffett), Margaret (m. John Carson.

8. James—son of 7—C: James M., Ellen J. (m. 1. Alexander Smiley, 2. James Berry).

9. William—bro. of 1—C: James.

10. James—son of 9—d. 1778—m.Lydia ——————C: William, Alice, Martha, Mary, Samuel (m. Betsy Lowry), Robert, John.

11. John T.—son of 5—b. 1783, d. 1857, m? Nancy Hanna, 1806—C: Susan M., Martha H., Jane T., Samuel W.

12. James—k. 1758.

13. James—m. Jane Reed, 1797.

McKeever.—1. Peter—m. Mary Brown, 1794. 2. Rachel—m. John Brown, 1818.

McKemy.—1. Alexander—m. Catharine Baker, 1799. 2. James—d. 1826—m. Deborah ——— —C: Madison, Sally, Margaret, Polly, John, Betsy (m. ——— Mitchell), Joseph K. 3. James and John—bro.-in-law to James Cooper. 4. John—m. Hannah McCampbell, 1803. 5. William E.—b. 1782, d. 1848, m. Elizabeth ———, b. 1805, d. 1865. 6. ——— —m. Polly Montgomery by 1837.

McKenry—1. Betty—m. Archelaus Mitchell, 1819. 2. Edward—m. Polly Montgomery, 1821. 3. John—m. Lucy Mitchell, 1821.

McKinney.—1. Alexander—m. Mary McClure, 1795. 2. John—m. Margaret Wallace, 1785. 3. Mary—m. Francis Doty, 1788.

McKinzey.—Daniel—d. 1824—C: Polly (m. John Anderson, 1809), Betsy (m.—Flint).

McLaughlin.—1. Charles—m. Elizabeth Young, 1810. 2. Dorothy—m. Charles Wright, 1812. 3. Edward—m. Jane Hughart of James, 1796. 4. Edward J. b. 1788, d. 1858—m. Elizabeth Nesbitt, 1814—C: William (b. 1827, d. 1898). 5. Elizabeth—m. Frederick Oyler, 1802. 6. Hugh—d. by 1772—C: Hugh (b. 1758), James. 7. Jean—m. Samuel Kirkpatrick, 1812. 8. Joseph—m. Polly McGuffin, 1821. 9. Martha—m. John Wright, 1810 10. Thomas —b. 1774—bound to Thomas Lackey, 1788. 11. William—m. Sarah Turner, 1812.

McNight.—1. John—b. 1729, d. 1801. 2. —— ——m. Betsy Paxton by 1827. 3. Timothy —b. 1739—m. Eleanor Griffin—C: John (s), Robert (m. in Mexico), Thomas (m. 1. Fanny Scott, 2. Cornelia Hempstead), William (m. Elizabeth Meek), Jane (m. Dudley Jones), Nancy (m. John Youell), Mary (m. Robert McCutchen), Margaret (m. William Jameson), Rebecca (m. William McCutchen).

McManamy.—1. Ann—m. William Goul, 1820. 2. James—m. Sophia Wyant, 1815. 3. Polly—m. Christian Brownfield, 1820. 4. Sarah—m. Thomas Stanage, 1797. 5. William —m. Lydia McCormick, 1802. 6. ——— —m. Sally Welch by 1821.

McMath.—1. James—d. 1794—C: William, Sarah, Jenny, Mary, Susan. 2. Nancy—m. James S. Mackey, 1822. 3. Polly—m. Samuel Carrick, 1804. 4. Sally—m. John Winst, 1793. 5. Susan—dau. of 1—b. 1774, d. 1857, m. Thomas Johnston. 6. William—m. Sally Scott, 1810.

McMillen.—1. Daniel—m. Elenor Ferguson, 1795. 2. John—m. Polly Lefler, 1791. 3. Margaret—m. Joseph Hill, 1799.

McMullen.—1. Edward—m. ——— ———, 1759. 2. Peggy—m. James Plunkett, 1815. 3. ——— —lived near Robert Stuarts mill, 1745, in which year a dau. was m.

McMurray.—Samuel C.—b. Ireland, 1767, d. 1855, s.

McMurtry.—Samuel—b. 1759—orphan of Alexander—Matthew Lyle, admr.

McNabb.—1. Alexander—m. Mary Siders, 1819. 2. Catharine—in suit, 1747. 3. James— d. 1810—C: John, Alexander, Mary, Rebecca, Saly, Isabel, one other dau. 4. Jane—m. John McCollem, 1785. 5. John—m. Elizabeth Skeen. 1804. 6. Martha—m. John Moore, 1791. 7. Mary—m. Gabriel Morgan, 1795.

McNauton.—John—d. 1798—m. Mary Taylor, 1791—C: Elizabeth (m. ——— Taylor).

McNutt.—1. Alexander—s—bro to 11. 1x. Alexander—1748. 2. Alexander—m. Rachel Grigsby, 1790. 3. Elizabeth—m. Thomas P. Edmondson, 1820c. 4. Elizabeth—m. David Williams, 1793. 5. Elizabeth—m. John Hamilton, 1816. 6. Francis—proves importation, 1771—C: James, John, Francis, Agnes, Isabella 7. George—m. (1) Isabella Callison, (2) Katharine Kain, (3) Jeanette Anderson—C: Isabella (b. 1780, m. Moses White), William, Jennie (m. John McFarland), Rebecca (m. John Webb), Nannie (b. John Jack), Asenath (m. Robert Lindsay), James (m. Mary Fleming), Mary (b. 1793, dau. of 2d w., m. William McFarland), George. 8. George—son of 7—b. 1798 of 3d w.—m. Malinda Houston. 9. James —estate, 1749, $133.10—C: James, Robert. 10. James—officer under Matthew Arbuckle. 11. John—d. 1818—m. Mary ——— —bro. to Joseph, Benjamin, William (has John), Alexander (has Ruth), Elizabeth (see 3). 12. John—m. Catharine Anderson—C: Alexander (father of Alexander G.). 13. John—m. Polly Laird, 1807. 14. Joseph—m. Peggy Boyd, 1807. 15. Patsy—m. John Glasgow, 1815. 16. Peggy—m. Elisha Paxton, 1809. 17. Susanna —m. David Dickson, 1790. 18. William—son of 7—b. 1783, d. 1842, m. (1) Elizabeth B. Dewitt, (2) Margaret V. Gillespie. 19. William—bro. to 7.

McPheeters.—1. Betsy—m. James McClung, 1791. 2. John—m. Mary Anderson, 1787. 3. Rebecca—m. Robert Culton, 1796. 4. William—b. 1775c—m. Rachel Moore—C: Rachel

(m. John Logan, 1797). 5. William—tanner, 1759. 6. William—m. Margaret Caruthers, 1789. 7. William—m. Elizabeth Wardlow, 1795.

McQuean.—1. Jane—m. William Fuller, 1812. 2. Sally—m. Thomas Jarvis, 1816.

McQuiltin.—1. Jean—m. John Hoffman, 1809. 2. Margaret—m. John Weeks, 1808.

McSpaden.—Thomas—admr. for Robert Edmondson, 1750.

McTeer.—1. Samuel—m. Mary ——— —d. 1810—C: Samuel, Betsy, Mary, Sarah, James, William. 2. William—m. Nancy Kirkpatrick, 1806.

McVey.—1. Samuel—m. Jane Paxton, 1794. 2. Samuel—m. Margaret Stephens, 1820. 3. William—m. Polly Lowry, 1805.

Meek.—John—d. 1774—m. ——— —C: Henry (has land in Botetourt), William.

Michael.—1. Ann—m. John Walker, 1810. 2. George—m. Catharine Rust, 1816.

Miles.—1. John—m. Elizabeth Tooly, 1806. 2. Margaret—m. Hugh Keys, 1791. 3. Mary —m. Stephen Brown, 1804.

Miley.—Jacob—b. 1807, d. 1882—m. Lucy ———, b. 1809, d. 1886.

Miller.—1. Agnes—m. William McKnight, 1812.

2. Andrew—m. Jean Archibald, 1798.
3. Andrew—m. Elizabeth Plott, 1805.
4. Andrew—m. Ann Armentrout, 1817.
5. Betsy—m. Randolph Ross, 1810.
6. Catharine—m. Frederick Dice, 1818.
7. Daniel—m. Mary Groves, 1785.
8. Deborah—m. James Davis, 1786.
9. Eleanor—m. John Shaver, 1822.
10. Elizabeth—m. John Cook, 1811.
11. Elizabeth—m. William Paxton, 1803.
12. Elizabeth—m. Archibald Burford, 1804.
13. George—m. Basha Downs, 1820.
14. Henry—d. 1797—m. Rebecca ——— —C: John, Rebecca, Samuel, 4 other dau.
15. Henry—d. 1826—m. Catharine Montgomery, 1816—C: Joseph, Matilda, Lavinia, Jacob, Betsy.
16. Henry—m. Nancy Jackson, 1810.
17. James—m. Sally Trimble, 1820.
18. Jean—m. Thomas Ocheltree, 1796.
19. John—m. Jean Neely, 1795.
20. John—m. Ann Leech.
21. Joseph—m. Polly Booker, 1812.
22. Judith—m. James Bordin, 1795.
23. Margaret—m. David Leech, 1788.
24. Mary—m. Robert Martin, 1791.
25. Nancy—m. Reuben Ross, 1810.
26. Oliver—m. Jennet Youel, 1793.
27. Patsy—m. James Holmes, 1822.
28. Polly—m. Adam Solomon, 1815.
29. Rachel—m. John Alexander, 1791.
30. Rebecca—m. William Ramsay, 1798.
31. Rebecca—m. John Richey, 1801.
32. Rebecca—m. Samuel Russell, 1811.
33. Robert—m. Margaret A. Simonds, 1823.
34. Robert—m. Margaret Brown, 1799.

MISCELLANEOUS DATA   511

35. Samuel—d. 1816—m. Elizabeth ——— —C Susanna.
36. Samuel—m. Nancy Lawson, 1808.
37. Samuel—m. Ann Brawford, 1786.
37x. Sarah—b. 1771, d. 1858, m. John P. Ackerly.
38. Sophie—d. 1836—C Isaac.
39. Susanna—d. 1831—sister to Samuel, John, James.
40. Susan—m. Thomas Clifton, 1818.
41. Thomas L.—m. Elizabeth Miller, 1817.
42. William—b. in Pa. 1753, came to Rbg, 1770c, living, 1832.
43. ——— —m. Anne Welch by 1821.
44. ——— —m. Catharine Montgomery by 1837.

Millikin.—1. Charles—in N. C., 1761. 2. John—m. Isabella Doak, 1786. 3. Robert—m. Betsy Wiley, 1809. 4. William—m. Nancy Patton, 1812. 5. William—d. 1796c—m. Martha ——— —C: Elizabeth (d. 1815), Mary, James, Rachel, John, William (has Eliza, 1815).

Mills.—1. John—m. Priscilla Madison, 1780. 2. Weston—m. Polly Taylor, 1806. 3. ——— —m. Janette Hays by 1751.

Mitchell.—1. Alexander—d. 1822—C: George, James, Polly.
2. Andrew—m. Mrs. Andrew Cunningham, 1747c.
3. Archelaus—m. Betsy McKenry, 1819.
3x. Andrew—m. Elizabeth Snodgrass, 1811.
4. Andrew—m. Polly Orenbaum, 1822.
6. Betsy—m. Thomas Flynt, 1812.
7. Eleanor (widow)—lived near John Tate, 1747—C: John.
8. Elizabeth—m. Henry Shields, 1790.
9. Esther—m. Richard Cunningham, 1810.
10. Hannah—m. Ezra Tankery, 1797.
11. John—d. 1771—m. Elizabeth ——— —C: Thomas, Robert, John, James, Eleanor (m. —— Wilson), Mary (m. —— Wright). Elizabeth.
12. John—d. 1790—m. Margaret ——— C: Thomas, William, Hannah, John, Mary, Jane, Margaret.
13. Lucy—m. James McKenry, 1821.
14. Mary—m. Andrew McClure, 1789.
15. Samuel—m. Hana Gillis, 1792.
16. Samuel—m. Catharine Litten, 1807.
17. Thomas—m. Rachel Crawford, 1799.
18. Thomas—m. Margaret Callison, 1788.
19. Thomas—m. Ann Calbraith, 1798.
20. William—m. Agnes Brownlee, 1785.
21. William—m. Margaret McDowell by 1753.
22. ——— —m. Elizabeth Beard by 1769.
23 ——— —. —— Hutchinson (woman) by 1806—C: Robert.
24. ——— —m. Margaret Porter by 1780.

Moffett.—1. James—m. Mary Stuart, 1789. 2. Jane—m. Joseph Culton, 1795. 3. Magdalene—m. James Cochran, 1793. 4. Martha—m. Robert Kirk, 1786. 5. Rachel—m. James McKee, 1820. 6. Solomon—Moffetts Cr. 1740. 7. William—m. Mary McClenachan, 1791.

Mohler.—1. Frederick—d. 1834—C: Betsy, Joseph, Frederick, John, Jacob, Philip, —— (m. Philip Hoilman), Mary (m. Paul Butler, 1808). 2. Jacob—m. Ella. b. in Loudoun. 1777, d. 1856. 3. James B.—b. 1830c—g'son to Frederick, Sr. 4. John—b. 1772, d. 1830,

m. Magdalena Ryanback, 1799. 5. John—m. Elizabeth Amick, 1810. 6. Samuel—m. Margaret Shuey, 1821.

Moneymaker.—Lewis—d. 1812—C: Jacob, Mary (m. —— Strickler), John, Betsy, Saly, Daniel, Christianna, William, Doley.

Montgomery.—1. Catharine—m. Henry Miller, 1816.

2. Elizabeth—m. Thomas J. Flournoy. 1819.

3. Humphrey—d. 1798—m. Jean Gay—C: Polly (b. 1781, d. 1859, m. John McCorkle, 1800), Jean (m. James Johnston, 1807), Elizabeth (m. Cathey Sehorn, 1812x, Samuel (b. 1791, d. 1861, m. Mary Bailey, 1814, Sarah Haynes, 1839,. Patsy (s). Molly (b. 1798).

4. James—m. Martha Hall, 1807.

5. John—m. Esther Houston—C: John, Mollie (m. —— Edmondson), Ann (m. —— McCroskey), James (m. Margaret Weir, 1779), Dorcas (m. —— Lowry), Jane (m. Samuel Newell), Robert (m. —— Colville), Esther (m. Samuel Doak), Alexander (unknown), Isabella (m. —— Buchanan).

6. John—son of 5—b. 1752, d. 1818, m. Agnes Hughart, 1782—C: Esther (m. James C. Wilson), John, Thomas (m. Juliet Dalhouse). William H. (d. 1826), Isabella (m. Eugenio Irvine), Hughart (d. 1844), Estelline (s).

7. John—son of 6—b. 1788, d. 1829, m. Elizabeth Nelson.

8. Nancy—m. William Johnson, 1805.

9. Nancy—m. James C. Hutton.

10. Robert—d. 1827—m. Martha Crawford? who d. 1837—C: Thomas, Samuel, James, Alexander (m. Margaret ——), Catharine (see 1), Polly (m. —— McKemy), Davis by 1809).

11. William—m. Margaret Greenlee—C: James, Alexander, Mary (m. William Davis by 1809).

Moody—1. Anness—m. Dennis Donoho, 1787. 2. Betsy—m. Joseph Pullen, 1801. 3. Catharine—m. Thomas Robertson, 1808. 4. Mary—m. Samuel Cain, 1798.

Moore.—1. Agnes?—m. James Cunningham by 1780.

2. Alexander—d. 1766.

3. Alexander—b. 1728, living, 1805—bro. to David of Borden Tract.

4. Alexander—d. 1749—seems to be bro. to Alexander, Samuel, James, John, William.

5. Andrew—d. 1791—m. Martha —— —C: William, Mary, Samuel, Sally (m. John M. Wilson), 1 other dau.

6. Andrew—C: William (b. 1701 (?), d. 1771, m. Mary (——), David (b. 1722, d. 1783, m. Mary ——), John, Quintain, James, Samuel, Alexander (m. Margaret ——, b. 1729, d. 1784).

7. Anna—m. Robert Allen, 1805.

8. Betsy—m. Smith Scott, 1801.

9. David—C: David (orphan, b. 1752).

10. David—m. Mary Evans—C: William (b. 1748c, d. 1841, m. Mary McClung), Andrew (b. 1752).

11. David—d. 1748—bro. to Mary (m. —— Edmondson..

12. David—1768—g, father to Henry Gay.

13. David—d. 1783—m. Mary —— —C: Isabell, Sarah, Mary, Jennet, David.

14. David—m. Janet McClung, 1782.

15. David—m. Jane DePriest, 1788.

16. David—m. Anna Ewing, 1800.

17. David—m. Elizabeth Porter, 1820.
18. Elizabeth—m. Jessee White, 1820.
19. Eliazbeth—m. Samuel McCown, 1803, Samuel.
20. Isabella—m. Moses McCown, 1823.
21. James—m. Jane Walker—C: James.
22. James—son of 21—m. Martha Poage—k. 1786—C: Mary (b. 1777, d. 1824, m. Samuel Brown, 1798).
23. James—d. 1791—m. Jinet ——— —C: John, James, Joseph, Mary, Rachel, Jean.
24. James—orphan of David, 1803.
25. James—d. 1813—m. Mary ——— —C: James, Samuel, John, Sarah (m. William Hall), Elizabeth (m. Smith Scott, 1801), Hugh, William.
26. James—son of Samuel, 1808.
27. James—d. 1826—m. Mary ——— —bro. to Robert, William, Elizabeth (m. Jesse White, 1823), Addison C., Sarah, Margaret (m. Robert McDowell, 1792).
28. James—m. Hannah Barclay, 1791.
29. James—m. Mary Kirkpatrick, 1797.
30. James—m. Barbara Taylor, 1797.
31. Jenny—m. Samuel Forsythe, 1802.
32. Jenny—m. Hugh Kelso, 1794.
33. Jenny—m. Thomas Orbison, 1807.
34. John—in Ohio, 1812.
35. John—d. 1838—m. Elizabeth Cunningham, 1801—C: James C. C. (m. Jane Gilmore), William T. (m. Nancy W. Wilson), Abner W. (m. Mary J. Campbell), Jane (m. Preston Dunlap), Polly (m. William C. Gilmore), Patsy (m. James F Harper).
36. John—witnessed will of Robert Kirkham, 1748.
37. John, Sr.—d. 1802—C: James, Robert, Jean, ——— (m. Florence ———).
38. John—m. Margaret Steel, 1787.
39. John—m. Martha McNabb, 1791.
40. John—m. Elizabeth McClintock, 1793.
41. John—m. Elizabeth Dingledine, 1817.
42. John—m. Margaret Moore, 1788.
43. Joseph—Ky., 1801.
44. Juliana—m. Hugh Paxton, 1798.
45. Margaret—m. Robert Logan.
46. Margaret—m. John Allen, 1787.
47. Margaret—m. James Black, 1818.
48. Mary—m. Samuel Paxton.
49. Mary—m. Samuel Eakin, 1787.
50. Mary—m. Hugh Wilson, 1806.
51. Mildred—m. McCampbell, 1806.
52. Moses—m. ——— Risk—1766.
53. Moses—d. 1758.
54. Nancy—m. William W. Chittum, 1821.
55. Nancy—m. Henry Armentrout, 1819.
56. Peggy—m. Samuel Humphreys, 1812.
57. Peter—m. Sally McCray, 1823.
58. Polly—orphan of James, 1791.
59. Polly—m. Hugh Fulton, 1812.

60. Prudence—m. James Finley, 1785.
61. Rebecca—m. William E. Weir, 1823.
62. Robert—witnessed will of Robert Kirkham, 1748.
63. Robert—d. by 1800—m. Elizabeth ———, d. 1801—C: Sarah, John, Robert, William, James, Peggy (m. Robert McDowell, 1792).
64. Robert—m. Ann McElheny, 1787.
65. Robert—m. Sarah Pollock, 1793.
66. Sally—m. Thomas Anderson, 1819.
67. Sally—m. William Hall, 1799.
68. Samuel McD.—b. 1796, d. 1875—son of Andrew of 10.
69. Samuel—d. 1753—C: Elizabeth, David.
70. Samuel—d. 1808c—bro. to Mary (see 59), Sally, Martha, William.
71. Samuel—m. Phebe Paxton, 1790.
75. Samuel—m. Mary Thomas, 1801.
73. Samuel—m. Sally Scott, 1800.
74. Samuel—m. Elizabeth Snodgrass, 1806.
75. Samuel—m. Ann Hayslett, 1820.
76. Samuel R.—m. Mary S. Willson, 1823.
77. Sarah—m. John A. Chitham, 1823c.
78. Thomas—k. 1757.
80. Thomas—m. Mary Crouse, 1810.
81. Timothy—son of Andrew—b. 1784, d. 1858, m. M——— ———.
82. William—d. 1791—C: John, William, Quintin, Samuel, Jane, Mary, Margaret.
83. William—d. 1799—m. Sarah ——— —C: William, Samuel, Sally, Margaret, John, Nancy, Julian (dau.).
84. William—m. Agnes ——— —1786.
85. William—son of 10—C: Samuel, David, John, Eliab, Jane, Isabella, Elizabeth, Nancy.
86. William—m. Margaret McCown, 1795.
87. William—m. Nancy Jack, 1801.
88. William—m. Sassandra Paxton, 1808.
89. William—m. Christena Dods, 1812.
90. William—m. Sally Scott, 1818.
91. William—m. Mary Norris, 1820.
92. ——— —m. Jane Walker by 1797.

Moran.—Dominic—m. Elizabeth ——— by 1780.

Morehead.—1. John—d. 1834c—had C. 2. James—m. Jane Paxton, 1820.

Morgan.—1. Andrew—d. 1820—son of Francis—C: Benjamin, William, Frances (m. Nathaniel Wells), John. 2. Charity—m. George Cress, 1790. 3. Gabriel—m. Mary McNabb, 1795. 4. Jacob—m. Elizabeth McClure, 1807. 5. John—b. Elizabeth Smith. 1799. 6. John —m. Peggy Vance, 1809. 7. Luther—m. Nancy Dold, 1798. 8. Sarah—m. John McBride, 1799.

Morris.—1. Alexander—m. Peggy Till, 1802. 2. David—m. Elizabeth Aires, 1789. 3. Elijah—m. Jean Vansandt, 1801. 4. Elizabeth—m. John Beaty, 1798. 5. Elizabeth—m. John Bennington, 1818. 6. Isaac—m. Sarah McCutchen, 1787. 7. James—m. Sally Entsminger, 1817. 8. John—m. Agnes Ward, 1792. 9. John—m. Elizabeth Highman, 1792. 10. Mark—b. 1781, d. 1857, m. Margaret Hinkle, 1801—son of Mark and Ann. 11. Mary— m. Joshua Vinzant, 1794. 12. Peggy—m. Heyburn Rowlinson, 1799. 13. Polly—m. Jacob

MISCELLANEOUS DATA

Henkle, 1811. 14. Sally—m. Peter Nick, 1817. 15. Sarah—m. William Geerhart, 1801. 16. Thomas—m. Nancy Nick, 1807. 17. Thomas—m. Rachel Smith, 1823. 18. Richard—pension witness, 1832. 19. William—m. Anne Guinn, 1799 20. David—m. A. Bickett, 1823. 21. Patsy—m. John Plaugher, 1823.

Morrison.—1. Eleanor—m. William Henry, 1787. 2. James—m. Frances Brown, 1820. 3. James D.—b. 1833, d. 1902, m. Laura Chapin—son of William—C: William, Kenneth, Isaac.

Morter.—Jacob—d. 1838—m. Katharine Replogle, 1809—C: David, John, Sarah, Polly, Barbary A., Katharine, Elisa.

Morton.—Andrew—m. Mary Harper by 1802—doctor.

Murphy.—1. James—m. Susannah Harper, 1785 2. John—d. 1809—uncle to John and to Agnes Evans. 3. John, Joseph, William—orphans of Hugh Allen, 1805. 4. John—m. Elizabeth Lawson, 1799. 5. Joseph—m. Belinda Wall, 1815. 6. Nancy—m. Robert Evans, 1792. 7. William—m. Jean Allen, 1796. 8. William—m. ——— Culloch—neighbor to James Hall, 1800—C: John.

Muterspaw.—1. F——— —m. Christiana Agnor by 1824. 2. George—son of Philip and Nancy—b. in Md., 1781, d. 1856—m. Tiny ———. 3. Catharine—m. Henry Siders, 1810. 4. Mary—m. Abraham Cox, 1809

Myers.—1. Francis—m. Rebecca Wyse, 1803. 2. James—m. Polly Wilson, 1800. 3. John —d. 1787. 4. Sarah—m. James Howard, 1811.

McCown.—1. John—d. 1783—m. Agnes ——— —C: John, James (m. Jane ———), Malcolm (s), Mary (m. ——— Black), Agnes (m. ——— Sloat), Elizabeth (m. ——— Mayse); will names Walker, James, Agnes, Sloat, Eales, John.

2. John—son of 1—b. 1755, d. 1817—m. (1) Nancy Kinnear, (2) Eleanor McCampbell, 1794—C: John, Moses, Nancy R. (m. 1. David Orbison, 1817, 2. Christian Goul, 3. James Wilson), Andrew (m. Margaret Anderson), Ann G. (m. James Wilson, 1822), James G.

3. John—son of 2—b. 1784, d. 1850c—m. Mary Culton, 1810—C: John K., Robert C. (s), Nancy K. (b. 1815, d. 1894, m. Joseph K. Kirkpatrick, 1834), Jane E. (b. 1822, d. 1900, m. John H. Stuart, 1835).

4. John K.—son of 3—b. 1811, d. 1892, m. Mary M. Wilson, 1835—C: John W. (s), Sarah J. (m. Samuel W. Wilson, 1879), Mary A. (s), Martha E. (s), William H. (m. Ida K. Niswander of Rockingham Co.), Samuel W. (m. Anne K. McClure), Emma M. (m. John A. McNeil).

5. Moses—son of 2—d. 1854—m. Isabella Moore, 1823—C: William M. (m. 1. Sarah McCurdy, 2. Nancy Matheny).

6. James G.—son of 2—b. 1804, d. 1874, m. Mary Sprowl—C: Andrew G., Nancy A., Jane E., James W., John A., Samuel T.

Other Names: 7. Alexander—1752. 8. Francis—d. 1761—m. Margaret ——— —C (minors): George, Francis, Malcolm, James, Margaret, Katrine, Isble, Agnes. 9. George— Lincoln Co., Ky., 1811. 10. George—m. Sarah McCulloch, 1811. 11. James—b. 1731, living, 1805. 12. James—m. Mary Trotter, 1789. 13. Joseph—soldier, 1777. 14. Moses—bro. to John—m. ——— ———, 1765. 15. Margaret—m. William Moore, 1795. 16. Patrick—m. Nancy Stevens, 1789. 17. Patrick—d. 1772c. 18. Samuel—m. Elizabeth Moore, 1803. 19. Samuel—b. 1763, d. 1853. 20. ——— —m. Jane Hamilton.

Neely.—1. John—1751, 1786—m. Elizabeth ———. 2. William—d. 1782—m. Hannah ——— —C: James, Elizabeth, post.

Neil.—1. Hamilton—in Greene Co., Tenn., 1816. 2. Isabella—m. Samuel Patterson, 1802. 3. Patrick—d. 1802—m. Mary ——— —C: Mackinion, James, Patrick (Mary D. Beers, 1800), Hamilton, Hulker, Isabella (m. ——— Paten), Daniel, Graham. 4. Stoddard—m. Peggy Collins, 1807.

Nelson.—1. Elizabeth—b. 1790c—m. John Montgomery. 2. James—m. Agnes Henry, 1787. 3. John—m. Janet ———, by 1787.

Nesbit.—1. Samuel—b. 1754. 2. William—d. 1794—m. Margaret ——— —C: William, John, Andrew, Mary, Agnes, Margaret, Jean, Elizabeth.

Newcomer.—1. Elizabeth—m. Philip Hull, 1816. 2. Margaret—m. Stephen Leget, 1791. 3. William—m. Elizabeth Smith, 1820.

Newell—1. Henry—m. Patsy ——— by 1787. 2. Margaret—dau. of Robert—m. Duncan Campbell by 1812. 3. Samuel—m. Jane Montgomery—b. 1760c.

Newton.—1. Betsy—m. David White, 1817. 2. James—m. Phœbe Paxton, 1818.

Nicholas.—1. Barbara—m. Edward Gaylor, 1789. 2. Elizabeth—m. John Price, 1810. 3. Peter—m. Margaret E Goul, 1783. 4. ——— —m. Magdalene Coswell by 1805.

Niçely.—1. Barbara—dau. of Jacob and Margaret—b. in Shenandoah, 1782, d. 1856—m. James Bradds. 2. David—m. Peggy Wetter, 1812. 3. Jacob—m. Elizabeth Cook. 4. Michael—m. Elizabeth Sizer, 1808.

Nichols.—1. John—m. Elizabeth Hogshead, 1798. 2. Selina—m. John Irvine, 1821. 3. William—m. Ann ——— —Mecklenburg Co., N. C., 1779.

Knuckles—1. Rosanna—1789. 2. William—b. 1783.

Ocheltree.—1. Elizabeth—m. James Agnew, 1801. 2. James—d. 1803—C: Janet, John, James, Thomas, Nancy, Clency, Martha (m. William Ramsay, 1796). 3. James—m. Caty Paxton, 1818. 4. Jane—m. George Leyburn, 1815. 5. Jinny—m. John Alexander, 1803. 6. Michael—m. Betsy Findley, 1798. 7. Thomas—m. Jean Miller, 1796.

O'Friel.—Daniel—son of Morris—m. Agnes ——— by 1804.

Ogden.—1. Cornelius—m. Susanna Diehl, 1799. 2. Joseph—m. Sarah Wiars, 1806. 3. Sarah—m. Christian Roads, 1809.

Ogle.—1. Eleanor—m. John Campbell, 1799. 2. Samuel—m. Polly Caldwell, 1811.

Orbison.—1. David—m. Nancy K. McCown, 1811. 2. Eleanor M.—m. William M. Wilson—b. 1812c. 3. Elizabeth—m. William McCampbell, 1807. 4. Polly—m. John Gilmore, 1808. 5. Thomas—m. Jenny Moore, 1807. 6. Thomas—son of 7—C: Cassandra (m. ——— Mansfield), David, Samuel, William, Elizabeth, James. 7. John—d. 1829—m. Elizabeth ——— —C: Thomas (m. ——— McCampbell), Henry.

Ornbaum.—Lewis—d. 1818—m. Eve ——— —C: George, Andrew, James, Michael, Henry, Lewis, Polly (m. Andrew Mitchell, 1822), Betsy (m. Frederick Albright).

Otey.—1. Isaac—m. Elizabeth Matthews, 1789. 2. Jane—m. Walter Lockard, 1814. 3. Nancy—m. James Kemsey, 1807. 4. Nancy—orphan of William—1807. 5. Thomas—d. 1828—C: Panina, Joshua, Phebe, Solomon, Ruth, Hannah (m. ——— Bratton). 6. Thomas —m. Peggy Shuey, 1814.

Owens.—1. Peter—m. Polly Watkins, no date. 2. Peter—m Nancy Patterson, 1819.

Oyler.—1. Frederick—m. Elizabeth McGlockland, 1802. 2. Polina—m. William Wilmoth, 1820.

Painter.—1. Frederick—m. Elizabeth Beggs, 1815. 2. George—m. Mary Sorrels, 1820.

Palmer.—1. John—m. Nancy Crawford, 1790. 2. John—m. Mary Rodes, 1802. 3. Robert —m. Polly Gregory, 1817.

Paine.— ——— —m. Ann Gay by 1815—C: William, Robert G.

Parks.—1. James—m. Jean Buchanan, 1786. 2. John— b. 1714, d. 1793—m. Rebecca McCampbell?—C: Margaret (m. ——— Steele), Rebecca (m. ——— Evans). 3. Joseph —. Elizabeth Davis, 1795. 4. Joshua—m. Dorky Sweet, 1816. 5. Martha—m. William McComb, 1806. 6. Mary—m. Abraham Evans, 1788.

Parker.—1. Elizabeth—m. Matthew Shaw, 1791. 2. George—doctor, 1793. 3. Polly— m. Edward Bryan, 1790. 4. ——— —m. Sophia Harper by 1806.

Parsons.—1. David—m. Jean Pettigrew, 1817. 2. Elizabeth—m. John Fitzgerald, 1819.

3. George—m. Esther Anderson, 1805. 4. Nancy—m. Sylvanus Rowlinson, 1813. 5. Richard —m. Nancy Lants, 1805. 6. Richard—m. Jane Rowlinson, 1815.

Patterson.—1. Abigail—m. Jacob Caulk, 1793.
 2. Adam—m. Sophia Jones, 1796.
 3. Andrew—1764.
 4. Frances—m. Peter Bratton, 1794.
 5. Isabella—m. John Dixons, 1794.
 6. James—m. Agnes Berryhill, 1794.
 7. Jane—m. John Patterson, 1794.
 8. Jamiston, H.—m. Polly Hight, 1821.
 9. Jinny—m. Lewis Quigley, 1814.
 10. John—d. 1749—m. Agnes ——, related to Joseph Lapsley—C: John, Agnes, George.
 11. John A.—bro.-in-law to James Willson, 1837.
 12. Joseph—m. Jean Walker, 1791—Cedar Co., Ky., 1810.
 13. Mary—m. Alexander Stuart.
 14. Nancy—m. Peter Owens, 1819.
 15. Patty—m. William Watkins, 1816.
 16. Robert T.—1864.
 17. Sally—m. John Craig, 1795.
 18. Sally—m. John Silling, 1798.
 19. Samuel—d. 1803—C: William, James, Samuel.
 20. Samuel F.—son of Samuel—b. 1799, d. 1874—N. C.
 21. Samuel—b. 1769, d. 1841.
 22. Samuel—m. Polly Finley—C: Finley, Andrew.
 23. Thomas—m. Precilla Garrison, 1794.
 24. William—m. Rebecca Campbell, 1823.
 25. William—m. Sally Steele, 1795.
 26. William—b. 1765, d. 1842.
 27. —— —m. James McChesney.
 28. —— —m. Mary Martin by 1770.

Patton.—1. Betsy—m. David Wilson, 1799.
 2. Elizabeth—m. Benjamin McFall, 1794.
 3. Isbel—m. Archibald Alexander, 1795
 4. James—d. 1814—m. Sarah Wilson—C: John (d. 1802), Matthew, William (d. 1837), James, Elizabeth (m. —— Wilson), Nancy (m. —— Jameson), Margaret (m. David Wasson, 1811), Isabella (m. —— Ireland), Mary (m. Nathaniel Taylor, 1791), Sarah (m. Thomas McDowell, 1808, d. 1820c).
 5. John—d. 1757—m. Agnes —— —C (minors): William, James, Margaret, Isabel, Agnes.
 6. John—d. 1809—m. Martha —— —C: Jane, Nathan, John, Thomas, Nancy, Nathaniel, Patsy, Polly.
 7. John—m. Phebe Taylor, 1812.
 8. Joseph—m. Ann Brown, 1810.
 9. Joseph M.—m. Elizabeth Patton, 1818.
 10. Martha—m. James Campbell, 1800.
 10x. McClung—b. 1795, d. 1865—m. Elizabeth ——.
 11. Mary—m. John McKee, 1797.
 12. Nancy—m. Jesse Davis, 1806.
 13. Nancy—m. William Milligan, 1812.
 14. Nancy—m. Joseph Wilson, 1820.

518   A HISTORY OF ROCKBRIDGE COUNTY, VIRGINIA

15. Nathan—m. Jean Campbell, 1809.
16. Nathaniel—m. Polly Robison, 1797.
17. Patsy—m. William Hopkins, 1805.
18. Polly—m. Charles Kirkpatrick, 1803.
19. Samuel—m. Jenny McClung, 1789.
20. Sarah—m. Thomas McDowell, 1808.
21. Thomas—m. Peggy Ewin, 1805.
22. Thomas—m. Jenny Glasgow, 1805.
23. William—d. 1830—m. Nancy ——— —C: John, Joseph d. 1837), Isabel (see 3), James, William, Matthew, David, Ann, Nancy. Polly (d. 1820c), Samuel, Margaret (m. ——— Clung).
24. William—b. 1743, living, 1806.
25. William—d. 1793—m. 1740c, Mary Beaty in Ireland—C: John.
26. William—m. Sally Elwood, 1802.
27. William—m. Martha Bailey, 1803.
28. ——— —m. Isabella Neil by 1802.
29. ——— — m. Rachel Kincaid by 1824.

Paul.—1. Andrew—d. 1833—C: James. 2. Ann—b. 1758, d. 1828—m. (1) James Taylor, 1768, (2) William McCorkle, 1802. 3. Audley—b. 1731, d. 1800c—C: Ann (see 2), ——— (m. George Taylor), Audley, Jr. 4. Audley—son of 3—b. 1770c, living 1839—m. Agnes Cochran by 1805. 5. Elizabeth—m. Archer Defries, 1796. 6. Esther—1828. 7. George M.—m. Sally Wilson, 1810. 8. Hugh—b. 1707—m. Jane Lynn—C: John, Audley (see 3), Polly (m. George Mathews), ——— (m. John Stuart of Greenbrier). 9. Isabella—m. James Beaty, 1789. 10. Jean—d. 1826—m. ——— McClung. 11. Jenny—m. James Anderson, 1806. 12. John—m. Elizabeth Reed, 1823. 13. John—Agnes ———, b. 1763, d. 1795. 14. Samuel—m. Phœbe Bates, 1796. 15. William—d. 1757—exr.—Charles Hays, James Moore. 16. ——— — m. Nancy Porter by 1794.

Paxton.—1. James—d. 1745—m. Elizabeth Alexander—C: John, Joseph (d. 1755's), Samuel, Thomas, William.

2. John—son of 1.b. 1716, d. 1787—m. Mary Blair, 1742c—C: John, Isabel (m. John Lyle), Joseph (m. Margaret Barclay), William, Elizabeth (m. Samuel Houston), Hannar M. (m. James Caruthers, 1793), Mary (m. Thomas Conn, 1787), James.

3. John—son of 2—b. 1743, d. 1787, m. Phœbe Alexander, 1767—C: John (b. 1768, m. Elizabeth Logan, 1789), James, Margaret (s), Archibald, William (m. Nancy Logan), Joseph (m. Elizabeth Paxton, 1804), Isabella (m. Hugh Paxton, 1802), Polly (b. 1784, d. 1859, m. William Paxton), Alexander (s).

4. James—son of 3—b. 1770, d. 1838, m. Nancy Dickson, 1808—C: Thomas N., Sarah A. (m. ——— Risk), Elizabeth, Lucinda.

5. Samuel—son of 1—b. 1730, d. 1756, m. Mary Moore—C: Samuel (b. 1754, d. 1824, m. Margaret Thompson.

6. Thomas—son of 1—b. 1719, d. 1788, m. (1) Elizabeth McClung, 1746, (2) Mary Barclay, 1774—C: John, Samuel, William, James (m? ——— Edmondson), Thomas (m. Rebecca Hogshead, 1790), Sarah (David Edmondson), Mary (m. John Tedford), Jean (m. Andrew Cummings), Joseph (d. 1817); by 2d w.—Joseph (s), Hugh (m. Isabella Paxton, 1802), Hannah (m. Cornelius Goodwin, 1796), David, Isaac, Elizabeth (m. Joseph Paxton, 1804), Rachel (m. Joseph Blair).

7. John—son of 6—b. 1747, d. 1832, m. Sarah Walker—C: Elizabeth (m. David Hall, 1794), Thomas, Nancy (m. John Donald, 1813), Joseph (m. Sarah Edmondson, 1803), Mary (m. David Rice, 1804), John (m. John Cowan, 1815), John D. (b. 1784, d. 1868, m. 3 times), Samuel, James H. (m. Elizabeth S. Houston).

8. Joseph—son of 7—C: Thomas P., David P. (s), John W., Joseph W., Samuel H., James T. (m. in Ky.), William F. (d. 1862).

9. Thomas P.—b. 1803, d. 1893, m. (1) Phœbe McCluer, (2) Elizabeth H. Sterrett—C: Sarah P. (by 1st w.), Alexander S. (m. 1. Mamie Hall, 2. Mary F. Tapscott), Joseph McC., Emma L. (m. Robert L. McCulloch), James H. (m. Fannie C. Jones, David E. (m. Carrie L. Boyd), Reubenia A. (m. John T. Campbell).

10. Samuel—son of 6—b. 1748, d. 1807—m. (1) Sarah Coalter, (2) Jane Smiley—C (all by 1st w.): William (b. 1803, d. 1879, m. Sarah P. Burks), Frances J. (s), Agnes A. (m. Alfred Douglass), Hannah E. (m. William Crawford, 1829).

11. William—son of 6—b. 1757, d. 1838, m. Jane Grigsby, 1787—C: Joseph (m. Elvira Bagby, 1815), Elizabeth (m. Alexander T. McClure, 1808), Martha (m. Joseph Steele), Phœbe (m. John Grigsby), Sally (m. Robert Templeton, 1829), Rachel (s), Thomas, John (s), Samuel (s), Benjamin P., William, Frances J. (s), Agnes A. (m. Alfred Douglas), Hannah E. (m. William Crawford, 1829).

12. Hugh—son of 6—C: Lucinda (m. 1. Thomas C. Poague, 1821, 2. William B. Sterrett, 1830), Aurelia R. (m. 1. Peter A. Salling, 2. Jacob Mohler), Mary J. (m. Edwin Jordan), Margaret (m. Cornelius C. Baldwin, 1837), Hannah, John A. (b. 1819, m. Hannah McClelland), Elizabeth A. (m. B—— J. Jordan).

13. William—son of 1—b. 1733, d. 1795, m. Eleanor Hays—C: Joseph (m. Esther Lyle, 1787), Polly (m. Samuel Greenlee, 1798), Sarah (m. N—— Prior), John, Susannah (b. 1772, m. Joseph Gilmore, 1793), Elizabeth (m. David Sawyers, 1794), Isabella (m. Andrew Alexander, 1800), William, James, Elisha.

14. William—son of 13—b. 1777, d. 1853, m. Polly Paxton, 1804—C: Archibald S. (s), Mary E. (3d w. of Alexander T. Barclay), James H., Phœbe A. (m. James W. McClung), Margaret P. (b. 1817, d. 1892, m. Samuel R. Houston), William B. (m. in Ky).

15. James H.—b. 1812, d. 1902, m. Katharine A. Glasgow, 1862—C: Nellie, Kate G., Archibald H., Robert, William T., James H., J. Gordon.

16. James—m. Catharine Jordan, 1817—commandant of arsenal.

17. Elisha—m. Margaret McNutt, 1809—C: James G. (b. 1822, d. 1870), William H., Alexander McN., Andrew J., John G., Rachel G. (m. —— Buckner), Elisha F.

18. Elisha F.—b. 1829, d. 1863—C: Matthew W. (m. Mary L. Hopkins), John G., Frank.

18. William—son of 2—b. 1751, d. 1817, m. Elizabeth Stuart, 1773—C: John (d. 1874), James, Elizabeth, William (m. Sarah G. McDowell), Jean (m. Alexander S. Hall), Joseph (m? Sarah Edmondson).

20. James—son of 19—b. 1790—m. (1) Elizabeth Blair, 1814, (2) Eliza Poague Gibson—C (by 1st w.): William (m. Julia Moffett, 1835), Elizabeth S. (m. John B. Poague, 1835), Jean A. (m. David Guthrie), Elvira H. (m. John F. Shields), James (s), Robert S.—by 2d w.—Adaline (m. John Guthrie), Amanda R. (m. Thomas Mann), Isabella C. (m. John R. Guy), John H. (k. 1863), Margaret C. (m. in Miss.), Emma L., Horace A. (s), Rice P. (s).

21. Joseph—son of 2—widow m. —— Gilliland—C: Cassandra (m. William Moore, 1808), Mary (m. George Coulter, 1809), Hannah (m. David Edmondson), Harriet (m. Horatio Philpot).

22. James—b. 1762, accidentally k. by David Grinstead, 1788—m. Phœbe McClung, 1786—C: James A. (b. 1788, d. 1825, m. Maria Marshall).

23. Thomas—bro. to 1—b. 1690c, d. 1762—m. Sarah —— —C: Thomas, Elizabeth, Samuel, Elizabeth (m. —— Eakin).

24. Thomas—son of 23—b. 1713c, m. Jane Eakin—C: Martha (b. 1753, m. Robert Crawford), Margaret (m. D—— McGregor), Elizabeth (m. —— McCune), Thomas (b. 1769, m. Jane Crawford, 1800c.

25. Elizabeth—dau. of 23—m. (1) Thomas Taylor, (2) Nathaniel Robinson.

26. Samuel—d. 1756—m. Mary —— —C: Samuel, 1 other.

Other Names:—27. Betsy—m. Charles Cartright, 1812.
28. Catharine—m. James Ocheltree, 1818.
29. Catharine—m. Malachi Staley, 1818.
30. Elizabeth—m. Joseph Blair, 1812.
31. Elizabeth—m. John Stephenson, 1788.
32. Hannah—m. Cornelius Goodwin, 1796.
33. Hannah—m. Robert McCormick, 1817.
34. Hannah—m. John Moore, 1797.
35. Hugh—m. Julian Moore, 1798.
36. Hugh—m. Ibby Paxton, 1802.
37. Jane—m. Samuel McVey, 1794.
38. Jane L.—m. Alexander L. Hall, 1818.
39. John L.—m. Esther Cummins, 1812.
40. John—m. Martha Blair, 1730c.
41. Jonathan—b. 1777, m. Nancy Gilmore, 1799—C: Martha (m. Robert Gilmore, 1818).
42. Joseph—son of William—C. Hester (m. Benjamin Higgenbotham), Mary J. (b. 1791, m. Robert S. Campbell, 1814), Sallie (m. Samuel Cummings, 1809).
43. Joseph—d. 1756—cousin to Thomas Jackston—see 1.
44. Joseph—m. Jane McClure, 1792.
45. Joseph—m. Nancy Scott, 1801.
46. Nancy—m. Samuel C. Whiteside, 1818.
47. Nathaniel—son of 23?—m. Hannah —————C: Nathaniel (m. Jane Gilmore), John, Samuel, Andrew.
48. Nathaniel—son of 47—C: James G. (m. Betty Adair), Sarah (m. David Hart), Nathaniel (m. Margaret Hart), Jane (m. George McCullough).
49. John—son of 47—d. 1784, m. Mary ————C: Isaac, Sarah, T. Fergus, John, Mary (m. Samuel Fergus), Martha (m. John Paxton), William.
50. Samuel—son of 47—m. Agnes ————C: Mary, Samuel, Margaret, Jean.
51. Andrew—son of 47—C: James (m. ———— Biggerhead).
52. Patsy—m. Jacob Steel, 1817.
53. Patsy—C (1801): Martha, Phœbe.
54. Phœbe—m. Samuel Moore, 1790.
55. Phœbe—m. Joseph Newton, 1818.
56. Polly—m. John Corbit, 1798.
57. Polly—m. James Greenlee, 1812.
58. Polly—orphan of John, 1804.
59. Sally—m. Samuel B. Graham, 1816.
60. Sally—m. John Shaw, 1796.
61. Samuel—C: Thomas, John (m. Jane Wilson, 1797), David, Margaret (m. Moses Whiteside, 1797), William (m. Elizabeth Wilson).
62. Samuel—m. Rachel ———— —C: John, Samuel, Thomas.
63. John—son of 62—C: Nathaniel (m. ———— McFarland).
64. Samuel—m. Rachel Whiteman, 1798—C: Samuel (m. Esther Wilson).
65. Thomas—son of 62—b? 1739—m. (1) Isabella Quate, (2) Martha White—C: Roert (m. Adoris Archer), Isabella (m. John Ramsay), Nancy (m. ———— Smith), Margery (m. S———— Hutchinson), Jane (m. Owen Todd), Bettie (m. John Donnell), Sarah (m. Robert Orr), Mary (m. David Snider), Rebecca (m. Silas J. Jack), Samuel (m. ———— Weller), Thomas (m. ———— Barbour); by 2d w.—Jane, Isabella, Nathaniel, Hugh, George, Benjamin, Robert, Moses, David, Joseph, Grizel, Sarah (m. ———— Whitman), Mary (m. John Torbet).

MISCELLANEOUS DATA 521

66. Thomas—son of 61—b. 1764, d. 1839—m. Martha Steele, 1781—C: Thomas (b. 1801, d. 1885, m. Polly Edley), Samuel (m. Nancy McCorkle, 1825), John S. (m. Margaret Steele of Monroe Co.), William (m. Isabella Kirkpatrick), Martha (m. Samuel D. Smiley), Jane (m. James Morehead, 1820), Phœbe (m. James Newton), Alexander (m. Nancy W. Switcher, 1836), David (m. Jane Paxton).

67. Samuel—m. Catharine Atkinson, 1790—b. 1766, d. 1841.
68. Samuel—m. Rachel Whiteman, 1798.
69. Samuel—m. Isabella Taylor, 1800.
70. Samuel—m. Susanna Smiley, 1816.
71. Samuel—m. Agnes ——— —1781.
72. Samuel—d. 1834—m. Jean ——— —C: James, Samuel, David C., William, John W., Sarah (m. Thomas Dixon), Betsy (m. ——— McKnight).
73. Samuel—d. 1763.
74. Samuel—b. 1736—son of Thomas.
75. Samuel—b. 1766—son of Elizabeth.
76. Sarah—m. Thomas Dixon, 1809.
77. Sarah—m. Thomas Dunaway, 1792.
78. William—m. Elizabeth Miller, 1803.
79. William—m. Jean Grigsby, 1787.
80. William—m. Elizabeth Miller, 1803.
81. ——— ——. Daniel Lyle.

Peck.—1. Garret—m. Peggy Croddy. 2. Jacob—m. ——— Coursey by 1814—C: Jacob.

Peebles.—1. Thomas—m. Simpson, 1800. 2. William—m. Elizabeth Edmondson by 1761—neighbor to Nathan, or Nathaniel.

Peerman.—1. Michael—m. Catharine Gaylor, 1792. 2. Michael, Jr.—m. Polly Riley, 1817.

Peery.—1. Thomas—k. 1761. 2. ——— —m. Margaret Martin by 1801.

Parry.—1. Esther m. William Watkins, 1801. 2. James—m. Polly Smith, 1799. 3. Martha—m. ——— Hannah by 1815. 4. Mary—m. Robert C. McClure—b. 1820c.

Peters.—1. Barbara—m. Samuel Burgess, 1800. 2. Catharine—orphan of Jonas, 1801. 3. Catharine—m. Christopher Rader, 1801. 4. John—m. Sally Steele, 1821. 5. John—m. Nancy Liptrap, 1821. 6. Mary—m. Adam Seaglor, 1788. 7. Polly—m. James Littel, 1823. 8. Sally—m. Alexander McCorkle, 1822.

Pettigrew.—1. Ann—m. Peter Barger, 1816. 2. Betsy—m. James Kent, 1806. 3. James —d. 1795—m. Jean ——— —C: James, Samuel, Robert, William, Elizabeth. 4. Jane—m. David Parsons, 1817. 5. Robert—m. Martha McCalmon, 1806. 6. Robert—m. Jane Grigsby, 1818. 7. Samuel—m. Peace W. Buchanan, 1812. 8. Samuel—m. Hannah Gamble, 1817.

Phillips.—1. Sarah—m. John Albright, 1807. 2. ——— ———m. Mary Lusk by 1771.

Pine.—1. Agnes—m. James Harvey, 1788. 2. Edward—m. Polly Watts, 1788. 3. Robert —m. Mary Cammock, 1795.

Pinkerton.—1 Elizabeth—m. Walter Currice, 1810. 2. James—m. Mary Foster, 1788. 3. Mary—m. John McCampbell, 1797.

Plott.—1. Abraham—m. Polly Gaylor, 1823. 2. Elizabeth—m. Andrew Miller, 1805. 3. Henry—m. Catharine Entsminger, 1791. 4. Joseph—1803. 5. Mary—m. Andrew Entsminger, 1791. 6. Peggy—m. Jacob Hosteter, 1814. 7. Polly—m. Gasper Thomas, 1823.

Plunkett.—1. James—m. Peggy McMullen, 1815. 2. Mary—m. Thomas Rickett, 1811. 3 Thomas—d. 1831—m. Polly——— .

Poague.—1. Anne—m. Alexander Wood, 1789.
2. Elizabeth—m. John Allen, 1801.
3. Isabella G.—m. Richard Gibbs, 1819.
4. James—m. Anne ——— by 1770.

5. James—m. Nancy Hogshead?—d. 1817—C: Amy, John G., Thomas, William, James M., Eli, Rebeckah (m. Thomas Dryden, 1803).
5. James—m. Mary Henry, 1793.
6. Jean—m. Matthew Whiteman, 1806.
7. Jenny—sister to 16—m. Joseph Allen, 1800.
8. John—m? Mary Crawford, 1751—Forks.
9. John—d. 1803—C: William, Grisel, James, Thomas, Rebekah.
10. John—m. Martha Rankin, 1798.
11. John—m. Rachel Barclay Crawford, 1792.
12. John—m. Mary Boils, 1796.
13. John B.—m. Elizabeth S. Paxton, 1835.
14. Jonathan—m. Martha Baggs, 1794.
15. Nancy—m. Alexander T. Barclay, 1819.
16. Polly—m. William Houston, 1805.
17. Rebecca—m. Thomas Dryden, 1803.
18. Robert—m. Martha Crawford, 1791.
19. Robert—d. 1779—m. Margaret ———.
20. Robert, Sr.—m. Elizabeth ——— —1753.
21. Robert—m. Jean Somers—C: Jonathan, Ann (m. Isaac Caruthers), Martha (m. James Moore), 7 others.
22. Sally—m. Thomas Lackey, 1820.
23. Thomas—1765.
24. Thomas—son of Robert (immigrant)—m. Polly McClenahan—C: Elijah, Robert, William, Elizabeth, Ann, Polly, Agnes, John (see 11).
25. Thomas C.—m. Lucinda Paxton, 1821—d. 1773—n. c.
26. ——— —C: William d. by 1813), John (d. by 1813; C: Rebecca, Sarah), James (has Ann), Jonathan (has John, James, Jonathan).

Pollock.—1. James—C: James, William, ———, Isabella (m. ——— Handly). 2. James —son of William (above)—b. 1742—C: Isabella (see Poague, 3), 3. James—m. Margaret ——— —1786. 4. Sarah—m. Robert Moore, 1793.

Porter.—1. Agnes—m. John McCutchen, 1789.
2. Alexander, Sr.—d. 1811—m. Mary ——— —C: Elizabeth, Agnes, Martha, Mary, Sarah, David, Rebecca.
3. David—m. Polly Culton, 1803.
4. Elizabeth—m. David Moore, 1820.
5. Elizabeth—m. William McCampbell, 1804.
6. James—b. 1727c, living, 1798.
7. Jean—m. Nathaniel McClure, 1795.
8. John—d. 1805—m. Hannah ——— —C: Nancy (m. ——— Paul), Jane (m. ——— Wilson), William, John.
9. John—m. Rebecca Stuart, 1809.
10. Letty—m. Andrew Wilson, 1789.
11. Robert—m. Elizabeth Blair, 1790.
12. Samuel—m. Nancy Culton by 1826.
13. William—d. 1782—m. Gene ——— —C: John, William, Margaret (m. ——— Mitchell), Mary (m. ——— Mackey).
14. William—d. 1804—m. Mary ——— —C: Agnes (see 1), William, Jean (see 7), Mary (m. ——— Sharp), Lilly (m. ——— Wilburn), John, David, Charles, Elizabeth, Joseph, Stephen, Samuel, Ross.
15. William—m. Fanny Tharp, 1796.
16. William—m. Esther McCorkle, 1799.
17. ——— —m. Esther Mackey by 1810.

Potter.—1. Barbara—m. James Smiley, 1823. 2. David—m. Susanna Ballard, 1822. 3. John—m. Lucy Sharp, 1803. 4. Margaret—d. 1819—C: Patty, Letty, Eve, Barbaray, Charles. 5. Philip—d. 1834—m. Kathine —————— —C: David (b. 1783, d. 1855), Sophy (m. —————— Mais). 6. Philip—m. Betty Hart, 1804.

Pressly.—1. Mary—m. John Davies, 1788. 2. William—d. 1801—m. Mary —————— —C: William (has William, Samuel), James, Eliner, Nancy, Patsy. 3. William—m. Sarah Beach, 1787.

Price.—1. Jean—m. James McCroskey, 1808. 2. Sally H.—m. Robert Scott, 1805. 3. William—d. 1818. 4. —————— —m. Elizabeth Campbell by 1754.

Pryor.—1. John—m. Sally Margrave, 1812. 2. N—————— —m. Sally Paxton by 1796.

Pullin.—1. Elizabeth—m. William Bogins, 1801. 2. Joseph—m. Betsy Moody, 1801. 3. Sophia—m. James Kingan, 1797. 4. Thomas—m. Elizabeth Grove, 1809.

Quigley.—1. Jane—m. John Wallace, 1817. 2. Lewis—m. Jinny Patterson, 1814.

Rader.—1. Christopher—m. Rebecca Neece, 1801. 2. Christopher—m. Catharine Peeters, 1801.

Ramsay.—1. Hugh—m. Frankey Shepherd, 1803. James—m. Jane Lyle—doctor. 3. James—m. Keziah Davis, 1798. 4. James—d. 1759c. 5. James—m. Mary Kerr, 1794. 6. Jennett—m. Edward Cryden, 1786. 7. John—m. Elizabeth Campbell, 1792. 8. John—in court, 1803. 9. Peggy—m. George Adair, 1808. 10. Robert—d. 1759. 10x. Robert—m. —————— Beard by 1812. 11. Sally—m. John Hogan, 1809. 12. Sarah—m. James McKehen, 1795. 13. Samuel—m. Polly Ramsay, 1819. 14. William—m. Polly Carter, 1798. 15. William—d. 1789—m. Jane —————— —C: William, Samuel, James, Fanny (m. —————— Scott), Jane (m. —————— Lyle), Sarah, Elizabeth, Mary. 16. William—m. Martha Ocheltree, 1796. 17. Will—m. Rebecca Miller, 1798. 18. —————— —m. Mary McConkey by 1812.

Rapp.—1. Anthony—b. 1798, d. 1835, m. Sarah J. ——————. 2. Anthony—m. Polly Holden, 1822. 3. John—m. Elizabeth Oiler, 1796. 4. Mathias—d. 1818—m. Margaret —————— —C: Henry, George, Joseph.

Reany.—William—m. Jane Armstrong—C (1837): McKee, Martha J., Rebecca A., Mary, John A.

Reardon.—John—b. 1757c—m. Elizabeth Hall, 1797—C 1815c): 6.

Reed.—1. Alexander—d. 1816—m. Martha —————— —C: Robert, James, Hugh, Nancy, Mary (m. —————— Goodwin), Barbary, Rebecca (m. —————— Kiger), Betsy. 2. Daniel—d. 1815—m. Margaret —————— —C: Daniel, Andrew W., Ann (m. —————— Taylor), Adam, Elizabeth (m. —————— Bunten), James, William, John, Nancy (m. —————— Willey), Daniel. 3. Joseph—d. 1798—m. Mary McClure—C: Thomas, James, Jean. 4. Manuel—m. Catharine Dice by 1830. 5. Peter—m. Sally Miller, 1799. 6. Philip—d. 1819—m. Mary —————— —C: Immanuel, Philip, Betsy, Susannah. 7. Robert—m. Isabella Walker, 1790. 8. Robert—m. Sarah Notfield, 1790. 9. Thomas—m. Polley Smiley, 1799. 10. William—uncle to James—d. 1819—m. Agnes ——————. 11. —————— —m. Elizabeth Fulton by 1799.

2. Adam—d. 1789—m. Barbara —————— —C: William, Daniel, Katron (m. —————— Wilson); Adam, a g'son.

3. Andrew—m. Magdalene McDowell—C: Magdalena, Ann A., Sally (m. Moore), Elizabeth, Alexander (has Agnes), Margaret M. (m. William H. Venable, 1823), Mary (m. John McCampbell), Samuel McD., 1 other son, 2 dau.

4. Andrew—C: Agnes A. (m. William Alexander).
5. Betsy—m. John Alexander, 1815.
6. Catharine—m. Robert Smith, 1796.
7. Daniel—m. Letitia Scott, 1816.
8. Downey—m. Ailse Dihart, 1788.
9. Flora—m. John Lyle.
10. Frederick—son of Jasper and E—————— —b. in Pa., 1759, d. 1855.

11. George—m. Martha Fulton, 1792.
12. Isabel—m. Henry Ayres, 1788.
13. James—m. Peggy Kirkpatrick, 1818.
14. Jane—m. Samuel W. Venable, 1821.
15. John—m. Mary Scott, 1819.
16. Martha—m. Abraham Smith, 1823.
17. Michael—d. 1832—m. Ann K. ——— —C: Benjamin, Elizabeth (m. —— Wiseman).
18. Philip—m. Mary Scott, 1819.
19. Polly—m. John McCampbell, 1806.
20. Sally—m. Andrew Trout, 1821.
21. Samuel McD.—son of 3—m. Sarah E. Hare—C: Mary L. (m. James J. White), Agnes (m. J. DeHart Ross, Culpeper)—b. 1790, d. 1869.
22. Thomas—d. 1821—uncle to Thomas.
23. ——— —m. Betsy ——— —C: Gasper (d. 1825), Christopher, Polly, Andrew, William, Sally.
24. ——— —m. Margaret Kilpatrick by 1823.

Renick.—1. Robert—k. 1757—C: William, Robert, Thomas, Joshua, Betsy, 2 others. 2. Samuel—m. Jane Lindsay, 1823.

Replogle.—Balsor—d. 1810—m. Barbara ——— —C: Elidabeth, Mary (m. Charles Ayres, 1818), Catharine, Hannah (m. Daniel Eyres, 1816), Susanna (m. James Anderson, 1814), Sarah, Barbara, Margaret (m. John Carter, 1821), David, Jacob, John.
 2. Catharine—dau. of 1—b. 1788, d. 1858, m. Jacob Morter, 1809.

Reynolds.—1. James—d. 1749. 2. Johnson—m. Elizabeth Blair, 1821. 3. Polly—m. William Armentrout, 1820. 4. Michael—m. Nancy Tools, 1798. 5. Richard—m. Elizabeth ——— by 1767.

Rhea.—1. Archibald—d. 1776c—C: William, Hugh, John. 2. Archibald—m. Ann Humphries, 1798. 3. Elizabeth—m. Richard M. Wilson, 1807. 4. Elizabeth—m. Martha Koiner, 1792. 5. George—m. Mary ———, 1816, b. 1794. 6. Hugh—m. Rebecca Smiley, 1796. 7. Jane—m. Abraham Dick, 1782. 8. Jean—m. Benjamin Larew, 1808. 9. John—m. Sally Standoff, 1809. 10. Martha—m. Samuel Workman, 1785. 11. Robert —. Patsy Adams, 1818. 12. William—d. 1777—m. Elizabeth ——— —C: John (m. —— Turk of Thomas), Alexander, Nancy (m. Joseph Ritchy), Elizabeth (m. Robert Rhea), James (out of county), Thomas, Margaret, Hannah, Polly, Martha, Jane, Archibald (see 1), Ann (m. —— Lockridge). 13. ——— —m. Mary Gay 1781—C: Agnes.

Rhodes.—1. Abraham—m. Elizabeth Thomas, 1810. 2. Catharine—m. George Gale, 1800. 3. Catharine—. Andrew Lair, 1803. 4. Christian—m. Sarah Ogden, 1809. 5. Eve—m. Philip Syler, 1790. 6. Jean—m. George Good, 1799. 7. Margaret—b. 1758, d. 1830. 8. Mary—m. John Palmer, 1802.

Rice.—1. Benjamin H.—m. Martha Alexander, 1814. 2. David—m. Polly Paxton, 1804—C: Catharine, Sally.

Richardson.— ——— —m. Arnot (woman)—Clarke Co., Ky., 1758c.

Rickett.—1. John—m. Elizabeth Hall, 1804. 2. Sally—m. William Haislet, 1823. 3. Thomas—m. Mary Plunkett, 1811.

Riddle.—1. John—m. Catharine Dial, 1809. 2. John—m. Nancy Fenter, 1816. 3. ——— —m. George Campbell, 1789.

Riley.—1. Barbara—m. Zachariah Woods, 1823. 2. Betsy—m. John Hight, 1815. 3. Elizabeth—m. James Sweet, 1807. 4. Margaret—m. James Elder, 1790. 5. Mary—m. Andrew Benson, 1790. 6. Nancy—m. Robert McPherson, 1801. 7. Polly—m. Michael Pearman, Jr., 1817.

Ripley.—1. Betty—m. John Waskey, 1801. 2. Catharine—m. George Barger, 1807. 3. Christian—m. Polly Waskey, 1807. 4. Henry—m. Abigail Banning, 1797. 5. John—m.

MISCELLANEOUS DATA

Mary Waskey, 1802. 7. Matthias—d. 1814—m. Barbara ———, d. 1824—C (partly minors in 1812) : Jacob, Betsy, John, Polly, Catharine, Ann, Sally, Peggy, William, Valentine.

Risk.—1. Elizabeth—dau. of William and M——— —b. 1775, d. 1855. 2. James—m. Elizabeth Risk, 1785. 3. James—m. Jane Fulton, 1813. 4. John—m. Jannett Brown, 1786. 5. John—m. Sarah Henderson, 1796. 6. Mary—m. John Lynch, 1795. 7. ——— —m. Sarah A. Paxton by 1839.

Ritchey.—1. Abel—m. Mary Wasson, 1806. 2. James—d. 1797c—m. Jain ——— C: ——— (m. John Smith), Margaret (m. ——— Evans), Jain (m. ——— Boils), Mary (m. ——— Mecartin), Able, Ann, James. 3. James—b. 1777, d. 1826. 4. James—m. Isabella Crawford. 1798. 5. John—d. 1812—m. Rebecca ——— —C: Robert (in Botetourt), Nancy (m. John Moore), Jenny (m. William Greenwood), Peggy (m. Duncan McCahan). 6. John—d. 1780 —estate, $423.68. 7. John—m. Rebecca Miller, 1801. 7x. Joseph—m. Nancy Rhea by 1777. 8. Mary—m. Andrew McCaslin, 1790. 9. Robert C.—m. Ann Richey, 1797. 10. William, Sr., and Jr.—1769. 11. ——— —m. Mary Campbell by 1777.

Roach.—1. Charles—m. Elizabeth Croddy, 1804. 2. Robert—m. Rebecca McFarland, 1787. 3. ——— —m. Betsy Ptomey by 1833.

Robertson.—1. Elizabeth—m. William Stuart, 1804. 2. James—d. 1754—Martha, admr —C: George, Alexander, post. 3. John—m. Nancy Hall, 1804. 4. Thomas—m. Catharine Moody, 1808.

Robinson.—1. Ann—m. Jacob Icenhower, 1808.

2. Eleanor—m. Alexander Hamilton, 1812.

3 Eleanor—d. 1826—sister to Elizabeth McCutchen—cousin to William Willson, Jr., Uriah Gillam, Betsy McCutchen (dau. of Samuel), Betsy, Willson, Betsy Benson, Betsy (m. John McCutchen, Jr.), Nancy (m. Samuel McCutchen), Nancy (m. Joseph McCutchen), Catharine Hodge, Drusilla Hodge, Polly Hodge, Eleanor McCutchen.

4. James—d. 1748c—m. Hannah ——— —James, admr.

5. John—d. 1789—m. Sarah ——— —C: John, David, Isabella (m. ——— Kerr), Mary, Rebecca, Sarah, Jean, Hannah.

6. John—m. Margaret Bennett by 1779.

7. John—d. 1817—m. Eleanor ——— —C: Sally, John, David, ——— (m. James Robinson), Mitchell.

8. Margaret—m. Stephen Worley, 1812.

9. Mary—m. William Hutson, 1785.

10. Nathaniel—m. ——— Paxton by 1762.

11. Peggy—m. James Hamilton, 1804.

12. Polly—m. Nathaniel Patton, 1797.

13. Polly—m. James Oliver, 1807.

14. Rachel—m. Robert Short, 1811.

15. Samuel—d. 1822—bro. to Thomas.

16. Samuel—m. Hannah ——— —Washington Co., 1779.

17. Thomas—m. Nancy Paxton—b. 1805c—g'son of Matthew.

18. William—d. 1765—m. Isabella—C: John.

19. William—m. ——— McCalpin by 1789.

20. ——— —m. Margaret Wallas—C (1779) : William.

Rogers.—1. Anniel—m. Rachel Campbell by 1826. 2. Betsy—m. ——— Carson, 1810. 3. David—d. 1809—m. Elizabeth ——— —C: Jeremiah, 4 "darters." 4. David—m. Elizabeth Olingar, 1798. 5. Irene—m. James McCormick. 6. James—d. 1760—Ann, admr. Walter Smiley on bond—estate, $114.42. 7. John—d. 1813—C: Thomas, Irene, Margaret. 8. Milly—m. William Griffith, 1822. 9. Robert—m. Sally Starke, 1796. 10. ——— —m. Peggy Culton by 1826. 11. ——— —m. Mary Davidson by 1834.

A HISTORY OF ROCKBRIDGE COUNTY, VIRGINIA

Rollin.—James—stepson to Charles Boyles, who married the widow, Rebecca, by 1794.

Ross.—1. Randolph—m. Betsy Miller, 1810. 2. Rebecca—m. James Gore, 1790. 3. Reuben—m. Nancy Miller, 1817.

Rowan.—1. Thomas—m. Susanna Donahow, 1789. 2. William—m. Elizabeth Occroman, 1814. 3. —— —m. Mary Davies by 1786.

Rowlison.—1. Heyburn—m. Peggy Morris, 1799. 2. Jane—m. Richard Parsons, 1815. 3. Nathaniel—d. 1839—C: Lang, Lavina (m. John Dold, 1816), Rachel (m. —— Short), Margaret (m. Peter Lance), Mary (b. 1781, d. 1859, m. Adam Beats, 1801),—m. Ann ——. 4. Sylvanus—m. Mary Parsons, 1813. 5. Sylvanus—m. Mary Smith, 1822. 6. William—d. 1836—. Keziah —— ——C: Aseriah, Elsey (dau.) Ann, Jane, Sylvanus.

Ruff.—1. Catharine—m. David Hall, 1794. 2. Elizabeth—m. John Dalton, 1796. 3. Jacob—d. 1799c—C (by 1st w.): Peter, Henry, George, John, Peggy, 5 other dau.— (by 2d w.): Andrew, Jacob, Sally. 4. John—son of 3—b. 1783, d. 1858, m. Hennetta ——. 5. John—m. Martha Wallace—C(1836): Samuel W., Amanda (m. Jacob G. Sheltman), Jacob M., Rebecca (m. Henry Imboden), Magdalen C. (m. Joseph Spriggs), Elizabeth G., Martha, Susan P., Jane, John A., William. 6. Mathias—m. Mary Cawful, 1796. 7. Sally—m. Peter Eagle, 1809.

Ruley.—1. Jacob—C (1821): 5. 2. Jacob T.—m. Sarah Marlin, 1805. 3. Jacob T.—m. Ann Irvine, 1821. 4. Matulda—m. Ann Hart, 1821. 5. William—m. Catharine Cohenower, 1813. 6. William W.—b. 1816, d. 1876—m. Rebecca G. Thomas, 1840—C: John F., Nancy J., Burtnoy W., Sarah E., Zachary A., William J., James A., David K., Hugh P., Thomas M., Julia A., Robert L.

Russell.—1. Florence—m. William Brooks, 1798. 2. James—m. Margaret Wilson, 1791. 3. Joshua—m. Elizabeth Ager, 1822. 4. Martha—m. James Brown, 1786. 5. Mary—James Robertson, 1789. 6. Matthew—m. Jane Henderson, 7. Polly—m. Samuel Mays, 1811. 8. Samuel—m. Rebecca Miller, 1811. 9. Samuel—d. 1832—m. Hannah ——, 1827. 10. Stephen—m. Sally Dean, 1818. 11. William—1778.

Rust.—1. Catharine—m. George Michael, 1816. 2. Philip—d. 1808—m. Mary ——. 3. —— —m. Elizabeth Coswell by 1805.

Ryan.—1. Charles—m. Sally Griffith, 1822. 2. Sally—m. Daniel Baggs, 1801.

Salling.—1. George—d. 1788—m. Hannah —— —C: William, Henry, George, John, Peggy, 5 other dau. 2. George—m. Tilly Carter, 1791. 3. Henry—1. 1834c—m. Lucy Darst, 1815. 4. John—g'son of 5. John P.—l. 1755—m. Ann —— —C: George A., John, Catrine (m. Henry Fuller by 1751), Mary E. (m. Joseph Burton, 1755). 6. Magdalen—m. John Booker, 1797. 7. Feter—m. Rebecca Holmes, 1787. 8. Polly—m. Byrd Goodwin, 1804.

Saunders.—1. Jacob—m. Malinda Douglass, 1820. 2. Mary—m. William Williams, 1811. 3. Nancy—m. Thomas McCullough, 1820.

Saville.—1. Abraham—m. Martha Keebler—C: George (m. Betsy Bogan, 1808), Robert (m. Martha Skeen, 1810), Abraham (m. Elizabeth J. Whiteman, 1817), Joseph (m. Polly Skeen, 1822), William (m. Jane Skeen, 1816), Samuel (m. Ann Saville, 1816), Jacob (m. 1. Phebe Skeen, 1818, 2. Susanna Leech, 1823, 3. Nancy Snater, 1828), Mary (m. John McHenry).

2. George—son of 1—C: John (m. Sue Shafer, 1832).

3. Jacob—son of 1—C: Susan (by 2d m.); by 3d m.—Margaret A., Sarah E., Lianna, Nancy M., Mary K., Martha J., Emily, Drusilla, Hannah V., John L., William, Joseph, Jacob.

4. Joseph—son of 8—C: William, J. Sidney, Charles, Narcissa, Janetta, Francis C., Virginia.

5. Margaret—m. Lawrence Roberts, 1803.

6. Nancy—m. William Leighton, 1812.

7. Patsy—m. William Struthers, 1816.
8. Robert—son of 10.
9. Robert—son of 1—C: Abraham (m. 1. Elizabeth Deisher, 1842, 2. Harriet Deisher), Joseph (m. Frances M. Circle, 1846), Samuel (m. Mary Turpin), William (m. out of county), Robert (m. Jane A. Wilson, 1856), John (m. out of county), Mary (m. Mathias Rapp, 1834), Martha (m. J. Frank Wilson, 1851).
10. Samuel—C: Abraham (see 1), Robert.

Sayers.—1. David—m. Elizabeth Paxton, 1794. 2. John—d. 1789—m. Elizabeth ——— —C: William, Mary (m. —— Bater), Priscilla (m. —— Gore). 3. Robert—d. 1756—bro. to David—C: Robert. 4. ——— —m. Susanna Thomas by 1827.

Scott.—1. Andrew—d. 1824—C: John, Jesse (has Andrew, Mary), Jean (m. Aron Beaty), Robert (has Nancy), Elizabeth, Andrew F.), Andrew.
2. Andrew—son of 1—C: Polly, William, David.
3. Andrew—m. Agnes Leach, 1791.
4. Ann—m. Jacob Ford, 1813.
5. Ann—m. David Hopkins, 1818.
6. Hannah—m. William Lyet, 1792.
7. Hugh—d. 1807—C: Hendray, Moses, Nancy, Sally, Ebley, Ann, Hannah, Molly.
8. Isabella—m. David Bagges, 1790.
9. Jacob—b. 1748—orphan of John.
10. Jane—m. John Smith, 1821.
11. James—d. 1818—m. Mary ———.
12. John—m. Esther Houston, 1795.
13. John—m. Martha Cumins, 1814.
14. John—m. Rebecca Davies, 1816.
15. John—m. Ann McCampbell, 1816.
16. Joseph—d. 1808—C: John, Hannah, Patsy.
17. Margaret—m. Addison Gilmore, 1823.
18. Margaret—m. Thomas Leech, 1810.
19. Margaret—m. David Lyle, 1819.
20. Mary—m. Philip Reed, 1792.
21. Mary—m. John Reid, 1819.
22. Matilda—m. John Sprowl, 1820c.
23. Nancy—m. James McKee, 1807.
24. Nancy—m. Joseph Paxton, 1801.
25. Phoebe—m. Benjamin Kirkpatrick, 1792.
26. Robert—m. Sally H. Price, 1805.
27. Sally—m. William M. McMath, 1810.
28. Sally—m. Samuel Moore, 1800.
29. Sally—m. William Moore, 1818.
30. Smith—m. Betsy Moore, 1801.
31. Thomas—d. 1797—m. Sarah ——— —C: Andrew, Sarah, Margaret, John, Harrison, Smith, Thomas.
32. Thomas—m. Rebecca Leech, 1822.
33. Thomas—m. Elizabeth Mullen, 1807.
34. William—m. Margaret Alexander, 1790.
35. William—m. Nancy Bogle, 1793.
36. William H.—m. Ann Houston, 1804.
37. ——— —m. Fanny Ramsay by 1789.

38. ——— —m. Elizabeth Moore by 1808.
39. ——— —m. Betsy Finley—C (1816): Betsy, Mary.

Sea.—1. George—d. 1752—estate, $530.62. 2. James—d. 1759—appraisers, James McCowen, Isaac Anderson, Jacob Anderson, Alexander Walker. 3. Martin—d. 1807—m. Margaret Stokes, 1785—C (by 1st w.): John, Dolly (m. ——— Kender), Mary (m. ——— Lemons), John Nalus Coonrod, George.

Seacott.—1. Charles—m. Nancy Kirkwood, 1796. 2. Peggy—m. Mark Jacobs, 1796.

Sehorn.—Cathy—b. 1789, d. 1831, m. Elizabeth Montgomery, 1812—C: Martha (m. ——— McClintic), Marion (b. 1817, M. Rebecca Wallace), Masillon (m. Jane Rapp), Montgomery (s), Lafayette (b. 1825, m. 1. Jean Johnston, 2. Sarah M. Johnston).

Shainor.—William—son of George and Elizabeth—b. in Pa., 1774, d. 1858—m. Elizabeth Crawford, 1801.

Sharp.—1. Joseph—d. 1803c—C: Lucp. 2. ——— —m. Mary Porter by 1803. 3. ——— —m. Jenny Johnston by 1818. 4. ——— —m. Polly Welch by 1821.

Shaver.—1 Dolly—m. William Bargar, 1822. 2. John—m. Christiana Troxall, 1806. 3. John—m. Eleanor Miller, 1822. 4. Polly—m. John Croddy, 1822.

Shaw.—1. Catharine—m. Richard Pattison, 1795. 2. David—m. Margaret West, 1789. 3. Esther—m. Daniel Matthews, 1801. 3x. George—m. Nancy Maiss, 1796. 4. James—m. Judy Davis, 1817. 5. John—m. Sally Paxton, 1796. 6. John—m. Isabel McCalpin, 1816. 7. John L.—m. Sally Davidson, 1803. 8. Polly—m. Edward Bryan, 1819. 9. Susanna—m. Daniel Davis, 1816.

Sheltman.—1. Jacob G.—Amanda Ruff. 2. Sarah—m. John Smith, 1817.

Shields.—1. Alexander—m. Phebe Caruthers, 1796—C: George W., John N., Ann C., Mary.
2. Ann—m. Peter Larew, 1795.
3. Ann C.—m. John A. Cummings, 1818.
4. Catharine—m. Richard W. Chandler, 1819.
5. Elizabeth—m. James Creag, 1792.
6. Esther—m. James Barclay, 1795.
7. Henry—m. Elizabeth Mitchell, 1790.
8. James—d. 1749c—estate, $337.51—m. Jane ——— —C: John, ward of John.
9. James—d. 1808c—m. Rachel ——— C: Rachel (m. John McCullock), John (has Rachel), Patsy, Joseph, Sally, William, Polly (m. John Sloan); a dau. m. John Camden.
10. James—m. Kizia Bane, 1811.
11. James—m. Rachel Anderson, 1786—d. 1808c—C: Rachel (m. John McCullock). John (has Rachel), Patsy, Joseph, Sally, William T., Polly (m. John Sloan); a dau. m. John Camden.
11. John—m. Margaret ——— d. 1775—C (1749): John, William, Thomas, Robert, Patrick (?) Mary.
12. John—m. Pamela Camden, 1822.
13. Patsy—m. Robert Moderwill, 1809.
14. William—m. Eleanor Black, 1787.
15. William—m. Mary Thompson, 1797.
16. man—m. ——— Hoffman—C (1817): Catharine.

Shirley.—1. Elizabeth—m. Samuel Patterson, 1787. 2. Mary—m. James Gardner, 1788.

Short.—1. Adam—m. Elizabeth Asly, 1798. 2. John—m. Nancy Downs, 1820. 3. Robert—m. Rachel Robinson, 1811. 4. ——— —m. Rachel Rowlinson by 1839.

Shultz.—1. Adam—m. Sally Hoffman, 1815. 2. Henry—m. Elizabeth Nephews, 1819. 3. ———— —m. Mary Stoner by 1826.

Simonds.—1. John—m. Rebecca Thompson, 1798. 2. Magdalena G.—m. Rebecca Miller 1823. Margaret, Sr.—d. 1815. 4. Richard—m. Nancy Hart, 1812. 5. Susanna—m. John McKee, 1798.

Sisson.—1 Caleb—d 1807—w. and C. 2. Stanley—m. Catharine Kirkwood, 1796.

Sizer.—1. Catharine—m. Conrode Siders, 1811. 2. Elizabeth—m. Michael Nicely, 1808. 3. Margaret—m. John Wilhelm, 1819.

Skeen.—1. Elizabeth—m. John McNabb, 1804. 2. Henry—d. 1810—C: Polly, Peggy, Matty. 3. James—m. Matty Millikin by 1815. 4. Jane—m. William Saville, 1816. 5. John m. Elizabeth Ford, 1798. 6. Martha—m. Charles Ayres, 1812. 7. Matty—m. Samuel Mateer, 815. 8. Phoebe—m. Jacob Sabille, 1818. 9. Polly—m. Joseph Savill, 1822. 10. Robert—d. 1795—m. Barbara ———— —C: William, Henry, Joseph, Jonathan, Martha, Robert, Elizabeth (m. ——— Spear). 11. Robert—m. Polly Hart, 1817. 12. William—d. 1817 —C: Robert, William, Jonathan, Joseph, James, Samuel (b. 1802c), Rhoda, Martha (m. ——— ———). 13. William—m. Elizabeth Priestly, 1790. 14. William—d. 1831—m. Jane Kincaid, 1822—bro. to Robert—C: James, Isaiah, Samuel.

Sloan.—1. John—d. 1830—m. Polly Shields—C: Alexander, James, Mary, Robert, Jackson, Rachel, Matthew, John. 2. Mary—dau. of James and Rachel—b. 1784, d. 1857, s. 3. Rosanna—m. William McClintic, 1796.

Sly.—1. Henry—m. Rachel Tankersly, 1822. 2. Jonathan—m. Ann Good, 1811.

Smiley.—1. Alexander—d. 1748c—m. Mary ——— —minor C. 2. Eleanor—m. John Winegar, 1812. 3. J——— —m. Sally ———, b. 1782, d. 1858. 4. James—m. Barbara Potter, 1823. 5. James—m. Polly Finley, 1802. 6. James—m Susanna Garner, 1805. 7. Jane—m. Samuel Paxton. 8. Jean—m Richard Denton, 1791. 9. John—m. Jean Steele. 1809. 10. John—m. Hannah McClure—b. 1750c. 11. Mary—widow—1784. 12. Polly—m. Thomas Reed, 1799. 13. Rebecca—m. Hugh Rhea, 1796. 14. Robert—m. Mary Armstrong by 1837. 15. Susan—b. 1790c—m. Samuel Moore. 15x. Samuel D.—m. Martha Paxton. 16. Susanna —m. Samuel Paxton, 1816. 18. Walter—d. 1817—m. Ann ———, d. 1823—C: Walter, James, Archibald, Rebekah (see 13), Ann, Polly m. ——— Rhea), Eleanor (see 2)— Daniel, admr.

Smith.—1. Abraham—m. Polly Gore, 1822.
2. Abraham—m. Juliet Lyle by 1793.
3. Barbara—m. Charles Keller, 1789.
4. Edward—m. Harriet Allen, 1821.
5. Elizabeth—m. William Newcomer, 1820.
6. Elizabeth—m. Abraham Edmondson, 1815.
7. Francis R.—m. Peggy Holmes, 1822.
8. George—m. Mary Garvin, 1803.
9. George—m. Rachel Church, 180.
10. Grace—m. James Lawrence, 1811.
11. James—m. Caty Letshaw, 1821.
12. James—m. Betsy Ayres, 1817.
13. Jennet—m. Alexander Campbell, 1786.
14. Jeremiah—m. Rachel Parrat, 1805.
15. John—d. 1802c—C (minors): Grace, John, William
16. John—m. Peggy Forehand, 1820.
17. John—m. ——— Richey by 1797.
18. John—d. 1822—m. Elener ——— —C: Henry, James, Thomas.

19. John—m. Jane Scott, 1821.
20. John—m. Peggy Gore, 1822.
21. John—m. Nelly Gaylor, 1791.
22. John—m. Sarah Sheltman, 1817.
23. Joseph—m. Peggy Kirkpatrick, 1818.
24. Levi—m. Ann Counes, 1814.
25. Martha—m. Hugh Barclay, 1792.
26. Mary—m. James Bridget, 1786.
27. Mary—m. John Campbell, 1788.
28. Nancy—m. Sylvanus Rowlinson, 1822.
29. Nancy—m. James Willson, 1823.
30. Rachel (widow)—m. William Adams, 1821.
31. Rachel—m. Thomas Morris, 1823.
32. Rachel—m. Charles Dean, 1818.
33. Robert—m. Catharine Reid, 1796.
34. Robert—m. Catharine Reid, 1796.
34. Sally—m. Enoch Keller, 1821.
35. Samuel—m. Jean Cunningham, 1806.
36. Samuel—m. Mary Dunn, 1808.
37. Samuel—m. Elizabeth Thornton, 1810.
38. Samuel R.—m. Margaret Fuller, 1818.
39. Seth—m. Mary Hostetter, 1814.
40. Theophilus—m. Rachel Gill. 1797.
41. Thomas—k. 1757—C: John (captive).
42. William—m. Mrs. —— Steel—d. 1756—C: Post.
43. William—m. Hannah Mould, 1787.
44. William—m. Nancy Taylor, 1799.
45. William—m. Mary McCalpin, 1799.
46. William—m. Polly Foran, 1814.
47. —— —m. Mary McDonald by 1757.
48. —— —m. Nancy Paxton.

Snider.—1. David E.—b. at Winchester, 1770, d. 1855. 2. Frederick—1833. 3. Isaac—m. Lee Watkins, 1806. 4. John—d. 1838—m. Barbara —— —C: John, Daniel, Elizabeth (m. Jacob Kern), Rebecca, Mary A. 5. Susan—m. Daniel Werner, 1808.

Snodgrass.—1. Elizabeth—m. Samuel Moore, 1806. 2. Elizabeth—m. Andrew Mitchell, 1811. 3. Nancy—m. John Houston, 1815. 4. Robert—d. 1795—m. Elizabeth —— —C: Robert, Elizabeth, 1 other. 5. Robert—m. Mary White. 6. Samuel—m. Elizabeth Adair, 1792. 7. —— —m. Agnes McClung by 1812.

Solomon.—1. Adam—m. Polly Miller, 1815. 2. John—m. Elizabeth Martin, 1789. 3. Mary—m. Peter Dagger, 1794.

Speer.—1. Jenny—m. William Keller, 1820. 2. John—m. Mary Harbarger, 1792. 3. John—m. Mary Houston, 1797. 4. Robert—m. Agnes Williams, 1796.

Spence.—1. Esther—d. 1808. 2. Grizzy—m. Robert McCalpin, 1811. 3. John—m. Isabella McCormick, 1786. 4. Robert—m. Nancy Edley, 1816. 5. William—m. Polley Anderson, 1793.

Sprowl.—1. James—m. Catharine —— by 1786. 2. William—m. Rebecca Baker, 1800. 3. William—d. 1798—m. Elizabeth —— —C. 4. William—m (1) Jane ——, 1757, (2) Susanna ——, 1773—C (by 1st w): James, Alexander (m. Jane Beard, 1781), William; (by 2l w.—Joseph, Oliver, John (m. Matilda Scott, 1820c), Charles, Samuel, Jane

(m. John Weir, 1793), Silney (m. Joseph Beard, 1799), Mary (s), Martha (m. Robert Hutchinson), Fanny, Nancy. 5. ——— —C (1806): William, James, Joseph, Elizabeth.

Standoff.—1. Ann—m. James Forl, 1800. 2. Catharine—m. John Connor, 1810. 3. Elizabeth—m. Thomas Connor, 1800. 4. Jenny—m. George Black, 1806. 5. John—m. Mary ——— —C: Hannah (b. 1780, d. 1855, m. George Armentrout), 6. Margaret—m. David Hosteter, 1806. Polly—m. Valentine Hart, 1795. 8. Sally—m. John Ra, 1809.

Starke.—1. John—Polly Whiteside, 1802. 2. Sally—m. Robert Rogers, 1796.

Steele.—1. Adam—m. Christina Wyand, 1798.
2. Andrew—C (1749): Samuel (b. 1738).
3. Catharine—m. John Thompson, 1787.
4. David—d. 1747—C: Robert, Nathaniel. Martha (m. ——— Teas), Jane, Isabella (m. Moses McClure, 1745c, d. 1797), Rebecca, Janet.
5. David—d. 1809—C: Samuel, Joseph, Isaac.
6. David—in Washington Co., 1777.
7. David—m. Agnes Trimble, 1789—C: Joseph.
8. Eleanor—m. John Allen, 1790.
9. Elizabeth—m. John Martin, 1798.
10. Jacob—m. Patsy Paxton, 1817.
11. James—b. 1735, d. 1802, m. Sarah Wright—C: Andrew (b. 1766, d. 1832, m. Elizabeth Tate, 1795), Sarah (s) Martha (m. Daniel Henderson), Samuel (m. Fanny Hunter), John (s).
12. James—m. Nancy T. Hall, 1798.
13. James W.—m. Betsy Anderson, 1818.
14. Jane—dau. of David of 28—m. George McCormick.
15. Jean—m. John Smiley, 1809.
16. Jean—m. William Bodkin, 1808.
17. Jean—m. Bernard Kayton, 1794.
18. Jenet—m. Richard Cowden, 1799.
19. Jenny—m. Peter Alexander, 1787.
20. John—m. Mary Morris, 1791.
21. Margaret—m. David Buchanan, 1789.
22. Margaret—m. John Moore, 1787.
23. Martha—m. Robert Cooper, 1789.
24. Mary—m. Nathaniel Cox, 1812.
25. Nancy—m. John McClure, 1775c.
26. Nathaniel—d. 1796—m. Rosanna ——— —C: Eleanor (m. David McClure), Rosanna (m. Samuel McClure, 1782), Mary (m. Halbert McClure), ——— (m. Archibald Blackburn), Martha (m. Robert Cooper, 1789), Nathaniel (d. 1802).
27. Nathaniel—m. Jean McCleland, 1802.
28. Robert—son of 2—d. 1800—C: Mary, Eleanor (see 8), Martha (m. Thomas Paxton), John (had John), William, David (b. 1755c, m. Mary Steele of Samuel).
29. Robert—m. Jane ——— by 1768.
30. Robert—m. Elizabeth Johnston, 1823.
31. Sally—m. John Peters, 1821.
32. Sally—m. William Patterson, 1795.
33. Samuel—m. ——— Campbell by 1753—C: James.
34. Samuel—m. Sarah Trimble by 1816—C: John.
35. Samuel—d. 1808—C: Robert, Samuel, William, Polly (m. ——— Beard), Margaret (see 21), Sally (see 32).

36. Samuel—d. 1821—bro. to Joseph—m. Betsy L. ——— —C: David T.
37. Samuel—m. Sally Gum, 1811.
37x. Samuel—b. 1709, d. 1790, m. ——— Fulton—C: James (see 11), Samuel (b. 1736, d. 1808—m. Sarah Hunter), Andrew (b. 1743, d. 1800, m. Mary ———), Mary (m. David Steele, see 28), Margaret (see 21), Martha, Sarah.
38. Thomas—Giles Co. Tenn., 1802—C: Samuel, Jane, David.
39. Thomas W. D.—m. J ——— E. McChesney, 1818.
40. Thomas—d. 1761c—C: David.
41. William—m. Rebecca McClung—C: Elizabeth.
42. ——— —m. Agnes Coalter by 1784.
43. ——— —m. Margaret Parks by 1793.
44. ——— —m. Jane Leech by 1821.
45. ——— —m. Elizabeth Taylor by 1828—C: Ann.

Stephenson.—1. Andrew—m. Sarah ——— by 1766. 2. James—m. Jane? ———. 3. John—m. Elizabeth Cloyd, 1830. 4. John—m. Elizabeth Paxton, 1788. 5. Joseph—m. Susanna McClure, 1794. 6. (Man) m. ——— Walkup by 1787—C: Joseph, Jean, Mary, Margaret.

Sterrett.—John—m. Polly Maynought, 1795. William B.—m. Lucinda Paxton, 1830—C: Isabella (m. Joseph G. Steele, Jr.), Emaline (m. Charles Dodd), William (m. Lizzie McCorkle), Aurelia (m. Douglass McCorkle).

Stevenson.—1. John—m. Martha Warwick, k. by Indians—C: Thomas (k. at Blue Lick, 1782), Samuel. 2. Samuel—son of 1—b. 1744—m. Jean Gay—C: James (b. 1772), John.

Stighleather.—1. George—m. Nancy Gordon, 1807. 2. Peter—d. 1821—m. Eve ———, d. 1828.

Stoner—Henry—d. 1828—m. Eve ——— —C: Jacob, Betty (m. ——— Snider), George, Katharine (m. ——— Stricklin), Eve (m. ——— Cox), Mary (m. ——— Shultz).

Stoops.—1. Betty—m. John Clyburn, 1815. 2. David—m. Abigail Williams, 1795. 3. Jane (or Ann)—m. Strother L. McElheny, 1817. 4. Philip—m. Ann McCormick, 1789. 5. Rachel—m. Patrick Naylor, 1798. 6. Robert—d. 1797—m. Rachel Milor, 1786—C: Thomas, Betsy, Nancy, James, David, John, Robert, post.

Strickland.—1. Mary—m. William Carpenter, 1786. 2. William—m. Christiana Hart, 1812. 3. ——— —m. Nancy Tooly by 1804. 4. ——— —m. Catharine Stoner by 1826. 5. ——— Strickler—m. Mary Moneymaker by 1812.

Strother.—1. James—m. Elizabeth Savile, 1819. 2. William—m. Patsy Savile, 1816.

Stuart.—1. Alexander—m. Polly Walker by 1797.
2. Alexander—m. Mary Patterson by 1763.
3. Alexander B.—b. 1796, d. 1886, m. Elizabeth A. ———.
4 Archibald—d. 1759—m. Janet Brown—C: Thomas (b. 1732), Alexander (b. 1735), Eleanor, Benjamin.
5. Benjamin—son of 4—C: Archibald (b. 1757, d. 1831), Robert, Alexander, James.
6. Elizabeth—b. 1755, d. 1826, m. William Paxton.
7. Elizabeth—(widow)—d. 1825—C: John, Walker, ——— (m. William Walker)—Ann E., a g'dau.
8. James—servant to John McKee, 1779.
9. James—m. ——— Montgomery by 1779.
10. John—m. Elizabeth Walker by 1797.
11. John—Jane McCown.
12. John—m. Jenny Wardlaw, 1790.

13. John—d. 1831—m. Elizabeth Walker—C: James, John, Robert, Margaret, Hugh, Alexander, Walker, Mary—a dau. m. William Walker—Ann E., a g'dau.
12. John—b. 1740, living, 1806c.
13. Julia A.—b. 1755c—dau of Thomas—m. William Lyle, 1784.
14. Mary—m. John McClung, 1788.
15. Mary—m. James McLaughlin, 1786.
16. Mary b. 1732—m. John Hamilton, 1748.
17. Mary P.—d. 1834—a sister to John M., Betsy (m. —— McClure).
18. Polly—m. Edward Hull.
19. Polly (widow)—d. 1838—sister to w. of 11 and Alexander Walker.
20. Rebecca—m. John Porter, 1809.
21. Robert—m. Betsy McClung—son of 5—C: John, —— (m. William Walker) Walker, Dolly.
22. Robert—d. 1827—C: Alexander, Mary P. (see 16), Elizabeth (m. —— McClure), Jane, Isabella.
23. Robert—m. Polly Armstrong, 1792.
24. Susanna—g'dau. to Andrew Kinnear—1809.
25. Thomas—m. Margaret Wasson, 1804.
26. Walker—m. Mary —— C: Mary, John, Alexander, James, William.
27. William—m. Elizabeth Robertson, 1804.
28. ———— —m. William Lyle, 1770c.

Summers.—1. Adam—m. Mary Kiddy, 1802. 2. Jane Somers—m. Robert Poage.

Sutton.—1. Hugh—merchant, 1790. Martin—m. Mary Smith, 1787.

Sweet.—1. Dorcas—m. Joshua Parks, 1816. 2. Elizabeth—m. Thomas Hatfield, 1812. 3. James—m. Rosey Gibson, 1792. 4. James—m. Elizabeth Riley, 1807

Swisher.—1. Henry—m. Susan Trout, 1812. 2. Jacob—son of George and N———of Aug. Co.—b. 1780, d. 1857, m. Catharine S. ——. 3. Nancy W.—m. Alexander Paxton, 1836.

Swoope.—George—son of Peter—b. in Pa. 1776, d. 1853.

Syders.—1. Conrad—m. Catharine Sizer, 1811. 2. Elizabeth—dau. of Frederick—b. 1779, d. 1860, m. John Tribbett. 3. Henry—m. Catharine Motherspel, 1810. 4. John—m. Margaret Aigner, 1811. 5. Nancy—m. Alexander McNabb, 1819. 6. Polly—m. Henry Frush, 1818. 7. —— —m. Susannah Agnor by 1824.

Sylor.—1. Margaret E. ——. James Flint, 1809. 2. Philip—m. Eve Rodes, 1790. 3. Polly—m. Robert Campbell, 1812. 4. Sarah—m. William Tidd, 1802.

Tapley.—Elizabeth—servant of James Greenlee, 1750.

Tapscott.—1. Allison—m. Margaret Eply, 1812. 2. Robert—m. Jane Taylor, 1810.

Tankersley.—Richard—d. 1821—m. Nancy Leech, 1800—C: Polly, Rachel.

Tate.—1. Eliza—m. Allison Ford, 1803. 2. John—k. 1781—m. Sarah ——, who later m. Hugh Fulton—C: Thomas, John (m. Jane ——). 3. John—b. 1752, d. 1834. 4. Mary—m. John Fullen, 1809. 5. Robert—m. Margaret McClung—C: Ellen, Phoebe, Rebecca. 6. Samuel—m. Elizabeth Alexander, 1785. 7. Thomas—m. —— Campbell, 1780c. 8. William—m. Nancy McCormick, 1809.

Taylor.—1. Aaron—m. Elizabeth Maupin, 1821.
2. Abigail—m. John Harvey, 189.
3. Abigail—m. John Tolly, 1809.
4. Andrew—m. Ann Wilson, cousin—C: Nathaniel.
5. Andrew—orphan of Daniel, 1810.
6. Andrew—b. in Ireland, 1795, d. 1879.

7. Archibald—m. Nancy McCorkle, 1812.
8. Barbara—m. James Moore, 1812.
9. Daniel—d. 1809—uncle to John and William—m. Mary ——— —C: Andrew, Isaac.
10. Daniel—b. 1775c—m. Ann ———.
11. Daniel—d. in Ohio, 1815c.
12. David—d. 1825—C: James, David, Peggy (m. Dickey Beard, 1800).
13. David—b. 1785, d. 1827.
14. Elizabeth—g'dau. of Mary Mackey, 1810.
15. Elizabeth (widow)—d. 1799—C: Jemima, Isabella, William, Thomas (d. 1799).
16. Elizabeth—m. Andrew Amice, 1810.
17. Fanny—m. Amos Thomas, 1808.
18. George—d. 1801—m. Letty ——— —bro. to Susanna and Nancy—C: Mark, Silas George, Sally, Betsy, Polly (b. 1780c), Nancy.
19. Hugh P.—bro. to Elizabeth Steele, Nancy Thomas—1834.
21. Isabella—witness, 1747—surety, Isaac.
22. Isabella—m. Samuel Paxton, 1800.
23. James—m. Catharine McClure, 1800c.
24. James—d. 1801—m. Annfl Paul, 1768—C: Nathaniel (same as 38?), James (see 25x), William M. (Tenn.), Phœbe (m. John Patton, 1812), Nancy (b. 1788, d. 1833, m. Amos Thomas), Audley, Caufleld, Elizabeth (m. ——— Steele), Hugh P. (s), Stuart Tenn?).
25. James—son of 38—(1) Ann Reid, 1801, (2) Elizabeth McCorkle, 1805, (3) (see 50), John (see 32), Rebecca (see 45), Archibald (see 7), Andrew, Catharine McClure, 1808.
26. James—son of David and Grace—b. 1778, d. 1858.
27. Jane—m. Robert Tapscott, 1810.
28. Jemima—m. Thomas Lackey, 1801.
29. John—d. 1777—estate, $50.
30. John—m. Nancy Cunningham, 1806.
31. John—m. Esther ——— —d. 1770—C: John, 10 others.
32. Mary—m. James Lawson, 1810.
33. Mary—m. John McNaughton, 1791.
34. Nacy—m. John Gore, 1815.
35. Nancy—m. William Smith, 1799.
36. Nathaniel—b. 1772, d. 1816—son of 4—m. Mary Patton, 1791.
37. Patsy—m. John Nowel, 1808.
38. Peggy—m. William Cunningham, 1807.
39. Peggy—m. Peter Lowry, 1806.
40. Phoebe—m. John Patton, 1812.
41. Polly—m. Charles Bodkin, 1820.
42. Polly—m. Weston Mills, 1806.
43. Rebecca—m. Henry Green, 1799.
44. Robert—m. Agnes McCroskey, 1795.
45. Sally—m. John Elliott, 1798.
46. Sally—m. William Tolley, 1800.
47. Samuel—m. Catharine Walker, 1793.
48. Stewart—son of 24—b. 1795, d. 1874—m. Martha E. Hickman, 1819—C: William,

Mary, Eliza J., James, Archibald, Rebecca, Andrew, Hulda, Rachel, Christy A., John.
49. Thomas—k. by tree, 1749c—estate, $105.33—m. Elizabeth Paxton.
50. William—m. Susan McDowell.
51. William—d. 1807—m. Ruthy —————C: John, William, Polly, Peggy, Betty, Sarah (see 45).
52. William—d. 1768—C: Isaac, William, James, 1 minor son—will mentions Andrew, Martha, Esbel, Jemima.
53. William—m. Jean Guffey, 1792.
54. William—m. Elizabeth Bodkins, 1819.
55. Capt. ———— —m. ———— Campbell, 1790c.
56. ———————m. Ann Reed by 1815.
57. ————— —C: George (m. ———— Paul), James (m. Ann Paul), William Caufould, John (see 31).

Tedford.—1. Alexander—d. 1793—m. Mary ——————C: James, Elizabeth, Robert, William, David, Alexander, Jean (m. James McKee, 1782).
2. Alexander—m. Mary McCampbell, 1787.
3. Alexander—d. 1781—bro. to John—m. Jane ———— —C (minor): Sarah.
4. Alexander—m. Elizabeth McClung, 1797.
4x. Andrew Telford—m. Priscilla Robertson, 1777.
5. David—d. 1784—m. Eleanor —————— —C: James, John, Agnes.
6. Hugh—at Falling Springs, 1740c.
7. James—b. 1763—son of Alexander.
8. James—m. Maty McCroskey, 1785.
9. James—m. Jane McCroskey, 1789.
10. James—m. Agnes Dickson by 1797.
11. Martha—m. James Alexander, 1794.
12. Mary—m. Samuel Dickson, 1789.
13. Robert—d. 1791—m. Sarah —————— —C: George, James, Robert, Mary.
14. Sarah—g'dau. to James Edmondson, 1782.
15. Sarah—m. Elihu Barclay, 1796.
16. Samuel—m. Elizabeth Cull, 1786.
17. William—m. Rebecca McClung, 1798.

Temple.—1. Boston—d. 1830—m. Mary A. ———— C: Peter, Catharine, Elizabeth, Mary A., Eve M., George, Henry, John, Boston, William. 2. John—m. Jenny Wardlaw, 1790. 3. John—b. 1795, d. 1841.

Templeton.—1. David—m. Mary McClure, 1791. 2. David—m. Betsy Grigsby, 1818. 3. David—d. 1824. 4. Ellen—m. Rudolph Hawp, 1819 5. James—d. in Henry Co., Ind. 1829. 6. James—m. Elizabeth Edmondson, 1792 7. John J.—b. 1785, d. 1857, m. Sally Wilson. 8. Robert—son of John and M————b. 1781, d. 1857—m. Sarah ————. 9. Robert —m. Patsy Dickson, 1809. 10. Sarah—m. Jemison Cochran, 1821.

Tennant.—1. Elizabeth—m. Elijah West, 1798. 2. Mary—m. John Marshall, 1803. 3. Nancy—m. Charles Coehorn, 1799.

Tharp.—1. Fanny—m. William Porter, 1796. 2. William—m. Polly Clark, 1813.

Thomas.—1. Amos—m. Fanny (or Nancy) Taylor, 1808—C: Elvira (m. Coleman Dempsey), Elizabeth (m. Charles Daniels), Lorissa (m. James Reed), Polly (m. James Rowsey), Ann (m. John Bowyer), Rebecca G. (m. William W. Ruley, 1840), Rachel (m. Joseph Milan), James. 2. Casper—d. 1828—m. Magdalene —————— —C: Peter, Susanna (m. ———— Sayer), John, Elizabeth (m. Abraham Roads, 1810), Rebecca (m. ———— Beaver), Esther (m. John Beaver, 1810). 3. Catharine—m. Benjamin Davis, 1808. 4. Gasper—m.

Polly Plott, 1811. 5. Isaac—m. Harriet Watkins by 1838. 6. Mary—m. Samuel Moore, 1801. 7. Peggy—m. David Beaver, 1818. 8. —— —m. Polly McKamon, 1810.

Thompson.—1. Dolly—m. Samuel Kinnerly, 1812.
2. Elizabeth—m. James Riley, 1795.
3. Harriet—m. Adam Holden, 1819.
4. Henry—m. Jenny Campbell, 1788.
5. Isaac—m. Mary Duff, 1786.
6. James—d. 1795—m. Elizabeth ——— —C: Thomas, Mary, Rebecca.
7. John—d. 1802—m. Jean ——— —C: Thomas, Rebecca (m. John Symonds, 1798).
8. John—d. 1807—m. Catharine ———.
9. John—m. Catrene Steele, 1787.
10. John—m. Margaret McCormick, 1798.
11. Mary—witness in court, 1747.
12. Mary—m. Samuel Weir, 1779c.
13. Mary—m. William Blain, 1797.
14. Mary—m. Thomas Brown, 1792.
15. Mary—m. William Shields, 1797.
16. Mary—m. William Hamilton, 1815.
17. Polly—m. Simon Hoylman, 1808.
18. Rachel—m. Alexander Berryhill, 1786.
19. Rebecca—m. Robert Kirkpatrick, 1816.
20. Susanna—m. John Evans, 1807.
21. Thomas—d. 1810—m. Dolly ——— —son of John, who d. before 1804.
22. Thomas—d. 1760.
23. Thomas—m. Elizabeth Forcan, 1807.
24. William—b. 1735, d. 1800.
25. William—d. 1801—m. Margaret ——— —C: John, William, James, Mary, Agnes.
26. William—son of 25—b. 1783, d. 1855—m. Nancy B. ——.
27. William—guardian of Martha Campbell, 1747.
28. William—m. Sally Caruthers, 1806.
29. ——— —m. Rosanna Davies by 1786.
30. ——— —m. Rebecca Gay by 1785—C: Henry.
31. ——— —m. Margaret Cloyd—C: David, James.

Thornton.—1. Coats—m. Mary King, 1787. 2. Ebenezer—murdered 1807—m. Elizabeth Hamilton, 1807. 3. Elizabeth—m. Samuel Smith, 1810. 4. Samuel—m. Nancy Cook, 1806.

Tidd.—1. Charles—b. 1820c. 2. William—m. Sarah Sylers, 1802.

Todd.—1. Jenny—m. Thomas Crawford, 1794. 2. John—m. Agnes Todd, 1794. 3. Maria—g'dau. to Joseph Walker, 1818. 4. Samuel—m. Jane ——— —C: William. 5. Sarah—m. John Houston.

Tolley.—1. Abbe—dau. of James and Mary—b. 1786, d. 1857. 2. Christopher—d. 1806 m. Patience ——— —C: Samuel, John, Joseph, Christopher. 3. Elizabeth (widow)—d. 1805—C: Nancy (m. ——— Stricklin), George, John, Charles. 4. Elizabeth—m. James Taggart, 1809. 5. James P.—g'son to Joseph, 1832. 6. John—m. Abigail Taylor, 1809. 7. Joseph—d. 1833—C: John, Elizabeth, Ezekiel, Christopher V., 2 others. 8. Polly—m. John Nick, 1822. 9. William—m. Sally Taylor, 1800.

Tooley.—1. Charles—m. Polly Cummings, 1805. 2. Elizabeth—m. John Miles, 1806. 3. Judith—m. John Gabbert, 1792. 4. Nancy—m. Thomas Eubanks, 1795. 5. Polly—James B. Craig, 1815. 6. Sally—m. James McColgan, 1822

Toomey (Ptomey).—1. Jane—m. Moses Keys, 1810. 2. John P.—d. 1823—C: James

MISCELLANEOUS DATA 537

N., Polly, William, George, Michael, John (m. Rebecca Beason, 1822c), Alexander (m. Mary Timberlake, 1816), Betsy (m. —— Roach. 3. Robert P.—. Nellie McElwee.

Trevy.—1. Joseph—b. 1760, d. 1825—m. Susanna ——, b. 1761, d. 1831—C: Jacob, Joseph Y., Susan, Diannah (m. Daniel Hoylman), Adam, Andrew. 2. Joseph Y.—son of 1.—b. 1795, d. 1859, m. Rebecca ——. (m. Andrew McCartney), Lydia (m. Jacob Higgins, 1820).

Trimble.—1. Alexander—d. 1817—m. Martha Grigsby, 1793—C: (by 1st w.) Jane (m. William McClure), James, Rachel (m. Joseph Caruthers), Agens (m. David Steel, 1789), Sarah (m. Samuel Steele).

2. Isaac—m. Mary Graham, 1787.

3. James—d. 1776c—m. Sarah Kersey—C: John (d. 1783), Agnes—or Jean—(m. McClure), Sarah, Isaac, James, Moses, Alexander, William, Rachel—estate $566.25.

4. John—son of 3—m. Mary McClure, 1780c—d. 1783—C: James.

5. Mary—m. Lewis Jordan, 1785.

6. Mary—m. McCord Bready, 1795.

7. Moses—d. 1784c.

8. Moses—d. 1821—m. Mary ——— —C: James, Susanna, Elizabeth, Sally (m. James Miller, 1820).

Trotter.—1. Mary—m. James McCown, 1789. 2. Sarah—m. James Campbell, 1793.

Trout.—1. Andrew—m. Sally Reid, 1821. 2. Christian—m. Elizabeth Geehart, 1795. 3 Susan—m. Henry Swisher, 1812.

Troxal.—Abraham—d. 1812—m. Anna E. Hoylman, 1794—C: John, Margaret, Sally.

Turk.—Anthony—slaveholder—d. 1837.

Turner.—1. Mahala—m. Archibald Beard, 1822. 2. Martha—m. James McMullon, 1788. 3. Robert—m. Mary Thompson, 1787. 4. Sarah—m. William McGlothlin, 1812. 5. Susanna—m. George Wens, 1810. 6. William—m. Nancy Alexander, 1806.

Underwood.—John—m. Mary —— —related to Mary Whiteside—1756—C (?) Elizabeth, Joseph.

Unrew.—1. Jacob—d. 1829—m. Catharine Wilhelm, 1816—C: John, Jacob. 2. —— — m. Christina —— by 1826.

Utter.—Valentine—m. Mary —— —servants of John Paxton, 1756—set free for $40.

Vance.—1. Catharine—m. Henry Spitzer, 1793. 2. Elizabeth—m. William Davidson, 1790. 3. Hugh—m. Sarah Law, 1803. 4. Patrick—b. 1780—son of Dr. Patrick—m. Keziah Robertson.

Vansandt.—1. Jean—m. Elijah Morris, 1801. 2. Joshua—m. Mary Morris, 1794. 3 Mary—m. William McCoy, 1803.

Venable.—1. Samuel W.—m. Jane Reid, 1821. 2. William H.—m. Margaret M. Reid, 1822—C: Magdalena.

Verner.—1. Charles—m. Sally Wallace, 1820. 2. Christian A.—m. Barbara Ruff, 1796. 3. William—m. Elizabeth Edmiston, 1817.

Vernon.—1. Elizabeth—m. John Boyd, 1787. 2. John—m. Elizabeth Hunter, 1782. 3. John—m. Elizabeth Mathews, 1797. 4. Lydia—m. Lawson McCullough, 1790.

Vineyard.—1. George—m. Mary Campbell, 1790. 2. John—d. 1758—Barbara, admr.

Waddell.—1. David—m. Sally Edsal, 1802. 2. James—m. Ann Stephenson, 1786. 3. Jane—m. Edward Erwin, 1791. 4. John—m. Elizabeth Erwin, 1791.

Wade.—George W.—b. 1789, d, 1876, m. Mary ——.

Walker.—1. Alexander—d. 1820—m. Jane —— —C: Archibald, Jane (m. —— Kelso), Frances (m. —— Ficklin), Mary, Alexander, Margaret, John, Joseph.

2. Alexander—d. 1771—bro. to John, Martha (m. ——— Minerly).
3. Alexander—d. 1777—m. Martha ———, who later m. ——— Grimes—C: Jane, Elizabeth.
4. Alexander—d. 1784—m. Janet ——— —C: **Alexander, Joseph,** Jean, Ketrane, David. ——— (m. James Walker).
5. Alexander—d. 1785—m. Jean ——— —C: Eleanor, John, Rebecca, Joseph.
6. Alexander—d. 1794—C: Isabella (m. Robert Reed, 1793), Barbara, Margaret (m. Thomas Conolly).
7. Anderson—m. ——— Willson by 1805.
8. Andrew—m. Elizabeth Houston, 1810.
9. Ann E.—g'dau. of Elizabeth Stuart, 1825.
10. Archibald—son of 1—C (1816): Eleanor, Elizabeth, Priscilla, Melinda.
11. Archibald—colonel, 1840.
12. Catharine—m. Samuel Taylor, 1793.
13. Charles—m. Catharine Dyal, 1798.
14. Elijah—m. Mary M. Dial, 1800.
15. Elizabeth—m. Thomas Berry, 1788.
16. James—m. Mary ——— —1763.
17. James—m. Mary ———, d. 1802—C: Mary (m. Hugh Kelso), Jean (m. ——— Moore), Elizabeth (m. John Stuart).
18. James—m. Peggy Baily, 1815.
18x. James—m. Margaret Woods, 1773.
19. Jane—m. Samuel Barclay, **1795.**
20. Jane—m. Andrew. 20. Jane—m. Andrew McMahan, 1793.
21. Jean—m. Gabriel Cummings, 1787.
22. Jean—m. Joseph Patterson, 1791.
23. Jennet—m. George Icenhower, 1810.
24. John—m. Catharine Rutherford—C: John, James, Samuel, Alexander, Joseph, Jane (m. James Moore), 1 other.
25. John—b. 1748.
26. John—d. 1814—m. Margaret ——— —C: Alexander, John, William, Hugh, Thomas, Peggy, Betsy (m. Hugh Stuart), Polly (m. Alexander Stuart).
27. John—d. 1816—bro. to Joseph, William, Jane, Polly, Besty.
28. John—d. 1797—m. Margaret ——— —C: William, Alexander, Joseph, John (d. by 1797), Samuel, Mary (m. ——— Graham), Margaret (m. ——— Phresher), Jean (b. ——— Reagh—d. by 1797).
29. John—d. 1800—mother living—m. Mary ——— —C: Alexander, John (d. 1816), James, Joseph, William, Jenny, Polly, Betsy.
30. John—d. 1801—m. Mary ——— —C: Charles, Elijah, Philip.
31. John—m. Ann ——— —1746.
32. John—m. Ann Michal, 1810.
33. John—m. Sally Crawford, 1799.
34. Joseph—son of 24—b. 1722—m. Nancy McClung, 1749—C: Sarah (b. 1750, d. 1839, m. John Paxton), Margaret, Janet, Betsy, Joseph (b. 1759), Nancy, Suckey, James (b. 1766), Samuel (b. 1768).
35. Joseph—d. 1815—m. Jean Moore—C: Margaret (b. 1771, d. 1854, m. Samuel Houston, 1794), Jinny (m. Samuel Barclay), Polly (m. Richard Bernard, 1798), Martha M. (m. John Donihoo, 1811).
36. Joseph—m. Kitty Kelso, 1794.

37. Joseph—m. Mary Hayse, 1789.
38. Margaret (widow?)—d. 1827.
39. Margaret—m. Robert Anderson, 1791.
40. Mary—m. John Dickey, 1801.
41. Matthew—m. —— Lackey by 1825.
42. Nancy—m. Isaac Hughes, 1818.
43. Philip—m. Jean McDaniel, 1795.
44. Polly—m. Isaac Hughes, 1818.
45. Polly—m. —— Stuart—sister to Capt. Alexander and Mrs. Betty Stuart—1838.
46. Sally—dau. of John—m. William Cunningham by 1821.
47. Susan—m. William Lyle, 1807.
48. William—m. —— —Walker by 1825.
49. William—d. 1837—C: John, Joseph, James, Peggy, Ann E.—a dau. m. William Brown.
50. William—m. Mary ——, who later m. James Stuart—1757.
51. William—m. Mary —— —C: William, George, John, Betsy (see 15) Jane (m. —— Buchanan), Susanna (see 47), Hugh (d. —— had Mary, William).
52. —— —m. Priscilla Culton by 1824.
53. —— —m. Esther McCroskey by 1797.
54. —— —C: Margaret (d. 1287), Alexander, Thomas H., Polly (see 45), Hugh.

Walkup.—1. Andrew—d. 1817—m. Nancy Willson, 1795—C: Eleanor (m. —— McCoy), Margaret (m. Benjamin Logan, 1822), Elizabeth, Peggy, James.
2. Arthur—d. 1834—m. Esther Mackey, 1797—C: Mary M., James, Betsy B. (m. David D. Berry, 1821c), Samuel.
3. Barbara—m. John McElheny, 1821.
3x. John—m. Margaret Fulton Blair—C: William (m. Sarah McCoy), Joseph (b. 1778), Jane (m. Jesse Paxton), Martha (m. David Stewart), Isabel (m. David Chambers), Margaret (s), Jane (m. Alexander Dunlap), Rebecca (m. John Sims), John.
4. John—m. Jane Allen, 1816.
5. Joseph—d. 1787—m. —— Graham of Christopher—(m. Margaret Risk), C: John Christopher, Robert (has Nathaniel), Jean, Ann R., Margaret; a dau. m. William Elliott —Matthew, Christopher, Robert, are g'c.
6. Joseph—m. Lettice Bell, 1803.
7. Joseph—m. Eleanor Wilson, 1810.
8. Matthew—d. 1785—estate, $150.96.
9. Sally—m. William Dixon, 1823.
10. Samuel—m. Maria T. Houston, 1821—C: Samuel A. (Louisa E. Banks, Pittsylvania Co.), John A., Joseph W. (m. in Richmond), Matthew H. (m. in Monroe Co.), James D. (Tenn.), S—— H. (m. in Richmond).
11. —— —m. Jane Allen by 1825.

Wallace.—1. Anderson—m. Margaret Calbreath, 1796.
2. Andrew—son of 10x—m. Jane Blair, 1812—C: William A., Samuel A., Susan W. (m. James Ward).
3. Andrew—m. Elizabeth Graham—C: John (b. 1784, d. 1853, m. Elizabeth Graham, 1809).
4. Elizabeth—m. John Caskey, 1819.
5. James—m. Betsy Hoffman, 1801.
5x. James—m. —— Bogan by 1825—C: Jenny.

6. John—d. 1782—m. Rebekah ———— —C: James, Rebekah (m. ———— Campbell), Robert.
8. John—m. Margaret Graham, 1785.
9. John—m. Jane Quigley, 1817.
10. John—b. 1807, d. 1870, m. Nancy ————.
10x. John—son of 12—d. 1786—m. Rebekah ———— —C: Elizabeth, Martha, James, William, Andrew, post.
11. Margaret—m. John McKenny, 1785.
12. Peter—d. 1784—m. Martha Woods—C: Andrew (k. 1781), Samuel, John, James, Malcolm, Adam (k. 1781), Janet, Susanna, Elizabeth (m. John Gilmore).
13. Robert—m. Margaret Hughes, 1800.
14. Robert—m. Elizabeth Merriam, 1815.
12x. Rebecca—m. James Grigsby, 1786.
15. Sally—m. Charles Varner, 1820.
16. Samuel—son of 12—d. 1786c—m. Rebecca ———— —C: James, Andrew (see 2), Elizabeth (m. Charles Grigsby), Martha (m. John Ruff), William (s), Anderson (post).
17. Samuel—d. 1746c—m. Elizabeth ————.
18. Samuel—m. Jane ———— —1758.
19. Samuel—m. Mary Tate, 1794.
20. Samuel—m. Lydia Lowry, 1804.
21. William A.—son of 2—b. 1816, d. 1899, s—"Big Foot."
22. William Wallace—d. 1795—bro. to Margaret (m. ———— Robinson), Martha, Frances, Samuel, dau. (m. ———— Brawford).

Ward.—1. John—m. Agnes ———— —1761 2. John—m. Mary Bennett—Elk Cr. 1779. 3. John—m. Sally Coots, 1792. 4. William—m. ———— ————, 1761. 5. William—m. Rebecca Wallis, 1800.

Wardlaw.—1. Elizabeth—m. William McPheeters, 1795. 2. Elizabeth—m. David McMaster, 1818. 3. Hugh—m. Elizabeth Culton? 1763. 4. James—b. 1745. 5. Jenny—m. John Temple, 1790. 6. Robert—1793. 7. William—d. 1762—m. Jeannot ———— —C: John, James, Hugh, Joseph, William, Margaret, Robert. 8. William—b. 1747, d. 1819, m. Mary ————, b. 1751, d. 1808—C: Jenny (m. John Stuart, 1790), Joseph, Timothy, Betsy, Margaret, Hugh.

Warwick.—William—m. Elizabeth Dunlap—C: Jean (m. James Gay), Martha (m. John Stevenson), John (m. Eleanor Crouch), Jacob (m. ———— Vance of John).

Waskey.———— —Margaret ————, d. 1817—C: John (m. Betsy Ripley, 1801), George (m. Patsy Kelly, 1811), Christopher (m. Polly Ripley, 1807), Nancy (m. ———— Kepler by 1811), Polly (m. John Ripley, 1802).

Wasson.—1. Alexander—m. Elizabeth Pairy, 1791. 2. David—m. Margaret Patton, 1811. 3. Ellen—b. 1772, d. 1857, s. 4. John—d. 1832—m. Ellin ———— —C: Mary (m. Abel Ritchey, 1806), James, Isabella (m. ———— McClain), Jane (m. ———— Shipley), David, Samuel, Esther (m. ———— Willson), Matthew. 5. Margaret—m. Thomas Stuart, 1804. 6. Mary —m. Philip Entsminger, 1792. 7. Sarah—m. William Morley, 1796. 8. Thomas—m. Rebecca Cowan, 1803.

Watkins.—1. Betsy—m. Coleman Clayton, 1818. 2. Henry M.—m. Martha Thompson, 1823. 3. John—d. 1838c—C: Harriet (m. Isaac Thomas), Polly (m. John Wilcher), Paulina (m. Lewis Collins), Eliza (m. James Withrow). 4. Lea—m. Isaac Snider, 1816. 5. Polly—m. Peter Owens. 6. Rachel—m. Thomas Bennington, 1812. 7. William—m. Esther Perry, 1801. 8. William—m. Polly Patterson, 1816.

Watson.—1. Elizabeth—m. George Till, 1802. 2. James L. —m. Sally Greenlee—doctor, 1838.

MISCELLANEOUS DATA 541

Watts.—1. Polly—m. Edward Pines, 1788. 2. William W.—m. Mary S. Leyburn by 1831.

Weaver.—1. George—m. Jane Wilbur, 1822. 2. Henry—m. Susanna Winters, 1817. 3. Polly—m. Obadiah Rinehead, 1823. 4. Sarah—d. 1835—sister to Hannah, Seibert, Mrs. Margaret Davis, Mrs. Lydia Gorgas—aunt to Mary Simpson.

Webb.—1. John—m. Catharine Icenhower, 1807. 2. Sarah—m. George Karnes, 1819.

Weeks.—1. James—m. Catharine Hogg, 1817. 2. John—m. Margaret McQuilten, 1808. 3. Margaret—m. Patrick McCorkle, 1804.

Weir.—1. Adolphus—m. Mary Caruthers—n. c.
   2. Andrew—d. 1822—m. Polly Grigsby, 1793—C: Patsy, Andrew, Benjamin G. (m. Catharine S. ———), Adolphus G., Frances (m. in Miss.), Mary A., Hannah M., Martha R. (m. in Ky).
   3. Andrew—m. Patsy Weir, 1814.
   4. Anne—m. Patrick Campbell by 1777.
   5. George—d. 1781—m. Jean ——— —C: Thomas.
   6. Hugh—d. 1779—estate, $1296.67—C: Jonathan, Abraham, James, George, Hugh, John, Joseph, Samuel, Jean (m. James Cunningham), Margaret (m. James Montgomery, 1779), Mary (m. —— Walker), Susanna (m. —— Buchanan). John has a son, John.
   7. James—m. —— Campbell by 1777.
   8. James—m. —— Montgomery by 1785.
   9. James—d. 1801—m. Mary —— —C: Robert, James, Ketron, Roanna.
   9x. James—m. Mary Telford, 1799.
   10. Jane—m. Cornelius Allen.
   11. John—m. Jane Sprowl, 1793.
   12. John—d. 1800—m. Mary —— —C: John, Polly, Nancy.
   13. John—m. Agnes —— —1787.
   14. Margaret—m. John Cowan, 1796.
   15. Mary—m. —— McKee—d. 1822.
   16. Mary—m. John Wilson, 1817.
   17. Polly—d. 1830—sister to John, aunt to Hugh and Samuel.
   18. Sarah—m. Joseph Ogden, 1806.
   19. Sarah—m. William McCalpin, 1807.
   20. Susanna—m. John McCampbell, 1789.
   21. William E.—nephew to 17—b. 1798, d. 1852, m. Rebecca Moore.
   22. ——— —C: Hugh (m. Mary ———), Aaron (has Hugh), Polly, Elizabeth (m. —— Houston), John (has William).
   17x. Robert—m. Sarah McCampbell, 1791.
   23. ——— —m. James Montgomery—b. 1760c.
   24. ——— —m. Nancy Mathews by 1834.

Welch.—1. Benjamin—b. 1792, d. 1797.
   2. Betty—d. 1822c—m. Henry Decker, 1797.
   3. Elizabeth—m. Reuben Harris, 1818.
   4. Elizabeth—m. Benjamin Darst, 1800.
   5. Jenny—m. Benjamin Holmes, 1806.
   6. John—m. Sarah Wilson, 1799.
   7. John—m. Polly Logan, 1809.
   8. Milly—m. Alexander McCorkle, 1793.
   9. Nancy—m. William McCorkle, 1799.
   10. Rachel—m. Thomas Wilson, 1810.

11. Robert—m. Susanna Aps, 1794.
12. Rosanna—m. William Cunningham, 1801.
13. Samuel—d. 1822—m. Nanny —————C: Mildred (see 8), Betty (see 4), John, Anne (m. ——— Miller), Polly (m. ——— Cunningham).
14. Thomas—m. Phebe Dean, 1817.
15. ——————m. Sarah Grigsby by 1792.
16. ——————m. Mary Logan by 1821.

Wence.—1. Catharine—m. David Anderson, 1808. 2. George—m. Susanna Turner, 1810. 3. John—m. Sally McMath, 1793. 4. Sophia—m. James Anderson, 1811.

West.—1. Elijah—m. Elizabeth Tennant, 1798. 2. John—m. Sally Coots, 1791. 3. Margaret—m. David Shaw, 1789. 4. Nancy—m. Hugh Elliott, 1808. 5. Polly—m. Peter Kerlin, 1811. 6. William—m. Jenny Carson, 1796.

White.—1. Ann H.—m. William H. Caruthers, 1805c. 2. Ann R.—m. John P. Caruthers, 1823. 3. David—m. Betsy Newton, 1817. 4. Hofel—d. 1760c. 5. Isaac—m. Campbell by 1754. 6. Jesse—m Elizabeth Moore, 1823 7. John—m. Katharine Evans, 1740c—C: Robert, John (b. 1757, d. 1793), James, William, Nathaniel (m. Margaret McFarland), Mary (m. Robert Snodgrass), Rebecca (m. William McFarland), Margaret, Jane, Esther. 8. Joseph—d. 1816, going to Ky.—m. Ann ——————C (minors): John, Zachariah, Ann (m. ———Caldwell), Hannah, Eliza, William. 9. Joseph—m. Peggy Gordon by 1821. 10. Robert —b. 1775, d. 1851, m. Margaret Johnston, 1802—C: James N. (dy), Zachariah J., Robert L. 11. Sarah—m. Lawrence Green, 1820. 2. William—servant of David Hays, 1754.

Whiteman.—1. Elizabeth—m. Abraham Saville, 1817. 2. Matthew—m. Jean Poage, 1806. 3. Nancy—m. Isham Thomas, 1820. 4. Samuel—d. 1817—C: Nancy (m. William McDonnel, 1799), Elizabeth (m. Matthew McDonald, 1802), Sarah, Jain, Samuel P. (m. Elizabeth Woods, 1805), Robert, Rachel (m. Samuel Paxton, 1798), Margaret (m. James Graham, 1815). 5. Susanna—m. John Deal, 1809.

Whiteside.—1. James—in Rutherford Co., N. C. 1782. 2. James—m. Polly Dougherty by 1796. 3. John—m Jean Hopkins, 1788. 4. Mary—m. Ephriam Lewis, 1795. 5. Moses— d. 1795—m. Margaret ——————C: Thomas, Moses, John, James, Mary, Margaret, 1 other dau. 6. Moses—m. Margaret Paxton, 1797. 7. Phœbe—m. Elias Lewis, 1810. 8. Polly— m. Ann Thompson, widow, by 1761.

Whitley.—1. Ann—m. Thomas Baggs, 1786. 2. Jonathan—m. Sarah Cunningham, 1773. m. John Starke, 1802. 9 Samuel C.—m. Nancy Paxton, 1818. 10. Samuel P.—m. Elizabeth Thomas, 1822. 11. William—m. Mary ——————, related to Richard Burton—1756. 12. William 3. Samuel—m. Sarah Baggs, 1782. 4. Paul—d. 1772—m. Jane ——————C (minors): Michael, Sarah, Moses, Thomas, Anna, Samuel, Paul. 5. Sarah—m. James Fallen, 1772. 6. William —b. in Rbg, 1749, k. 1813—m. Sarah Fuller.

Wiggenson.—Peter—given legacy by David Martin, 1789.

Wiley.—1. Alexander—d. 1804—C: John, others. 2. Alexander—m. Elizabeth Kirkpatrick, 1806. 3. James—m. Polly Smith, 1802. 4. John—d. 1748—C: George, Jean, Margaret. 5. John—d. 1802—m. Jinny ——————C: Margaret, Robert, Andrew, John, Joseph. 6. John—m. Mary Cooper, 1791. 7. Joseph—m. Mary McCampbell, 1791. 8. Margaret—m. John Cooper, 1809. 9. Nancy—m. James Adams, 1823. 10. Robert—m. Martha Cooper, 1794.

Wilhelm.—1. Adam—d. 1823—m. Elizabeth ——————C: John (m. Margaret Sizer, 1819), Adam, George, Jacob (m. Elizabeth Hosteter, 1817), Michael (m. Susanna Unrow, 1819). 2. Catharine—m. Jacob Unrow, 1816. 3. Elizabeth—m. John Egner, 1820. 4. Michael—b. 1757, living, 1832.

Williams.—1. Agnes—m. Robert Speer, 1795. 2. David—m. Elizabeth McNutt, 1793.

MISCELLANEOUS DATA

3. John—m. Susanna Harnest, 1804. 4. William—d. 1821—C: William. 5. William—m. Lilly Teller, 1789. 6. William—m. Mary Saunders, 1811.

Williamson.—1. John—d. 1801—estate, $112.25. 2. Richard (Ann)—Collierstown, 1783.

Wilson.—1. Agnes—m. Andrew Walkup, 1795.
  2. Andrew—uncle to Pheby A., James C.—d. 1837.
  3. Andrew—m. Lettie Porter, 1789.
  4. Betty—m. Samuel Hight, 1792.
  5. David—d. 1793c—C: Seth.
  6. David—m. Betsy Patton, 1799.
  7. David—m. Margaret Kinnear, 1819.
  8. Eleanor—m. Joseph Walkup, 1794.
  9. Elizabeth—m. William Paxton.
  10. Elizabeth—m. James Blair, 1786.
  11. Elizabeth—m. William Harper, 1813.
  12. Elizabeth—m. John Lindsay, 1791.
  13. Elizabeth—m. William Withrow, 1802.
  14. Hannah—orphan of William, 1802.
  15. Hannah (widow)—d. 1822—C: Elizabeth (m. —— ——), Sally (m. James L. Mackey), Robert.
  16. Hugh—d. 1828—m. Sarah —— —C: William, John, James, Hugh L., Thomas.
  17. Hugh—m. Elizabeth Miller, 1792.
  18. Hugh—m. Mary Moore, 1806.
  19. James—d. 1824—C: James, John, Peggy (m. —— Mackey), Jenny, —— (m. Joseph ——).
  20. James—C: Mary (d. 1834), James, Nancy (m. —— Walkup), William (has Mary E.
  21. James—son of 20—C: John F., Eleanor.
  22. James Willson—d. 1838—M. —— Patterson—bro. to Nancy—C: William, Janetta, Margaret, Isabella, Cynthia A., James A., John P.
  23. James—b. 1740c, living, 1811.
  24. James—d. 1809—m. Rebecca —— —C: Matthew, Andrew, Sarah, Robert, Samuel, David, Elis (m. —— Campbell), Rebecca (m. —— Henderson), William (has James, b. 1800c), John, Moses, Thomas, James (d. 1800c).
  25. James—m. Martha —— —1781.
  26. James—d. 1814—C: James, Elizabeth, Polley, William, James.
  20x. James—C: John (d. 1817), James, William (has Mary E.), Nancy (m. Andrew Walkup), Mary (d. 1834), Martha (m. —— —Hastings, Ireland), Eleanor (d. by 1817).
  27. James—m. Ann McCown.
  28. James—m. Nancy Smith, 1823.
  29. James—m. Agnes McKee, 1788.
  30. James—m. Hannah Hicks, 1809.
  31. James—m. Sally McCorkle, 1814.
  32. James C.—m. Esther Montgomery—n. c.—minister.
  33. Jane—m. Henry McCormick, 1821.
  34. Jean—m. John Henry, 1801.
  35. Jenny—m. John Paxton, 1797.
  36. Jinny—m. William Caruthers, 1798.
  37. Jinny—m. Joseph Davidson, 1805—C: Sally William.

38. John—m. Sarah Alexander, 1786c.
39. John—d. 1754—m. Anna Adair.
40. John—d. 1814—C: Polly, Elly, William, James.
41. John—m. Anna——— (2d w.)—C (minors): Mary, Sarah, James, William.
42. John—servant to Francis Beaty, 1746.
43. John—d. 1740c—C: Martha, Matthew, William, John, Sarah, Elizabeth.
44. John—d. 1826—C: James C. (has Rachel), Samuel (has John and others), Elizabeth (m. ——— McClung).
45. John—m. Elizabeth Miller, 1792.
46. John—m. Sally Miller, 1795.
37. Jinny—m. Joseph Davidson, 1805—C: Sally, William.
48. John—m. Mary Aschew, 1803.
49. John—m. Mary Weir, 1819.
50. John M.—b. 1782, d. 1851, m. Sally Moore, 1809—C: William M. (b. 1811, m. Eleanor M. Orbison, 1835), Mary M. (m. John K. McCown, 1833), Andrew J. (m. Jane E. McGuffin, 1842), Samuel (m. Drusilla F. Larew), John.
51. Jonathan—m. Nesbitt, 1812.
52. Joseph—m. Mary Johnston, 1802.
53. Joseph—m. Betsy Wilson, 1819.
54. Margaret—m. James Russell, 1791.
55. Martha—m. John Buchanan, 1796.
56. Mary—m. Richard Davis, 1803.
57. Mary (widow)—d. 1820—C: Sally (m. Alexander Johnston), Robert (m. Betsy ———, (has Mary).
58. Mary S.—m. Samuel R. Moore, 1823.
59. Matthew—witnessed will of Nathan Patterson, 1752.
60. Matthew—d. 1830—m. Nancy ——— —C: Phoebe A., Ann C.
61. Matthew—m. Elizabeth Douglass, 1811.
62. Moses—d. 1826—m. Elizabeth ——— —C: Thomas, James, Matthew, John, William.
63. Nancy—b. 1779, d. 1857—dau. of William and Ann Caruthers.
64. Nancy—m. James Bradford, 1810.
65. Nancy W.—m. William T. Moore.
66. Nathaniel—d. 1818—m. Eleanor ——— —C: Elizabeth, David, Thomas, Jenny, Rhoda, Nathaniel, Matthew, Polly, Sally, Robert, Samuel, Eleanor, Rebeckah, William.
67. Nathaniel—m. Mary Wilson, 1801.
68. Peggy—m. John Macky, 1810.
69. Polly—niece to Robert Weir, 1828.
70. Polly—James Mayers, 1800.
71. Polly—m. James Collins, 1804.
72. Polly—m. David Davis, 1810.
73. Polly—m. William McClelland, 1809.
74. Richard M.—m. Elizabeth Rea, 1807.
75. Robert—m. Elizabeth Wilson, 1801.
76. Robert—m. Eleanor Frush, 1815.
77. Sally—d. 1829.
78. Sally—m. John Hall, 1791.
79. Sally—m. John Templeton, 1814.

MISCELLANEOUS DATA 545

80. Sally—m. George M. Paul, 1810.
81. Samuel—bro. to Robert, cousin to Samuel and Thomas.
82. Samuel—m. Eleanor Alexander, 1790c.
83. Samuel—d. 1808—m. Mary ——— —C: Robert, Betty (see 12), Sally (m. ———
Johnston), Hugh.
84. Samuel—d. 1826—C: Elizabeth (see 13), John, Thomas (w. and C), Samuel, Mary
(m. ——— Davidson), Sarah (see 79), Jane (see 33).
85. Samuel—m. Peggy Johnson, 1804.
86. Samuel—m. Betty Hanna, 1806.
87. Sarah—m. John T. Howard, 1799.
88. Sarah—m. John Logan, 1792.
89. Sarah—m. James Macky, 1807.
90. Sarah—m. John Welch, 1797.
91. Seth—orphan of David, 1794.
92. Thomas—d. 1818—m. ———Peebles—came from Cowpasture.
93. Thomas—b. 1794, d. 1857, m. Elizabeth ———, b. 1801, d. 1854.
94. Thomas—d. 1773c—m. Martha ——— —C: Matthew, Samuel, Nathaniel, Rebecca,
Martha, Elizabeth, Rhoda, Sarah.
95. Thomas—m. Ann R. Johnson, 1823.
96. Thomas—m. Jennet Wallace, 1788.
97. Thomas—m. Peggy Caruthers, 1811.
98. Thomas—m. Rachel Welch, 1810.
99. William—d. 1808—C: Joseph, William, Thomas, James, Peggy, Samuel.
100. William—m. Eleanor Lackey, 1791.
101. William—m. Ann McClelon, 1805.
102. William—m. Jean Macky, 1806.
103. William H.—m. Jean McCampbell, 1811.
104. ——— —m. Eleanor Mitchell by 1771.
105. ——— —m. Agnes Kirkpatrick—C 1777) : Lettie.
106. ——— —m. Mary Mackey by 1810.
107. ——— —m. Katron Reid by 1787.
108. ——— —m. Esther Wasson by 1832.
109. ——— m. Elizabeth Hannah by 1815.
110. ——— —m. Betsy McCroskey by 1839.

Windle.—1. Betty—m. Joseph Hoffman, 1811. 2. Catharine—m. James Dryden, 1796.
3. Mary—m. Christopher Hoffman, 1809. 4. ——— —m. Mary ———, d. 1815—C: Andrew,
Matilda, Nancy (m. Anderson Johnston, 1810), Sally (m. Blackburn Jones), William,
Catharine (see 2), Mary (see 3).

Winegar.—1. Betsy—m. Samuel Lapsley, 1814. 2. Henry—m. Nancy Campbell, 1815.
3. John—m. Elenor Smiley, 1812. 4. Moses—m. Patsy Wilson, 1823. 5. Sarah—m. Daniel
Hull, 1812.

Winters.—1. Nancy—m. John G. Young, 1821. 2. Susanna—m. Henry Weaver, 1817.

Wise.—1. Ann—m. Samuel McDonald, 1812. 2. Christopher—m. Catharine Beets, 1813.
3. Christopher—m. Elizabeth Hamilton, 1818. 4. Hugh—m. Polly McCroskey, 1797. 5. Rebecca—m. Francis Myers, 1803. 6. Sally—m. John Woods, 1811. 7. Sarah—m. Nathaniel
Doughorty, 1812.

Withrow.—1. James—m. Eliza Watkins by 1838. 2. Jane—m. James M. Beard, 1821.
3. John—b. 1804, d. 1878, m. Sarah ———. 4. William—m. Elizabeth Wilson, 1802.

Wood.—1. Elias—m. Franky Chesham, 1822. 2. George—m. Jenny Curry, 1791.

Woods.—1. Catharine—m. John Campbell, 1816. 2. Charles—d. 1761—C (minors): Samuel, Arthur, Elizabeth, Esther—wards of Richard Woods and Magdalena McDowell. 3. Elizabeth—m. Samuel Whiteman, 1805. 4. James M.—m. Margaret Caruthers, 1815c. 5. John—d. 1763—Samuel McDowell, admr. 6. John—m. Elizabeth Campbell by 1750. 7. John—m. Sally Wise, 1811. 8. John—m. Sarah Christ, 1819. 7. Magdalena—m. (1) John McDowell, (2) Benjamin Borden, Jr. (3) John Bowyer. 8. Michael—m. Esther Caruthers, 1795. 9. Rebecca—m. Alexander Culton, 1782. 10. Richard—d. 1778—estate, $4,545—m. Jenny ———— —C: Benjamin, Samuel. 11. Richard—m. Elizabeth ———— —C: ———— (m. Richard Woods). 12. Richard—in Green Co., N. C., 1791. 13. Sally—m. John Allison, 1815. 14. Searight—m. Ann McCoskey, 1797. 15. Samuel—d. 1804c—m. (?) Jane Green, 1778—C: John, Elizabeth. 16. Zachariah—m. Sally Foran, 1814. 17. Zachariah—m. Barbara Riley, 1823. 18. ———— —C: Magdalena (see 7), Martha (m. Peter Wallace), Sarah (m. Joseph Lapsley).

Worley.—1. Caleb—d. 1791c—Caleb, Malcom, admr. 2. Sarah—m. John Johnson, 1803. 3. Stephen—m. Margaret Robinson, 1812—C: James W.

Woodsell.—John—d. 1763—Samuel McDowell, admr.

Wright.—1. Ann—m. William Arnold, 1787. 2. Charles—m. Dorothy McGlothlin, 1810. 3. Daniel—m. Peggy Davis, 1799. 4. Fanny—m. Samuel Frazure, 1823. 5. John—m. Martha McGlothlin, 1810. 6. Peggy—m. James Cowan, 1806. 7. Thomas—d. 1814. 8. ———— —m. Mary Mitchell by 1771.

Wyant.—1. John—m. Sally McMath, 1793. 2. Sophia—m. James McManamy, 1815.

Yeats.—1. Stephen—m. Mary Hampton, 1803. 2. William—m. Peggy Hampton, 1803.

Youell.—William—d. 1834—m. Elizabeth ———— —C: John (m. Agnes McKnight), Jane (m. Robert Miller), Margaret (m. William Allen, 1808), Nancy (m. Joseph McCutchen), Elizabeth (m. John McCutchen, 1810), Christiana (m. Andrew Lockridge). NOTE: The will of William Youell mentions Christian, who married an Anderson.

Young.—1. Alexander—m. Catharine Redy, 1803.

2. Andrew—m. Jenny McBride, 1799.

3. Elizabeth—m. Charles McLaughlin, 1810.

4. George—d. 1829.

5. Hannah—m. William Cosby, 1792.

6. James—d. 1760c—m. Sarah ———— —C: James (b. 1755), Robert.

7. James—d. 1829—m. Margaret Kenady, 1802—C: Suanah, Jane, James, Thomas, Robert.

8. Jean—m. William Allison, 1789.

9. John—d. 1747c—bro. to James.

10. John G.—m. Nancy Winters, 1821.

11. Margaret—m. Robert Anderson, 1786.

12. Patrick—d. 1761c—m. Isabella ———— —C: Sarah (b. 1751), James (b. 1752), Jennet, Else.

13. Polly—m. John Agnor, Jr., 1822.

14. Polly—m. James Allen, 1788.

15. Robert—b. 1744.

16. Robert—d. 1765c—m. Agnes ———— —C: William, Hugh, Joseph.

17. Robert—m. Isabella Hutton, 1795.

18. William—m. ———— Hillis by 1795.

19. William—m. Peggy Fuller, 1805.

20. William—m. Susan Bane, 1818.

Zollman.—William—d. 1804—m. Mary ———— —C (minors): Henry, Alexander, Adam, Charles, James M., Margaret C.

APPENDICES

ROCKBRIDGE ATTORNEYS

The date following a name indicates the year in which we first find mention of the attorney in the order-book. When the date is starred, it shows the year in which he qualified.

Alexander, William A.—1852
Allen, John—1794
Baldwin, John B.—1852
Baldwin, Robert C.—1853
Barclay, Elihu—1822
Bell, Henderson M.—1849
Booker, Samuel—1812
Bowyer, John Jr.—1792
Bowyer, Henry M.—1825
Bowyer, John C.—1826
Brockenbrough, John B.—1860
Caldwell, Joseph W.—1848
Caruthers, Madison—1817
Coalter, George—1807
Davidson, James D.—1831
Davis, Abram W.—1836
Dickenson, Henry C.—1852
Dilworth, Joseph—1805
Dorman, James B.—1845
Doyle, John—1839*
Eskridge, Alexander P.—1829
Fisher, John S.—1845
Frazier, William—1835
Glasgow, William A.—1845
Glasgow, Joseph—1845
Hancock, John—1785*
Harman, William H.—1859
Hays, Andrew—1817
Lee, Richard H.—1817
Letcher, John—1839*
Letcher, Samuel F.—1850*
Loving, John—1794
Lyle, James Jr.—1792
Martin, Frederick A.—1854
Massie, James W.—1851
Mayers, James—1804
McCampbell, James—1794
McCampbell, William—1828
McLaughlin, William—1851
Moore, David E.—elected prosecuting attorney, 1843
Moore, Andrew—1854
Patterson, David M.—1822
Paxton, John G.—1843
Paxton, Elisha F.—1848
Poague, William T.—1861
Preston, Thomas L.—1805
Richardson, William S.—1832
Risque, James—1794
Shafer, Jacob K.—1845
Skillern, William P.—1801
Steele, Joseph G.—1853
Sterrett, John D.—1851
Stuart, Thomas J.—1817
Stuart, Alexander H. H.—1828
Tate, Caleb—1805
Taylor, William—resigned as prosecuting attorney, 1843
Tidd, Samuel—1811
Trimble, James—1801
Tutwiler, Thomas H.—1864
Walker, Alexander—1804
Wilson, William A.—1856
Woodward, Augusta E. B.—1794
Yelliott, Coleman—1865

AN APPRAISEMENT OF 1761

Appraisement of Patrick Young's personalty by Richard Woods, William Hall, John Paxton, John Willy (Wiley), June 9, 1761; recorded, August 1, 1761.

one Gray horse—12p
one sorrel Mare—6p—10s

one Dark Bay Mare—4p
one chestnut young Mare—4p—5s
one White Mare—6p
one Bell and Coler—2s—6d
one Roand horse—5p
one Soral Mare—2p
one colt—1p
one Brown Cow & Calf—2p
one sorel Colt—3p
one Brindled Cow & Calf—2p
one Red & White Cow & Calf—2p
one Young Black Cow—1p—15s
one Black Bull—1p
one large Year old Steer—1p
one Red Steer—1p—10s
one Brown haffer two Year old—1p
one Year old haffer—12s
one Year old haffer—12s
Two Sows & nine pigs—1p
one Cow Bell & Coller—6s
172 pounds of iron at 4½d per pound—3p—4s—6d
one Set of Cart boxes—5s
One Weaver Loom and tacklings—12s
One Riffel Gun—2p—10s
One Smal Round Bored Gun—12s
One skillet—3s—6d
Three pails—2s—6d
Nine Plates & Six Spoons—6s
3 old Basons and one Smal Dish—7s
Ten Smal Tins—5s
One Iron Candlestick—6d
One Spinning wheel—3s
One flower Cask & one Riddle & Sieve—2s—3s
One old Bible & two old Testaments—2s—6d
One fring pan 2-6 one faling ax 4- and one Mattock 4- —10s—6d
two old Sickels 1- and one hilling hoe 3- —4s
8 pound of Wool 8- and one Barrel 1-3—9s—3d
1 Sadle and one Bridle—1p
ten pounds of flax—6s—3d
1 Chest—4p
1 Bed & Cloaths—1p—5s
2 pair of Shoes and one pair of buckels—5s
1 patorn for a jacot and Buttons—6s
two pair of Stockings and one pair of Leggins & Razor—4s—3d
one fine hat—8s
old Body Cloths—2p
one Churn—4s
plow Irons—1p
Six old Sheep & four Lambs—2p—15s

1 Deer Skin—2s
Seven Acres of Grain—5p
Cash—2p
One Smal Bel
ten dozen of Yarn—12s—6d
600 weight of flower—3p
four bags—14s
five Bushels and a half of Rye—8s—3d
Six Acres of Rye and Barley—3p—12s
one grinding stone—12s
one pair of Sadle Bags—7s—6d
one Raw Hyde—2s
one hilling hoe—3s
Insolvent—8p—14s—10d
against Mathew Young Insolvent—10p
against Halbert McClure, Solvent—15s
Book Debt—7s

THE PATENT FOR BORDEN'S GREAT TRACT

George the second by the grace of God, of Great Britain France and Ireland King Defender of the Faith & etc.

To all to whom these presents shall come greeting KNOW Ye that for divers good causes and considerations but more especially in consideration that Benjamin Borden late of the Province of East Jersey now of the County of Orange in Virginia hath lately caused to be imported and settled on the land hereinafter mentioned one family for every 1000 acres WE HAVE given granted and confirmed and by these presents for us our heirs and successors do give grant and confirm unto the said Benjamin Borden and to his heirs and assigns forever One certain Tract or parcel of land containing 92,100 acres situate lying and being on the west side of the Blue Ridge in the county of Augusta and on the north and northeast branches of James River between the Blue Ridge and North Mountain and bounded as followeth (to wit)

Beginning at three hiccories and four red oaks on the west side of the northeast branch of James River it being a corner to Beverly Manor Tract and running from the said corner south 73 degrees west 84 poles near a white oak southwest 140 poles to a hiccory, southeast 48 poles to a white oak on the east side of the road to John McDowell's southwest 1108 poles crossing two branches of James River southeast 40 poles southwest 466 poles to a black oak, white oak and spanish oak saplings on both sides of the road northwest 64 poles southwest 166 poles crossing a branch to a large black oak a hiccory saplin and a black oak saplin south 25 degrees east 68 poles to a black oak south 13 degrees east 206 poles to a hiccory and black oak west 45 poles to a black oak and white oak saplins north 55 degrees west 166 poles to a black oak and hiccory south 66 degrees west 397 poles crossing two branches to a white oak north 30 degrees west 78 poles to a large black oak and white oak saplin on the south side of the bark cabin branch north 30 degrees west 34 poles to a black oak on the side of a hill south 50 degrees west 350 poles to an Ash and a poplar on the east side of the Wood's Spring branch then down the branch south 18 degrees east 508 poles to a white oak near a spring east 52 poles to a white oak and a hiccory saplin south 18 degrees east 220 poles to a hoopwood and two sugar trees on the west side of the northeast branch of James River then down the said branch as followeth south 60 degrees west 324 poles south 30 degrees east 46 poles south 20 degrees west 82 poles south 60 degrees west 14 poles to a sycamore and white walnut tree on the east side of the said branch south 60 degrees west 330 poles to a black oak on the edge of a bottom south 30 degrees east 68 poles to two black oaks on the side of a ridge south 50 degrees west 374 poles to a pine south 70 degrees west 310 poles to white oak saplin and a hiccory saplin in a bottom south 27 poles to two white oaks south 80 degrees west 195 poles to a black oak and white oak near a spring branch south 44 poles to a white oak and two black oaks south 55 degrees west 196 poles to a gum and two white oaks near a spring in a bottom north 30 degrees west 24 poles to three poplars on the east side of the north branch of James River about 100 poles below where the northeast branch comes into the north branch of the said river then crossing the said river north 30 degrees west 129 poles to a white oak and a hiccory on a ridge south 70 degrees west 56 poles to a hiccory and white oak north 40 degrees west 14 poles north 70 degrees west 608 poles crossing Borden's Creek and three other branches to three white oaks south 20 degrees west 182 poles to a black oak and a hiccory north 60 degrees west 84 poles south 75 degrees west 350 poles to three white oaks on a hill south 30 degrees west 178 poles crossing a branch of Wood's Creek to two white oaks on hill south 60 degrees west 148 poles to a mulberry and a hiccory north 78 degrees west 462 poles north 30 degrees east 320 poles to a black oak and two white oaks north 43 degrees west 540 poles south 85 degrees west 202 poles crossing two branches of Buffalo Creek to a white oak gum and hiccory north 43 degrees west 220 poles to a chestnut oak and a hiccory on a ridge north 20 degrees east 668 poles crossing four branches to two hiccory saplins and two white oak saplins on a spur of the House Mountain north 40 degrees east 1944 poles crossing nine branches to a pine and black oak south 50 degrees east 110 poles to three black oaks north 40 degrees east 908 poles crossing the river to three hiccories north 50 degrees west 52 poles to a chestnut oak and a dogwood 200 degrees east 354 poles to five chestnuts out of one stump northeast 156 poles crossing a branch to two white oaks and two poplars north 20 degrees east 108 poles to a dogwood and poplar on a branch north 80 degrees east 112 poles to two black oaks on a high ridge on the west side of Hays Creek northeast 288 poles north 47 and ½ degrees east 930 poles to a white oak and a spanish oak on the side of Hay's Creek east 640 poles crossing the said creek to three white oak saplins north 20 degrees east 230 poles crossing a branch of Moffett's Creek to a black oak and a chestnut north 60 degrees east 150 poles to a blazed white oak north 20 degrees east 104 poles near a white oak north 80 degrees east 436 poles crossing a branch of Sherando to two white oaks in Beverly's line south 1840 poles crossing four branches of James River to two hiccories two chestnuts and a white oak near a spring of James River south 56 degrees east 630 poles crossing a branch of Sherando to a black oak north 56 degrees east 322 poles crossing two branches of James River and south 56 degrees east 232 poles to the beginning, with all woods underwoods swamps marshes low grounds meadows feedings and his due share of all veins mines and quarries as well discovered as not discovered within the bounds aforesaid and being part of the said quantity of 92,100 acres of land and the rivers waters and water courses therein contained together with the privileges of hunting hawking fishing fowling and all other profits commodities and heriditaments whatsoever to the same or any part thereof belonging or in wise appertaining to have hold possess and enjoy the said tract or parcel of land and all other the before granted premises and every part thereof with their and every of their appurtenances unto the said Benjamin Borden and to his heirs and assigns forever to the only use and behoof of him the said Benjamin Borden his heirs and assigns forever to be held of us our heirs and successors as of our Manner of east Greenwich in the county of Kent in free and common socage and not in Capite or by knights service yielding and paying unto us our heirs and successors for every 50 acres of land and so proportionably for a lesser or a greater quantity than 50 acres the free rent of one shilling yearly to be paid upon the feast of St. Michael the Arch Angel and also cultivating and improving three acres part of every fifty of the tract above mentioned within three years after the date of these presnts provided allways that if three years of the said fee rent shall at any time be in arrear and unpaid or if the said Benjamin Borden his heirs or assigns do not within the space of three years next coming after the date of these presents cultivate three acres part of every fifty of the tract above mentioned then the estate hereby granted shall cease and be utterly determined and thereafter it shall and may be lawful to and for us our heirs and successors to grant the same lands and premises with the appurtenances unto such other person or persons as we our heirs and successors shall think fit in witness whereof we have caused these our letters patent to be made witness our trusty and well beloved William Gooch Esquire our Lieutenant Governor and Commander in chief of our said colony and dominion at Williamsburg under the seal of our said colony the sixth day of November one thousand seven hundred and thirty nine in the thirteenth year of our reign.

WILLIAM GOOCH.

ROAD PRECINCTS OF 1841

(As Described by the County Court.)

1. County line at George Barger's to Cedar Creek.
2. Cedar Creek to Eli Poage's.
3. Eli Poage's to bridge on Buffalo.
4. Stage road near Matthew Houston's to county line near John McNight (Skidmore's Ferry road.)
5. Galbraith's to Natural Bridge.
6. Back road near William Shield's, crossing stage road near William Moffett's, to the Bridge Road.
7. Natural Bridge to Gilmore's mill on James River.
8. James River at Greenlee's Ferry up Arnold's Valley to county line.
9. Gilmore's mill to county line near Richard H. Burk's.
10. Alexander Paxton's on James River to Gilmore's mill.
11. Wallace's mill to Boatyard mill on Buffalo.
12. Fancy Hill to Weaver's Forge and mills.
13. Stage road at east end of John Moffett's lane to Falling Spring church.
14. Boatyard to head of the canal.
15. Mouth of Buffalo to ford above Bunker Hill mills.
16. Ford at Bunker Hill mills to stage road at Douglass's.
17. Back road at Miller's to stage road near Laird's.
18. County line on Back road to Captain William Shield's.
19. William Shield's to John P. Ackerley's smith shop.
20. Stage road at William L. Burk's to Ackerley's on back road.
21. John P. Ackerley's smith shop to Buffalo at Zollman's mill.
22. Redbud in Opossum Hollow to center Buffalo bridge.
23. Zollman's mill to top of the hill on the stage road at Elliott's.
24. Redbud in Opossum Hollow to town limits.
25. James S. Mackey's on Back road to Bolivar Mills.
26. Stage road in Bowyer's lane, passing McKee Harper's to Buffalo ford.
27. Bolivar Mills to Lindsay's ford on Buffalo.

28. Forks of the road south of A. B. Davidson's to the fork of Buffalo Creek, and up the creek to the intersection of the Dagger Spring road near Zollman's field.
29. Lindsay's ford on Buffalo to Joseph Wilson's.
30. Thomas Wilson's mill, passing B. F. Porter's, to John Chandler's.
31. Joseph Wilson's up north fork of Buffalo to county line.
33. Bolivar Mills to Henry McCorkle's store.
34. Ford at McCorkle's to Tolley's sawmill.
35. Addison Gilmore's ford to Ezekiel Hayslett's.
36. From turnpike crossing Collier's Creek and up the creek to Thomas Goodbar's.
37. Fork below Tribbett's on Collier to Adam Hick's.
38. Ford by way of Gravelly Hill to Hall's mill.
39. Turnpike at Shanklin McClintic's (Scott's old place) to Adam Unroe's.
40. Mackey's on turnpike to Lindsay's ford on Buffalo.
41. Town limits to Campbell's and Karley's mill.
42. Turnpike at Robert Wilson's, passing Weir's, to Kerr's Creek road at James Wilson's.
43. Nathaniel Gaylor's to Cumings and Carter's, intersecting Gilmore's road.
44. Campbell and Karley's mill to Kerr's Creek turnpike.
45. Kerr's Creek turnpike to Henry Hayslett's.
46. Town limits to John Chandler's.
47. Town limits to stake in Steele's lane.
48. Fork of road at John Thompson's to stake in Steele's lane.
49. Fork of road at John Thompson's to North River at Boatyard.
50. Fork at John Thompson's, passing Ben Salem, to Jennings' old ford.
51. Ford at Hart's Bottom, (excepting road from fork at Colonel Paxton's to ford at Jennings' old place,) to junction at Boatyard road near Samuel McCorkle's.
52. Kerr's Creek road at John T. McKee's to Robert Gilmore's.
53. Town to North River, and from the fork below the spout to the bridge.
54. Moore and Dunlap's store to Peter Hull's.
55. Bryan's Forge to Rock Forge.
56. Kerr's Creek road above S. W. McKee's to Lindsay's ford.
57. Barley's mill to landing on North River down Kerr's Creek.
58. Top of poorhouse hill to North River bridge, and to make the route along Sterrett's fence at the end of Lyle's old lane above the turn.
59. Spout at the stage road passing Winnis to McCorkle's road.
60. Cooper's shop at Contention Falls, crossing South River, to Robert Glasgow's sawmill.
61. Potter's lane to top of poorhouse hill.
62. Brownsburg to Potter's.
63. Bridge at North River to Patton's smith shop.
64. Patton's shop to George Ireland's.
65. Ireland's to William R. Morris's smith shop.
66. Moore's shop to county line.
67. Samuel Lyle's mill to Lindsay's.
68. Fairfield to Whitmer's mill.
69. Brownsburg road, by John A. Cross's, to Fairfeld road.
70. Beard's lane on Augusta line to Brownsburg.
71. Tye River turnpike to Archibald McClung's.
72. Whitmer's mill to Strickler's Springs.

APPENDICES 553

73. Strickler's Springs to mouth of John Taylor's lane.
74. Taylor's lane to North River.
75. Top of mountain at White's Gap to McClure's mill.
76. McClure's mill to Reid's mill.
77. Reid Alexander's mill to Timber Ridge meeting house.
78. Mrs. Patton's at signpost to Augusta line.
79. Fairfield to McClung's mill.
80. Brownsburg, by Samuel Wilson's mill, to ridge road on Nevius's land.
81. Brownsburg to Captain Alexander Walker's mill.
82. Whitmer's mill to Walker's mill.
83. Walker's mill up Walker's Creek to Augusta line.
84. Whitmer's mill to stage road near Norcross's.
85. Cedar Grove to mouth of Robert Hutcheson's lane.
86. Mouth of Hutcheson's lane, next to Culton's, to Moffett's Run near New Providence church.
87. White's house, by Swoope's, to Walker's Creek. (New road).
88. Mouth of Walker's Creek to White's mill.
89. Weaver's Bell farm to Augusta line, passing Joseph Kelso's.
90. Mrs. Davis's to Tree Road at Sea's old place.
91. Weaver's turnpike up the big river to the county line.
92. Bath line to Augusta line on the Tree Road.
93. Mouth of Bratton's Run to Millboro turnpike.
94. Panther Gap to James McCutchen's on Big Calfpasture.
95. Midway, by Kennedy's mill, to New Providence and Moffett's Creek.
96. Reid Alexander's mill to top of mountain at Irish Creek Gap.

PRICES, 1745-1853

(Period 1745-1775)

Muslin, per yard ....$ 2.50	Greatcoat 6.25
Cambric, per yard 1.50	Quilted petticoat 1.45
Osnaburg, per yard .... .17	Flannel Gown 2.85
Velvet, per yard 3.33	Woman's hood 85
Linen, per yard ....50 to 1.25	Woman's jacket 1.75
Ribbon, per yard .... .32	Shoebuckles, silver 3.33
Bed Ticking, per yard .... .39	Shoes 1.25
Calico per yard ....42 to 1.04	Pumps 2.00
Broadcloth, per yard ......3.00 to 3.58	Stockings ....83 to 1.17
Cotton Cloth, per yard ....50 to .83	Broadcloth coat 5.75
Sacking, yer yard .... .25	Silk bonnet 1.83
Tablecloth 1.33	Quilt 1.33
Bed Sheet 2.08	Leggings 1.04
Thread, per pound .... .26	Boy's hat .... .83
Wool, per pound ....11 to .33	Plaid hose .... .33
Silk, per hank .... .11	Club .... .50
Blankets ....2 08 to 2.50	Fine hat 6.67
Dutch blanket ....1.25 to 1.67	Bonnet 15.00
Kid Gloves .... .58	Morocco shoes 1.75
Buckskin gloves .... .44	Umbrella 8.00

554 A HISTORY OF ROCKBRIDGE COUNTY, VIRGINIA

Item	Price
Indian gaiters, belt, and pair of moccasins	3.33
Flour, per barrel	2.67 to 8.00
Middlings, per barrel	2.54
Tea	1.58 to 2.00
Coffee	.24
Bottled honey, 1 lb	.31
Butter	.08
Bacon	.07
Beef	.02½ to .14
Potatoes, per bu.	.19
Allspice, per lb.	1.08
Pepper, per lb.	.31 to .58
Cinnamon, per oz.	.42
Cloves, per lb.	.42
Nutmegs, each	.02 to .05
Madder, per lb.	.42
Indigo, per oz.	.17 to .25
Rye brandy, per gal.	.33
Rum, per gal.	.75
Whiskey, per gal.	.50
Gunpowder, per lb.	.46 to .67
Lead, per lb.	.12½ to .50
Shot, per lb.	.08 to .10½
Flints, per doz.	.10½
Building a house	30.00
Laying a barn floor	2.50
Splitting rails, per 1000	5.00
Making and nailing clapboards per 1,000	1.46
Making table with 4 divisions in the drawer	2.50
Common labor, per day	.33
Horse hire, per day	.17
2 horse shoes and putting them on	.42
Picking and husking corn, per day	.25
Driving cattle, per day	.58
Maintenance per day while driving cattle	.10½
Door lock and putting it on	.71
Hauling corn, man and 2 horses, per day	.50
Dressing a deerskin	.33
Buckskin	1.25
Bringing salt from Richmond, per bu.	.83
Cooking and washing, per mo.	1.00
Burial charges	4.17
Lining a coat and jacket	.75
Labor, per mo.	6.67
Wagon	13.33 to 18.00
Iron-tooth harrow	2.00
Scythe	1.25
Broadaxe	1.25
Saddle	1.67
Common Axe	.58
Grindstone	1.00
Gimlet	.12½
Hammer	.25 to .33
Sickle	.29
Bell and collar	1.25
Steelyards	2.33
Brass candlestick	.71
Iron Candlestick	.11
Auger, ¼ inch	.25
Iron, per lb.	.05½
Ten penny nails, per 1000	1.50
Eight penny nails, per 1000	1.10
Four penny nails, per 1000	.46
Shingles, per 1000	3.71
Cupboard hinges, per pair	.50
Window lights, per doz.	2.00
Loom	5.00
Trunk	5.00
Tumblers, per doz.	3.33
Glasses, per doz.	1.00
Comb	1.33
Thimble	.08
Iron Pot	1.17
Nutmeg grater	.88
Saucepan	.75
Brass kettle	2.50
Mortar and pestle	1.25
Spinning wheel	1.67
Silver teaspoon	.42
Flatiron	.17 to .50
Funnel	.50
Feather bed	7.50
Looking glass	.38 to 1.42
Pepper mill	.50
Frying pan	.67
China plates, per doz.	4.50
Pewter plate	.20
Knives and forks, per doz.	1.46
Pewter porringer	.83

APPENDICES 555

Brass wire and riddle	.55
Needles, per doz.	.16
Pins, per 1000	.33
Large Bible	5.00 to 7.50
Testament	.33
Bradley's Dictionary, 2 vol.	3.00
Pine plank, 100 feet	1.04
Large still and worm	123.59
Gingseng, per lb.	.25 to 1.25
Candle mould	.12
Brimstone, per lb.	.17
Pewter, per lb.	.17
Tobacco, per lb.	.07½ to .10½
Paper, per quire	.42
Penknife	.10½
Beaver skin	.83
Tallow, per lb.	.02
Candles, per lb.	.08
Bearskin	.67
Saltpeter, per lb.	.24
Camphor, per oz.	.33
1 acre standing wheat	.83
Cutlass	.41
Cowhide	.80
Necklace	.33
Turpentine, per bottle	.55
Razor	50

Period 1775-1825

Copper boiler, 100 gal	75.00
Fanning mill	15.00
Loom	10.00
Robinson's History of America	3.75
History of Virginia	1.00
Pike's Arithmetic	1.00
Wesley's Sermons	.92
To Richmond and return, 1802	21.40
Butter, per firkin (56 lb.)	4.83
Straw bonnet	1.67
Broken flax, per lb.	.04¼
Wheat, per bu.	.67
Rye, per bu.	.55
Corn, per bu.	.50
Flour, per barrel	3.54
Cassimere, per yd	2.00
Domestic plaid, per yard	.20
Red flannel, per yard	.23
Letter paper, per quire	.20
Breakfast plates, per doz.	.50
Loaf sugar, per lb.	.20
Calico, per yd.	.20
Gunflints, per 100	.60
Wineglasses, per doz.	.60
Plow and doubletree	6.00
Coffee	.30
Cinnamon, per lb.	.75
Ginger, per oz.	.17
Broken chocolate, per oz.	.04
Rice, per lb.	.04
Handsaw file	.22
Brass knife and fork	.21
Packsaddle	.50
Pocketbook	.33
Basin	.37½
Bell and collar	1.25
Horseshoe	.17
Thimble	.11
Casteel soap, per pound	.33
Calomel, per ounce	.67
Court plaster, per roll	.33
Chalk, per pound	1.00
Frying pan	1.25
Goose	.42
Fishhooks, per dozen	.12
One beaver skin	.83
China bowl	.33
Making a jacket	1.00
Blanket	3.67
Tobacco, per pound	.10 to .14

LYNCHBURG MARKET, 1853

Bacon	.08
Sugar	.07 to .12
Butter	.13
Wheat	.75
Flour, per 100 lb.	.75 to .80
Mountain Whiskey	.30

MINISTERS IN ROCKBRIDGE·

A

(Those Qualifying Before the County Court Prior to the War of 1861)
Baker, John F.—Presbyterian—1858
Baldridge, William—1795.
Blain, Daniel—1817.
Brown, John—1785.
Brown, Samuel—1797
Brown, Henry—Presbyterian—1830
Buckingham, Nathan E.—Methodist—1847.
Campbell, John—1793
Edwards, Francis M.—Methodist—1861
McCarthy, Florence—Baptist—1858
Graham, William—1788.
Houston, Samuel—1789.
Landstreet, John—Methodist—1851.
Linn, Joseph H.—1838
Marshall, Robert T.—Methodist—1857
Mason, Gilbert—Baptist—1853
Mason, Emmet T.—Baptist—1857
Filler, Samuel—Lutheran—1843
McCorkle, Alexander B.—Presbyterian—1836
McCune, Robert L.—Presbyterian—1858.
Moore, John H.—Baptist—1864
Preston, Thomas L.—Presbyterian—1861
Ramsay, John B.—Presbyterian—1854.
Reid, Joseph—Presbyterian—1807
Richardson, John C.—Baptist—1855
Smith, Edward—Methodist—1826.
Taylor, Robert J.—Presbyterian—1852
Trimble, William M.—Presbyterian—1844
Waggoner, John—1801.
Walkup, Joseph W.—Presbyterian—1863
Young, John—1794

B

(Natives of Augusta; According to a List Compiled by William G. McDowell)

PRESBYTERIAN

Alexander, Archibald, D. D., LL. D.
Arnold, Edward P.
Baxter, Joseph F.
Beard, W. S.
Blain, Samuel W.
Brown, James M., D. D.
Brown, Joseph, D. D.
Brown, Samuel, D. D.

Brown, William, D. D.
Brown, Henry
Brown, Cyrus G.
Campbell, W. G.
Campbell, Samuel D.
Campbell, Samuel B., D. D.
Campbell, Isaac N.
Campbell, James T.

APPENDICES 557

Campbell, Robert F.
Campbell, W. A.
Crawford, Edward
Davidson, Andrew B.
Finley, David H.
Freeman, Adam
Gilmore, J. Harvey
Gilmore, Robert C.
Glasgow, Samuel McP.
Goul, John M.
Graham, Jacob
Greenlee, James F.
Grigsby, Benjamin F.
Hendron, John, D. D.
Houston, James
Houston, Matthew
Houston, Samuel
Houston, Samuel R.
Houston, W. W.
Junkin, Daniel P.
Laird, Henry P.
Laird, Alexander F.
Laird, W. R., D. D.
Lapsley, Joseph B.
Leyburn, John, D. D.
Leyburn, George W.
Leyburn, Edward R.
Lockridge, Andrew Y.
Lyle, John (1)
Lyle, John (2)
Lyle, Matthew
McClung, James C.
McCorkle, Alexander B.
McCorkle, Emmett W., D. D.
McCown, J. Harry
McCown, John W.
McCutchen, John S.
McMasters, Robert B. McK.
Miley, William H., D. D.
Morrison, William W.

Morrison, William McC., D. D.
Myers, Harry W., D. D.
Ocheltree, William H.
Paine, James
Paine, Henry H.
Paxton, John, D. D.
Paxton, Thomas R.
Paxton, James H.
Paxton, James T.
Pinkerton, John D.
Pittman, Francis W. L.
Poague, James W.
Preston, Thomas L., D. D.
Preston, John A.
Price, Joseph J.
Ramsay, Samuel G.
Reveley, John G.
Reveley, William A.
Ruff, Andrew W.
Ruff, John
Ruff, William W.
Ruffner, W. Henry, D. D., LL. D.
Smith, Jacob H., D. D.
Smith, James H.
Smith, Josiah M.
Strickler, Givens B., D. D., LL D.
Stuart, Robert
Stuart, Ebenezer
Taylor, Robert J.
Templeton, Alexander
Thomas, Joseph A.
Thompson, William McQ.
Walker, Robert C.
Walkup, Joseph W.
Wilson, William
Wilson, Robert
Wilson, James P., D. D.
Wilhelm, William F.
Womelsdorf, Carlyle R.

METHODISTS:

Buchanan, R. C. A.
Dolly, William L.
Fultz, Robert L.
Green, S. H.
Hamilton, Alexander L., D. D.

Mitchell, John W.
Taylor, William—Bishop
Taylor, Andrew
Vanderslice, George C.
White, G. Dorsey

EPISCOPALIANS:

Campbell, William S.
Davidson, Charles B.
Gibbs, George

McDowell, William G.
Moore, James

BAPTISTS:

Beach, William M.
Harris, J. H.
Margrave, William

McLaughlin, J. T.
Richardson, J. C.
Root, Erastus C.

C

MINISTERS REPORTING MARRIAGES, 1782-1818, INCLUSIVE

The first date is that of the first marriage reported. The second is that of the latest marriage. The numbers following are those of the number of marriages reported by the various ministers.

Baldridge, William, 1796-1809 109
Baxter, George A., 1799-1817 224
Bell, John, 1817 1
Blain, Daniel, 1801-1812 266
Brown, John, 1782-1797 166
Campbell, John P., 1793-1795 21
Carrick, Samuel, 1786-1791 25
Crawford, Edward, 1785-1791 15
Cree, John, 1799-1803 23
Cumings, Charles, 1793 2
Dameron, William, 1795 1
Davidson, A. B., 1815-1817 55
Duncan, William, 1811 2
Ewing, John D., 1813-1818 11
Graham, William, 1785-1797 132
Graham, J. L., 1812 1
Hammond, Benjamin, 1811 1
Harper, James, 1801-1803 22

Hemphill, Andrew, 1806 1
Heron, Andrew, 1817 5
Holmes, John, 1801 1
Houston, Samuel, 1790-1818 319
Lanier, Edmund, 1809 1
Lindsay, John, 1791 1
Lyle, Matthew, 1796 2
McConnell, James, 1787 22
Miers, J. W., 1811 1
Mitchell, Edward, 1792 2
Montgomery, John, 1800-1805 7
Reid, Joseph, 1808-1810 8
Shanks, William, 1816 1
Vansandt, Elijah, 1794-1805 39
Ward, James, 1801 (Methodist) 1
Wilson, Robert, 1814 1
Young, John, 1796-1799 30

G

ROCKBRIDGE LEGISLATORS

Other counties forming a senatorial district with Rockbridge are the following: 1778-1818, Augusta, Rockingham, and Shenandoah, Pendleton and Bath being added in 1788 and 1790, respectively; 1818-1830, Augusta and Pendleton; 1830-1852, Augusta; 1852-1865, Bath and Highland; 1865-1869, Nelson; 1869-1879, Alleghany and Bath; 1879-1904, Alleghany, Bath, Botetourt, and Highland; since 1904, Bedford. The following is a complete list of the senators.

1778-1781—Sampson Mathews
1783-1786—Thomas Adams.
1786-1789—Alexander St. Clair.

APPENDICES 559

1790-1791—Simpson Mathews
1792-1793—Alexander St. Clair.
1794-1796—John Oliver
1797-1800—Archibald Stuart
1800—Andrew Moore
1800-1806—James Allen, Moore having resigned to become a United States marshal in 1801.
1806-1810—Daniel Smith
1810-1826—Chapman Johnson
1827-1839—David W. Patterson
1839-1845—John H. Peyton
1845-1847—Samuel McD. Moore
1847-1851—William Kinney
1852-1858—James H. Paxton
1859-1861—James G. Paxton
1861-1865—William Frazier
1865-1867—David S. G. Cabell
1869-1873—William A. Anderson
1873-1877—John L. Eubank
1877-1880—Joseph H. Sherrard, Jr.
1881-1884—William A. Glasgow
1885-1896—Charles P. Jones
1897-1898—S. H. Fletcher
1899-1900—C. E. McCorkle. Mr. McCorkle died December 14, 1899, and A. Nash Johnson was chosen to fill the vacancy.
1901-1904—George A. Rivercomb
1904-1906—J. Lawrence Campbell
1908-1910—J. Randolph Tucker
1912-1914—W. T. Paxton and J. Randolph Tucker
1916-1918—A. Willis Robertson

DELEGATES

Alexander, Andrew*,—1798-99, 1800-01, 1801-02, 1803-04, 1804-05, 1805-06, 1806-07, 1818-19, 1819-20, 1820-21, 1821-22. Mr. Alexander became surveyor in 1806 and was succeeded by Thomas L. Preston.

Anderson, Francis T.—1861-62, 1862 (April and September), 1863 (January)

Anderson, William A.—1883-84, 1884 (August), 1887-88, 1918

Anderson, William C.—Convention 1901-02.

Armentrout, Charles, 1874 (January), 1874-5.

Arnold, Jacob W.—1885-86, 1887 (March).

Barclay, E. H.—1899-1900.

Bowyer, John, 1778, 1782, 1784-85, 1785-86, 1789, 1790, 1791, 1792, 1793, 1794, 1795, 1796, 1799-1800, 1800-01, 1801-02, 1810-11, 1812-13, 1814-15, 1815-16, 1816-17, 1817-18, 1818-19, 1819-20, 1820-21, 1821-22, 1822-23, 1823-24, 1824.

Campbell, Charles—1781-82, 1783, 1788.

Caruthers, James—1798—99.

---

*Whether the following dates are to be shared between an elder and a younger Andrew is not known with compiler. And so with other instances in the list.

Caruthers, John—1796.
Craig, J. S.—1895-96, 1897-98, 1908.
Donald, William A.—1871-72, 1872-73.
Dorman, Charles P.—1833-34, 1834-35, 1835-36, 1836-37, 1839 (January), 1839-40, 1840-41, 1841-42, 1846-47, 1847-48.
Dorman, James B.—Convention, 1861; House, 1848-49, 1849-50, 1850-51.
Doyle, Robert L.—1855-56.
Dunlap, Robert K.—1881-82.
Dunlap, John T.—1891-92.
Edmondson, J. K.—1893-94.
Frazier, James A.—1877-78, 1879-80.
Frazier, James B.—1881-82.
Gilmore, Joseph, 1852 (January).
Gold, William M.—1845-46.
Graham, A.—1865-66, 1866-67, 1869-70, 1870-71.
Grigsby, Joseph—1804-05, 1805-06, 1806-07, 1807-08, 1808-09.
Grigsby, Reuben—1811-12, 1812-13, 1813-14, 1815-16.
Harper, James F.—1845-46, 1846-47, 1847-48.
Hays, John—1784-85.
Johnston, James M.—1889-90.
Johnston, Zachariah—1792, 1797-98.
Jordan, Charles F.—1885-86, 1887 (March).
Kirkpatrick, John—1853-54. ,
Lady, John B.—1877-78, 1879-80, 1881-82.
Leech, W. B. F.—1875-76, 1876-77, 1881-82, 1895-96, 1899-1900.
Letcher, Greenlee D.—1889-90, 1891-92.
Letcher, John—1875-76, 1876-77.
Leyburn, Alfred—1835-36, 1838 (January), 1839 (January), 1839-40, 1840-41, 1841-42, 1852 (January).
McCampbell, John—1809-10.
McClelland, Thomas S.—1802-03, 1803-04.
McDowell, James—1796.
McDowell, James—1830-31, 1831-32, 1832-33, 1833-34, 1834-35, 1838 (January).
McDowell, Samuel, 1778, 1780-81.
McKee, John T.—1887-88.
McKee, William—1779, 1886-87, 1787-88, 1788, 1789, 1790, 1791, 1793, 1794.
McLaughlin, W.—1869-70.
Massie, James W.—1857-58.
Mitchell, R. G.—1904, 1906.
Moore, Andrew—1780-81. 1781-82, 1782, 1783, 1785-86, 1786-87, 1787-88, 1799-1800.
Moore, David E.—1842-43, 1843-44, 1844-45.
Moore, Samuel McD.—1825-26, 1826-27. 1827-28, 1828-29. 1829-30, 1830-31. 1831-32, 1832-33, 1836-37.
Morrison, James D.—1874 (January), 1874-75.
Morrison, S. B.—1869-70, 1870-71.
Patterson, Andrew—1849-50, 1850-51, 1855-56- 1859-60. 1861 (January).
Paxton, J. G.—1848-49, 1857-58.
Paxton, Matthew W.—1883-84, 1884 (August).
Paxton, R. G.—1893-94.

APPENDICES

Paxton, William—1816-17, 1817-18.
Poague, William T.—1871-72, 1872-73.
Preston, Thomas L.—1806-07, 1807-08, 1808-09, 1809-10, 1910-11.
Quisenberry, John M.—1901-02.
Reid, Samuel McD.—1859-60, 1861 (January), 1861-62, 1862 (April and September), 1863 (January), 1863-64, 1864-65.
Rogers, Andrew—1813-14, 1814-15.
Stuart, Alexander, 1779.
Taylor, James McD.—1853-54, 1865-66, 1866-67.
Taylor, William—1822-23.
Waddy, Charles W.—1901-02.
White, Hugh A.—1910, 1912, 1914, 1916.
White, Robert—1823-24, 1824-25, 1825-26, 1826-27, 1827-28, 1828-29, 1829-30, 1842-43, 1843-44, 1844-45.
White, Robert J.—1863-64, 1864-65.
Wilson, John—1797-98.
Winborne, R. W.—1897-98.

Remarks: W. McLaughlin resigned, 1869, and was succeeded by A. Graham. S. B. Morrison resigned in 1869. In 1881 R. K. Dunlap was unseated in favor of J. A. Frazier, and W. B. F. Leech in favor of J. B. Lady.

Hugh W. Sheffey was President of the Senate, 1863-65.

Thomas Lewis and Samuel McDowell represented Augusta in the State Convention of 1776.

William McKee and Andrew Moore represented Rockbridge in the Convention of 1788, which ratified the Federal Constitution.

In the Constitutional Convention of 1829-30, Rockbridge was represented by Samuel McD. Moore; in that of 1850-51, by John Letcher.

Samuel McD. Moore and James B. Dorman represented Rockbridge in the Secession Convention of 1861.

William McLaughlin represented Rockbridge, Bath, and Highland in the State Convention of 1867-68; William A. Anderson and J. W. Gilmore in that of 1901-02.

CENSUS FIGURES AND VITAL STATISTICS

(Population by Decades)

Year	Population	Year	Population
1790	6,548	1860	17,248
1800	8,945	1870	16,058
1810	10,318	1880	20,003
1820	11,945	1890	23,062
1830	14,244	1900	21,799
1840	14,284	1910	24,416
1850	16,045		

In 1790 there were, of all ages, 3,069 white males and 2,756 white females. The number of those not less than sixteen years of age were 1,517 males and 1,429 females. The totals were 5,825 whites and 723 blacks.

(From the Census of 1850)

Whites	11,848	Libraries, other than private	2
Slaves	4,197	Volumes in such libraries	3,200
Families	1,972	Wheat, bushels	198,553
Dwellings	1908	Rye, bushels	10,017
Births among the white and free colored	290	Corn, bushels	372,705
Births among the slaves	95	Barley, bushels	2,345
White marriages	105	Buckwheat, bushels	2,019
Deaths of whites	97	White potatoes, bushels	14,226
Deaths of slaves	60	Sweet potatoes, bushels	980
Public schools	18	Flax fiber, pound	8,925
Teachers in the same	21	Flaxseed, bushels	657
Pupils in the same	430	Acres in farms	104,638
School funds, public	$1,352	Acres unimproved	155,233
School funds from other sources	$5,329	Farms, cash value	$3,207,030
Total of school funds	$6,681	Farm machinery, cash value	$99,346
Colleges	2	Horses	3,071
College teachers	16	Mules and asses	189
College students	186	Working oxen	94
College funds, endowment	$14,610	Milch cows	3,453
College funds, public	$75,000	Sheep	1,262
College funds, other than endowment or public	$3,000	Hogs	20,937
Total of college funds	$93,110	Livestock, cash value	$436,149
Attending school, males	800	Hay, tons	7,626
Attending schools, females	679	Tobacco, pounds	78,298
Foreigners	none	Butter, pounds	178,384
Illiterate adults, white males	110	Cheese, pounds	17,051
Illiterate adults, white females	126	Maple sugar, pounds	1,728
Illiterate adults, native born	221	Honey and wax, pounds	6,298
Illiterate adults, foreign born	15	Livestock, cash value	$436,149
		Value of animals, slaughtered	$89,525
		Homemade manufactures, value of output	$22,018

(From the Census of 1860)

Real property	$8,290,943	Property	$14,461,132
Personal property	6,170,188	Families	2,379
Total of real and personal		Free population	13,263

(From the Census of 1870)

People not less than 70 years of age:

White males	83	Total of males	109
White females	100	Total of females	132
Colored males	26	Grand total	241
Colored females	32		

APPENDICES

Persons between the ages of 5 and 21:

White	4,369	Total	5,861
Colored	1,492	Total negro population	3,890

Towns. Districts, etc., 1890 and 1910

White population, 1890	17,931	1910	20,471
Colored population, 1890	5,131	1910	3,944
Buffalo District, 1890	3,072	1910	2,617
Kerr's Creek District, 1890	2,757	1910	2,238
Lexington District, 1890	4,418	1910	4,378
Natural Bridge District, 1890	4,539	1910	4,182
South River District, 1890	3,977	1910	4,096
Walker's Creek District, 1890	3,255	1910	3,660
Lexington (town)	3,059	1910	2,931
Buena Vista		1910	3,245
Glasgow		1910	405
Goshen, 1900	253	1910	165

(From the Census of 1910)

Males	12,095	Acres improved	161,710
Females	12,321	Land value, per acre	$12.96
Dwellings	4,767	Horses	6,607
Families	4,954	Mules	141
Males of voting age	5,922	Cattle	14,073
Illiterate voters, white	622	Sheep and goats	14,817
Illiterate voters, colored	345	Hogs	10,659
Persons of foreign birth	59	Wheat, acres of	23,661
Persons of foreign or mixed parentage	133	Wheat, bushels	284,703
		Oats, acres of	2,548
Naturalized voters of foreign birth	15	Oats, bushels	40,098
Aliens of voting age	9	Corn, acres of	22,978
Foreign born with first naturalization papers only, or naturalization status unknown	10	Corn, bushels	658,402
		Hay, acres of	17,163
		Hay, tons	15,857
Natives of Scotland	5	Potatoes, acres of	492
Natives of Italy	4	Potatoes, bushels	55,258
Natives of Austria	4	Percentage of farms operated by tenants	21.7
Natives of Greece	3		
Natives of Hungary	2	Value of all farm property, including implements and animals	$9,779,232
Natives of other countries	4		
Farms	1,944		

According to the returns on file in the office of the County Clerk, there were, for the period 1913-1916 inclusive, a yearly average of 188 deaths among the white people and fifty among the negroes. For the whites the rate is not quite 9.2 per 1,000 of population. For the colored people it is about 12.5 per 1,000, the mean for the two races being about 9.6.

During the years 1915 and 1916, diseases of the respiratory organs caused 122 deaths, tuberculosis being responsible for 57 and pneumonia for 50. Affections of the cerebral system occasioned 45 deaths, 37 being due to apoplexy or paralysis. From disorders of the circulatory system the deaths were 51, 41 being attributed to diseases of the heart. There were 49 deaths from urinary complaints and 25 from diseases of the digestive organs. Diseases peculiar to childhood caused 57 deaths, constitutional ailments 27, female disorders 16, old age 4, and accidents 8. There were 19 stillbirths and in 31 instances the cause of death was not known.

In 1915, 4 deaths were reported from gunshot wounds and 4 from grip. In 1916, cancer was the cause of 14 deaths and blood poisoning of 5. In 1915, 44 of the deaths were of children less than a year old; 36 were of persons between the ages of 1 and 21; 84 were of persons between the ages of 21 and 70. 48 men and women died between the ages of 70 and 80, 25 between the ages of 80 and 90, while 3 whites and 1 negro were 90 years old or upward, the oldest, 98 years of age, being a white.

COUNTY OFFICERS

County Clerks

Andrew Reid—1778-1831
Samuel McD. Reid, son of Andrew
   Reid—1831-1852
C. Chapin—1852-1863
James K. Edmondson—1863-1865

Andrew Agnor—military ap-
   pointee—1865-1870
J. P. Moore—1870-1893
Initials to be supplied—Shields—1893

Circuit Clerks

Andrew Reid—1809-1831
Samuel McD. Reid—1831-1858

J. G. Steele—1858-1864
J. C. Boude—1864-1865 and 1870-1893

Surveyors

James McDowell—1778-1785
Alexander Campbell—1785
Andrew Alexander—1806
William Paxton—Resigned, 1831

Edward J. McLaughlin—1831-1845
James C. C. Moore—1845-1852
Andrew M. Lusk—1858-1864

Sheriffs

Archibald Alexander—1778
John Bowyer—1779
Samuel McDowell—1780
John Greenlee—1785
John Houston—1786
Joseph Moore—1788
James Buchanan—1791
Joseph Walker—1792
James Gilmore—1794
William Moore—1795
Samuel Keys—1796
David Edmondson—1798
Matthew Hanna—1800

James Caruthers—1802
Alexander Shields—1806
Charles Campbell—1809
John Wilson—1811
James McDowell—1812
William Lyle—1813
John Leyburn—1816
William Moore—1819
James Caruthers—1820
Joseph Gilmore—1824
James Moore—1826
Joseph Allen—1828
John McClelland—1830

APPENDICES 565

Robert White—1832
John Alexander—1834
William Paxton—1836
Joseph Cloyd—1839
John McCorkle—1840
John Bowyer—1842
James Davidson—1844
Joseph Bell—1845

Reuben Grigsby—1845
John Ruff—1850
ELECTIVE
John T. Shields—1852-1854
John A. M. Lusk—1854-1858
William F. Poague—1858-1860
David J. Whipple—1860-1864

JUSTICES, 1778-1852

NOTE.—A star following a name shows that there is no express statement that the person qualified. A star following a date shows that the person was in commission later than the year given.

Alexander, Andrew—1826
Alexander, Archibald—1778
Alexander, John—1807-1827*
Allen, Joseph—1807-1827*
Anderson, Robert B.*—1850
Barclay, Alexander T.—1829
Barclay, Hugh—1838-1851*
Barton, Robert R.—1829
Bell, Alexander N.—1836
Bell, Joseph, Jr.—1817-1843
Bowyer, John—1778-1827*
Buchanan, James—1778-1801c
Campbell, Addison H.*—1842
Campbell, Charles—1778-1801*
Campbell, John—1798
Campbell, Robert L.—1829
Caruthers, James—1790-1827
Caruthers, John—1791
Caruthers, John T.—1830
Cloyd, Joseph—1807-1827*
Compton, James*—1850
Culton, Alexander—1809
Cumings, John A.—1827-1843*
Davidson, James—1809
Davidson, John—1806
Davis, William C.—1848
Edgar, Thomas—1784
Edmondson, David—1784-1801*
Edmondson, David—1839
Finlay, Andrew—1803
Gay, John—1778-1801*
Gilmore, Addison*—1840
Gilmore, John—1778-1801*
Gilmore, Joseph—1804
Gilmore, Paxton—1839

Gilmore, William*—1827
Glasgow, Alexander M.—1843
Gold, William M.—1838
Greenlee, John—1778-1801
Grigsby, Joseph—1797-1801*
Grigsby, Reuben—1817-1827*
Hanna, Matthew—1789-1801*
Harper, James F.*—1840
Hays, John—1778*
Houston, John—1778-1801
Houston, William—1837
Ingles, William—1834
Johnston, Alexander*—1840
Johnston, James—1817
Jordan, Samuel F.—1837
Keys, Samuel—1784-1801*
Lackey, William—1840
Leech, John S.*—1835
Lewis, William C.—1840
Leyburn, Alfred—1834
Leyburn, John—1802-1827*
Lusk, William—1829
Lyle, John—1778
Lyle, Samuel—1778
Lyle, William—1802
McChesney, Zachariah J.*—1827
McCleland, John—1807-1827*
McClung, Benjamin—1827
McConkey, John—1797-1801*
McCorkle, John—1809
McCutchen, William M.*—1850
McDowell, James—1791-1827*
McDowell, James, Jr.*—1827
McDowell, Samuel—1778
McGuffin, Jamison D.*—1840

McKee, William—1778-1797*
Milleland, John—1807
Montgomery, John—1817
Moore, Andrew—1797-1801*
Moore, James—1807
Moore, Joseph—1778-1801*
Moore, William—1784-1801*
Moore, William R.—1843
Patterson, Samuel—1817-1827*
Patton, William—1836
Paxton, Joseph (1)*—1806
Paxton, Joseph (2)*—1806
Paxton, Thomas—1837
Paxton, Thomas L.*—1842
Paxton, Thomas S.*—1850
Paxton, William (1)—1778
Paxton, William (2)—1807-1827*
Poague, James A.*—1835
Reid, Andrew—1778
Ruff, Jacob M.—1843
Ruff, John—1828
Shields, Alexander—1793-1827*

Stevens, William—1836
Stoner, George—1838
Stuart, Alexander—1778
Stuart, Hugh*—1806
Templeton, David—1807
Todd, Samuel—1782
Trimble, John—1778
Walker, Archibald B.—1834
Walker, John M.*—1806
Walker, Joseph—1778-1801*
Walker, Thomas H.*—1827
Wardlaw, Hugh B.*—1827
White, Joseph—1810
White, Robert—1807-1827*
White, William G.*—1850
Wilson, David*—1806
Wilson, John—1795-1801*
Wilson, Samuel M.*—1840
Wilson, Thomas—1839
Wilson, William—1802
Withrow, John*—1806

JUSTICES, ELECTIVE

1852

The starred names are of those present on opening day, July 5th.

Barton, Robert R.*
Brown, Daniel*
Bryan, Matthew*
Cummings, John A.*
Eubank, John S.
Gilmore, Addison*
Gilmore, William C.
Gold, William M.*
Hamilton, John G.*
Hamilton, John G.*

Harper, James F.*
Lackey, William*
Leech, John S.*
Lewis, William C.*
Lindsay, Andrew*
Luster, John*
Mackey, Hugh W.*
McKemy, John*
Moore, William R.*

Poague, William F.*
Steele, Joseph (president)
S———, Moses*
Sterrett, Robert*
Varner, Charles*
Walker, Joseph*
White, William*
Wilson, Thomas*
Wilson, William B.*

1856

Brown, Daniel
Davidson, James G.
Davidson, Lewis C.
Gilmore, Paxton
Gold, William M.
Hamilton, Andrew J.
Harper, James F.
Hatcher, Henry M.
Humphreys, Meriwether A.

Johnston, Samuel
Jordan, William (resigned)
Lackey, William
Lewis, William C.
Lindsay, Andrew
Lusk, William (president)
Mackey, Hugh W.
Mackey, John P.
McClintic, Shanklin M.

McCorkle, Theodore M.
McCutchen, William M.
McKemy, John
Paxton, William
Poague, William F.
Varner, Charles
Walker, Joseph
White, William (resigned)
Withrow, Andrew

James Campbell was elected in place of White in 1857, and William Dold in place of Varner in 1859.

1860

Bradley, Schuyler	Johnston, Samuel	McKemy, John
Brown, Daniel	Kirkpatrick, William M.	Moore, Nathan G.
Campbell, James	Laird, John G.	Poindexter, George B.
Chapman, John P.	Lewis, William C.	Updike, James G.
Davidson, Lewis C.	Lusk, William (president)	Walker, Joseph
Echols, Edward	Mackey, Hugh W.	Willson, William B.
Gibson, John A.	McClintic, Shanklin M.	Wilson, James W.
Hamilton, John W.	McCutchen, William M.	Wilson, William A.

In 1861, William C. Gilmore was elected vice Laird, Hobson Johnson vice Echols, and William R. Moore vice Lusk. In 1862, William A. McDonald was elected vice Bradley, John S. Leech vice J. W. Wilson, and James Compton vice Jacob M. Ruff, who seems to have filled an earlier vacancy. William C. Lewis was president, 1862.

1864

Brown, Daniel	Johnston, Samuel	Moore, Nathan G.
Campbell, James	Kinnear, John A.	Patterson, Robert T.
Dold, William	Kirkpatrick, Thomas M.	Patterson, Andrew
Donald, William A.	Kirkpatrick, William M.	Pettigrew, James M.
Forsythe, William E.	Lenter, John	Sandford, Henderson
Gibson, Henry S.	McClintic, Shanklin M.	Templeton, John M.
Gilmore, William C.	(resigned)	Updike, James G.
Hamilton, John W.	McKemy, John (president)	White, William
Hatcher, Henry M.		

George W. Houston was elected vice Templeton, deceased, 1864. William F. Poague was elected vice McClintic, 1865.

REORGANIZED COURT, 1865

First District: Hugh Barclay, William Dold, Samuel Vanderslice, William White.

Second District: Samuel Cowan, John W. Hamilton, Henry M. Hatcher, James C. C. Moore.

Third District: James Campbell, John Luster, Nathan G. Moore, William F. Poague.

Fourth District: Charles Armentrout, James J. Hill, Thomas McCorkle, Robert T. Patterson.

Fifth District: William C. Gilmore, William Kirkpatrick, John McKemy, William A. Wilson.

Sixth District: Daniel Brown, Samuel A. East, William M. McCutchen, and James A. Walker.

Seventh District: James S. Gibson, H. F. Lyle, J. W. Mackey, James T. Patton.

Brown and McKemy were refused commissions. The oath was administered by William White, one of the commissioners to hold the election.

J

A DEGREE FROM WASHINGTON COLLEGE IN 1841

PRAESES ET CURATORES
COLLEGII WASHINGTONIENSIS
IN VIRGINIA
OMNIBUS SINGULISQUE HAS LITERAS LECTURIS
SALUTEM IN DOMINO

NOTUM SIT, Quod, Secundum Institutum ab antiquis Collegiis derivatum, alumnos disciplinae suae bene meritos adorandi insignibus eruditionis et doctrinae, et eo modo eos secernendi a rudibus ARTIUM LIBERALIUM:
NOBIS PLACET, auctoritate, Republica Virginiensi nobis commisa MITCHELL D. DUNLAP cadidatum, PRIMUM IN ARTIBUS GRADUM a nostro Collegio competentum, examine sufficiente previo approbatum, titulo graduque

ARTIUM LIBERALIUM BACCALAUREI

adornare; cujus sigillum commune huic membranae affixum, nominaque nostra subscripta, testamonium sint.
Datum COLLEGII WASHINGTONI EN SIS,
 viseccimo-quarto die Junii, Anno Domini   Henry Ruffner   Praeses
MDCCCXLI

JOHN D. EWING
A. T. BARCLAY
ANDW. ALEXANDER
A. B. DAVIDSON
ROBT. WHITE
SAM. McD. REID
J. ALEXANDER
R. GRIGSBY
HORATIO THOMPSON
JAS. McDOWELL
JAMES MORRISON
WM. TAYLOR
ROB. R. BARTON

(Seal)

SUPPLEMENTARY ITEMS

Brownsburg was established on the land of Robert Wardlaw and Samuel McChesney by act of assembly, November 23, 1793. In 1798 lot owners were given five mere years in which to build, and in the same year the Brownsburg Library Corporation was incorporated.

Fairfield was established December 24, 1800. The original trustees were James McDowell, Samuel Keys, John McClung, Samuel Preston, Samuel Moore, Isaac Robinson, and Andrew Scott.

An act of January 22, 1810 authorized John Jordan and James Moorehead to bridge North River and to charge the following tolls: man on horse, 6¼ cents; sheep or hog, one-half cent; cart or turmoil, twenty-five cents; riding carriages, per wheel, 6¼ cents.

The Lexington arsenal was established by 1819, and in 1824 a roofing of zinc was ordered.

Elizabeth Preston Allan, wife of Colonel William Allan, was born at Lexington, December 22, 1848. She wrote stories for children, edited Sunday school literature for the Southern Presbyterian Church, and the *Life and Letters of Margaret J. Preston,* her stepmother. Colonel Allan wrote *The Army of Northern Virginia, Jackson's Valley Campaign,* etc.

William McCutchen Morrison, son of James L. and Mary A. (McCutchan) Morrison, was born November 10, 1867, was graduated from Washington and Lee 1887, and in 1896 was ordained and sent to Luebo on the Congo. One of his journeys in that river valley was of 700 miles. He reduced the Baluba tongue to writing. On behalf of the Congo natives he appeared before the British Parliament. He was sued for libel, but acquitted.

Thomas Plunkett was pensioned $60.00 a year in 1817, and Samuel Kirkpatrick $120.00 a year in 1818.

Hans Peter Stalley arrived in America 1732. He was then under sixteen years of age.

ERRATA

Several errors of very little importance are not included in the list below:

Page 65, line 9—For "precipating," read "precipibating."

Page 62, line 12—Supply "were" after "burials."

Page 90, line 5 (above bottom): For "phonographic," read "phonologic."

Page 92, line 10 (above bottom): After "English," read "and neither could his son, George II."

Page 96, lines 9 and 12 (above bottom): Omit brackets.

Page 96, line 12 (above bottom): For "not known" read "know that."

Page 178, line 12 (above bottom): After "Lewis" supply "son of."

Page 178, line 9 (above bottom): For "chapel of care," read "chapel of ease."

Page 179, line 6 (above bottom): For "Beth Heron," read "Beth Horon."

Page 182, line 21: At end of line supply "oaths."

Page 191, line 24: After "Hoge" supply "Houston."

Page 240, line 5: For "competent" read "component."

Page 259, line 3: For "Dockor" read "Samuel R."

Page 339, line 13 (above bottom): For "Adams" read "Adam."

Page 405: Under "Section XI" supply "Roster of Confederate Soldiers."

GENERAL INDEX

NOTE: Since the arrangement of lists in this book is alphabetical, any particular name may readily be found, except so far as cross-indexes might be used.

Academies 188, 212
Agriculture 38, 109, 168
Alexander, Archibald 244, 301
Alexander Family 229, 244
Alexander, Robert 188
America in 1716 .... 16, 17
Anderson Family 245
Anderson, Isaac 229
Anderson, William A. 245
Animals, Wild 5
Ann Smith Academy 207
Appendices 547
Augusta, subdivision of 76
Augusta Resolutions 1775 95
Balcony Falls 9, 165
Baldwin, John C. 246
Baldwin, Joseph, Jr. 301
Ballagh, James C. 301
Baptists in Rockbridge 178
Baxter, George A. 246
Buclay, Elihu H. 246
Bell, John 229
Ben Salem 176
Benton, Thomas H. 230, 303
Bethesda 176
Blair, James 303
Booms of 1889-90 .... 136, 153
Borden, Benjamin, Jr. 28
Borden, Benjamin, Sr. 22
Borden, Joseph 31
Borden Litigation 30, 32
Borden's Great Tract 26, 343
Botetourt, formation of 76
British Invasion, 1781 97
Brockenbrugh, John W. 246
Brown, John 247
Brown people 146
Brown, Samuel 247
Brounlow, William G. 250
Brownsburg 156
Buena Vista, town of 153

Cadets, V. M. I. 123, 124, 203
Calfpasture Families 88
Calfpasture Land Grant 86
Calfpasture, settlement of 87
Campbell, Alexander 302
Campbell, Charles 302
Campbell, John L. 301
Campbell, Samuel R. 268
Caruthers Family 248
Caruthers, William A. 249, 301
Church Buildings, Sundry 179
Churches of Lexington 149, 176, 177
Civil Government 45
Classes, Social 33
Climate 3, 4
Cold Sulphur Spring 160, 303
Collierstown 157, 176
Conditions, 1844 109
Confederate Soldiers, roster of .. 125, 405
Convention of 1861 .... 119, 120
Cornstalk, murder of 78
Costello, Fannie K. 230
Costume 25, 106
Council of War, 1756 67
County Court 47
Courthouses 148
Crockett, Davy 303
Crystal Spring 11
Deeds 50
Dale, Samuel 225
Davidson, Andrew B. 249
Daviess, Joseph H. 301
Deserters 131
Disestablishment 105
Donally's Fort, relief of 81
Dorman, Charles P. 249
Dunlap, Alice W. 291
Dunlap Family 249
Dunlap, Richard G. 303
Dunmore War 74

Dyes 107, 135
Early Settlement 23, 27, 28, 36, 37, 464
Echols, Edward 251
Edmondson Family 252
Education 51
Emancipation 143, 146
Emigration from Rockbridge 224
Episcopal Church 178
Estill Family 226, 252
Fairfield 157
Falling Springs 176
Fancy Hill 158
Farming, early 38
Federal Incursions 127
Fincastle Resolutions, 1775 94
Finlay, John 302
Fire of 1796 148
Flax and Hemp 38, 107, 168, 461
Forts, pioneer 66, 158
Franklin Society 199, 214
Free School System 184
Free Negroes 143, 145
Moore, S. McD. 120, 268
Frontier, American 18
Gardens 108
Garfield, death of 137
Gray Family 253
Genealogic Data 470
Geology 3
German Duke, visit by 109
Gibbs, James E. A. 229, 304
Glasgow Family 253, 304
Glasgow, town of 155
Goshen 157
Goshen Pass 9
Graham, William 254
Greenlee Family 254
Greenlee, John F. 255
Greenlee, Mary 254
Grigsby Family 256
Hardships, 1861-1865 131
Hardships in Revolution 101, 104
Health 4
Hepburn, Charles M. G. 302
House Mountains 10
Houses, pioneer 37
Houston Family 258
Houston, Rev. Samuel 258
Houston, Gen. Samuel 256

Houston, Samuel R. 258
Hunter's Raid 129
Indian Meadows 37, 63, 161
Indian Mounds 61, 300
Indian Occupancy 61
Indian Paths 161
Indians, relations of with settlers.... 63
Inventions, sundry 334
Ironworks 170
Jackson, Gen. T. J. 233
Johnson, James 230
Jordan, John 259
Jump Mountain 10
Junkin, George 260
Kerr's Creek Names 460
Kerr's Creek Raids 69
Laird Family 260
Land Grant Methods 26
Laws, colonial 49
Lee, George W. C. 261
Lee, Henry 238
Lee, Robert E. 239
Lee, Sarah P. 261
Letcher, John 261
Letter of 1781 152
Lewis, John 19, 20
Lexington Arsenal 199
Lexington, disturbance at, 1861 121
Lexington, founding of 147
Lexington Gazette 217
Lexington in Middle and Recent
  Periods 149, 150
Lexington, residents of, 1796 462
Leyburn, John 262, 302
Liberty Hall 189
Liquor Habit 180
Living 108
Locher, Charles H. 231, 262
Log Houses 37, 107
Logan, John A. 231
Long Hunters 74
Lusk, William 263
Magisterial Districts .... • 5
Manufactures 169
Marriage Procedure 51
Massacre at Middle River 66
Maury, Matthew F. 263
McCorkle, Charles E. 289
McCorkle, Emmett W. 290

GENERAL INDEX 573

MacCorkle Family 278
McCorkle, Henry H. 291
McCorkle, Walter L. 280
MacCorkle, William A. 287
McCorkle, William H. 288, 291
McCormick, Cyrus H. 229, 307
McCoy, Daniel 231
McDowells, coming of 21
McDowell Fight 64
McDowell, James L. 265
McDowell, James, Jr. 265
McDowell, John 264
McDowell Family 263
McNutt, Alexander 266
McNutt, Alexander G. 266
McNutt Family 266
Meetings, 1860-1861 ....115, 118, 121
Methodism 177
Middle and Recent Periods 104
Middle Period, features of 104
Midway 157
Miley, Michael 231
Military Organizations, 1861-1865..124, 125
Militia Officers 396
Militia System 221
Mills 40, 168
Money 52
Montgomery, Humphrey 267
Moore, Andrew 267
Moore Family 268
Morrison, James D. 268
Morrison, William M. C. 304
Mountains 1, 2
Mount Pleasant Academy 188
Mulberry Hill 190
Muster Days 223
Names, geographical 5
Natural Bridge 6, 160
Naturalizations 456
Negro Property 146
Nelson, Alexander L. 268
New Monmouth 175, 462
New Providence 173
Newspapers of 1804 217
Newspapers, extracts from, 1860-
 1861 ....115, 116, 118, 120
Nichols, Edward 268
Old Field Schools 183

Old Providence 183
Order, public 41
Order-books, Augusta, extracts
 from 54, 299, 458
Order-books, Botetourt, extracts from 59
Order-books, Orange, extracts
 from 54, 299, 456
Order-books, Rockbridge, extracts
 from 81, 132
Ordinaries 52, 463
Oxford 176
Padget, Frank 252
Parsons, Henry C. 269
Pastures, the 85
Patents and Conveyances for Land,
 early 343, 351, 355
Patterson, S. F. 231
Paxton, Alexander S. 270
Paxton, Elisha F. 270
Paxton Family 269
Paxton, James 199, 269
Paxton, James H. 269
Paxton, John D. 269
Paxton, John G. 302
Pension Statistics, 1832 101
Pennsylvania, colonial 17, 21
Pennslvania Road 36
Petticrew Tragedy 110
Plant Life 4
Poague, William T. 270
Politics, colonial 45
Politics Since 1865 137
Pontiac War 68
Posey, Thomas 232
Position, Size, and Form of County..1, 5
Postal Rates 163
Presbyterianism 172
Presidential Campaign, 1860 114
Preston, John T. L. 270
Processioning 50, 467
Railroads 166
Rankin, Adam 203
Raphine 158
Reaper, the McCormick 306
Recent Period, changes in 138
Reconstruction Period 136
Reid Family 271
Reid, Samuel McD. 271

Remick Affair 67
Resources, Natural 5
Revolution, causes of 92
Roads, public 162, 164, 300
Robinson, John 271
Rockbridge; Act Establishing County 77
Rockbridge Alum 159, 303
Rockbridge Baths 159
Rockbridge County News 220
Rockbridge Notables 225
Rocky Spring Church 87
Rosters, Military 66
Ruffner, Henry 196, 271
Ruffner, William H. 272
Salling, John P. 19, 272
Saville Family 273
Scenery 6
Schools of Lexington 149
Schools, pioneer 87
Servants and Indentures 33
Sewing Machine, the Gibbs 329
Slavery 141, 145
Smith, Ann 208, 210, 211
Smith, Francis H. 201, 274
Society, frontier 35, 36, 39, 41, 42, 52
Soils 3
Soldiers of Revolution 402
Spottswood's Expedition 18
Sports and Frolics 108
Springfield 157
Staunton 40, 48
Sterrett, John D. 232
Sterrett, John R. S. 304
Strathclyde and Ulster 12-16
Stories 40, 108
Streams 2
Strickler, Givens B. 302
Stuart Family 274
Surnames, Present 388
Surnames, Rockbridge 340
Taxpayers, 1841 378
Taylor Family 274
Taylor, Stuart 275

Taylor, William 275, 302
Teachers, early 184, 186
Temperance Societies 181, 182
Timber Ridge 175, 189, 459
Tin Mine 171
Tithables, 1778 365
Tithables, 1782 370
Toleration, religious 51
Toryism and Disaffection 100
Tucker, Henry St. G. 276
Tucker, John R. 276
Turnpikes 163
Valley Star 218
Values, colonial 42
Vestry 48
Vethake, Henry 277
Virginia in 1716 17
Virginia in the Revolution 96
Virginia Military Institute, history of 201
Virginia Military Institute, organization of 200
Virginia Military Institute, restoration of 206
Wallace, Hugh C. 303
Wallace, William A. 277
War, French and Indian, incidents of 68
War of 1861, causes 111
War of 1861, beginning of 123, 131
War of 1861, close of 136
War of 1914, causes 139, 293
War of 1914, Local Incidents 294
Washington Academy 193
Washington and Lee University 197
Washington College 194
Washington College, presidents of 195, 300
Waterways 165
Wanchope, George A. 302
White, Robert 277
Whitley, William 226
Wills 41, 44, 176
Wilson's Spring 158
Wolves 39
Woods Family 277

www.ingramcontent.com/pod-product-compliance
Lightning Source LLC
Chambersburg PA
CBHW071132300426
44113CB00009B/953